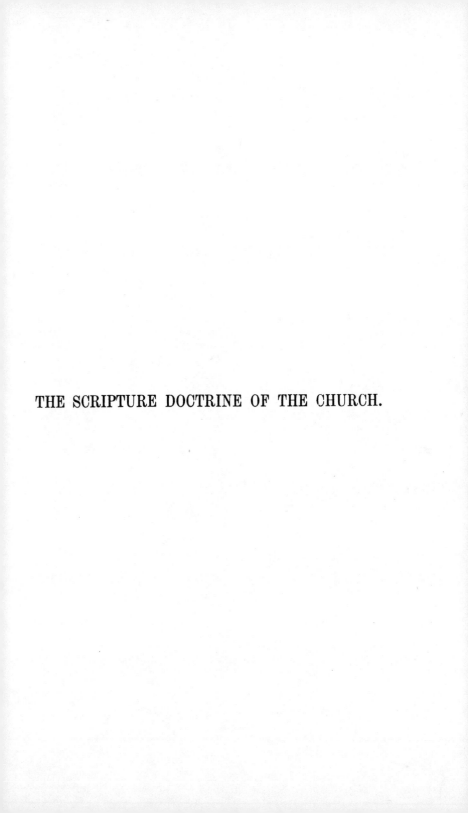

THE SCRIPTURE DOCTRINE OF THE CHURCH.

THE SCRIPTURE DOCTRINE

OF

THE CHURCH

HISTORICALLY AND EXEGETICALLY CONSIDERED

The Eleventh Series of the Cunningham Lectures.

BY THE

REV. D. DOUGLAS BANNERMAN, M.A.,

SOMETIME "CUNNINGHAM FELLOW," NEW COLLEGE, EDINBURGH.

BAKER BOOK HOUSE
Grand Rapids, Michigan

Reprinted 1976 by
Baker Book House

Reproduced from the
edition issued in Edinburgh
in 1887

ISBN: 0-8010-0656-2

PHOTOLITHOPRINTED BY CUSHING - MALLOY, INC.
ANN ARBOR, MICHIGAN, UNITED STATES OF AMERICA
1976

CONTENTS.

—o—

PART I.

THE CHURCH IN THE TIME OF ABRAHAM.

CHAPTER I.

ABRAHAM'S POSITION IN SCRIPTURE; THE GOSPEL PREACHED BEFOREHAND TO HIM.

CHAPTER II.

THE COVENANT MADE WITH ABRAHAM.

CHAPTER III.

THE CHURCH VISIBLY SET UP.

PART II.

THE CHURCH FROM THE TIME OF ABRAHAM TO THAT OF THE EXILE.

CHAPTER I.

THE CHURCH IN ITSELF.

CHAPTER II.

CHIEF NAMES AND EXPRESSIONS USED IN OLD TESTAMENT TO DENOTE THE FELLOWSHIP OF THE COVENANT PEOPLE AND THEIR RELATIONS TO GOD.

CHAPTER III.

BASIS AND PRINCIPLES OF ORGANIZATION IN THE FELLOWSHIP OF THE COVENANT PEOPLE.

PART III.

THE CHURCH FROM THE TIME OF THE EXILE TO THAT OF OUR LORD.

CHAPTER I.

THE JEWISH DIASPORA OR DISPERSION ; HELLENISM AND THE HELLENISTS.

CHAPTER II.

THE PROSELYTES.

PART IV.

THE CHURCH IN OUR LORD'S TEACHING.

CHAPTER I.

CHRIST'S TEACHING REGARDING THE CHURCH IN EXPRESS UTTERANCES.

PART VI.

FROM ANTIOCH TO ROME——THE GENTILE CHRISTIAN CHURCH.

CHAPTER I.

PREPARATION AND TRANSITION.

CHAPTER II.

THE GENTILE CHRISTIAN CHURCH IN ITSELF—ITS LIFE AND WORK AND GENERAL CHARACTERISTICS.

CHAPTER III.

WORSHIP OF GENTILE CHRISTIAN CHURCH.

CHAPTER IV.

PART I.

THE CHURCH IN THE TIME OF ABRAHAM.

CHAPTER I.

ABRAHAM'S POSITION IN SCRIPTURE; THE GOSPEL PREACHED BEFOREHAND TO HIM.

MANY definitions of the Church have been given, but all of them agree in this, that according to Scripture the Church is a company of men, a society or fellowship of some sort; and that, as the leading terms for it (קָהָל, ἐκκλησία) indicate, the Scripture conception of the Church involves that of "calling," "calling out," or "choosing," and implies that the call has been, so far, an effectual one, that it has been, to a certain extent at least, obeyed. Further, there is general agreement that one great bond of union in this society or fellowship is a common faith or belief of some kind, with respect to God, that the Church is a fellowship of believers, "a congregation of faithful men,"—of whatever sort the belief may be which binds them together, and to whatever relations to God and to each other it may give rise. Hence a favourite starting-point with the old divines of the Reformed Church in their treatises *De Ecclesia* was the fourteenth verse of the seventeenth chapter of Revelation.[1] They held that the words which the angel spoke to the apostle in his vision set before us briefly and clearly what the Church of God is and has been in all ages. It means "those that are with the Lamb, who is Lord of

---

[1] Τὸ Ἀρνίον . . κύριος κυρίων ἐστὶ καὶ βασιλεὺς βασιλέων καὶ οἱ μετ᾽ αὐτοῦ κλητοὶ καὶ ἐκλεκτοὶ καὶ πιστοί, Rev. xvii. 14.

lords and King of kings, and they that are with Him are
called, and chosen, and faithful." [1]

Looking back, then, over the history of revelation with
this general idea in our minds, we can hardly help pausing
at the point near the beginning, where those three " notes of
the Church," which we have named, are seen for the first
time to stand out together in a pre - eminent degree, and
where the inspired narrative, hitherto so brief and condensed,
suddenly changes its character, and broadens as from a rivulet
to a river.

Of Abraham those three memorable words are .spoken
again and again, " called, and chosen, and faithful." He is
the first in Scripture history to whom they are all applied.
They are applied to no other with like frequency and
emphasis, save to One, greater than Abraham, " whose day "
the patriarch " rejoiced to see " afar off, " and he saw it and
was glad." [2]   " Thou art the Lord, the God who didst choose
Abram, and broughtest him forth out of Ur of the Chaldees,
and gavest him the name of Abraham, and foundest his heart
faithful before Thee, and madest a covenant with him."   " By
faith Abraham, when he was called, obeyed to go out unto
a place which he was to receive for an inheritance ; and he
went out, not knowing whither he went." [3]

The call of Abraham is not spoken of in Scripture as that
of an individual merely.   Over and over again, both in the
Old Testament and the New, the children of Abraham are
told to look back to him as their head and representative, to
see themselves called and chosen in him, and to follow the

---

[1] So, for instance, Heidegger, in what Krauss in his valuable work, *das protestantische Dogma v. der unsichtbaren Kirche* (Gotha 1876, S. 73), declares to
he " the *opus palmare* of the orthodox theology of the Reformed Church : "
" Proprie et auguste ecclesia est cœtus seu collectio hominum electorum, voca-
torum, et fidelium, quos Deus per Verbum et Spiritum e statu peccati in statum
gratiæ ad æternam gloriam vocat.   Ita finit ipse angelus, ecclesiam indigetans
eos qui cum Agno seu Domino dominorum et Rege regum militantes sunt κλητοί
καὶ ἐκλεκτοὶ καὶ πιστοί, Apoc. xvii. 14."   Heidegger, *Corpus Theol. Christianæ*,
locus xxvi. 6.

[2] John viii. 56.

[3] Neh. ix. 7 ; Heb. xi. 8.   Throughout these lectures I quote, as a rule, from
the Revised Version (1881–1885), and use the Revisers' Greek text as given by
Palmer (Oxford 1881).

example of his faith and obedience. "Hearken to me, ye that follow after righteousness, ye that seek the Lord: . . . Look unto Abraham your father, and unto Sarah that bare you; for when he was but one, I called him, and I blessed him, and made him many." "But thou, Israel, my servant, Jacob whom I have chosen, the seed of Abraham my friend; thou whom I have taken hold of from the ends of the earth, and called thee from the corners thereof, and said unto thee, Thou art my servant, I have chosen thee, and not cast thee away; fear thou not, for I am with thee; be not dismayed, for I am thy God." "So then, they which be of faith are blessed with the faithful Abraham." [1]

The more we study what is said in Scripture of Abraham and the events of his life, the more we shall be struck with the peculiarity and loftiness of the position which he holds. His name stands out from the first as a mighty landmark in the history of redemption. It has been calculated that in the later books of the Old and New Testament there are about one hundred references to the covenant made with Abraham, as compared with some eight or ten references to the covenants with Adam and with Noah.[2] Those earlier covenants were very great and momentous transactions. Adam comes before us as the first natural head of the human family, and is dealt with as such by God, both before and after the Fall. Noah is treated as the head and representative of our race in the Divine covenant after the Flood, regarding the stability of the ordinances of nature. Yet the covenant with Abraham is referred to at least ten times as often in the later Scriptures. And of all Old Testament names, with perhaps the single exception of that of Moses, Abraham's occurs oftenest in the Gospels, the Acts, and the Epistles. More is made of the brief narrative of his life in the teaching of our Lord and His apostles, than of the chapters and books devoted to the history of Joshua, Samuel, David, and all the kings of Israel and Judah put together. In two long sections of his two great theological Epistles, —Romans and Galatians,—the Apostle Paul draws or illus-

---

[1] Isa. li. 1 f., xli. 8–10; Gal. iii. 9.
[2] Stuart Robinson, *Discourses on Redemption*, 2nd ed. p. 76.

trates his reasonings about the most vital doctrines of the
Christian faith from what is said in Genesis of Abraham.
James, the Lord's brother, and the author of the Epistle to
the Hebrews do the same.

How are we to explain this ?

Not from personal achievements. Abraham founded no
kingdom. He wrote no part of Scripture. He is called "a
prophet;" but no prophetic utterance has come down to us
under his name.[1] Nor can we find the explanation in Abraham's personal character or holiness of life. He does not
stand out in the history as a perfect man. His faith was not
always strong. Something of that tendency to craft and
falsehood which came out so plainly in several of his descendants is seen also in Abraham. Other lives recorded in
Scripture, such as those of Joshua and Daniel, are more
blameless than his.

Undoubtedly there is much that is striking about Abraham's
character. We see in him a noble simplicity and strength of
faith, a generosity and unselfishness, a spiritual greatness,
well suited to the great position which he holds in the
history of revelation. But these things are not the reason of
that position.

The explanation becomes clear when we read the history
of Abraham in the light of those New Testament passages,
to some of which reference has already been made; especially when, to use a vivid image of Calvin's, we "follow
Paul, going before us with his torch held up."[2] In that light
certain things stand out plainly which have a direct bearing
on the subject of these lectures.

I. "The Gospel" was "preached beforehand unto Abraham," and received by him. The apostle's whole argument
with the Galatian Christians, in the third chapter of his
Epistle to them, is, that if they do not know Abraham's
Gospel, they do not know the Gospel of God's grace at all.

[1] Gen. xx. 7 ; Ps. cv. 15. It may have been through Abraham, as Dr. Dykes
suggests, that Rebekah "inquired of Jehovah," as recorded in Gen. xxv. 23,
and received the brief enigmatic oracle concerning the future of her two sons,
then unborn ; but this cannot be said to be more than a conjecture, although a
probable one. Dykes, *Abraham, the Friend of God*, 3rd ed. p. 315.

[2] "Nisi facem nobis prætulisset Paulus." Calvin, *Comment. in Gen.* xv. 5.

He reasons to a like effect throughout the fourth chapter of Romans.

II. The covenant which God made with Abraham and his seed was the very covenant of grace and peace whereby we also, if we are true believers, inherit the promises. "The blessing of Abraham," Paul tells the Galatians, "has come upon the Gentiles in Christ Jesus." We are heirs of the blessing only as we are "Abraham's seed, heirs according to the promise" given to him and his.[1] If we are not in that "covenant confirmed beforehand by God," [2] we are not in the covenant at all.

III. In the history of Abraham we see a little company of believers gathered together on the ground of God's gracious word and covenant, in the world, yet not of it, united for common worship and witness-bearing, with work to do for God, which has relation to a future of blessing, in which, through them, all the world is to share, with a solemn sacrament of admission into this fellowship applicable both to themselves and to their infant seed. In other words, the Church of God, built upon the Gospel and the covenant of grace, was distinctly and visibly set up in connection with God's dealings with Abraham.

In these facts we have the key to the unparalleled position assigned to Abraham both in the Old and New Testament; and under these three heads we may consider the chief "momenta" for the Scripture doctrine of the Church which appear in the patriarchal period of the history of revelation.

It is worth noting for a moment at this point how, as the centuries of that history roll on, the call and the obedience of Abraham stand out more and more clearly, as forming in many respects the greatest epoch between the Fall and the coming of the Saviour.[3] At each great step taken afterwards

---

[1] Gal. iii. 14–19, 29.

[2] Gal. iii. 17. The εἰς Χριστόν, "with respect to Christ," of the Textus Receptus in this verse is no doubt, critically considered, a gloss, and is rightly excluded from the text by the R. V. But the whole context and scope of the passage show as clearly that it is a correct *interpretation*.

[3] As it has been well put by an honoured father of our Church, the Moderator of last General Assembly, "The transmission of the true religion, and all the salvation which the world will ever experience, shall yet be traced back, with

in the development of God's purposes of grace towards men there is some reference to the revelation made to Abraham. At each great revival of spiritual life among God's people, at each turning-point in their history, there is a fresh taking hold of the covenant made with Abraham, and of the promises given to him and to his seed.

When Israel cried to God from the iron furnace of Egypt, "God heard their groaning, and God remembered His covenant with Abraham, with Isaac, and with Jacob. And God saw the children of Israel, and God took knowledge of them." His first word concerning Himself to Moses at the bush was: "I am the God of thy father, the God of Abraham, the God of Isaac, and the God of Jacob. . . . Thus shalt thou say unto the children of Israel, Jehovah, the God of your fathers, the God of Abraham, the God of Isaac, and the God of Jacob, hath sent me unto you; this is my name for ever, and this is my memorial unto all generations." [1]   It is here that Moses finds his chief argument when pleading for the people in the crisis brought about by their sin beneath the mountain of the law: "Remember Abraham, Isaac, and Israel, Thy servants, to whom Thou swarest by Thine own self. . . . And the Lord repented of the evil which He said He would do unto His people." [2]   So in the parting charge of Joshua to the children of Israel in Canaan; so in the religious movements under Jehoshaphat and Hezekiah; [3] so repeatedly in the words of psalmists and prophets, whether speaking to Israel in their own land or to Israel in the exile. [4]

The same thing comes out strikingly in connection with the new beginnings of national and religious life after the return from Babylon under Ezra and Nehemiah. Listen to the magnificent doxology in which the feelings of the time found expression: "Stand up and bless the Lord your God from everlasting to everlasting: and blessed be Thy glorious name, which is exalted above all blessing and praise. . . . Thou

---

wonder, gratitude, and joy, to that morning dawn when 'the God of glory appeared unto our father Abraham, when he was in Mesopotamia, before he dwelt in Haran.'" Principal Brown of Aberdeen, *Romans*, ed. 1883, p. 42.

[1] Ex. ii. 23; iii. 6, 15.   [2] Ex. xxxii. 13 f.

[3] 2 Chron. xx. 7; xxx. 6.   [4] Ps. xlvii. 9, 10; cv. 6-10, 42.

art the Lord the God who didst choose Abram and broughtest him forth out of Ur of the Chaldees, and gavest him the name of Abraham ; and foundest his heart faithful before Thee, and madest a covenant with him . . . and hast performed Thy words, for Thou art righteous." [1] Pass on to the final stage of revelation ; the very first sentence of the first Gospel takes us back to Abraham. This is the life of " His seed, which is Christ." " The Book of the generations of Jesus Christ, the son of David, the son of Abraham." [2]

When the birth of the Saviour was first announced to those who " waited for the consolation of Israel," and the Spirit gave them utterance, they saw and said that this was the performance of the covenant made with Abraham, the fulfilment of the " good tidings preached beforehand " unto him. " My soul doth magnify the Lord," Mary says, " and my spirit hath rejoiced in God my Saviour. . . . He hath holpen Israel His servant, that He might remember mercy (as He spake unto our fathers) toward Abraham and his seed for ever." [3]

" Zacharias was filled with the Holy Ghost, and prophesied, saying, Blessed be the Lord, the God of Israel; for He hath visited and wrought redemption for His people . . . to remember His holy covenant, the oath which He sware unto Abraham our father, to grant unto us that we, being delivered out of the hand of our enemies, should serve Him without fear in holiness and righteousness before Him all our days . . . to give knowledge of salvation unto His people in the remission of their sins." [4]

So, too, when the Holy Ghost had come in power upon the apostles at Pentecost, it is noteworthy how often they turn in their first public addresses to Abraham and the Church in his house. As the master builders of the Church of God, under the New Testament dispensation, they seem carried back over all the temporary peculiarities of the Sinaitic legislation to build afresh on the broad lines of the covenant of grace with Abraham and with his seed for ever. Listen to Peter on the day of Pentecost speaking to repentant children of Abraham,

---

[1] Neh. ix. 5, 7 f.   [2] Matt. i. 1 ; Gal. iii. 16.
[3] Luke i. 46 f., 54.   [4] Luke i. 67 f., 72-77.

"devout men, Jews and proselytes. Repent ye and be baptized every one of you in the name of Jesus Christ, unto the remission of your sins; and ye shall receive the gift of the Holy Ghost. For to you is the promise, and to your children, and to all that are afar off, even as many as the Lord our God shall call unto Him."[1] Listen to the same apostle in the temple after the healing of the lame man: "The God of Abraham, the God of our fathers, hath glorified His Servant Jesus. . . . Ye are the sons of the covenant which God made with your fathers (τῆς διαθήκης ἧς διέθετο ὁ Θεὸς πρὸς τοὺς πατέρας ὑμῶν), saying unto Abraham, ʻAnd in thy seed shall all the families of the earth be blessed.' Unto you first God, having raised up His Servant, sent Him to bless you in turning away every one of you from your iniquities."[2] Hear Stephen, "full of the Holy Ghost," speaking before the Sanhedrin: "Men, brethren, and fathers, hearken. The God of glory appeared unto our father Abraham, when he was in Mesopotamia before he dwelt in Haran. . . . And He gave him the covenant of circumcision; and so Abraham begat Isaac, and circumcised him the eighth day."[3] Listen to Paul in his first recorded address to Jews and proselytes in the synagogue of Antioch in Pisidia: "Brethren, children of the stock of Abraham, and those among you that fear God, to us is the word of this salvation sent forth. . . . And we bring you good tidings (εὐαγγελιζόμεθα τὴν πρὸς τοὺς πατέρας ἐπαγγελίαν γενομένην, we preach unto you the Gospel) of the promise made unto the fathers, how that God hath fulfilled the same unto us their children in that He raised up Jesus. . . . Be it known unto you, therefore, brethren, that through this Man is proclaimed unto you remission of sins; and by Him, every one that believeth is justified from all things, from which ye could not be justified by the law of Moses."[4]

Let us, too, go back for a little, as the apostles loved to do, to that great "beginning of the Gospel of Jesus Christ," when

---

[1] Acts ii. 38 f. Comp. the words of another apostle: "That upon the Gentiles might come the blessing of Abraham in Christ Jesus, that we might receive the promise of the Spirit through faith," Gal. iii. 14.
[2] Acts iii. 13, 25 f.   [3] Acts vii. 2, 8.
[4] Acts xiii. 26, 32 f., 38 f.

"your father Abraham," as the Lord said to the Jews, "rejoiced to see my day; and he saw it, and was glad."[1]

Of course with respect alike to the Gospel, the covenant, and the Church of God in Abraham's time, we must expect to find all the three reduced, so to speak, to their first elements. The foundation truths stand out alone in their massive strength. The picture is sketched on the canvas of Scripture in grand and simple outlines, with a glow of noble colouring over all. We see little or nothing of the details. These were to be filled in afterwards.

What was "the Gospel," of which the apostle speaks in Gal. iii. 8, which was "preached beforehand unto Abraham," or in other words—for the two things are evidently equivalent —what was "the blessing of Abraham" spoken of in ver. 14 of the same chapter, which afterwards "came upon the Gentiles in Christ Jesus"? Let us consider, first, what this Gospel or blessing was; and secondly, how was it received by Abraham?

1st. The Scripture, foreseeing that God would justify the Gentiles (τὰ ἔθνη) by faith, preached the Gospel beforehand unto Abraham, saying: "In thee shall all the nations (τὰ ἔθνη, the Gentiles) be blessed." The last clause plainly refers to those passages in Genesis, from the twelfth to the twenty-second chapter, in which "the blessing of Abraham" is spoken of. Turning to these, and putting together what they say, we find that it amounts to this.

1. First and most prominent of all, emphatically repeated in different forms from the earliest to the latest recorded revelation to Abraham, comes the promise of God's blessing to him and his. "Jehovah said to Abraham, I will bless thee, and make thy name great, and be thou a blessing; and I will bless them that bless thee, and him that curseth thee will I curse: and in thee shall all families of the earth be blessed."[2]

Observe how emphatic and comprehensive the wording of the promise is here. "It passes from the simple futures through the cohortative to the imperative as the strongest

<hr>

[1] John viii. 56.   [2] Gen. xii. 2 f.

expression of the gracious will of God. Everything is summed
up in וֶהְיֵה בְּרָכָה ; one who is blessed of God and blessed of
men, a receiver of blessing and a dispenser of it for all other
men. . . . The promise rises higher still in ver. 3 : ' I will
bless those that bless thee, and him that insulteth thee (*dich
schmähet*) will I curse.' The blessing shall not be merely
an external or alien possession (*ein fremdes Eigenthum*), which
passes through the hands of Abram to others; it shall be
so united with his person that blessing and curse for men
depend henceforth upon the position which they take up
towards Abram." [1]

This was the first and fundamental charter of the children
of Abraham. These words of promise " lie at the foundation
of the whole after history : step by step their fulness of
meaning came to be unrolled,—first, in the successive dis-
closures made to Abraham himself; next, in the long experience of his posterity. The wealth of blessing which lay
folded up in this germ took more than two thousand years to
ripen into fruit. But from the very first God left it in no
doubt that, when the fruit of that chosen vine should at last
be ripe, it should be for all nations." [2] The nature of the
blessing is further shown in the central passage (chap. xvii.),
by its being put in this form : " I will establish my covenant
between me and thee, and thy seed after thee throughout their
generations for an everlasting covenant, to be a God unto thee
and to thy seed after thee." The last recorded revelation to
Abraham repeats the assurance given in the first, but with

---

[1] Delitzsch, *Commentar über die Genesis*, 3te Ausg. S. 348. Delitzsch, Dillmann,
and some other good exegetes prefer the reflexive rendering in the last clause of
ver. 3 : "bless themselves," as being the proper force of the Niphal וּנִבְרְכוּ.
The R. V. gives only the passive rendering in Gen. xii. 3, but puts the
reflexive in the margin at xxii. 18. The rendering of the A. V. and R. V. (text)
is the translation of the LXX. (cf. Rom. iv. 13, 16) and Vulgate, and seems on
the whole preferable. As regards meaning there is no substantial difference.
"All families of the earth shall bless themselves in thee," would mean "shall
wish for themselves the blessedness which Abram possesses, shall recognise that
as the only true blessedness, and use Abram's name as a formula and synonym
for blessing." Dillmann, *Genesis*, 4te Ausg. S. 208 ; comp. Zech. viii. 13 : "As
ye were a curse among the nations, O house of Judah and house of Israel, so
will I save you, and ye shall be a blessing."

[2] Dykes, *Abraham, the Friend of God*, 3rd ed. p. 33.

additional solemnity, and with the significant change that, with regard to the future development of the blessing, Abraham's "seed" takes the place of himself.[1] "By myself have I sworn, saith the Lord . . . that in blessing I will bless thee . . . and in thy seed shall all the nations of the earth be blessed; because thou hast obeyed my voice."[2]

Such was the first part of the good news declared to Abraham. It was summed up in a promise from God, sealed by a special sign, and confirmed with an oath, that God would bless him indeed, that He would be his God for ever and the God of his seed, and that this blessing was to spread in the future from him and his seed to all the nations of the earth.[3]

2. A promise was given to Abraham that his seed should be like the stars of heaven or the sand by the sea-shore for multitude, that he should be "a father of many nations."[4]

3. A promise was made by God to Abraham : "I will give unto thee and to thy seed after thee the land of thy sojournings, all the land of Canaan for an everlasting possession; and I will be their God."[5]

This promise was significantly worded, expressed in such a way as to invite inquiry into the full meaning of it. "God

---

[1] Cf. Robson, *The Bible; its Revelation, Inspiration, and Evidence*, Lond. 1883, p. 44.

[2] Gen. xxii. Comp. Rainy, *Delivery and Development of Doctrine*, p. 48 f.

[3] I have not thought it necessary, in citing the passages in Genesis which bear upon the history of Abraham, to refer to the different views held by competent scholars regarding the materials from which the book is framed, and the method of its composition. Questions as to the sources from which the history in Genesis is drawn, and as to the different threads of narrative which may be woven together in it, are interesting and important in their own place. But they are quite distinct from and independent of the question of the inspiration and Divine authority of the book as it comes to us now. Comp. Bannerman, *Inspiration of the Holy Scriptures*, p. 536 f. It would be altogether foreign to my present purpose to enter here on the field of critical inquiry as to the authorship and editing of the Pentateuch. I take the narrative in its present form as a reliable record of the facts of Divine revelation with which I have to do in the first portion of these lectures. For a clear and temperate statement in popular form of the results arrived at by the more sober section of recent Biblical critics as regards the sources of Genesis, see Dods, *Genesis*, Edin. 1882, Introd. pp. viii.–xiv.

[4] Gen. xiii. 16 ; xv. 5 ; xvii. 4 f. ; xxii. 17.

[5] Gen. xvii. 8.

gave him," Stephen says in his speech before the Sanhedrin, adverting to this very point, "*none* inheritance in the land, no, not so much as to set his foot on: yet He promised that He would give it to *him* in possession, and to his seed after him;" as if he would say: surely there is something more here than lies on the surface. What does this Scripture *see?* To what does it look?[1]

These were the three main parts of "the blessing of Abraham," "the Gospel preached beforehand unto him." We can hardly fail to notice how large a place in it is filled by what is purely spiritual. We see this at once as regards the deep and broad foundation of the whole,—the emphatic, all-embracing assurance that God would bless him indeed, that He would be his God and the God of his seed in an everlasting covenant, and that this blessing should spread through his seed to all nations. But we have distinct Scripture authority

---

[1] Acts vii. 5. It has often been pointed out that in many respects Stephen seemed to live again in Paul. This is one illustration of it. Their methods of interpreting the significance of Old Testament history are closely akin. The striking metaphor used by the apostle in Gal. iii. 8 (προϊδοῦσα δὲ ἡ·γραφὴ . . . προευηγγελίσατο τῷ 'Αβραάμ) may have been drawn from the phraseology of the Jewish schools of his day; but it is quite in accordance with the manner and spirit of Stephen's speech. He felt that God's dealings with Abraham, the promises given, the form of the covenant, the precise language in which it was recorded, were all moulded and fixed by a Divine foresight of the way in which, hundreds of years afterwards, salvation should be revealed to the Gentiles. It was no dead Scripture this in which he read these things, but the living word of God, instinct throughout with His wisdom, and grace, and foreknowledge. The apostle embodies his feeling in this powerful figure. He personifies the Scripture—"The Scripture, foreseeing that God would justify the Gentiles by faith, preached the Gospel beforehand unto Abraham, saying: 'In thee shall all the nations be blessed.'" Some of the rabbinical teachers of the better class, after Paul's time, although far inferior to the apostle in clearness of insight, had something of the same feeling, and expressed it in a similar phrase. After citing some weighty verse they say: מָה רָאָה הַכָּתוּב, "What did the Scripture see?" They felt that the inspired word was looking at something beyond what might be seen at the first glance. They sought to look with it, and to see what it saw. Gamaliel may have spoken so when Saul of Tarsus sat as an eager listener at his feet in Jerusalem. Schöttgen remarks on the phrase: "Formula Judæis admodum solennis est. . . . Proferemus ex innumeris quædam exempla. *Sifra*, fol. 186, 2. מה ראה הכתוב Quidnam cogitavit Scriptura ut inter festa præcipua, Paschatis scil. et Pentecostes, novum annum et festum expiationis interponeret?" *Horæ Hebraicæ et Talmudicæ*, Dresd. et Lipsiæ, 1733, i. p. 732.

for saying that there was a spiritual element also in the other two parts of the blessing, and that this was apprehended in some measure even by Abraham himself.

What were the other two parts ? They were the promise of a countless seed, and the promise of a future inheritance which should be really *his* as well as theirs, and which was to be an everlasting possession. Look at the inspired commentary on both of these things in the fourth chapter of Romans. The new name " Abraham," " the father of a multitude," was given to the patriarch in connection with the promise of a countless seed, "a multitude of nations," and of an everlasting inheritance to him and them, and in connection with the ordinance of circumcision.[1] Now, that ordinance, the apostle tells us, was " a sign and seal of the righteousness of the faith which he had while he was in uncircumcision, that he might be the father of all them that believe, though they be in uncircumcision,"—that is to say, not Hebrews at all, not of the natural seed of Abraham. " For the promise that he should be heir of the world"—this is the apostle's interpretation of the inheritance ; not restricting it to Canaan, which was only an earnest or pledge of something more and higher—" was not to Abraham or to his seed through the law, but through the righteousness of faith. . . . For this cause it is of faith that it may be according to grace, to the end that the promise may be sure to all the seed ; not to that only which is of the law, but to that also which is of the faith of Abraham, who is the father of us all, as it is written, ' A father of many nations have I made thee.' " [2]

As to the insight of the patriarch himself into the meaning of the promised inheritance, look at the eleventh chapter of Hebrews: " By faith Abraham became a sojourner in the land of promise, as in a land not his own, dwelling in tents with Isaac and Jacob, the heirs with him of the same promise ; for he looked for the city which hath foundations, whose builder and maker is God. . . . These all died in faith, not having received the promises, but having seen them and greeted them from afar, and having confessed that they were strangers and

---

[1] Gen. xvii. 4–8.
[2] Rom. iv. 11–16. Comp. Candlish, *Genesis*, Edin., 2nd ed. i. pp. 271–276.

pilgrims on the earth ; . . . wherefore God is not ashamed of
them to be called their God, for He hath prepared for them
a city." [1]

In further confirmation of this, it may be noted that in the
passages in Genesis which speak of the seed and the inheritance, the temporal elements in the blessing are so joined with
the spiritual as to show that the former were of subordinate
value. Twice over, with special solemnity the promises of
the seed and of the land are given and sealed by sacrifice and
sacrament ; and on both occasions they are introduced by
words from God specially fitted to raise the thoughts of
Abraham to the higher and spiritual blessing. In the fifteenth
chapter the vision opens with the voice of Jehovah, saying :
" Fear not, Abram ; I am thy shield ; and thy reward shall
be exceeding great." [2]   Then comes the promise of an
innumerable seed, and of the land which *he* should inherit,
although he is presently told that even his *seed* shall not
receive it for more than four hundred years. " And," we read,
" Abram *believed in Jehovah ;* and He counted it to him for
righteousness." That is the connection of the pregnant
sentence which is taken up and dwelt on by the Apostle Paul
in his two great doctrinal Epistles, as conveying the very sum
and substance of the Gospel.

[1] Heb. xi. 9–16. Even the Jewish Rabbis saw immortality and the resurrection of the dead in the promise made to Abraham touching the land of Canaan.
Comp. Fairbairn, *Typology*, 6th ed. i. p. 399 f. "The mere land of Canaan was
never in itself all that was understood either by those to whom it was promised
or by God who promised it, when it was named as Israel's heritage. The
patriarchs and people certainly looked to the possession of the land, but the
idea they attached to it or the light in which they regarded it was that of a
settled place of abode with God, where He would be fully present, and where
they would find repose in His fellowship. All those religious ideas, dimly
perhaps, yet in longing and imagination, clustered about it, which we now
attach to the heavenly world. The possession of the land, though an essential
part of Israel's happiness and a true part of its inheritance from God, and neither
merely a symbol of spiritual blessings present nor a type of spiritual blessings to
come, always depended on the spiritual relations of Israel to God, and its meaning lay in its being a fitting sphere for those in fellowship with God." Davidson,
Hebrews, p. 99. Comp. Schürer, *Hist. of Jewish People*, Edin. 1885, ii. p. 13.

[2] Gen. xv. 1. The marginal rendering of the R. V. seems preferable here.
Abram's answer (ver. 2) shows that he understood the promise to refer to a
definite reward to be given him by the Lord. So Dillmann, Delitzsch, and most
interpreters.

The seventeenth chapter, again, begins: "And Jehovah appeared to Abram, and said unto him, I am God Almighty, walk before me, and be thou perfect." Then come the change of name, and the reason for it; then the great central promise: "I will establish my covenant between me and thee, and thy seed after thee, throughout their generations for an everlasting covenant, to be a God unto thee, and to thy seed after thee." Then, and not till then, the promise is renewed, to *him* and to his seed, of the land "for an everlasting possession; and" (this is the conclusion of all) "I will be their God."[1]

We gather, in short, from the whole narrative that "the Gospel preached beforehand unto Abraham" carried with it—as the Gospel always has done—"a promise of the life that now is," as well as of "the life which is to come." It included both temporal and spiritual blessings. But the former, although more prominent than in New Testament times, were put, as we have now seen, in the second place, not in the first. They did not form the great or essential part of "the blessing of Abraham," with which all the nations of the earth should be blessed.

2nd. Consider how the blessing was received by Abraham.

Look at the apostle's discussion of this very point in the fourth chapter of Romans and the third of Galatians.

He starts in both cases from that memorable verse: "Abraham believed God, and it was reckoned unto him for righteousness;"[2] and his conclusion is: "It was not written for his sake alone that it was reckoned unto him, but for our sake also, unto whom it shall be reckoned, who believe on Him that raised Jesus our Lord from the dead, who was delivered up for our trespasses, and was raised for our justification."[3] In other words: These events, these dealings of

---

[1] Gen. xvii. 1–8.

[2] Rom. iv. 3; Gal. iii. 6. The apostle follows the LXX.: Καὶ ἐπίστευσεν Ἀβραμ τῷ Θεῷ καὶ ἐλογίσθη αὐτῷ εἰς δικαιοσύνην. In the Hebrew of Gen. xv. 6 we read: "And he believed in Jehovah, and He counted it to him (for) righteousness," וְהֶאֱמִן בַּיהוָה וַיַּחְשְׁבֶהָ לּוֹ צְדָקָה The same phrase is used in reference to Phinehas in Ps. cvi. 31 with the insertion of the preposition לְ before צְדָקָה.

[3] Rom. iv. 23 f.

God with Abraham, are not put on record in Scripture simply
as so many historical facts, but as embodying great moral and
spiritual principles, as showing God's way of salvation by
faith, which has been in substance one and the same in all
ages.   It is traced as with a sunbeam in the record of
Abraham's history.   All the circumstances in the narrative
were Divinely ordered for this end.   Let no Jew or Jewish
Christian think within himself: "We have Abraham to our
father; and what the Scripture says of his faith and blessing
holds only of the circumcised."   Nay, look a little more
closely,—*when* was it that the Gospel was preached and the
promises were given to Abraham?   It was when he was yet
uncircumcised, when he was on the same level with the
Gentiles in that matter.   Therefore it is plain that these
blessings can have no necessary connection with the ordinance of circumcision.   Abraham was a justified man, according
to the Scriptures, years before he received it.   "The sign of
circumcision" was given to him and his as "a seal" or
confirming token of the (justifying) righteousness, the
righteousness by faith which he had *before* he was circumcised;[1] "in order that," as it has been well put, "he might
stand forth to every age as the parent-believer, the model
man of justification by faith, after whose type, as the first
public example of it, all were to be moulded, whether
Jew or Gentile, who should hereafter believe to life everlasting."[2]

In the third chapter of the Epistle to the Galatians, Paul
adduces the case of Abraham for the same general purpose.
These warm-hearted but unstable Christians in Galatia were
in great danger of going off Gospel ground, and so losing
Gospel blessings.   Note the apostle's clear and powerful
reasonings with them.   Did they receive the Spirit at their
conversion in connection with a message about salvation by
works or by *faith?*   Should they not go on as they had
begun in the Christian life?   Let them consider the facts
before their own eyes now.   The power of the Spirit of God
was still manifest among them in Christ-like lives, in special
gifts and miracles.   Were these found in connection with a

[1] Rom. iv. 3-12.   [2] Principal Brown, *Romans*, Edin. 1883, p. 41.

Gospel of works and legal righteousness, or in connection with the message of salvation by faith in Christ crucified and risen? They all knew that it was where the old Gospel was preached and received that the old power was seen. God was supplying the Spirit still, just as He had given the Spirit among them at the first. Did not these facts show that the Gospel which Paul preached among them then was the true Gospel of Christ, from which there was great danger lest they should now be led away by Judaizing teachers to a different Gospel, which was not really another, which was no good tidings of the grace of God in Christ at all?

Nay, let them go back to the beginning of the Gospel, not in their experience merely, but in the earliest times of God's revelation of His grace to sinful men. Did not Abraham believe God, and it was reckoned unto him for righteousness? "Know ye, therefore, that they which be of faith, the same are sons of Abraham. And the Scripture, foreseeing that God would justify the Gentiles by faith, preached the Gospel beforehand unto Abraham, saying, In thee shall all the nations be blessed. So then they which be of faith are blessed with the faithful Abraham." If you would inherit his blessing, imitate his faith. The work of Christ in redeeming His people from the curse of the law was for this very end, "that upon the Gentiles might come the blessing of Abraham in Christ Jesus, that we (Jews and Gentiles alike) might receive the promise of the Spirit through faith." [1]

What, then, was the faith of Abraham? What was its nature, and of what did it lay hold?

"Abraham," says the apostle, quoting from the Greek version of the Old Testament, as he wrote to a Greek-speaking Church,—"Abraham believed God, and it" (namely, his faith in God) "was reckoned unto him for righteousness ($\epsilon\lambda o\gamma i\sigma\theta\eta$ $a\dot{v}\tau\hat{\omega}$ $\epsilon i\varsigma$ $\delta\iota\kappa a\iota o\sigma\acute{v}\nu\eta\nu$)." Not that we are to suppose the act of believing was a substitute for complete obedience; that would be to make a "work" of it, and a ground of merit. It would be to run counter to the whole scope of the apostle's argument in the passage, and is not in the least required by the words he uses.

[1] Gal. iii. 1-9, 13 f.

Two interpretations of the phrase ἐλογίσθη αὐτῷ εἰς δικαιοσύνην are possible and natural:—

(1) We may take it as an instance of the " accusative of
the predicate," as in Rom. ii. 26 : " Shall not his uncircumcision be reckoned for circumcision ? " (εἰς περιτομὴν λογισ-
θήσεται); shall it not be counted as being such virtually
and in effect ? [1]   In that case the statement of the apostle is
that Abraham's faith in Jehovah, his whole attitude of reliance
on God as now revealing Himself to him in grace, was
reckoned unto him as righteousness, so that he himself in this
crucial instance of his real relation to Jehovah was accepted
and treated as righteous.[2]

Or (2)—and this interpretation corresponds perhaps somewhat more closely with the precise course of the apostle's
argument—we may take the phrase εἰς δικαιοσύνην as an
instance of the " accusative of destination or purpose."   The
meaning will then be, not that Abraham's faith was reckoned
" as righteousness," or " in place of righteousness," but " unto
righteousness," with a view to righteousness, to his being
received and accounted as righteous with God.   The apostle
uses a similar phrase in the tenth chapter of the Epistle to the
Romans : " With the heart man believeth unto righteousness "
(εἰς δικαιοσύνην), i.e. in order to his becoming righteous, so as
to obtain righteousness with God.[3]

How Abraham's faith came to have this effect, to be the fit
instrument for this end, we see more clearly when we consider its nature and object.   " Abraham believed in Jehovah,"
we read in Genesis, " and He counted it to him for righteousness."   In other words, Abraham received Jehovah's testimony
to him, and trusted Jehovah Himself for more than He had
yet said.   He received the word of promise, and passed on

---

[1] Comp. Winer-Moulton, *Grammar of N. T. Greek*, 3rd ed. p. 285 f.   Bp.
O'Brien, *Nature and Effects of Faith*, 2nd ed. p. 453 f.

[2] So Luther takes it : " Quomodo igitur acquisivit justitiam ?   Hoc solo modo,
quod Deus loquitur, et Abraham loquenti Deo credit.   Accedit autem Spiritus
Sanctus, testis fide dignus, hoc ipsum credere, seu hanc ipsam fidem esse justitiam, seu imputari ab ipso Deo pro justitia et haberi pro justitia," *In Genes.*
xv. 6.   Comp. Candlish, *Genesis*, 2nd ed. i. pp. 235–240.

[3] Comp. Winer-Moulton, 3rd ed. p. 495 f.   Hodge, *Romans*, ed. 1864, pp.
108–111.   Cunningham, *Hist. Theol.* ii. p. 49.

from it to Him who spake it, resting himself upon Him. Now, that is just the sum and substance of saving faith still.

"Abraham believed in the Lord;" he trusted in Him as his shield and portion; he believed that from Him his reward would be exceeding great; he received the Lord as He offered Himself to him in covenant to be his God; he believed in His blessing as covering everything needed by him and his for life and death, for this world and for the world to come. Abraham did, in substance and reality, just what we do now, when, to use the familiar words in which our children learn what saving faith is, "we receive and rest upon the Lord Jesus Christ alone for salvation as He is offered to us in the Gospel." [1] And so his faith in God was "reckoned to him"—God reckoned it to him—"unto righteousness," so that he received a righteousness from God, and entered on the blessedness of a man justified, forgiven, accepted, and brought into fellowship with God. Faith was the hand by which Abraham laid hold of God Himself to be the Lord his shield and portion, in one word, to be "his God," according to His own promise, "in an everlasting covenant."

"We do not say," as Calvin puts it, "that Abraham was justified because he laid hold of the one little word concerning his having a seed, but because he embraced God as his Father. Nor, indeed, does faith justify us for any other reason save that it reconciles us to God; nor is this brought about by any merit in the faith itself, but by our thus receiving the grace offered to us in the promises of God, so that we become assured of God's love toward us as His children, and obtain a sure hope of eternal life." [2]

"The LXX.," says a later interpreter, "translate here καὶ ἐπίστευσεν Ἄβραμ τῷ θεῷ. It would have answered better to have used here, and in like passages, one of the New Testament phrases, πιστεύειν εἰς τὸν θεόν, or ἐπὶ τὸν θεόν, or ἐπὶ τῷ θεῷ, or ἐν τῷ θεῷ. For האמין בה denotes faith, not as *assensus*, but as it were, in accordance with its inmost perfected nature (gleich

---

[1] Westminster Shorter Catechism, Qu. 86.

[2] Calvin, *Comment. in Gen.* xv. 6. Comp. Bp. O'Brien, *Nature and Effects of Faith*, 2nd ed. pp. 119 ff., 441-456. Buchanan, *Doctrine of Justification*, p. 379 f.

seinem innersten vollendeten Wesen nach), as *fiducia* or
acquiescentia. It is not simply said that Abram believed
the testimony of Him who promised, but that he cast himself
upon the person of Him who promised, and rested trustfully
on Him. . . . 'Credere in Deum,' Augustine says, in reference to the ביהוה of our text, 'est credendo amare, credendo
in eum ire, credendo ei adhærere et ejus membris incorporari.
Per hanc fidem justificatur impius, ut deinde ipsa fides incipiat
per dilectionem operari.'" [1]

Thus it was that Abraham received the Gospel, the good
tidings of God's grace made known to him. Thus it was
that "he believed in the Lord," so revealing Himself to him,
and "his faith was reckoned unto him for righteousness."
And so likewise in all ages "they which be of faith are
blessed with the faithful Abraham." [2] Consider him now for
a little as a believer, living in right relation to the good news
received. We see in his history—as will be pointed out in
more detail presently—how the Church of God was set up
as a separate fellowship on earth, in the world but not of it.
We may see in his own personal life and character what the
members of that fellowship ought to be, what manner of
persons really receive the blessing of Abraham, and what it
makes them in all holy living and godliness.

The whole character of Abraham as a religious man might
be summed up in two words: faith and obedience. We have
in his life, as recorded in Scripture, true religion reduced
to its simplest elements, faith in the living God as a God
of redemption, and obedience to Him by His grace, and
according to the light which He gives.[3] Abraham believed
in the Lord as the great Living One, living and seeing, the

---

[1] Delitzsch, *Genesis*, 3te Ausg. S. 368 f. Comp. Fairbairn, *Typol.* i. p. 360 f.
6th ed.

[2] Gal. iii. 9.

[3] Comp. Peter's words to Cornelius : "In every nation he that feareth God
and worketh righteousness is acceptable to Him," Acts x. 35 ; and the conclusion of Ecclesiastes : "Fear God, and keep His commandments ; for this is
the whole duty of man." It is to be remembered in both cases that "the fear
of God," in the Old Testament sense, implied faith in Him as revealed. It was
"the fear of the Lord, wherein is strong confidence, and His children have a
place of refuge," Prov. xiv. 26.

God of heaven and earth, the Almighty, the Most High, the Everlasting God;[1] One who was as real a Person as he himself, who spoke to him, and with whom he could speak as a man with his friend; One who was always to be trusted, and loved, and worshipped, and loyally obeyed. It was this faith that gave him that dignity and freedom which so impress us in the narrative of his life. He moves before us there as a man walking in the presence and before the face of the Almighty God,[2] fearing Him only, trusting Him absolutely, knowing with whom he walked, although not knowing the path, knowing whom he trusted, although not seeing how His words should have their fulfilment.[3]

We see in Abraham noble features of character in his relations to others. He proves himself disinterested, free-handed, courageous, faithful to friends and allies. But all these characteristics had their roots in his faith in God. Because of this he sat loose to earthly things, and let Lot choose. With God for his shield, he ventured himself with his little band against the four eastern kings and their host when flushed with victory. With his reward in store with

---

[1] Gen. xiv. 22; xvi. 13 f.; xvii. 1; xxi. 33; xxii. 14; xxiv. 3, 7. Comp. Dykes' note on the Divine names in Genesis, *Abraham, the Friend of God*, 3rd ed. pp. 334-338.

[2] Gen. xvii. 1.

[3] Physical science in our time has been teaching us many wonderful lessons concerning the greatness and wisdom, the eternal power and Godhead of Him whom we profess to worship. There are other lessons as to the greatness of God, and as to the spirit of reverence and faith in which we ought to serve Him, which form a weighty part of the contribution offered by the Old Testament Church to the religion of the present day. "We have great cause to seek the conversion of the Jews," a Scottish theologian of the 17th century wrote, in reference to the increase of light and blessing among the Gentiles when Israel shall be gathered in; "surely we shall be much the better of them," Geo. Gillespie, *Miscell. Quest.* c. x. Certainly we have great need in the religious life of our time of not a few elements of strength and stedfastness which we see in the spiritual history of Abraham, and of those in the Hebrew Church in after days, who followed most closely in his footsteps. To use the words of a distinguished living interpreter of the Old Testament Scriptures: "There is another strife beginning, and we need Israel's — that is, God's champion's help. . . . God grant that before the conflict rages fiercely, the Christian may learn to read the New Testament more in the light of the Old, and the Israelite the Old Testament more in that of the New." Dr. T. K. Cheyne, "The Jews and the Gospel," in *Expositor*, 3rd series, i. p. 417. Comp. Rainy, *Delivery and Development of Christian Doctrine*, Edin. 1874, p. 68 f.

God, he could refuse the spoil, trusting his Divine Friend, and waiting His time to give. His fearlessness and freedom before men arose from this, that he lived in the fear of God, in trustful childlike reverence before Him, as His willing servant in all things.[1]

Wherever Abraham has a direct word of God to obey, he is always true to it and strong. He is weak, as in Egypt and Gerar, when he has no direct word to guide him, and goes on, without seeking counsel of the Lord, in ways of his own devising.[2] But these are exceptional instances. In his life as a whole, the obedience of faith is not less striking than the faith itself. It was a faith which approved itself by works; and " by works was the faith made," and shown to be, " perfect." Hence St. James finds in Abraham's history as fitting illustrations for his main purpose as St. Paul does for his. " Was not Abraham our father justified by works, in that he offered up Isaac his son upon the altar? Thou seest that faith wrought with his works, and by works was the faith made perfect; and the Scripture was fulfilled which saith: ' And Abraham believed God, and it was reckoned unto him for righteousness;' and he was called ' the friend of God.' "[3]

Abraham thus stands out in the inspired history as the great Old Testament example of true and fruitful faith, as the father of all who thereafter should believe in God. His figure seems at first to fill the whole foreground of the picture; but it is worth noting how the same spirit

---

[1] Comp. a fine passage in Ewald on the fear of God as a high ennobling power. " The Greek has no such short word with the same distinct idea. Islamism leaves so little to moral freedom and spontaneity that it calls religion ' guidance.' . . . The Hebrew expressed it by ' the fear of Jahveh,' or more fully, ' the knowledge and the fear of Jahveh.' What this knowledge is, whether scanty or abundant, whether more or less clear and reliable, depends, according to biblical teaching, upon obedience in the fear of God to what is known as God's will. Indeed, all true religion essentially consists in continual and anxious attention to all real knowledge of God's will, with a view to ordering the life more perfectly and happily in conformity to it. Abraham is the highest example of this in the Old Testament." Ewald, *Revelation; its Nature and Record*, E. Tr., Edin. 1884, pp. 30–34.

[2] Comp. Dykes, p. 76.

[3] Jas. ii. 21–23. Comp. Candlish, *Genesis*, 2nd ed. i. pp. 369–371.

of faith and obedience is seen, if we look more closely, in her who stands beside him, and was heir with him of the same promises. "Look unto Abraham your father," the evangelical prophet says to those in Israel, "who feared the Lord, and obeyed the voice of His servant," and "followed after righteousness and sought the Lord;" "look unto Abraham your father, and unto Sarah that bare you."[1] She, too, was strong in faith when she left her country and kindred and her father's house in days when life was full of hope and brightness at home, and followed her husband at God's word across the great river into the uncertain future and the unknown land. About her also there was something of the loftiness and dignity which we saw in Abraham. She was a princess in bearing and spirit, as well as in name. She had her faults, indeed, and infirmities, as in the matter of Hagar. But hers was a life of faith; and she is fitly joined with Abraham in the Epistle to the Hebrews in the list of those "who by faith wrought righteousness, obtained promises, out of weakness were made strong."

"By faith," Sarah too, when the call of God came, "obeyed to go out into a place which they were to receive for an inheritance; and she went out, not knowing whither she went. By faith she became a sojourner in the land of promise" all these long years with Abraham. "By faith Sarah herself received power to conceive seed when she was past age, since she counted Him faithful who had promised." And in faith she died, "not having received the promises, but having seen them, and greeted them from afar."[2] Her picture is set thus in the great gallery of Scripture, the first in the long array of believing women who are held up there for an example and pattern to the women of the Church in all time. "After this manner, in the old time," the Apostle Peter says, speaking of Sarah, "the holy women, who trusted in God, adorned themselves." After this manner they lived and died. Christian women in all the Churches of the dispersion, in Pontus, Galatia, Cappadocia, Asia, and Bithynia, had become daughters of Sarah as well as of Abraham,

[1] Isa. li. 1 f. [2] Heb. xi. 8-13.

although not of Hebrew descent, when first they joined themselves by faith to the Israel of God. The apostle bids them be like her in her spirit of reverent obedience on the one hand, and of believing courage on the other: "Even as Sarah obeyed Abraham, calling him lord, whose daughters ye are become (ἧς ἐγενήθητε τέκνα), doing well and not being afraid with any terror." [1]

---

[1] 1 Pet. iii. 5 f.   Comp. Dr. Candlish's lecture, "The Death and Burial of a Princess," *Genesis*, ii. pp. 216–240, and 22–37.

CHAPTER II.

THE COVENANT MADE WITH ABRAHAM.

NOT only was the Gospel preached beforehand unto Abraham, but God's covenant was established with him and his.

That weighty and pregnant word "covenant" meets us constantly, both in the Old Testament and the New, in connection with the name and position of Abraham in the history of revelation. Illustrations of this have already been given.[1] God's promises to Abraham are indeed scarcely ever adduced in the later Scriptures without some reference to the fact that they are covenant promises. They did not come to him in word only, but were made sure and doubly sure to his faith by a solemn engagement entered into by God, sealed by sacrifice, confirmed with an oath, and with a visible sign and seal of the covenant annexed to it. This aspect of God's dealings with Abraham is especially dwelt upon by the Apostle Paul in the latter part of the third chapter of Galatians, and by the author of the Epistle to the Hebrews in the end of his sixth chapter. Let us consider briefly the nature of the covenant, the parties with whom it was made, and the significance of the tokens or signs connected with it.

1st. It is plain that the nature of the blessing of Abraham determines the nature of the covenant. The great purpose of the latter was to guard the former, and to secure its full realization in the end. The covenant sealed and made sure the promises in connection with which it was established.

"A covenant," to use the words of an eminent living interpreter of the Old Testament, "is properly an agreement between two parties who bind themselves by certain conditions with the view of attaining some object. A covenant

---

[1] See above, pp. 3, 6–9.

may be between equals, as that between Abraham and
Abimelech, or between parties of whom one is superior to
the other, as that between Joshua and the Gibeonites.[1] The
covenant relation between God and men is of the latter class,
for God imposes the covenant. None the less both parties
lay themselves under obligations and contemplate an object
by the covenant. A covenant between God and men cannot
possibly have any other meaning than that He will be their
God and they His people.[2] . . . The general idea of a
covenant was that God was drawing near to the people in
grace. This general fact demanded, as its correlative, on the
part of the people the general attitude towards God of faith
and hope" (and, it might be added, of obedience, or willingness to obey. Comp. Gen. xviii. 19 ; xxii. 18 ; Ex. xix. 5–8 ;
xxiv. 3–8). "Within this general attitude the personal life
of the individual might be a very chequered one, full of
imperfections, and marked even by sins that were voluntary.
These were great evils which the covenant relation sought
more and more to overcome, but they did not involve suspen-
sion of this relation itself. Only unbelief like that in the
wilderness, or idolatry, had this consequence."[3]

---

[1] Gen. xxi. 32 ; Josh. ix. 6, 20.   [2] Heb. viii. 8–10.

[3] Davidson, *Hebrews*, Edin. 1882, p. 162 f. See the whole of the valuable
and suggestive "Note on the Two Covenants" (pp. 161–168). In one or two points
only I would be disposed to dissent from particular statements or expressions.
Thus, for instance, Prof. Davidson says (p. 162) : "The Epistle does not speak
of a covenant with Abraham, as the Pauline Epistles do (Gal. iii. 15, 17); it
knows of promises to Abraham (vi. 13, vii. 6) which the first covenant was
ineffectual to realize (xi. 39), which, however, are realized through the second
(ix. 15)." He adds in a note : "The promises made to Abraham do not refer to
either of the covenants, but to something lying beyond them both, to the
attaining of which both covenants are but means."

Now it is true that the Epistle does not use the word covenant to describe the
Divine engagement to Abraham, but it speaks of the engagement itself to the
same effect as the Pauline Epistles do. The very passage first cited by Prof.
Davidson—Heb. vi. 13–20—refers not so much to promises as to the solemn
transaction or engagement "wherein God, being minded to show more abundantly unto the heirs of the promise the immutability of His counsel, interposed
with an oath, that by two immutable things in which it is impossible for God
to lie we may have a strong encouragement." The fact on which the writer to the
Hebrews lays special stress here is the way in which the promises were established
and made sure to Abraham, "the oath for confirmation ;" in other words, what he
emphasizes is just the covenant with Abraham, as the Apostle Paul repeatedly

Now we have already seen[1] that the promises made to Abraham were primarily of a spiritual kind. It follows that the covenant must correspond in its essential nature to the promises which it made sure. If "the blessing of Abraham," as the apostle tells us, " has come upon the Gentiles in Christ

styles it in Gal. iii., when referring to the same passage in the patriarch's history. Similarly, in Luke i. 72 f., "God's holy covenant" and "the oath which He sware unto Abraham our father" are identified.

Further, this covenant is represented as one in which believers now have an interest. The "two immutable things" on which it rested—namely, the Promise and the Oath of God, or "God the Promiser and God the Surety, brought in by the Promiser," as Prof. Davidson well puts it, p. 127—were thus established "that we may have a strong encouragement, who have fled for refuge, to lay hold of the hope set before us." It does not seem fair to limit the promises to Abraham, contemplated in Heb. vi. 12-18 (as Prof. Davidson appears disposed to do, p. 126), to the one regarding a numerous seed in the literal sense ; whereas the promises with respect to which "God interposed with an oath" begin and end with the comprehensive assurance of Divine blessing in the fullest sense, and that this blessing should in Abraham's seed reach all the nations of the earth, Gen. xxii. 18 ; Gal. iii. 14 ; Heb. vi. 14. No doubt "the promises made to Abraham do not refer to" the special covenant made with Israel in the wilderness, "in the day when God took them by the hand to lead them forth out of the land of Egypt" (Heb. viii. 9) ; and, no doubt, the full "attainment" of that to which they refer is in the future even to Christians now. But the Apostle Paul distinctly teaches that the covenant with Abraham and his seed was the covenant of grace in Christ, revealed before to the patriarch and revealed anew in the Saviour, which the law and the legal covenant, coming four hundred and thirty years after, could not disannul nor introduce into it any new conditions (Gal. iii. 15-18). "The blessing of Abraham has come upon the Gentiles in Christ Jesus" (ver. 14). The covenant revealed in Him was a *new* covenant as compared with the Sinaitic one with its temporary elements which decayed, waxed old, and vanished (Heb. viii. 13). Yet in another aspect it was "old, and men had it from the beginning." It was the everlasting covenant of God's grace, through which all spiritual blessing had come to His people from the first (Heb. ix. 15 ; xiii. 20). The "Epistle to the Hebrews," Prof. Davidson says, "conceives religion, or the relation of God and His people, under the idea of a covenant. A covenant is a realized state of relation between God and men, in which He is their God and they His people (viii. 10). . . . And the object of the Epistle is to show that in Christianity this covenant state has come into existence, and exists truly and for ever" (p. 36). But this "realized state of relation between God and men" is just what is expressly comprehended in the central promise made by God to Abraham and established by His covenant with its sign and seal (Gen. xvii. 7 f.). And this is just the promise which, in the closing utterances of Revelation, sums up the final blessedness of all believers. "Behold, the tabernacle of God is with men ; and He will dwell with them, and they shall be His people, and God Himself shall be with them, and be their God" (Rev. xxi. 3).

[1] *Supra*, pp. 12-15.

Jesus," [1] the covenant must have some reference to Him in
whom the blessing is summed up, and of whom God said
afterwards by the lips of the evangelical prophet : " Behold
my servant whom I uphold, my chosen in whom my soul
delighteth . . . I will give Thee for a covenant of the people,
for a light of the Gentiles, that Thou mayest be my salvation
unto the end of the earth." [2]   The first and the last word of
grace from God to Abraham, as we saw before, was an all-
embracing one.   It comprehended all things that pertain unto
life and godliness : " I will bless thee, and be thou a blessing."
The central promise of all those guarded by the covenant was that
which is given in Gen. xvii. 7 : " I will establish my covenant
between me and thee, and thy seed after thee, throughout
their generations, for an everlasting covenant, to be a God unto
thee, and to thy seed after thee."   Now, that is the essential
promise of the covenant of grace. [3]   It sums up the fulness
of the blessing of the gospel of Christ.   As such it runs
through the whole of the Scriptures from the first book to
the last, appearing always afresh at every new stage in the
development of God's gracious redemptive purposes, very
often in direct connection with some reference, express or
implied, to the covenant.   This promise is repeated, for
example, in all the great cardinal passages with respect to
God's covenant of grace and peace in Isaiah, Jeremiah,
Ezekiel, and Hosea. [4]   It appears in special prominence in the

---

[1] Gal. iii. 14.   [2] Isa. xlii. 1, 6 ; xlix. 6–8.

[3] " Uno hoc verbo clare docemur spirituale hoc fuisse fœdus, non præsentis
tantum vitæ respectu sancitum, sed unde spem æternæ salutis conciperet
Abraham, et in cœlum usque evectus solidam perfectamque beatitudinem
apprehenderet. . . . Notemus ergo hoc esse præcipuum fœderis caput
quod se filiis Abrahæ Deum fore promittat Is qui viventium Deus est, non
mortuorum," Calvin, In Genes. c. xvii. 7.   The gracious character of the
covenant with Abraham is indicated in the very wording of the original in the
chief passage—above referred to—in which its nature is described : " And I
will give my covenant (וְאֶתְּנָה בְרִיתִי) between me and thee."   It is " as a
favour bestowed by a superior, not a bargain between equals " (Dods in loc.).
It is the same phrase that is used in reference to the covenant with Noah
(Gen. ix. 12), where the absence of all conditions on the human side makes the
Divine graciousness the more evident, and in reference to God's favour to
Phinehas : " Behold, I give unto him my covenant of peace " (Num. xxv. 12).

[4] Isa. xli. 8 ff. ; xliv. 5 ; Jer. xxxi. 31–34 ; xxxii. 38 ff. ; Ezek. xxxvi. 24–28 ;
xxxvii. 26 f. ; Hosea i. 9 f. ; ii. 18, 23.   Comp. the way in which the author of

closing visions of the Apocalypse: " I heard a great voice out
of the throne saying, Behold, the tabernacle of God is with
men, and He shall dwell with them, and they shall be His people,
and God Himself shall be with them, and be their God. . . .
And He said unto me, I am the Alpha and the Omega, the
beginning and the end.   I will give unto him that is athirst of
the fountain of the water of life freely.   He that overcometh
shall inherit these things; and I will be his God, and he shall
be my son." [1]   Our thoughts cannot rise beyond that promise.
Its full meaning will open up to us through all the " days of
heaven," if indeed we are found worthy to obtain that world and
the resurrection from the dead.   As an old Scottish commentator on the passage puts it: " Not as if now God did begin to
be their God, which, as to His own, was true in all ages.   But
they get now the possession of Him who in right and title was
their portion before.   They know what it is to have God as their
God, when He becometh all in all to them, and they are filled
with His fulness, and see Him as He is.   This saith, that the
fruit and substance of that great covenant promise : ' I will be
their God, and they shall be my people,' is never well known
nor taken up till they be in heaven, that being the place wherein
the fulness of this promise streameth out to believers." [2]

   " Let it observed," Dr. Rainy says in a suggestive note on
the Abrahamic covenant, " how the condescension implied
in entering into covenants brought a new element in and
constituted a step towards the great condescension which
crowns the ways of God with men.   God not only reveals
what He has fully resolved to do, but He binds Himself in a
covenant.   He assumes a position in relation to Abraham in
which reciprocal obligations are recognised ; He has made an
agreement which must be fulfilled ; He has conferred on
Abraham an interest in His own future procedure,—a right
which may be pleaded to claim the benefits engaged for.

the Epistle to the Hebrews adverts to the *gracious manner* and *purpose* of God's
covenant with Abraham : " God, *being minded to show more abundantly* unto
the heirs of the promise the immutability of His counsel, interposed with an
oath " (Heb. viii. 17).   " The Divine promise in the N. T. is always ἐπαγγελία,
not ὑπόσχεσις, 'pollicitum' not ' promissum,' a gift graciously bestowed, and
not a pledge obtained by negotiation."   Bp. Lightfoot on Gal. iii. 14.

   [1] Rev. xxi. 3, 6 f.
   [2] Durham, *Revelation*, Glasg. 1788, p. 771.   Comp. Dykes, *Abraham*, p. 156.

"Now the early Scriptures speak, and theologians have reasoned much, of the 'Angel of the Lord,' the 'Angel of the covenant.' Very considerable difficulties attach to the complete explanation of all the passages, and gather about the question, how much the old believers attained to think about this Angel, and what impressions they cherished in connection with Him. But let it be observed at all events, that in the very fact of entering into covenant, Jehovah does silently assume to Himself the character of an angel—one sent. He takes office; He binds Himself to ministries which must be certainly and punctually discharged; He takes on Him obligations, which He is henceforth to be seen fulfilling. God is the sender forth of all angels. But here—if it may be reverently so expressed—we see Him becoming at the same time the Sent, sending Himself along a prescribed path of long-suffering Divine dealings. In that path He is thereafter seen proceeding, year after year, age after age, not only with the majesty of Divine decrees, but with the patient faithfulness of one who—shall I say—executes the commission which He has taken on Him in behalf of Abraham His friend.

"It does not seem wonderful that henceforth in the faith of the Church, along with the impression of the mighty and gracious One who sends out all powers and agencies that work in all the world, there is an impression also of One who follows His people in a holy unfailing attendance, in the attitude of one who executes a charge. It does not seem unreasonable to read the remarkable texts concerning the 'Angel of the Lord' in the light of this general impression. 'The God before whom my fathers Abraham and Israel did walk . . . the Angel which redeemed me from all evil, bless the lads.'"[1]

The fact that temporal promises were also given to Abraham and confirmed by covenant, is not in the least inconsistent with what we have said as to the essential nature of the Gospel declared to him, and as to that of the covenant by which it was made sure. The relation of the primary to the

---

[1] Rainy, *Delivery and Development of Christ. Doct.* p. 336 f. As Principal Rainy notes, a good statement of the opinions regarding the Angel of the Lord may be found in Oehler's *Theologie des A. T.*, Tübingen 1873, i. S. 199, E. Tr. Edin. i. pp. 188-191. Comp. Westcott, *Introd. to Study of Gospels*, 5th ed. p. 146 f.

subordinate elements in the blessing of Abraham, and in God's
covenant with him and his seed, has often been discussed in
connection with the Scripture argument for the Baptism of
the infant seed of believers now.   For a fuller treatment of
the subject, and for satisfactory replies to the allegations of
Anti-Pædobaptists to the effect that the Abrahamic covenant
was of an essentially carnal and temporary character, I may
refer to Dr. Wardlaw on *Infant Baptism,* and to Dr. Bannerman's work on the *Church of Christ.*[1]

2nd. As to the parties with whom the covenant was made :
God makes or establishes His covenant with Abraham and
his seed.

It is clear at once that the principle of representation
comes in here as in the previous covenants with Adam and
Noah.   Abraham is dealt with by God, not as an individual
merely, but as standing for all those who are included under
the term " thy seed."   The phrase is often repeated in Scripture when reference is made to the covenant with Abraham.

Thus, for instance, in Isa. xli. 8 f. we read : " And thou,
Israel, my servant, the seed of Abraham my friend, thou whom
I have taken hold of from the ends of the earth, and called
thee from the corners thereof, fear thou not, for I am with
thee ; be not dismayed, for I am thy God."   The words were
evidently in the mind of the author of the Epistle to the
Hebrews when he wrote : " He taketh not hold of angels, but
He taketh hold of the seed of Abraham."[2]   Mary, the mother

---

[1] Wardlaw, *Infant Baptism,* 3rd ed. pp. 21-34, 42 ff.   Bannerman, *Church of
Christ,* ii. pp. 69-75.   It may be noted that the force of the reasoning of these two
writers is not really impaired by the fact that they use the gloss εἰς Χριστόν in Gal.
iii. 17 as if it formed part of the genuine text.   As already observed, these two
words simply summarize the apostle's argument in the passage.   "The main thing,
the substance and marrow of that covenant which God made with Abraham and
the other patriarchs was the covenant of grace, which is continued in these days
of the Gospel and extends to all his spiritual seed, of the Gentiles as well as Jews.
But yet that covenant with the patriarchs contained other things that were
appendages to that everlasting covenant of grace, promises of lesser matters,
subservient to the grand promise of the future seed, and typical of things apper-
taining to Him."   Jon. Edwards, *Works,* Lond. 1834, i. p. 462.

[2] Σπέρματος Ἀβραὰμ ἐπιλαμβάνεται, Heb. ii. 16.   Comp. the LXX. of Isa. xli. 8 :
σπέρμα Ἀβραὰμ ὃν ἠγάπησα, οὗ ἀντιλαβόμην.

of our Lord, in her song of praise hails the birth of her Son
as the fulfilment of God's promises of help and mercy " to
Abraham and to his seed for ever." [1] This brings us to consider the Apostle Paul's memorable exposition of this point in
Romans and Galatians : " To Abraham were the promises
spoken, and to his seed. He saith not ' and to seeds,' as of
many, but as of one, ' and to thy seed,' which is Christ." [2]

I agree in substance here with the careful ,exegesis of the
late Principal Fairbairn. [3] It is plain that if we are to follow
the apostle's guidance, the seed referred to in the covenant
with Abraham must be regarded as essentially of a spiritual
kind, a *believing* seed, not taking in all his natural descendants
on the one hand, and not limited to them on the other.

Not only is this unquestionably the Apostle Paul's interpretation of the original transaction, but it is the only one
which is in accordance with the subsequent history as recorded
in the Old Testament, and with the principles of the Divine
procedure brought out there and referred to in the New Testament. One of Paul's arguments, for example, in the fourth
chapter of Romans, is based upon the time when the promises
were made to Abraham, and the blessing pronounced upon him
by God. It was when he was yet, as it were, on Gentile ground,
among the uncircumcised : " not in circumcision, but in uncircumcision ; and he received the sign of circumcision, a seal of
the righteousness of the faith which he had while he was in
uncircumcision, that he might be the father of all them that
believe, though they be in uncircumcision, that righteousness
might be reckoned unto them ; and the father of circumcision
to them who not only are of the circumcision, but who also
walk in the steps of that faith of our father Abraham which
he had in uncircumcision. For not through the law was the
promise to Abraham, or to his seed, that he should be heir of
the world, but through the righteousness of faith." [4]

This view as to those who were primarily contemplated in
the covenant, and who constituted the true seed of Abraham,
is illustrated and confirmed by the whole subsequent history.

---

[1] Luke i. 54 f.
[2] Gal. iii. 16. Comp. Rom. iv. 13, 16.
[3] Fairbairn, *Typology*, 6th ed. i. pp. 457-460. [4] Rom. iv. 10-13.

Action is taken on these lines from the very first. Abraham was bidden by God to administer circumcision, the sign of the covenant, not only to Ishmael and Isaac, his lineal descendants, but to " all who were his." " He that is born in thy house, or bought with money of any stranger which is not of thy seed [by natural descent], must needs be circumcised; and my covenant shall be in your flesh for an everlasting covenant. . . . In the self-same day was Abraham circumcised, and Ishmael his son. And all the men of his house, those born in the house, and those bought with money of the stranger, were circumcised with him." [1]

The whole house or family of Abraham, all who were one with him, to whom he stood in the position of being their head and representative, whether they were of one blood with him or not, were from the first in a certain sense " reckoned for a seed." [2] " In him," provided only that they came to be in some true sense *in him*, " all families of the earth were blessed," receiving the higher elements of the blessing just in proportion to the closeness and reality of their union with Abraham.

So it was also in all the subsequent stages of the history. The whole of the legislation regarding " the stranger within thy gates," the " sojourners " in Israel, the proselytes of later times, bears upon this point in a very interesting way. In substance it came to this, that whoever heartily cast in his lot with the children of Abraham and with the God of Abraham, of whatsoever seed or tongue, was received within the pale of the covenant as regards its most essential provisions, and had a right to its sign and seal. [3]

In the ninth chapter of Romans the apostle shows that the true blessing of Abraham and of Israel, " whose is the adoption and the covenants and the promises," was to descend through grace by faith. " For they are not all Israel which are of Israel; neither because they are Abraham's seed are

---

[1] Gen. xvii. 12 f., 26 f., LXX.: πάντες οἱ ἄνδρες τοῦ οἴκου αὐτοῦ, καὶ οἱ οἰκογενεῖς αὐτοῦ, καὶ οἱ ἀργυρώνητοι ἐξ ἀλλογενῶν ἐθνῶν.

[2] Rom. ix. 8.

[3] This subject is treated more in detail in Part III. chap. ii., under the head, "The Proselytes."

they all children; but in Isaac shall thy seed be called.
That is, it is not the children of the flesh that are children of
God, but the children of the promise are reckoned for a
seed." [1]

This 'again corresponds to the words of our Lord when
dealing with the claims put forth by the Jews: "We be
Abraham's seed, . . . our father is Abraham." Jesus saith
unto them, " If ye were Abraham's children, ye would do the
works of Abraham. But now ye seek to kill me, a man that
hath told you the truth, which I heard from God; this did
not Abraham. Ye do the deeds of your father. . . . Ye are
of your father the devil, and the lusts of your father it is
your will to do." [2]

The same principles underlie a striking utterance of our
Lord's great forerunner, John the Baptist: "When he saw
many of the Pharisees and Sadducees coming to his baptism,
he said unto them, Ye offspring of vipers, who warned you to
flee from the wrath to come? Bring forth therefore fruit
worthy of repentance, and think not to say within yourselves,
We have Abraham to our father; for I say unto you, that God
is able of these stones to raise up children unto Abraham." [3]

As has been pointed out by my distinguished predecessor
in this lectureship, John here "indicates that he regarded the
kingdom of heaven which he proclaimed as the fulfilment of
God's ancient promise to Abraham. This seems to show that
John regarded the establishment of the kingdom of God as a
matter of grace, not, as the Pharisees thought, to be merited
by obedience to the law, but bestowed by God in pursuance
of His free promise to Abraham. The expression is in the
line of such passages as Deut. ix. 4 f.; Ps. cv. 8–12, 42–45;
and points towards Paul's argument against the legalists, in
which he goes back from the law given at Sinai to the free
promise to Abraham four hundred years before." [4]

The promises of temporal blessing which were given along
with those that bore on the higher elements of the blessing of
Abraham, and were confirmed to him and his in the covenant,
took for granted spiritual conditions on the part of Abraham's

[1] Rom. ix. 4, 6–8.
[2] John viii. 33, 39–44.
[3] Matt. iii. 7–9.
[4] Candlish, *Kingdom of God*, p. 368 f.

seed as a whole. The land of promise, for example, was won
and kept by faith and obedience. It was lost through unbelief
and disobedience.[1]

"He saith not, 'And to seeds,' as of many, but as of one,
'And to thy seed,' which is Christ. . . . The law was added
because of transgressions, till the seed should come to whom
the promise hath been made."[2] Much needless controversy
has been waged regarding the force of the apostle's argument
from the expression "seed." The objection has been urged,
that the plural of the Hebrew term זֶרַע could only mean
"grain" or "crops." A complete and satisfactory reply has
been given by Tholuck, Fairbairn, and others. It is well
summed up, so far, by Bishop Lightfoot: "The very expression in St. Paul which starts the objection supplies the
answer also. It is quite as unnatural to use the Greek σπέρματα with this meaning as to use the Hebrew זְרָעִים. No
doubt by a forced and exceptional usage σπέρματα might
be so employed as in Plato, Legg. ix. 853 C., ἄνθρωποί
τε καὶ ἀνθρώπων σπέρμασι νομοθετοῦμεν; 4 Macc. § 17, ὦ
τῶν Ἀβραμιαίων σπερμάτων ἀπόγονοι παῖδες Ἰσραηλῖται;
but so might the corresponding word in almost any language.
The fact points to St. Paul's meaning. He is not laying
stress on the particular word used, but on the fact that a
singular noun of some kind, a collective term, is employed
where τὰ τέκνα or οἱ ἀπόγονοι, for instance, might have been
substituted.

"Avoiding the technical terms of grammar, he could not
express his meaning more simply than by the opposition, ' not
to thy seeds, but to thy seed.' A plural substantive would
be inconsistent with the interpretation given ; the singular
collective noun, if it admits of plurality (as it is interpreted
by St. Paul himself, Rom. iv. 18, ix. 7), at the same time
involves the idea of unity. . . . With a true spiritual
instinct, though the conception embodied itself at times in
strangely grotesque and artificial forms, even the Rabbinical
writers saw that ' the Christ' was the true seed of Abraham.

[1] Cf. Wardlaw, *Infant Baptism*, 3rd ed. pp. 70-74. Fairbairn, *Typology*,
6th ed. i. pp. 369 f., 385.
[2] Gal. iii. 16, 19.

In Him the race was summed up, as it were. In Him it
fulfilled its purpose, and became a blessing to the whole
earth. . . . Thus He was not only the representative, but
the embodiment of the race. In this way the people of
Israel is the type of Christ; and in the New Testament,
parallels are sought in the career of the one to the life of
the other. (See especially the application of Hosea xi. 1 to
our Lord in Matt. ii. 15.) In this sense St. Paul used the
'seed of Abraham' here." [1]

Some further remarks lead to the same general conclusion
as that arrived at by Tholuck and Fairbairn, viz. that the
" seed of Abraham " also means " Israel after the spirit," or
Christ's people as well as Himself. But Dr. Lightfoot speaks
somewhat vaguely of " the Jewish nation denoting the Christian Church," and does not bring out so clearly and effectively
as is done by the other two exegetes named, the precise
interpretation which corresponds to the apostle's argument in
the relative passages in Romans and Galatians. In Paul's
view, Abraham's seed of blessing in the promise are his
believing posterity, "those who are his" in the unity of
faith, whether his descendants in the literal sense or not.
And this brings out the consistency of the apostle's statements in the eighth and sixteenth verses of the third chapter
of Galatians. He limits the seed of blessing in the latter
instance to Christ, in the very same sense in which, in the
former, he limits it to Abraham. " In the one case he
identifies Abraham with all the posterity of blessing, and in
the other Christ ; in both cases alike the two heads compre-
hend all who are bound up with them in the same bundle of
life. 'The Scripture foreseeing,' he says at ver. 8, 'that
God would justify the heathen through faith, preached before
the Gospel unto Abraham, saying: In thee shall all nations
be blessed.' *In thee*, combining the blessing of Abraham
and all his spiritual progeny of believers into compact
unity ; he the head, and those who spiritually make one
body with him, being viewed together and blessed in the

---

[1] Lightfoot, *Galatians*, 5th ed. p. 142 f. Comp. Cremer's thorough and satisfactory treatment of this point, *s.v.* σπέρμα, *Biblico-Theol. Lexicon of N. T.
Greek, with Supplement*, Edin. 1886, p. 911 ff.

same act of God. In like manner, when at ver. 16 the
apostle passes from the parent to the seed, and regards the
seed as existing simply in Christ, it is because he views
Christ as forming one body with His people; in Him alone
the blessing stands as to its ground and merit; and in Him,
therefore, the whole seed of blessing have their life and
being. So that the term 'seed' is still used collectively
by the apostle. It is applied to Christ, not as an individual,
but to Christ as comprehending in Himself all who form with
Him a great spiritual unity,—those who in this same chapter
of Galatians are said to have 'put on Christ,' and to have
become 'all one in Him' (a personal mystical unity), ver.
27 f." [1]

The idea of the "seed," in short, in this aspect of it, as
seen by the apostle in New Testament light, corresponds to
that which he embodies in other passages of his writings,
which we shall have occasion to consider at a later stage in
these lectures. It corresponds to the conception, developed
in the Epistles to the Ephesians and Colossians, of "the
Church which is Christ's body," or to that in 1 Cor. xii.
12 f.: "As the body is one, and hath many members, and
all the members of the body being many are one body, so
also is Christ," that is, He and His people together.[2] "For
in one Spirit were we all baptized into one body, whether
Jews or Greeks."

The covenant, then, was made by God with Abraham,
but not with him as an individual merely. It was with

---

[1] Fairbairn, ib. p. 460; see also Rainy, Delivery and Development of
Christian Doctrine, pp. 338–340. Comp. Pfleiderer, Hibbert Lect. 1885, p. 126:
"This line of argument (as to the promise to Abraham having reference to
Christ as his seed) seems surprising at first sight; but the strangeness of it
is lessened when we consider that in Paul's view Christ was not a mere
individual like others, but the archetypal Head of the sons of God generally,
and thereby the one Representative of all those for whom the Divine promises
of grace are intended."

[2] Comp. Principal Edwards on this verse: "Christ is here regarded as the
personal subject, the 'Ego' whose body is the Church. In modern form the
apostle might have said: As the person is one, while the members of his body
are many, so also Christ is One, but the members of His mystical body, the
Church, are many." First Corinthians, 2nd ed. p. 324 f.; see also Godet in
Expositor, 3rd series, i. p. 293 f.

Abraham as one with "his seed, which is Christ." He was "the son of David," as the first Gospel says in its first sentence, "the son of Abraham." But just as David's Son was David's Lord, according to the psalm by which Christ put the Pharisees to silence; so Abraham's seed was Abraham's Lord as well. "Verily, verily, I say unto you, before Abraham was born, I am (πρὶν Ἀβραὰμ γενέσθαι, Ἐγώ εἰμι)."[1] And so, as the old divines of the Reformed Church loved to point out from this passage, the covenant, in one aspect of it, was made with Him before it was made with Abraham. It was "a covenant confirmed beforehand by God"[2] to Christ in the eternal counsels of peace that were betwixt them both in the beginning, ere ever the world was.

But looking now at the covenant as specially revealed and confirmed to Abraham, we see that it was between God as a God of grace on the one hand, and on the other the patriarch as a believing man and a representative of believers, laying hold by faith of the promises of God to him and his, laying hold of God Himself to be his God and theirs in an everlasting covenant.

3rd. The tokens or signs of the covenant.

When Abraham thus "believed in the Lord, He reckoned it to him for righteousness." The covenant of Divine acceptance and friendship was formed then; and God in gracious condescension bound Himself to perform all that it implied, and gave a visible sign of this, a token for Abraham's faith to grasp, by making His glory to pass between the sacrifices which the patriarch at His command had prepared. It was the first time since the fall that the visible presence of God —the Shekinah, as the Jewish teachers called it—had been manifested to men. The appearance, as of "a smoking furnace and a flaming torch," recalls "the flame of a sword, turning every way, to keep the way of the tree of life."[3] In both revelations there was an element of majesty and terror as well as of grace, as afterwards in the pillar of cloud and fire.

[1] John viii. 58.   [2] Gal. iii. 17.   [3] Gen. iii. 24; xv. 16-18.

Again, when, some thirteen years afterwards, that fuller and more explicit proclamation of the covenant came, of which we have the record in the seventeenth chapter of Genesis, Abraham and all who were his received, as the apostle says, "the sign of circumcision, a seal of the righteousness of the faith which he had while he was in uncircumcision." [1] Thereby Abraham, for himself and all whom he represented, formally accepted his side of the covenant, binding its obligations upon himself and them. What the special significance was of circumcision as a token of the covenant may be more suitably considered under the next head, when we look at it as the appointed ordinance of admission into the covenant fellowship. Meanwhile observe that in thus openly and deliberately taking hold of God's covenant, Abraham acted, in the first place, only for himself and those of his family, whose covenant standing was by reason of age and position bound up for the time with his own.

But, as the apostle shows so fully in the passages on which we have been dwelling, in another aspect of the transaction all the faithful are to recognise Abraham as their representative in the covenant. He is "the father of all them that believe." "If ye are Christ's, then are ye Abraham's seed, heirs according to promise;" [2] in other words, if we are of the same faith, we are in the same covenant, and heirs of the promises which it made sure. Only we have to transact for ourselves, separately, with the Lord, the Author and Administrator of the covenant, the same in Abraham's days and in ours, as to our own personal interest in it.[3] We have to do, in short, just as Gentile sojourners had to do before they could receive that ordinance which was the sign and "seal of the righteousness of faith." They had to come first "to put their trust under the wings of the Lord God of Israel," to "join themselves unto the

---

[1] Rom. iv. 11.   [2] Rom. iv. 11; Gal. iii. 29.

[3] As Augustine says of those who entered in by the door into the sheepfold before Christ came in the flesh: "The times are diverse, not the faith" (Tempora variata sunt, non fides). Aug. *In Joannis Evangel. Tractatus,* xlv. 9.

Lord," to "love the name of the Lord," before they received the token of the Lord's covenant with Abraham and his seed.[1]

Christians now, as the apostle's words teach us, get to Abraham and to Abraham's covenant-standing and blessing through Christ, not to Christ through Abraham. Members of Abraham's family by natural descent, such as Esau, although circumcised as children, when one with their father from age and position in the house, might by their own act separate themselves afterwards from the blessing. All the children of Abraham were not "reckoned for a seed," but "in Isaac shall thy seed be called." Only to "those who were of faith" was the ordinance of circumcision what it was to Abraham himself, and to Isaac, not only a sign but a seal of the righteousness of faith and of the covenant of spiritual blessing.

It is worthy of note in this connection how, once and again, when some man or woman had come to our Lord in faith for bodily or spiritual healing, He emphasized in their case that very relation to Abraham which He denied, as we have seen, in the case of the Jews who prided themselves on their natural descent from him. "Ought not this woman, being a daughter of Abraham, to have been loosed from this bond on the day of the Sabbath?" "To-day is salvation come to this house, forasmuch as he also is a son of Abraham; for the Son of man came to seek and to save that which was lost."[2]

"The God before whom Abraham and Isaac did walk, the angel that redeemed them from all evil," has been made known to us in the Lord Jesus Christ. In Him the Gospel and the covenant are brought nigh to us. "Behold my servant, whom I uphold; my chosen, in whom my soul delighteth: I have put my Spirit upon Him; he shall bring

---

[1] Ruth ii. 12; Ex. xii. 48; Isa. lvi. 3, 6. In the Rabbinical writings circumcision in the case of proselytes and their children is called "the seal of Abraham" (חותמו של אברהם), or "the seal of the holy covenant" (חותמו של ברית הקדש), Shemoth rabba, c. 19. Weber, *System der altsynagogalen Palästinischen Theologie aus Targum, Midrash u. Talmud dargestellt*, Leipzig 1880, S. 75.

[2] Luke xiii. 16; xix. 9 f.

forth judgment to the Gentiles. . . . I the Lord will keep thee, and give thee for a covenant to the people, for a light to the Gentiles." "That the blessing of Abraham might come upon the Gentiles in Christ Jesus; that we might receive the promise of the Spirit through faith." [1]

The covenant with Abraham was thus sealed on both sides by sacrifice and shedding of blood. God Himself came forward in this way, as we have seen, at the first great ratification of the covenant, when His glory passed between the divided sacrifices.[2] Abraham, on his part, from the first offered sacrifice. "The lamb for the burnt-offering" was the form of sacrifice in the worship of God with which his children and his servants were most familiar.[3] Sacrifice always meant *giving* something. In the sacrifice of the lamb *life* was offered to God, the life of one of those creatures which He had "given" to man "for food,"—and life with the blood, the special vehicle and representative of the life, which had a peculiar sacredness, because by the covenant with Noah and his seed it had not been given for food, but solemnly reserved in some sense for God.[4] But in the supreme crisis in the history of Abraham as a believing man, he was taught that sacrifice meant giving to God, not only something, not only what was of value, but what was absolutely best. It meant giving what included everything, what was dearer to him than his own life.

And it was when Abraham's faith came forth victorious in that supreme trial, when his heart was found right with God, withholding nothing from him, that the heart of God was most fully revealed to Abraham. It was on Mount Moriah that the covenant of blessing was most strongly confirmed. It was there that "God, being minded to show more abundantly unto the heirs of the promise the immutability of His counsel, interposed with an oath, that by two immutable things," the word and the oath of the covenant, they "might have strong encouragement." [5] The Promiser became the Surety. "By myself have I sworn, saith the

---

[1] Gen. xlviii. 15 ; Isa. xlii. 1, 6 ; Gal. iii. 14.
[2] Gen. xv. 17.   [3] Gen. xxii. 5-8.
[4] Gen. ix. 1-7.   [5] Heb. vi. 17 f.

Lord ; because thou hast done this thing, and hast not withheld thy son, thine only son : that in blessing I will bless
thee, and in multiplying I will multiply thy seed as the
stars of the heaven, and as the sand which is upon the sea-
shore ; and thy seed shall possess the gate of his enemies :
and in thy seed shall all the nations of the earth be blessed ;
because thou hast obeyed my voice." [1]

What Abraham himself saw of " the day of Christ " from
this " mount of the Lord " we cannot tell. That he did see
something of that day afar off, and rejoiced in it, our Lord
Himself assures us.[2] But no Christian can fail to see the
light of that day thrown before in this wonderful history of
the offering of Isaac. In the cross of our Lord Jesus Christ
we see the heart of God revealed. We hear Him saying to
every sinner who has believed in the love of God manifested
in that great sacrifice, and has made that Saviour his : " By
myself I have sworn, that in blessing I will bless thee." " It
is God that justifieth ; who is he that shall condemn ? " " He
who spared not his His own Son, but delivered him up for us
all, how shall He not also with Him freely give us all
things ? " [3]

---

[1] Gen. xxii. 16–18.   [2] John viii. 56.

[3] Rom. viii. 32 f. "Judaism sees in the offering or the binding of Isaac
(עקדת יצחק) a transaction full of meritorious efficacy for all times, and availing
with God for the good of Israel. Where the Church prays : 'For the sake of
the sufferings and death of Jesus Christ,' the synagogue prays : 'For the sake
of the binding of Isaac.' This greatest temptation (נסיון) of Abraham is held by
her to be the banner (נס) of Israel ; and it is so in truth, but only in the light
of its antitype which the synagogue still disowns." Delitzsch, *Genesis*, 3te
Ausg. S. 418.

CHAPTER III.

IN the history of Abraham we see the Church of God visibly set up, built upon the Gospel declared to him, and the covenant made with him and his seed.

There had been believing men and " preachers of righteousness " before Abraham. Abel offered sacrifice in faith, and obtained witness from God that he was righteous in His sight. Enoch walked with God and bore witness for Him, and " had this testimony, that he pleased God." Noah " became heir of the righteousness which is according to faith." There had been altars raised before the flood ; men had " called upon the name of the Lord," as it seems, in common worship.[1] But now, for the first time in the record of revelation, we find God by His word and providence distinctly separating to Himself a little company of men " called, and chosen, and faithful."

At a time when the dark history of the world before the flood threatened to repeat itself, when the clouds seemed gathering again over the future of mankind, God makes His bow of promise to appear in the cloud. He calls and separates to Himself this little fellowship of believers together with their children, not for the destruction of the world, but that, in the end, the world through them might be saved. " To Abraham and to his seed are the promises spoken,"— promises which comprise, as we have seen, the very same Gospel of salvation which was to be made known afterwards to the Gentiles in Jesus Christ. God establishes these promises by solemn covenant made, not with Abraham only nor with Abraham as a representative of believers only, but

---

[1] Heb xi. 4-7 ; Gen. iv. 26 ; comp. Candlish, *Genesis*, 2nd ed. i. p. 281 ff.

with " his seed, which is Christ." As Abraham himself was
" the father of all them that believe," so " the Church in his
house " with its simple Gospel " preached beforehand " to him
and his, with its sacrament of admission common to the
believer and his infant seed, with its worship under the open
heaven beside the altar of sacrifice, with its testimony for
God and its influence on all around, was the true mother
Church of all the Churches in which those " called of God
and chosen and faithful " have been joined together in all
ages and all lands for common worship and spiritual fellowship, for work and witness-bearing,

If we turn to the symbolical books of Reformed Christendom for their most careful definition of " the visible Church
Catholic," we find that it " consists of all those throughout
the world that profess the true religion, together with their
children," and is " the house and family of God." [1] We can
hardly fail to recognise what answers closely to this definition
in the picture which Scripture gives of Abraham and his
household and of his relations with all, such as Melchisedec,
in whom the knowledge and the fear of God were found in
his time. The lines of likeness stand out the more clearly
the more we look into the history, using especially the light
which apostolic interpretation throws upon it.

Bishop Lightfoot shows in an interesting way how Paul
in this matter avoids the errors fallen into, in opposite
directions, by Alexandrian Judaism on the one hand and
Palestinian Judaism on the other, and how he combines
all that was true in the teaching of both. After a careful
examination of the references to Abraham's life and character
in the writings of Philo, the great representative of the
Alexandrian school of Jewish theology, Dr. Lightfoot concludes: " If we look only to the individual man, faith
with Philo is substantially the same as faith with St.
Paul. The lessons drawn from the history of Abraham by
the Alexandrian Jew and the Christian apostle differ very
slightly. Faith is the postponement of all present aims and
desires, the sacrifice of all material interests to the Infinite
and Unseen. But the philosopher of Alexandria saw no

[1] Westminster Conf. xxv. 2.

historical bearing in the career of Abraham. As he was severed from the heart of the nation, so the pulses of national life had ceased to beat in him. The idea of a chosen people retained scarcely the faintest hold on his thoughts. Hence the only lesson which he drew from the patriarch's life had reference to himself. Abraham was but a type, a symbol of the individual man. The promises made to him, the rich inheritance, the numerous progeny, had no fulfilment except in the growth of his own character. The Alexandrian Jew like the heathen philosopher was exclusive, isolated, selfish. With him the theocracy of the Old Testament was emptied of all its meaning; the covenant was a matter between God and his own spirit. The idea of a *Church* did not enter into his reckoning. He appreciated the significance of Abraham's *faith ;* but Abraham's *seed* was almost meaningless to him.

"On the other hand, Judaism proper was strong where Alexandrian Judaism was weak, and weak where it was strong. The oppressive rule of Syrians and Romans had served only to develop and strengthen the national feeling. ' We are Abraham's sons; we have Abraham to our father : ' such was their religious war-cry, full of meaning to every true Israelite. It was a protest against selfish isolation. It spoke of a corporate life, of national hopes and interests, of an outward community, a common brotherhood, ruled by the same laws and animated by the same feelings. In other words, it kept alive the idea of a *Church.* This was the point of contact between St. Paul's teaching and Rabbinical Judaism. But their agreement does not go much beyond this. With them, indeed, he upheld the faith of Abraham as an example to Abraham's descendants. But while they interpreted it as a rigorous observance of outward ordinances, he understood by it a spiritual state, a stedfast reliance on the unseen God. With them, too, he clung to the fulfilment of the promise, he cherished fondly the privileges of a son of Abraham. But to him the link of brotherhood was no longer the same blood but the same spirit; they only were Abraham's sons who inherited Abraham's faith." [1]

[1] Lightfoot, *Galatians,* 5th ed. p. 163.

Consider for a little the worship of the patriarchal Church, its ordinance of admission, the gracious character of its fellowship with God, and the practical fruits in it of the Gospel preached beforehand to Abraham and received by him and his.

1st. Its worship.

"Abraham," as Calvin says finely, "bore with him everywhere an altar in his heart."[1] That spirit of faith in God and reverence before Him, which so marks the patriarch's life, found natural expression in those simple altars which he built wherever his tents were pitched, under the tree of Moreh, by the well of the oath, beneath "the oaks of Mamre which are in Hebron." With these altars Abraham took possession of the land for God. These with "the lamb for a burnt-offering"[2] formed the centre of the worship of his great household when he gathered them together to "call upon the name of the Lord, the everlasting God," and to "command his children and his household to keep the way of the Lord, to do justice and judgment, to the end that the Lord might bring upon him" and them "that which he had spoken."[3]

"Nothing is more characteristic," says a great German interpreter, "of the spirit of the worship of Abraham and his descendants than the custom of everywhere raising simple altars, without images or temple, under the open heaven. These were enough where men believed in an unseen God in the heavens, and corresponded in their simplicity with a religion as true as it was simple." Ewald adds one of his many memorable sayings, full of characteristic insight, to the effect that Monotheism is the most *natural* faith, just because of its truth. The man who really meets with God *knows* that it is *One* Power that meets him.[4]

[1] "Ferebat ipse altare in corde suo," Calvin, *In Genes.* xiii. 18.
[2] Gen. xxii. 5–8. The words of Abraham to the servants show that "worship" to him and them implied sacrifice ; those of Isaac seem to indicate what he looked for at any altar, what was the most common form of sacrifice in his father's house.
[3] Gen. xxi. 33 ; xviii. 19.
[4] Ewald, *Geschichte des Volkes Israel*, 3te Ausg. i. S. 459 f. E. Tr. i. p. 320.

" Abram passed through the land," we read in reference to
his first setting foot in that country which God promised
to give him for an inheritance, " unto the place of Shechem,
unto the oak of Moreh. . . . And the Lord appeared unto
Abram, and said, Unto thy seed will I give this land : and
there builded he an altar unto the Lord who appeared unto
him.   And he removed from thence unto the mountain on
the east of Bethel, and pitched his tent, having Bethel on the
west and Ai on the east ; and there he builded an altar unto
the Lord, and called upon the name of the Lord." [1]

" The Lord appeared unto Abram."   This, as has been
noted,[2] is the first Theophany recorded in Scripture since the
time when " Adam and his wife heard the voice of the Lord
God walking in the garden in the cool of the day, and hid
themselves from the presence of the Lord amongst the trees of
the garden."   The previous call of Abraham, like the revelations to Noah, is represented as having taken place in the
way of a word coming from the Lord, — an inward voice,
it may be, which he who heard it knew beyond question
to be from God Himself.   " The Lord *said* unto Abram "
—" the Lord had *spoken* unto him." [3]   But now, in yet more
condescending grace, the Lord *appears ;* and Abram builds
his first altar in the promised land " to the Lord who
appeared unto him."   It is striking that it should have
been in that very " place of Shechem " where, hundreds of
years afterwards, our Lord, " the son of David, the son of
Abraham," said to the woman by the well : " The hour
cometh when neither in this mountain nor in Jerusalem
shall ye worship the Father.   But the hour cometh, and
now is, when the true worshippers shall worship the Father
in spirit and in truth ; for such doth the Father seek to be
His worshippers.   God is a Spirit, and they that worship
Him must worship in spirit and truth." [4]

God had sought and found such worshippers long ago in
Shechem, in Abraham and his house.[5]   " They which be of

[1] Gen. xii. 6–8. [2] Delitzsch, *in loco.*
[3] Gen. xii. 1, 4. [4] John iv. 23–25.
[5] There, too, Jacob " came in peace," and there he dug the well that bore his
name ever after, and "drank thereof, himself, and his sons, and his cattle ;" "and

faith," — the whole household of faith in all lands, — so worship Him to-day and are accepted and "blessed with the faithful Abraham."[1]

2nd. Consider the ordinance of admission into this fellowship of faith.

This was touched upon under a previous head,[2] but may be taken up more fully now.

1. Circumcision, as the appointed sign of God's covenant with Abraham and his seed, corresponded, of course, with the nature of that covenant itself and of the blessings which the covenant made sure; that is to say, it had primarily a spiritual meaning and force. It was designed and suited for the purposes of such a fellowship as was set up on the basis of the Gospel and the covenant revealed to Abraham.[3] That the ordinance was not a mere Jewish one is plain at first sight from the very time of its institution. "Circumcision," our Lord said to the Jews, "is not of Moses, but of the fathers."[4] When taken up into the later economy, it retained its essential character. Hence, both in the Old Testament and the New, stress is laid upon its spiritual significance. "And now, Israel, what doth the Lord thy God require of thee, but to fear the Lord thy God, to walk in all His ways, and to love Him, and to serve the Lord thy God with all thy heart, and with all thy soul, to keep the commandments of the Lord, and His statutes, which I command thee this day for thy good? . . . Only the Lord had a delight in thy fathers to love them, and He chose their seed after them, even you above all peoples, as at this day. Circumcise therefore the foreskin of your heart, and be no more stiff-necked." "And the Lord thy God will circumcise thine heart, and the heart of thy seed,

---

he erected there an altar, and called it El-elohe-Israel," Gen. xxxiii. 18-20; John iv. 10.

[1] Gal. iii. 9.　　　　　　　　　　[2] See above, pp. 32 f., 39.

[3] Attempts have been made, chiefly by Anti-Pædobaptist writers, to prove circumcision to be a mere carnal ordinance connected with purely temporal promises. It is unnecessary to refer to these in the text. For a full reply to them, see Bannerman, *Church of Christ*, ii. pp. 81-89, 96-99. Wardlaw, *Infant Baptism*, 3rd ed. pp. 25-89.

[4] John vii. 22.

to love the Lord thy God with all thy heart, and with all thy soul, that thou mayest live." "For he is not a Jew which is one outwardly; neither is that circumcision which is outward in the flesh : but he is a Jew which is one inwardly; and circumcision is that of the heart, in the spirit, not in the letter; whose praise is not of men, but of God." "He received the sign of circumcision, a seal of the righteousness of the faith, which he had while he was in uncircumcision, that he might be the father of all them that believe."[1]

2. As to the special meaning of the rite of circumcision, it is clear that it spoke emphatically of purity. Abraham and all who should be "heirs with him of the same promises" were to "cleanse themselves from all defilement of flesh and spirit, perfecting holiness in the fear of God."[2]

The first appointment of circumcision was introduced by a fresh revelation of God in His majesty and holiness: "The Lord appeared to Abram, and said unto him, I am God Almighty; walk before Me (under My eye, as conscious of My Presence), and be thou perfect (blameless). And I will make My covenant between Me and thee."[3] Then follow the promises of the covenant (vv. 4-9). Then the sign and seal of it is appointed: "This is My covenant which ye shall keep, between Me and you, and thy seed after thee; every male among you shall be circumcised. It shall be a token of a covenant betwixt Me and you. My covenant shall be in your flesh for an everlasting covenant. . . . And the uncircumcised male, who is not circumcised in the flesh of his foreskin, that soul shall be cut off from his people; he hath broken My covenant."[4]

The ordinance thus solemnly established spoke to all who received it both of privilege and responsibility. It spoke to them of a covenant fellowship with God and with His people, in which they "had to do with higher powers and higher objects than those of corrupt nature," in which they were called to "walk in His presence and be blameless." It spoke of "nature purged from its uncleanness, nature raised above

[1] Deut. x. 12-16 ; xxx. 6 ; Jer. iv. 4 ; ix. 25 f. ; Rom. ii. 28 f. ; iv. 11. Comp. Fairbairn, *Typology*, 6th ed. i. p. 368 f.
[2] 2 Cor. vii. 1. [3] Gen. xvii. 1 ff. [4] Gen. v. 10 f., 13 f.

itself, in league with the grace of God, and bearing on it the distinctive impress of His character and working."[1] "It implied that nature was impure, and could not produce the promised seed. It was a sign at once of the unfitness of nature to generate its own Saviour, and of God's intention to give this saving and blessing seed. Nature must be cut off, renounced, if God's gift is to be received. As a seal of the covenant it was handed down from father to son, and so kept the whole series and each individual in an unbroken connection with the original establishment of the covenant, so that each might feel, It is to *me* God's promise is made."[2]

3. Circumcision by Divine appointment was administered to the infant seed of Abraham, as well as to all who were "the men of his house" and worshippers of his God. This fact, of course, raises for those who hold an individualistic theory of the way of salvation, all the difficulties which have been felt by some in connection with the Baptism of the infant children of believers under the Christian dispensation. "The sign of circumcision," the apostle expressly tells us, was "a seal of the righteousness of faith."[3] Yet it was administered to infants incapable of faith. It pledged him who received it to obedience to God's revealed will. "I testify," the same apostle writes, "to every man that receiveth circumcision, that he is a debtor to do the whole law."[4] Yet it was dispensed to an unconscious child, eight days old, who could do neither good nor evil, and could in his own person undertake no obligation to do anything.

Such difficulties are at once removed by recognising here the application and embodiment of that principle of representation which runs through all God's dealings with men from the beginning of the history of revelation onwards. The Church of God on earth is not merely "the sum of individual converts." The grace of God and the blessings of His covenant are not confined to the one channel of conscious intelligence. "The Gospel," which was "preached beforehand unto Abraham," was to bring blessing, not to individuals only, but to "all the families of the earth." Its central promise,

---

[1] Fairbairn, *ut supra*, i. p. 368.   [2] Dods, *Genesis*, p. 76 f.
[3] Rom. iv. 11.   [4] Gal. v. 3.

the sum of the everlasting covenant revealed to Abraham, was, " I will be a God to thee, and to thy seed after thee." It was in express and direct connection with that promise that the sign of circumcision was appointed "as a token of the covenant." [1] And accordingly, as administered to infants such as Isaac, this " seal of the righteousness of faith " spoke unmistakeably of blessing to the infant members of the family through their believing head and representative, and on the ground of his faith. The ordinance testified to the existence by Divine appointment of a fellowship of believers on earth to which all who had faith in the God of Abraham were to join themselves, to which the promises of blessing were made, and in which the infant children of His people had a special place and standing. Their connection with that fellowship was to be recognised then by circumcision, as it is recognised now by Baptism.[2]

" If indeed," as it has been well expressed by one whose name will ever be held in honour in our Church, and who was the first lecturer under this Trust, " the visible Church were a mere voluntary association,—a union formed by men of their own accord,—the idea of a transmitted right or a transmitted duty might seem unreasonable and unfair. To make me a member of such a body in my infancy, and without my consent, might be held to be an unwarrantable infringement on my freedom of choice. But if the visible Church be God's ordinance, and not a mere contrivance or expedient of man, there is no absurdity and no injustice in the arrangement. If, while yet unconscious and incapable of consenting, I am enrolled and registered, stamped and sealed, as one of the household of God, visible on earth ; if with His sanction and by His authority I am marked out from the womb as peculiarly His—His, in the same sense in which the Christian profession of my parents makes them His— His, by privilege, by promise, and by obligation,—no wrong is done to me, nor is any restriction put on me, more than by the circumstance of my being born in a home of piety and peace rather than in a haunt of profligacy and crime.

" If God makes me by birth the scion of a noble stock, the

[1] Gen. xvii. 7, 10. [2] Comp. Fairbairn, *ut supra*, i. p. 373.

child and heir of an illustrious house, then by my birth I am
necessarily invested with certain rights, and I am bound to
certain duties.   In so far, I have no discretion.   When I am
old enough to understand my position in society, I find it in
a great degree made for me, and not left for me to make.   I
may refuse to take the place assigned to me ; I may never
avail myself of its advantages ; I may never realize my
rank, or imbibe the spirit and enter into the high aims of
my honourable calling.   Still if I live not according to
my birth, the fault is my own, and my responsibility is
great.   And still, whether I take advantage of it or not,
my birth, in the plan and purpose of God's providence, had a
meaning which might have actually stood me in good stead,
if I had so chosen and so willed it.   So also in regard to
circumcision or Baptism.   If God makes me, by such an
initiatory rite, such a seal or pledge of grace, imparted to me
in infancy, a member of the society on earth which bears His
name, I may never be in reality what that rite should
signify me to be.   But not the less on that account has the
rite a significancy as implying a spiritual title and spiritual
benefits, which are in themselves intended and fitted for my
good.   And if afterwards I wilfully refuse them or cast them
away, with the badge of them upon my person, it is with
aggravated guilt, and at my own increased peril." [1]

Anti-Pædobaptists have declared that " the Gospel has
nothing to do with infants, nor have Gospel ordinances any
respect to them ; " that " the salvation of the Gospel is as
much confined to believers as Baptism is," that " by the Gospel
no infant can be saved." [2]   Such statements must apply to
another and a narrower Gospel than that which was " preached
beforehand unto Abraham."   " As we understand it," says an
eminent American divine of the present day, " the Gospel is
much more and better than the proclamation of the terms
on which God will save those who are capable of believing."
(It includes that, but it includes much more.)   " It is the
declaration of His infinite love to a fallen world, the revelation of the way in which He seeks and saves that which was

---

[1] Candlish, *Genesis*, 2nd ed. i. p. 287 f.
[2] Carson, *Baptism in its Mode and Subjects*, Lond. 1844, p. 173.

lost. We deny that any one, infant or adult, is regenerated by the proclamation of the Gospel. We are born again by the Holy Spirit, whose influences, the purchase of Christ's death and intercession, are not confined to words nor to any outward means, but, like the wind which bloweth where it listeth, works when and where and how He wills." [1]

"The blessing of Abraham," as the apostle tells the Galatians, had special reference to "the promise of the Spirit" which "came upon the Gentiles in Christ Jesus," a promise which was "unto them and to their children." "And if ye are Christ's, then are ye Abraham's seed, heirs according to promise." [2] To limit "those who are Christ's," who form "His seed, the travail of His soul, which He saw and was satisfied," to "those whom we can see, and from whom we can hear the confession of their faith, is to bound the vision and the purpose of Christ by our finite senses. The only restrictions we are authorized to put upon redeeming grace are those which God Himself has expressly imposed. We may not exclude any whom He has not excluded. He has excluded those who hear the Gospel and believe not. But He has not excluded any infants as such. Here the silence of Scripture is profoundly significant, and it is exactly analogous as it is co-extensive with their silence in regard to the Baptism of infants. Their Baptism and their salvation rest upon the same broad foundations. The silence in both cases is underlaid and pervaded by a multitude of good and necessary inferences, and re-echoes with the sweetest utterances of the still small voice of God. It is a silence and an infinitude like that which we feel on the seashore, where the waves that murmur and break at our feet are as nothing to the fulness which stretches in our thoughts beyond the bounds of our horizon.

> 'There's a wideness in God's mercy
> Like the wideness of the sea.'" [3]

---

[1] Van Dyke, "The Scripture Warrant for the Baptism of Infants," a very able article in the *Presbyterian Review* for Jan. 1885, p. 56 f.

[2] Gal. iii. 14, 29 ; Acts ii. 38 f.

[3] Van Dyke, *ut supra*, p. 58 f. To the objection which might be suggested, "Why then not baptize all infants dying in infancy?" Dr. Van Dyke

But if the silence of Scripture speaks thus graciously concerning all infants dying in infancy, much more do its express utterances in word and sign speak in special grace to God's believing children concerning their little ones. For them, ever since He established visibly a Church for Himself in the world, God has given special promises and tokens for good, and has assigned to them a special place in the covenant-fellowship of His people on earth. The rite of circumcision in the patriarchal Church, like the later sacrament which the apostle calls " the circumcision of Christ,"[1] might be defined as a holy ordinance of Divine appointment, "wherein by sensible signs" the blessings of God's grace and covenant " were represented, sealed, and applied" to believers and their infant seed.[2]

Before leaving this point, we may note the significant and, as it has been rightly called, " sacramental" change of name which took place in the case both of Abram and Sarai in connection with the institution of circumcision and the formal establishment of the covenant-fellowship of which it was the token. We are not warranted probably to lay much stress upon the suggestion of Delitzsch, that the import of the change is to be found in its being made by combining the fundamental letter of the name יהוה, " the star and centre of the wondrous future which lay before them and theirs," with the names which Abram and Sarai had hitherto borne.[3] But undoubtedly the change carried significance with it. This also was a token of God's covenant and of the gracious fellowship established by Him with the patriarch and all who were his. And whereas, from the nature of the ordin-

---

might probably answer that he would feel warranted in doing so if he knew certainly that they were to die, and so to be cast simply on the Fatherhood of God in Christ. Compare a suggestive passage in Dr. John Owen's treatise, " Of Infant Baptism and Dipping," which is referred to by Dr. Van Dyke, *Works* (Goold's ed.), xvi. p. 259 f.

[1] Col. ii. 11 f.

[2] Westm. Shorter Catech. 92. Comp. Dr. Candlish's remarks on the sacramental terms used in Genesis and the N. T. in reference to circumcision and the cup in the Lord's Supper; also what he says regarding the wilful neglect of ordinances involving exclusion from the visible Church, *Genesis*, 2nd ed. i. p. 280 f.

[3] Delitzsch, *Genesis*, 3te Ausg. S. 382. Comp. Dods, *in loco*.

ance, circumcision extended only to the males of Abraham's family,—the women being held to be represented by them, in this as in many other instances in Old Testament history, on the general principle that "the head of the woman is the man,"[1]—as regards the change of name, Sarah, as being one with Abraham in faith and in the covenant, received a like sign and seal from God. "She" too "counted Him faithful who had promised,"[2] and received, along with her husband, this abiding sacramental pledge from the great Promiser that their faith was not in vain.

"The sacramental character of a name, as of an institution or ordinance, consists," to use the words of a writer who has studied "the Personal names of the Bible" with much care, "in its Divine appointment to represent, commemorate, and testify some special grace and blessing, and so to be a permanent pledge of its bestowal. . . . It was this property of perpetuity and of constant daily use which rendered a proper name so peculiarly suitable as a medium by which the gracious purposes and promises of God might be exhibited and remembered. It was a sign and seal of what the Lord had spoken, which was necessarily understood and recognised as such by all. It became therefore a token of profession of faith or of gratitude on the part of those who bore it, and of those connected with them who were interested in its significance. . . . It was God's testimony of Himself, or of His will to and by those who were His, and their testimony concerning Him to the world."[3]

The covenant name Abraham, "father of a multitude," according to what seems the most probable interpretation,[4] commemorated the promises, the import of which we have already considered, that the patriarch should be "the father of many nations," "a great multitude that no man could number," and that "in him and his seed all nations of the earth should be blessed." The name Sarah, "princess" or

---

[1] 1 Cor. xi. 3.   [2] Heb. xi. 11.

[3] Wilkinson, *Personal Names in the Bible*, Lond. 1866, p. 313 ff.

[4] "Vater einer dröhnenden Menge," Delitzsch. The author of the apocryphal book known as "Ecclesiasticus" seems to favour the rendering, "high father of a multitude," Ἀβραὰμ μέγας πατὴρ πλήθους ἐθνῶν, Ecclus. xliv. 19.

"queen," was associated with God's promise, given in connection with the establishment of His covenant and its token in the ordinance of circumcision : "I will bless her, and she shall be a mother of nations ; kings of peoples shall be of her." [1]

It was doubtless from this significant event in the history of Abraham and Sarah, and of Isaac as the child of promise, that the custom arose among their descendants of giving the child its name, or at least publicly declaring the name already given at the time of its circumcision. We have instances of this in New Testament times in connection with the circumcision of John the Baptist, and that of our Lord Himself. The name of the child, as of one who was now formally and publicly recognised as belonging to the fellowship of the house of Abraham, was fitly associated with the solemn religious ordinance which had marked the beginning of that fellowship in the covenant made by God with his great forefather and his seed for ever, and in connection with which a new and covenant name had been given both to Abraham and Sarah.

3rd. Look now at the character of the fellowship between God and man seen in the history of Abraham, and enjoyed on the footing of God's grace revealed and His covenant established with him and his. Compare it with the relation of God to the highest and most religious minds among the heathen. To them He is "the unknown God," standing over against man, obscure, invisible, inarticulate, silent.[2] But here God "appears" to Abraham, speaks with him and his ; and they speak with God as a man with his friend, as children with a father. Think of those marvellous pictures in Genesis,

---

[1] Gen. xvii. 16. Comp. Wilkinson, *ut supra*, pp. 316–322.

[2] See a fine passage in Ewald, *Revelation*, E. Tr. p. 3 ; and the memorable words of Pascal : "La Divinité des chrétiens ne consiste pas en un Dieu simplement auteur des vérités géométrique et de l'ordre des éléments ; c'est la part des paiens. Elle ne consiste pas simplement en un Dieu qui exerce sa Providence sur la vie et sur les biens des hommes pour donner une heureuse suite d'années à ceux qui l'adorent ; c'est le partage des juifs. Mais le *Dieu d'Abraham et de Jacob*, le Dieu des chrétiens est un Dieu d'amour et de consolation ; c'est un Dieu qui remplit l'âme et le cœur qu'il possède. . . . Qui fait sentir à l'âme qu'il est son unique bien, que tout son repos est en lui." *Pensées*, 2me Partie, art. xv. 2.

so matchless in their simple dignity, which show us how
Abraham met with God by the tent door under the shadow
of the great oak trees of Mamre; how, on the height eastward
from Hebron, he stood and pleaded with Him for Sodom,
while the angels were passing down the valley on their errand
of mercy and of judgment.   In two other periods only in
Scripture history do we see something which may be placed
beside that wonderful, reverent, yet familiar intercourse between Abraham and the Lord.   It recalls the time before the
Fall, when man could "hear the voice of the Lord God
walking in the garden in the cool of the day," and could meet
with Him gladly and fearlessly in Paradise.   It recalls also
the intercourse of the risen Saviour with His disciples, when
the chosen witnesses did eat and drink with Him after He
rose from the dead, and He spoke with them of the things
concerning the kingdom of God, but when, mingling with all
the joyful and gracious fellowship, there was such Divine
majesty seen on His part, and such holy reverence on theirs.
"Touch Me not, for I am not yet ascended to my Father."
"None of the disciples durst ask Him, Who art Thou? knowing that it was the Lord."   "Thomas answered and said
unto Him, My Lord and My God."   "And they worshipped
Him." [1]

In the periods that followed the patriarchal, God seemed
again to withdraw Himself.   Only prophets and priests could
draw near to His immediate presence, and receive direct communications from Him.   Nay, even among them there were
distinctions.   Some things were only vouchsafed to prophets
of a special eminence, or to the high priest alone, once in the
year.   In a profound passage in the book of Numbers, God
Himself is represented as pointing out such differences between the higher and lower ranks even of true prophets of

[1] Gen. ii. 15–25; iii. 8; xviii. 1–33 ; Acts i. 3 ; x. 41 ; John xx. 17, 28 ; xxi. 12 ;
Luke xxiv. 52.   " In the commencement of the period of the law, which taught
men the infinite distance between the holy God and His sinful creatures, the
warning went forth to Moses from the burning bush : 'Draw not nigh hither.
Put off thy shoes from off thy feet.' The patriarchal period has more of the
evangelical spirit ; as the time before the law, it is a foretaste of the time after
the law." Delitzsch, *Genesis*, S. 392. Comp. Fairbairn, *The Revelation of Law
in Scripture*, Edin. 1869, p. 76 f.

Jehovah: " If there be a prophet among you, I the Lord will make Myself known unto him in a vision. I will speak unto him in a dream. My servant Moses is not so; he is faithful in all Mine house; with him will I speak mouth to mouth, even manifestly, and not in dark speeches; and the form of the Lord shall he behold." [1]

Abraham was like Moses in this. The Lord so spake with him " mouth to mouth, even visibly, and not in dark speeches; and the form of the Lord did he behold." He also, like Moses, is called emphatically by God Himself " My servant." [2] And whereas the relation of friendship with God is but once suggested in the case of Moses, to Abraham that high title, " the friend of God," is expressly applied three times in Scripture. [3] In this, too, Abraham was the father and pattern of all them that believe. We see the same gracious relations of fellowship with God subsisting, although taken advantage of in a less eminent degree, in the case of Isaac and Jacob, " the heirs with him of the same promise."

In the Church of the Old Testament, in short, as set up in patriarchal times, we find the true spirit of " the Gospel preached beforehand unto Abraham." We see, in substance, the New Testament priesthood, with its direct access to God, with its liberty of prayer and intercession, with its reverent, childlike confidence in drawing near to God as a covenant God and Father. It was a fair and gracious dawn of the Gospel day. Clouds came over it through sin and unbelief in the children of Abraham; but the light from heaven never wholly passed

---

[1] Num. xii. 6-8. So in the note at end of Deuteronomy: "There hath not arisen a prophet since in Israel like unto Moses, whom the Lord knew face to face," xxxiv. 10. Comp. Cox, *Balaam*, p. 135.

[2] Gen. xxvi. 24; Ps. cv. 6, 42.

[3] Ex. xxxiii. 11; Isa. xli. 8; 2 Chron. xx. 7; Jas. ii. 23. The LXX. of Gen. xviii. 18 has: " I will not hide from Abraham, My servant (or ' My child,' τοῦ παιδός μου), what I do." Philo seems to have read here τοῦ φίλου μου; Delitzsch, *in loco*. Certainly the title " friend " expresses the spirit of the passage. It is the name by which Abraham is still known through all the Mohammedan world. It clings to that ancient city, " built seven years before Zoan, in Egypt," where the covenant was made and promises were given to Abraham, whence he went out to battle against the kings, where he buried Sarah, where he himself and his son and his son's son were buried. Hebron is still known in the native Semitic speech of the Holy Land only as Beit el Khulîl, " the House of the Friend."

away. It shone out again in full glory in that "day of Christ" which the patriarch saw afar off, and which we see reflected beforehand in his own.   Then for the first time since it was given to Abraham was that name "the friend of God" vouchsafed again to men, not now spoken through prophets merely, but directly from the lips of the Son of God Himself. " Henceforth I call you not servants; for the servant knoweth not what his lord doeth: but I have called you friends; for all things that I have heard of My Father I have made known unto you.   Greater love hath no man than this, that a man lay down his life for his friends.   Ye are My friends, if ye do the things which I command you."[1]

4th. Notice some of the fruits of the Gospel which was preached to Abraham, as manifested in himself and the Church in his house.

The fellowship with God, which we see exemplified in the history of Abraham and those who were his, was a fellowship not of faith only, but of obedience.   Its practical results were righteousness and godly living.   The great central promise of the covenant, " I will be a God unto thee and to thy seed," was sealed by a sacramental ordinance.   It was fulfilled in a pure and blessed family life.

We recognise Abraham's spirit of faith and obedience in Sarah, in Isaac, in Eliezer, "the elder of his house, who ruled over all that he had," whose conduct in all the weighty business of finding a bride for the heir is such a model of how work should be done by a believing man, "not with eye-service as men-pleasers, but in singleness of heart, fearing God."[2]   We see the same spirit in that band of trusty and willing household servants, "born in his house," whom Abraham "drew as a sword from the sheath," as the graphic words of the original imply, in the sudden emergency which sent him forth to battle against the kings of the east.[3]

---

[1] John xv. 13 ff.   [2] Gen. xxiv. 2–61.

[3] וַיָּרֶק, Gen. xiv. 14.   The word is used elsewhere of drawing a sword or spear from its sheath, or arrows from a quiver, Ex. xv. 9 ; Ps. xxxv. 3, etc.   These servants were "his approved ones (אֶת־חֲנִיכָיו), being born in his house," as distinguished from slaves bought from strangers, in whom he could place less

We see the effects of Abraham's training and influence even in those members of his family who were not altogether one with him in spirit. Hagar and Ishmael are cast out; yet, in the desert, "God hears the voice of the lad," —remembering, as it seems, in his time of need how his father had taught him to pray,—and sends deliverance, and answers the prayer of Abraham also in behalf of his wayward son: "As for Ishmael, I have heard thee; behold, I have blessed him, and I will make him fruitful. . . . And God was with the lad." [1]

In all this we see what the Church of God was to be and to do for those within its pale, and especially how the Church in the family (ἡ κατ' οἶκον ἐκκλησία) was fitted and designed to be the firm foundation of the Church in the city, and in the land, and throughout the world. From the very first period in the history of the Church on earth, wherever "two or three have been gathered together in the Lord's name," His gracious Presence has been felt in the midst of them, and His blessing has made them rich. "Who are the two and the three met in His name?" Chrysostom asks; "Is it not the father, and the mother, and the child?"

From this centre of believing fellowship in the family, in the wider "household," we behold in the patriarchal history the power of the true religion going forth mightily all around for moral and spiritual ends. The faith of Abraham and his household was known by its fruits. It "made for righteousness" on every side. "His true greatness," as Ewald says, "was that he not only held fast to the purer knowledge of the true God in his own personal life and conduct, but that he knew also how to make that knowledge an abiding reality in his mighty household and tribe. And nothing shows more clearly the genuine and noble way in which the fear and the blessing of God were manifest in his

confidence. Dillmann and Delitzsch render "seine Erprobten oder Bewährten." " Vocat servos istos חניכים non qui ad rem militarem edocti formatique essent, ut sentiunt plerique, sed potius, meo judicio, qui educati fuerant sub ejus manu et ejus disciplina a pueris imbuti, ut animosius sub fide et auspiciis ejus bellarent, et quidvis discriminis subire parati essent ejus causa." Calvin, in loco.

1 Gen. xvii. 18 ff.; xxi. 17-20.

life than the fact that the most powerful and the most religious men among foreign nations could not but own openly that God was with him, and so sought eagerly for his friendship and blessing, Gen. xxi. 22 ; xiv. 18 ff." [1] We are expressly told in Scripture that it was for such ends that God had chosen and called Abraham, and established His covenant of grace and gracious fellowship with him: "All the nations of the earth shall be blessed in him; for I have known him (*i.e.* elected him [2]), to the end that he may command his children and his household after him, that they may keep the way of the Lord to do justice and judgment; to the end that the Lord may bring upon Abraham that which He hath spoken of him." [3]

This is just the great work of the Church of God in all ages, to bring about, through the saving knowledge of God and of His will for men, a pure and blessed social state, in which all men in personal, family, and all other relations, should keep the ways of the Lord, and do righteousness and judgment, that the Lord might bring upon them all the blessings of which He has spoken. "I will bless thee, and be thou a blessing." "In thee and in thy seed shall all the families—the nations—of the earth be blessed." [4] We see the essential nature of the blessing in what is said of Abraham and his house in their relations to God. Human history can end in nothing better and higher than that God should indeed dwell among men and be their God, and they His people. It forms the crowning vision of the Apocalypse when the apostle saw the new heaven and the new earth, and the holy city, New Jerusalem, coming down out of heaven from God, and heard Him that sitteth on the Throne proclaim: "Behold, I make all things new." [5] The Gospel preached beforehand unto Abraham with its covenant promises shall be fully realized then.

No doubt there was a childlike implicitness in Abraham's

---

[1] Ewald, *Gesch. Israel*, 3te Ausg. i. S. 456 ; E. Tr. i. p. 318. Comp. Candlish, *Genesis*, 2nd ed. i. p. 344 f.

[2] Comp. the reference given by the Revisers : "You only have I known of all the families of the earth," Amos iii. 2 ; also Hosea xiii. 5.

[3] Gen. xviii. 18 f.   [4] Gen. xii. 2 f.; xxii. 18.   [5] Rev. xxi. 1-8.

faith, a great vagueness in his hope for the future. With what feelings and anticipations he looked towards the day of Christ from afar we cannot say. But we know that he did look towards that day with expectation of some glorious and blessed state of things, not limited by this life merely, not for himself and those of his line alone, but one in which, through his seed, and by the grace and goodness of his covenant God, all nations of the earth were to share. "Your father Abraham," our Lord tells the Jews, "rejoiced to see My day, and he saw it, and was glad." "With Isaac and Jacob, the heirs with him of the same promise, he looked for the city which hath foundations, whose builder and maker is God. . . . Wherefore God is not ashamed of them, to be called their God; for He hath prepared for them a city."

It may be well, before passing from this part of our subject, to recall briefly some of the "momenta" in relation to the Scripture doctrine of the Church, which come out especially in that portion of the history of revelation which we have been considering.

I. God is revealed in His greatness and majesty, as the Almighty, the Most High, the Everlasting One, and yet at the same time as a God of grace and redemption, as One ready to meet with man in real and blessed fellowship, One to be absolutely trusted and willingly obeyed. "Abraham believed in Jehovah, and He counted it to him for righteousness." In face of all difficulty "he obeyed His voice," and received the fulfilment of His promises.[1] Faith in God and obedience to His revealed will form the keynote of the whole history.[2]

---

[1] Gen. xv. 6; xxii. 18.

[2] This is brought out in the well-known hymn, "The God of Abraham praise." It is brought out with at least equal power in that noble prayer which belongs to the oldest part of the synagogue service, the first of the blessings of the "Shemoneh Esreh," which many competent authorities hold to have been in use, in substance at least, in our Lord's time. Certainly it breathes the true spirit of the Old Testament Church in its deep reverence, its faith in the living God, and its hope in a Redeemer—a Goel—sent not "for the piety of the fathers," but "in love" and "for His name's sake:" "Blessed be Thou, O

II. God is revealed as making an election in a way of sovereignty, for reasons in Himself. Some of these we may gather from the circumstances and the results; others of them remain inscrutable to man. We see God choosing and passing by "according to the counsel of His will." He calls and separates to Himself certain persons out of the general company of men.

The chief names used in Scripture for the Church of God (קְהַל יְהוָֹה, ἐκκλησία τοῦ θεοῦ) suggest, as already noted,[1] the essential truths regarding it, that its foundations are laid in the sovereign grace of God, that its existence depends upon a Divine choosing and calling, or calling out, and on a human response to that call. These truths meet us from the very first in the facts and experiences recorded in the history of Abraham and his house. We see "the election of grace," the ἐκκλησία, and the κόσμος out of which that election is made. Some are called, and chosen, and faithful. Others are left. Others, again, being outwardly called, prove unfaithful.

III. The election is for world-wide ends of a gracious sort. Abraham is called and blessed of God in order that he may "be a blessing" from the first to all around, that "in him and his seed," ultimately, "all nations of the earth may be blessed." "The immediate particularism is for the sake of an ultimate universalism."[2] It was for the ends which the Apostle Paul expounds so powerfully in his epistles, to which another inspired descendant of Abraham had pointed before when he called upon all nations to rejoice in "the Lord Most High,

Lord our God, and the God of our fathers, the God of Abraham, the God of Isaac, and the God of Jacob, the great, the mighty, the terrible God (הָאֵל הַנּוֹרָא), the Most High God (אֵל עֶלְיוֹן), bountifully dispensing benefits, the Possessor of all things (קֹנֵה הַכֹּל), who rememberest the piety of the fathers, and wilt send a Redeemer (וּמֵבִיא גּוֹאֵל) unto their children's children, for Thy name's sake in love.

"Remember us for life (i.e. to grant us life), O King, who delightest in life; and write us in the book of life for Thine own sake, O God of life." [This is added during the "Ten Days of Penitence."]

"O King, who art a Helper, and a Saviour, and a Shield! Blessed art Thou, O Lord, the Shield of Abraham!" Comp. Gen. xiv. 18-22; xv. 1; Ps. xlvii. 2.

[1] See above, p. 1. [2] Fairbairn, *Typol.* 6th ed. i. p. 345.

who is terrible " (יְהֹוָה עֶלְיוֹן נוֹרָא), to " sing praises to God with understanding as the King of all the earth," and saw in prophetic vision how God was to reign over all the nations, and "the princes of the peoples were to be gathered together to be the people of the God of Abraham." [1]

IV. This election is carried out, and its results developed, on the principle of representation or covenant headship. We find one man standing for many, who are identified or counted one with him, to certain effects and on certain conditions, in the sight of God in connection with His promises and covenant.

V. There is visibly set up on earth by Divine guidance and appointment a Church or fellowship of believing men, together with their children, gathered together on the ground of God's word and in obedience to His call, brought into a gracious covenant relation with Himself, which has a Divinely appointed sign and seal, with special promises vouchsafed for all who are in this fellowship, special responsibilities laid upon them, and special work given them to do for God in the world.

[1] Ps. xlvii. 2, 7-9.

PART II.

THE CHURCH FROM THE TIME OF ABRAHAM TO THAT OF THE EXILE.

CHAPTER I.

THE CHURCH IN ITSELF AS SEEN IN SCRIPTURE FROM THE TIME OF ABRAHAM TO THAT OF THE EXILE.

THE general conception of the Church which we reached in last lecture was that of a fellowship of those who are called of God, and chosen, and faithful, as Abraham was,—a fellowship built upon the Gospel and the covenant revealed to him, and established in the world for the great purposes which were to be answered by him and his. Keeping this conception before us, let us glance at the subsequent history.

Many illustrations meet us from the first of what we have already gathered as to the essential nature of the fellowship, and the principles on which God dealt with those who were connected with it. "All the children of Abraham were not counted for the seed." Some, as Ishmael, the sons of Keturah, and Esau, received the sign of the covenant in childhood, and were associated with the chosen family for a certain time. Then they were separated, or separated themselves from it. These all showed a spirit more or less alien to that of Abraham. Some of them were manifestly "sensual, having not the Spirit;" they went out from the fellowship because they were not of it.[1] Others again, such as Jacob, with perhaps less attractiveness of natural character, and giving manifold proof of human sin and

---

[1] Jude 19 ; 1 John ii. 19 ; Gal. iv. 29 f. ; Heb. xii. 16 ff.

infirmity, are yet seen as to the main purport of their lives to "walk in the steps of that faith of their father Abraham, which he had being yet uncircumcised." [1]

All along it is plain that there is an election within the election. "All are not Israel who are of Israel." [2] This becomes the more manifest as the number of Abraham's descendants in the line of promise multiplies. We see them pass rapidly, in the time of Jacob and his sons, from the position of a family or tribe to that of a nation. Coincident with this change, and correspondent to it, there is a marked difference in the tone and character of God's dealings with them. There is no more the old familiar intercourse of patriarchal days between God and man, as of friend with friend. There is a long silence during the sojourn in Egypt. With the first words spoken to Moses, as noticed in last chapter,[3] there comes a revelation of the terrible majesty of God, of the distance between Him and sinful men; and a warning is given against drawing near to Him rashly and without warrant. Yet He who thus speaks, reveals Himself at the same time expressly as "the God of Abraham, and Isaac, and Jacob," the same, and not another. Grace is still reigning through righteousness. The voice of Divine Majesty, and of the law, coming after, does not disannul the promises so as to make them of none effect.[4]

Then we come to the redemption of the chosen people from Egypt, to the giving of the law, and the long discipline of Israel under it. Many difficult, but most interesting, questions arise here as to the relation of the two covenants, the Abrahamic and the Sinaitic, to each other and to the life and experience of Israel, as to the import and effect of the revelation of law and of grace, of sin and atonement, of the whole ceremonial and sacrificial system which centred in the tabernacle and the temple, and as to the two classes of men— the priests and the prophets—who held so close a relation to the system of worship, and to the progressive revelation of the righteousness and the grace of God. These questions, again, are complicated by critical problems regarding the date of particular books, or of certain elements in them, which

---

[1] Rom. iv. 12.   [2] Rom. ix. 6.   [3] Pp. 57–59.   [4] Gal iii. 17.

cannot be regarded as fully solved. Fortunately, our subject does not require us to enter upon this wide and difficult field.

"The gifts and calling of God are without repentance" (ἀμεταμέλητα, are not repented of (R. V. Marg.): once given, they are not recalled).[1] Through all these centuries of chequered history, the Gospel preached beforehand to Abraham remained for the faith of his true children. Its central promise: "I will be a God unto thee and to thy seed," emerges, as we have seen, unfailingly in prophecy and Psalm as a great light shining through all darkness. The original charter of the Church of God, "the covenant made with Abraham and his seed for ever," was neither "disannulled nor altered by adding new conditions." Certain temporary ordinances and statutes were superinduced upon it; but the foundation of God remained sure, having the former seals.[2]

This becomes the more clear as we use again the light which the apostle Paul holds up to us. We learn from his teaching, in particular, that that institution of the law, which fills so great a place in the history of Israel, whose uses, as Paul himself teaches, were so manifold, was after all essentially secondary to the other revelation made before unto Abraham. "The law came in beside" (νόμος δὲ παρεισῆλθεν), he tells the Roman believers, "that the trespass might abound." "Through the law cometh the knowledge of sin."[3] The period of the law in Israel was, as it were, a long parenthesis in the history of redemption, interposed between the promise to Abraham and its fulfilment in Christ. "For if the inheritance," the apostle says again, "is of the law, it is no more of promise; but God hath granted it to Abraham by promise. What then is the law? It was added because of transgressions, till the seed should come to whom the promise hath been made. . . . Is the law, then, against the promises of God? God forbid; for if there had been a law given which could make alive, verily righteousness would have been of the law. Howbeit the Scripture hath shut up all under sin, that the promise by faith in Jesus Christ might be given to them that believe."[4]

---

[1] Rom. xi. 29.
[2] Comp. Bannerman, *Church of Christ*, i. p. 75 f.
[3] Rom. iii. 20; v. 20.
[4] Gal. iii. 18 ff.

God had many lessons to teach in the school of the law, concerning Himself and concerning man, of sin, and righteousness, and judgment, and Israel was slow in learning.

Paul of Tarsus, who had learned so much himself in that school, never for a moment in his most impassioned arguments for Gospel freedom speaks slightingly of God's law as given to Israel. To him it was "spiritual, holy, just and good." He sought that men should "use it lawfully." " Do we make the law of none effect through faith? (διὰ τῆς πίστεως, 'the faith' spoken of, which 'justifies apart from the works of the law'). God forbid; nay, we establish the law." [1]   But all the while, behind the majestic figure of the law there rose to his eyes the yet loftier and fairer form of the grace of God in the Gospel preached beforehand to Abraham, to which the law was visibly to give place when "the seed should come to whom the promise was made." "Before faith came" (ἡ πίστις, the "faith in Jesus Christ," spoken of in the verse immediately preceding) "we were kept in ward under the law, shut up unto the faith which should afterwards be revealed.   So that the law hath been our tutor to bring us unto Christ, that we might be justified by faith. But now that faith is come, we are no longer under a tutor. For ye are all the sons of God through faith in Christ Jesus. For as many of you as were baptized into Christ did put on Christ. . . . And if ye are Christ's, then are ye Abraham's seed, heirs according to promise." [2]

Without embarrassing the treatment of our subject with needless details, we may note that certain things which have an important bearing upon it stand out with increasing clearness as this period of the history of revelation passes on.

1st. There emerges more and more distinctly the conception of a people of God, separated from other peoples, called and chosen of God to special fellowship with Him and with

---

[1] Rom. iii. 28, 31 ; vii. 12-14 ; 1 Tim. i. 8.

[2] Gal. iii. 19, 23-29.   Comp. Litton, *Church of Christ*, Lond. 1851, p. 109 f., and especially the interesting chapter on "the spiritual operation of the Mosaic law," pp. 128-143.

each other for high ends, bound by covenant obligations to faithfulness and obedience to Him.

To this people of God, consisting of the seed of Abraham in the line of promise with all who identified themselves with them, special promises are given for themselves, and assurance of blessing through them to others. So in the fundamental oracles vouchsafed by Jehovah to Moses at Sinai : " Thus shalt thou say to the house of Jacob, and tell the children of Israel : Ye have seen what I did unto the Egyptians, and how I bare you on eagles' wings, and brought you unto Myself. Now therefore, if ye will obey my voice indeed, and keep my covenant, then ye shall be a peculiar treasure unto Me from among " (or " above," Marg.) " all peoples : for all the earth is Mine. And ye shall be unto Me a kingdom of priests, and a holy nation." [1]

In connection with such promises, Israel, as a whole, is in many respects treated " as one personality," just as before the covenant was with Abraham and his seed in him. We find this expressed in striking utterances of Jehovah Himself : " Israel is My son, even My first-born." " When Israel was a child, then I loved him, and called My son out of Egypt." [2] Israel is dealt with as a son through much stubbornness and rebellion. In the beautiful words of the Westminster Confession respecting " adoption," he is " pitied, protected, provided for, and chastened by God as a Father, yet never cast off." [3]

2nd. Through all the changeful history there comes out more and more clearly the spiritual character of those who really belonged to the true people of God ; the family likeness to Abraham proves their right to be regarded as the seed of promise. They show the faith and do the works of their father.

Now and again for a time the influence of this true seed so prevails in the nation that Israel, as a whole, seems indeed

---

[1] Ex. xix. 3-6.   Comp. Candlish, *Kingdom of God*, Edin. 1885, p. 50 ff.
[2] Ex. iv. 22 f. ; Hosea xi. 1 ; Jer. iv. 19 ; xxxi. 9.
[3] Conf. c. xii.   Comp. Lev. xxvi. 40-45; Deut. xxx. 1-7; 1 Sam. xii. 22 ; Ps. lxxxix. 26-34 ; xciv. 14 ; Jer. xlvi. 28 ; Amos ix. 9, 14 f.

to be " called, and chosen, and faithful." But for the most part it is not so. " All are not Israel which are of Israel ; neither because they are Abraham's seed are they all children. . . . Not the children of the flesh are children of God, but the children of the promise are reckoned for a seed." " Except the Lord of hosts had left unto us a very small remnant " (" had left us a seed," as the apostle quotes it, following the LXX.), " we should have been as Sodom, we should have been like to Gomorrah." [1] The true representatives of the cause and people of God have to struggle against enemies and hostile influences which are often too strong for them. Sin and shortcoming in themselves, foes to the highest interests of Israel among their own countrymen, national tendencies to evil of every sort, all these things led to depression, some-times well-nigh to despair. " The whole head was sick, and the heart faint." Hopes of national blessing in things spiritual and outward seemed ever doomed to be disappointed and deferred, till they almost died out altogether.[2]

This painful experience wrought for good in God's hand. The believing seed of Abraham were thrown back more and more on the central blessing of the covenant, on God Him-self as their God, their shield and portion, from whom their reward should be exceeding great. They learned to claim Him as their Father and Redeemer, apart even from outward connection with Abraham by natural descent, and although feeling themselves separated in spirit and sympathy from the great majority of their fellow-countrymen. " Doubtless Thou art our Father, though Abraham knoweth us not, and Israel doth not acknowledge us : Thou, O Lord, art our Father, our Redeemer (גֹּאֲלֵנוּ) ; from everlasting is Thy name." [3]

We have an illustration of this in a remarkable crisis in the history of Israel in the time of Isaiah, to which reference is made in an early section of his prophecies (chap. vi. to viii.).

---

[1] Rom. ix. 6–8, 29 ; Isa. i. 9.

[2] Some of the thoughts and possibly even expressions in this passage are due, I believe, to remembrances of Principal Rainy's lectures, which I had the privilege of attending in New College, Edinburgh, some twenty years ago. Comp. his *Delivery and Development of Christian Doctrine*, p. 346 ff.

[3] Isa. lxiii. 16.

A sublime vision of God in His holiness and glory in the temple brings upon the prophet an overwhelming sense of his own sinfulness and that of his people. This is removed, so far as his own case is concerned, by the cleansing touch of fire from the altar of sacrifice. Then a message is given him to Israel. If this is rejected, the result is to be desolation for the land and banishment for its people. The vision ends with words in which judgment and grace are mingled : " And if there be yet a tenth in it, it shall again be eaten up : as a terebinth and as an oak whose stock remaineth " (or " whose substance is in them," Marg.) " when they are felled " (or " cast their leaves," Marg.) ; " so the holy seed is the stock thereof." [1]

In the prophecies recorded in the two following chapters the meaning of these words is shown. " When King Ahaz," as Professor Candlish says in his interesting exposition of the passage, " instead of trusting in Jehovah, sought help by calling in as an ally Tiglath-pileser, king of Assyria, the doom of his kingdom was sealed. Once drawn into the vortex of Eastern politics and brought within the range of Assyria's ambitious plans, there was no hope of such a small and poor kingdom retaining its independence. Jehovah would bring upon Judah as an overflowing flood that very empire of Assyria from which they now sought help (Isa. vii. 17 ; viii. 10). Seeing the king and people bent on this infatuated course, Isaiah is instructed by God to hold aloof from their confederacies and fears, and to wait on the Lord even when He was hiding His face from the house of Israel. He and his children and disciples form a little band, fearing and trusting Jehovah ; and among them the testimony and instruction that God has given, but the nation has rejected, is to be bound up and sealed, i.e. kept safely, and handed down to the time when it would be received by the people (viii. 11–20).

" This event marks a turning-point in the history of Israel. A society or Church is formed within the nation, having faith in God for its uniting principle, and treasuring His word as its guide ; and the existence of this prophetic party, nourish-

[1] Isa. vi. 13.

ing its faith on God's revelation, is what made it possible that the religion of Jehovah should survive the utter destruction of the nation. This was actually in history the stock of Israel formed by the holy seed, *i.e.* the presence and recognition of the Holy One in the midst of it, which made it possible that a new and better kingdom of God should spring up after the earthly one fell." [1]

Those children of Abraham who thus sought refuge with the Lord God of their fathers found no disappointment there. God was not ashamed to be called their God. Their reward from Him was exceeding great. Hence we find not a little spiritual light and strength and freedom enjoyed by many of the godly in Israel even in dark and troublous days. More and more their hearts came to lay hold of what was best and highest in the Divine covenant with Abraham, of the spiritual blessings comprised in the Gospel preached beforehand unto him,—the forgiveness of sins, deliverance from inward evils, "the clean heart and stedfast spirit," "the joy of God's salvation" and of His Presence,—and to find that these were given to faith even when outward mercies were withheld. "Who is a God like unto Thee, that pardoneth iniquity and passeth by the transgression of the remnant of His heritage? He retaineth not His anger for ever, because He delighteth in mercy. He will turn again and have compassion upon us; He will tread our iniquities under foot" (" will subdue our iniquities," Marg.); "and Thou wilt cast all their sins into the depths of the sea. Thou wilt perform the truth to Jacob and the mercy to Abraham, which Thou hast sworn unto our fathers from the days of old." [2] We meet much that recalls what we saw in Abraham, a strong implicit faith in God as a God of grace and redemption, a trustful reverence before Him, a joy in obedience, and in the will of God revealed in His law for obedience. This is signally manifest in the Psalms. In them we hear the answer of the believing seed to God's teaching in the law and

---

[1] Candlish, *Kingdom of God*, Edin. 1884, p. 73. Comp. Prof. Davidson's remarks on the same crisis in the religious history of Israel, *Hebrews*, p. 67 f.

[2] Ps. li. 10-12; Micah vii. 18-20.

by the prophets, the voice of spiritual life in the Church of the Old Testament.

3rd. Especially and increasingly, through centuries of Divine training and Providence, the hope of the true Israel came to concentrate itself in the better Seed of promise, the Coming One, and the blessings in store for God's people in connection with Him.

There was to be "a Prophet raised up like unto Moses," One who was to be "a Priest for ever, after the order of Melchisedec," a King to reign in righteousness and peace on the throne of David, of whose kingdom there should be no end, a "Servant of Jehovah," an ideal "Israel," a Prince with God, to be and do all that the earthly Israel had been called to aim at, but had failed to attain. In Him both Israel and all the nations of the earth should be blessed.[1] Fresh and fuller light concerning Him was ever breaking out in new forms through prophet and Psalmist, from sign and ordinance. It spread more and more in the general spiritual consciousness of Israel.

---

[1] Deut. xviii. 15–19 ; comp. xxxiv. 10 ; Ps. cx. 4, 72. See Rainy, *Delivery and Development of Doctrine*, pp. 62–64. Westcott, *Introd. to Study of Gospels*, 5th ed. pp. 92–94, 125–133, 152–154. Orelli, *alttestamentliche Weissagung von der Vollendung des Gottesreiches*, Wien 1882, pp. 166–209, 303–318, 345–349, 429–462. E. Tr., Edin. 1885, pp. 106–188. Schürer, *Hist. of Jewish People*, ii. pp. 135–187. Stanton, *Jewish and Christian Messiah*, pp. 97–111, 147–154. Castelli, in his careful discussion of the subject of "the Messiah according to the Hebrews," is sufficiently ready himself to apply rationalistic solvents to Messianic passages in the Psalms and prophets ; but he admits frankly that these passages were almost all taken in a Messianic sense, not only by Christian interpreters, but by the oldest Jewish exegetes, while the later ones, often men of a less religious spirit, show a strong polemic interest in their efforts to minimize the Messianic references which had been taken advantage of by Christians. "Abbiamo veduto, ed avremo luogo di vederlo anche in seguito, che le interpretationi messianiche dei passi biblici non sono per la maggior parte una invenzione cristiana ; ma trovano invece quasi sempre il loro eco nella tradizione ebraica. Ed è molto notevole la reazione che avviene negli interpreti ebrei posteriori ; i quali mossi da spirito di polemica, e non di rado ancora da un latente e inconscio razionalismo, si affaticano a dimostrare che moltissimi, se non tutti, di questi cosi detti luoghi messianici si riferiscono ad altri tempi del regno israelitico," *Il Messia secondo gli Ebrei*, Firenze 1874, p. 54 f. Comp. Canon Westcott's interesting table of Old Testament prophecies quoted as Messianic by our Lord, or by New Testament writers, with the corresponding interpretations by Jewish commentators, *Introd. to Gospels*, 5th ed. pp. 155–158.

The way by which the God of Abraham led His children was to end in this great consummation of blessing. And so the closing words of Old Testament prophecy bid God's people remember His law, with its statutes and judgments, and wait in faith and obedience for the Coming One.   " Behold, I send My Messenger, and He shall prepare the way before Me ; and the Lord, whom ye seek, shall suddenly come to His temple ; and " (or " even," Marg.) "the Messenger " (or "Angel," Marg.) " of the covenant, whom ye delight in : behold, He cometh, saith the Lord of Hosts." [1]

[1] Mal. iii. 1 ; iv. 4.

CHAPTER II.

IN considering this part of the subject we must carry with
us the results arrived at in last chapter, the conception
of the people of God, the fellowship of Israel, called, and
chosen, and separated unto the Lord from the other peoples of
the world; the conception of the true and holy seed in the
midst of Israel after the flesh; and, lastly, their faith and
hope in the Coming One, through whom the covenant
blessings promised to Abraham were to come to them and to
all nations of the earth. Turning back now to the first of
the three, observe that certain names and phrases denoting
the fellowship itself, or bearing specially upon its relations to
God, emerge throughout the history. As we follow its course,
we find them used with an increasing fulness and definiteness
of meaning; and they pass with us into the New Testament.
The most important of these names or phrases are:—

The house of Abraham, of Jacob, or of Israel;[1] the house
of God or of the Lord, the tabernacle, the tent of meeting,
the temple or sanctuary of the Lord;[2] the congregation

---

[1] Gen. xiv. 14; xvii. 23, 27; xviii. 19; xlvi. 27; Ex. xix. 3; Lev. x. 6;
xvii. 3, etc.; Ps. cxiv. 1; Isa. ii. 5. Frequent in Amos, Jeremiah, and Ezekiel.
Luke i. 33; Matt. x. 6; Acts ii. 36.

[2] House of God or of the Lord: Gen. xxviii. 17–22; Ex. xxiii. 19; xxxiv.
26; Josh. ix. 23; Judg. xviii. 31; xx. 18. Frequent in Kings, Jeremiah, and
Chronicles. Ps. lii. 8; lxxxiv. 10; Isa. ii. 3; Matt. xii. 4; xvii. 3, 15; Heb.
x. 21. Tabernacle, Tent of Meeting, etc.: Ex. xxv. 8 f.; xxix. 42–46; xxx.
16 ff.; xxxiii. 7–11; xl. 1 ff., 34 ff.; Lev., Num., and 1 Chron. *passim.*
Ps. xv. 1; xx. 2; xxvi. 8; xxvii. 5 f.; lxi. 4; lxiii. 2; lxxiii. 17; lxxvii. 13;
cxiv. 2; Isa. viii. 14; xvi. 12; Ezek. xi. 16; xxxvii. 27; xlvii. 12; Jer. xvii.
12; Heb. viii. 2; ix. 2–11.

(עֵדָה) of Israel, of the people, or of the Lord;[1] the assembly or Church (קָהָל) of Israel, of the people, or of the Lord.[2]

We may take the first and second groups together; doing the same with the third and fourth.

1. The common Hebrew word for "house" (בַּיִת), besides denoting an ordinary material dwelling-place, is employed in two special senses in the Old Testament. It often means (1) A family or household, whether in the narrower sense of a man's descendants, or in the wider one of all who are identified with his fortunes and theirs, although not originally of the same stock. (2) The place of God's special presence on earth.

(1.) In the first sense, the word is used repeatedly in Genesis of the family of Abraham, including all who were his, although by other ties than those of blood relationship; as when we read: "Every male among the men of Abraham's house (בְּאַנְשֵׁי בֵּית אַבְרָהָם, ἐν τῷ οἴκῳ 'Αβραάμ, LXX.) was circumcised. . . . All the men of his house, those born in the house and those bought with money of the stranger, were circumcised with him." "I have known him to the end that he may command his children and his house (וְאֶת־בֵּיתוֹ) after him." "And Abraham said unto his servant, the elder of his house, that ruled over all that he had."[3] It is worth noting that the LXX. translate here not by οἶκος but οἰκία, indicating a distinction in Hellenistic Greek which is not made in the Hebrew, but to which we shall have occasion to refer again. It was not over the "house" or "family" in the narrower sense, the wife and children of Abraham, that Eliezer the Damascene presided. He was the "major-domo," having charge of the servants and establishment of Abraham generally, his goods and household affairs.[4]

---

[1] עֵדָה, Ex. xii. 6 ; xvi. 3 ; xix. 47, etc.; Num. xxvii. 17 ; xxxi. 16 ; Lam. i. 10 ; 1 Chron. xxviii. 8 ; 2 Chron. v. 6 ; vi. 3, etc.

[2] קָהָל, Ex. xii. 6 ; Lev. iv. 14 ; xvi. 17, 33, etc.; Num. xvi. 3 ; Deut. xxiii. 1-4, 8 ; Ps. cvii. 32, etc.

[3] Gen. xvii. 23, 27 ; xviii. 19 ; xxiv. 2.

[4] It may be added that the same distinction between these two words seems to be repeatedly made by the LXX. in this same chapter (Gen. xxiv.). Thus

The word "house" in the sense of family, both in the narrower and wider sense, is constantly used in the later Scriptures, alike in narrative and prophetic portions, to denote the descendants of Abraham in the line of promise, or his posterity along with all those who identified themselves with them. "I shall be destroyed," Jacob says to his sons; "I and my house" (ὁ οἶκός μου, LXX.). "All the souls of the house of Jacob (οἶκος Ἰακώβ) were seventy souls." "Thus shalt thou say to the house of Jacob (οἶκος Ἰακώβ), and tell the children of Israel."[1]

(2.) The house of God or of Jehovah.

The phrase first occurs in the twenty-eighth chapter of Genesis in connection with the dream of Jacob, when God revealed Himself to him as "Jehovah, the God of Abraham his father," and repeated to him the central promises of the Abrahamic covenant when on his way to Laban; and it is associated with an instance of the other use of "house:" "And Jacob awaked out of his sleep, and he said, Surely the Lord is in this place, and I knew it not. And he was afraid, and said, How dreadful is this place! this is none other but the house of God, and this is the gate of heaven. . . . And he called the name of that place Beth-el" (*i.e.* "The house of God." The LXX. give simply the translation: ἐκάλεσε τὸ ὄνομα τοῦ τόπου ἐκείνου οἶκος θεοῦ) . . . "And Jacob vowed a vow, saying, If God will be with me, and will keep me in this way that I go, and will give me bread to eat, and raiment to put on, so that I come again to my father's house in peace (εἰς τὸν οἶκον τοῦ πατρός μου, LXX.), then shall the Lord be my God, and this stone

---

Abraham speaks of the Lord taking him "from his father's house, and the land of my nativity" (ἐκ τοῦ οἴκου τοῦ πατρός μου, ver. 7); on learning whose daughter Rebekah is, the servant gives thanks to God for leading him "to the house of my master's brother" (εἰς οἶκον τοῦ ἀδελφοῦ τοῦ κυρίου μου), and Rebekah runs "to tell her mother's house" (τὸν οἶκον τῆς μητρὸς αὐτῆς, ver. 28 f.). But when Laban accosts the steward standing at the head of his band of servants and camels, it is with the words: "I have prepared the house" (τὴν οἰκίαν, the household or establishment generally, for the reception of such a caravan), "and room for the camels; and the man came into the house (εἰς τὴν οἰκίαν), and ungirded the camels, and he gave straw and provender for the camels," etc. (ver. 31 f.).

[1] Gen. xxxiv. 30; xlvi. 27; Ex. xix. 3. See other illustrative references in note above, p. 75.

which I have set up for a pillar shall be God's house (ἔσται μοι οἶκος θεοῦ); and of all that Thou shalt give me, I will surely give the tenth unto Thee." [1]

In this striking passage it is manifest that it was the presence of God revealed in His grace and majesty which made the place for Jacob to be "the house of God." So also on his return from Padan-Aram: "God said unto Jacob, Arise, go up to Beth-el, and dwell there; and make there an altar unto God, who appeared unto thee when thou fleddest from the face of Esau thy brother. Then Jacob said unto his house (אֶל־בֵּיתוֹ, τῷ οἴκῳ αὐτοῦ, LXX.), and to all that were with him, Put away the strange gods that are among you, and purify yourselves, and change your garments; and let us arise and go up to Beth-el, and I will make there an altar unto God, who answered me in the day of my distress, and was with me in the way which I went." [2]

From the period of the wilderness sojourn onwards, the tabernacle and the temple are constantly referred to both in the historical and prophetic books as the "house of God," or "of the Lord." "The tent which He pitched among men," the place where His immediate presence was to be recognised, where His glory was to be seen, and where especially He met with men and spoke to them in grace. [3] Yet ever and anon such references were accompanied with an emphatic testimony to the fact that God's presence was also in every place, and that the heavens and the earth were full of His glory. [4]

---

[1] Gen. xxviii. 16-22.   [2] Gen. xxxv. 1-4, 6 f.

[3] See the references at p. 75.   Of the two names tabernacle and temple, the first (מִשְׁכָּן, from שָׁכַן, to dwell) means literally dwelling-place.   It is closely allied to the impressive name used in the Targums and by the Jewish Rabbis, for the glory in the midst, the visible manifestation of the Divine Presence, or for God Himself as dwelling in the Tabernacle or Temple, viz. the Shekinah (שְׁכִינָה).   Tabernacle (מִשְׁכָּן) is a loftier and more poetic word in itself than "tent" (אֹהֶל), which is often translated "tabernacle" in our A. V. "Temple," again (הֵיכָל), conveys the thought that the "tent," the "house," is royal, the dwelling-place of "the great king."   Comp. Dean Plumptre on the word and its synonyms in his art. "Tabernacle," in Smith's *Dictionary of the Bible.*

[4] Ex. xx. 24 ; xxxiii. 9 ff., 14-23 ; xxxiv. 5-9 ; 1 Kings viii. 27-30 ; Deut. x. 14-17 ; xii. 11 ; 2 Chron. vi. 18-21 ; Isa. vi. 1-5 ; lxvi. 1.

Compare the striking answer of one of the wiser Rabbis when pressed to solve

This brings us to that weighty and pregnant expression—
"the tent of meeting." Among the many good services done
by the Old Testament Company of Revisers, not the least is
this, that they have in great measure removed the obscurity
which the A. V. left resting for English readers over what it
called "the tabernacle of the congregation" (אֹהֶל מוֹעֵד), but
which is now recognised as "the tent of meeting."[1] The
significance of the great revelation in Ex. xxix. 42–46,
stands out now in a much clearer light. The tent or tabernacle was to be known as "the tent of meeting," because
there Jehovah said, "I will meet with you to speak there
unto thee. There I will meet with the children of Israel:
and the tent shall be sanctified by My glory. And I will
sanctify the tent of meeting and the altar; Aaron also and
his sons will I sanctify to minister unto Me in the priest's
office. And I will dwell among the children of Israel, and
will be their God."

the difficulty of God's working on the Sabbath day—"May not a man walk
through his own house on the Sabbath ? The house of God is the whole realm
above and the whole realm below."—Cited by Westcott on John v. 17.

[2] The resources of the English language were probably inadequate to carry
the Revisers farther on the right road without aid from a humbler sister-tongue.
But the Hebrew verb from which the substantive מוֹעֵד comes (יָעַד, in Niphal
and Hiphil נוֹעַד and הוֹעִיד) suggests especially the idea of meeting *by appointment* or *mutual agreement*. "The Scottish Revisers," one of their number tells
us, "often regretted that the old word 'tryst,' still well known in their
country, was inadmissible ; it expresses so shortly and precisely what is wanted.
And, moreover, it would have conducted us straight to the best conceivable
rendering of another noun of the same family (with עֵדָה, to which the writer
has been referring), namely מוֹעֵד, grossly mistranslated in the extremely
frequent expression 'tabernacle of the congregation,' whereas its meaning is
'trysting tent' or 'tent of tryst,' according to the promise, There I will meet
with thee (וְנוֹעַדְתִּי לְךָ שָׁם), namely, by appointment, Ex. xxv. 21 ; xxix. 42 f. ;
xxx. 6, 36 ; Num. xvii. 4. Not being able to employ this word, we took 'tent
of meeting,' this noun answering to the verb in these verses quoted. But this
was the smaller part of our difficulty and cause of regret." The Reviser goes
on to show "what a flood of light" this word tryst would have thrown for
English—or at least Scottish—readers, on the whole subject of the "feasts of
the Lord," headed by the weekly Sabbath, in the Old Testament.—Principal
Douglas, "Revision of the English O. T.," in *Monthly Interpreter*, Aug. 1885,
p. 255 ff.

There is an evident reference in these words to the great central promise of the covenant made by God with Abraham. This was the nearest typical fulfilment of it which could be given at that stage in the history of redemption. It was a sort of sacramental pledge and foretaste of what should be afterwards, an outward sign through which faith laid hold of the thing signified.

God's Presence was visibly revealed in majesty and yet in grace over the mercy-seat in the tent of meeting. Each man of Israel was encouraged to bring his own oblation (קָרְבָּנוֹ, his corban) to the door of the tent of meeting "that he might himself be accepted before the Lord," if his oblation was a burnt-offering (עֹלָה); that his oblation might be "of a sweet savour before the Lord," if it was a meal-offering (מִנְחָה), or a peace- or thank-offering (זֶבַח שְׁלָמִים). Careful provision was made that an acceptable offering in some form of all the three different classes was within easy reach of the poorest among the people.[1] Each man for himself, in bringing the primary sacrifice which Abraham used, was "to lay his hand upon the head of the burnt-offering, and it shall be accepted for him to make atonement for him. And he shall kill it before the Lord; and the priests shall present the blood, and sprinkle the blood round about upon the altar that is at the door of the tent of meeting."[2] There the priests, representing the people, drew near to God continually in the ritual of the daily oblations, and of the sin and trespass-offerings, with incense and the blood of sacrifice. Yet more special access into the immediate presence of the Lord was vouchsafed to Israel once a year in the person of their chief representative, the High Priest, who entered within the veil into the Holiest of all with the blood of sin-offerings on the great day of Atonement "for himself and for his house, and for all the assembly of Israel."[3]

Through these means the true Israel attained a large

---

[1] Lev. i. 3, 10, 14; ii. 1 f., 4 f., 7.   Comp. Bonar, *Leviticus*, pp. 12–15.   Cave, *Sacrifice*, Edin. 1884, p. 468 f.

[2] Lev. i. 4 f.

[3] וְכִפֶּר בַּעֲדוֹ וּבְעַד בֵּיתוֹ וּבְעַד כָּל־קְהַל יִשְׂרָאֵל, Lev. xvi. 17.   Comp. David-son, *Hebrews*, p. 172 f.

measure of spiritual fellowship with God, which was good
for the time then present, and which was an earnest of
better things to come. Many a believing spirit among the
children of Abraham turned in after times towards " the tent
of meeting," and grasped the promises which the God of
their fathers had given in connection with it. In many a
Psalm we hear the longings and the joy of their faith,—

> "One thing I of the Lord desired, and will seek to obtain,
> That all days of my life I may within God's house remain;
> That I the beauty of the Lord behold may and admire,
> And that I in His holy place may reverently inquire.
> For He in His pavilion shall me hide in evil days,
> In secret of His tent me hide, and on a rock me raise.
> And now, even at this present time, mine head shall lifted be
> Above all those that are my foes, and round encompass me :
> Therefore into His tabernacle I'll sacrifices bring
> Of joyfulness : I'll sing, yea, I to God will praises sing."

> "My table Thou hast furnished in presence of my foes ;
> My head Thou dost with oil anoint, and my cup overflows.
> Goodness and mercy all my life shall surely follow me ;
> And in God's house for evermore my dwelling-place shall be." [1]

To God thus revealed in His house the faith of the Hebrew
exiles looked, as they prayed, like Daniel, with " the windows
open in their chamber toward Jerusalem." [2] Their heart's
desire and prayer were that they " might see His power and
His glory so as they had looked upon Him in the sanctuary,"
as " they had thought upon His loving-kindness in the
midst of His temple," that " this God should be their God
for ever and ever, that He should be their guide even unto
death." [3]

The answer to such prayers of faith was given in such
assurances as the exiles received from the lips of Ezekiel.
In a vision, recorded in the eleventh chapter of his book,
the prophet is taken to " the east gate of the Lord's house "
in Jerusalem. He is made to see the ungodliness that

---

[1] Ps. xxvii. 4–6 ; xxiii. 5 f., Scottish Metrical Version. Comp. xv. 1 f. ;
xxvi. 8 ; lxi. 4 ; lxxvi. 2 ; lxxviii. 60 ; lxxx. 1 f. ; lxxxiv. 1–5, 10 f. ; xcii. 13 f. ;
xcix. 1 ff. ; c. 4 f. ; cxxxii. 7 f.

[2] Dan. vi. 10.   [3] Ps. lxiii. 2 ; xlviii. 9, 14.

prevailed among the remnant of Israel there, and how evil counsels were given in the city, and scornful words spoken by the inhabitants of Jerusalem concerning the community of the exiles,—the Dispersion in distant lands, with whom Ezekiel himself was specially identified,—as being "far 'from the Lord" and from His house. To that fellowship of the Dispersion, "them of the captivity," "thy brethren, the men of thy kindred (גְאֻלָּתֶךָ, 'of thy redemption'), and all the house of Israel," this message of comfort is now sent: "Thus saith the Lord God, Whereas I have removed them far off among the nations, and whereas I have scattered them among the countries, yet will I be to them a sanctuary for a little while (or, as margin of R. V., which is the rendering of Ewald and many good authorities: 'Yet have I been to them a sanctuary') in the countries where they are come." And then follows one of the most gracious republications, which we find in all Scripture, of the promises made, and the Gospel preached beforehand to Abraham: "Thus saith the Lord God, I will gather you from the peoples, and assemble you out of the countries where ye have been scattered, and I will give you the land of Israel. . . . And I will give them one heart, and I will put a new spirit within you; and I will take the stony heart out of their flesh, and will give them a heart of flesh; that they may walk in My statutes and keep Mine ordinances, and do them: and they shall be My people, and I will be their God." And the vision closes with "the glory of the Lord," the Shekinah, departing from the midst of the city of Jerusalem, and moving towards the east. "And the Spirit lifted me up, and brought me in the vision by the Spirit of God into Chaldæa, to them of the captivity. Then I spake unto them of the captivity all the things that the Lord had showed me." [1]

"The house of Israel" met with God in "His house." His Presence was "the glory in the midst of Jerusalem, and a wall of fire round about." [2] More and more clearly through the teaching of God's word and Providence His people learned practically that it was the Lord's Presence only

---

[1] Ezek. xi. 1 ff., 13–25.   [2] Zech. ii. 5, 10 ff. ; Isa. iv. 5.

which made the place holy and glorious, that the Lord Himself *was* the sanctuary, and that wherever He revealed Himself in grace, there was "the House of God and the gate of heaven." The ancient promise gathered a new breadth and depth of meaning: "In every place where I record My name (or 'cause My name to be remembered,' Marg.), I will come unto thee, and I will bless thee."[1]

The Lord made His name to be remembered among them in strange lands. He promised and proved Himself "to be a sanctuary to the house of Israel" in all countries in which they sought His Face. It is not yet expressly said that wherever a company of true believers were gathered together in His Name, there He was in the midst of them, that the house of Israel in truth *were* the Lord's house. In such passages as those last cited, it is evident how closely the two conceptions were approaching each other. Not perhaps till we reach New Testament ground can we say that they absolutely coincide.[2] But there they unmistakeably do so. One memorable utterance of the wilderness period—already cited in part in another connection—marks the transition. In the twelfth chapter of Numbers we hear how Aaron and Miriam sought to place themselves on a level with Moses as regards closeness of relation with God. "Hath the Lord indeed spoken only with Moses? Hath He not spoken also with us?" A vindication of the superiority of Moses was given. The Lord appeared in a pillar of cloud at the door of the tent of meeting, and as the three stood before Him, He said: "If there be a prophet among you, I the Lord will make Myself known unto him in a vision, I will speak unto him in a dream. My servant Moses (ὁ θεράπων μου, LXX.) is not so; he is faithful in all Mine house (ἐν ὅλῳ τῷ οἴκῳ μου). . . . Wherefore then were ye not afraid to

---

[1] Ex. xx. 24. Comp. Ps. xc. 1.

[2] In one Old Testament passage (Hosea viii. 1), according to the most probable interpretation of it, Israel seems to be spoken of as "the Lord's house," in the sense of being the family among the nations which belongs specially to Him. But they are spoken of by this name only to be told that they are cast off by the Lord, "because they have transgressed My covenant, and trespassed against My law. . . . Now are they among the nations as a vessel wherein is no pleasure."

speak against My servant, against Moses ? " [1]   This declaration
as to the position of Moses in the house of God is expressly
cited by the author of the Epistle to the Hebrews, who
then proceeds : " Moses indeed was faithful in all His house,
as a servant (ὡς θεράπων), for a testimony of those things
which were afterward to be spoken ; but Christ as a Son
over His house ; whose house are we (οὗ οἰκίς ἐσμεν ἡμεῖς),
if we hold fast our boldness and the glorying of our hope
firm unto the end." [2]

Again, in the First Epistle to Timothy we read : " These
things write I unto thee . . . that thou mayest know how
men ought to behave themselves in the house of God, which
is the Church of the living God, the pillar and ground of
the truth.   And confessedly great," the apostle goes on,
bringing into the closest connection with the house of God
that Divine Presence in the midst of it which is its glory,
as the Shekinah was "the glory of the former house,"
" is the mystery of godliness : He who was manifested in
the flesh, justified in the spirit, seen of angels, preached
among the nations, believed on in the world, received up in
glory." [3]

The conclusion, then, to which we are led by our examination of Scripture teaching on this point is this, that the
Church of God or the fellowship of believers, as fully established in privilege, and receiving " the blessing of Abraham
in Christ Jesus, the promise of the Spirit through faith," [4]
is that which the tent of meeting and the temple, " the
holy and beautiful house of the Lord," [5] under the old
economy, typified, and for which they prepared the way.
The Church under the New Testament is the special abode
of God's gracious Presence as revealed in Christ ; it is
" builded together in Him for an habitation of God (εἰς
κατοικητήριον τοῦ θεοῦ) through the Spirit ;" and it is

[1] Num. xii. 2-9.

[2] Heb. iii. 2-6.   Comp. x. 21, "Having a great Priest over the house
of God."

[3] 1 Tim. iii. 14 ff.   Comp. 2 Cor. vi. 16 with the reference there to the sum
of God's gracious promises to Israel in the wilderness, after the LXX. rendering
of Lev. xxvi. 11 ff.

[4] Gal. iii. 14.

[5] Isa. lxiv. 11.

there that "spiritual sacrifices" are offered by the New
Testament priesthood, "acceptable to God through Jesus
Christ," "the High Priest of our confession," "a minister
of the sanctuary, and of the true tabernacle which the Lord
pitched, not man."[1]

Having been led at this point to trace the Biblical use of
the phrases "house of Israel" and "house of God" beyond the
limits of the Old Testament, it may be suitable to say something here regarding a distinction between two words for
house, family, or household (οἶκος and οἰκία), which has already
met us in the Greek version of the Old Testament Scriptures,
and which emerges also in the New Testament.

We saw before[2] that the Alexandrian translators, generally
referred to as the LXX., in their rendering of the Hebrew
term for house, made a distinction — not perhaps invariably
observing it, but as a rule — between οἶκος and οἰκία. This
same distinction is observed to a similar extent by the New
Testament writers.

"The meanings of the two words οἰκία and οἶκος," says an
eminent English scholar, "are very distinct in the original,
and ought not to be confounded. Οἰκία is the material house,
the actual building. It occurs ninety-four times in the New
Testament, and only in four of these is it used to signify a
family, according to the common metaphor by which the
name of a place is transferred to the persons who are in it.
These four passages are in Matt. x. 13; xii. 25 (where Luke
xi. 17 has οἶκος); Mark iii. 25; and 1 Cor. xvi. 15.

"Οἶκος occurs one hundred and ten times in the New Testament, and only in one of these is it used to signify a material

[1] Eph. ii. 19–22; 1 Pet. ii. 3; iv. 17; Heb. iii. 1; viii. 1 ff. In Luke xiii.
25–29, the "house" into which Christ exhorts all men to strive to enter, the
door of which will one day be shut by the Master of the house (οἰκοδισπότης),
is represented as equivalent to "the kingdom of God," in which Abraham,
Isaac, and Jacob, and all the prophets have their place. Cremer is right,
as against Delitzsch, who says "that בֵּית ה, οἶκος τοῦ θεοῦ, is the invariable Biblical designation of the Church of God" (Hebräerbrief, S. 481), in
stating that "its use to denote the Church occurs first in the New Testament
because the ἐκκλησία is that which the temple in the Old Testament typified,
the abode of God's Presence." Biblico-Theol. Lexicon of New Testament Greek
3rd ed., Edin. 1880. Sub voce οἶκος.

[2] Supra, p. 76 f.

house like οἰκία, namely, in Luke xii. 39 : 'would not have
suffered his house (τὸν οἶκον αὐτοῦ) to be broken through,'
where Matt. xxiv. 43 has οἰκίαν. And even here the idea
intended by St. Luke to be conveyed by the word οἶκος is
probably not that of a mere house, but the house with all
its contents, 'his house and goods;' just as it is used in
Homer, e.g. :—

'Οὐ γὰρ ἔτ' ἀνσχετὰ ἔργα τετεύχαται, οὐδ' ἔτι καλῶς
   Οἶκος ἐμὸς διόλωλε.'—*Odyss.* ii. 64, and elsewhere.

"The general use of οἶκος in the New Testament exhibits
two principal significations, under each of which some varying
shades of meaning are to be found:—

"1. The most frequent meaning of οἶκος is 'a family' or
'household,' with a more or less distinct reference to the
house as containing it.

"Thus in Matt. ix. 6, the first place in which the word
occurs, ὕπαγε εἰς τὸν οἶκόν σου means, Go to thy family and
friends at home, which explanation is actually added in Mark
v. 19: εἰς τὸν οἶκόν σου πρὸς τοὺς σούς. Hence the word is
sometimes very properly translated 'home,' as in this place
of St. Mark, 'Go home to thy friends ;' as also in 1 Cor. xi. 34,
xiv. 35, and elsewhere. From this it followed that οἶκος was
the word to signify 'house' in the sense of a family of
descendants or a separate race, as 'the house of Israel,' Matt.
x. 6 ; 'the house of David,' Luke i. 27.

"2. The second meaning of οἶκος nearly resembles that of
the Latin 'ædes' in the singular, and signifies an apartment,
hall, or building appropriated to some special purpose, particularly a *sacred* purpose. Thus in Luke xiv. 23 : 'that my
house may be filled,' where οἶκος is the hall or room in which
the guests were assembled ; in Matt. xi. 8 : 'in kings' houses,'
ἐν τοῖς οἴκοις τῶν βασιλέων, in the halls or palaces of kings.
So in Acts x. 30, Cornelius says: 'I was praying in my
house' (ἐν τῷ οἴκῳ μου), meaning the apartment to which,
doubtless, he retired to pray. Hence οἶκος is the word always
used for 'house' in a religious sense, as applied to the Jewish
temple; as in Matt. xxi. 13 : 'My house shall be called a
house of prayer' (ὁ οἶκός μου οἶκος προσευχῆς κληθήσεται) ;
John ii. 16 : 'My Father's house' (τὸν οἶκον τοῦ πατρός μου) ;

while 'in my Father's house,' in a different sense, is ἐν τῇ οἰκίᾳ τοῦ πατρός μου. ... So also οἶκος is employed in speaking of the Christian Church under the similitude of a sacred building or spiritual temple, as in 1 Tim. iii. 15 ; 1 Pet. ii. 5.

"Now this word οἶκος, never οἰκία, is the one always used in the New Testament as the common name of the places where Christians met for religious purposes. The 'upper room,' where the apostles and their earliest adherents after the Ascension ' continued with one accord in prayer and supplication,' is probably meant by 'the house (τὸν οἶκον) where they were sitting' in Acts ii. 2 ; and the word is afterwards indisputably applied to places of Christian worship in nine other passages: Acts ii. 46 ; v. 42 ; viii. 3 ; xx. 20 ; Rom. xvi. 5 ; 1 Cor. xv. 19 ; Col. iv. 15 ; Titus i. 11 ; Philem. 2." [1]

My own examination of the question leads me in substance to agree with Dr. Jacob. I believe that the line of distinction which he points out is a real one, although not, I think, so invariably observed as his statements would seem to imply. There are certainly cases where in parallel accounts of the same incident or passage in our Lord's teaching the two words appear to be used interchangeably.[2] These, however, are instances in which the wider sense includes the narrower. Generally speaking, the two words do seem to be used with a quite appreciable difference of meaning. It may be put in this way : οἶκος, both in the material and metaphorical sense, expresses more of unity and closeness of connection than οἰκία. Thus, when the two words are used in the literal or material sense, οἶκος denotes either the *home* as such, the *family* abode, or the dwelling room of the family, the hall or chief apartment of the house, where the members of the family are most at home ; οἰκία, on the other hand, denotes rather the

---

[1] Jacob, *Ecclesiastical Polity of the New Testament*, Lond. 1871, p. 191 f.

[2] Thus, *e.g.*, besides the exception admitted by Dr. Jacob (Matt. xxiv. 43 compared with Luke xii. 39), we have in Matt. x. 13 f.: "As ye enter into the house (τὴν οἰκίαν), salute it ; and if the house (ἡ οἰκία) be worthy, let your peace come upon it. ... As ye go forth out of that house (ἔξω τῆς οἰκίας) or that city." The corresponding words in Luke x. 5–8 are : "Into whatsoever house (οἰκίαν) ye shall enter, first say, Peace be to this house (τῷ οἴκῳ τούτῳ). ... And in that same house (οἰκίᾳ) remain. ... Go not from house to house (ἐξ οἰκίας εἰς οἰκίαν)."

"establishment" and material surroundings of the family, the "house and offices," as we might say, the whole group or combination of dwellings, large and small, which meet the wants of an Oriental household.[1]

When the two words are used in the metaphorical sense, οἶκος means the "family," regarded as a unity, closely knit together in relations of common privilege and responsibility under a common representative head; οἰκία again denotes the "household" in a wider sense, the domestic establishment of servants, etc., the suite of a nobleman or prince, where the union is of a much looser sort, and individuality is more recognised.[2]

2. We have seen how the two conceptions of the "house of Abraham" and "of Israel" on the one hand, and of the "house of God" or "of Jehovah" on the other, drew nearer and nearer to each other in the consciousness of God's people under the discipline of His Providence and the guidance of His Word and Spirit, but that they can hardly be said to coincide until we reach New Testament ground in the teaching of our Lord and His apostles. We have now to examine two

---

[1] Thus, e.g., Luke i. 40 : "Mary entered into the house (οἶκον) of Zacharias," i.e. the family room in which her kinswoman Elizabeth was to be found. But Mark i. 29 : "They entered into the house (οἰκίαν) of Simon and Andrew, with James and John." It was not the home of a single family, but, according to Eastern fashion, an abode where several households lived together, united by kinship or common interests. Cf. Luke v. 7, 10, "partners with Simon." In Luke vii. 6–10 : "When not far from the house" (οἰκίας, i.e. the centurion's quarters), "he sent unto Him friends . . . and they, returning into the house (εἰς τὸν οἶκον,"—probably the family room in which the servant lay, "dear unto the centurion," and called by him "my child," ὁ παῖς μου, ver. 7). In Luke xiv. 23 the master of the house (οἰκοδισπότης) bids the servant "compel them to come in, that my house" (ὁ οἶκός μου, my hall for the banquet) "may be full." So Acts xi. 12 f., etc.

[2] Thus, e.g., Mark vi. 4 : "A prophet is not without honour save in his own house" (οἰκία), i.e. in such a circle of relatives and comrades as dwelt in the οἰκία of Simon and Andrew, with their partners James and John in Capernaum, Mark i. 29. The prophet, like our Lord Himself and the Baptist, might often have no family (οἶκος) of which he was the natural head, or in which he commonly lived. In John iv. 53 : "The nobleman believed and his whole household" (οἰκία, i.e. the servants and others who formed his suite). It is not said that the child (τὸ παιδίον, ver. 49), who belonged to his family (οἶκος) in the narrower sense, believed, or was capable from age of doing so. So in Phil. iv. 22 : "All the saints salute you, especially they that are of Cæsar's household" (ἐκ τῆς Καίσαρος οἰκίας). It is not members of the emperor's family in the closer sense who are meant, but slaves or freedmen of the Imperial household.

other important expressions, in which the conceptions of relationship between the members of the chosen people on the one side, and of their relationship to God on the other, were from the first combined, although there was manifest progress and development of thought as to the proper contents of the conceptions and the true nature and effects of the twofold relationship. The expressions to which I refer are עֵדָה and קָהָל, "congregation" and "assembly" or "Church," used especially in the phrases "the congregation of Israel" or "of the Lord,"[1] and "the assembly or Church of Israel," or "of the Lord."[2]

All through the Old Testament from Exodus onwards, alike in the historical, legislative, and prophetic portions, the community of Israel as a whole, and its meetings for worship or the transaction of affairs connected with religious, social, or political life, are constantly referred to under these expressions. They meet us in the Gospels, the Acts, and the Epistles in the form in which they were rendered by the Alexandrian translators of the Old Testament.[3] It is obvious that we cannot be in a position rightly to estimate the meaning of these words in the New Testament unless we know something of their previous history and use.

The precise force of these two important terms עֵדָה and קָהָל has been repeatedly discussed by able and learned exegetes. The first complete and satisfactory investigation was made by Vitringa in his great work *De Synagoga Vetere*, and was conducted by him with such thoroughness and discrimination

---

[1] עֲדַת יִשְׂרָאֵל and עֲדַת יְהֹוָה, or simply הָעֵדָה, Ex. xii. 3-6 (כֹּל קְהַל עֲדַת־יִשְׂרָאֵל, the whole assembly of the congregation of Israel); xix. 47; xvi. 1 f., 9 f., 22, etc. ; Num. xxvii. 17 ; xxxi. 16 ; Josh. xxii. 17, etc.

[2] קְהַל יִשְׂרָאֵל and קְהַל יְהֹוָה, or simply הַקָּהָל, Ex. xii. 6 ; xvi. 3 ; Lev. iv. 13 f., 21 ; xvi. 17, 33 ; Num. x. 7 ; xiv. 5 ; xv. 15 ; xvi. 3, etc. ; Deut. xxiii. 1-3, etc. It is worth noting that עֵדָה does not occur in Genesis ; קָהָל, on the other hand, occurs four times in the patriarchal period : in three of these the word is used in express reference to the blessing of Abraham (Gen. xxviii. 3 ; xxxv. 11 ; xlviii. 4), while in the fourth instance there is a reference to it implied by way of contrast (xlix. 6).

[3] Matt. iv. 23 ; vi. 2 ; ix. 35 ; x. 17 ; xvi. 18 ; xviii. 17, etc. ; Acts v. 11 ; vi. 9 ; vii. 38 ; viii. 1 ; ix. 2, 31, etc. ; Rom. xvi. 1-4 f. ; xvi. 23 ; 1 Cor. i. 2, etc.

that his conclusions have been generally accepted by the most competent modern interpreters, such as Archbishop Trench, Cremer, and (in substance) Schürer.[1] The distinction arrived at by him, which may be taken, I think, as substantially established, is to this effect,—I translate from Vitringa, condensing slightly :—

"The term קהל is used in a more specific and restricted sense than the term עדה. The former denotes properly the whole body of any people, united by common bonds in one society, and constituting some kind of republic or commonwealth. The word עדה, again, simply indicates any meeting or assembly of men (cœtum vel conventum), whether larger or smaller in extent, but more especially a *fixed and appointed meeting ;* not necessarily of the people as a whole (although the scope of the word is wide enough to admit of that application also), but it may be of certain persons from among the people, as when magistrates meet in council. Hence עדה may be used of any definite meeting within a society, to which קהל would by no means apply. Take, for example, any Sanhedrin of twenty or thirty members ; take any meeting of men from among the people for the performance of this or that action whether in things sacred or civil,—עדה would apply to them, but not קהל ; for the latter term always denotes a number of persons so joined together as to form a unity, such as a city or a commonwealth.

"When used in its wider sense, קהל signifies just what the Hebrews and the Romans expressed by עַם, 'populus,' and sometimes also by עִיר, 'civitas.' Cicero's words may be suitably adduced here : 'Populus est non omnis cœtus multitudinis, sed cœtus juris consensu et utilitatis communione sociatus.'[2] . . . Again, קהל taken more strictly denotes very often the whole body of the people called together to consider regarding the most important affairs of the common-

---

[1] Trench, *Synonyms of the N. T.* p. 3 ff.   Cremer, *Biblico-Theol. Lex. of N. T. Greek*, 3rd Eng. ed., *sub voce* ἰκκλησία.   Schürer, *History of Jewish People*, E. Tr. 1885, ii. p. 59.   Köstlin makes עדה "an assembly in general, and קהל an assembly for Divine worship," art. "Church" in Schaff's *Relig. Encyclop.* (based on Herzog).

[2] *De Republica*, quoted by Augustine, *De Civit.* ii. 21. 2.

wealth. The Romans had their 'comitia calata,' which corresponded closely to the Hebrew conception of קהל in the
stricter sense. Thus we read in Lev. xvi. 33 of עַם הַקָּהָל, 'the
people of the assembly.' The most illustrious instance of this
in the history of Israel was the assembly at Sinai when God
gave them commandments and laws, בְּיוֹם הַקָּהָל (Deut. ix. 10),
'die calatorum comitiorum,' ἡμέρᾳ ἐκκλησίας, as the LXX.
rightly translate. It is to this that Stephen refers when he
says of Moses : 'This is he who was in the assembly in the
wilderness (ἐν τῇ ἐκκλησίᾳ ἐν τῇ ἐρήμῳ).'[1] . . . Every convocation or comitium is of course an עדה, a coetus or meeting,
and may be called so. But the term עדה in itself, and without
aid from the context, never indicates the whole body of any
people or community. The term קהל, on the contrary, always
does so. What is done in the comitia of the people may be
said to be done in a meeting or gathering (in coetu) ; but
it would be a wrong conclusion from this that the words
meeting and comitia do not differ in meaning.[2] . . .

   " The term 'kahal' may be used of any species of people
if only that species is considered as a whole, as forming some
sort of unity or society in itself. Suppose we have a thousand
Dutchmen living in Constantinople, men of one and the same
species of people. Let them all meet together to consult and
take action, either in spiritual or civil matters, with a view to
their common interests in the place. They would, in that
case, constitute a 'kahal,' a comitium, just as much as the
many thousands of Dutchmen formed into a community
elsewhere, and holding council in the interests of the commonwealth of Holland. So, too, the people of each of the seven
Provinces, if viewed separately as forming a community, may
with equal right be called a 'kahal.' So also if in any Province there are men belonging to a distinct political or ecclesiastical party, who are bound together by certain laws and form
one body, these again may be designed by the same name
'kahal.' . . . The Jews to this very day use the phrase τὰς ἁγίας
ἐκκλησίας (קְהִלּוֹת) in reference to the community of believers
in the Jewish faith as existing in different localities. Thus,

[1] Vitringa, *De Synagoga vetere*, Franequeræ, 1696, i. p. 80 f.
[2] *Ib.* p. 83.

too, we find them designating the place where their religious books are printed : ' Here in the holy Church of Cracow ' (פהקהלא קרישא קראקא), or ' in the holy Church of Frankfort ' (בקהלא קדישא ורנקבורט).   The thing is so well known that there is no need to dwell upon it.   So also in Codex Bera-koth (fol. ix. col. 11), a sentence of R. Jose Ben Eliakim is recorded, which is pronounced ' in the name of the Holy Church which is at Jerusalem ' (משום קהלא קדישא דברושלים). And although the word קהל does not occur in the Plural in the Hebrew text of the Old Testament, yet the Jews are quite accustomed to speak in their writings of ' the Holy Churches ' (קהלות קדושות), just as the apostles use the term ἐκκλησία in the Plural.[1] . . .

"The Hebrew עדה corresponds to the Greek συναγωγή as קהל does to ἐκκλησία.   It seems very clear, therefore, why Christ and the apostles prefer to speak of the company of Christians under the name ἐκκλησία rather than that of συναγωγή.   It was not so much in order to distinguish the Christian Church from the Jewish, as some of later times have supposed, for the Jews themselves were wont to call their meetings ἐκκλησίας, as we have shown ; but because the word ἐκκλησία was in itself much more suitable for setting forth the conception which they desired to express.   Συναγωγή, like עדה, always means a meeting assembled or congregated, although possibly bound together by no special tie ; but ἐκκλησία, like קהל, denotes a number of persons who form a people, joined together by laws and other bonds, although it may often happen that they are not assembled together, and that it is impossible that they should be so. When, for example, believers are scattered through different parts of a country, so that they have no opportunity of meeting together, then indeed they cease to be an עדה, a συναγωγή ; but they do not cease to be a קהל, an ἐκκλησία.   In other words, they do not, in such a case, cease to form one body, which is united together in the very closest bonds by the Holy Spirit and faith." [2]

---

[1] Vitr. p. 86 f. So in modern translations of the N. T. into Hebrew, ἐκκλησίαι is always rendered by קְהִלּוֹת. See, e.g. Delitzsch's excellent translation, ספרי הברית החדשה, 1885.

[2] Vitr. p. 88.

That there is a clear distinction in meaning between these two Hebrew synonyms, and that it must be in substance to the effect above stated, is further proved by the action of the Alexandrian translators in this matter.

Two Greek words seem to have presented themselves to them as the most suitable renderings for the Hebrew עדה and קהל, namely, συναγωγή and ἐκκλησία. With the previously established meanings of both they were perfectly familiar. Συναγωγή is a term seldom used in classic Greek,—meaning there, when it does occur, according to its etymology, a collection or gathering of any kind. But it was a household word with every Alexandrian Jew at the date of the Septuagint, as the ordinary name for the stated religious meetings of his fellow-countrymen on Sabbaths and other appointed times. It had probably already come by an easy transition to denote also the place of meeting, the building in which a Jewish congregation met, as it frequently does in the New Testament. The term ἐκκλησία, on the other hand, was equally familiar in all Greek - speaking countries as the designation of "the lawful assembly in a free Greek city of all those possessed of the rights of citizenship for the transaction of public affairs. That they were *summoned* is expressed in the latter part of the word ; that they were summoned *out of* the whole population, a select portion of it, including neither the populace nor yet strangers, nor those who had forfeited their civic rights, this is expressed in the first." [1]

Having these two well-known words before them, the Alexandrian translators—to judge from their practice—seem to have laid it down as an absolute rule that the rendering for עדה should be συναγωγή, and that in no case whatever should it be translated by ἐκκλησία. In point of fact, עדה is rendered by συναγωγή about one hundred and thirty times in the canonical books of the Old Testament; and it is never once rendered by ἐκκλησία. Συναγωγή occurs, besides, some sixteen times in the Apocrypha. The LXX. appear to have been equally clear in their opinion that the best rendering for קהל was ἐκκλησία. They translate it so about seventy times.

[1] Archbishop Trench, *Syn. of N. T.* p. 1 f.

Ἐκκλησία occurs also twenty times in the Apocrypha. But the LXX. were not equally decided, as in the case of עדה, in rejecting other renderings; for קהל is translated by them συναγωγή about thirty-seven times in the Old Testament.[1] In like manner the Targums translate עדה always by כנישתא, the Aramaic for συναγωγή; and, for the most part, put קהלא for קהל.

Our A. V. is still more inconsistent, inclining on the whole to render קהל by "congregation," but wavering both as regards that word and עדה between "congregation" and "assembly." A decided benefit is conferred on the English reader by the change introduced here by the Revisers—with them as a rule עדה is "congregation," and קהל "assembly."[2]

"In many cases," writes a distinguished member of the Old Testament Company of Revisers, "the two words might come to have little or no difference in the way in which they were practically used. Yet theoretically always, and practically often, there was a distinct difference. For קָהָל was the fitting word for the people of God, actually or potentially assembled; עֵדָה for any orderly and appointed

---

[1] " Verum est paraphrastas illos Septuaginta το קהל aliquando transtulisse per συναγωγή, idque hanc ob causam, quia vere omnis קהל seu ἐκκλησία sano sensu vocari potest συναγωγή, quatenus innuit plurium hominum coitionem ad constituendam rempublicam vel de summâ reipublicæ deliberandum. Satius tamen fuisset, ut opinor, si το קהל semper reddidissent per ἐκκλησία quia hæc notio formata videtur in linguâ Græcâ ad clare exprimendum Hebræum קהל. Omnis enim קהל semper et ubique locorum est ἐκκλησία." Vitr. p. 84. Archbishop Trench states that עדה is rendered by συναγωγή "more than a hundred times," and קהל by the same word, "in all some five-and-twenty times" (N. T. Syn. 3). This is an under-estimate. According to the list of instances given in Trommius, Concordantiæ Græcæ Versionis LXX., Amstelodami 1718, the numbers should be as above, viz. 130 and 37. It may be added that ἐκκλησίαι occurs twice in the LXX. for מַקְהֵלִים or מַקְהֵלוֹת in Ps. xxvi. 12; lxviii. 26 (both ἅπ. λιγ. in the Old Testament), and ἐκκλησία for לְהָקַה, per metathesin for קְהָלָה, in the phrase, "the company of the prophets," 1 Sam. xix. 20. The verb ἐκκλησιάζω is used repeatedly for הַקְהִיל, generally with συναγωγήν or λαόν, "to assemble the congregation" or "the people." Krauss is wrong in stating that the LXX. use ἐκκλησία to translate עדה as well as קהל, and equally wrong in attributing the statement to Cremer, Prot. Dogm. v. der unsichtb. Kirche, S. 124. Cremer's statement, sub voce ἐκκλ., is to the very opposite effect, and is perfectly correct.

[2] A good illustration of the uncertainty of the old translation and the greater clearness introduced by the R. V., is to be found in Lev. iv. 13 f.

meeting, naturally a good word for a swarm of bees under their queen, Judg. xiv. 8." [1]

" Both the Hebrew designations of the community of Israel," Cremer says in summing up his careful examination of the terms which we have been considering, " plainly expressed something more than their collective unity springing from natural causes. They implied that the Israelitish community as an ἐκκλησία was based on a special idea, that it was established in a special way and for a special end. . . . The use of these words was determined by something else than the mere thought of *national* unity ; and it is self-evident that the underlying thought is the function of the people in the plan of salvation, of a *religious* position which is confirmed, especially in the case of קָהָל, by its application to festive and Sabbath assemblies. The same thought lies at the root of the word as used by Christ, so far as it was suggested by the Old Testament. . . . When Christ says, οἰκοδομήσω μου τὴν ἐκκλησίαν, we are scarcely reminded that ἐκκλησία denoted in profane Greek the place of assembly as well as the assembly itself, but rather that the Old Testament community was ' the House of Israel.' " [2]

We need not concern ourselves here with the precise way in which the community of Israel was organized at different times, the manner in which meetings of the assembly were called and conducted, the matters dealt with and the powers exercised. In connection with many of these points our information is scanty, and questions of considerable difficulty arise. It may be enough to note that all through the history, from the period of the exodus to that of the Maccabees, through all changes of outward circumstances and political constitution, " the congregation " and " the assembly " " of Israel " and " of the Lord " hold a prominent place. Alike in the times of the wilderness, of the judges, of the kings, and of the restoration after the exile, these names appear unchanged, embodying the conceptions of unity and fellowship on the part of the chosen people with God and with each other. Through all that eventful history these names

---

[1] Principal Douglas in letter to the author, of date June 24, 1885.

[2] Cremer, *s. v.* ἐκκλησία.

gathered round them sacred associations, closely akin to those which the second of them—the ἐκκλησία τοῦ Θεοῦ, the Church of God—has for ourselves, and became fraught with a deeper meaning to the mind of the thoughtful and believing portion of the seed of Abraham, "the house of Israel."

This was especially the case in connection with the changes brought about at the memorable epoch of the Babylonian exile and the return.   These changes were full of moral and spiritual significance.   A consideration of them brings us at once to the borders of the New Testament time.   They bear very directly upon the position and character of the fellowship of Israel when our Lord came.

It may be well, however, before passing the boundary of the exile, and without entangling ourselves in needless or uncertain details of the kind to which reference has been made above, to note how, even on the most cursory survey of what is said of the fellowship of Israel from the time of Moses to that of Ezra, certain things stand out clear and unmistakeable, as to the general nature and principles of its organization.

CHAPTER III.

BASIS AND PRINCIPLES OF ORGANIZATION IN THE FELLOWSHIP OF
THE COVENANT PEOPLE.

1. THE Eldership.

Among the Hebrews, as with every tribe or people among whom a patriarchal system prevails, we find the eldership existing as a recognised institution from the earliest times, and forming the basis for all common counsel and action.[1] It is not always easy to distinguish in such cases between the honour accorded to age and experience, and that given to a distinctly official position. But "the elders of Israel" appear at the time of the Exodus as a body of men whose position among the people is perfectly well known, and whose authority is acknowledged on all hands. They form "the presbytery of Israel" (ἡ γερουσία Ἰσραήλ), as the Alexandrian translators repeatedly render the Hebrew words (אֶת־זִקְנֵי יִשְׂרָאֵל) in cases where the reference is to common action.[2] They are the natural and acknowledged representatives of the people, entitled to speak and act in their name. As such they appear again and again in the subsequent history. It is through the elders in Egypt that the ordinance of the Passover is given by God to "the whole assembly of the congregation of Israel." [3] When there was fear in the desert lest "the whole assembly perish with hunger,

---

[1] The first mention of the term is in the case of Abraham's faithful steward or overseer, "the elder of his house (זְקַן בֵּיתוֹ) that ruled over all that he had," Gen. xxiv. 2. The LXX. translate: τῷ πρεσβυτέρῳ τῆς οἰκίας αὐτοῦ, τῷ ἄρχοντι πάντων τῶν αὐτοῦ, uniting the two names, so familiar in every Hellenistic synagogue, of presbyter and archon or ruler. Comp. Gen. xxiii. 10 ; l. 7.

[2] ἐλθὼν συνάγαγε τὴν γερουσίαν τῶν υἱῶν Ἰσραήλ . . . καὶ εἰσελεύσῃ σὺ καὶ ἡ γερουσία Ἰσραήλ. πρὸς Φαραώ, Ex. iii. 16-18 ; iv. 29 ; xii. 21, etc.

[3] בֹּל קְהַל עֲדַת־יִשְׂרָאֵל Ex. xii. 3, 6, 21.

and the manna has been given, the rulers of the congregation
(οἱ ἄρχοντες τῆς συναγωγῆς, LXX.) tell Moses what has been
done about it by the people.[1]   Seventy of the elders of
Israel are called along with Moses and Aaron with his two
sons to meet the Lord in the Mount, in connection with
the solemn covenant made by sacrifice between God and the
people.[2]

It is needless to multiply instances of this kind.   Many
points of difficulty may be raised as to the different capacities
in which we find elders acting, as representatives of the
nation in civil and religious matters, " elders of Israel " or
" of Judah ; " as local or tribal rulers, " elders of the land,"
" of the city," " of the gates ; " and as to their relations to
other constituted authorities at different periods.[3]

On questions of this sort we need not enter here.   But
it is of importance to note and carry with us the broad
facts bearing upon our subject which meet us in this field,
and about which there can be no dispute.   They are such as
these : that in connection with this fundamental institution
of the eldership, which formed, so to speak, the natural and
permanent basis of all other organization in Israel, there
grew up among the people generally a spirit of reverence
for law and justice, and for lawful and constituted authority.
This spirit was educated and deepened by the teaching of the

---

[1] Ex. xvi. 3, 22.

[2] Ex. xvii. 5 f. ; xxiv. 1-11.   Comp. Dr. Stuart Robinson in *Proceedings of
First General Presbyterian Council,* p. 64 f.   Dr. Stuart Robinson speaks in this
paper for the vigorous High Church Presbyterianism of the Church of the
Southern States.   But without accepting all the inferences drawn from the
facts regarding the Hebrew eldership by Dr. Robinson and older writers of the
same school, we are bound to note the facts themselves, and to recognise in
them a Providential preparation by the hand of God in history for the future
polity of the New Testament Church, and to mark the establishment and
illustration of principles to be afterwards embodied in other forms.

[3] "Judges"(שֹׁפְטִים)and "officers"(שֹׁטְרִים) are mentioned along with the elders
in several passages (Ex. v. 14, 9 ; cf. iv. 29 ; Num. xi. 16–24 ; Deut. xxi. 2 ;
xxxi. 28 ; Ezra x. 14).   "The two orders of officials must be regarded as in
any case distinct, but probably only to this extent, that the 'judges' were those
among the elders to whom the administration of justice was especially entrusted.
Similarly the 'officers' are to be regarded as belonging also to the number of
the 'elders,' their special function being to take charge of the executive department."   Schürer, *Hist. of Jewish People,* i. p. 150.

prophets as preachers of righteousness in the name of the
Lord; but alike in its origin and growth it owed much to the
character of the institution by which primarily order and
righteousness and the fear of God were practically represented in Israel. The king might be distant. Prophets
were not always raised up. The priests might seldom leave
the priestly cities. But every village and district had its
eldership.

The office of the elder in Israel implied by its very name
that those only should be set to judge others and take the
oversight who were fitted for it by experience and gifts.
" Our teachers have handed down to us," was a saying of
the Rabbis, " that no one is an old man " (or elder, זקן) " unless
he who has gotten to himself wisdom; and the reason why
the Scripture expresses the idea of wisdom by the word elder
is because a wise youth sees through his wisdom what an old
man sees through the multitude of his years."[1] " One ought
to deal with an elder," it was said, " as with a prince (מנהג
נשיאות). . . . At all times it is the elders who maintain Israel
in existence." " Moses imparted the Holy Spirit to the
elders. Thenceforward each lighted his lamp from that of
the other." " Where judges give righteous judgment, there
is the Shekinah, the Presence of God Himself. . . . Their
responsibility is the very greatest. Over them hangs a
sword; beneath them Gehinnom is always open. . . . For
this very reason a *college* of elders is established, in order that
the responsibility may be shared between them."[2]

The sense of what was required for righteous dealing

---

[1] Rabbi Levi in Vitringa. He cites Maimonides and others to the same
effect. *De Syn. Vet.* pp. 616 ff., 554.

Boyd of Trochrig, discussing the subject of Church Government in one of
the many able and learned dissertations which lie buried in the huge tome of
his Latin lectures on Ephesians, speaks thus of what is implied in the name
"presbyter :" "Ab ætate et dignitate desumitur, quo nimirum innuitur huic
tam sancto muneri, tamque præclaro Episcopatus operi, seniores quam juniores
esse magis idoneos ; aut certe, si ætate juniores sunt qui ad illud advocantur,
senilem saltem prudentiam, gravitatem, et auctoritatem in ipsis requiri." *Præ-
lectiones in Epist. Pauli ad Eph.*, Genevæ 1661, p. 500*b*.

[2] Tanchuma, Behaal 11 ; Shemoth rabba, c. iii. ; Sanhedrin 13 ; Tosefta
Sota, c. xiii., in Weber, *System der altsyn. Palästin. Theol. aus Targum,
Midrasch u. Talmud dargestellt*, Leipzig 1880, S. 122 f., 140.

between man and man, both in civil and religious matters, was further educated in Israel by the fact referred to in the last quotation, namely, that the authority was vested not in *one* elder, but in several, acting in a collective capacity. The elders of the gate, as afterwards of the synagogue, always met together. Witnesses were brought forward. Both sides were fairly heard in each other's presence; and the judgment was the mind of the elders upon the evidence and the law. The idea was thus planted deep in the general consciousness of the Hebrew people, that there ought to be united counsel regarding all affairs of weight, and that the decision in the end should be the consensus of the wisest and fittest to decide.

Again, the existence and influence of the eldership fostered the principle and the habit of self-government in Israel. Each village and town had its little body of natural representatives in the elders of the place. As soon as we get definite information — as we shall see presently when we come to consider the synagogue system — we find them chosen to office by the people, or at least appointed with their full concurrence.

When all other national institutions went down in the overthrow of the two kingdoms, that of the eldership alone survived. It had its roots too deep in the life of Israel, even from patriarchal times, to be destroyed.

We see it in the records of the captivity. The elders gather round Ezekiel. "Certain of the elders of Israel" come once and again to the prophet to inquire of the Lord; and the prophet's message of warning and exhortation from God to "the house of Israel" is given through the elders.[1] To them first, "unto the residue of the elders of the captivity," Jeremiah addresses his letter from Jerusalem in the name of the Lord, "unto all the captivity, whom I have caused to be carried away captive from Jerusalem to Babylon," sending gracious promises, and bidding them "seek the peace of the city whither I have caused you to be carried away captive, and pray unto the Lord for it; for in the peace thereof shall ye have peace."[2]

[1] Ezek. xiv. 1–6; xx. 1–5, 27 f. [2] Jer. xxix. 1, 4–7.

How the institution of the eldership rose in fresh life, and with a more fully developed organization in the synagogue system after the exile, we shall see presently. Meanwhile observe,—

2. In connection especially with the eldership, but appearing also in many other ways in the life and action of Israel as a people under the special guidance of God's word and Providence, we find the principle of representation, and the sense of unity to which practical expression is given by means of it.

Illustrations of this have been furnished already in several of the passages lately cited. The people are spoken to and speak through their elders. What is done by the elders is described as done by the people, or "the congregation" whom they represent.[1] What "the princes of the congregation," those "called to the appointed meeting" (נְשִׂיאֵי־הָעֵדָה, קְרִיאֵי מוֹעֵד), do, binds the congregation even when the act is disapproved of by the latter, although, in deference to a general expression of disapproval, the effect of the decision may be somewhat modified by the rulers.[2]

An interesting glimpse of the elements composing the congregation of Israel is afforded by the incident recorded in the seventh chapter of Joshua. We see there the different sections which were recognised as having a certain unity of their own within the congregation—a "kahal" within the "kahal," as Vitringa would express it; the "tribe," the "family," the "household," and the individual with his "house."[3] All of these were represented severally by their heads, natural or elected; as the whole congregation were by "the elders of Israel."

---

[1] Num. xxxv. 12, 24 f. The manslayer is to "stand before the congregation (עֵדָה) for judgment." They are to "judge between the smiter and the avenger of blood," and give the former, if found free from deliberate purpose to kill, an asylum in the city of refuge till the death of the high priest. But this is done, according to Josh. xx. 4 f., with express reference to an earlier statute by the hand of Moses, by the manslayer "declaring his cause in the ears of the elders of that city," and being judged by them. Comp. Ex. iv. 29 ff. ; xii. 3, with ver. 21 ; Josh. xxiv. 1 with vv. 2, 19, 21 ; and 1 Sam. viii. 4 with vv. 7, 10, 19 ff.

[2] Josh. ix. 15–21 ; Num. xvi. 2.   [3] Josh. vii. 14–18, 24.

In the eleventh chapter of Numbers we see an important step taken in the representative organization of the community by the appointment of seventy chosen men out of those who were already "elders of the people, and officers [1] over them," to "bear the burden of the people with Moses, that he should not bear it himself alone." [2] This selected company seems to have formed a sort of standing executive, as distinguished from the general body of the eldership, or those "called to the assembly." They are solemnly set apart to their special functions by Divine command at the tent of meeting in the presence of the Lord, and fitted for their work by His "taking of the Spirit which was upon Moses, and putting it upon them." Their first installation into this new position was signalized by prophetic gifts being conferred upon them for a time. "It came to pass that when the Spirit rested upon them they prophesied, but they did so no more." [3]

It is unnecessary to give further instances of this kind from the later Scriptures, or to refer to methods and details of organization at different periods in the community of Israel, so far as these can be traced with any certainty by Old Testament scholarship. I would simply draw attention to the fact that in this whole field we meet with constant illustrations of the sense of unity pervading the fellowship of the children of Abraham, and of the way in which that

---

[1] שֹׁטְרִים, prefects or overseers, from שָׁטַר, to write, the art of writing having a special importance in public and legal proceedings in primitive times. Hence the LXX. render it here by the familiar term "scribes," πρισβύτεροι τοῦ λαοῦ καὶ γραμματεῖς αὐτῶν. We read in Ex. xviii. 13-27 of a previous step of a similar kind being taken on the suggestion of the father-in-law of Moses, with the approval of God ; "able men, such as fear God, men of truth, hating unjust gain," were appointed "out of all Israel to be heads over the people, rulers of thousands, of hundreds, of fifties, and of tens," in the smaller matters of judgment between man and man. These may have been the "officers of the people," from whose number this smaller representative body was now chosen. Comp. the parallel passage in Deut. i. 9-18, where the share of the people in the election and appointment of men to be "heads" and "officers" among their brethren is distinctly brought out.

[2] Num. xi. 16 f.

[3] Num. xi. 16-25. Much significance was afterwards attached to this event by Jewish writers, who saw in it the original institution of the Sanhedrin.

feeling was strengthened, and found practical expression through the application of the principle of representation.

Under the guidance of the great "Shepherd of Israel," His people were led to learn more and more how common rights and interests should be dealt with by common counsel and action of the wisest and most godly of their brethren; how what concerns all should be done, as far as may be, with the knowledge and consent of all; and how in "the assembly of Israel," which was also "the assembly of the Lord," all Israel were to be represented, and the voice of Israel as well as the voice of God heard there.

In all this we cannot but trace something of a "Præparatio Evangelica" for what after centuries were to bring. We see the hand of God in the history of Israel preparing the soil for a future harvest, and planting in it seeds which were destined to grow and bear fruit over all the world and in all time.

PART III.

THE CHURCH FROM THE TIME OF THE EXILE TO THAT OF OUR LORD.

A S already said, when we come to the great epoch of the captivity and the restoration, we find certain important changes taking place with respect to the fellowship of Israel and the forms in which that fellowship was realized and embodied. To these changes we must now turn our attention. They naturally group themselves under three heads:—

I. The Jewish Diaspora.

II. The Proselytes.

III. The Synagogue System.

CHAPTER I.

THE JEWISH DIASPORA OR DISPERSION; HELLENISM AND THE HELLENISTS.

The Diaspora had its first centre in Babylonia and the countries round about. It consisted of those children of the captivity (בְּנֵי נָלוּתָא)[1] who remained in foreign lands after the return of their brethren in the times of Ezra and Nehemiah. The position of these descendants of the first exiles, who were now permanent settlers, and who often rose to wealth and influence in the countries where they dwelt, soon became that of a "sojourning" or "colony" (a μετοικεσία or ἀποικία), rather than that of captives (αἰχμαλωσία), or of

---

[1] Ezra vi. 16. So גָּלוּת in Jer. xxiv. 5; xxviii. 4; xxix. 22, etc.,—from נָלָה, to be, or to make naked.

men bereaved and stripped bare, as the emphatic Hebrew and
Aramaic words used in Jeremiah and Ezra with respect to them
imply. This is reflected in the language used regarding them
in the LXX. The expressive name, "the Diaspora," ultimately
established itself over all others.[1] Originally a word of dark
associations, as conveying God's judgment upon Israel for
disobedience, it soon ceased in general use to carry any sound
of reproach. Occasionally it might be used with a touch of
contempt by the Jews of Palestine : "Will He go unto the
Dispersion among the Greeks, and teach the Greeks ?"[2] On
the lips of earnest and pious men, "Hebrews of the Hebrews,"
it might express a sense of disadvantage and loss of privilege,
but of faithfulness to the truth notwithstanding, to which all
sympathy and honour were to be accorded. It is in this
spirit that Paul speaks of "our twelve tribes earnestly
serving God night and day" (τὸ δωδεκάφυλον ἡμῶν ἐν ἐκτενείᾳ
νύκτα καὶ ἡμέραν λατρεῦον).[3] The old separation between
the northern and southern kingdoms was lost in the sense of
a higher spiritual unity. The "two houses of Israel" became
one again under God's hand in the Diaspora.[4]

It was thus that Gamaliel wrote : "To the sons of the
Dispersion in Babylonia, and to our brethren in Media
. . . and to all the Dispersion of Israel."[5] The very name
itself, "the Diaspora," seemed to suggest how the seed of the
scattered nation was springing up by the blessing of the God
of their fathers in all lands for some great harvest of blessing
in the future.

The growth of Israel in the Dispersion was something
marvellous. Wherever that seed was cast after the captivity,
it seemed to spring up and multiply "thirty, sixty, and even
an hundredfold." And cast it was, as by an unseen Hand, in
every country of the known world. The wars of Alexander
the Great, the colonizing policy of the heirs of his Empire,

---

[1] Διασπορά is used by the LXX. in Deut. xxviii. 25 and Jer. xxxiv. 17 for
the Hebrew זַעֲוָה, which is rendered by the R. V. "tossed to and fro."

[2] John vii. 35.   [3] Acts xxvi. 7.

[4] Isa. viii. 14 ; Ezek. xxxvii. 16–28. Comp. Binnie, *The Church*, p. 14.

[5] Frankel, *Monatschrift*, 1853, S. 413, as cited by Westcott, art. "Dispersion," in Smith's *Dict. of Bible*, i. p. 441.

the persecutions of Antiochus Epiphanes, the campaigns of the Romans in Syria, were among the forces that led to this. They were like mighty winds of God, blowing from the four quarters of the heaven to scatter the seed over all the earth.[1] Gentler but not less powerful influences worked for the same end. Foremost among these was the awakened genius of the nation for commerce and finance, with the scope offered for this by the social and political circumstances of the time.

This impulse sent the Jews along all the great thoroughfares, and to all the seats of trade throughout the civilised world. And everywhere they rose to positions of wealth and influence in a way that drew the eyes of men to them and their religion. Especially was this seen along all the shores of the Mediterranean, and in the mighty commercial centres of Ephesus, Alexandria, and Rome.

"A new vital power and a new courage awoke in the nation. Material comforts supplied the place of national independence. Increase in goods and in offspring kept pace with each other. The people multiplied within a few generations to an almost incredible extent. They came everywhere to have means, and especially to have credit, and thereby to wield power and carry weight. In place of an almost purposely limited horizon, there came a world-citizenship such as antiquity had never seen hitherto in the same degree. And for its sake the Jews were willing to sacrifice even their language. Only *not* their religion."[2]

The list of those who heard the apostle Peter speak in Jerusalem on the day of Pentecost[3] brings out three facts with equal clearness: *first*, how at the Christian era the Diaspora was represented in all parts of the Roman Empire and beyond it; *secondly*, how, wherever they went, the members of the

---

[1] "They have come already into every city," a Greek geographer wrote regarding the Jews, speaking of a time nearly a century before that of our Lord, "and it is not easy to find a place in the inhabited world which has not received this race, and is not occupied by them." Strabo in Josephus, *Antiq.* xiv. 7. 2.

[2] Reuss, *Gesch. der heiligen Schriften A. T.*, Braunschweig 1881, S. 528.

[3] Acts ii. 9–11. This list has an interesting parallel in the letter of Agrippa to the emperor Caligula, preserved by Philo : "Jerusalem is the capital not only of Judæa, but of most countries, by reason of the colonies which it has

scattered people held fast their religion and their sense of the unity of the religious fellowship of Israel, and looked to the house of God at Jerusalem as its centre ; and *thirdly*, how this sense of unity was both manifested and constantly strengthened by the regular resort of Jewish pilgrims from all parts of the Dispersion to Jerusalem at the great yearly religious festivals. In the words of a contemporary of our Lord's, a Hellenist of the Dispersion in Alexandria : "Many thousands of persons, from as many thousands of towns, repair at every feast to the Temple, some by land and some by sea, from the east and the west, the north and the south." [1]

Other practical embodiments of this unity were not wanting. The nature and significance of the synagogue system are to be considered under another head. But so much may be noted here : In the synagogue, as its very name showed, the idea of the congregation of Israel meeting at an appointed time (עֵדָה = συναγωγή) was embodied and localized throughout the whole world. Its other familiar name, the proseucha, or house of prayer (בֵּית הַתְּפִלָּה, οἶκος τῆς προσευχῆς), testified to the spiritual bond by which all the true Israel were united,—a bond which included many in the synagogues of the Diaspora who were not of the seed of Abraham after the flesh. It recalled the words spoken to the exiles by the greatest of the prophets in the name of the Lord : " My house shall be called an house of prayer for all peoples. The Lord God which gathereth the outcasts of Israel saith, Yet will I gather others to Him, besides His own that are gathered." [2] If the synagogue system did not actually originate in the Diaspora, as some hold, it was there at least that it first reached its full development and made its influence most widely felt. From the worshippers in every synagogue of the Dispersion, from faithful Jews in places where no synagogue could be con-

---

sent out into the neighbouring lands of Egypt, Phœnicia, Syria, Cœlosyria, Pamphylia, and Cilicia, into most parts of Asia as far as Bithynia, and into the most distant corners of Pontus ; also to Europe, Thessaly, Bœotia, Macedonia, Ætolia, Attica, Argos, Corinth, and the most and best parts of the Peloponnesus. . . . Also the most important islands, Eubœa, Cyprus, Crete, to say nothing of the lands beyond the Euphrates. All . . . have Jewish inhabitants." Philo, *Legat. ad Caium*, § 36.

[1] Philo, *De Monarchia*, ii. 1.   [2] Isa. lvi. 7 f.

stituted, and not even two or three could meet for prayer, the yearly offering of the half-shekel came up to Jerusalem with a regularity like that of the Imperial revenues. It was the boast of the Jewish writers that the free-will offerings of their people came year by year without fail from regions where the Roman tax-gatherer had no power.[1]

What effect this wonderful Providential movement, the Dispersion of the Jews, had upon the moral and spiritual life of the nations among whom they were scattered, we shall see to some extent in next chapter. Meanwhile reference may be made in a few sentences to the effects produced upon the members of the Dispersion themselves by contact with the nations beyond Palestine. These effects may be summed up in two words, which meet us in Jewish literature almost as soon as we cross the limits of the Hebrew canon, and have a notable place both in the Apocrypha and in the New Testament, "Hellenism" and "the Hellenists."

The phrase "Hellenists," or "Grecian Jews," denoted those members of the community of Israel, whether ordinarily resident in the Diaspora or in parts of the Holy Land, such as Joppa, Cæsarea, and Tiberias, who had adopted to a certain extent the habits and the speech of Greek civilisation; and the word "Hellenism" meant this tendency both in its process and results.[2]

Not that the Hellenistic Jews abandoned their religion like the apostates in the time of Antiochus, with reference to whom the term is used in the history of the Maccabees. They gave up for the most part or altogether the use of their own Hebrew or Aramaic speech, adopting in its place a dialect of

---

[1] Joseph. *Antiq.* xvi. 6. 5, 6; xviii. 9. 1; *Bell. Jud.* vii. 6. 6. Vitr. p. 810 f. Cf. Cicero, *Pro Flacco*, 28. Schürer, ii. pp. 288–290.

[2] "There took place," says an apocryphal writer, speaking of the fruits of Jason's high-priesthood in the time of Antiochus Epiphanes, "a kind of culmination of Hellenism and a going over to a foreign manner of life" (ἀκμή τις Ἑλληνισμοῦ καὶ πρόσβασις ἀλλοφυλισμοῦ), 2 Macc. iv. 13. Comp. the account of Aristotle's interview with a cultured Jew who was ἑλληνικὸς οὐ τῇ διαλέκτῳ μόνον ἀλλὰ καὶ τῇ ψυχῇ. The incident took place about the middle of the fourth century B.C. It is recorded by Clearchus, a disciple of Aristotle, in his book on sleep, from which Josephus takes it. *Contra Apion.* i. 22.

the Greek, which was now the common language not only of
the educated throughout the whole civilised world, but of the
great mass of the population in all the chief centres of trade
and commerce. In dress and manner, in many outward habits
of life, the Jews of the Dispersion became citizens of the
world. They learned to understand the feelings and character
of the Gentile nations with whom they mingled, to respect
and sympathize with the moral and religious aspirations of
the higher spirits among them, to tolerate at least many things
which would have met with little tolerance at the hands of
their more rigid Palestinian brethren. Yet, notwithstanding
all this, essentially and at heart Israel in the Dispersion was
Israel still. With them Hellenism did not mean apostasy ;
on the contrary, it was often combined with an enthusiastic
devotion to the religion and the people of their fathers, which
no Hebrew of the Hebrews could have surpassed. It meant
simply the fellowship of the true religion, adapting itself to
new circumstances, clothing itself to a certain extent in a
new garb, but breathing the same spirit, cleaving to the
same hopes, and guiding itself by the same Divine revelation
spoken to the fathers by the prophets, and written now for
their children in the Scriptures of truth.[1]

The Jewish-Greek, which was the language of the Hellenists, and of which we have an imperishable monument in
the Alexandrian version of the Old Testament and in the
writings of the Evangelists and Apostles, reflects in a
striking way the true nature of the Hellenism of which
we have been speaking. "Its characteristic," as Canon
Westcott points out in his valuable article on the subject,
" is the combination of a Hebrew spirit with a Greek
body, of a Hebrew form with Greek words. The conception
belongs to one race and the expression to another. Nor is it
too much to say that this combination was one of the most
important preparations for the reception of Christianity, and

---

[1] " Der gesammte Hellenismus voller Beweglichkeit und Verschiedenheit ist
ein sprechender Beweis für die Entwickelungsfähigkeit und demnach zugleich
für die selbstandige Existenz des Judenthums," Kuenen, *Volksreligion u. Weltreligion*, S. 172. Comp. Stanton, *Jewish and Christian Messiah*, p. 105 f.
Rendall, *Theology of the Hebrew Christians*, Lond. 1886, pp. 51–56.

one of the most important aids for the adequate expression of
its teaching.   On the one hand, by the spread of the Hellenistic Greek, the deep theocratic aspect of the world and life
which distinguishes Jewish thought was placed before men at
large ; and, on the other, the subtle truths which philosophy
had gained from the analysis of mind and action, and en-
shrined in words, were transferred to the service of revelation.
In the fulness of time, when the great message came, a language was prepared to convey it; and thus the very dialect
of the New Testament forms a great lesson in the true philosophy of history, and becomes in itself a monument of the
providential government of mankind. . . . The adoption of a
strange language was essentially characteristic of the true
nature of Hellenism.   The purely outward elements of
the national life were laid aside with a facility of which
history offers few examples, while the inner character of the
people remained unchanged. . . . As the Hebrew spirit made
itself distinctly visible in the new dialect, so it remained
undestroyed by the new conditions which regulated its action."[1]

It was from the heart of the Diaspora at Alexandria that
the Old Testament Scriptures were first given to the world in
the world's tongue.   The Word of God in a language understood by all men,—that was to interpret Israel to inquirers
from among the heathen.   Jew and Gentile began to draw
near to each other once again as brethren in the Jewish
" houses of prayer ; " and over the written message from the
one God and Father of all which was " read in the synagogues
every Sabbath day." [2]   In all these events and institutions and
movements of mind among the nations, we can see now that
in the manifold wisdom and grace of God a bridge was being
built by which " the blessing of Abraham " was to pass over
to " all the families of the earth." [3]   One might say that the
Hellenistic Jews formed the first arch in the bridge, and
the Proselytes the second.

---

[1] Westcott, art. " Hellenists," in Smith's *Dict. of Bible*, i. p. 783 f.

[2] Acts xv. 21.

[3] "Dieses Judenthum der Zerstreuung bildete die natürliche Brücke zu einem
Vordringen der wahren Religion unter den Weltvölkern."   Schulz, *A. T. Theol.*
2te Ausg. S. 779.

CHAPTER II.

THE PROSELYTES.

PHILO, the famous Hellenistic teacher of Alexandria, defines the word proselyte as meaning "one who had drawn near to the new and God-loving polity."[1] We may use the term for convenience in that broad sense as denoting all those strangers in race who had come in varying degrees to hold the faith and adopt some at least of the usages of the children of Abraham.

Room and provision had been made for such in "the house of Abraham" from the first. In the history of the patriarch himself we have seen how many "born in his house, or bought with his money of the stranger," had become one with him and his.[2]

In the first gathering of "the congregation of Israel" in Egypt, when the ordinance of the Passover is given, the "gêr" has a place, which he may lose by transgression. "Whosoever eateth that which is leavened, that soul shall be cut off from the congregation of Israel, whether he be a sojourner or one that is born in the land."[3] We recognise the

---

[1] προσήλυτος, ἀπὸ τοῦ προσεληλυθέναι καινῇ καὶ φιλοθέῳ πολιτείᾳ, cited by Leyrer, art. "Proselyten," in Herzog, *Real-Encycl.* vol. xi.

[2] See above, pp. 33, 76 f.

[3] בֵּגֵּר וּבְאֶזְרַח הָאָרֶץ, Ex. xii. 19. Comp. vv. 43–49 and Num. ix. 14 ; xv. 15 f. "For the assembly (הַקָּהָל) there shall be one statute for you and for the stranger that sojourneth with you (לַגֵּר הַגֵּר), a statute for ever throughout your generations ; as ye are, so shall the stranger be before the Lord. One law and one ordinance shall be for you and for the stranger that sojourneth with you." The LXX. in these and other passages generally renders גֵּר by προσήλυτος ; sometimes, as in the first verse cited above, using the word γειώρας, from the Aramaic גִּיּוֹרָא.

presence of such strangers, and the unfavourable influence
which they might often exert, in what is said of "the mixed
multitude" who went up with the Israelites out of Egypt.
The spirit in which proselytes of the better class were
welcomed may be seen in the words of Moses to Hobab the
Kenite, and the greeting of Boaz to Ruth the Moabitess.[1]
In the vivid picture drawn in Deuteronomy of "the covenant
which the Lord commanded Moses to make with Israel in the
land of Moab, beside the covenant which He made with them
in Horeb" in "the day of the assembly," the stranger has
his special place.   He also forms a recognised part of the
collective unity of the assembly of Israel which enters into
"the covenant of the Lord thy God, and into His oath, which
the Lord thy God maketh with thee this day."   He is
addressed as "thou," and bidden to claim the central blessings of the covenant vouchsafed to "thy fathers, to Abraham, to Isaac, and to Jacob."   "Ye stand this day all of you
before the Lord your God; your heads, your tribes, your
elders, and your officers, even all the men of Israel, your little
ones, your wives, and thy stranger that is in the midst of thy
camps, from the hewer of thy wood unto the drawer of thy
water; that thou shouldest enter into the covenant of the
Lord thy God, and into His oath, which the Lord thy God
maketh with thee this day; that He may establish thee
this day unto Himself for a people, and that He may be
unto thee a God, as He spake unto thee, and as He sware
unto thy fathers, to Abraham, to Isaac, and to Jacob.
Neither with you only do I make this covenant and this
oath; but also with him that is not here with us this day . . .
lest there should be among you man, or woman, or family, or

---

[1] Ex. xii. 38 ; Num. xi. 4–10, 29 ; Ruth ii. 11 f.   Another interesting
instance of this kind seems to be presented by the case of Caleb.   He
was the representative of the tribe of Judah among the twelve spies.   In
the division of Canaan he "received a portion among the children of
Judah, according to the commandment of the Lord to Joshua" (Josh. xv. 13).
But he was a Kenezite, a descendant apparently of Kenaz of the line of
Edom, and therefore not an Israelite by natural descent at all, although "he
wholly followed the Lord God of Israel."   Comp. the art. "Caleb," by the
Bishop of Bath and Wells, in Smith's *Dict. of Bible.*   Schulz, *A. T. Theol.*
2te Aufl. S. 781.

tribe, whose heart turneth away this day from the Lord our God." [1]

The numerous statutes recorded in Scripture which bear upon the position of the sojourner and the stranger within the gates of Israel, form a most interesting study. But on this subject we cannot even touch here, save only to note the fact that, as if to counterbalance certain disadvantages attaching to the stranger's position as to marriage and inheritance in the land, he was placed under the special shield of the law in other ways. His right to special sympathy and interest is strongly enforced. His cause is ranked with that of the fatherless and the widow. In some respects he is to share in the peculiar privileges of the Levite. Psalmists and prophets give repeated utterance to the gracious spirit of the Hebrew law as regards the stranger in the land. They rebuke wrongs done to him, recognise his place in the religious fellowship of Israel, and press his claims to love and kindly help at the hands of all God's people.[2]

In the prophetic visions of future blessings for Israel, a large ingathering of converts from all the nations always forms a part.[3]

Under the monarchy, when Israel was powerful, individuals from this class, such as Doeg the Edomite and Uriah the Hittite, rose to high position at court. Mercenary motives, as in the case of the first named, might be largely operative at such a period in bringing men of other nationalities into

---

[1] Deut. xxix. 1, 10–15, 18. "The protected stranger is still known in Arabia. Among the Hodheil at Zeimeh I found, in 1880, an Indian boy, the orphan child of a wandering Suleimâny or travelling smith, who was under the protection of the community, every member of which would have made the lad's quarrel his own. The *dakhîl*, as he is called, is as it were adopted into the tribe, and his lack of relations to help him is supplemented by the whole community. So no doubt in early Hebrew times the Gêr is in process of conversion into an Israelite." Robertson Smith, *Old Testament in Jewish Church*, Edin. 1881, p. 434.

[2] Ex. xxii. 21 ff.; xxiii. 9, 12 ; Lev. xix. 10, 33 f.; xxv. 35 ; Deut. x. 8 ; xiv. 29 ; xxiv. 17 ff.; xxvi. 12 ; xxvii. 19 ; Ps. xciv. 5 ff.; cxv. 9–14 ; cxlvi. 9 ; Isa. lvi. 3, 6–8 ; Jer. vii. 6 ; xxii. 3 ; Ezek. xxii. 7, 29 ; xlvii. 22 ; Zech. vii. 10 ; Mal. iii. 5.

[3] Ps. lxxii. 87, etc. ; Isa. ii. 2–4 ; xi. 9 f. ; xiv. 1 ; xlii. 6 f. ; xlix. 6–23 ; liv. 1–5 ; lx. 10 ; lxi. 5 ; Micah iv. 1–3.

outward fellowship with Israel, while they had little or no sympathy with its religion. On the other hand, "strangers" under David and Solomon had heavy burdens laid on them in the shape of forced labour and other compulsory services from which the native Israelites were free.

It concerns our subject more especially to realize the position of the proselytes after the captivity, and from that epoch onwards to New Testament times. They now become a much more important and significant element in connection with the fellowship of the people of God than in previous periods. There were no longer the same outward inducements to lead men to associate themselves with the hopes and fortunes of Israel as in the palmy days of the monarchy. Those who threw in their lot with the despised and persecuted Jews in the time of the exile and the return, were likely to do so from motives of a higher and purer kind than those of wealth and worldly advancement. And such higher inducements were not wanting. God had been seen to be with Israel in their captivity. He Himself, according to His promise, "had been to them a sanctuary in all the countries whither they were come." [1] Words of grace and power had been spoken by the lips of His prophets in the gatherings of the exiles by the rivers of Babylon. Some of the inhabitants of the land had mocked; but others, whether of the ruling race or fellow-captives from other countries, had passed from the standpoint of mere curiosity to feelings of interest and sympathy in what they heard and saw.[2] The good hand of the Lord had been manifestly with individuals and families among the children of the captivity, as well as with His people as a whole, now working special deliverances for them, now blessing them through the ordinary channels of His Providence and grace. Lives like those of Ezekiel, Daniel, Ezra, and Nehemiah must have carried power with them, and led to moral and spiritual results in ever widening circles of influence.

Hence it came about, as has often been noted, that among the company of those who returned to Palestine, there was a

---

[1] Ezek. xi. 16.
[2] Lam. i. 7 ; Ezek. i. 1 ff.; iii. 10-15 ; xvi. 24 f.; Ps. cxx., cxxvi., cxxxvii.

comparatively large number, besides the seed of Israel, of those "who had separated themselves from the peoples of the lands unto the law of God, their wives, their sons, and their daughters, every one that had knowledge and understanding."[1] These entered under the guidance of Ezra and Nehemiah into the solemn religious covenant by which the house of Israel and the house of the Lord were built up again in Jerusalem, in close accordance with the great precedent of "the days of the assembly" in Horeb and in the plains of Moab. The number of foreign names among the Nethinim or Temple servants has been noted as indicating that the zeal of the new converts led them especially to consecrate themselves to the service of the Lord's house.[2]

Then came the period of the growth and spread of the Diaspora as already described. In every centre of the Dispersion, the same moral and spiritual influences as had been felt in connection with the exiles during the seventy years, were in some measure at work. The blood of the martyrs in the persecutions under Antiochus Epiphanes spoke with its unfailing power. A faith worth suffering and dying for, and that with such noble constancy and such "hope of a better resurrection,"[3] must have seemed to many an earnest and thoughtful Gentile to be worthy at least of inquiry and consideration. The children of the persecuted were eager to spread the truth for which their fathers died. And some two generations before this time, in the Providence of God, the Greek Version of the Hebrew Scriptures had issued from Alexandria, opening the secret of the martyrs' faith and hope to all who were willing to read and understand. These were "the holy books which we (the Maccabees) have in our hands to comfort us, so that we need nothing else."[4]

---

[1] Neh. x. 28. See below, p. 124. As to the spirit of hope and enthusiasm which marked this "period of Israel's renaissance at the close of the exile," see the fine passage in Prof. Davidson's *Hebrews*, p. 87 f.

[2] Neh. vii. 46–60. See Dean Plumptre, art. "Proselytes," in Smith's *Dict. of the Bible*, ii. p. 941a.

[3] Heb. xi. 35 ; comp. 2 Macc. vii. 7–12 ; xiv. 29, 36.

[4] ʽΗμεῖς οὖν ἀπροσδεεῖς τούτων ὄντες, παράκλησιν ἔχοντες τὰ βιβλία τὰ ἅγια τὰ ἐν ταῖς χερσὶν ἡμῶν, 1 Macc. xii. 9. That the Jews at Alexandria also had been

From all these causes, and others on which we cannot dwell here, for several generations before the Christian era there had been a large and steady increase of proselytes to the faith and fellowship of Israel. The fact forced itself upon the notice of the historians and philosophers of Rome. "The superstitions of this wretched people," they said with haughty wonder, "are received throughout the whole world; the conquered have given laws to their conquerors."[1]   The frequent references to the subject made by the Latin satirists attest the same thing, and are in perfect accordance with the statements and allusions which bear upon it in the New Testament narratives.[2]

Proselytism had its bad as well as its good side.   After the Maccabean wars of freedom, Judaism was often spread as well as defended by the sword.   Josephus records how circumcision was forced upon the Idumæans by John Hyrcanus, and upon the Ituræans by Aristobulus, and how fanatical zeal among his own followers sought expression in similar ways.[3]   Where violent means were not within reach, recourse was had to other unscrupulous expedients, such as fraud, sorcery, exorcisms, and base inducements as to relief from previously existing social and moral obligations.[4]   Such were the methods of the scribes and Pharisees to which our Lord refers in the indignant words: "Woe unto you, scribes and Pharisees, hypocrites! for ye compass sea and land to make one proselyte; and when he is

persecuted on religious grounds, and had continued stedfast in the faith at an earlier period than that of Antiochus, seem to be the historical facts that underlie the legendary narrative of 3 Maccabees.   Such sufferings in the cause of their religion must have drawn the more attention in Egypt as well as elsewhere to the sacred books in which it was set forth.

[1] "Usque eo sceleratissimæ gentis consuetudo convaluit ut per omnes jam terras recepta sit; victi victoribus leges dederunt."   Seneca, as cited by Augustine, *De Civit. Dei*, vi. 11.

[2] Comp. Schürer, *History of Jewish People*, E. Tr., Edin. 1885, Div. II. vol. ii. pp. 304–313, with the copious references given by him.

[3] Joseph. *Antiq.* xiii. 9. 3; xi. 3; *Life*, c. 23; *Bell. Jud.* ii. 11. 10. Horace's "Veluti Judæi, cogemus" (*Sat.* i. 4. 142) seems to imply, as Dean Plumptre observes (art. "Proselytes"), that "they sometimes ventured on employing such violent measures even in Rome."

[4] Leyrer, *Proselyten*, S. 239. Plumptre, "Proselytes," in Smith, ii. p. 941. C. Taylor, *Sayings of the Jewish Fathers*, Cambridge 1877, p. 35 f.

become so, ye make him twofold more a son of hell (υἱὸν γεέννης) than yourselves."[1]

The character of such proselytes in whom "the vices of the Jew were engrafted on the vices of the heathen," explains though it does not justify many a contemptuous utterance regarding proselytes generally in the Rabbinical writings. They are "like the leprosy in Israel." They "hinder the coming of the Messiah." It became a proverb: "Do not trust a proselyte unto the twenty-fourth generation."[2]

That the better aspect of the movement predominated in our Lord's time and the generation preceding, we may gather with some certainty from the results which appear in the Gospels and Acts. Such men as the Roman centurions with their households at Capernaum and Cæsarea, such circles of "God-fearing men," "devout proselytes," "devout women of honourable estate which were Greeks," as Paul found in connection with every synagogue of the Dispersion, had certainly been attracted by what was best and highest in the faith and life of Israel.[3]

The Talmudic distinction of "proselytes of the gate" and "proselytes of righteousness" does not occur in the New Testament, and was probably formulated only at a much later date, along with a multitude of other minute rules and

---

[1] Matt. xxiii. 15. Comp. what Justin Martyr says to his Jewish opponent of the proselytes in the first half of the second century: "The proselytes not only do not believe, but twofold more than yourselves blaspheme Christ's name, and wish to torture and put to death us who believe in Him; for in all points they strive to be like you." *Dial. cum Tryph.* cxxii. in *Ante-Nicene Library,* ii. p. 253.

[2] Jalkuth Ruth, f. 163*a*, in Leyrer, S. 240. This applies, Leyrer says, to the "half and half proselytes," "inter utrumque viventes," of whom Commodianus speaks:—

> " Quid in synagoga decurris ad Pharisæos,
> Ut tibi misericors fiat quem denegas ultro?
> Exis inde foris; iterum tu fana requiris,
> Vis inter utrumque vivere, sed inde peribis."
> *Instruct. adv. Gentium Deos,* xxiv. 317–320.
> *Patrol. Lat.* ed. Migne, v. p. 219.

Comp. Weber, *System der altsyn. Palästin. Theol.* S. 76. Schürer, *Hist. of Jewish People,* ii. p. 32 f.

[3] Luke vii. 1–9 ; Acts x. 1 f., 22–24 ; xiii. 16, 43 f., 48–50 ; xvii. 4, 12, etc.

distinctions devised by the Rabbis.[1]   But the fact is established from many sources, that there were proselytes who
stood in the two different degrees of nearness to the community of Israel indicated by that formula, and that there
were two views held by Jewish teachers in New Testament
times and previously as to the necessity of circumcision in
such cases, in order to a saving relation to the God of Israel.
It is plain, for example, that Cornelius the centurion, although
recognised as a " righteous " and " devout man, who feared
God with all his house," who was " well reported of by all
the nation of the Jews," and kept the stated hours of prayer
and other Jewish usages, was yet to the Jewish mind
essentially " a Gentile," a " man uncircumcised," and " of
another nation " ($\dot{a}\lambda\lambda\acute{o}\phi\nu\lambda o\varsigma$), to whom it was " unlawful
($\dot{a}\theta\acute{e}\mu\iota\tau o\nu$) for a Jew to join himself or to eat with him." [2]
So also in the synagogue of Antioch in Pisidia " the devout
proselytes," although " fearing God," and worshipping statedly
along with the " children of the stock of Abraham," seem yet
to be referred to as " Gentiles." [3]

With respect to such proselytes, we see from the sayings
of those Rabbis in whom the better and higher spirit of
Judaism found expression, that a wise caution was exercised
in testing their motives for seeking admission, and in
instructing them carefully as to what was implied in joining
the fellowship of Israel, but that a gracious and kindly
welcome was given them, and special consideration of their
feelings after admission was enjoined upon all who were
Israelites by birth.   " Proselytes were instructed in the
commandments, and concerning the reward for keeping them
and the penalties for transgressing them.   Their conversion
is therefore called a ' coming to this rule of life ' (בא
למדה זו, Jebamoth 47a). . . . After instruction there followed
the formal admission by circumcision (מילה) and Baptism
(טבילה, Berakoth 47b, Jebamoth 46b, and repeatedly).   Women

---

[1] As Dean Plumptre truly says : " In proportion as they ceased to have
any power to make proselytes, they dwelt with exhaustive fulness on the
question how proselytes were to be made."

[2] Acts x. 1 f., 22, 28 ff., 45 ; xi. 2 f., 18.

[3] Acts xiii. 16, 26, 42-48.   Comp. Jacob, *Church Polity of N. T.*,
p. 49 f.

were admitted simply by Baptism (see Tanchuma on Way-yikia Sinai 3).[1] The bath served for purification from heathen impurity. Circumcision was the sign that the proselyte had entered into the covenant of Abraham ; hence it is called 'the seal of Abraham' (חותמו של אברהם, Shemoth Rabba, c. 1), or 'the seal of the holy covenant' (הותמו של ברית הקדש). By circumcision a proselyte is separated from all national and religious fellowship with the heathen, and is made a member of the Jewish people. . . . He has come under the wings of the Shekinah (קרב תחת כנפי השכינה, Aboda sara 13b, Shabbath 31a)." [2] " A new Jewish name was given to the proselyte at circumcision, but, according to some authorities, he remained a Gentile (גוי) until he was baptized. Little children were baptized (and circumcised if males) with their parents or with the surviving one if either were dead (Bab. Gem. on Ketubh, § 11)." [3]

" According to Jalkut on Bereshith lech lecha 66a, to convert a heathen is as much as to re-make him. Such proselytes have all the predicates which are ascribed to Israel. Their descendants may even attain to the priesthood. . . . Nay, a proselyte is in a certain sense dearer to the Lord than a 'son of Israel ;' for Israel stood at Mount Sinai and received there the great impressions that led him to believe ; but the proselytes have attained to faith without such advantages (Tanchuma on Bereshith lech lecha). . . . God's will is that the proselyte should be treated with tenderness, and that for ten generations nothing should be said in his presence against the Gentiles, lest he should be reminded of his own Gentile origin, and so be vexed (Sanhedrin, Chelek 21)." [4]

[1] So long as the Temple worship continued, there was also required a sacrifice. Schürer, *Hist. of Jewish People*, ii. p. 319 f. Leyrer, art. "Proselyten," in Herzog, xi. S. 242. From this valuable monograph Dean Plumptre's art. "Proselytes," in Smith's *Dict. of the Bible*, is, as he states, largely drawn.

[2] Weber, S. 75.

[3] Leyrer, *Proselyten*, S. 242. The subject of Jewish Proselyte Baptism is one of considerable interest and importance. Questions regarding the manner and date of its origin have been discussed with much learning and at great length, in connection especially with the Anti-Pædobaptist theory, since the close of the 17th century. See Schürer, ii. pp. 319–324, and remarks on the subject below, Part iv. chap. ii. 1st, 2, note.

[4] Weber, S. 75 f.

Simon ben Gamaliel said : " Our wise men teach that if a Gentile seeks to enter the covenant, we should reach out the hand to him, and bring him under the wings of the Lord." [1]

Such utterances spoke the feelings of the more generous and spiritually - minded of the Jewish teachers. Many sayings, however, as already stated, might be quoted of a different kind, expressing contempt and dislike for the proselytes.[2]

The general result of this whole movement of things which we have been considering, as regards the religious fellowship of Israel after the exile, both in the Holy Land and in the Dispersion, was a widened and widening membership. But of far greater importance were the widening and elevation of thought, the increase of spiritual insight on the part of Israel, into the gracious purposes of the God of Abraham, who was also " the God of the whole earth." There rose before their eyes the vision of a mighty fabric, like that of the temple of old rising without sound of axe or hammer, " a spiritual house," a great fellowship of brethren, speaking different tongues, dwelling in different and distant lands, but united by the strongest bonds in faith and life, having all been drawn by the God of Abraham to Himself and to His true people, forming one great Ecclesia Dei (קהל יהוה), although its members only met together from Sabbath to Sabbath in their little appointed meetings (עדה, συναγωγή) in widely separated parts of the earth, remembering each other then, but never all to see each other's faces in one assembly at Jerusalem.

The striking words of the last of the prophets are best interpreted by the facts of the Diaspora, which were familiar to every Jew of that generation. Malachi spoke from that standpoint. There was much before his eyes in the Jerusalem of the returned exiles which was discouraging to a spiritual mind, and which called for rebuke in the name of the Lord. It was a far more hopeful sight that opened to the prophet as he looked beyond the narrow limits of Jewish Palestine, to those communities of his fellow-countrymen now spreading in such a marvellous way into all the lands of the known

---

[1] Leyrer, S. 242. Comp. Ruth ii. 12.   [2] See above, p. 117

world, where Gentiles were drawn to "join themselves to the Lord" and to His people, and where in humble meeting-places believing hearts were lifted up with one accord to God in prayers and praises, which were "to Him as incense and as the evening sacrifice."[1] It was an earnest of a glorious future for all the earth. "For, from the rising of the sun, even unto the going down of the same, My name is great among the Gentiles; and in every place incense is offered unto My name, and a pure offering; for My name is great among the Gentiles, saith the Lord of hosts."[2]

Many a "devout proselyte" rejoiced to offer this incense and pure offering to God in that great and wonderful Name which he learned to know from the representatives of the true Israel in the Dispersion. For them—to use the words of a distinguished German interpreter of the Old Testament—"a certain fence of outward rites still narrowed the entrance into the full privileges of citizenship in God's kingdom; but the conception of that kingdom rose more and more above merely national limitations. The religion of Israel and its requirements, no longer natural descent from the fathers of the nation, formed the conditions of being a child of God and a member of the kingdom of heaven (die Bedingung um ein Kind Gottes, ein Glied des Himmelreichs zu sein). A world-wide community of God must have presented itself before the eyes of the godly in Israel, and that no longer a national kingdom of the Messiah to which the other nations brought homage and were in subjection, but a Messianic kingdom of a religious kind, in which all who received the

---

[1] Ps. cxli. 2 ; comp. some of the sayings of the Jewish teachers : "He who prays in a synagogue is regarded as though he had presented a pure 'mincha,'" Jer. Berachoth 3. "The study of the Torah is greater than the bringing of the 'Tamid offering,'" Megilla 4, etc., cited in Weber, *altsyn. Palästin. Theol.* S. 39. The hours of prayer were arranged so as to correspond with those of the daily sacrifices in the temple.

[2] Mal. i. 11, 14. It makes no difference in meaning whether we translate with the Revisers' text : "is great," or with their margin : "shall be great." The eye of the prophet saw the future in the present. He spoke of it in terms of present or past experience, so speaking to the mind and heart of his own generation to whom he bore God's message. Comp. Dods on "The Prophets and Prophecy," in his introduction to the *The Post-Exilian Prophets*, Edin. 1879, pp. 27–32.

true religion could become true and fully privileged members. All the sound impulses of this period point to a breaking down of the Old Testament walls of partition, to the transition from a national to a universal religion." [1]

This movement, fraught with such moral and spiritual significance, and carrying in it such wonderful powers of growth and expansion, found organization and permanence in the synagogue system.

[1] Schulz, *A. T. Theol.*, 2te Ausg. S. 782.

CHAPTER III.

1. *Origin and general Characteristics.*

IN apostolic times the synagogue system was regarded as one of venerable antiquity. "From generations of old" (ἐκ γενεῶν ἀρχαίων), one of the leaders of the Hebrew Christian Church at Jerusalem said in the assembly of the apostles and elders there, "Moses hath in every city them that preach him, being read in the synagogues every Sabbath day."[1]

How far back do these "generations" go? Vitringa, in the first book of his great work, *De Synagoga Vetere*, considers with characteristic thoroughness all the references to worship in the Old Testament from the creation onwards, and searches diligently for the synagogue in connection with each of them.[2] He discusses especially the way in which the Sabbath was kept, the position of the priests and Levites in Israel, the injunction given in Deuteronomy to "the priests and all the elders of Israel" to read the law to the people once in seven years.[3] He inquires carefully into the special means for religious instruction used by Jehoshaphat, and into the meetings of a religious kind with prophets like Elisha, on Sabbaths and new moons, but fails to find the synagogue anywhere before the exile.[4] We may recognise a preparation for

---

[1] Acts xv. 21.　　　[2] Vitringa, pp. 271–413.　　　[3] Deut. xxxi. 9-13.

[4] In Ps. lxxiv. 8 we read, "They have burnt up all the synagogues of God in the land" (כָּל־מוֹעֲדֵי־אֵל, all the places of tryst, or appointed meeting). The LXX. render καταπαύσωμεν τὰς ἑορτὰς κυρίου ἀπὸ τῆς γῆς. Vitringa, like most other competent interpreters, regards this reference as too obscure in meaning and too uncertain in date to form the basis of any decided conclusion (pp. 396–405). Calvin and others are disposed to assign the Psalm to the time of the Maccabees. One difficulty in connection with that view is, that, strangely enough, as

the synagogue system before that date, that the same objects
were sought and attained by other means in a partial and
preliminary way; but not until the time of the return from
the captivity do we find what seems the origin of the institution itself.

In the eighth chapter of Nehemiah, in the striking scene
of the gathering of the people "as one man" for worship,
and the reading of the law "in the broad place that is before
the Water Gate" at Jerusalem, all the elements of a synagogue
service present themselves. We have public prayer and
thanksgiving "in the congregation," for which the ancient
and sacred term (קהל, ἐκκλησία) is used, and which consists
of "men and women and all that could hear with understanding."[1] We have the people themselves taking earnest
part in the service, and answering "Amen" at the close of
the prayers. We have the reading and explanation of the
Scriptures by Ezra and other teachers from a raised pulpit or
platform of wood, with marked impression and spiritual
results among the audience.[2]

Here, in all likelihood, we see the commencement of the
synagogue system. Like many other great things, it began
in a very simple way. The returned exiles naturally took
steps to continue, in different places and on a smaller
scale, those gatherings of the congregation, which they found
so profitable in those memorable days of the seventh month
in Jerusalem, to which they had been led under the guidance

Vitringa points out (p. 416 f.), we find no mention of synagogues as places of
worship in the books of the Maccabees, and the author of the first of these
books makes no allusion to the destruction of synagogues in his list of the
calamities of the time (1 Macc. i. 38–51, 54–57). A proseucha or house of
prayer is mentioned as being erected at Ptolemais (in Egypt) in 3 Macc. vii. 20,
and a statement is made in one of the "Psalms of Solomon" (63–48 B.C.)
which probably refers to the age of the Maccabees: "Those who loved the
assemblies of the saints (συναγωγὰς ὁσίων) wandered (reading ἐπλανῶντο) in
deserts," Ps. Sol. xvii. 19.

[1] "Ezra brought the law before the congregation (לִפְנֵי הַקָּהָל)," Neh. viii. 2,
ἐνώπιον τῆς ἐκκλησίας, LXX. Comp. the covenant with God made by the congregation with the religious services recorded in the two next chapters, c. ix. x.
It was a fresh beginning of the religious life of the community of Israel, as in
"the Church in the wilderness" in the day of the assembly at Horeb.

[2] Neh. viii. 1–12, 18; ix. 2–5.

of men Divinely raised up, and on whose action in this matter it was plain that the blessing of God had signally rested. " It obviously met a want which had begun to make itself felt during the captivity. The captives longing for home had awakened in them the outcasts' thirst for God ; and on their return to their fatherland they longed to hear that which alone made it home to them, the voice of their Father. Listening to this voice, articulate in ample promises and in minute arrangements for their welfare, they felt as they had never felt before, that in the reception of that voice lay their true unity as a people. And when they scattered once more through the land, when no master's voice broke the stillness of the Sabbath morning, could anything be more natural than the wish that again they might listen to the Word of their Deliverer and King ? It was this desire which gradually formed the meetings associated with the name of the synagogue, the greatest and most beneficial of Jewish institutions." [1]

Once begun in such circumstances as attended the religious gatherings at Jerusalem under Ezra and Nehemiah, it is easy to understand how the synagogue system spread rapidly. This was especially the case in all the centres of the Dispersion both in the East and West. The germs of such stated meetings for worship and instruction may already be seen in the gatherings of elders and others, during the captivity, to hear God's word from prophets such as Ezekiel.[2] The seed would spring up into vigorous life under the tidings of the religious movement at Jerusalem, and of the arrangements for worship and the study of the law which had been adopted there.[3]

For some time, indeed, the synagogue system spread and

---

[1] Dods, *Presbyterianism older than Christianity*, Edin. 1873, p. 13 f. Vitringa has some suggestive remarks on the different causes which probably combined to give rise to the synagogue system at this time, p. 425.

[2] Ezek. viii. 1 ; xiv. 1 ff. ; xx. 1-4, 27-31 ; xxxiii. 30-32.

[3] Kuenen and others are disposed to hold that the synagogue system arose independently in Babylonia, "whether before the end of the captivity or among those who then remained behind." Kuenen, *Volksreligion und Weltreligion* (Hibbert Lect.), Berlin 1883, S. 171.

prospered more in foreign lands than in Palestine. In the latter, where the returned exiles formed for a long time a comparatively small community, religious interest centred visibly in the restored temple and within the walls of Jerusalem, rebuilt with such special effort under Nehemiah. Meetings for worship were naturally held in the temple courts, or, as the first had been, in the broad places near the gates of the city. This would lead to few or no synagogues — in the later sense of "houses of prayer"—being erected through the country for a considerable time, and may explain the fact, to which I have adverted above, that the books of the Maccabees make no mention of such structures as existing in the Holy Land, nor any reference to their destruction as taking place among the other disasters of the period.[1] But in the regions of the Diaspora it was otherwise. There the necessity of a separate place of meeting, however simple, was felt from the first. The temples used by the heathen, and their buildings for civil purposes, were of course not open to the Jews. Sometimes, therefore, by river-sides, under the open sky, sometimes in groves, sometimes in a large room or hall in the house of some wealthier member of their community, the little congregations of the Dispersion met to worship the God of their fathers and to hear His word.[2]

In such centres as Alexandria and Antioch, where the Jews were strong in numbers and influence, and could count on the forbearance or favour of the civil authorities, separate buildings were erected by them at an early date. These were sometimes of large size and splendidly furnished; and in connection with them probably the transition took place by which the word "synagogue" ($\sigma \upsilon \nu \alpha \gamma \omega \gamma \acute{\eta}$), which in the canonical

---

[1] See note at p. 123 f. As there pointed out, the only "house of prayer," apart from the Temple, to which the books of Maccabees refer, is one erected at Ptolemais in Egypt.

[2] The apocryphal book known as "Susanna," or "the Judgment of Daniel," in Theodotion's revision of the LXX., speaks of such a hall in the house of Joiakim, a wealthy Jew at Babylon, serving as a place of meeting for his fellow-countrymen, in which elders preside and disputes are heard and settled. The work is a sort of religious romance, but no doubt reflects the customs and experiences of the Jews of the Dispersion at the time when the apocryphal additions to Daniel took shape. Hist. of Susanna, 4–7.

writings of the Old Testament always means the congregation itself, came by the time of Josephus and the New Testament writers very often to denote also the building or place of worship in which the congregation met.[1]

Long before the Christian era every little town in Palestine had its synagogue. In Jerusalem itself, "according to one tradition (Shir Rabba 20), there were in the time of the second temple four hundred and eighty synagogues. According to another tradition (Echa Rabba 52a), each of these synagogues had attached to it a school for the exposition of the Holy Scriptures, and for the Mishna."[2] This no doubt is an immense exaggeration; but that different nationalities of the Dispersion had different synagogues of their own at Jerusalem in our Lord's time is evident from what is said in the sixth chapter of the Acts as to Stephen's opponents coming from five different Hellenistic synagogues in the city.[3]

In the chief seats of the Diaspora also there were several synagogues, sometimes, as in Alexandria, where there were "many of them," Philo writes, "in each division of the city," regularly united under a common government. To use the words of Strabo, already cited, "it was not easy to find a place in the habitable world which had not received this race of the Jews, and was not taken possession of by them." And everywhere the sign of their infeftment in it was the establishment of a synagogue or a place of prayer. It was not, indeed, without risk that they thus raised the banner of their religion and drew public attention to their position in the town. Hated as the Jews generally were by the populace throughout the Roman Empire for their success in money-

---

[1] Josephus tells us that the successors of Antiochus Epiphanes bestowed everything of brass among the spoils taken by him from the Temple of Jerusalem upon the Jews of Antioch, to be placed by them in their synagogue (εἰς τὴν συναγωγὴν αὐτῶν ἀναθέντες), and allowed them to have equal rights of citizenship with the Greeks. *Bell. Jud.* vii. 21. The splendours of the chief synagogue of the Jews at Alexandria (μεγίστη καὶ περισημοτάτη) are referred to by Philo, *Leg. ad Caium*, § 20. They are celebrated by the Talmudic writers in their usual exaggerative style.

[2] Weber, S. 38. "Scripta quidem," as Vitringa says of similar statements, "ut Judæi solent, ὑπερβολικῶς, sic tamen ut veritas per fictiones eorum facile pelluceat," p. 428.

[3] Acts vi. 9.

making, their usurious practices, and especially for what was counted intolerable religious pride and bigotry, a Jewish synagogue was, as Reuss calls it, "a sort of natural lightning conductor for sudden storms of popular feeling." And "the magistrates often shared the prejudices of the mob, or were willing to pander to them from some petty regard to temporary advantage."[1] A good illustration of this may be seen in the way in which the charge is brought against Paul and Silas at Philippi by the owners of the slave girl: "These men, being Jews, do exceedingly trouble our city, and set forth customs which it is not lawful for us to receive or observe, being Romans;" and in the easy success which so vague an accusation met with at the hands of the prætors, in the belief that the accused were only Jews.[2]

The word "synagogue" (συναγωγή), as already observed, primarily denotes the congregation itself, or the meeting of the congregation, just as the word "Church" (ἐκκλησία) does, although both came in time by a natural transition to mean also the building in which the congregation met. The names more properly used by the Jews for the place of worship were "the house of meeting" (בֵּית־הַכְּנֶסֶת) and "the house of prayer" (בֵּית־הַתְּפִלָּה), with their Greek equivalents in Hellenistic congregations (οἶκος τῆς συναγωγῆς and οἶκος or τόπος τῆς προσευχῆς). These latter phrases soon became shortened in Greek-speaking communities to "synagogue" and "proseucha" (συναγωγή and προσευχή), as we find constantly in Josephus and other writers of his time.[3]

---

[1] Reuss, *Gesch. der heil. Schriften A. T.*, S. 528. Different synagogues in one city were often designated from the locality in which they were built, or, as in Acts vi. 9, from the nationality in the Diaspora which they represented. Thus we find at Rome "the synagogue of them of the Suburra" (Σιβουρησίων), "of them of the Campus Martius" (Καμπησίων), "of the Hebrews" (Αἰβρέων). In the last of these, doubtless, the Scriptures were still read in the original, not as elsewhere in the Alexandrian translation.

Sometimes, again, synagogues received graceful and significant names, "the synagogue of the Olive," "of the Vine" (συναγωγὴ Ἐλαίας, כנישתא דנופנא). Comp. Schürer, ii. pp. 74, 247 f.

[2] Acts xvi. 19–23; cf. 37–39.

[3] "Proseucha" seems often to denote a smaller or less formal erection than a synagogue. It might mean four walls by a river-side under shade of trees, or beneath the open sky, such as the "place of prayer" at Philippi may have

These two simple but expressive names, "the house of meeting" and "the house of prayer," embody the leading ideas of the institution of the synagogue. It provided a place where "the whole congregation of Israel," "the congregation of the Lord," in all its separate parts, met with God in prayer and in His Word at appointed times, and met also with each other for mutual profit.

The arrangements within these houses of prayer were of the simplest kind. A chest or press at one end of the building to hold the rolls of the law and the prophets, a teacher's seat on a slightly raised platform, or "pulpit of wood made for the purpose,"[1] seats for the congregation, lamps for evening meetings, two collecting-boxes, one for local objects and one "for the land of Israel,"—these were all the requirements.[2] It was in a village synagogue, with such simple furnishings, that our Lord worshipped week by week for nearly thirty years with His earthly parents and "His brethren and sisters" at Nazareth. It was thither that "He entered in, as His custom was, on the Sabbath day," after His public ministry had begun, and His fame as a teacher in the synagogues of Galilee had spread abroad; and there, at the fitting point in the service, He "stood up to read; and there was delivered unto Him a roll of the prophet Isaiah."[3]

---

been in which the Gospel was first preached by Paul in Europe (Acts xvi. 13, 16). But Josephus speaks of the synagogue in Tiberias, "a very large edifice, and capable of holding a great multitude," as a proseucha. On the whole, Schürer's conclusion seems correct, that "no material distinction can be established between the two expressions." *Hist. of Jewish People,* ii. p. 73. Comp. Vitringa, pp. 115–133. Leyrer, art. "Synagogen," in Herzog, xv. S. 303.

[1] Neh. viii. 4 ; ix. 4.

[2] See Vitringa, pp. 174–212. Schürer, ii. p. 74 f. Ten was said to be the quorum of worshippers needful for a synagogue. According to the Rabbis, a synagogue must not be set up in any Jewish community unless there could be found there ten "men of leisure" (בטלנים). What stores of learning have been lavished on the elucidation of this phrase may be seen—by those who are themselves men of leisure—in the treatises of Rhenford and Vitringa, *De decem otiosis synagogæ,* Franequeræ 1686, and *De decemviris otiosis,* do. 1687 both writing against Lightfoot in his *Horæ Hebraicæ.*

[3] Luke iv. 15 ff.

2. *The Worship of the Synagogue.*

The worship of the synagogue was essentially just what it was in the great religious gatherings under Ezra and Nehemiah, in which, as we have seen reason to believe, the institution took its rise.   The reading and exposition of the Scriptures, with prayer and praise, formed the centre and substance of the whole.   In this the power and solemnity of the synagogue meetings were felt to lie by all the worshippers who, like Simeon, were " righteous and devout, waiting for the consolation of Israel," [1] and by all the more spiritually-minded of the Jewish teachers.   " Wherever ten persons pray together," it was said, " there the Shekinah is in the midst of them."   " Wherever Israel prays and studies in its synagogues and schools, wherever the wise men, the elders, and the prophets are, there the Shekinah is also present to bless them." [2]   We must beware of taking our impressions of the synagogue system from the dreary follies of the Talmud,[3] and from the spiritual deadness, the chilling formality and irreverence which too often characterize the modern Jewish synagogue.   In its best days it was very different.   In our Lord's time, in particular, there can be no doubt that, with whatever intermixture of lower elements, all that was deepest and highest both in the intellectual and religious life of Israel centred in the synagogue.

Its plan of worship and instruction, while making sufficient provision, as we shall see presently, for order and central control, was characterized by an admirable spirit of freedom. Although the synagogue liturgy as a whole cannot be assigned to a very early date, several elements in it can be traced back with considerable certainty to the New Testament period. Foremost among these is the recitation of the " Shema," as a sort of simple and popular creed or confession of faith in the unity of God, and in Jehovah as the God of Israel, to be

---

[1] Luke ii. 25.

[2] Berakoth 6*a* ; Pesikta 193*a*, *b* ; Vayyikra rabba 11, cited in Weber, S. 182.

[3] " The ocean of the Talmud," as the Rabbis called it, is one whose waters cast up not a little mire and dirt.   Its pearls and precious things are few and far between, however well they may look when drawn from their native surroundings and grouped together by a skilful hand.

acknowledged with love and thanksgiving as the God of redemption, "who brought them out of the land of Egypt to be their God." This is distinctly referred to by Josephus.[1] Round this centre-point the rest of the Hebrew liturgy gradually grew up. Some of the oldest prayers, such as the "Kaddish" and the "Shemoneh Esreh," seem to have early assumed a fixed shape, and to belong, at all events in substance, to the time of our Lord. Two at least of the petitions in the prayer which He taught His disciples appear to be taken from the striking formula of the "Kaddish," with which they were in all probability familiar from childhood.[2] For materials of praise recourse was naturally had to the treasury of the Hebrew Psalter.[3]

Along with this permanent element in the synagogue service, room was given for free prayer, both by the congregation in silence and by those who led their devotions. The usual

---

[1] Josephus, *Antiq.* iv. 8. 13. Schürer, ii. p. 84 f. The Shema includes the three passages, Deut. vi. 4–9 ; xi. 13–21 ; and Num. xv. 37–41.

[2] The first -and second petitions. Compare the beginning of the Kaddish : "May His great name be magnified and hallowed in the world which He hath created according to His will. May His kingdom come in power " (lit. be made to reign) " in your life and in your days, and in the life of all the House of Israel speedily and in a short time. And say ye, Amen " (רַבָּא שְׁמֵהּ וְיִתְקַדַּשׁ יִתְגַּדַּל

בְּעָלְמָא דִּי־בְרָא כִרְעוּתֵהּ וְיַמְלִיךְ מַלְכוּתֵהּ בְּחַיֵּיכוֹן וּבְיוֹמֵיכוֹן וּבְחַיֵּי דְכָל בֵּית

יִשְׂרָאֵל בַּעֲגָלָא וּבִזְמַן קָרִיב וְאִמְרוּ אָמֵן). Hamburger, *Real-Encycl. für Bibel u. Talmud*, art. "Kaddisch," ii. S. 603 ff. Vitringa, pp. 962, 1077 f., 1098 : "Sanctissima illa precationis formula, quæ in initio et fine actuum quorumque sacrorum recitabatur, et forte omnium, quas synagoga hujus temporis habet, precationum antiquissima ; Chaldaice concepta ut a plebe ignarâ Hebrææ linguæ et ab ipsis quoque gentibus Syriacè peritis intelligeretur, et omnes inde perciperent quæ Judæorum de futurâ sanctificatione et glorificatione Divinæ nominis in orbe terrarum spes sit." Schürer gives a translation of the "Shemoneh Esreh," sometimes called κατ' ἐξοχήν "the Prayer " (התפלה), ii. pp. 85–87. It is to be found, as well as the "Kaddish," in all prayer-books of the orthodox Jews. Dr. Edersheim points out how closely the hymn of Zacharias corresponds in several points with the "Shemoneh Esreh." *Life and Times of Jesus the Messiah*, i. p. 159. Zunz, *Ritus des synagogalen Gottesdienstes*, Berlin 1859, S. 2 f., and his *Gottesdienstliche Vorträge*, S. 366 ff.

[3] Compare Philo's account of the responsive singing of the Essenes in their Sabbath services. "They sing hymns to the praise of God, composed in different kinds of metre and verse, now with one mouth, now with antiphonal hymns and harmonies." *De Vita contempl.* p. 901, ed. Frankof. Art. "Antiphon," in *Dict. of Christ. Antiq.* i. p. 94.

practice was to pray standing, with the face turned towards
Jerusalem, or to the Temple. None of the prayers were
repeated by the members of the congregation generally, but
by some one acting as the mouthpiece of the rest. But
the congregation made certain brief responses, uniting audibly
in particular in the " Amen " at the end of the prayer, in
accordance with Scripture precept and example.[1] Some of
the Jewish teachers in the first century—possibly influenced
by the example of greater freedom and gifts of utterance in
the Apostolic Church—saw danger in the growth of the liturgical
element in the synagogue worship. Rabbi Eliezer of Lydda
(circa 80–115 A.D.) taught that no form of prayer was binding
in the public services, and urged that the leaders of prayer in
the synagogue should give up even the well-known " eighteen "
blessings or prayers,—the " Shemoneh Esreh,"—and should
pray from the heart as they might be enabled at the time.[2]

After the reading of the law and the prophets, either by an
official of the synagogue or by some qualified person or
persons in his place, there followed an exposition of Scripture, or " word of exhortation," as it was called by the rulers
of the synagogue at Antioch when they invited Paul and
Barnabas to speak to the congregation there.[3] The rulers of
the synagogue, or their president as representing them, were
themselves responsible for this part of the service. But the
address might be entrusted by them to any suitable person
among the audience, as in the case at Antioch now mentioned.[4]
" Thus "—in theory at least—as Dr. Dods put it, " every man's
gift became available for the whole congregation. No knowledge, no happy interpretation of Scripture, no significant

---

[1] Deut. xxvii. 15 ; 1 Chron. xvi. 36 ; Neh. viii. 6 ; Ps. xli. 13 ; lxxii. 19 ;
cvi. 48 ; 1 Cor. xiv. 16. Comp. Schürer, ii. p. 77 f. Zunz, Ritus, S. 15.

[2] See Leyrer, art. " Synagogen," in Herzog, Real-Encycl. xv. S. 307. " In
later times the leaders in prayer (die Vorbeter) claimed the רִשׁוּת (the dis-
cretionary or alterable elements in the service) as a free sphere for their own
unfettered utterances (für eigene Produktion)."

[3] Acts xiii. 14 ff.

[4] In Philo's interesting picture of a synagogue Sabbath service in his time the
address or exposition of Scripture is given by " one of the priests who may be
present, or one of the elders," and is of considerable length. τῶν ἱερέων τις ὁ παρὼν
ἢ τῶν γερόντων εἷς ἀναγίνωσκει τοὺς ἱεροὺς νόμους αὐτοῖς, καὶ καθ᾽ ἕκαστον ἐξηγεῖται
μέχρι σχεδὸν δείλης ὀψίας. Fragment in Eusebius, Præpar. Evang. viii. 7. 12 f.

religious experience, was retained as private property, but they had all things in common; every one who could contribute to the common stock of edification being at liberty to do so. The synagogue thus skilfully and fearlessly absorbed into itself all the talent, all the intellectual and religious life of the locality." [1]

It is plain that such freedom was liable to great abuse, and might lead to signal disorders, if there were no central authority in existence to regulate its exercise, or if that authority were not suitably used, or did not meet with general support from the congregation. Of the nature of the disorders likely to arise some indications are given in what is perhaps the oldest portion of the New Testament. James, the Lord's brother, writing to Jewish Christians who met· like their fathers in a synagogue,[2] gives the significant exhortation : " My brethren, do not many of you turn teachers ($\mu\grave{\eta}$ $\pi o\lambda\lambda o\grave{\iota}$ $\delta\iota\delta\acute{a}\sigma\kappa a\lambda o\iota$ $\gamma\acute{\iota}\nu\epsilon\sigma\theta\epsilon$), knowing that we shall receive heavier judgment. For in many things we all stumble. If any stumbleth not in word, the same is a perfect man. . . . The tongue can no man tame : it is a restless evil, full of deadly poison." [3] In the fourteenth chapter of First Corinthians we have a vivid picture of the sort of abuses hinted at by James. Apart from the special character of the gifts possessed by members of the Church at Corinth, this is just the state of things which would naturally arise in an ill-regulated synagogue. When the congregation met, " each one had a Psalm, had a teaching, had an interpretation." Several would rise to speak at once, and none of them was ready to give place to his brethren. Things were not " done unto edifying." They were done neither " in seemly form nor according to order." [4]

Such abuse of freedom was no argument against its lawful use in the synagogue. But it showed the need of a wise and efficient provision for order and control in connection with it. And such there was. This brings us to consider more closely :

---

[1] Dods, *Presbyterianism older than Christianity*, p. 16 ; comp. Vitringa, pp. 695–711 ; Schürer, ii. p. 65.

[2] Jas. ii. 2.   [3] Jas. iii. 1 f., 8.   [4] 1 Cor. xiv. 26–33, 40.

3. *The Organization of the Synagogue.*

The synagogue, as we have seen, was just in name and in reality the "congregation of Israel" localized. It represented especially that congregation meeting in its highest capacity as a religious fellowship in covenant with the God of Abraham, "called, and chosen, and faithful," as an "ecclesia" or "kahal." "Συναγωγή," as Schürer says, "designated the congregation more on the side of its empirical reality; ἐκκλησία more on that of its ideal signification; συναγωγή being the associated congregation as constituted in some one place; ἐκκλησία, on the other hand, the assembly of those called by God to salvation, especially, like קָהָל, the ideal Church of Israel." [1] It is interesting, accordingly, to observe how the principles of the congregation of Israel, learned in past centuries of its history, and the sense of unity which had grown and gathered strength through all the trying experience of the Exile and the Dispersion, found expression in the organization of the synagogue system. With a true instinct, it laid hold at once of the ancient institution of the eldership. This alone had strength and elasticity enough for the purposes to be served. It formed the keystone of the whole fabric, as the membership of the synagogue congregation itself formed the foundation.

(1.) The eldership or presbytery of the synagogue. [2]

There is universal agreement among all competent scholars who have studied this subject, that the whole authority of the synagogue in every normal instance was in the hands of a small body or consistory of elders. [3] These were either chosen directly by the people, as seems to have been the rule in the congregations of the Dispersion, or nominated by

---

[1] Schürer, ii. p. 59.

[2] בֵּית הַזְּקֵנִים ,זִקְנֵי הַכְּנֶסֶת. ﬁﬂﬂﬁ, ἡ γερουσία.

[3] The two things conjoined by the author of one of the later Psalms always went together in the synagogue system, "the assembly of the people and the seat of the elders," Ps. cvii. 32 (בִּקְהַל עָם וּבְמוֹשַׁב זְקֵנִים), LXX.: ἐν ἐκκλησίᾳ λαοῦ καὶ ἐν καθέδρᾳ πρεσβυτέρων).

the Sanhedrin of the nearest town, or the Great Sanhedrin in
Jerusalem, with concurrence of the congregation, as appears to
have been done in Palestine. The general principle acted
upon in all cases is laid down as follows in the Codex
Berakoth (f. 55a) : " Rabbi Isaac says : They appoint no one
as a shepherd " (פרנם = ποιμήν, pastor) " over any congregation
without first consulting it (בצבור אלא אם כן נמלכין)." [1]

Where teaching functions were required of an elder, he
was formally set apart to office by the laying on of hands
(סמיכת ידים). This was done by the eldership of the place.
There was no anointing with oil, as in the consecration of
priests. " When a wise man has attained sufficient knowledge of the law, and is called by a congregation to be
their president or pastor (מפרנם), in order to his entering
on the exercise of his office he receives the imposition of
hands or ordination. Three elders are required for the
ceremony," Tos. Sanhedr. 1.[2] The quorum of the smallest
court by which any judicial sentence could be pronounced
was three. It was known as the "Beth Din," or house of
judgment in each Jewish community, and one of its members
at least must be " a disciple of the wise " (תלמיד חכם), i.e.
trained in the knowledge of Scripture law and its interpretation.[3] In exceptional cases, where from the smallness
of the Jewish population three suitable men could not be

---

[1] Vitringa, pp. 828–835. Wünsche, der Babylonische Talmud, Leipzig
1886, S. 67. Weber, altsyn. Paläst. Theol. S. 137. There is an interesting
passage in the Life of Alexander Severus, by Aelius Lampridius, in which it is
stated that the Emperor was accustomed to consult the people, and seek their
consent, in the appointment of governors and rulers of different sorts in the
provinces, giving as his reason for this "that the Christians and the Jews were
wont to act thus in the nomination of their priests for ordination (in prædi-
candis sacerdotibus qui ordinandi sunt), and that the rule should much more
be observed in the appointment of rulers to whom the goods and lives of men
were to be entrusted." Scriptores Hist. August. (Herm. Peter's ed.), Lipsiæ
1884, i. p. 283 ; c. xlv. 7. Comp. c. xix. p. 261, as to the Emperor's practice
in the appointment of senators.

[2] Weber, S. 130. Leyrer in his art. "Synagogen," in Herzog (xv. S. 312),
gives an excellent summary of the position and functions of the synagogue
elders. Their names of office, as grouped together by him, are especially noteworthy from their close correspondence with the names of the office-bearers of
the apostolic Church as seen in the New Testament.

[3] The distinction between the ordinary elders and the trained teachers with

found for office, a single teacher might preside in a synagogue; but he could give no authoritative decision, either
on doctrinal or practical questions, until colleagues were
associated with him. "An individual Rabbi can decide
nothing."[1] One passage alone in the New Testament, and
that of uncertain interpretation, may possibly refer to a case
of a single ruler only being found in a synagogue.[2]

Among the rulers of the synagogue was one known as
the "legate" or "deputy of the congregation" (שְׁלִיחַ צִבּוּר).[3]
His special duty was to lead in the public prayers of the
synagogue. Whether this, however, was assigned in early
times to one distinct official may be questioned. Certainly
the office of "Sheliach Tsibbur" seems to have varied considerably in respect of dignity at different periods, being sometimes united with that of "Chazzan" or synagogue attendant,
while at other times his position is described in high terms
as being one to which a peculiarly representative character
belonged.[4] The importance attached to his functions would
naturally increase in proportion to the growth of the liturgical element in the synagogue services. It is Maimonides

whom they were associated is frequently brought out. We have it, *e.g.*, in an
Imperial enactment of Honorius and Theodosius, inscribed, "To the teacher
and elders of the Jews ('Didascalo et Majoribus Judæorum ')," Vitringa, p. 590;
cf. Hausrath, *N. T. Times*, i. p. 8. In the modern Jewish synagogue a
single Rabbi or teacher is often associated with a body of 'Parnasim' (lit.
shepherds) or elders, representatives of and chosen by the people, in whose
hands the management of the affairs of the synagogue congregation is placed.
This consistory of Parnasim can meet without the Rabbi, but if present he
presides *ex officio*. They are chosen yearly, but may be re-elected, Vitr. pp.
513 ff., 578 f., 605 f. It is plain how closely this arrangement corresponds
to the "Deacons' Court" of our own Church, and to the joint meetings of elders
and deacons in the Dutch and other branches of the Reformed Church.

[1] Weber, SS. 131–140. Schürer, i. p. 323. Vitringa, pp. 549–565, 573 f.,
590. Litton gives a clear summary of the general conclusions arrived at by
Vitringa, *Church of Christ*, Lond. 1851, p. 252 f.

[2] Luke xiii. 14. This may be just such a case as that referred to in the
note above, where the teaching elder (the "didascalus") is distinguished from
the rest as the president or head of the synagogue, ὁ ἀρχισυνάγωγος.

[3] According to Schürer, this word צִבּוּר, which is frequent in the Mishnah,
generally denotes the Church or Congregation, "not as a community, but only
as an aggregate in contrast to the individual," ii. p. 59.

[4] Dr. Dods suggests, as the best rendering for "Sheliach Tsibbur," the phrase
"representative elder," and identifies him pretty decidedly with "the angel

and other late writers who make most of his position, and
of its pre-eminently representative character. In their time
it was held to be of vital importance that every word and
syllable of the prescribed prayers and readings should be
given in exact accordance with the traditional rules. The
" Sheliach Tsibbur," as head of the liturgical department, was
responsible for this.[1]

It is worthy of note that a Jewish priest as such had no
special place or rights in the synagogue. If suited in other
respects to be an elder or teacher in the congregation, he
might be chosen to that position ; but his priesthood in
itself (with one exception, to be noted immediately) gave him
no peculiar privileges. It was expressly enjoined that " no
one was to presume to wear the dress of a priest in the
service of the synagogue." [2] The only exceptional mark of
honour paid in the synagogue to the priesthood rested on the
ancient rule that " the priests, the sons of Aaron, were to
bless the people." If one or more members of a priestly
family were present at the service, they were asked to come

---

of the Church" in the Revelation, *Presbyterianism*, p. 17. In this latter
view he agrees with Vitringa, pp. 911-913. Bishop Lightfoot, on the other
hand, regards the legate of the synagogue as " an inferior officer,"—which he
certainly was in the first century at least,—and prefers an ideal interpretation of
the apocalyptic ἄγγελος τῆς ἐκκλησίας, *Philippians*, 3rd ed. p. 197 f. Schürer
seems to go to an opposite extreme in being disposed to deny the separate
existence of such a functionary altogether, although it may be true that
" whoever said the prayer in the name of the congregation was called the שְׁלִיחַ
צִבּוּר, the 'plenipotentiary of the congregation,' " ii. p. 67. There were no
doubt, as Vitringa shows, ordinary and occasional leaders in prayer, pp. 893,
903-908. Leyrer's conclusion is marked by his usual discrimination : " A
function which at an earlier period any qualified member of the college of
elders undertook, namely, to be the mouth of the congregation in prayer and
in reading the holy Scriptures, came in process of time to be transferred to a
qualified man specially appointed for the purpose, who was then called
'Sheliach ha-Tsibbur,' nuncius, legatus ecclesiæ, the deputy (Abgeordnete),
also the scribe of the synagogue. R. Gamaliel says : ' Legatus ecclesiæ fungitur
officio pro omnibus, et officio hoc rite perfunctus omnes ab obligatione liberat.'
. . . His importance grew with the development of the public worship of the
synagogue, and with the decrease of the knowledge of the Hebrew language,"
art. "Synagogen," in Herzog, *Real-Encyl.* xv. S. 313.

[1] It is to this that the passages from Maimonides, adduced by Dr. Dods in
support of his view, refer. Vitringa, pp. 893, 905.

[2] Schürer, i. p. 277.

forward and pronounce with uplifted hands the closing benediction : " The Lord bless thee and keep thee ; the Lord make His face to shine upon thee and be gracious unto thee ; the Lord lift up His countenance upon thee and give thee peace ;" to which the whole congregation answered, Amen.

If no one of priestly descent happened to be in the congregation, the blessing was spoken in the form of a prayer by one of the rulers of the synagogue, the Sheliach Tsibbur.[1]

(2.) The president of the eldership.

In the consistory or council of elders by which each synagogue was governed, one was appointed president or chairman. · He was called the head of the session or consistory (ראש ישיבה), or in the Hellenistic congregations the gerusiarch (γερουσιάρχης), from his presiding over the eldership or presbytery (γερουσία).[2] He appears generally to have held this position *ad vitam aut culpam*, but could be removed from it for a time or permanently by the votes of his

[1] Num. vi. 22–27. Vitringa, pp. 1114–1120. Schürer, ii. p. 82 f. If the high priest himself were in the congregation and rose to read, the roll was handed to him in token of permission by the president of the synagogue,—the archisynagogus or ראש הכנסת,—as in the case of any other member of the congregation held competent for the duty ; and he read standing. Schürer, ii. p. 64 ; comp. Luke iv. 16, "He stood up to read." As a matter of courtesy, precedence was also generally given to those known to be of priestly or Levitical descent in reading the Scriptures in the congregation. "The following things have been ordained for the sake of peace : the priest is first to read ; then the Levite ; then the Israelite, for the sake of peace," Gittin v. 8, in Schürer.

[2] Schürer, *Gemeindeverfassung der Juden in Rom in der Kaiserzeit*, Leipzig 1879, S. 18. This name seems to answer also to the "head of the synagogue" (ראש הכנסת) in Hebrew congregations, and possibly to the ἀρχισυνάγωγος of the N. T., although both of these words seem used also in a more general sense to denote any who held a prominent position among the elders of the synagogue, who were, *e.g.*, members of the Executive or Acting Committee of its eldership, commonly spoken of in Hellenistic synagogues as the archons (ἄρχοντες), from whom the president was usually chosen. This is especially clear as to the N. T. usage of archisynagogus. Thus in Luke viii. 41 and 49 the names ἄρχων τῆς συναγωγῆς and ἀρχισυνάγωγος are used interchangeably ; and there is repeated evidence of the existence of several archisynagogi in one congregation. In some of the inscriptions in Jewish cemeteries, on the other hand, the two titles archon and archisynagogus are conjoined, showing that a man might in some cases hold both positions, and that a distinction was recognised between the two. The archisynagogus may sometimes have been the chairman of the archons, as the gerusiarch was of the whole eldership, somewhat in the same way as the President of a large "General Committee," and the chairman of its

colleagues, subject, as it seems, to the intervention of the Sanhedrin, where the decision was not a unanimous one, or if the matter was referred to them from the inferior court.[1] The

Executive, or the Moderator of a Church Session, and the Convener of a Sessional committee, are often represented by different persons among ourselves.

Schürer inclines, chiefly on the ground of the Roman inscriptions discussed in his valuable monograph, to understand by the archisynagogus, in every case in which the term is used, one of the elders or archons specially entrusted with the charge of public worship, the "head of the synagogue" in that whole department. This is a feasible hypothesis as to the meaning of the word in some instances, but does not seem to correspond with the N. T. use of it, to which reference is made above. Bishop Lightfoot goes rather beyond the evidence of the passages which he cites, in saying : "In the New Testament, at all events, ἀρχισυνάγωγος is only another name for the elder of the synagogue (Mark v. 22 ; Acts xiii. 15 ; xviii. 8, 17 ; comp. Justin, *Dial. c. Tryph.* c. 137)." No doubt every archisynagogus was an elder, but it does not follow that every elder was an archisynagogus, nor that he was an archon. In the case of Jairus (Luke viii. 41–49), the names archon and archisynagogus are applied to the same person, apparently as equivalent in meaning, by an evangelist who is peculiarly accurate in his use of official titles ; but there is no N. T. instance of archisynagogus and elder being used as synonymous. Dr. Lightfoot admits that apart from the N. T. we seem to have instances of ἀρχισυνάγωγος denoting the president of the council of elders, *Philippians*, p. 205, note. Josephus and Philo, both contemporary with the N. T. writers, distinguish clearly between the general body of the Sanhedrin,—the βουλευται,—and the ἄρχοντες who formed its executive. The latter were οἱ πρωτεύοντες τῆς γερουσίας, *Bell. Jud.* vii. 10. 1 ; comp. ii. 16. 1, and 17. 1. Philo, *In Flaccum*, § 10. Schürer, *History of Jewish People*, ii. pp. 64 f., 251 f. Comp. Hausrath, *N. T. Times*, i. p. 86. Leyrer's view, founded on a very careful examination of the evidence, is that the president of the eldership in each synagogue was the ἀρχισυνάγωγος κατ᾽ ἐξοχήν, and that he was the person referred to as the "head of the synagogue, of the congregation, of the Church" (רֹאשׁ הַכְּנֶסֶת, הַקָּהָל 'ר, הַצִּבּוּר 'ר), M. Jom. vii. 1 ; Sot. vii. 7, etc. Art. "Synagogen," in Herzog, xv. S. 312. The curious term διάβιος (regarding which see note at p. 150) occurs in several Jewish inscriptions as indicating an official of the synagogue. Garucci (*Dissertazioni*, ii. p. 187, cited by Schürer) holds that the archisynagogus is referred to in such cases ; Schürer prefers to supply "archon." It appears from a Neapolitan inscription that such a διάβιος might at the same time be a γερουσιάρχης (Ti. Claudius Philippus dia viu et gerusiarches). In such a case, therefore, on Garucci's theory, the two distinct positions of President of the presbytery (gerusiarch) and Chairman of its Executive or Committee of Archons (archisynagogus) had been held by the same man, and it was desired to note the double honour upon his monument. On Schürer's view, the deceased had been an archon for life, and had also been president of the presbytery. Schürer, *Gemeindeverf.* S. 23 f.

[1] Schürer, ii. pp. 185 f., 370. Selden, *De Synedriis*, Londini 1655, lib. iii. c. 2, pp. 17-22, 37. Vitringa, pp. 832 f., 851 f.

same rule held in the case of the president of the great
Sanhedrin in Jerusalem, of which we shall speak presently;
only with this difference, that as the Sanhedrin was the
highest court, there was in it no room for reference or
intervention.[1]

As to the position and functions of the presidents of the
Jewish synagogue elderships, Vitringa sums up his careful
examination of the evidence bearing on this point as follows :
"There were presidents of this kind in those greater consistories which flourished both before and after the overthrow
of Jerusalem in Canaan, and in the more celebrated places
beyond Canaan such as Alexandria, Antioch, Damascus, and
in Babylonia. It is not to be denied that such a president
was distinguished by a dignity and authority beyond the
other presbyters who along with him constituted the synedrium.
But it is to be observed—

" (a) That the president of a council (senatus) of this kind
was always held to be of the same order and office (ordinis et
officii) with the rest of the council of which he was the most
distinguished member; and, what is more, that he was always
subject to the council, who could remove him from his office
at their pleasure (quotiescunque volebat). We must therefore compare this president of a Jewish presbytery with the
presidents of civil or legal courts, such as we find in many
countries. In such cases the dignity of the president's position
obtains for him a greater authority and honour with the
public, and gives him certain other prerogatives; but he is
not thereby removed from the order and class of the other
members of the court over which he presides. The rectors
of our modern universities supply an illustration of this.
Thus all the members of the great and venerable supreme
council in Jerusalem, the president not excepted, were alike
included under the names 'Sanhedrin,' 'House of Judgment,' Elders, Presbytery, Gerusia, and such other titles
proper to that court. It is therefore sufficiently clear that
each of those ecclesiastical councils of which we speak constituted a homogeneous body of men, of the same class and order
(ejusdem generis et ordinis). For any superior dignity attach-

[1] Comp. Vitringa, p. 832 f. Selden, *De Syned.* lib. iii. c. 1, p. 5 f.

ing to the president was reflected upon the whole council from whom he derived it.

"(b) In those ordinary ecclesiastical consistories (ישיבות) which existed in less populous places, the dignity of the head of the consistory (ראש ישיבה) was hardly greater than that of any of his colleagues. He was first in the consistory, and its standing chairman (præses perpetuus), but was of the same order and office with the rest of his colleagues, and of the same power, since he could do nothing save with them and through them. He was distinguished from them in point of dignity in no respect whatever, save that he held the first place among a body of men of his own order, rank, and office."[1]

(3.) Functions of the elders of the synagogue.

In each synagogue the duties of the eldership thus constituted under their president were comprehended under the two general departments of teaching and ruling. To the first of these some reference has already been made. It may be added here, that in connection with it a learned or professional class naturally grew up, known as the scribes (סופרים, γραμμα-τεῖς, νομικοί, νομοδιδάσκαλοι). These were men specially trained in the knowledge of Scripture law and its traditional

---

[1] De Syn. Vet. lib. ii. c. 12, p. 604. Schürer's investigations lead him to the same conclusion as to the gerusiarch who appears so often in the Jewish inscriptions at Rome and elsewhere: "Er wird unter der ἄρχοντες nur der primus inter pares gewesen sein," Gemeindeverf. S. 20. Vitringa goes on to indicate with his usual lucidity and fairness how these facts bear upon the ecclesiastical polity of the Christian Church, and how naturally such presidents of presbyteries developed in the early centuries by a gradual process into prelates or monarchical bishops. His conclusions on the subject are in substance those expressed in the following sentences from Bishop Lightfoot: "The Episcopate [Dr. Lightfoot means, of course, the prelatic or monarchical Episcopate] was formed not out of the apostolic order by localization, but out of the presbyteral by elevation; and the title (bishop), which originally was common to all, came at length to be appropriated to the chief among them. . . . The existence of a council or college necessarily supposes a presidency of some kind, whether this presidency be assumed by each member in turn or lodged in the hands of a single person. It was only necessary, therefore, for him [the Apostle John at Ephesus, according to Dr. Lightfoot's theory, of which again] to give permanence, definiteness, stability to an office which already existed in germ. There is no reason, however, for supposing that any direct ordinance was issued to the Churches." Philippians, 3rd ed. pp. 194, 205. Comp. Dods, Presbyterianism, p. 29 f.

interpretation. Ezra was at once a priest of the line of Aaron, and also "a ready scribe in the law of Moses, which the Lord the God of Israel had given."[1] But it is in the latter capacity that he is chiefly spoken of, and as such he was foremost in "bringing the Scriptures before all the congregation" in the great gatherings at Jerusalem after the restoration, "giving the sense and causing them to understand the reading."[2] But in later times the systematic study and exposition of the Scriptures, from causes on which we cannot dwell here, passed more and more into the hands of men who were not of priestly families, but sprung from the ranks of the people. Their influence grew with the spread of the synagogue system. The scribes were the natural leaders in a religious community. Their lives might often be unworthy of their position, but the theoretic value of their teaching was acknowledged by our Lord Himself : " The scribes and Pharisees sit in Moses' seat : all things therefore whatsoever they bid you, these observe and do ; but do ye not after their works : for they say, and do not. . . . They love the chief place at feasts, and the chief seats in the synagogues, and the salutations in the market-places, and to be called of men, Rabbi."[3]

As indicated in the words of Christ now cited, these trained teachers filled the highest places in the synagogue elderships. The scribe or scribes in every congregation were those among its elders specially qualified to speak on religious subjects, and ordinarily expected to do so when the Scriptures were read on sabbaths or week-days. "The lectures and exhortations in the synagogues were not indeed confined to appointed persons. Any one capable of doing so might stand up to teach in the synagogue at the invitation of the ruler. But as in the courts of justice the learned doctors of the law were preferred to the laity, so too in the synagogue their natural superiority asserted itself."[4]

By the influence and under the presidency of the scribes, schools for the regular instruction of the young in Scripture knowledge grew up in connection with almost every synagogue, where the most hopeful of the youth of Israel

---

[1] Ezra vii. 6.
[2] Neh. viii. 1–9.
[3] Matt. xxiii. 2 f., 6 f.
[4] Schürer, i. 328.

sat eagerly at the feet of the teachers of the law.[1] Touching instances are recorded of the thirst for sacred learning,
and of persistent self-denial in order to obtain it, in connection with the poorest families.[2]

Through the teaching of the scribes especially, both in the
school and the congregation, the synagogues became centres of
religious instruction and influence for the ends described
in such glowing terms by one of themselves. "What are
our houses of prayer ($\pi\rho o\sigma\epsilon\nu\kappa\tau\eta\rho\iota\alpha$) in every town," he
asks, "but places of instruction in prudence and manhood,
temperance and righteousness, piety and holiness, and
every virtue with respect both to things human and things
Divine?"[3]

The contrast which sometimes existed between the ideal
and the actual in this matter may be seen in the words
of an apostle who was contemporary with Philo, and who
had sat at the feet of Rabban Gamaliel, "the glory of the
Law:" "Thou bearest the name of a Jew and restest upon
the law, and gloriest in God, and knowest His will, and
approvest the things that are excellent, being instructed out
of the law, and art confident that thou thyself art a guide
of the blind, a light of them that are in darkness, an in-
structor of the foolish, a teacher of babes, having in the
law the form of knowledge and of the truth. Thou there-

---

[1] Schürer, ii. pp. 48 ff.   Schürer makes a curious slip here in quoting 2 Tim.
iii. 15: ἀπὸ βρέφους ἱερὰ γράμματα οἶδας, as a proof that "in *Christian* communities also children were instructed in the Holy Scriptures." No doubt that
is a fair inference; but Timothy was trained in a *Jewish* home. "Seeing
that the Jews," says the great scribe of Alexandria, "regard their laws as
utterances from God, and are instructed in this species of knowledge from
their earliest childhood (ἐκ πρώτης ἡλικίας), they bear the image of the things
enjoined upon them in their very souls. They are taught, as it were, from
their very swaddling-clothes (ἐξ αὐτῶν τρόπον τινὰ σπαργάνων) by their parents,
tutors, and teachers (παιδαγωγῶν καὶ ὑφηγητῶν), even before they are instructed
in the holy laws and the unwritten traditions, to believe in one God, the Father
and Maker of the world." Philo, *Legat. ad Caium*, p. 31.

[2] As, *e.g.*, in the story of Hillel sitting outside the window of the schools in
snow to hear the words of his teachers when he had not even the small sum
needful to pay the gate-keeper for admission. C. Taylor, *Sayings of the Jewish
Fathers*, Cambridge 1877, p. 34.

[3] Philo, *Life of Moses*, iii. p. 27. See on the whole subject of the scribes,
Schürer, i. pp. 312-328. Hausrath, i. p. 89 f.

fore that teachest another, teachest thou not thyself? . . .
Thou who gloriest in the law, through thy transgression of
law dishonourest thou God? For the name of God is blas-
phemed among the Gentiles because of you." [1]

Under the head of " ruling " in the synagogue came the
control of everything connected with the arrangements and
order of worship in the congregation, the administration of
discipline among its members, the management of its financial
affairs, and the care of the poor and afflicted in connection
with it.[2]

Meetings of the congregation and of the elders were held
not only on Sabbaths and fasts and festivals, but on Mondays
and Thursdays, the usual market days of the week, when the
country people came with their wares to the town, and
took the opportunity of joining in the services, hearing
religious questions discussed, and sometimes of bringing their
disputes before the elders in the synagogue.[3]

A vigorous discipline was exercised. Offending members
were dealt with in various ways, and in the last resort were
" cast out of the synagogue " or excommunicated. This infliction corresponded to the Old Testament penalty of being
" cut off from the congregation or assembly of Israel " and
" of the Lord," [4] and was deeply dreaded by every pious Jew.

[1] Rom. ii. 17–21, 23 f.

[2] Vitringa, lib. iii. c. 5, pp. 667 ff. Leyer, art. "Synagogen," in Herzog,
xv. S. 312.

[3] Hausrath, i. pp. 83, 86. Schürer, ii. p. 83. Dr. Hatch in his valuable
work, *The Organization of the early Christian Churches*, gives an interesting sketch of the Jewish communities in the apostolic age as "meeting
probably in the same place, in two capacities and with a double organization " (p. 58 f.). He seems to regard the week-day meetings as purely secular,
"for the ordinary purposes of a local court." But this is certainly incorrect.
See, to the contrary, Hausrath and Schürer as above, with the references
given by them. Compare also Luke xviii. 12 with the *Teaching of the Twelve
Apostles*, c. 8: "Let not your fasts be with the hypocrites, for they fast on
the second day of the week and on the fifth." "In the larger congregations
there were daily meetings at the times of sacrifice in the Temple." Leyrer, art.
"Synagogen," in Herzog, xv. S. 305. Zunz, *Ritus des syn. Gottesd.* S. 123.

[4] This was the opposite of "entering into the assembly of the Lord," *i.e.*
being received as a member in full standing in the religious fellowship of Israel.
See Deut. xxiii. 2 ff. etc. Compare the expression used of the pious dead,
"gathered to his people," Gen. xxv. 8, etc. ; and see Candlish, *Kingdom of
God*, p. 54. Bannerman, *Church of Christ*, i. p. 121 f.

It represented to his mind separation from the fellowship and privileges of the covenant people of God. The fear of it, as we read in the Gospels, kept many, especially among those in the better social positions, from acting upon their real convictions as to the Divine mission of Jesus of Nazareth. "Even of the rulers many believed on Him; but because of the Pharisees they did not confess it, lest they should be put out of the synagogue (ἀποσυνάγωγοι γένωνται)." Our Lord, in His last words of warning to His disciples regarding the trials in store for them after His departure, speaks of this as something which must needs be to them a specially bitter and painful experience. "These things have I spoken unto you that ye should not be made to stumble. They shall put you out of the synagogues (ἀποσυναγώγους ποιήσουσιν ὑμᾶς, they shall make you excommunicated men)." [1]

From the nature of the case, in a community such as that of the Jews in Palestine after the return, and in the wealthier Jewish congregations of the Dispersion, not only religious but social and civil losses of a serious kind followed inevitably from the fact of exclusion from the fellowship of the synagogue. But besides these more indirect results, fines and similar penalties sometimes formed part of the sentence itself, and punishments such as scourging were inflicted within the synagogue precincts. Another of our Lord's warnings to His followers referred to this: "They will deliver you up to councils" (εἰς συνέδρια, to Sanhedrin), "and in their synagogues they will scourge you." [2]

During the theocratic period in Israel, although Church and State might be distinguished in idea, yet practically they were allied in the most intimate way. A separation was made indeed, especially in the later stages of the history, between "the outward business over Israel for officers and judges," and "all the business of the Lord," between "all the matters of the Lord" and "all the king's matters." [3] There were

---

[1] John xii. 42; xvi. 1 f.; comp. ix. 22; Luke vi. 22. See also Schürer, ii. p. 60 ff. Vitringa, pp. 727-751, 768-782.

[2] Matt. x. 17.

[3] 1 Chron. xxvi. 29-32; 2 Chron. xix. 5-11. Comp. Deut. xvii. 8-12.

always sacred things with which the king in Israel dared not intermeddle, or did so at his cost, and a region into which the civil ruler as such must not enter.[1] But practically the connection between the two spheres was so close, and the representatives of the two in each local centre throughout the land were so often the same, that it is not to be wondered at that, when " the congregation of Israel " was reorganized on the lines of the synagogue system, the boundary between things civil and spiritual was not always very clearly drawn, and was often overstepped in practice. The elders of the town, where the community was purely Jewish, and the elders of the synagogue in the town, were often almost the same persons, although different gifts were required for the two departments, and different men came to the front in each respectively. They had to deal in both relations, in the civil and the ecclesiastical Sanhedrin, with the same individuals ; and the Divine law, in accordance with which they sought to do righteousness and judgment among their people, bore upon the whole sphere of man's life. Thus a decision given in the " Beth Din " on the Monday or Thursday about some secular dispute among the country people who came to the town market from the neighbouring district, might often be held without further question to settle the ecclesiastical position of some member of the congregation when the synagogue or its eldership met on Sabbath. And penalties such as fines and imprisonment, which might be suitable enough in the one sphere, were transferred *brevi manu* to the other.

We may note how in this matter the Providence of God seemed to prepare the way for the clearer teaching of the New Testament. In the Dispersion from the first, and in Palestine in ever-increasing measure as Rome strengthened her grasp upon the land, the power of the synagogue courts in secular matters was confined within very narrow limits. Criminal cases were taken out of their hands altogether. Practically, it came to be only in the way of voluntary arbitration that differences about civil matters were sub-

---

[1] 1 Sam. xiii. 8–14 ; 2 Chron. xxvi. 16–21. See Bannerman, *Church of Christ*, i. p. 121 f., and the whole section : "Non-identity of Church and State among the Jews."

mitted to the judgment of the synagogue elders.   They had
no power of enforcing their decision save by moral influence,
if the disputants did not agree to receive it as final.   But in
every Jewish community the elders of the synagogue were
the natural arbiters.   One of the commonest titles by which
those among them were designated who had special knowledge
of Scripture, and of the customs of their people, was that of
" wise men " (חכמים).   Their judgment on this ground carried
great weight, and was often useful in preventing litigation.[1]
It is to this, no doubt, that the apostle refers when warning
the Corinthian Christians against going to law before the
heathen.   The Church at Corinth, like almost all others of
whose origin we have any information in the New Testament,
had arisen out of the Jewish synagogue.   Could they not do
as the members of the synagogue did in like circumstances ?
" Is it so," Paul asks, " that there cannot be found among you
one wise man" (σοφὸς οὐδὲ εἷς, not one חכם) "who shall be able
to decide between his brethren, but brother goeth to law with
brother, and that before unbelievers ? "[2]

" The whole synagogue system," as a leading German
authority on the subject (Schürer) expresses it, " presupposes
above all things the existence of a *religious* community ; " and
in the Providence of God, from the very first, over by far the
greater extent of the field in which that system established
itself, it was to the moral and religious sphere that the action
of the synagogue eldership was practically limited.   And
even in those parts of Palestine,—the purely Jewish as distinguished from the Hellenistic districts,—where a certain
mixture of secular jurisdiction took place, this was more and

---

[1] An illustration of what has now been said is supplied by an edict of
Arcadius and Honorius, cited by Vitringa, in which, on the one hand, all
ordinary jurisdiction and power of inflicting punishments are expressly withheld from the Jews, "in his causis quæ tam ad superstitionem eorum quam ad
forum et leges ac jura pertinent;" but, on the other hand, recognition is
accorded to their custom of arbitration among themselves: "Si qui vero ex his
communi pactione ad similitudinem arbitrorum apud Judæos in civili duntaxat
negotio putaverint litigandum, sortiri eorum judicium jure publico non vetentur.
Eorum etiam sententias judices exequantur tanquam ex sententia cognitoris
arbitri dati fuerint." Vitringa, p. 817. Comp. Hatch, *Organization of Early
Christ. Churches*, pp. 67 f., 72.

[2] 1 Cor. vi. 5 f. ; comp. Acts xviii. 4–8.

more eliminated in the process of events, and the influence of
the elders came increasingly to depend upon their religious
character and position.[1]

The other officials of the synagogue were of a subordinate
kind. They consisted of an attendant, known as the
"chazzan" (חַזָּן), or, in the Hellenistic synagogues, the
ὑπηρέτης, whose duties were very much those of the modern
"Church officer" or "beadle,"[2] and one or two collectors of
alms and offerings (גַּבָּאִים or גַּבָּאֵי צְדָקָה),[3] in cases where that
work was not done by the chazzan.

It only remains to refer to the relations of the different
synagogues to each other, and to the position held by the
great Sanhedrin or supreme council at Jerusalem.

(4.) Relations of different synagogues to each other.

Where a synagogue stood alone it was governed, as we have
seen, by its own eldership. Where several synagogues arose
in one city or district, their relations to each other seem to
have varied considerably according to circumstances. In some

---

[1] Schürer discusses the point, "Whether in the time of Christ the civil and
religious community were so separated in Palestine that the latter possessed an
independent organization." There is no question that all the synagogues of the
Dispersion possessed it. With respect to Palestine, his conclusion is that there
was such an independent religious organization in every part of the Holy Land
where the Jews were either excluded from civic rights or shared these with non-
Jews. This was the case in all the Hellenistic towns and districts, e.g. in the
old Philistian and Phœnician regions, in Joppa, Cæsarea, Ptolemais, Damascus,
Gadara, Gerasa, Samaria, Antipatris, Cæsarea Philippi, Tiberias, etc.

As regards places with predominantly Jewish population the case is not so
clear. There may have been, in such instances, no definite distinction between
the elders of the town and those of the synagogue, and the old local Sanhedrin may
have had charge of the affairs of the synagogue congregation and appointed its
officials. "At least there was no urgent reason for the formation of a college
of elders for each separate synagogue, although with the scantiness of our
materials we have to concede the *possibility* of this being done. Nay, in one
case it is even *probable*, for the Hellenistic Jews in Jerusalem, the libertines,
Cyrenians, Cilicians, and Asiatics evidently formed separate communities,
having five synagogues." i. pp. 57–149. *The Hellenistic Towns*, ii. p. 55 ff.

[2] Vitringa, pp. 890–908. Schürer, ii. p. 66 f. As in the case of a capable
Church officer, especially in a small congregation, a great variety of work often
fell into the hands of the chazzan, from cleaning the lamps, and officiating in
the infliction of the "forty stripes save one," to teaching a sort of Sabbath school,
or reading the Scriptures and leading in prayer and praise in the congregation.

[3] Vitringa, lib. i. Pars 1, c. 10 ; lib. iii. Pars 1, c. 13, pp. 211 f., 811-814.
Leyrer, "Synagogen," in Herzog, xv. S. 313 f.

cases each synagogue, with its body of office-bearers, was apparently established on an independent footing, and we have no evidence of any formal or organic connection subsisting between it and the neighbouring congregations.   In other cases, the collective eldership of all the synagogues in question seems to have formed the presbytery (γερουσία or πρεσβυτέριον) of the city or district, and exercised authority and oversight over all the congregations.

In the Jewish community at Rome, for example, under the Cæsars, we have abundant evidence, as recently brought out by Schürer in his interesting monograph, of a thorough congregational organization on a Presbyterian system.   Each synagogue had its own session or consistory of elders (ἡ γερουσία); its president of the consistory, or moderator of session (ὁ γερουσιάρχης); its executive, or acting committee of session (οἱ ἄρχοντες); its ἀρχισυνάγωγος,—possibly in the Roman synagogues the elder specially in charge of the department of worship, or else the chairman of the executive;[1] its synagogue attendant (ὑπηρέτης).   "But no trace has been found as yet," Schürer writes, "of a general united organization of the whole Jewish community at Rome under one γερουσία.   This is a very remarkable phenomenon when we compare it, for instance, with the organization of the Jews at Alexandria.   The Jewish community there, although much more numerous than at Rome, was united in a most complete organization, in the earlier period with an ethnarch at its head (Strabo in Josephus, *Antiq.* xiv. 7. 2), at a later date under a γερουσία (Philo, *In Flacc.* § 10).   This was possible at Alexandria, where the Jews took from the first a much more dominant position than at Rome. . . .   Here they were obliged to content themselves with the more modest position of individual religious societies (*collegia*, or clubs)."[2]

In every Jewish presbytery of any size, whether it had the oversight merely of one congregation or of several, the plan was usually adopted of having an executive or acting committee for the more efficient transaction of business.   This was obviously in itself a reasonable arrangement.   It corre-

---

[1] See note above, p. 138 f.

[2] Schürer, *Gemeindeverf. der Juden in Rom*, S. 15, 18–25.   Vitringa, p. 559 f.

sponded to the well-known threefold division of the Greek communes (δῆμος, βουλή, ἄρχοντες); and it was commended to the Jewish mind and feeling by such precedents from the history of Israel as that of the seventy men chosen from the general eldership of the people to bear the burden along with Moses, and that of the central board appointed by Jehoshaphat.[1] The members of this executive were chosen from time to time by the congregation from the general body of the elders.

There was thus a distinction which appears repeatedly in the inscriptions on Jewish tombs between one who was merely an elder of the synagogue,—which seems to have been a position held *ad vitam aut culpam*,—and one who, in addition, was an "archon," or member of the executive of the eldership or presbytery.

The election of archons was usually an annual one, being held as a rule in September, which was the beginning of the civil year with the Jews, and also the season of their greatest religious fast and festival, the day of Atonement and the feast of Tabernacles.[2] Any archon might be re-elected; and the appointment was sometimes for a period of years, or even, as it seems, for life. Such a mark of confidence on the part of the members of the synagogue was naturally held to be a special honour, to be noted as such in the inscription on the tomb of the office-bearer who had enjoyed it.[3]

---

[1] See above, p. 110.

[2] Schürer quotes a passage on this point from a Homily ascribed to Chrysostom, which specially refers to the state of matters in Italy under the Emperors: "Inter hæc intuendæ sunt temporum qualitates et gesta morum; et primum perfidia Judæorum, qui semper in Deum et in Mosem contumaces exstiterunt, qui cum a Deo secundum Mosem initium anni mensem Martium acceperunt, illi dictum pravitatis sive superbiæ exercentes mensem Septembrem ipsum novum annum nuncupant, *quo et mense magistratus sibi designant quos archontas vocant.*" *Hist. of Jewish People,* ii. p. 250.

[3] Inscriptions such as the following often occur: δὶς ἄρχων, ἄρχων πάσης τιμῆς, ἄρχων διὰ βίου or διάβιος. The last-named phrase Schürer interprets with considerable probability to mean that the archon in question had held office for life. *Gemeindeverf.* S. 23. *Hist. of Jewish People,* ii. p. 250 f. See note above, p. 139. Dr. Hatch points out that in some Greek cities the executive of the βουλή was known as the γερουσία, and that the two bodies seem sometimes to have had separate chairmen, the βούλαρχος and the προστάτης γερουσίας. Hatch, p. 64.

Among the synagogues of Palestine itself, as was to be expected, we find a more fully developed organization. At the head of all stood the high court of the Sanhedrin at Jerusalem.

(5.) The great Sanhedrin at Jerusalem.

As to the historic origin of this body, much uncertainty prevails. The name "Sanhedrin" (from the Greek συνέδριον) probably points to the Macedonian period as that during which the institution first arose;[1] there are other grounds for the same conclusion. The first mention of it by Josephus occurs in connection with the reign of Antiochus III. (223–187 B.C.).[2] But there is reason to believe that it had been in existence before the time of that king, and had probably taken definite shape during the eighty years or more when Palestine was under the favouring sway of the Ptolemies (from 301 to about 218 B.C.). A council of elders or presbytery (γερουσία) at Jerusalem appears thrice in the religious romance of Judith, and repeatedly in the historical books of the Maccabees.[3]

In the New Testament history frequent reference is made to the Sanhedrin in Jerusalem as a well-known and influential body, composed of priests, scribes, and elders of the people, under the presidency of the high priest. It is repeatedly spoken of under its technical designation "the Presbytery," "the Presbytery of the People" (i.e. of Israel), or "the Sanhedrin," especially by the N. T. writer who is most careful in his use of official and technical names and titles.[4]

Its members are spoken of under the general name of

[1] Livy mentions that the members of the Macedonian senate were called "Synedri." "Pronuntiatum quod ad statum Macedoniæ pertinebat senatores quos *synedros* vocant, legendos esse, quorum consilio republica administraretur," xiv. 32.

[2] *Antiq.* xii. 3.

[3] Judith iv. 8; xi. 14; xv. 8; 1 Macc. xii. 6, 35 f.; comp. vii. 33; xi. 23; xiv. 20; 2 Macc. i. 10; iv. 44; xi. 27. Reuss puts the date of Judith "in the evil days that followed the death of Simon" (i.e. *circa* 140–130 B.C.), and regards the reference in this work to the synedrium as the first mention of it by a contemporary writer, although "the establishment of such a senate or college of elders may well belong to a time a century or more earlier." *Gesch. der heil. Schriften A. T.*, S. 610–615.

[4] τὸ πρεσβυτέριον τοῦ λαοῦ, πᾶν τὸ πρεσβυτέριον, οἱ ἀρχιερεῖς καὶ τὸ συνέδριον ὅλον, Matt. xxvi. 59; Mark xiv. 55; Luke xxii. 66; Acts xxii. 5; iv. 15; v. 21, 27, 34, 41; vi. 12, 15; xxii. 30; xxiii. 1, 6, 15, 20, 38; xxiv. 20.

" councillors " (βουλευταί).[1] More specifically they are "the
chief priests, elders, and scribes " (ἀρχιερεῖς, πρεσβύτεροι,
γραμματεῖς, or with scribes before elders),[2] the archons,
elders, and scribes (ἄρχοντες, πρεσβ., γραμμ.),[3] or " the chief
priests and archons " (ἀρχιερεῖς κ. οἱ ἄρχοντες).[4] Sometimes
the term Sanhedrin (συνέδριον) is used to denote a meeting
of the council (a " session " or " sederunt") as well as the
council itself.[5]

It is evident that the Sanhedrin was thus a thoroughly
representative body, in which three elements were combined :
first, the chief priests, including the past and present
occupants of the chair of the high priest, and also probably
the heads of the twenty-four priestly " courses;" secondly,

---

[1] Luke xxiii. 50 ; Mark xv. 43.

[2] Matt. xxvii. 41 ; Mark xi. 27 ; xiv. 43-53 ; xv. 1.

[3] Acts iv. 5. Comp. ver. 8 : "Archons of the people and elders ;" and ver. 23,
" chief priests and elders."

[4] Luke xxiii. 13 ; xxiv. 20.

[5] Thus, e.g., in John xi. 47, the priests and Pharisees held a Sanhedrin
(συνήγαγον συνέδριον). In Acts v. 21 we have the peculiar expression, "they
called the Sanhedrin together, and all the eldership of the children of Israel
(τὸ συνέδριον κ. πᾶσαν τὴν γερουσίαν τῶν υἱῶν Ἰσραήλ)." Reuss regards this as a
" singular tautology which betrays a narrator who stands far from the events
which he records " (Gesch. der heil. Schr. A. T., S. 616). Archdeacon Farrar
finds the phrase " somewhat perplexing, because we know nothing of any Jewish
' senate' apart from the Sanhedrin, and because if γερουσία be taken in an
etymological rather than a political sense, the Sanhedrin included the elders "
(St. Paul, i. p. 106). Schürer, too, finds some difficulty in the words. He
rightly says that the natural explanation of them is that "the author of the
Acts supposed that the συνέδριον was of a less comprehensive character than the
γερουσία," but thinks that this supposition was erroneous on his part, ii. p. 172.
But the historian of the Acts was more familiar than his critics are with the
methods and practice of a " Presbyterianism older than Christianity," and from
a Presbyterian standpoint his phrase presents not the slightest difficulty. No
doubt " elders" were included in the Sanhedrin ; "the elders," as distinguished
from "the chief priests " and "the scribes," formed one of its three constituent
sections ; but not "all the elders of the children of Israel," not even all the
elders of all the synagogues in Jerusalem. Only a certain number of elders
were ordinary members of the high council ; but it was open to the Sanhedrin
on special occasions to ask the presence of others as assessors for the time,
" even the whole eldership of the sons of Israel," in and around Jerusalem.
Nothing is more common at this day in all the Reformed Churches which hold
the Presbyterian system, when a Presbytery, Synod, or General Assembly takes
up some subject of practical importance and general interest, than for the court
to invite to its aid in conference "all ministers and elders not members," in
other words, " the whole eldership " of the city or district.

the scribes or professional teachers of the law, the experts in Scripture knowledge, and in the traditions of the Jewish schools of sacred learning; and thirdly, the elders, a certain proportion of leading and representative men taken probably from the eldership of the different synagogues in Jerusalem, and it may be from other parts of the country.[1] The total number of the members of the Sanhedrin in Jerusalem was seventy-one; in what proportion the three constituent sections were respectively represented we do not know.

Under this supreme court, and connected with it more or less closely, were several local or provincial Sanhedrin of smaller size and less authority. In Jerusalem itself, according to the Talmud, there were two such subordinate courts of twenty-three members each. Every town containing more than one hundred and twenty Jewish heads of families had the right to have such a Sanhedrin established in it. We hear also in Josephus and elsewhere of local Sanhedrin, in which the quorum was seven, and from which cases were referred to the Sanhedrin in Jerusalem, when the judges in the local council could not agree among themselves.[2]

The great Sanhedrin at Jerusalem unquestionably held an imposing position in the eyes of every member of the fellowship of Israel. It exercised a powerful authority not only over the synagogues of the Holy Land, but by letters and deputies over all the synagogues of the Dispersion. To it they all looked, e.g. for authoritative information as to the

---

[1] The word συνέδριον is sometimes employed in Hellenistic and other Greek in a general way to denote any assembly or corporate body. But, as Schürer points out, "it is comparatively seldom that it is used to denote civic councils, which are mostly designated by the terms βουλή and γερουσία. It is more frequently employed to denote *representative* assemblies composed of *deputies* from various constituencies. We have, for example, the συνέδριον of the Phœnicians usually convened in Tripolis (Diodor. xvi. 41); the κοινόν συνέδριον of ancient Lycia, which was composed of representatives from twenty-three different towns (Strabo, xiv. 3. 3); and the συνέδριον κοινόν of the province of Asia. . . . The senators of the four Macedonian districts, who, according to Livy, were called συνέδροι, were deputies representing an entire *regio* (see Marquardt's *Staats Verwaltung*, 1881, i. S. 317)." Schürer, i. p. 170.

[2] Schürer, i. pp. 151–154, 184–190. Weber, *alt. Synag. Paläst. Theol. S.* 137. Hausrath, *N. T. Times,* i. p. 83 f. Isaac Abendana, *Discourses of the Eccles. and Civil Polity of the Jews,* Lond. 1706, pp. 6–10. Josephus, *Antt.* iv. 8. 14.

reckoning of new moons and festivals. Thither, at the time of the yearly pilgrimages, innumerable questions of a religious, social, and legal kind were sent up for settlement. Round the Sanhedrin in Jerusalem old traditions of civil and religious independence and self-government gathered. It was the " Presbytery of the People." It spoke in the name and with the voice of the elders of Israel. More than any other assembly on earth it represented to the pious Jew the congregation and assembly of Israel and of the Lord. " From the Sanhedrin," it was said, " the Torah goes forth for all Israel." [1]

So much is clear. But when we proceed to inquire as to the way in which members of the Sanhedrin were appointed, the modes in which its authority was exercised, the manner in which it could be invoked, and all the matters of which the Talmud in its tract on the Sanhedrin speaks with such confidence and precision, and which are dealt with in such laborious fashion by Selden through the three volumes of his great work, *De Synedriis Hebræorum*, we find ourselves in no little difficulty. The actual state of the case is pithily stated by Reuss : " This only we may regard as certain, that the Sanhedrin was a supreme judicial council, with a number of smaller local ones existing along with it (Matt. v. 22), and that it watched over the observance of the Law and of everything which could be held as flowing from the Law. . . It meets us in the Gospel history as an institution which was well known, and which so to speak explained itself ; and yet at bottom everything about it— its origin, organization, jurisdiction—is indefinite while we keep to the older sources, and the later ones underlie the suspicion of giving us only theories instead of facts." [2]

---

[1] Sifre 104*b*, in Weber, S. 131.   "The members of the Sanhedrin are, as regards their personal qualifications, 'wise men' (חכמים) ; but as regards their official position they are called 'elders.' Their legislative power is that they determine by authoritative interpretation of the law what shall be held in Israel as right and lawful."   *Ib.*

[2] Reuss, *Gesch. der heil. Schr. A. T.*, S. 615, 617. On the whole subject of the Sanhedrin, see Schürer, i. pp. 163–195.

4. General results of the Synagogue System in its relation to the Scripture doctrine of the Church ; principles embodied in and illustrated by it.

These may be summed up as follows :—

1. A transition from the symbolical in worship to the real, from the vicarious to the direct.

We can hardly overestimate the practical importance of the change for the great body of the ordinary members of the fellowship of Israel, when it came to be to the synagogue and not to the temple that their minds naturally turned when they thought of the worship of God. It was a visible and tangible transition from outward symbols to spiritual realities, from worship in the hands of a human priesthood, a distinct religious caste, to worship by the members of the congregation themselves, led by men whom they chose for themselves, without regard to Levitical or priestly descent, as their best qualified representatives, " elder brethren," acting and speaking for them and with them.[1]   There was ordinarily no reading or exposition of Scripture in the temple until the synagogue and its teachers, as it were, took possession of its courts.   There were no altars, no incense, no separate priesthood, no material sacrifices of any kind in the synagogue, and no place within its walls more holy than another through any visible symbol of the presence of God.

The tabernacle and the temple served great religious purposes in their time.   What some of these were we saw before.[2]   Psalmists and prophets taught the spiritually-minded in Israel to rise from the signs to the things signified in the material " house of God " with its temporary priesthood, " its ordinances of Divine service, and its sanctuary which was of this world." [3]   But now in history and Providence the Lord of the sanctuary taught these lessons in a yet

---

[1] As to the reading and rendering adopted by the Revisers in Acts xv. 23, on which Dean Burgon pours out the vials of his wrath in such characteristic fashion in the *Quarterly Review* (July 1885), we may have something to say at a later stage. The phrase " the elder brethren " at all events well expresses the feelings of a pious Israelite towards those who presided and took the lead in the synagogue congregation in which he worshipped from week to week.

[2] *Supra*, pp. 78–85.   [3] Heb. ix. 1.

more effective way for the great mass of the members of the house of Israel. God had " of old time spoken unto their fathers by divers portions and in divers manners (πολυμερῶς καὶ πολυτρόπως)." Now " at the end of these days He was to speak to them in His Son." [1] " That which was perfect " was at hand, and therefore "that which was in part," and which by reason of its imperfection and outwardness had become a snare to many, was to pass away. It did so gradually, the new rising out of the old by a steady but at the time almost imperceptible development, and carrying with it all that was best and highest in the former order, according to the analogy of God's working in other fields of nature, Providence, and grace.

" For those who dwelt far from Jerusalem, the temple with its stately services remained doubtless the mysterious place of the Divine Presence and of accepted sacrifice, the expression for all the great religious conceptions of forgiveness of sins, consecration to God, and communication from God to His people. But it became more of a symbol. On the other hand, there stood daily before their eyes a worship of God without Levitical priests, without sacrifices, without mystery or symbol, a worship the central point in which was the edification of the heart through the holy Scriptures and common prayer." [2] We note a corresponding effect on the Temple worship itself, and in the attitude observed towards it by devout Israelites in Jerusalem. In the priestly and legislative portions of the Pentateuch, which so abound in rules about material offerings and purifications, there is scarcely a single express precept as to prayer, or express conjunction of prayer with sacrifice. [3] But the very earliest scene in the

---

[1] Heb. i. 1 f.

[2] Schultz, *A. T. Theol.*, 2te Ausg. S. 784. "It was the synagogue," he adds, "that turned the scale in favour of the scribe as against the priest, the Pharisee as against the Sadducee." Compare an admirable statement regarding the relation of the synagogue to the temple, and of both to the Christian Church, in Nitzsch's reply to Möhler's *Symbolism. Protestantische Beantwortung der Symbolik Möhler's*, Hamburg 1835, S. 204 f.

[3] The Jerusalem Talmud says : "Prayer is not a word of the Torah :" תפילה אינ' דבר תורה, Berakoth i. 5, cited by Taylor, *Sayings of Jewish Fathers*, p. 27.

New Testament writings is of "the whole multitude of the people praying without at the hour of incense," while the priest entered into the Temple.   The appointed times when the burnt-offerings and meat-offerings were offered daily in the Temple have become to the people "the hours of prayer" rather than "of sacrifice." [1]

2. A transition from the local and national to the universal.

This simple synagogue worship was everywhere possible, and in it the true worshippers everywhere alike received God's blessing, and knew that they had received it.   The poorest Jewish widow in the Suburra of Rome or by the docks of Alexandria, when she came with her children after sunset on the Sabbath to the "house of meeting," did not even need to bring with her a dove or a handful of fine flour, as in the Temple courts of old, to be assured that she and her little ones were "accepted before the Lord," who was "the Father of the fatherless and the Judge of the widows in His holy habitation."   She heard His gracious words read and explained in the synagogue, and felt that they were fulfilled there for her.   "God setteth the solitary in families; He bringeth out the prisoners into prosperity." [2]

Week by week in the Jewish "places of prayer" the poor and the afflicted found fellowship at once with the God of Abraham and with His people.   They saw the faces of brethren and sisters in the faith of the one living and true God, the Possessor of heaven and earth, the God of grace and redemption.   They joined with them in praise and prayer. Seasonable counsel and kindly help were received from the hands of the elders of the synagogue.   That its aspect was humble, and that it stood in the poorest part of the city, made its doors the more accessible for the poor.   For the sojourners of the Dispersion the synagogue system was like a return to the days when Abraham raised his simple altar wherever for the time he pitched his tent, and called there upon the name of "the Lord the everlasting God;" and through that system the blessing of Abraham was visibly passing to all the families of the earth.   Round the synagogue in every centre of the Diaspora, as already noted, proselytes

[1] Luke i. 10 ; Acts iii. 3.   [2] Ps. lxviii. 5 f.

gathered of every tongue and nation, coming to " put their trust under the wings of the Lord God of Israel."

We have before referred to a striking utterance by the last of the prophets, who spoke with the synagogue system and its fruits already forming a feature of his times. " From the rising of the sun, even unto the going down of the same, My name is great among the Gentiles ; and in every place incense is offered unto My name, and a pure offering ; for My name is great among the Gentiles, saith the Lord of hosts." [1] Doubtless many a devout worshipper, whether of Hebrew or Gentile descent in the synagogues of the Dispersion, was encouraged to lay hold in faith of such a Divine assurance.

> " As incense let my prayer be accepted in Thine eyes,
> And the uplifting of my hands as the evening sacrifice." [2]

It was a practical anticipation of the words spoken afterwards in Samaria by One greater than all the prophets.   The alien woman by the patriarch's well might be held a picture of the Gentiles coming with mingled motives to the wells of blessing opened for them in a dry and thirsty land by the Jewish houses of prayer, and finding far more than they dreamed of seeking.   " Jesus saith unto her, Woman, believe Me, the hour cometh, when neither in this mountain, nor in Jerusalem, shall ye worship the Father. . . . Salvation is from the Jews.   But the hour cometh, and now is, when the true worshippers shall worship the Father in spirit and in truth : for such doth the Father seek to be His worshippers." [3]   The synagogue system made such common worship possible for earnest and believing souls everywhere.   It provided a basis and a centre for it in all parts of the civilised world.

3. The central place in the sphere of worship was given to the written revelation of God's grace and His will for men,— to the holy Scriptures.

---

[1] Mal. i. 11.

[2] Ps. cxli. 2, Scottish Metrical Version.   Justin Martyr, in his discussion with Trypho the Jew, refers to this interpretation of the prediction of Malachi as current among the Jews of his time : Λέγετε ὅτι τὰς διὰ τῶν ἐν τῇ διασπορᾷ τότε δὴ ὄντων ἀπὸ τοῦ γένους ἐκείνου ἀνθρώπων εὐχὰς προσίεσθαι Αὐτὸν εἰρηκέναι, καὶ τὰς εὐχὰς αὐτῶν θυσίας καλεῖν.   *Dial. cum Tryph.* cap. cxvii.

[3] John iv. 21–23.

It was, as we saw, from a general desire among the returned exiles to hear and understand God's Word that the synagogue services first took their rise. And round this centre everything else gathered. With all the faults of the scribes as a class, their position and influence in the fellowship of Israel from the time of Ezra to that of Gamaliel testified powerfully to the reverence for the Word of God felt by the people as a whole, and to their strong conviction as to the vital importance of systematic instruction in the Scriptures by trained and qualified men. Such teaching going on for generations in Jewish homes, in the synagogue schools, and in the congregation, had this result among others, that in New Testament times the general level of intelligence and education was far higher among the Jews both in the Holy Land and the Diaspora than among any other people in the Roman Empire, the art of reading, in particular, being far more widely diffused even among the poorest.[1] The audiences to whom Christ and His apostles spoke in the synagogues, whether these consisted exclusively of Jews or also of proselytes (in the stricter or looser sense) from the Gentiles, were as a rule thoroughly conversant with the historical and prophetical books of the Old Testament. They were able to test every statement of the speaker by that standard, and "to examine the Scriptures daily, whether these things were so."[2] The amount of Scripture knowledge which the apostle Paul, *e.g.*, is able constantly to take for granted on the part of those to whom he speaks or

---

[1] Schürer, ii. p. 50.

[2] Acts xvii. 11. Comp. John v. 39. It is worth noting that a precisely similar state of matters is taken for granted in the Mishnah as regards the general familiarity of its hearers or readers with the Old Testament Scriptures. The Mishnah, as Dr. Schiller-Szinessy states in his valuable article on the subject in the *Encycl. Brit.*, is "the fundamental document of the oral law of the Jews." It was not brought substantially into its present form until the third century of our era; but it was compiled in a part of Palestine where, from special circumstances, the tradition of Jewish customs and beliefs was peculiarly strong and unbroken. There is general agreement among the best authorities that "in substance and spirit the position of the Jews in the Mishnah is that of the Jews in the first century." Now, it is a significant and suggestive fact that "the Mishna never states the text it is discussing, but assumes that the reader will be so familiar with it as to know from the discussion itself what point is under consideration." Bennet, *The Mishna as illustrating the Gospels*, Camb. 1884, pp. 23 f., 103. Art. "Mishnah," in *Encycl. Britann.* 9th ed. pp. 502-504.

writes is surprisingly great.   And those whom he addressed
were "not many rich, not many noble, of this world," but for
the most part artisans and slaves, the poor and the despised of
the earth.   The Jewish historian did not go beyond the facts
of the case when he boasted that the synagogue system had
made the law of God the common possession of all the people,
and that, whereas Roman procurators and proconsuls could
not trust to their own knowledge of the laws of Rome, but
had to carry jurists in their train, in a Jewish household even
the servant girls knew from the teaching in the synagogues
what their Divine law enjoined in every matter.[1]

4. The rights and duties of all individual members in the
congregation were strongly emphasized.

In the synagogue there was no hierarchy and no caste.
Every member of the congregation, who was not put out of
communion or suspended from privilege temporarily for some
offence, had a recognised place and voice in the congregation.
Its office-bearers were chosen without regard for Levitical or
priestly descent.   None were appointed "without consulting
the people."   The humblest Israelite with gifts, piety, and
application might and often did rise to the highest seat in the
synagogue.   On the other hand, the rule that every Rabbi or
scribe, from whatever rank in society he sprang, should
become master in his youth of some handicraft, ensured that
the professional teachers should have some sympathy by
practical experience with the feelings and circumstances of the
great mass of their hearers, who were obliged to labour with
their hands for daily bread.[2]   The very name corresponded
closely with the spirit of the institution; it was a "house of
meeting" as well as a "house of prayer."   The people themselves, the believing children of Abraham, and those of the
Gentiles who had joined themselves to the Lord, meeting with
one accord to worship the God of Abraham and Israel, to hear
His Word and learn His will, *made* the עֵדָה, the קָהֵל, the
συναγωγή and ἐκκλησία.

---

[1] Josephus, *Cont. Apion.* ii. 17, 18, 19.

[2] Hausrath, i. p. 91 f.   Comp. the proverb quoted in the Babylonian Talmud
regarding a famous teacher who was a smith : "Better is the sentence of the smith
(R. Isaac) than that of the smith's son (R. Jochanan)."   T. B. Sanhedrin 96a.

5. A simple but strong and elastic organization of a Presbyterian and representative kind was developed and brought into practical operation in every part of the civilised world.

In the synagogue system at its best, we see a democratic government of the highest type, acknowledging the aristocracy of the wisest and fittest to rule, combining a vigorous executive with a full and fair expression of the mind and feelings of the people. It was by this Presbyterian organization, on a broad and popular basis, which united strength with elasticity and capability for adaptation to varied circumstances, that the Diaspora were enabled to hold their ground everywhere throughout the Empire in the face of general dislike and frequent persecution. What Dio Cassius says of the Jewish community in Rome was exemplified all over the known world: "Often crushed down, they yet grew again mightily (αὐξηθὲν δὲ ἐπὶ πλεῖστον), so that they even succeeded in fighting out for themselves (ὥστε καὶ ἐκνικῆσαι) the free exercise of their peculiar laws."[1] It was the synagogue organization which formed in great measure the secret of their success.

6. The collective unity of the religious fellowship of Israel was more clearly brought out both in idea and in practical development.

The sense of that unity had been formed and fostered, as we saw, by many forces, direct and indirect, in the past history of Israel as the covenant people of God. The synagogue system led to its being more strongly felt and more constantly acted upon. In the synagogue the conception of the congregation of Israel was localized but not limited. To the pious Jew the Sabbath gatherings in the places of prayer all over the earth represented the congregation of Israel in its highest capacity, as the congregation of the Lord, assembled together with one accord in His name on His holy Day to meet with Him in worship, to confess His name before men, to hear His promises of blessing to His people, and to learn His will for daily life. They felt their oneness with all who held a like faith and hope as they thus met with the Lord, and with

[1] Dio Cass. xxxvii. 17.

"those who feared Him and thought upon His name" in the synagogue. It was a fellowship of "all who professed the true religion," in which that which was best and highest in Israel visibly drew to itself all who were of the best and noblest among the Gentiles.

The synagogue system embodied and strengthened this sense of religious unity,—of a real world-wide fellowship of faith and obedience. It also supplied the means for giving it effective practical expression. The unity of each congregation was represented and expressed by its own eldership. Where neighbouring synagogues stood towards each other on an independent footing, their elders met, as opportunity offered, more or less formally, for consultation and co-operation in matters of common interest. The elders from every synagogue in great and prosperous Jewish communities, such as that of Alexandria, met in a common presbytery (γερουσία), under a common president, as a court of authority and oversight for all the congregations represented. The sense of unity throughout all the fellowship of Israel was further strengthened by the constant resort of pilgrims, "devout men," in whom the spiritual life of the synagogues was fully represented, to Jerusalem at the three great yearly festivals. References and questions bearing on religion went up with them continually to "the elders of Israel" in Jerusalem, and decisions and replies went forth by the same channels, or by special messengers of the Sanhedrin (apostoli) into every land. The high council of the elders, "the presbytery of the people," meeting under the shadow of the holy and beautiful house of the Lord in Jerusalem, was looked upon as the highest representative of the unity of all the synagogues, and of the scattered people of God in all countries.

What did all these things mean ? What light do they throw upon the mind of God for His Church under the new dispensation for which such centuries of Providential preparation had been made in so many converging lines? The answer is to be found in the teaching and action of our Lord and His apostles as recorded in the New Testament, alike in what they say and do, and in what they refrain from saying and doing.

PART IV.

IN seeking to learn what is the mind of Christ respecting any subject, especially one which is many sided and has important practical aspects, it is obvious that we must have regard not only to His express utterances but to His actions. We shall try accordingly to study His conception of the Church, both in what He said regarding it and in what He did with a view to its establishment and progress in the world.

Without attempting to draw an absolutely distinct line between our Lord's teaching on this subject by word and His teaching by institution, we may divide our discussion of it into two general heads: first, Christ's teaching regarding the Church in express utterances; and, secondly, His teaching regarding it in institutions or appointments.

CHAPTER I.

CHRIST'S TEACHING REGARDING THE CHURCH IN EXPRESS UTTERANCES.

In two important passages in the first of the synoptic Gospels we find the word Church ($\dot{\epsilon}\kappa\kappa\lambda\eta\sigma\acute{\iota}a$) used by our Lord.

1st. " Now when Jesus came into the parts of Cæsarea Philippi, He asked His disciples, saying, Who do men say that the Son of Man is (or, that I, the Son of Man, am)? And they said, Some say John the Baptist; some Elijah; and others Jeremiah, or one of the prophets. He saith unto them,

But who say ye that I am? And Simon Peter answered and said, Thou art the Christ, the Son of the living God.

"And Jesus answered and said unto him, Blessed art thou, Simon Bar Jonah; for flesh and blood hath not revealed it unto thee, but My Father which is in heaven. And I also say unto thee, That thou art Peter, and upon this rock I will build My Church; and the gates of Hades shall not prevail against it. I will give unto thee the keys of the kingdom of heaven: and whatsoever thou shalt bind on earth shall be bound in heaven; and whatsoever thou shalt loose on earth shall be loosed in heaven," Matt. xvi. 13–19.

Before considering the words themselves, let us notice at what stage in our Lord's ministry they were spoken. Both of Christ's great utterances regarding His Church, recorded by Matthew, belong to the same period, and seem to have been made within a few days of each other. It was about the middle of the last year of His public ministry, the year which has been called that of "opposition," as distinguished from the one of general "public favour" which went before it. The training of the twelve apostles was now considerably advanced, and they had had some experience of separate evangelistic work.[1]

Our Lord's own teaching and His mighty works were now well known throughout all Galilee and Judæa. He had already given expression to the feelings with which He looked upon the general results of His Galilæan ministry in the woes pronounced against Chorazin, Bethsaida, and Capernaum.[2] The tidings of the death of His forerunner John the Baptist after a long imprisonment had reached the Saviour, and been recognised by Him as significant for Himself.[3] His feeding of the five thousand, recorded by all the evangelists, had been followed by that memorable discourse in the synagogue of Capernaum on the bread of life, recorded by John only, which led to such a dispersion of the crowds of professed followers who had been drawn to Him chiefly by carnal and worldly motives. "Upon this many of His disciples went back and walked no more with Him." But His true disciples, who felt in their inmost souls—the Spirit of God bearing witness with

---

[1] Matt. x.   [2] Matt. xi. 20-24.
[3] Matt. xiv. 12 f.; comp. xi. 16 ff.

their spirits—that He was " the Holy One of God," and that He had " the words of eternal life," proved faithful in this testing time. They drew the closer to their Master, and He to them.[1]

Attention has been rightly called to "the changed aspect of our Lord's ministry" from this time forward. He devotes Himself now with a special earnestness to the apostles and the circle of true disciples beyond the number of the twelve, who, with whatever shortcomings and mistakes, really and at heart " understood Him, and were capable of being the adherents of a spiritual enterprise." [2] With them He now makes long journeys in remoter districts, withdrawing Himself, as much as may be, from public view, and teaching His own disciples many things in private. It was on one of these journeys, and in this inner circle of the disciples, that the words now to be considered were spoken.

Signs of an open collision between our Lord and the religious leaders in Israel had been multiplying and growing more ominous. A good while before this, in connection with one of His many references to the Rabbinical perversions of Scripture teaching regarding Sabbath observance, the Pharisees had unitedly " taken counsel against Him how they might destroy Him." [3] It was evident that the attention of the Sanhedrin had been seriously turned to the question of His claims. Deputations from Jerusalem appear in Galilee to dog the steps of the Saviour, to inquire into and challenge His attitude and that of His followers to the traditions of the elders. These hostile proceedings were met on our Lord's part by a clear exposure of the error and superstition which marked much of the teaching generally received in the synagogues, and by stern denunciation of the hypocrisy of the teachers. His disciples came to Him privately in alarm at the irritation on the part of His opponents caused by His words, but received only fresh warnings against the spirit

---

[1] John vi. 60–69.

[2] Stalker, *Life of Jesus Christ*, ed. 1885, p. 163.

[3] Συμβούλιον ἔλαβον, Matt. xii. 14. The phrase is repeatedly used by the first two evangelists for what seems to have been a conference of private meeting of the members of the Sanhedrin or its executive, Matt. xxii. 15 ; xxvii. 1, 7 ; xxviii. 12 ; Mark iii. 6 ; xv. 1. In Acts xxv. 12, συμβούλιον is used to denote the privy council or assessors, πάριδροι, of the Roman governor.

and principles of the Pharisees and Sadducees.[1]   All these
things show clearly that a crisis was approaching in the
relations between our Lord and the representatives of the
Jewish Church of His day, and that this was very specially
present to His own mind when He uttered those memorable
words to Peter which we are now to consider.   Observe also
that they are immediately followed by the significant statement: "From that time began Jesus to show unto His
disciples, how that He must go unto Jerusalem, and suffer
many things of the elders, and chief priests, and scribes, and be
killed, and the third day be raised up." [2]   These names, as
we have seen, are those of the three well-known sections of
the Sanhedrin at Jerusalem.   The purport of our Lord's
words, therefore, as understood by His disciples, was that He
was to be formally and finally rejected by that great assembly
of " rulers of the people and elders," [3] who were to their minds
and to those of all devout Jews the highest representatives
of the congregation or Church of Israel and of the Lord, the
קהל ישראל, the קהל יהוה, the ἐκκλησία τοῦ θεοῦ.

It was in this light that Christ's followers were to read
His promise concerning a congregation or Church, an ἐκκλησία,
which He was to build for Himself, and against which the
mightiest powers of opposition should not prevail.   His rejection
by what was in profession the Church of Israel and of God,
His death itself, formed in His eyes no unexpected barrier
crossing His path.   They were to be no hindrance whatever
to His building His Church on a rock-fast foundation, so that
it should defy all assaults of all possible enemies in the future.
It was in this light also that the disciples were to understand
the instruction given to them shortly after, and recorded in
the eighteenth chapter of Matthew, concerning the principles
on which offences were to be dealt with when they arose
within the pale of this Church of Christ, and the promise
concerning His presence in every gathering of His disciples

---

[1] Matt. xv. 1–20 ; xvi. 1–12.

[2] Matt. xvi. 21.   There is the same connection between the scene at Cæsarea
Philippi and Christ's prediction of His rejection by the rulers, death, and
resurrection, in Mark viii. 27–32.

[3] Acts iv. 8.

in His name wheresoever that gathering might take place, and however small a number it might comprise.[1] Immediately after this second great utterance regarding His Church had been given forth by our Lord, we read: "It came to pass, when Jesus had finished these words, He departed from Galilee, and came into the borders of Judea beyond Jordan."[2] He set forth, in fact, upon His last journey up to Jerusalem, in the course of which He repeatedly warned His disciples in the plainest language that His rejection by the representatives of Israel and His death and resurrection were close at hand.[3]

The language which our Lord uses regarding His Church in these two passages is in perfect accordance with the circumstances now indicated. It has its starting-point in the present, but it looks unmistakeably to something in the future. In the first passage this is expressly stated: "I *will* build . . . I *will* give;" in the second it is implied with equal clearness in the nature of the promise, given in close connection with the rule about offences among brethren in the Church, regarding Christ's spiritual Presence in the midst of every little group of His disciples, wheresoever they might meet in His name.

The immediate occasion of the first utterance was the confession of Peter. Our Lord had asked His disciples, "Who do men say that I, the Son of Man,[4] am?" In other words: Whom do they generally suppose Me, as the Son of Man, to be?

The name "the Son of Man" (ὁ υἱὸς τοῦ ἀνθρώπου) was specially familiar to the Jews of our Saviour's time, from its use in Daniel's sublime vision, in which the Messiah appears

---

[1] Matt. xviii. 15–20.   [2] Matt. xix. 1.

[3] Matt. xx. 17–19, 22 f., 28 ; xxi. 37–39 ; xxvi. 11 f. ; xxi. 24–31, with the parallel passages in the other Gospels.

[4] Matt. xvi. 13. The R. V. prefers: "Who do men say that the Son of Man is?" omitting the μι, but notes in the margin that the reading of the A. V. is supported by "many ancient authorities," and by the parallel passages in Mark viii. 27 and Luke ix. 18, where we have: "Who do men (or 'the multitude') say that I am?" Meyer's reasons for retaining the reading of the Textus Receptus seem to me satisfactory. *Matthew*, E. Tr., Edin. 1883, i. pp. 408–413.

as "One like unto a Son of Man (כְּבַר אֱנָשׁ) coming with the clouds of heaven."[1]   Jesus had constantly used that name Himself in His public teaching.[2]   How did the people usually understand it?   In what sense did they hold it to be applicable to Him, and what view did they take of His claims and position generally?

Then, after eliciting a statement of various popular theories regarding Himself, our Lord went on: "But you (ὑμεῖς δέ)? Who say ye that I am?"   From those who had been now so long time with Him, and seen so much of His glory, higher views and deeper spiritual insight were to be expected. Knowing well, as we have seen, how great a crisis was immediately before Him and them, their Master sought to draw them forward to a clear and full confession of the faith that was in them.   It was good for the disciples to make such a confession now.   It was a timely refreshment to the spirit of their Lord, as "the Son of Man," to see that they were able to make it from the heart.

The question had been put to all the disciples.   But Peter, "the mouth of the disciples and the leader of their band," as Chrysostom calls him,[3] was as usual ready to speak for the rest.   He answers in the name of all: This is what we say, Thou art the Christ, the Son of the living God (ὁ Χριστός, ὁ υἱὸς τοῦ θεοῦ τοῦ ζῶντος).   In other words: Thou art the Messiah, the Anointed of Jehovah, called and chosen of Him, and fully fitted for all the work which the prophets foretold that the Lord's Anointed One should do.   We have seen it done by Thee, and have believed in Thee, as sent by God for these great ends. And Thou art not only the Son of Man, the Messiah, but the Son also of the living God; that is to say, *the* Son, in a sense wholly unique and unapproachable, the Son of God in His essential nature.   "Both elements combined," as Meyer says well, "the work and the Person of Christ together,

---

[1] Dan. vii. 13.   Comp. Matt. xxiv. 30 ; xxvi. 64.

[2] Matt. viii. 20 ; ix. 6–10, 23, etc.   Comp. Meyer's full discussion of the point, *Matthew*, E. Tr. pp. 257–261.

[3] Στόμα τῶν μαθητῶν καὶ κορυφὴ τοῦ χοροῦ, *Homil. in Joann.* lxxxviii. 1, ed. Migne, tom. viii. p. 478.

constituted then, as they do always, the sum of the Christian confession." [1]

The manner of the apostle's utterance is as noteworthy as the substance of it. Peter makes his confession, not as if merely stating a general conclusion to which he and his fellow - disciples have come, and which they regard as probably correct, but as a man speaking what he believes and knows surely, and what he *feels* from the bottom of his heart. There is a tone of loving reverence and worship in the words: "Thou art the Christ, the Son of the living God." They answer to our Lord's picture of the spiritual experience of His disciples in His great intercessory prayer: "I manifested Thy name unto the men whom Thou gavest Me out of the world: Thine they were, and Thou gavest them Me; and they have kept Thy word. Now they know that all things, whatsoever Thou hast given Me, are from Thee: for the words which Thou gavest Me I have given unto them; and they received them, and knew of a truth that I came forth from Thee, and they believed that Thou didst send Me."

The apostle had made a solemn and pregnant confession of his faith and that of his fellow - disciples. His Lord's answer is given in like manner with a peculiar solemnity and emphasis: "Jesus answered and said unto him, Blessed art thou, Simon Bar Jonah: for flesh and blood hath not revealed it unto thee, but My Father which is in heaven."

It was not from man in his human weakness that such truth had come to Peter. It was not in the exercise of his own human faculties merely that he had so received and could so confess it. There had been in the full sense a revelation to him (ἀπεκάλυψέ σοι) from without and from above. The Most High God, "My Father which is in heaven," had drawn near in grace to the apostle, unveiling and making known to him the truth concerning the Lord

---

[1] Meyer, *in loco*, E. Tr. i. p. 415. "Estque gradatio," as Bengel notes, "nam cognitio de Jesu, ut est Filius Dei, sublimior est quam de eodem ut est Christus." Comp. Bruce, *Training of the Twelve*, 2nd ed. p. 161 f.

[2] John xvii. 6 f.

Jesus, opening his heart and mind to receive the truth in the love of it. It was the special testimony of the Father at the Jordan, in the hearing of John the Baptist, when Peter was among his followers there. It was to be repeated within a few days by the Voice from heaven from the most excellent glory, heard by Peter and two other favoured disciples on the mount of transfiguration.[1] That seed of the Word had fallen on the good soil of an honest and true heart, and had borne this good fruit. This our Lord first of all recognises in words that breathe a solemn joy and thanksgiving, as when " He rejoiced in the Holy Spirit " over the seventy disciples returning from their first successful mission work in His name, and said, " I thank Thee, O Father, Lord of heaven and earth, that Thou didst hide these things from the wise and understanding, and didst reveal them unto babes." [2]

Christ goes on to give a great promise, and to utter a great prediction : " And I also say unto thee." Peter had made a solemn declaration respecting His Master ; and He in turn (κἀγώ) has this to say respecting him and the position which he in the name of his brethren has thus boldly taken. " And I also say unto thee, that thou art Peter, and upon this rock will I build My Church, and the gates of Hades shall not prevail against it. I will give unto thee the keys of the kingdom of heaven, and whatsoever thou shalt bind on earth shall be bound in heaven, and whatsoever thou shalt loose on earth shall be loosed in heaven."

" Thou art Peter (σὺ εἶ Πέτρος),"—not, " thou shalt be called " so. The name " Petros," " Kephas," had been given to him by his Master when he first became a disciple of Jesus. It had been confirmed when he was set apart to be an apostle.[3] But its suitableness was now signally proved. Our Lord's words seem to amount to this : " Yes, thou art indeed what thy name implies, ' Petros,' ' a man of rock,' when speaking with such strong and stedfast faith

[1] Matt. iii. 17 ; Mark i. 11 ; Luke iii. 23 ; John i. 34, 41 ; Matt. xvii. 4 f. ; 2 Pet. i. 17 f.

[2] Luke x. 21.   [3] John i. 43 ; Mark iii. 16.

in Me, holding so firmly the truth which My Father hath revealed to thee concerning what I am, and what I am anointed and sent to do; and upon this rock (ἐπὶ ταύτῃ τῇ πέτρᾳ) I will build My Church."

It is clear, I think, that there is here a certain personal and official reference to Peter himself, which cannot be fairly set aside by supposing, for example,—as is done by Augustine and others,—that our Lord made some gesture pointing to Himself as the Rock on which the Church was to be built, nor by making the rock to be the truth concerning Christ embodied in Peter's confession. It is equally clear, on the other hand, that it is on Peter only as thus believing and confessing, and as doing so in the name and as the spokesman of the other apostles and of the disciples generally, that the Church is to be built. It is to him only as the representative of such faith and such a confession that the blessing and the promise of Christ are given.

How little Peter's personal position secured to him, apart from faith, is very evident from the stern rebuke by the name of "Satan" which he receives from our Lord in the verses which immediately follow this passage. And how little warrant we have here for attributing to him any peculiarity of official position as compared with the other apostles, is plain from the facts that they as well as Peter are described elsewhere in the New Testament as forming the foundation of the Church,—in the subordinate sense in which alone that can be said of any save Christ Himself,—and that the keys of the kingdom of heaven, or the powers of binding and loosing, are declared in the eighteenth chapter of this Gospel to be given also to the rest of the twelve, nay, as we shall see presently, to the Church or congregation itself, that is, to the whole company of Christ's disciples as such.[1]

---

[1] Matt. xvi. 23 ; xviii. 18-20 ; Eph. ii. 20 ; Rev. xxi. 14. Beyschlag, in his interesting and suggestive chapter on our Lord's idea of the Church (die Gemeindeidee Jesus), holds that there is no reference here to Peter's official position, but that "he is regarded solely as the first New Testament believer in the full sense of the expression, the first complete member of the Church of Jesus Christ." "So ists lediglich der erste Glaübige, der erste Bekenner den Jesus in ihm aus zeichnet. . . . So ist er der erste wahrhaft neutestamentlich Glaübige, der erste rechte Gemeindeglied Jesu. Was ist natürlicher als dass dieser Erstling der

But Peter stands out in this memorable scene as the first public representative in the Gospel history of true and saving faith in the Person and work of our Lord as the Messiah and the Son of the living God. He speaks in that spirit of faith which in the apostles and in the membership of the apostolic Church was destined to overcome the world, against which all the power of the enemy should not prevail. "Who is he that overcometh the world," a fellow-apostle wrote afterwards, "but he that believeth that Jesus is the Son of God?"[1] Peter stands out here, in short, on New Testament ground much as Abraham does in the Old Testament, as the representative of true faith, a pattern and model to all who hereafter should believe in Christ Jesus.

Further, we see from our Lord's reply to Peter's confession that He was looking forward in a special way at this time into the future of His disciples after His death. In that future this apostle again stood out before His eyes as we see him in the history of the day of Pentecost, and the years that followed, as the first and for long the most powerful preacher of the faith, as the chief instrument in founding and building up the Church in Jerusalem, and as the first also to open the door of faith to the Gentiles. To Peter therefore as representing all this, both in his personal and official capacity, as one who had himself by Divine grace and teaching attained to what was the secret of spiritual strength and stability, the rock-fast foundation for a Church against which the gates of Hades should not prevail, and who was to be a chief instrument in Christ's hand in founding and building up the Church thereupon,—to him our Lord speaks these words of blessing and of promise : " Blessed art thou, Simon Bar Jonah,

Glaübigen der Grundstein wird, auf den Jesus den weiteren Bau errichten will, und durch das Glaubenszeugniss desselben am ersten Pfingsttag in der That errichtet hat ; dass Er, im Hinblick auf die nahe Zukunft, da Er selbst nicht mehr persönlich auf Erden das Himmelreich aufschliessen wird, diesem ersten Bekenner die Schlüssel des Himmelreichs übergeben will. d. h. Sein Wort und Seinen Geist, und in denselben die Macht den Menschen das Himmelreich weiter hin zu erschliessen?" *Christliche Gemeindeverfassung im Zeitalter des N. T.*, 1874, S. 20. But this, although true and well put, seems hardly to do justice to the full meaning of the passage viewed both in itself and its connection.

[1] 1 John v. 5.

for flesh and blood hath not revealed it unto thee, but my Father which is in heaven. And I also say unto thee, That thou art Peter, and upon this rock I will build my Church; and the gates of Hades shall not prevail against it." [1]

"I will build My Church"—I will build it for Myself (οἰκοδομήσω Μοῦ τὴν ἐκκλησίαν). There is a slight but significant emphasis upon the pronoun.[2] Full before our Lord's mind at this time, as we see from His very next recorded words to His disciples, was the thought of His approaching rejection by the highest representatives of the congregation and Church of Israel. It was a thought which was surrounded with dread and difficulty for His most devoted followers, which Peter himself could not yet receive. "Be it far from Thee, Lord," he said: "this shall never be unto Thee." [3] Against that dark background the Saviour bids them set this bright and inspiring promise. The Church of Christ shall never fail, whatever powers of opposition may array themselves against it in the future. "On this rock will I build for Myself My Church; and the gates of Hades shall not prevail against it." The darkest storms might gather and break upon it. But the rock should stand fast, and the Church built upon the rock by the Lord's own hand.

[1] The dilemma in which a conscientious Roman Catholic priest is placed by the discord which prevails among the Fathers over this text is well brought out by Archbishop Kenrick of St. Louis in his speech prepared for the Vatican Council. Like many other speeches designed for that assembly, it was not delivered there, but was published at Naples in 1870. In it he states that there are five different patristic interpretations of Matt. xvi. 18 : (1) *Seventeen* Fathers teach that St. Peter is the Rock. (2) *Eight*, that the Apostolic College, represented by Peter, is the Rock. (3) *Forty-four*, that St. Peter's faith is the Rock. (4) *Sixteen*, that Christ is the Rock. (5) *Several*, that the Rock is the whole body of the faithful. But every Roman Catholic priest swears at his ordination in accordance with the Creed of Pope Pius IV., " that he will never interpret Scripture *except according to the unanimous consent* of the Fathers." How then were members of the Vatican Council to interpret the text : Tu es Petrus, etc., which they read inscribed in gigantic letters of Mosaic high above their heads in the dome of St. Peter's ? Littledale, *Plain Reasons against joining the Church of Rome*, Lond. 1881, ii. p. 26 f. Stillingfleet, *Doct. and Pract. of Church of Rome* (Cunningham's ed.), p. 135 ff.

[2] Meyer, *in loc.*   [3] Ver. 22.

" I will build My Church" (Μοῦ τὴν ἐκκλησίαν).   There
can be no doubt as to the general meaning which that well-
known term would convey to the minds of the disciples who
heard it thus used by their Master.   As Rothe expresses
it : " The conception of the Church in its most general
outlines had already grown up on the soil of the Old
Testament.   The theocratic community of the people of
Israel regarded itself in that capacity as the ἐκκλησία τοῦ
θεοῦ (קָהָל, עֵדָה יְהֹוָה, מִקְרָא), i.e. as the holy congregation chosen
by God out of all other nations of the world, and called to be
His peculiar people (Deut. v. 22 ; Ps. xxii. 23 f. ; xxvi. 12 ;
Acts vii. 38).   And the Redeemer appropriates to Himself
this conception of the Church, inasmuch as He declares that
He will build for Himself an ἐκκλησία over which the gates
of Hell shall not prevail." [1]   Cremer, in his careful examination of the use of the term ἐκκλησία in the New Testament,
speaks to the same effect with still greater precision :
" Ἐκκλησία denotes the New Testament community of the
redeemed in its twofold aspect : First, the entire congregation
of all who are called by and to Christ, who are in the fellowship of His salvation, the Church.   That the application of
the word to the Church universal is primary, and that to an
individual Church secondary, is clear from the Old Testament
use of the word, and from the fundamental statement of
Christ in Matt. xvi. 18. . . . Secondly, the New Testament
Church as confined to particular places. . . . When Christ
says οἰκοδομήσω Μοῦ τὴν ἐκκλησίαν, we are scarcely reminded
that ἐκκλησία denoted in profane Greek the place of assembly
as well as the assembly itself, but rather that the Old Testament community was ' the house of Israel.' " [2]

The powerful and impressive figure of " the gates of
Hades " would naturally suggest the idea of mighty forces
coming from the realm of the unseen, the kingdom of death
and the world of spirits, marshalled by deliberate counsels
such as were held in the gates of Eastern cities.[3]

---

[1] Rothe, Dogmatik, Heidelberg 1870, iii. 2te Th. 2te Abth. § 2, S. 17.

[2] Cremer, Lexicon of N. T. Greek, E. Tr., Edin. 1880, p. 334.

[3] There seems to be no sufficient reason for departing from the usual exegesis
of the words πύλαι ᾅδου οὐ κατισχύσουσιν αὐτῆς, the gates of Hades shall not

The general conviction, therefore, which the promise was fitted to convey to the minds of the disciples was to this effect, that the congregation or Church of Israel, the fellowship of God's covenant people, was to be built up by the Son of God Himself in their time upon a rock-fast foundation, and that no powers of evil from the unseen future and the unseen world, the region of death and destruction, should ever prevail against it.[1]

"I will give unto thee the keys of the kingdom of heaven: and whatsoever thou shalt bind on earth shall be bound in heaven; and whatsoever thou shalt loose on earth shall be loosed in heaven."

The Future, as in "I will build," points to a time when

prevail against or overpower the Church. Meyer admits that this interpretation is equally correct with his own in point of grammar, and that it is given by the great majority of exegetes, but prefers a different one. He renders: "The gates of Hades will not be able to resist it, will not prove stronger than it," and holds that the main idea is that of a comparison between the strength of the Church and the strength of Hades, without any direct reference to attack or effort on either side. Hades is the embodiment of strength and impregnability. Yet the Church of Christ as now to be built upon the rock shall prove to be yet stronger. Its members in Hades shall be brought out, and the iron gates burst open. In the name of Jesus the things of the world below shall do homage, Phil. ii. 10. But this appears a somewhat artificial and far-fetched interpretation, and much less suitable to the context. It is adopted also by Weiss, *Biblical Theol. of N. T.*, 3rd ed., E. Tr., 1882, i. pp. 140, 156, note.

[1] The exposition of this passage given by Krauss is a superficial and unsatisfactory one. According to him, Peter is the rock, "Peter as confessing Christ, but still Peter." Therefore the ἐκκλησία must be one actually built on the confessing Peter, and what is to happen after his death the passage does not indicate; whether we are to look for a successor to Peter, a college of presbyters, a number of independent congregations, or a free development of life in different forms. "We must go back to the historical sense of the words, and explain them in relation to the historical circumstances in which they were spoken." Certainly, and therefore it is a bad omen for the success of Professor Krauss's inquiry that he begins with a blunder as to the historical sense and use of עֵדָה and קָהָל (pointed out above, p. 94), and goes on to commit himself to the assertion that "Jesus spoke these words looking only to the position of things *at that moment* (im Hinblick auf den augenblicklichen Stand der Dinge)." How then account for the use of the *future:* "I will build, I will give," and for the comprehensive character of the promise: "that the gates of Hades should not prevail in the future against this Church, which was yet to be built"? *Protestantische Dogma v. der unsichtbaren Kirche*, S. 124–128.

Christ should no longer be present with His disciples as He was now, and the phrase carries on the metaphor implied in οἰκοδομήσω. It indicates the position of things which would arise in His Church when He, the Master of the house (ὁ οἰκοδεσπότης), as He describes Himself in several of His parables,[1] should have departed from it for a season, giving authority to His servants in the house, and to every man his work, until He should return. The Church of Christ—here spoken of as one with, or at least most closely related to, "the kingdom of heaven"—is referred to as a house in which Peter is to hold the position of steward or overseer (οἰκονόμος or ταμίας), and in token of this "the keys," a familiar Old Testament symbol for authority and government, are to be entrusted to him. He is to decide in His Master's name who are to belong to the household, and who are to be excluded from it; who may enter freely into the house, and against whom its doors must be closed.[2]

"And whatsoever thou shalt bind on earth shall be bound in heaven; and whatsoever thou shalt loose on earth shall be loosed in heaven."

This clause confirms the power conveyed in the gift of the keys, and explains the nature of it. The decisions of the steward in the house, as given in the Master's name, are to carry His full authority. When thus given on earth, they

---

[1] Luke xii. 42 ff. ; xix. 12 ff.

[2] Comp. Isa. xxii. 15–23. Shebna, "the steward which is over the house" (הַסֹּכֵן אֲשֶׁר עַל־הַבָּיִת, ὁ ταμίας, LXX.), has become unworthy of his office, "the shame of his Lord's house." The prophet, in the name of Jehovah, declares that he is to be removed from office, and a worthier man, Eliakim, the servant of the Lord, set in his place. "I will commit thy government" (τὴν οἰκονομίαν σου, LXX.) "into his hand, and he shall be a father to the inhabitants of Jerusalem and to the house of Judah. And the key of the house of David will I lay upon his shoulder; he shall open and none shall shut, and he shall shut and none shall open." Compare also what Christ says of the scribes and Pharisees sitting in Moses' seat, but not like him faithful servants in all the house of God : "Ye shut the kingdom of heaven against men," Matt. xxiii. 13. In the parallel passage in Luke xi. 52, this is described as their "taking away the key of knowledge." In Rev. iii. 7 our Lord speaks of Himself as "He that hath the key of David, that openeth and none shall shut, and that shutteth and none openeth." He has not merely the keys of the house of David, but of David himself. It is no vicarious authority, but that of the οἰκοδεσπότης himself, direct and supreme.

shall be at that very moment ratified and registered ·in heaven.[1]

The phrase to bind and loose (אָסַר and הִתִּיר, δέειν and λύειν) was a familiar one in the Jewish synagogues and schools, in the sense of to forbid and to allow. There can be no doubt, I think, that that is its meaning here. It was the one in which the first disciples, accustomed from their earliest youth to the phraseology of the synagogues, would naturally understand the words.[2] The steward in Christ's house and kingdom, using the power of the keys, is to decide authoritatively what is to be forbidden and what allowed within it; in other words, he is to settle the conditions of membership and the rules of the house.

As to the nature of the things forbidden and allowed, and as to the way in which the authority is to be exercised, whether by the steward alone or in conjunction with others, nothing is said here. Only this much is evident from the words themselves, that the authority is a delegated and ministerial one. It is the power of a man who is himself " under authority," of a " steward," not of the master of the house. Further, as we saw, Peter had spoken as the representative of the rest of the disciples. We may infer, therefore, that he is addressed as such by their Lord. Fuller light is given on some of these points by Christ's teaching in the passage which we have now to consider.

2nd. "And if thy brother sin against thee, go show him his fault between thee and him alone : if he hear thee, thou hast gained thy brother. But if he hear thee not, take with thee one or two more, that at the mouth of two witnesses or three every word may be established. And if he refuse to hear them, tell it unto the Church : and if he refuse to hear the Church also, let him be unto thee as the Gentile and the

---

[1] Ἔσται δεδεμένον . . . λελυμένον, "shall be already a thing bound . . . loosed." The two transactions, below and above, absolutely coincide. As we look up from what has taken place in the Church on earth, behold, it is already done in heaven also. Comp. Meyer, *in loco.*

[2] See Vitringa, p. 754 f. Hausrath, *N. T. Times*, i. pp. 97–104. Meyer, E. Tr. i. p. 423 f. Julius Müller's arguments against the general consensus of interpreters on this point do not seem at all conclusive. *Dogmatische Abhandlungen*, Bremen 1870, S. 504–513.

publican. Verily I say unto you, What things soever ye shall bind on earth shall be bound in heaven; and what things soever ye shall loose on earth shall be loosed in heaven.

"Again I say unto you, That if two of you shall agree on earth as touching anything that they shall ask, it shall be done for them of My Father which is in heaven. For where two or three are gathered together in My name, there am I in the midst of them," Matt. xviii. 15–20.

These words were spoken shortly after our Lord's first great utterance concerning His Church. They belong to the very close of His Galilæan ministry, to the time just before His last journey to Jerusalem. The disciples had come to Him with questions as to high position in the kingdom of heaven. In reply, Christ spoke to them concerning the spiritual conditions needful in men ere they could enter into that kingdom at all, concerning occasions of stumbling given to little ones who believed on Him, and concerning the love and care of His heavenly Father and theirs for such little ones.[1] He passes on now by a natural transition to speak upon a kindred subject, namely, in what spirit and by what method sins and occasions of stumbling among fellow-believers should be dealt with by His disciples.

"If thy brother shall have sinned against thee." "Thy brother" (ὁ ἀδελφός σου). The generic use of the article, as in the subsequent phrase, "the Gentile and the publican," shows that the reference is to a whole class. It is a typical case that is described, not limited to the special section of brethren above referred to, the μικροί, but including any fellow-believers, whether high or low as regards position in the brotherhood. Suppose an offence given by any one within the fellowship of Christ's disciples to any other of its members, an offence which is in the nature of it a sin (ἐὰν ἁμαρτήσῃ εἰς σέ), what is the right course to be followed by the brother offended?[2]

---

[1] Matt. xviii. 1–14.

[2] The emphasis is on the fact of the *sin* (ἁμαρτήσῃ), not on its personal reference (εἰς σέ). But there seems no sufficient reason, from external or internal considerations, for omitting the εἰς σέ, as is done by Drs. Westcott and Hort, and by Jul. Müller, *Dogmat. Abhandl.* S. 513 f.

The trespass, whatever it be, has some special bearing on the brother who is

The first step to be taken is this: Go to him in a frank and brotherly spirit. Do not speak to others about it until you have spoken first of all with himself. Do not wait for him to show signs of repentance and to make any approach to you. Seek a personal interview as between brother and brother. And let it be strictly in private. " Go, show him his fault " (ἔλεγξον αὐτόν, convince him by brotherly reasoning) " between thee and him *alone*. If he hear thee (ἐάν σου ἀκούσῃ), if he will be persuaded to listen to this kindly reasoning and brotherly admonition, and to act accordingly, thou hast gained thy brother (ἐκέρδησας τὸν ἀδελφόν σου); thou hast won him back to the fellowship of the kingdom of heaven, from which he had separated himself by his sin;[1] thou hast gained him again as a brother, in the full sense of the word, to thyself, as one of the believing members of that fellowship. And therein thou hast a full reward for all thy pains in this matter."

But suppose the efforts thus made fail; then a second stage of admonition must follow. " If he hear thee not, take with thee one or two more, that at the mouth of two witnesses, or three, every word may be established."

The dealing with the offender is still of a brotherly kind, and is carried on in hope of the best results. But it is now assuming a more formal character, and it looks to the possibility of a further step being needful. The " one or two more" whom the disciple against whom the sin has been committed is now to associate with himself are, of course, brethren also, and take part, as is evident from ver. 17, and that probably now the leading part ("If he shall refuse to hear *them* "), in the friendly reasoning with him. But there

---

first called to deal with the offender. This may be through personal injury and loss sustained by him, through some special relation to the person sinning, or simply through the scandal coming specially under his eye and appealing in a special way from Providential circumstances to his Christian feeling and conscience. In one way or other it is, and he feels it to be, a sin εἰς αὐτόν.

[1] Comp. the apostle's words : "To the Jews I became as a Jew, that I might gain (κερδήσω) Jews. . . . I am become all things to all men, that I may by all means save (σώσω) some," 1 Cor. ix. 20 ff. "That if any obey not the word, they may without the word be gained (κερδηθήσονται) by the manner of life of their wives," 1 Pet. iii. 1.

is a further end to be secured by their presence. They
are to serve also, if need be, as witnesses when the case
goes before the Church. They are present now in order
that (ἵνα) at the mouth of two or three witnesses every
word may be fully attested (σταθῇ πᾶν ῥῆμα, may be made
to stand); that is to say, in order that there may be no
subsequent evasion or denial on the part of the offender as
to what he actually said and did at this second interval,
and as to the statements made to him or in his presence;
in order that the whole facts of the case may be brought
before the tribunal, to which appeal may yet have to be made,
in a thoroughly clear and reliable form.[1]

"And if he refuse to hear them, tell it unto the Church (εἰπὲ
τῇ ἐκκλησίᾳ)."

What Church is here referred to? It must either mean
the existing Jewish Church as represented by the synagogue,
or the Church of which our Lord had recently spoken to
Peter with such solemnity and emphasis. Against the
former view there are very strong and, I think, conclusive
considerations to be urged. The Jewish synagogue of that
time, although no doubt still representing so far the Old
Testament ἐκκλησία to the minds of the disciples, as it did
to those of their fellow-countrymen, is never called by this
name elsewhere in the New Testament. Still more conclusive against this interpretation are such considerations
as these: that our Lord could never have assigned such
weight to the decisions of the synagogue on a question of
moral and spiritual offence, as to bid His disciples regard
the man who would not hear it as a heathen and a publican;

---

[1] This was in exact accordance with the practice—or at least the rules—of the
Jewish synagogue courts, and with the Scripture law concerning offences or
sins in the congregation or assembly of Israel and of the Lord, the ἐκκλησία of
the Old Testament. "Both the men between whom the controversy is shall
stand before the Lord, before the priests and the judges which shall be in those
days, and the judges shall make diligent inquisition." "One witness shall
not rise up against a man for any iniquity or for any sin that he sinneth; at
the mouth of two witnesses or at the mouth of three witnesses shall a matter be
established" (στήσεται πᾶν ῥῆμα, LXX.), Deut. xix. 15 ff. The apostle Paul
gives special injunctions that this rule shall be strictly observed in the case of
office-bearers in the Church: "Against an elder receive not an accusation except
at the mouth of two or three witnesses," 1 Tim. v. 19.

that the whole connection of this passage, as in the case of
the utterance in the sixteenth chapter, points to a time still
future, although in the near future, when Jesus Himself
would no longer be in the midst of His disciples, save after
a spiritual sort, when they might be meeting in little
separate groups of two or three assembled in His name,
with His unseen presence equally to be realized wherever
they met. While Christ was yet with them they needed
to appeal to no other tribunal in matters of dispute among
themselves. No other voice of authority could be sought so
long as He expounded to them the things concerning the
kingdom of God. But soon it was to be otherwise with
them; and this was the course to be followed then.

The reference, therefore, is clearly to the Church already
spoken of, the society or fellowship of believers in Jesus as
" the Christ, the Son of the living God," which He was to
build for Himself upon the rock as His Church; more
particularly the reference is to that ἐκκλησία as represented
in the place where the sin in question has been committed
and where the case has taken shape, which is (*ex hypothesi*) in
process of being dealt with. We see here, in short, the קָהָל
or ἐκκλησία of Christ's former utterance localized. It is seen
and becomes accessible in the local Church; just as for the
pious Israelite the congregation of Israel and of the Lord was
represented in the synagogue congregation of the place in
which he lived.[1]

"There is nothing," as Meyer says, "to warrant the
assumption of an historical *prolepsis* (De Wette, Jul. Müller),
for the truth is the קהל of believers was actually existing.
. . . But as Jesus had already spoken of *His* קהל, it was

---

[1] "In this part of His discourse Jesus had in view the future rather than the
present. Contemplating the time when the kingdom, that is, the Church,
should be in actual existence as an organized community, with the twelve
exercising in it authority as apostles, He gives direction for the exercise of
discipline for the purity and well-being of the Christian brotherhood, confers
on the twelve collectively what He had already granted to Peter singly, the
power to bind and loose, that is, to inflict and remove Church censures (this
seems rather too limited an interpretation). . . . His aim throughout is to
ensure beforehand that the community to be called after His name shall be
indeed a holy, loving, united society." Bruce, *Training of the Twelve*, 2nd
ed. p. 200.

impossible for the disciples to misunderstand the allusion.
The warrant for regarding the judgment of the Church as
final in regard to the ἔλεγξις, lies in the moral power which
belongs to the unity of the Holy Spirit, and consequently
to true understanding, faith, earnest effort, prayer, etc., the
existence of all which in the Church is presupposed.   It is
not inconsistent with this passage to suppose that under
the more developed circumstances of a later period, when
local congregations sprang up as offshoots from the קהל, there
may have been some *representative body* composed of individuals chosen for the purpose of maintaining discipline; but
the choice would necessarily be founded on such conditions
and qualifications as were in keeping, so far as it was possible
for man to judge, with the original principle of entrusting
such matters only to those who were actual believers, and
had been truly regenerated." [1]   It may be added that such
an administration of discipline by the representatives of the
Church in its name would the more naturally be suggested
to the first disciples by Christ's words, inasmuch as it was
the ordinary and indeed apparently — so far as we have
evidence—the *only* method in use in the Jewish synagogue; [2]
and, as we saw at an earlier stage in our investigations, the

---

[1] Meyer, *Matthew*, E. Tr. ii. p. 12 f.   There is a slight ambiguity in Meyer's
reference to the original conditions of admission to the Church which need
not detain us here.   I may add, however, that I cannot agree with his view
that "there is here no allusion to individual congregations in different
localities, since these could come into existence only at a later period" (p.
12).   The whole passage evidently, as already shown, refers to a future, when
the קהל, of which our Lord spoke in xvi. 18, should be built on the rock,
and authority in the Master's house given to His servants to bind and loose,
and when believers should be meeting κατ᾽ οἶκον (comp. Acts ii. 46; Rom.
xvi. 5, etc.) in little groups of two or three assembled in Christ's name,
with His promised presence in the midst of each separate assembly.   Julius
Müller sums up the meaning of the passage in this respect more correctly:
"Christus hat bei diesem Ausspruch seine Kirche, wie sie sich bilden wird
nach seinem Hingang zum Vater, im Auge.   Es ist dieselbe Kirche wie die
deren Erbauung er, Matt. xvi. 18, vorausgesagt hat, aber wie sie als
Gemeinde an dem einzelnen Orte, sei es mit vielen oder wenigen Mitgliedern
bestehen wird."   *Dogm. Abhandl.* S. 517.

[2] "There is at least no trace of any direct deliberation and determination of
the whole congregation in individual cases of discipline and government of
the kind which we meet with in the Christian Church at Corinth.   In the
Jewish community, on the contrary, these were administered by appointed

term "assembly" (קָהָל, ἐκκλησία) is often used in the Old Testament Scriptures, where what is meant, as appears from the context, is not all the members of the assembly, but their representatives, "the elders of the congregation."[1]

"But if he shall refuse to listen even to the Church (ἐὰν δὲ καὶ τῆς ἐκκλησίας παρακούσῃ), let him be unto thee as the Gentile and the publican."

In the absence of the Lord Himself, in the form in which His disciples had been wont to bring their difficulties to Him, this was the last and highest resort on earth for the decision of such a case of offence between brethren.

Let the disciple, therefore, who has sinned, and who, after brotherly admonition, first absolutely in private, and then by two or three together, is still unrepentant, be brought before the Church. Let the case be fully stated on both sides in his own presence and before witnesses. Let him be dealt with by the Church, or its appointed representatives in its name, in the same spirit of brotherly love and faithfulness as before, but now with a voice of distinct authority. "And if he shall refuse to hear even the Church," let your attitude towards him henceforth, until he repents, be like that of the synagogue towards the Gentile and the publican; that is to say, let him be treated as one who is excluded from all close fellowship with you in religious things, as one who by his own conduct has placed himself, for the time at least, in the position of an alien and not of a brother.[2]

officials, the elders of the congregation. In particular, the latter were very probably competent to exercise that most important act of religious discipline, the infliction of excommunication or exclusion from the congregation." Schürer, ii. pp. 59 f., 62. Comp. Tertullian's account of the exercise of discipline in the Church in the second century : "With a great gravity is the work of judging carried on among us . . ., and it is a very grave anticipation of the judgment to come when any one has so offended as to require to be severed from us in prayer, in the assembly, and in all holy fellowship. The most approved elders preside." *Apol.* 39.

[1] *Supra*, p. 101. "קהל kommt besonders im Pentateuch, in den Psalmen in den Büchern der Chronik, Ezra, Nehemia sehr oft vor für die Israelitische Volksversammlung, oft auch nur für die Versammlung seiner Vertreter, seiner Priester und Aeltesten." Jul. Müller, *dogm. Abhandl.* S. 497.

[2] A Gentile in the eyes of the Palestinian synagogue of our Lord's time was one who stood outside of the fellowship of the covenant people of God altogether ; a publican was one who, originally within its pale, had wilfully

The injunction is put in the Singular (ἔστω σοι); but it is plain from the whole connection, and in particular from the Plural immediately following (ver. 18), that what is said here to one disciple is said to all. It could not be the duty of an individual member of the Church to treat as a Gentile and a publican one whom the Church as a whole was entitled to treat as a brother in full standing. Nay, without an express injunction from Christ Himself, the disciple against whom the trespass had been committed, remembering the Master's teaching as to forgiveness of merely personal wrongs, might have thought that he at least was not warranted in making any difference in his attitude towards the offender. The action contemplated is clearly one on the part of the Church or congregation as such, in which all its members are to concur. It was in substance just the "cutting off from the congregation," the effects of which were so familiar to every Hebrew believer.[1] This was to have its place in the קהל, the ἐκκλησία of Christ, as it had in that of the Old Testament. It was to be carried out, of course, in the spirit of the Gospel as now fully revealed by our Lord, and in accordance with the principles and rules of His house elsewhere made known by Him. By natural inference, and according to the analogy of the synagogue system in like cases, there might be a reference made from the decision of the local Church or its representatives to a higher and more widely representative body.[2]

The prospect of having to take part in such an exercise of discipline in the Church, ending in a result so serious, might well awaken misgivings and fears in the hearts of the disciples as to their own fitness for such trying duty. To

---

forsaken the fellowship of Israel and cast in his lot with the alien. Neither of them was excluded from all share in public worship, either in temple or synagogue. In connection, e.g., with the Temple services there was "the court of the Gentiles," where the publican also might pray "standing afar off," Luke xviii. 13.

[1] See above, p. 144 f.

[2] See above, pp. 149–154. It seems little else than a dispute about words to discuss the question whether or not we have in this passage the institution of excommunication in the Church of Christ. On the one hand, the word excommunication is not mentioned. No formulæ are given for the exclusion of the offending brother or for his readmission to fellowship; and we are not told what precisely is implied, as regards the privileges of the Christian society, in

meet the feelings which might so naturally arise on their part, Christ now vouchsafes two great promises resting upon a great and most pregnant assurance. First, He repeats in this significant connection to all the disciples the promise which He had so lately given to Peter when speaking as their representative, that their decisions made, as now appears more distinctly, in the Church, or in the name of the Church, on earth, shall be ratified in heaven. Secondly, Christ promises that if two of them even shall agree together in prayer as touching anything,—any case, for instance, that may have to be dealt with, however difficult, any felt need of Christian wisdom, faithfulness, and love,—their request shall be granted. Thirdly, both of these promises are grounded upon one great fact, now revealed for the comfort and encouragement of Christ's disciples, that wherever two or three of them are gathered together in His name ($εἰς τὸ ἐμὸν ὄνομα$, with reference to it, to confess and invoke the name in which they meet), there He is in the midst of them.

"Verily I say unto you, What things soever ye shall bind on earth shall be bound in heaven; and what things soever ye shall loose on earth shall be loosed in heaven."

Our Lord passes here from the Singular to the Plural, from "thou" to "ye;" just as in the passage in the sixteenth chapter, already considered, He does the reverse, beginning with "ye" and changing to "thou." The natural inference is that drawn by Luther: "We see that what is said to one is said to all."

But who are the "all" in this case?

In the first Gospel the phrase "the disciples" ($οἱ μαθηταί$)

---

his being dealt with in the way described. On the other hand, we see here authority given by Christ to His Church to shut out obstinate and impenitent offenders from her fellowship, and to place them in the position of the Gentile and the publican; and we have distinct directions as to the different disciplinary steps which should be taken before a decision of so serious a kind is arrived at. If excommunication, taken generally, means, as the term itself indicates, an authoritative exclusion from the communion or fellowship of Christ's Church, that is surely what we have here. Meyer expresses himself on this point with characteristic caution when he remarks: "In this passage Christ says nothing as yet about formal excommunication on the part of the Church (1 Cor. v.); but the latter was such a fair and necessary deduction from what He did say as the apostolic Church in the course of its development considered itself warranted in making." *Matthew*, E. Tr. ii. p. 13.

means almost invariably "the twelve," not the disciples in a
more general sense.[1]   It was to the twelve, as we saw,
indicated by this designation, that Jesus put the question at
Cæsarea Philippi regarding their views about Himself.   Peter
made answer then in their name.   It was the twelve, in all
likelihood, who came to Jesus, as mentioned in the beginning
of this chapter, with the question, "Who is greatest in the
kingdom of heaven?"   It seems probable, therefore, that the
special reference is to the apostles also in the 18th verse, where
the power formerly assigned to Peter as representing the rest of
the twelve is now expressly given to them all.   "It is thereby
set," as Meyer says, "in its proper light, and shown to be of
necessity a power of a collegiate nature, so that Peter is not
to be regarded as exclusively endowed with it either in whole
or in part, but is simply looked upon as *primus inter pares*."[2]

But just as Peter represented the rest of the apostles in his
faith and confession, so the apostles represent the body of the
disciples in the wider sense, in so far as they rise to the same
faith and the same confession, and "what is said to one is said
to all."   So the promise to united prayer in ver. 19: "If two of
you shall agree on earth," while it may have special reference
to the apostles as the first office-bearers in Christ's Church,—
the stewards in the House with the power of the keys entrusted
to them,—on whom the burden of such exercise of discipline
would especially fall, certainly cannot be limited to them.
The whole Church has the responsibility of dealing with the
offending brother, for it is to the Church as such ($\tau\hat{\eta}$ $\dot{\epsilon}\kappa\kappa\lambda\eta\sigma\dot{\iota}\alpha$)
that the appeal is made.   And any two or three believers
gathered together in Christ's name, for the purposes for which
that name has been revealed to them, are called to realize His
Presence in the midst of them, and to claim the promises
made in connection with it.[3]

Again, while the "you" in the 18th verse, like the "ye"
in Christ's question to the disciples in the 16th chapter,

---

[1] *E.g.* viii. 23; ix. 10 f., 14, 19; x. 1; xi. 1; xiii. 10; xiv. 15-20, 22, 26, etc.
[2] Meyer, *Matthew*, E. Tr. ii. p. 14.
[3] The $\dot{v}\mu\hat{\omega}\nu$, as Meyer notes, is not used in ver. 20.   The assembly to which
the promise is given is composed of any two or three believers gathered together
$\epsilon\dot{\iota}\varsigma$ $\tau\dot{o}$ $\dot{\epsilon}\mu\dot{o}\nu$ $\check{o}\nu o\mu\alpha$.   So also Müller, S. 520.

refers primarily to the apostles, it is perfectly clear that the
" thou " in the 8th and 9th verses, and in the passage
from the 15th to the 17th verse of this chapter, is spoken
to each believer as an individual. " The little ones who
believe in Jesus " are to receive this precept, and to have
this protection against any who may sin against them in the
Church, and who will give no heed to private remonstrance.
They are to make their appeal, first of all, to the one or
two brethren referred to in ver. 16, and then to the Kahal,
the ecclesia, the wider fellowship of the brethren, in the form
in which it may be most accessible to them. If it is to
brethren in office, such as the apostles, it is only as representing the Church and speaking in its name.

" Verily I say unto you, What things soever ye shall bind
on earth shall be bound in heaven." That is to say, Whatever you in the Church on earth pronounce to be unlawful
for a member of its fellowship, that will be held to be so in
the court of heaven. If—which the connection shows to be
the immediate reference—the judgment of the two or three
brethren, who have already dealt with the offending brother,
is sustained by the judgment of the Church before whom
the matter is brought, the offender is bound to receive this
as an authoritative decision on his case, and to obey it, to
acknowledge frankly that he has been in the wrong, and
to bring forth fruits meet for repentance. If he fails to do
so, his sin already committed is aggravated by such persistent obduracy, and he is cut off from the fellowship of
the Church by the exercise of the power of the keys.
It is taken for granted, of course, that this is a normal
case ; that the Church is acting in the spirit and on the
principles of the Gospel ; that being so, the sentence is confirmed in heaven.
" And what things soever ye shall loose on earth shall be
loosed in heaven." That is to say, What you in the Church
on earth pronounce to be a right and fitting spirit and mode
of acting for a member of its fellowship, that shall be held to
be so in heaven. Thus, for example, if the offending brother
in the case under consideration is brought by Divine bless-

ing on the effects of discipline to a better state of mind,
so that he repents and does the first works, the duty of
the Church now is to restore him formally to the fellowship from which he was shut out. And this step also will be
confirmed in heaven, and ought to be regarded accordingly by
all parties concerned in the case.

"Again I say unto you." The words introduce a second
promise, given by our Lord with the same solemnity and
emphasis with which He gave the first. It is fitted to meet
the sense of fear and insufficiency which the disciples might
still feel in prospect of having work of such difficulty and
delicacy to do alone. How should they ever be able to
reach a decision at all in such circumstances ? How should
their decision be such as would be ratified in heaven ? Their
Lord bids them go forward in faith and with prayer, and all
things needful shall be given them. "If two of you shall
agree on earth as touching anything that they shall ask, it
shall be done for them of My Father which is in heaven."

"For where two or three are gathered together in My
name, there am I in the midst of them."

This is the crowning assurance, the rock-fast foundation on
which the two foregoing promises were built. It draws back
the veil of the unseen, and reveals a great central fact of
the kingdom of heaven on earth, a fact which, once made
known, remains as a heritage for believers in all time. As
soon as the two or three disciples have met together in
their Lord's name, *before* they can agree together touching the
things to be asked, before at least the agreement can express
itself in words, Lo, He Himself is in the midst of them.

But in order to this, observe, the meeting must be no casual
one, but of a definite character, with a definite constituency, and
for a definite purpose. To recall for a moment the distinction
expounded in Part ii. chap. ii., the gathering must be a קָהָל,
not simply an עֵדָה, an "ecclesia," not merely a "cœtus." The
disciples must be "gathered together in My name" (συνηγ-
μένοι εἰς τὸ ἐμὸν ὄνομα), with express reference to My name,
trusting in it, and all that it implies for the ends of their
present meeting, whether it be for worship and edification, for
counsel, or for discipline in the Church. The disciples meet

as disciples, looking unto Jesus, trusting in Him as their Lord
and Saviour, owning in word and deed all that Peter's confession said, that this is indeed the Christ, the Son of the
living God. His name is the token and bond of union
between them as they meet thus together. His name makes
His Church. It is the attractive power of that name which
has drawn these disciples out of the world and brought
them into Christ's ἐκκλησία, the fellowship of those called,
and chosen, and faithful to Him. His name, revealed to them
as to Peter, not by flesh and blood merely, but by His Father
in heaven, has brought them into one and keeps them so.
They are the called and kept of Jesus Christ. His name is
the reason of this their present meeting, and the secret of
the solemnity and power which they feel breathing in it.
" For where two or three are gathered together in Christ's
name, there He is in the midst of them."

" These great words of our Lord," Dr. Dale says well,
" are no less true in our days than they were in the days
of the apostles. There is no limitation to suggest that they
were intended as a promise of exceptional honour and
blessedness to the Christians of the first century. Indeed
they are not a promise at all, but the revelation of a fact.
Christian men are so related to each other as well as to
Christ, that when they are ' gathered together in His name,'
He is ' in the midst of them.' They find Him when they
find each other." [1]

This explains the strange and at first sight startling authority ascribed by our Lord to the decisions of the Church
in this passage and some others. The power entrusted to
the disciples in their Church capacity is just because of and
in proportion to their loyalty to Christ Himself. They are
met as one with Him, gathered together in and unto His
name, pleading it in prayer.[2] Christ Himself is present with

---

[1] Dale, *Manual of Congregational Principles*, London 1884, p. 17. See the
whole of Dr. Dale's able and impressive treatment of this point, pp. 10–12,
17 f., 42 f.

[2] " Quodcunque petimus adversus utilitatem salutis non petimus in nomine
Salvatoris. Et tamen Ipse Salvator est non solum quando facit quod petimus,
verum etiam quando non facit ; quoniam quod videt peti contra salutem, non
faciendo potius se exhibet Salvatorem." See the whole of this passage in which

His believing people when thus met, even when they are but two or three. He is an Actor—the chief Actor—in what is done. The decision to which they are led in the exercise of faith and prayer, under the teaching of the Spirit sent by Christ to open to them the Word and the Providence of God, is His decision. Let all remember it, both those who are called to speak and act in such circumstances, and those on whom their decision specially bears.[1]

No doubt the promise in ver. 19 applies to all united prayer by believers. The two disciples who agree in their request may not be met in a *Church* capacity in the ordinary sense of the word. They may not be actually met at all, although they have agreed together touching the thing they would ask, and perhaps the time when they are to offer up their petition. But we are bound to remember that this promise is given by Christ in close connection with rules for discipline in His Church, and with the previous promise regarding the authority of Church decisions, and that the ground of both promises is one and the same, namely, the presence of Christ Himself where disciples are "gathered together in His name," not in the same sense and to the same effect where they are separately. The smallest possible assembly of disciples has express promises and encouragements from the Master which are not given to a solitary Christian. "For where two or three are gathered together in My name, there am I in the midst of them."

Augustine shows finely what it is to ask in Christ's name, *Tract. in Joann.* lxxiii. 3, ed. Migne, p. 1823 f.

[1] " 'There am I in the midst of them' (comp. 1 Cor. v. 4), as the Mediator through whom their prayer is heard, as the Giver of that which they ask, as the Confirmer of that which comes forth from them as a testimony either publicly or privately. Christ certainly speaks here already in the same sense as in John xiv. 13 f., and we have here already a prospective glance into the period of His heavenly Omnipresence, which in Matt. xxviii. 20 He promised when about to ascend to the Father. 'This must signify a spiritual presence or nothing, but it is a stupendous expression' (Pfenninger). . . . Could there be a severer judgment pronounced against all pseudo-Catholicism than is given in this word, and again a more friendly consolation, a stronger call to make use of this power, addressed to the weak Protestantism which seeks the invisible Church elsewhere than upon earth in the assembly of the faithful, which never remains invisible, from which the testimony of the 'There am I' goes forth ever anew to the world"? Stier, *in loco.*

We have already considered some of the Old Testament promises regarding the tabernacle, the tent of meeting, the house of God, the " place where His name was recorded," the Lord Himself being for a sanctuary to the exiles in all countries whither they came while the temple lay in ruins.[1] These promises received a fuller meaning now in this great utterance of Christ concerning His Church. Not in Jerusalem only, or in the temple henceforth, would the true worshippers fully realize their access to the Father.[2] " In every place where I record My name," God said of old to Israel, " I will come unto you, and I will bless you." [3] It was now revealed to the true Israel where that name was recorded in truth, even in every place where two or three of Christ's disciples should be gathered together in His name, the name of "the Christ, the Son of the living God." [4]

These weighty and pregnant utterances of our Lord, which we have now briefly considered, form, as has been well said, "the Magna Charta of His Church." [5] They set before us the great central facts concerning Himself, His work on earth, and His relations to God and men, on which the Church of Christ is built, and the great principles to be applied and acted on by the Church, through its office-bearers and members, in all the varying circumstances and emergencies of its history on earth. Let us now place alongside of these utterances another saying of our Lord's which has been very generally recognised as having a close relationship to them. It was addressed to the disciples in Jerusalem on the evening

---

[1] See above, pp. 79–85.

[2] " Wie könnte es auch anders sein," says Beyschlag, speaking of the powers of government and discipline entrusted to the Church, " da in dem ' mitten unter ihnen' des erhöhten Christus das Ideal des alten Bundes, das wahrhaftige und nicht mehr bloss symbolische Wohnungmachen Jehovah's in seinem Volke erfüllt ist, also der Geist des Herrn ausgegossen über alles Fleisch und Beide, Klein und Gross, von Gott gelehrt, die ganze Gemeinde ein Königreich von Priestern, da somit hier alle die Unterschiede principiell wegfallen, welche im alten Bunde zwischen Priestern und Volk, zwischen Propheten und Laien bestanden ?" *Christl. Gemeindeverf. im Zeitalter des N. T.*, S. 14.

[3] Ex. xx. 24.

[4] Comp. Weiss, *Biblical Theol. of N. T.*, E. Tr. i. p. 142 : " The Messianic Church."

[5] Beyschlag, S. 13.

of the day of the Resurrection, when for the first time Christ met with them as a company after He had risen from the dead.

3rd. " Jesus therefore said to them again, Peace be unto you : as the Father hath sent Me, even so send I you. And when He had said this, He breathed on them, and saith unto them, Receive ye the Holy Ghost. Whose soever sins ye forgive, they are forgiven unto them ; whose soever sins ye retain, they are retained," John xx. 21-23.[1]

Do these words convey the same authority as is implied in the power of binding and loosing, spoken of in the two passages in Matthew already considered ? They have been held to do so by many most competent interpreters of Scripture;[2] but on a careful examination of the three passages in question I find myself unable to adopt that view, at least in its full extent. It seems to me that, while all the three are related to each other, and throw light upon each other respectively, there is yet a distinct difference between the first two and the third, both as regards the parties primarily addressed by our Lord and the nature of the power conferred upon them.

The power to bind and to loose, as we saw, was given first of all to Peter, as representing the rest of the apostles in his faith and confession ; and then to all the apostles, as representing the Church or company of believers, and acting with it, in connection especially with the course to be adopted in dealing with offences arising within the Christian fellowship. The gift of power to bind and to loose was confirmatory and explanatory of the power of the keys, the power of a steward or overseer in the master's house. It meant a right to declare with authority in the Master's name the conditions of entrance and the rules of the household, to declare what was lawful for its members and what forbidden, what was and what was not compatible with a man's remaining within the

---

[1] With respect to the authenticity and historicity of the Fourth Gospel, see Dr. Salmon's masterly discussion of " the Johannine Books," *Introduction to the N. T.*, Lond. 1885, pp. 249-365 ; also Westcott, *St. John's Gospel*, Lond. 1882, pp. v.-lxxxvii.

[2] Among others, by Chrysostom, Theophylact, Luther, Calvin, Beza, Neander, Bleek, Olshausen, Jul. Müller, Bannerman (*Church of Christ*, ii. pp. 190 ff.).

house in full enjoyment of its privileges.   More than this, it seems to me, we are not warranted in saying that the words directly convey.[1]

But the connection of this with yet higher and deeper questions is very close.   From the essential nature of Christ's Church as a fellowship of believers in Him, as "the Christ the Son of the living God," of men trusting in Him as a Divine Saviour from sin in all its effects and consequences, this power of binding and loosing has to do with sins, with spiritual offences, sins against the brethren and against the laws which the Master of the house has given in the name of God, His Father in heaven.   It is conferred in direct and express connection with the rules for dealing with such sins within the Church (ἐὰν ἁμαρτήσῃ ὁ ἀδελφός σου); and one great aim in the exercise of this power is moral and spiritual restoration.   The object in view is not merely to keep the communion of the Church pure by casting out of it, if need be, in the last resort, those who in spirit and conduct have proved themselves alien from it, but especially, if possible, by brotherly yet authoritative admonition, to "gain" the erring brother,—either at the time when he is thus dealt with, or at a calmer hour after some experience of what it is to be shut out from privilege,—to win him back again for righteousness and the fellowship of Christ, so that the Church may gladly use the power of the keys for his restoration to brotherly communion, for "loosing" instead of "binding."

The question then naturally arises at once : What, in such cases, of the deepest effects of sin ?   The offending brother, on his hearing the Church, may be restored by the power of the keys to outward fellowship with the brethren against

---

[1] Beyschlag sums up their meaning well : "Es bedeutet nicht, wie früher in willkürlicher Combination mit Joh. xx. 23, und ohne hinreichende philologische Begründung angenommen ward, das Vergeben oder Behalten der Sünden, sondern nach einem unbestreitbaren Sprachgebrauch der sich aus den Rabbinen vielfach belegen lässt, das religiös - sittliche Verwehren oder Gestatten, bei den Jüngern Jesu also das Auslegen und Anwenden des Evangeliums in Bezug auf das Christlich-Zulässige oder Unzulässige in Lehre und Leben, eine Befugniss die—auch Matt. xvi. 19, mit dem Bauen der Kirche in Zusammenhang gesetzt —jedenfalls Alles in sich schliesst, oder im Gefolge hat, was man unter gesetz-gebender, ordnender Kirchengewalt begreifen kann," S. 13.

whom he had sinned. They have forgiven him, and gladly show it in their whole attitude and conduct towards him. All the more,—if he is at heart a true brother, and his repentance genuine,—he finds it hard to forgive himself, or to believe that God has forgiven him. What of the *real* forgiveness, the forgiveness he needs most, from the Lord "the Son of Man who" alone "hath power on earth to forgive sins"?[1] He is no more to be seen and heard on earth, saying,—and giving visible tokens of His right and power to say it: "Son, be of good courage. Thy sins are forgiven.thee, go in peace." Oh that I knew where I might find Him as of old, that I might hear His voice speaking so to me!

Turn now to the words in the twentieth chapter of John. The scene is in Jerusalem, in "the place where the disciples were," with "the doors shut for fear of the Jews," probably "the Lord's guest-chamber," the "large upper room furnished" (τὸ κατάλυμά Μου, ἀνώγεον μέγα ἐστρωμένον), in which Christ kept the last passover and instituted the Lord's Supper.[2] The time is the evening of the day of the resurrection. "The disciples" were gathered together, the general company of believers in Jerusalem, "the eleven, and they that were with them," as Luke expressly tells us in his description of the same scene.[3] Thomas, indeed, was absent, but otherwise the apostolic college—"the eleven" now, as formerly they had been "the twelve"—was fully assembled with the rest of their fellow-disciples in Jerusalem. The tidings of the resurrection have already been brought "to the eleven and all the rest" by the women, by Peter, and by the two from Emmaus.[4]

The members of that little company are gathered together in the name of "the Christ, the Son of the living God." Their hearts are filled with a new and wonderful hope, the meaning of which they can scarcely yet realize. Their faith is just

---

[1] Mark ii. 5–12.

[2] Comp. Mark xiv. 14 f.; John xx. 19, 26; Acts i. 13: τὸ ὑπερῷον οὗ ἦσαν καταμένοντες.

[3] εὗρον ἠθροισμένους τοὺς ἕνδεκα καὶ τοὺς σὺν αὐτοῖς, Luke xxiv. 33. Compare Paul's expression, "He appeared to Cephas, then to the twelve, then to James, then to all the apostles," 1 Cor. xv. 5–7. To Paul they had never been "the eleven."

[4] Luke xxiv. 9, 34 f.

grasping the fact that Jesus has indeed been " declared to be
the Christ, the Son of God with power, by the resurrection from
the dead." [1] He had been seen, not only by the women, but
" He has appeared to Cephas." *Peter* could not be mistaken.
The eager greeting from all sides to Cleophas and his companion before they could tell their tidings, was, " The Lord is
risen indeed, and hath appeared to Simon." [2]

Christ's disciples are gathered together in His name, and,
lo, according to His promise, " He is in the midst of them."
While they thus speak, confessing Christ risen, their eyes are
opened to see Himself standing in the midst. They see the
Lord, and are filled with joy as they realize, beyond all possibility of doubt, that it is indeed He Himself.

Twice over He speaks : " Peace be unto you," taking up again
His last words to the eleven, spoken probably in that very
room before He went out to the garden and the cross; [3] first,
fully establishing the personal faith of His disciples in Him
as the crucified and risen Saviour; and secondly, fitting them
for service in His name, and as His witnesses on earth.[4]

Both times the words are spoken without the slightest
limitation. They are evidently addressed, not to the ten
merely, but to " them that were with them," to all the disciples
present. " And when He had said this, He breathed on them,
and saith unto them, Receive ye the Holy Ghost (λάβετε
πνεῦμα ἅγιον)."

The absence of the Article has often been noted here. It
shows, as in like cases, that the reference is not to the Personal
Spirit of God Himself, but to a gift or special manifestation of
the Holy Spirit.[5] The disciples in the upper room received
from the risen Lord a breath of that quickening Spirit which

---

[1] Rom. i. 1.   [2] Luke xxiv. 34-36.   [3] John xiv. 27.

[4] John xx. 19 f., 21-23, " Il invite ses disciples à ouvrir leur cœur à la paix
de la réconciliation qu'il leur apporte en ressuscitant. 'Etant venu,' dit Paul
(Eph. ii. 17), 'il a annoncé la paix.' . . . Ce n'est plus seulement comme à des
croyants que Jésus veut leur donner la paix ; c'est en vue de leur vocation
future : Ce message de la réconciliation que Jésus leur apporte ils auront la
tâche de le prêcher au monde." Godet, *Evangile de Saint Jean*, 3me ed.
iii. p. 642 f.

[5] So, *e.g.*, in John vii. 39 : " οὔπω γὰρ ἦν πνεῦμα. For such a gift or outpouring of the Spirit was not yet, because Jesus was not yet glorified." See Westcott, *Gospel according to St. John*, Lond. 1882, pp. 123-295. Comp. John

dwelt in Him without measure. It was an earnest of, and
preparation for, the further gift of the Spirit at Pentecost,
which, like this one, was bestowed, not on the apostles only,
but on the whole company of the disciples gathered together
with one accord in one place. The first gift answers, as Godet
points out, to "the power of Christ's resurrection," the second
to "the power of His ascension." [1]

In connection with this first gift of the Spirit from the
risen Saviour two others were bestowed, and a promise already
given [2] was repeated, and the time of its fulfilment specified.
Christ gave His disciples understanding of the Scriptures in
reference especially to His sufferings, death, and resurrection,
and the fruits of His work for the world. He gave them
power to forgive and to retain sins, and He renewed the promise of the Advent of the Holy Ghost, bidding His followers
tarry for it in Jerusalem. "Then opened He their mind, that
they might understand the Scriptures, and He said unto them,
Thus it is written, that the Christ should suffer and rise
again from the dead the third day; and that repentance and
remission of sins should be preached in His name unto all the
nations, beginning from Jerusalem. Ye are witnesses of these
things. And behold, I send forth the promise of my Father
upon you; but tarry ye in the city until ye be clothed with
power from on high." [3] It was in connection with the first

---

i. 33 ; Acts viii. 15–19, of the gifts of the Spirit at Samaria ; xix. 2–6, Paul's
question to the disciples at Ephesus : *εἰ πνεῦμα ἅγιον ἐλάβετε πιστεύσαντες*, Did
ye receive any gift of the Holy Ghost when ye believed? literally, Did ye take
any gift? Canon Westcott notes, in reference to our Lord's use of the term in
John xx. 22, "that the choice of word seems to mark the personal action of man
in this reception. He is not wholly passive even in relation to the Divine gift."
The thought is suggestive from a practical point of view. Compare John
xii. 48 : "He that rejecteth Me, and *taketh not* My words (*μὴ λαμβάνων τὰ
ῥήματά μου*), hath One that judgeth him."

[1] "Cette expression (*λάβετε*) suppose une communication actuelle. Il ne
s'agit ici ni d'une simple promesse, ni de la pleine effusion de l'Esprit. Elevé
lui-même à un degré de vie supérieur, Jésus les élève, autant qu'il le peut faire,
à sa position nouvelle. Il les associe à son état de ressuscité comme plus tard
par la Pentecôte il les fera participer à son état de glorifié. . . . Cette communication préparatoire devra leur faire comprendre quand le vent de l'Esprit
soufflera que ce vent n'est autre que le souffle personnel de leur invisible Maître,"
iii. p. 644 f.

[2] John xiv. 16 f., 26 ; xv. 26 ; xvi. 7–15.   [3] Luke xxiv. 45–49.

or Paschal gift of the Spirit, and the subsequent opening of the mind of the disciples to understand the Scripture teaching as to the work of Christ and its results, and in view also of the second or Pentecostal gift of the Holy Ghost, soon to be bestowed, that the power or authority was also granted: " Whose soever sins ye forgive, they are forgiven unto them; whose soever sins ye retain, they are retained" (ἄν τινων ἀφῆτε τὰς ἁμαρτίας, ἀφίενται αὐτοῖς· ἄν τινων κρατῆτε κεκράτηνται).

The purport of these words cannot be better expressed than by Canon Westcott in his exposition of the passage. There is no stress laid, as he points out, on the " *ye* " in " ye forgive," " ye retain." " The pronouns in this case are unemphatic. The main thought which the words convey is that of the reality of the power of absolution from sin granted to the Church, and not of the particular organization through which the power is administered. There is nothing in the context, as has been seen, to show that the gift was confined to any particular group (as the apostles) among the whole company present. The commission, therefore, must be regarded properly as the commission of the Christian society, and not as that of the Christian ministry (comp. Matt. v. 13, 14). The great mystery of the world, absolutely insoluble by thought, is that of sin; the mission of Christ was to bring salvation from sin; and the work of His Church is to apply to all that which He has gained. Christ risen was Himself the sign of the completed overthrow of death, the end of sin, and the impartment of His Life necessarily carried with it the fruit of His conquest. Thus the promise is in one sense an interpretation of the gift. The gift of the Holy Spirit finds its application in the communication or with-holding of the powers of the new Life.

" The promise, as being made not to one but to the society, carries with it of necessity, though this is not distinctly expressed, the character of perpetuity; the society never dies (comp. ver. 21). In this respect the promise differs essentially from that to St. Peter (Matt. xvi. 18 f., see note), which was distinctly personal. And the scope of the promise differs from that formerly given to the society

(Matt. xviii. 18 f., see note), which concerns the enactment
of ordinances, and not the administration of that which is
purely spiritual.   At the same time this promise carries
that forward to a higher region.   As that promise gave the
power of laying down the terms of fellowship, so this gives
a living and abiding power to declare the fact, and the
conditions of forgiveness.   The conditions, as interpreted by
the apostolic practice, no less than by the circumstances of
the case, refer to character (comp. Luke xxiv. 47).   The gift,
and the refusal of the gift, are regarded in relation to
classes, and not in relation to individuals.   The use of the
plural appears in some degree to indicate this ($\H{a}\nu$ $\tau\iota\nu\omega\nu$,
$a\mathring{v}\tau o\hat{\iota}\varsigma$) ; and still more the necessity of giving to 'retain'
an application corresponding to that of 'remit.'   It is
impossible to contemplate an absolute individual exercise
of the power of 'retaining;' so far it is contrary to the
scope of the passage to seek in it a direct authority for the
absolute individual exercise of the 'remitting.'   At the same
time the exercise of the power must be placed in the closest
connection with the faculty of spiritual discernment, consequent
upon the gift of the Holy Spirit.   Comp. 1 John xi. 18 ff." [1]

We learn, therefore, from this passage that the treasure of
the Gospel of the grace of God, the good tidings of the

---

[1] Westcott, *Gospel of St. John*, p. 295.   Jul. Müller, in his elaborate discussion of this passage (*Dogm. Abhandl.* S. 512 f., 523–529), makes the power
of forgiving and retaining sins precisely equivalent to that of binding and
loosing, and holds that it was given to the apostles as such.   He fails to note
the facts brought out so well by Canon Westcott, that the declaration in John
xx. 23 is made to the company of disciples as a whole, not to "the eleven"
as distinct from the rest, and that the reference is to classes, not to individuals.
Müller comes, however, to the right conclusion on the general question, although
his premises, through the mistakes indicated, are weaker than they need have
been.   "Indem Christus das Recht welches er, Matt. xvi. 19, dem Petrus als
Repräsentanten der Apostel, John xx. 23, unmittelbar den Aposteln [?] ertheilt,
Matt. xviii. 18, zunächst auch den Aposteln, aber mit deutlicher Hinweisung
auf die ἐκκλησία ubergiebt, lässt er uns erkennen wen wir nach dem Hingange
der Apostel als den eigentlichen Inhaber dieses Rechtes, d. h. der Schlüsselgewalt anzusehen haben,—die Kirche.   Also berechtigte Erben des apostolischen
Rechtes sind nicht die von den Presbytern verschiedenen und ihnen vorgesetz-
ten Bischöfe als Nachfolger der Apostel, wie die Römische Kirche annimmt :
denn dergleichen Bischöfe hat die unmittelbar nachapostolische Kirche nicht
gehabt, aber auch nicht die Presbytern ; denn diese bestanden schon neben

forgiveness of sins for all who repent and believe in the name of the Christ, the Son of the living God, as revealed in His life, and death, and resurrection, is entrusted by our Lord Himself to the keeping of His Church as a whole, to the Christian society as such, the company of those who themselves profess to have received the Gospel. They are to have the power of declaring, with authority to others, in Christ's name, the conditions and the reality of the forgiveness of sins which they have first learned to know for themselves in living personal experience. They are to be "His witnesses of these things both in Jerusalem and in all Judæa and Samaria, and unto the uttermost part of the earth." And for these ends they are to "receive power when the Holy Ghost is come upon them." [1]

It confirms the interpretation of John xx. 23, now given, to observe that it is on the heart and conscience of the Church as a whole that the burden and responsibility of our Lord's great commission are laid. " All authority hath been given unto Me in heaven and on earth. Go ye, therefore, and make disciples of all the nations, baptizing them into the name of the Father, and of the Son, and of the Holy Ghost; teaching them to observe all things whatsoever I commanded you: and, lo, I am with you alway, even unto the end of the world." [2]

den Aposteln, ohne dass wir eine Spur haben dass sie an der Schlüsselgewalt auf eigenthumliche Weise Theil genommen ; dass aber auf sie von den Aposteln diese Gewalt ubergegangen dafür fehlt es uns gänzlich an urkundlichen Zeugniss ; sondern die Gemeinschaft derer die an Christum glauben," S. 527 f. Comp. Ritschl, *Christl. Lehre v. der Rechtf. u. Versöhnung*, ii. S. 486.

[1] Luke xxiv. 48 ; Acts i. 8. "Christendom," Luther wrote in 1528, in words which, like many of his utterances in a great crisis, were "half battles," "is not only among the Romish Churches or under the Pope, but in all the world. Christendom is scattered abroad under the Pope, among the Turks, Persians, and Tartars, and in every place in the body. But in the spirit it is gathered together in one faith and one Gospel, under one Head, who is Jesus Christ. . . . In this Christendom, wherever it is, there is forgiveness of sins ; it is a kingdom of grace and of the true absolution (des rechten Ablass). And out of this Christendom there is no salvation nor forgiveness of sins, but eternal death and condemnation ; ay, although there may be great show of holiness and many good works, yet all is lost notwithstanding (so ists doch alles verloren)." *Bekenntniss vom Abendmahl Christi, Werke* (Erlanger Ausg.), xxx. S. 369.

[2] Matt. xxviii. 18–20.

"The eleven," indeed, stand out in this passage with special prominence (ver. 16), as leading the movement into Galilee to meet the Lord there in "the mountain where He had appointed them." But the meeting itself was in all likelihood the one referred to by Paul as consisting of "upwards of five hundred brethren at once." [1] This explains the fact mentioned by Matthew, that at the interview in the mountain in Galilee "some doubted" (οἱ δὲ ἐδίστασαν).[2] We cannot suppose that such doubts existed at this stage in the minds of the eleven, although they might very naturally arise in the case of some individuals in so large a gathering of the disciples generally. The "them" in ver. 18 of Matthew's narrative must therefore be held to include all the disciples present at the appointed meeting in Galilee,[3] not merely the eleven, although no doubt with special reference to them from their representative and official position.

Moreover, this interpretation alone corresponds with what is said in the parallel passages in the other three Gospels. We have seen already that it was to the disciples generally that the words were spoken: "As My Father sent Me, even so send I you." The scene referred to in Mark xvi. 14, when the Lord "was manifested unto the eleven themselves as they sat at meat," is evidently to be identified with that in Luke xxiv. 37–43. It is in connection with that scene, both in the second and third Gospels, that the world-wide commission is recorded as given to the disciples then assembled.[4] But these, we are expressly told, were "the eleven, and they that were with them," as well as Cleophas and his unnamed associate, that is to say, the general company of the disciples.[5] These were bidden to tarry at Jerusalem until they should be clothed with power from on high by

---

[1] 1 Cor. xv. 6.　　　　　　　　　　　　　　[2] Matt. xxviii. 17.

[3] The knowledge of this meeting having been appointed was not confined to the eleven. The angel at the sepulchre said to the women : "Fear not ye, for I know that ye seek Jesus. . . . Go quickly and tell His disciples, He is risen from the dead, and, lo, He goeth before you into Galilee ; there shall ye see Him ; lo, I have told you," Matt. xxviii. 5 ff. Comp. ver. 10 and Mark xvi. 7.

[4] Mark xvi. 14-18 ; Luke xxiv. 33-49.　　　　　　　[5] Luke xxiv. 33.

receiving "the promise of the Father."   They tarried accordingly, being " a multitude of persons gathered together, about
a hundred and twenty." [1]   To them, not to the apostles
merely, the Holy Spirit is given at Pentecost.   " And they
went forth," the second evangelist says,—after recording that
" the Lord Jesus after He had spoken unto them " (giving the
great commission) " was received up into heaven,"—" They
went forth and preached everywhere, the Lord working with
them, and confirming the word by the signs that followed." [2]
It was certainly not " the eleven " alone who did this, and
received such tokens of the Lord's presence and blessing in
their work, as a glance at the narrative of the Acts and at
the apostolic epistles shows.   They who thus fulfilled the
Lord's commission were just those to whom it was first given,
or to whom it was handed on in the succession of faith.[3]

Many inferences might be drawn from our Lord's teaching
regarding His Church in the three pregnant passages which
we have now considered.   I shall refer here to one of these
only.

" Whose soever sins ye forgive, they are forgiven unto them ;
whose soever sins ye retain, they are retained."   It follows
surely that if this highest power is entrusted to the Church
or fellowship of believers as a whole, no lower ones essential
for the existence or well-being of that fellowship on earth can,
in case of need, be wanting to it.   The powers, for instance,
of appointment to office in the Church, and of administration
of ordinances, must in the last resort have their seat in the
Church or company of believers, as well as the power to
forgive and to retain sins.   The ordinary exercise of these
powers of appointment and administration may, not only for
the sake of order but by the will of Christ, be vested in the
office-bearers where such exist.   Yet, in case of need, it
follows by " good and necessary consequence," from our
Lord's gift and promise to His Church on the evening of His
Resurrection, that the Church itself, the " congregation of
faithful men," is fully entitled to recognise the special gifts

---

[1] Acts i. 15.   [2] Mark xvi. 19 f.
[3] Acts ii. 1-4, 17 f. ; iv. 31 ; vi. 8-10 ; viii. 4 f. ; xi. 19-21, etc. ; 1 Cor.
i. 4-7 ; Phil. i. 14-18 ; Col. i. 5 f. ; 1 Thess. i. 8 ; Heb. ii. 3 f.

and grace of Christ in some of its ordinary members, and to call and set them apart to office among their brethren.

The same conclusion may be drawn from our Lord's teaching in the two passages in the first Gospel, which have been under consideration. It is to the Church as such that the promise of perpetuity refers, not to the office-bearers. It follows, therefore, that the Church must have within herself at all times, by Christ's gift, power to do everything that is needful to perpetuate herself in strength and efficiency for her work and warfare on earth amidst all the opposition of the gates of Hades. It is to the Church as such—although no doubt with special reference to the work of discipline, in which, if it is to be done efficiently, the Church must speak and act to a great extent through representatives—that the promise is given of her Lord's unfailing presence, even although the gathering in His name be the smallest possible. Where Christ is in the midst of His disciples, and where they are truly gathered together in His name, what can be wanting that is really needed for the life and the successful working of His Church in this world ?

"The conclusion stands fast," as an eminent German theologian expresses it, "because Christ has reserved the government in His Church for Himself (Matt. xviii. 20 ; xxiii. 10), therefore the Church, which is spiritually and therefore freely [1] ruled by Him, is as such, in the last resort, the only lawful visible depositary of Church power,—of course on the basis of His name (Matt. xviii. 20), that is to say, His historic revelation of Himself, which must harmonize with the continuous revelation of Himself by the Spirit, in such a way that the two mutually attest each other. It was doubtless foreseen by Him that this self-government of the Church in His name and Spirit would, in accordance with the Divinely ordered nature of things and the diversity of gifts, seek and shape out its own forms.[2] But He who was not as

---

[1] On the principles and in the spirit of freedom (freiheitlich).

[2] What provision had been made for guidance in this field also has been shown above (Part II. chap. iii. ; Part III. chap. iii.) ; how it was used in the apostolic Church we shall see at a later stage (Part V. chap. iii. ; Part VI. chap. iv.).

Moses a giver of laws, but the Giver of life and of the Spirit, did not prescribe these forms beforehand, but—apart from the institutions of Baptism and the Lord's Supper, which are more than mere forms of Church life, which are the enduring memorials of His historic life, and pledges of His glorified working—confined Himself to the simple indication of general principles, and entrusted the application of these to the Spirit whom He was to send." [1]

In yet weightier and older words: "The visible Church, which is catholic, or universal, under the Gospel, consists of all those throughout the world that profess the true religion, together with their children. . . . *Unto this catholic visible Church Christ hath given the ministry, oracles, and ordinances of God* for the gathering and perfecting of the saints in this life to the end of the world, and doth by His own presence and Spirit, according to His promise, make them effectual thereunto." [2]

Besides these three great and outstanding passages in our Lord's teaching concerning His Church, there is much else in what He said which bears directly or indirectly upon our subject. It is impossible here even to indicate all the points to which reference might be made in a more exhaustive survey of the ground. The following passages, however, may be touched upon.

4th. Passages bearing on the unity of the Church in Christ's conception.

The nature and ground of this unity, and how it is manifested in diversity of time, place, and circumstances, are indicated, as already noted, in the two great fundamental passages for our Lord's doctrine of the Church which we have in the sixteenth and eighteenth chapters of Matthew's Gospel. In these passages we have plainly two aspects of the Church set before us, a catholic and a local one. There is first of all the Church which Christ will build upon the rock, against

---

[1] Beyschlag, *Christl. Gemeindeverf. im Zeitalter des N. T.*, S. 21 f.

[2] Westminster Conf. of Faith, xxv. 2 and 3. Comp. Bannerman, *Church of Christ*, i. pp. 262-275 : "The Primary Subject of Church Power;" Essay on "Sacerdotal Absolution," in Princeton Essays, Lond. 1846, i. pp. 352-366.

which the gates of Hades shall never prevail. It is clear that that promise is given to no local visible society existing at any particular time, but to the whole body of those who are chosen, and called, and faithful throughout the world and in all time. There is also, secondly, the local society in which that Church catholic takes shape and becomes accessible to the individual believer living at any given time and place. It is to it that the disciple who feels that a trespass has been committed against him by a brother, by one who is by profession a member of the same Christian fellowship, is to bring his case, after certain preliminary steps prescribed by Christ.

We have these two aspects of the Church set before us, the catholic and the local; but it is one Church in the mind and heart of the Lord Himself. It should be so also in the thoughts and feelings of His disciples. Wherein its unity consists is brought out by Him in many a deep saying and similitude. To some of these let us now turn.

1. In the ninth chapter of the fourth Gospel we read that Christ had healed one born blind at Jerusalem on the Sabbath day. The man thus healed is brought " to the Pharisees," met possibly, as it seems to have been on the Sabbath, in one of the synagogue courts, or as some commentators hold, in the great Sanhedrin itself,[1] to answer regarding the breach of the Sabbath alleged to have been committed in connection with his cure. He is examined as to the facts and as to his own view of the claims of Jesus, and is then remanded. His parents are called before the court and examined also. They know that the dominant party among the Jewish rulers have agreed among themselves that any one who confesses Jesus to be the Messiah shall be put out of the synagogue or excommunicated.[2] The father and mother naturally shrink from

---

[1] So Tholuck, Lange, Luthardt, and Brown. Certainly John refers to the Sanhedrin more than once in a general way as "the Pharisees," from their being the dominant party in it, and identified with it in the popular mind (vii. 47; xi. 46). Other exegetes, as Lücke and Westcott, hold that the reference in the text is to one of the two lesser Sanhedrin mentioned above, p. 153.

[2] ἤδη γὰρ συνετίθειντο οἱ Ἰουδαῖοι ἵνα ἐάν τις αὐτὸν ὁμολογήσῃ Χριστὸν ἀποσυνάγωγος γίνηται, John ix. 22.

exposing themselves to such a penalty, and while attesting
the fact that their son had been blind from his birth, decline
to give any opinion as to the manner or author of his cure.

The man himself is recalled and more closely dealt
with. The judges upbraid him with unfaithfulness to Moses,
and with being " a disciple of that man " (σὺ εἶ μαθητὴς
ἐκείνου). He answers boldly, adhering to what he had said
before, and declaring his faith in Jesus as One who was
" from God " (παρὰ θεοῦ), and had done what no sinner
could do. The result is that the accused is cast out of
the synagogue, and thereby authoritatively cut off from the
fellowship of the Jewish Church by its highest representatives, the elders of Israel acting as such.[1] But now another
voice interposes, " speaking with authority, but not as the
scribes ; " and another fellowship opens to the outcast : " Jesus
heard that they had cast him out, and finding him, He said,
Dost thou believe on the Son of God ? He answered and
said, And who is He, Lord, that I may believe on Him ?
Jesus said unto him, Thou hast both seen Him, and He it
is that speaketh with thee. And he said, Lord, I believe ;
and he worshipped Him." [2]

---

[1] There seems no reason to doubt that this " casting out " involved the excommunication which the Pharisees had before agreed (ver. 22 ; comp. xii. 42)
should be the penalty of such a confession as the man had now virtually made.
That he was of humble origin and unbefriended would make them have the less
hesitation in carrying out the resolution in his case, and doing so promptly and
roughly, suiting the action to the sentence. " Das aüssere Hinausstoszen des
Mannes (aus dem Gerichtsaal) war ohne Zweifel hier symbolisch, eine Bekräfti-
gung der Exkommunikation, des Ausstoszens (נָדַח, נֶרְדַּח = ἐκβάλλειν ἔξω, c. vi. 37 ;
xii. 31), welches voranging." Lange (comp. Luke vi. 22 ; 3 John 10). Godet
and Westcott hold that summary ejection from the place where the Pharisees
held their meeting is all that is meant, chiefly, as it appears, on the ground
that " such a body was not competent to pronounce a sentence of excommunication." But if the meeting was one of the Sanhedrin or even of the eldership of
a leading synagogue, this ground of objection is removed. See note on last
page. It is to be remembered also that it had been already resolved that such
an offence should be visited with the sentence of excommunication (ver. 22).
This resolution·had been arrived at apparently by the competent authority,
possibly in connection with the proceedings of the Sanhedrin recorded in chap.
vii. 32–53. The fact, at all events, was generally known and accepted by the
people as final. It only remained to carry out the agreement whenever a suitable instance arose. Comp. Trench, *Miracles*, 2nd ed. p. 305 f.

[2] John ix. 35–38. " He had neither pardon to ask nor petition to present.

It was in these circumstances that the words recorded in the tenth chapter of John were spoken. Over against these rulers of the people and elders of Israel, who were proving themselves to be blind to the highest duties of their position, who acted as hireling and evil shepherds, driving out of the fold such as this poor man in whom so much true faith and loyalty to truth were found, Christ sets Himself and His sheep and flock. He is the Door. By Him both shepherds —if they are to be true shepherds under Him—and sheep must enter into the fold. Round Him henceforth the true Israel are to gather in faith and obedience—whether hitherto, like this new follower, within the ancient fold of Israel, or beyond it, like those of whom He speaks in ver. 16. He Himself is the Good Shepherd (ὁ ποιμὴν ὁ καλός);[1] and His people are the sheep for whom He lays down His life and takes it again, whom He gathers one by one to Himself and to each other, so that, in accordance with Ezekiel's prediction, "they shall become one flock, with one Shepherd" (γενήσονται μία ποίμνη, εἷς Ποιμήν).[2]

Our Lord does not say here, it is to be observed, "they shall become one *fold*" (αὐλή). Rather, as with earthly shepherds when the flock is large, there may be many separate folds, and yet but one flock.[3] The eye of the

His kneeling, therefore, could only denote the homage of adoration, or at least of deep religious reverence. The word προσκυνεῖν, to prostrate oneself, is always applied in John to Divine worship" (iv. 20 ff. ; xii. 20). Godet, iii. p. 149.

[1] "Christ is not only the true Shepherd (ὁ π. ὁ ἀληθινός) who fulfils the idea of the Shepherd, but He is the good Shepherd who fulfils the idea in its attractive loveliness. The epithet implies the correspondence between the nobility of the conception and the beauty of the realization. The 'good' is not only good inwardly (ἀγαθός), but good as perceived (καλός)." Westcott, *in loco*.

[2] Ver. 16. Comp. Ezek. xxxiv. 23-31. "Dans ce passage ressort de nouveau de la manière la plus claire, l'idée de *l'unité organique* de l'ancienne et de la nouvelle alliance, idée dont Reuss et l'école de Tubingue prétendent ne pas trouver trace dans le quatrième évangile." Godet, iii. p. 164.

[3] "The translation 'fold' for 'flock' ('ovile' for 'grex ')," Canon Westcott well says, "has been most disastrous in idea and influence. The change in the original from fold (αὐλή) to flock (ποίμνη) is most striking, and reveals a new thought as to the future relations of Jew and Gentile. Elsewhere stress is laid upon their corporate union (Rom. xi. 17 ff.), and upon the admission of the Gentiles to the Holy City (Isa. ii. 3) ; but here the bond of fellowship is shown

Chief Shepherd here looks beyond the old Jewish fold and
" the lost sheep of the house of Israel," " whose own shepherds,"
as foretold in prophecy, " pitied them not," [1] to a great multitude which no man could number, scattered throughout all
the lands of heathendom, going astray like lost sheep, who
yet were His. " And other sheep I have, which are not of
this fold; them also I must lead (R. V. Margin, Κἀκεῖνα δεῖ
με ἀγαγεῖν), and they shall hear My voice, and they shall
become one flock, one Shepherd." Those " sons of peace,"
" the children of God scattered abroad" throughout the
world, for whom also Christ was to die,[2] were to hear His
voice, and follow Him whithersoever He led them. He
was to set Himself at their head as their Lord and Leader,
and in that sense first and chiefly to gather them together
into one.[3]   The unity is not that of outward organization,
but of a common spiritual relation to a common Lord and
Saviour.   It is not the external unity of the fold with its
encircling walls, but the living unity of the flock under the
one Shepherd.

2. In the fifteenth chapter of John we find the same
leading thought illustrated and enforced by Christ in a
different way.   If, as seems probable, the upper chamber in

to lie in the common relation to one Lord.   The visible connection of God with
Israel was a type and pledge of this original and universal connection. . . .
Nothing is said of one ' fold' under the new dispensation.   It may be added
that the obliteration of this essential distinction between the 'fold' and the
'flock' in many of the later Western versions of this passage indicates, as
it appears, a tendency of Roman Christianity, and has served in no small
degree to confirm and extend the claims of the Roman See."   *Gospel of St. John*,
p. 155 f.   See also " Additional Note," p. 162.

[1] Zech. xi. 5, 16 f. ; Ezek. xxxiv. 1–17 ; Jer. xxiii. 1–8.

[2] "Into whatsoever house ye shall enter, first say, Peace be to this house.
And if a son of peace be there, your peace shall rest upon him," Luke x. 5 f. ;
John xi. 52.

[3] Compare the ἀγαγεῖν of John x. 16 with the συναγαγεῖν εἰς ἓν of John xi. 52.
" La fin du verset (καί : *et ainsi* il y aura . . .) montre clairement que l'idée du
Seigneur est tout autre (than that of ' feeding,' as held by Meyer, Luthardt,
and Weiss) ; c'est celle *d'amener* ces brebis pour les joindre aux premières.   La
Vulgate traduit donc avec raison *adducere*. . . . C'est essentiellement l'œuvre
de Saint Paul, avec les travaux des missionnaires qui l'ont suivi jusqu'à nos
jours, qui décrit ce terme 'amener.'   Cette troisième similitude, annonçant l'appel
des païens, correspond ainsi à la première qui décrivait la sortie des croyants de
la synagogue."   Godet, iii. p. 178.

which He had instituted the Lord's Supper was left by Him and the eleven after the "Arise, let us go hence," with which the fourteenth chapter closes, these words must have been spoken while the little company were on their way to the garden beyond the Kidron. In that case, some vine on the terraced slopes on either side of the ravine may have suggested the image. Or if Christ led His disciples that night to Gethsemane, as some have thought, by the Courts of the Temple, the great golden vine on its gates, "which was at once the glory and the type of Israel,"[1] would afford a natural starting-point, according to our Lord's custom, for this discourse. In many a prophetic utterance the vine had been used as an emblem of the people of God in Old Testament times.[2] Its full significance is here interpreted by the Lord Himself.

Christ is the true, the ideal Vine (ἡ ἄμπ. ἡ ἀληθινή), and His disciples are the branches. Some, who are "in Him" in a sense, have but an outward and temporary connection with Him.[3] They bear no fruit, and are taken away, cast forth (ἐβλήθη ἔξω) as withered branches; "and they," whose office it is, "gather them and cast them into the fire, and they are burned."

Those disciples, on the other hand, who are in real and living union with the Lord Himself, abide in Christ, and He abides in them. There are chastenings and spiritual discipline appointed for them by the Father, even as the husbandman prunes and trains the fruit-bearing branches in the vine; but these things work, as they are designed, for good. Cleaving to the Lord, and receiving His words in faith and singleness of heart, such believers learn what to pray for and how to pray. They ask what they will and

---

[1] Westcott. Comp. Schürer, i. p. 253.

[2] Ps. lxxx. 8-14; Isa. v. 1-7; Jer. ii. 21; Ezek. xix. 10-14; Hosea x. 1.

[3] πᾶν κλῆμα ἐν ἐμοὶ μὴ φέρον καρπόν, αἴρει αὐτό, John xv. 2. "Si un exemple s'offre aux yeux de Jésus ce ne peut être que celui de Judas et de ces disciples qui avaient rompu au ch. vi. le lien qui les unissait a lui. En tout cas, il pense à l'avenir de son Eglise; il voit d'avance ces professants de l'Evangile qui tout en étant extérieurement unis à lui, n'en vivront pas moins séparés de lui intérieurement." Godet, iii. p. 423.

it is done for them.[1] They bring forth much fruit, and shall become more and more disciples of Christ indeed, lovingly owned by Him as such (καὶ γενήσεσθε ἐμοὶ μαθηταί).[2]

3. In all the Gospels, but especially in that of John, we find this great idea of the unity of the Church in Christ grounded in the idea of an election and gift of the Church by the Father to Him.

In such passages as those noted below,[3] we are led to look beyond the Church or company of believers as existing in the world at any given time, above and beyond even the vast multitude of "all those who have been, are, or shall be gathered into one in Christ" on earth, and to learn that all these separately and as a collective unity have from the beginning been chosen in Christ, and given to Him by the Father. The "calling" and the "faithfulness" of which men may take note in time, are the result of a gracious Divine "choosing" which goes back far beyond all time. And yet along with this high and mysterious truth, and in the closest connection with it, in almost every passage, it is as clearly taught that each believer has had his own separate spiritual history, his own free personal relations with the Lord Jesus, which have been different from those which have subsisted between Him and any other of His people. It is "a new name" of the Son of God that is written in

---

[1] As Godet says truly and beautifully: "Les paroles de Jésus méditées avec recueillement deviennent chez le fidèle l'aliment des saintes pensées et des pieux desseins, des célestes aspirations, et parlà la source des vraies prières. En les méditant il comprend l'œuvre de Dieu; il en mesure la profondeur et la hauteur, la longueur et la largeur, et il réclame avec ardeur l'avancement de cette œuvre, sous la forme déterminée qui répond aux besoins actuels. Une prière ainsi formée est fille du ciel; c'est la promesse de Dieu (la parole de Jésus) transformée en supplication; dans cette condition son exaucement est certain, et la promesse si absolue: ' Cela vous sera fait,' n'a plus rien qui étonne," iii. p. 428.

[2] "The dative ἐμοί is more emphatic and more tender than the genitive ἐμοῦ would have been. 'You shall belong to Me in a closer and closer bond as My own disciples.' We must always be *becoming* disciples of Christ; we are not made such once and for all." Godet, iii. p. 429.

[3] Matt. xx. 15 f.; xxii. 14; xxv. 34; Mark x. 40; xiii. 20–22, 27; Luke x. 20 f.; xii. 32; xviii. 7; John vi. 37 ff., 44; x. 16, 26–29; xv. 16, 19; xvii. 2, 6, 9, 11 f., 24; xviii. 9.

the life of each redeemed servant of His on earth, that
stands out on their foreheads in heaven, a name which no
one fully knows save only He who gives and he who receives
it. Each true disciple can say: "He loved me, and gave
Himself for me;" while all can join in the Church's united
utterance of praise and adoration: "Unto Him that loveth
us and loosed us from our sins by His blood, and made us
to be a kingdom, to be priests unto His God and Father; to
Him be the glory and the dominion for ever and ever. Amen."[1]

"All that which the Father giveth Me shall come unto
Me; and him that cometh to Me I will in no wise cast out,"
John vi. 37.

In that great unity made up of all the elect of God, all
the souls chosen in Christ and given to Him by the Father,
nothing shall be wanting in the end.

God will "accomplish the number of His elect."[2] All
who together make up the gift given from eternity by the
hand of the Father shall in the fulness of time reach the
hand of Christ; the "giving" is consummated, has its
perfect issue then. "All that which the Father giveth Me
($\pi\hat{\alpha}\nu$ $\hat{o}$ $\delta\dot{\iota}\delta\omega\sigma\dot{\iota}$ $\mu o\iota$ $\acute{o}$ $\pi\alpha\tau\acute{\eta}\rho$) shall come unto Me ($\pi\rho\grave{o}s$
$\acute{\epsilon}\mu\grave{\epsilon}$ $\acute{\eta}\xi\epsilon\iota$)." That is the blessed and final result, foreseen
and foreordained from the beginning, as regards the Church
as a whole. And then our Lord's words bid us mark how
in the case of each individual soul that result is attained
in time. The Saviour expresses it all in that simple but
most pregnant word, "Come unto Me," which on His lips
met the need of all souls on earth, from the case of
unconscious infants in their mothers' arms, to that of men
and women sunk to the lowest depths by years of sin:
"Suffer the little children to come unto Me;" "Come unto
Me, all ye that labour and are heavy laden, and I will
give you rest."[3] And for all souls, however brought, there

---

[1] Rev. ii. 17; iii. 12; xxii. 4; Gal. ii. 20; Rev. i. 5 f.

[2] Book of Common Prayer—Burial Service. Comp. Collect for All Saints'
Day, and Art. xvii.

[3] "And they brought unto Him also their babes ($\tau\grave{\alpha}$ $\beta\rho\acute{\epsilon}\phi\eta$), that He should
touch them; but when the disciples saw it, they rebuked them. But Jesus
called them ($\alpha\mathbf{\dot{\upsilon}}\tau\acute{\alpha}$ = the babes) unto Him, saying, Suffer the little children to
come unto Me, and forbid them not," Luke xviii. 15 f. ; Matt. xi. 28.

is the assurance here, "Him that cometh unto Me, I will in no wise cast out (τὸν ἐρχόμενον πρός με οὐ μὴ ἐκβάλω ἔξω);" him who is in that relation towards Me, who is in that attitude, drawn towards Me by the unknown love and the unseen hand of My Father in heaven, I will meet with more than welcome, with all blessing for time and for eternity.[1]

For this result, both in its collective and individual aspect, there is a twofold security, the gracious promise of Christ Himself, and the declared will of the Father who sent Him. "And this is the will of Him that sent Me, that of all that which He hath given Me (πᾶν ὃ δέδωκέ μοι) I should lose nothing, but should raise it up at the last day (μὴ ἀπολέσω ἐξ αὐτοῦ, ἀλλὰ ἀναστήσω αὐτό)." And then again our Lord sets the same truth before us on its personal and individual side: "For this is the will of My Father, that every one that beholdeth the Son and believeth on Him should have eternal life; and I will raise him (ἀναστήσω αὐτὸν Ἐγώ) at the last day."[2]

That this electing love of the Father had been revealed in the Old Testament Scriptures, and was to be recognised, not only in the grand result as regards the Church as a whole, but in the individual history of each true disciple, Christ goes on to show in the same discourse; and the truth taught received practical illustration both in the general company of the disciples and in the inner circle of the twelve. "No man can come to Me except the Father which sent Me draw him;[3]

---

[1] In the first clause of ver. 37, as Canon Westcott notes, "stress is laid upon the successful issue of the coming, the arrival (ἥξει, 'shall reach Me;' comp. Rev. iii. 3; xv. 4; xviii. 8); in the second, on the process of the coming (τὸν ἐρχόμενον, not τὸν ἐλθόντα) and the welcome."

[2] John vi. 39 f. "Christ speaks of it as a sublime certainty which men's refusals cannot frustrate; but He speaks of that certainty as taking effect only by men's voluntary advances to Him and acceptance of Him." Principal D. Brown, Comment. critical, experimental, and practical, Glasgow, p. 388.

[3] "Magna gratiæ commendatio," Augustine says on this verse, "nemo venit nisi tractus. Quem trahat et quem non trahat, quare illum trahat et illum non trahat, noli velle judicare, si non vis errare. Semel accipe et intellige. Nondum traheris? Ora ut traharis;" Tractat. in Joannis Evang. xxvi. 2.

and I will raise him up in the last day. It is written in the prophets, And they shall all be taught of God. Every one that hath heard from the Father and hath learned, cometh unto Me. . . . But there are some of you that believe not. For Jesus knew from the beginning who they were that believed not, and who it was that should betray Him. And He said, For this cause have I said unto you that no man can come unto Me except it be given unto him of the Father." [1]

"Upon this, many of His disciples went back and walked no more with Him. Jesus said, therefore, unto the twelve, Would ye also go away? Simon Peter answered Him, Lord to whom shall we go? Thou hast the words of eternal life. And we have believed, and know, that Thou art the Holy One of God. Jesus answered them, Did not I choose you the twelve (Οὐκ ἐγὼ ὑμᾶς τοὺς δώδεκα ἐξελεξάμην), and one of you is a devil? Now He spake of Judas, the son of Simon Iscariot, for he it was that should betray Him, being one of the twelve." [2]

Other sayings of our Lord in this Gospel bearing on the same subject would well repay study; [3] but we must content ourselves with a brief reference to the place which the election

---

[1] "Ergo et credere datur nobis; non enim nihil est credere. Si autem magnum aliquid est, gaude quia credidisti, sed noli extolli; quid enim habes quod non accepisti (1 Cor. iv. 7)"? *Ib.* xxvii. 7.

[2] John vi. 43–46, 64–71.

[3] See especially John x. 26–30, in connection with the passage already considered regarding the Shepherd, the sheep, and the flock. On ver. 29: "My Father which hath given them unto Me is greater than all," the R. V. notes in Margin: "Some ancient authorities read, 'That which the Father hath given unto Me is greater than all.'" This reading (ὃ δέδωκέν μοι πάντων μεῖζόν ἐστιν) is placed by Drs. Westcott and Hort in the text, with good reason, as it appears to me. As Canon Westcott remarks, "It has the most ancient authority, and is the most difficult (of the conflicting readings) and at the same time the most in accordance with the style of St. John. . . . His usage (vi. 39, 'All that which the Father hath given Me;' comp. ver. 37; xvii. 2, 'All that which Thou hast given Him') seems distinctly to point to the society of the faithful as the Father's gift; and this interpretation brings the clause into parallelism with those which have gone before." "The faithful, regarded in their unity as a complete body, are stronger than every opposing power. This is their essential character, 'and no one is able' . . . Comp. 1 John v. 4," *Gospel of John,* pp. 159, 162 f. Comp. also our Lord's great fundamental promise to His Church, that "the gates of Hades shall not prevail against it."

and vocation of His Church hold in His great High-Priestly prayer, in the seventeenth chapter of John.[1]

4. The Church in our Lord's High-Priestly prayer.

The time is the eve of the Betrayal. The eleven have passed out, as it seems, with their Master from the upper room where they had sat at meat with Him, in accordance with His "Arise, let us go hence."[2] They are on their way to Gethsemane. The Lord has spoken to them in the words recorded in the fifteenth and sixteenth chapters of John. He now turns to speak for them more than for Himself, to His Father and their Father, to His God and their God.

As to the precise place where this prayer was offered, we have no means of being certain. Canon Westcott makes an interesting suggestion on the point: " It is scarcely possible that chapters fifteen and sixteen could have been spoken in the streets of the city. It is inconceivable that chapter seventeen should have been spoken anywhere except under circumstances suited to its unapproachable solemnity. . . . One spot alone, as it seems, combines all that is required to satisfy the import of these last words, the Temple Courts. It may be true that there is nothing in the narrative which points immediately to a visit there ; but much in what is recorded gains fresh significance if regarded in connection with the seat of the old worship. The central object was the great Golden Vine,[3] from which the Lord derived the figure of His own vital relation to His people. Everything which spoke of a Divine Presence gave force to the promise of a new advocate. The warning of persecution and rejection found a commentary in the scenes with which the Temple had been associated in the last few days. Nowhere, as it seems, could the outlines of the future spiritual Church be more fitly drawn than in the sanctuary of the old Church. Nowhere, it is clear, could our High Priest more fitly offer His work and Himself and believers to the Father, than in the one place in which God had chosen to set His name.

" It may, indeed, have been not unusual for Paschal pilgrims

---

[1] John xvii. 1–3, 6, 12, 20, 26.

[2] John xiv. 31. Comp. Godet, *in loco*, iii. p. 418.

[3] Comp. Fergusson, *The Temples of the Jews*, p. 151 ff.

to visit the Temple during the night. At least it is recorded that at the Passover 'it was the custom of the priests to open the gates of the Temple at midnight ($\dot{\epsilon}\kappa$ $\mu\dot{\epsilon}\sigma\eta\varsigma$ $\nu\upsilon\kappa\tau\acute{o}\varsigma$).' [1] Such a visit, therefore, as has been supposed, is in no way improbable." [2]

This is an attractive suggestion. The chief objection to it seems to be that had the prayer been offered in the temple courts there would probably have been some reference by the Evangelist to the locality, as in other cases,—e.g. John vii. 14, 28 ; viii. 20.[3] If not in the temple courts, we may suppose the prayer to have been uttered by our Lord during a pause on the way to Gethsemane, with His disciples gathered round Him in some retired spot, perhaps just outside Jerusalem, and under the shadow of some projecting part of its walls, looking across the ravine towards the Mount of Olives, when the full splendour of the eastern heavens, lighted up by the Paschal moon, first broke upon the little company, before leaving the city behind them, they " went forth," descending the steep slope, and " crossing the winter-torrent of the Kidron " [4] to the place "where was a garden, into which He entered, and His disciples."

"These things spake Jesus ; and, lifting up His eyes to

---

[1] Josephus, *Antt.* xviii. 2. 2.

[2] Westcott, *Gospel of St. John*, p. 237. See, on the other hand, Godet, iii. p. 420 : " Rien de moins vraisemblable, me paraît il, que cette hypothèse."

[3] Godet's further objection, that the temple courts at night would not have afforded a place of sufficient retirement, does not seem valid. A pretty close examination of the ground, made some years ago at Jerusalem, both by day and night, leads me to disagree with Canon Westcott also in his statement that "the character of the descent to the Kidron and of the ground on the western side does not afford a suitable locality." It may be added that, admitting the suitableness of the associations of the temple, it was at least equally suitable that such a prayer should be offered under the open heavens. The disciples who heard it were soon to be cast out, as their Lord had warned them, from the temple and the synagogues where they had been wont to worship. But none of them could doubt henceforth that the closest and most blessed communion with God in prayer could be attained apart from consecrated buildings and temples made with hands. This prayer offered by the great High Priest in behalf of His people showed how not in Jerusalem only, or in the temple, but in all places, the true worshippers might worship the Father in spirit and in truth. See also Godet's remarks, given in next footnote but one, in reference to Christ's "lifting up His eyes to heaven" in this prayer.

[4] Ταῦτα εἰπὼν ὁ Ἰησοῦς ἐξῆλθε σὺν τοῖς μαθηταῖς αὐτοῦ πέραν τοῦ χειμάρρου τῶν Κέδρων, John xviii. 1.

heaven, He said, Father, the hour is come; glorify Thy Son, that the Son may glorify Thee: even as Thou gavest Him authority over all flesh, that whatsoever Thou hast given Him, to them He should give eternal life." [1]

Every one who has sought with any earnestness to enter into the meaning of these words, which are such as never man spake, must feel more and more how high they rise above us, how feeble and imperfect our interpretation is in comparison with what is here revealed of the mind of God in Christ.[2] We can but touch briefly on some points in one aspect of the prayer. In it, from beginning to end, the idea of the unity of the Church in its deepest and highest sense is brought out. This appears in all the three great divisions of the prayer: first, that in which our Lord refers specially to Himself and His work on earth as accomplished (vv. 1–5); secondly, that in which He prays for His first disciples in the circumstances in which they are now placed by His departure, and in view of the work given them to do in the world (vv. 6–19); and thirdly, that in which He prays for the whole fellowship of His disciples throughout the world and to the end of time, and for blessing for the world through them (vv. 20–26).

"As Thou gavest Him authority over all flesh in order that, whatsoever Thou hast given Him, to them He should give eternal life (ἵνα πᾶν ὃ δέδωκας αὐτῷ δώσῃ αὐτοῖς ζωὴν αἰώνιον)."

The authority or rightful power (ἐξουσία) over all flesh,— not Israel only, but all mankind as such,[3]—is for the sake of

---

[1] John xvii. 1 f. "Jusque-là Jésus avait contemplé les disciples en leur parlant. Elever les yeux vers le ciel, c'est un effort naturel de l'âme pour échapper à la prison de la terre, une aspiration à la contemplation du Dieu vivant, dont la gloire resplendit surtout dans la pure sérénité des cieux. Sans doute cet acte peut avoir lieu dans une chambre (Acts vii. 55); mais il se comprend mieux en plein air; comp. xi. 41; Mark vii. 34. Les mots: 'Et il dit' signalent le moment où, au travers de ciel visible son cœur a recontré la face de Dieu, et où dans le Dieu de cet univers il contemple son Père," iii. p. 476.

[2] Comp. Bruce, *Training of the Twelve*, 2nd ed. p. 437. Godet, ii. p. 514 f. "Quis non gaudeat," Bengel says, "hæc perscripta extare quæ cum Patre locutus est Jesus? Hoc caput in totâ Scripturâ est verbis facillimum, sensibus profundissimum."

[3] כֹּל בָּשָׂר. The phrase is frequent in the prophets. It denotes especially

His people whom He is sent to save. It is bestowed in
order that He should give to them eternal life. So in our
Lord's teaching elsewhere in the Gospels. "The field," in
which "the Son of Man" sows good seed, "is the world,"—
His field and His kingdom in fact as well as right in the end.
Yet not all in the world become His in the sense of being
willing subjects of the King. "In the end of the age (ἐν τῇ
συντελείᾳ τοῦ αἰῶνος) the Son of Man shall send forth His
angels, and they shall gather out of His kingdom all the
stumbling-blocks (πάντα τὰ σκάνδαλα), and them that do
iniquity, and shall cast them into the furnace of fire ; there
shall be the weeping and gnashing of teeth." "All authority
(πᾶσα ἐξουσία) is given to Me in heaven and on earth." Christ's
servants, therefore, are to go into all the world and preach the
Gospel to the whole creation, to make disciples of all the
nations. Yet some shall "disbelieve" and "be condemned." [1]

The order and connection of thought are noteworthy.
First we see the Church as a great collective unity in the
original gift of the Father to the Son (πᾶν ὃ δέδωκας αὐτῷ).
It is the unity (ἕν) spoken of in passages already considered,
in chap. x. 16 and xi. 52, and in ver. 23 of this chapter.
Then we see the several members of the Church as one by
one they receive the gift of eternal life from Christ, and so
are gathered into one in Himself, and drawn under His
teaching to know the only true God and Jesus Christ whom
He hath sent (ἵνα δώσῃ αὐτοῖς ζωὴν αἰώνιον).[2]

"I manifested Thy name unto the men whom Thou gavest
Me out of the world ; Thine they were, and Thou gavest them
Me, and they have kept Thy word." [3]

"mankind in their weakness and transitoriness as contrasted with the majesty
of God." Comp. the references given by Canon Westcott, in loco.

[1] Matt. xiii. 37–42 ; xxviii. 18 f. ; Mark xvi. 15 f. ; John iii. 16. Godet
compares Eph. i. 22 : "He gave Him to be Head over all things to the
Church ; " "c'est à dire," as he explains with characteristic point and clearness,
"comme son chef, qui est en même temps établi sur toutes choses en sa faveur,"
iii. p. 480. See also Prof. Bruce's answer to the question of the advocates of
universal restoration : "If Jesus has power over all flesh, is it credible that He
will not use it to the uttermost," Training of the Twelve, 2nd ed. p. 440.

[2] "The pronoun in the Plural individualizes the contents of the totality
which is the object of the gift," Godet.

[3] Ver. 6.

These first true disciples of the Lord Jesus became such by the gift of the Father, and the manifestation of the Father's name to them in Christ.[1] It was a progressive manifestation through the experiences of discipleship, through receiving Christ's words as they were able to bear them, following Him and learning of Himself who He was and what He was for them. He prays now for them ; not yet for the world, but for these disciples who are the Father's own children, and are so especially as having become Christ's true followers, from whom glory has arisen, and shall yet more arise to the Saviour.[2] He is now to leave them in the world; and for them this is His first petition :—

"Holy Father, keep them in Thy name which Thou hast given Me, that they may be one, even as We are (Πάτερ ἅγιε, τήρησον αὐτοὺς ἐν τῷ ὀνόματί σου ᾧ δέδωκάς μοι ἵνα ὦσιν ἕν, καθὼς ἡμεῖς)." [3]

"The unique phrase of address ('Holy Father,' comp. Rev. vi. 10 ; 1 John ii. 20 ; ver. 25, 'righteous Father') suggests the main thought. The disciples hitherto had been kept apart from the corruption of the world by the present influence of Christ. The revelation of holiness which He made had a power at once to separate and to unite. He asks that God, regarded under the separate aspects of purity and tenderness, may carry forward to its final issue ('that they may be one even as we are') that training which He had Himself commenced, and that too in the same way ('keep in My name,' comp. ver. 12). The name of the Father, the knowledge of God as Father, is regarded as an ideal region of security in which the disciples were preserved." [4] This name of the Father, given to the Son to reveal to men, has been manifested to the disciples already by Christ (ver. 6). He has shown them in some measure what God is for His own

---

[1] "De mundo sibi a Patre dicit Filius datos homines quibus alio loco dicit, 'ego vos de mundo elegi.' Quos Deus Filius de mundo elegit cum Patre, idem ipse homo Filius de mundo eos accepit a Patre ; non enim Pater illos Filio dedisset nisi elegisset." Augustine, *Tract. in Joann.* cvi. 5.

[2] Ver. 9 f. δεδόξασμαι ἐν αὐτοῖς, not merely ἐδοξάσθην. It is an abiding glory. The light shall shine in them, and from them to others, more and more unto the perfect day of heaven.

[3] Ver. 11.   [4] Westcott, *in loco.*

children, what He desires to be for the world.   Christ's last
utterance in this prayer pledges Him to continue this revelation
of the name of the Father to His disciples (ver. 26).

"That they may be one, even as We are."   Who can tell
all that these words foreshadow as to the final estate of the
Church of the redeemed ?   Christ's disciples shall be one
with each other, even as the Three who are most high in the
unity of the blessed Godhead.   They shall be one in heart
and will, in righteousness, holiness, and love, in the unity of
one new nature in Christ, and yet with no loss of personal
identity, with no obliteration of the diversity of personal
character, even as there are high and mysterious differences
between the Three who are One upon the throne in heaven,
"the same in substance, equal in power and glory." [1]

"While I was with them, I kept them in Thy name which
Thou hast given Me: and I guarded them, and not one of
them perished, but the son of perdition (εἰ μὴ ὁ υἱὸς τῆς
ἀπωλείας) ; that the Scripture might be fulfilled."   The "but"
(εἰ μή) here, as repeatedly elsewhere in the New Testament,
refers to the preceding verb, not to the preceding sentence as
a whole.   It is neither said nor implied that Judas was
among those whom the Father had given to Christ (vv. 2, 6, 9),
and whom He had guarded hitherto as such.   What is said
is simply that he "perished," in contrast to those whom the
Lord guarded, none of whom perished. [2]

In vv. 17–19 Christ prays that His disciples may be sanctified or consecrated in the truth, in the word of God (ἐν τῇ
ἀληθείᾳ· ὁ λόγος ὁ σὸς ἀλήθειά ἐστι), that being the great
means by which the work is to go forward in them, the

---

[1] "Non rogat Jesus ut Ipse unum sit cum Patre ; rogat ut credentes unum
sint.   Illa unitas est ex naturâ, hæc ex gratiâ : igitur illi hæc similis est, non
æqualis. Conf. καθώς, sicut, vv. 16, 18, et de eadem re v. 21. . . . Moses de Deo
et de se, vel ad Deum vel ad populum loquens, non poterat dicere : Nos."
Bengel.

[2] We have the same use of εἰ μή in Matt. xii. 4 ; Luke iv. 26 f. ; Gal. i. 19 ;
ii. 16 ; Rev. xxi. 27.   Judas was no more among the number of those given to
Christ and guarded by Him than Sarepta was a city of Israel, and James, the
Lord's brother, one of the twelve, or than David and his men were priests, or
those written in the Lamb's book of life among the unclean and the workers of
abomination and falsehood, who shall not enter into the city of God. See Winer-
Moulton, 3rd ed. pp. 566, 789.

element or atmosphere in which they are to be more and
more consecrated and made holy. He prays also that this
consecration may not be an outward one merely, but true and
complete, that His disciples, in all that they are and have,
may be set apart for service, and enabled truly to serve God,
even as Christ Himself did as the Representative and Example
of His people (καὶ ὑπὲρ αὐτῶν ἐγὼ ἁγιάζω ἐμαυτὸν ἵνα ὦσι καὶ
αὐτοὶ ἡγιασμένοι ἐν ἀληθείᾳ). He asks this on the ground of
His own work done for them (ὑπὲρ αὐτῶν), and for the sake
of the work which He is now to send them to do for Him and
His cause in the world (ver. 18).

In the third part of the prayer (vv. 20–26) we see how
the united company of the original disciples (ver. 11) is to grow
and gather more and more into itself, and so to do a world-
wide work. As our Lord spoke of His own work as already
accomplished (ver. 4), even while Gethsemane and the cross
were still before Him, so now He speaks of the members of
His Church in all future ages as already gathered to Himself
(τῶν πιστευόντων εἰς ἐμέ) through the proclamation of the
message entrusted to the first disciples. "That they may be
all one (ἵνα πάντες ἓν ὦσιν); even as Thou, Father, art in
Me, and I in Thee, that they also may be in us: that the
world may believe that Thou didst send Me." The unity of
believers now and in all future generations rests on their
inward real union with Christ and with God in Christ;[1] but
it is to show itself outwardly, so as to bear with victorious
power for spiritual ends upon those who have hitherto been
standing without the Church, upon the world.

"And the glory which Thou hast given Me I have given
unto them; that they may be one, even as We are One: I in
them, and Thou in Me, that they may be perfected into one
(τετελειωμένοι εἰς ἕν); that the world may know (γινώσκῃ)[2]

---

[1] "Sic itaque sunt in nobis vel nos in Illis, ut Illi unum sint in naturâ suâ,
nos unum in nostrâ. Sunt quippe Ipse in nobis tanquam Deus in templo suo;
sumus autem nos in Illis tanquam creatura in Creatore suo." Augustine, *Tract.
in Joann.* c. x. 1.

[2] Not the Aorist, which would imply a recognition of the truth all at once.
It is step by step, line upon line, that the great lesson is learned and the world
won for Christ. "This 'knowledge,' like the 'belief' above, cannot be taken
in any other general sense than that which is found in the other verses of the

that thou didst send Me, and lovedst them, even as Thou lovedst Me." [1]

The "glory" here spoken of seems to be especially the revelation of God in the Son of Man. It is the name of the Father as given to Christ to be made known to men (vv. 6, 12, 26), partially uttered in the "new name" given to each overcomer in the good fight of faith, "which no one knoweth but he that receiveth it," in "Christ's own new name," written with His own hand on each believer, the name which is seen on the foreheads of the saints in glory.[2] "Such divine glory leads to the unity of all being. The fulness of this glory is to be made known hereafter in the Lord's presence; but meanwhile it is partially presented in the different manifestations of Christ's action in believers through the power and beauty and truth of the Christian life. But the idea of 'the glory' cannot be limited to any one of these." [3] This gift of Christ to His people now and hereafter is given for three great ends: for the unity of the universal Church in all time, for the perfect development of that unity, and for the conversion of the world.

From the thought of this mighty and glorious work done in and by His Church militant on earth, our Lord passes to the thought of the final blessedness of His Church triumphant in heaven :——

"Father, that which Thou hast given Me, I will that where I am they also may be with Me ($\pi\acute{a}\tau\epsilon\rho$, δ $\delta\acute{\epsilon}\delta\omega\kappa\acute{a}\varsigma$ $\mu o\iota$, $\theta\acute{\epsilon}\lambda\omega$ $\acute{\iota}\nu a$, $\acute{o}\pi o\upsilon$ $\epsilon\acute{\iota}\mu\grave{\iota}$ $\acute{\epsilon}\gamma\acute{\omega}$, $\kappa\acute{a}\kappa\epsilon\hat{\iota}\nu o\iota$ $\hat{\omega}\sigma\iota$ $\mu\epsilon\tau$' $\acute{\epsilon}\mu o\hat{\upsilon}$); that they may behold My glory which Thou hast given Me: for Thou lovedst Me before the foundation of the world." [4]

Again, as in passages before considered, we see presented together first the Church in its collective unity as given to Christ, and then the individual members of whom it is made

---

chapter (ver. 8, etc.). It is the knowledge of grateful recognition, and not of forced conviction." Westcott, in loco.

[1] Ver. 22 f.

[2] Rev. ii. 17; iii. 12; xxii. 4. "Gloria *Unigeniti* effulget per *filios* Dei fideles," Bengel. Comp. the doxology in Ephesians: "Unto Him be the glory in the Church and in Christ Jesus unto all generations for ever and ever. Amen," Eph. iii. 21.

[3] Westcott, in loco.

[4] Ver. 24.

up. Our Lord brings His whole Church, as He received it from the Father, directly to Him in prayer, and does so with a singular majesty of tone, speaking as One who has all right to be heard, and whose will is done in heaven.[1] His will in behalf of His Church and all its members throughout all time is summed up in these two crowning petitions of this marvellous prayer: first, that they may have personal fellowship with Himself in heaven, there where He is *at home* — if we may say so reverently—with His Father and their Father, and can be best known in the fulness of His grace and love ; and secondly, that so they may behold His glory, which the Father has given Him according to the eternal counsels of His love, in all its height, and depth, and length, and breadth.

In the two closing verses, the Saviour makes reference to the great outstanding facts which have been brought out by His life and work on earth as to the world, as to Himself, and as to His disciples. With respect to them, it is to be noted that He speaks of a continuation of His own ministry in the world even after He should have returned to His original glory above. He is still to make known to His disciples on earth the Father's name as truly as when He was visibly in the midst of them in the days of His flesh.[2] And then "the last word of the Lord's prayer" taken along with "the last word of His discourses"[3] sums up the whole, and gives the key to all the future history of His Church : " Be of good cheer, I have overcome the world ; " "and I in them."[4] Christ, revealed by the Spirit, in His work for His people and His work in them, is the ground for Christian hope and courage in the darkest days. His presence with His disciples and in them is the earnest of the full inheritance of glory and blessedness. It is the pledge of endless victory for the Church of Christ on earth, and for every one of its true

---

[1] " Nunc incrementum sumit oratio : Volo ! . . . Rogat Jesus cum jure et postulat cum fiducia, ut Filius non ut servus. Conf. Ps. ii. ; Marc. x. 35 ; vi. 25." Bengel.

[2] How this was fulfilled, we shall see in Parts v. and vi. Comp. Acts i. 1.

[3] Westcott.

[4] Θαρσεῖτε, ἐγὼ νενίκηκα τὸν κόσμον, John xvi. 33 ; Κἀγὼ ἐν αὐτοῖς, John xvii. 26.

members in all the work and warfare appointed for them, " dum hic viat in patriam." [1]

5th. Passages bearing on the relation of the members of the Church to each other and to the world.

Several points which might have been brought under this head have been touched upon in connection with sayings of our Lord which have been already under consideration. As He was during His earthly life, so the members of His Church were to be, *in* the world and acting upon it powerfully for good, yet not *of* it. The servants were to be as their Master, the disciples as their Lord.

Few things are more striking in the Gospel history than the way in which Christ, while revealing and enforcing moral and spiritual truths and principles, which, wherever they were received could not but have the greatest and most far-reaching results in the field of social and political life, yet stood absolutely free from all entanglements in the politics of the day. Again and again His adversaries tried to induce Him to take a position, or give an opinion which would have brought Him into this region, but were invariably foiled.[2] The attempt to prove before the Roman governor and the tetrarch of Galilee that He had stirred up the people against the established civil authorities broke down utterly for want of even an appearance of evidence.[3]

As Christ was in this respect, in spirit, attitude, and action, so His Church ought to be in this world. His great cardinal utterances on this subject separate once and for all the two spheres so often and so hurtfully confounded with each other. " Render unto Cæsar the things which are Cæsar's, and unto God the things which are God's." " My kingdom is not of this world; if My kingdom were of this world, then would My servants (οἱ ὑπηρέται οἱ ἐμοί, My officers [4]) fight that I should not be delivered to the Jews; but now is My

---

[1] Wiclif.

[2] Matt. xxii. 15–22 ; Mark xii. 13 ff. ; Luke xiii. 1–5 ; xx. 1–8, 19–26.

[3] Luke xxiii. 4–15.

[4] "The use of the word ὑπηρέτης (here only of Christians in the Gospels ; comp. 1 Cor. iv. 1 ; Acts xiii. 5) corresponds with the royal dignity which Christ assumes." Westcott, *in loco.*

kingdom not from hence." Pilate therefore said unto Him, "Art Thou a king then? Jesus answered, Thou sayest that I am a king. To this end have I been born, and to this end am I come into the world, that I should bear witness unto the truth. Every one that is of the truth heareth My voice." [1]

In these and other sayings of Christ a broad and clear line of division is drawn between the field of things outward and civil, and that of things inward and spiritual, the things that belong to the moral and religious life; and it is clearly indicated that it is with the latter alone that His Church has directly to do. In full accordance with this, we find that the laws laid down by our Lord for the fellowship of His disciples are of a different sort, and are to be enforced by a different authority than in the case of the laws of the State. In the latter sphere it is the power of the sword that rules; in the former, the power of conscience, of love, and of a spiritual authority, "the power of the keys" in the House of God, administered in the name of Christ.

There is abundant evidence that our Lord's teaching in this respect was not fully understood or received by His disciples almost to the last moment of His intercourse with them.[2] After one instance of such misconception on the

---

[1] Matt. xxii. 21; John xviii. 36 f. The attempt made by one of the last Bampton lecturers to get over the testimony of this text against his own theory of Church and State is an instructive illustration of the process known to German exegetes as "hineinexegesiren." Canon Fremantle thinks that the emphasis must be laid strongly on "this," and that it must be held to mean "this sort of:" "My kingdom is not of *this* world;" "this present evil state of things in which empires are built up by fraud and violence." See p. 109 f. of *The World as the subject of Redemption, being an attempt to set forth the functions of the Church as designed to embrace the whole race of mankind.* Bampton Lect. for 1883, published London 1885. The book is an interesting and able work from the school of Arnold, Coleridge, and Kingsley, much, but not slavishly influenced by Rothe's *Ethik.* Canon Fremantle argues for a theory of Anglican Erastianism on a democratic basis, his ideal of the Church being the Elizabethan "Church and Realm of England" with some practical improvements. Apart from its Erastianism, the chief weakness of the book is the absence of any solid exegetical or theological foundation. Its author ignores entirely, as was to be expected, the distinction between the Church and the Kingdom of God so carefully handled by Professor Candlish.

[2] Matt. xvi. 21-24; xviii. 1-4; xx. 20-28; Mark ix. 31-35; x. 35-45; Luke ix. 46-48; xxii. 24-26; Acts i. 6.

part of two of the most favoured apostles, which occurred within a few days of His crucifixion, "Jesus called the twelve unto Him and said: Ye know that the rulers of the Gentiles lord it over them, and their great ones exercise authority over them. Not so shall it be among you; but whosoever would become great among you shall be your minister (διάκονος); and whosoever would be first among you shall be your servant (δοῦλος); even as the Son of Man came not to be ministered unto, but to minister (οὐκ ἦλθε διακονηθῆναι ἀλλὰ διακονῆσαι), and to give His life a ransom for many."[1]

Again and again, and with peculiar emphasis, Christ warned His disciples, in reference to the time when He should be no longer visibly in the midst of them, against all tendencies in the direction of a hierarchy, against allowing anything to grow up among them in the shape of "an authority thrusting itself between God and the soul, between the believer and his Saviour, even in the form which might seem the most innocent and natural, the authority of a teacher."[2]

The evils which might arise from misplaced reverence for religious teachers were sadly illustrated in the relations which generally prevailed between the common people and the scribes and Pharisees in our Lord's time. Again and again in His public teaching, especially towards the close of His ministry, He pointed to these relations and their results as forming beacons of warning for His Church in all ages. "Then spake Jesus to the multitude and to His disciples, saying: The scribes and the Pharisees sit in Moses' seat; all things therefore whatsoever they bid you, these do and observe;[3] but do not ye after their works, for they say and do not. . . . They make broad their phylacteries,

---

[1] Matt. xx. 25-28. Comp. the parallel passage in Mark x. 42-45. The same truths were specially enforced by our Lord both by word and action on the night on which He was betrayed. See Luke xxii. 24-27 ; John xiii. 3-17.

[2] Beyschlag, S. 15.

[3] Bengel notes the limitation implied in these words as to the extent to which the scribes' teaching was to be followed : "Hâc particulâ (οὖν) limitatur τό 'quæcunque dixerint,' ne putet populus traditiones Pharisaicas æque

and enlarge the borders of their garments, and love the chief place at feasts, and the chief seats in the synagogues, and the salutations in the market places, and to be called of men, Rabbi. But be not ye called Rabbi: for One is your Teacher (ὁ διδάσκαλος), and all ye are brethren. And call no man your father on the earth: for One is your Father, which is in heaven (ὁ οὐράνιος). Neither be ye called Masters (καθηγηταί): for One is your Master (ὁ καθηγητής), even the Christ. But he that is the greater among you shall be your minister (ὁ δὲ μείζων ὑμῶν ἔσται ὑμῶν διάκονος)." [1]

It does not indeed follow from this that there were not to be differences in position and honour in Christ's Church on earth. In fact, the closing words of the passage last quoted manifestly imply that such differences of "greater" and "less" were to exist in the fellowship of His disciples, and might therefore lawfully be recognised by suitable names.[2]

Other sayings of our Lord's put His mind in this respect beyond all question. There are greater and less in Christ's kingdom on earth, even as some of His servants hereafter shall be " set in authority over ten cities," and others " over

---

sibi esse servandas atque præcepta Mosis. . . . Mosaica, servanda, facienda." " Sedet in cathedra Mosis, qui non ex se ipso vel proprio sensu sed ex Dei auctoritate et verbo præcipit. Legitima vocatio hic notatur ; quia ideo audiri scribas jubet Christus, quod publici essent ecclesiæ doctores. . . . Hinc apparet Christum eatenus populum hortari ut scribis pareat quantisper in purâ et simplici legis interpretatione manent." Calvin, *in loco*.

[1] Matt. xxiii. 1-3, 5-11.

[2] Calvin's exposition of our Lord's words in the verse in question is a good instance of the masculine judgment and soundness of discrimination which characterize him as an interpreter of Scripture : " Hâc clausulâ ostendit se non sophistice litigasse de vocibus, sed rem potius spectasse, ne quis ordinis sui oblitus plus quam par est sibi usurpet. Pronuntiat igitur summam in Ecclesia dignitatem esse non imperium sed ministerium. Quisquis in hâc mensurâ se continet nec Deo nec Christo quicquam eripit, quocunque ornetur titulo. Sicuti rursum frustra servi elogio fucatur potestas, quæ Christi magisterio derogat. Quid enim prodest quod Papa tyrannicis legibus oppressurus miseras animas, se 'servum servorum Dei' præfatur, nisi ut palam insultet Deo, et hominibus probrose illudat ? Cæterum ut vocibus non insistit Christus, ita præcise hoc suis mandat ne altius aspirent vel conscendere appetant quam ut sub Patre Cœlesti æqualiter fraternam colant societatem, et qui honore pollent se aliis exhibeant ministros."

five cities" only.[1] The apostles under His training become as
"scribes made disciples unto the kingdom of heaven" (γραμματεῖς μαθητευθέντες τῇ βασιλείᾳ τῶν οὐρανῶν), as "heads
of households (οἰκοδεσπόται), bringing forth out of their treasure things new and old."[2] They and others like them are
to be sent thereafter in this capacity by the ascended
Saviour to their fellow - countrymen. Speaking to the
people and their religious leaders, the scribes and Pharisees,
in the temple courts at Jerusalem a few days before His
death, our Lord said: "Behold, I send unto you (ἐγὼ ἀποστέλλω πρὸς ὑμᾶς) prophets and wise men and scribes:
some of them shall ye kill and crucify; and some of them
shall ye scourge in your synagogues, and persecute from
city to city: that upon you may come all the righteous
blood shed on the earth, from the blood of Abel the
righteous unto the blood of Zachariah son of Barachiah,
whom ye slew between the sanctuary and the altar."[3]

Our Lord here uses the titles familiar in every synagogue, as

---

[1] Matt. v. 19; Luke xix. 11–26.   [2] Matt. xiii. 52.

[3] Matt. xxiii. 34 f. Comp. the parallel passage Luke xi. 49 ff. : "Therefore also said the Wisdom of God, I will send unto them (ἀποστιλῶ εἰς
αὐτούς) prophets and apostles ; and some of them they shall kill and persecute:
that the blood of all the prophets which was shed from the foundation of
the world may be required of this generation, from the blood of Abel," etc.
It is worth noting that "the Wisdom of God" is a name of Christ used by
Paul (1 Cor. i. 24), with whom Luke was so closely associated. Some hold
(e.g. Meyer, Lukas, 5te Aufl. S. 424) that Luke is citing here a previous
saying of Jesus, given by Matthew in more direct and original form, with this
formula of citation : "Therefore also said the Wisdom," etc. In that case
vv. 49–51 form a parenthesis, and the discourse of Christ is resumed in
the first person, according to Luke's own report in ver. 52. It seems more
natural, however, to take it all as Luke's own narrative. The evangelist
introduces this new section, with its solemn forewarnings of judgment, by
applying to Christ a name which his sense of the Divine power and insight
of the utterance made him feel to be peculiarly befitting: "The Wisdom of
God;" just as in ver. 39 we have "And the Lord said," in that tone of
authority and majesty which showed His right to the title.

Godet holds that our Lord refers here to the passage regarding the voice
of Wisdom in Prov. i. 20–31, and that He repeats the substance of it, both
as to promise and threatening ; only, "instead of the breath of the Spirit, which
God promises in that passage to send to the people to instruct and reprove
them, Jesus speaks of the living organs of the Spirit, His apostles and
prophets." L'Evangile de St. Luc, 2de éd. ii. p. 109 f. The explanation has
some attractions, but on the whole I prefer that given above.

applied to the Jewish teachers of the day, "wise men and scribes" (חכמים וספרים, σοφοὶ καὶ γραμματεῖς), as well as the title "prophets," which was held in yet higher honour as designating the ṣ ̣at teachers of the Church of the past. Such teachers Christ was now to send to Israel in His name, men who, from their gifts and commission, deserved even more respect and deference than what He bid His disciples and the multitude show to the scribes of their time, as "sitting in Moses' seat." And yet the treatment which they would receive from the synagogue authorities would be persecution, scourging, and martyrdom.

Teachers, therefore, there were to be in the fellowship of Christ's people, men worthy of at least the position and honour which the "wise men and scribes" of the synagogue were entitled to receive.[1] And from the nature of the case it was evident that 'here must be office-bearers of some kind, with functions of rule and administration as well as teaching, in the society of the disciples. Such office-bearers are needed in every society which has definite work to do. They were certainly needed in a society which had to discharge the duties expressly laid by Christ upon His Church on earth. The commands, for example, which we have already considered regarding offences within the pale of the Church (Matt. xviii. 15–18), carried with them the warrant by Christ's authority for all that was essential to their being put into execution. Now, it is perfectly obvious that for the orderly exercise of such government and discipline in the Church as our Lord there enjoined, it was essential that there should be office-bearers of some sort, men to act as leaders and representatives of their brethren.[2]

But all these differences in position and function in the Church of Christ, as contemplated by Himself, are of such a nature only as is compatible with the great fundamental truth

[1] It is clear, therefore, that "the prohibitions in vv. 8–10 have reference to the *hierarchical* meaning and usage which were at that time associated with the titles in question. The teacher's titles *in themselves* are as legitimate and necessary as his *functions* ; but the hierarchy in the form which it assumed in the (Roman) Catholic Church with 'the Holy Father' at its head is contrary to the spirit and mind of Jesus." Meyer, *in loco*, E. Tr. ii. p. 103.

[2] Comp. Binnie, *The Church*, p. 126 f.

that all His disciples are truly brethren, the children of one
Father in heaven, gathered into one by the power of His
Word and Spirit in Christ, the common Lord and Saviour.
Special gifts from God for loving service of the brethren and
of the Lord's cause, special diligence and zeal in using these
gifts, make the sole difference between them. "In one
word, the Church of Jesus was meant to be a 'communitas fratrum' (eine Brüdergemeinde) in the full sense
of the term (Matt. xviii. 15 ; xxiii. 9), in which He alone
governs, but that in a free fashion, ruling from within by His
Spirit of love; and in which all others seek in the same
Spirit of love to serve one another, and all together to serve
the world, in such a way that the individual member shall
be willingly subject to the whole body, and the individual
congregation to the whole Church, as to the more complete
and adequate organ of 'the Lord, who is the Spirit.'"[1]

[1] Beyschlag, S. 16.

CHAPTER II.

IN this chapter we shall consider, in their relation to our subject, the nature of the two sacraments appointed by Christ for His Church, the nature of the great commission entrusted to the Church by Him, and the special position and functions assigned by Him to His apostles.

The three first-named appointments stand in close relation to each other. It was in connection with Christ's great commission to His Church that the command to baptize, and the formula for Baptism, were expressly given by Him to His disciples. And in His words on the same occasion a reference to the Lord's Supper, as already instituted, seems clearly implied.[1]

1st. Baptism and the Lord's Supper.

What we have to do with at present is not, of course, the general subject of the sacraments, but only one particular aspect of it. In what relation do these two ordinances, and the command to preach the Gospel and make disciples, with which in their first institution they were closely linked, stand to the conception of the Church as it appears in our Lord's oral teaching, and what light do they throw upon it?

1. Both Baptism and the Lord's Supper emphasize to all

---

[1] Matt. xxviii. 19 f. : " Go ye therefore and make disciples of all the nations, baptizing them into the name of the Father, and of the Son, and of the Holy Ghost : teaching them to observe all things whatsoever I command you." His last command to them before His Passion had been : " This do in remembrance of Me," Luke xxii. 19 ; Matt. xxvi. 26 ff. ; Mark xiv. 22 ff. It was among the first things which the first converts were "taught to observe." "They continued stedfastly in the apostles' teaching and fellowship, in the breaking of bread and the prayers," Acts ii. 42.

who share in the ordinance, or witness its administration, the essential importance of a direct and personal relation to the Lord Himself. They embody this truth in speaking signs, and enforce it not to the ear only, but also through the avenues of the eye, and hand, and taste. The sacraments are "a visible word" from Christ Himself first of all, and most expressly concerning this. And this, as we have seen, lies at the very foundation of all our Lord's teaching concerning His Church.

"Jesus came and spake unto them,"—the assembled company of His disciples,—"saying, All authority hath been given unto Me in heaven and on earth. Go ye therefore and make disciples of all the nations, baptizing them into the name (εἰς τὸ ὄνομα) of the Father, and of the Son, and of the Holy Ghost: teaching them to observe all things whatsoever I commanded you; and, lo, I am with you alway, even unto the end of the world"[1] (the consummation of the age, ἕως τῆς συντελείας τοῦ αἰῶνος). Baptism was to be the sign and seal of admission into the fellowship of the disciples of Jesus among all the nations to the end of time. Any man, whether Jew or Gentile by birth, to whom the Gospel was preached, was "made a disciple" when he received Jesus Christ as his Saviour and Lord, confessing Him with heart and mouth as the Son of the living God and the Messiah foretold in the Scriptures. In token of that good confession, first expressly made by Peter, the convert was to be baptized into the name of God revealed in Christ. Hence in other forms of the great commission recorded by the evangelists—the substance of it being doubtless repeated by our Lord in different words at different times—we find the name of Christ only mentioned, in connection with the command to preach the Gospel and make disciples in all the world, and with the promises annexed to that command.[2] And so, too, in the subsequent history we see that Baptism "in" or "into the name of the Lord Jesus" was

---

[1] Matt. xxviii. 18–20.

[2] "Go ye into all the world, and preach the Gospel to the whole creation. He that believeth, and is baptized, shall be saved; but he that disbelieveth shall be condemned. And these signs shall follow them that believe: in My name shall they cast out devils," etc., Mark xvi. 15 ff. "That repentance and remission of sins should be preached in His name unto all the nations, beginning from Jerusalem," Luke xxiv. 47. "Ye shall be My witnesses both in Jeru-

held as equivalent to, or as a sufficient description of, Baptism
into the threefold name of God.[1]

2. In Baptism, therefore, we have an authoritative word
from Christ Himself concerning discipleship.

In this initial sacrament He speaks to each one who seeks
an interest in Him and His salvation as He spoke once to
Peter: " If I wash thee not, thou hast no part in Me." No
one can have place or name among My true disciples, unless
he has first come as a sinner to Me for cleansing. The sins
of his past life must be washed away. And there must be
not only a new beginning, but a new nature. There must be
created in him a clean heart and a right spirit. With man
this is impossible. But this ordinance of mine is a witness
to thee, that for all this I by the grace of God have made full
provision. I died for thy sins according to the Scriptures.
In this ordinance repentance and the forgiveness of sins are
preached now in My name unto thee; and power is offered
through the gift of the Holy Ghost that thou mayest become
one of My witnesses on the earth, created anew in Christ
Jesus unto all good works.[2]

Baptism is thus, as has been well said, " a glorious Gospel
in an impressive rite." [3] It is the very Gospel of the evening

salem, and in all Judæa, and Samaria, and unto the uttermost part of the
earth," Acts i. 8.

[1] ἐπὶ τῷ ὀνόματι Ἰησοῦ Χριστοῦ εἰς ἄφεσιν τῶν ἁμαρτιῶν ὑμῶν, Acts ii. 38.
" When they believed Philip preaching good tidings concerning the kingdom
of God and the name of Jesus Christ, they were baptized . . . baptized into
the name of the Lord Jesus (εἰς τὸ ὄνομα τοῦ Κ. Ἰ.)," Acts viii. 12–16 ; "baptized in the name of Jesus Christ (ἐν τῷ ὀν.)," x. 48 ; "baptized into the name of
the Lord Jesus (εἰς τὸ ὄν.)," xix. 5. So, too, in the recently discovered " Teaching
of the Apostles," we have the complete Baptismal formula given in the passage
where the subject is expressly treated (c. vii.) ; while elsewhere Christian
Baptism is simply described as " Baptism in the name of the Lord" (c. ix. 180).

[2] " Itaque quoties lapsi fuerimus repetenda erit Baptismi memoria, et hac
armandus animus, ut de peccatorum remissione semper certus securusque sit.
Nam etsi semel administratus præteriisse visus est, posterioribus tamen peccatis
non est abolitus. Puritas enim Christi in eo nobis oblata est ; ea semper viget,
nullis maculis opprimitur, sed omnes nostras sordes obruit et extergit. . . .
Quare nec dubium quin pii omnes toto vitæ curriculo, quoties vitiorum suorum
conscientiâ vexantur, sese ad Baptismi memoriam revocare audeant, ut se inde
confirment in illius unicæ ac perpetuæ ablutionis fiduciâ quam habemus in
Christi sanguine." Calvin, Instit. lib. iv. cap. xv. 3, 4.

[3] Dale, Manual of Congregational Principles, Lond. 1884, p. 138.

of the Resurrection, and of the great commission in all its forms.   And it is a Gospel summed up in Christ Himself, and embodied by Himself in this initiatory sacrament appointed for His people and their children.   The teaching of the ordinance is thus in full accordance with what we have already seen to be the teaching of our Lord as to the essential nature of His Church.   Only by union with Christ Himself can any enter it.   Only by abiding in union with Him can any really continue in His Church and be fruitful in it.

Viewed in this light, it is obvious that Baptism in the Church of the New Testament grew naturally, by more lines of development than one, out of the initiatory ordinance of the same Church under an older dispensation.   Circumcision also, as we saw before, was a sign and seal of the righteousness which is by faith.   It was a token of the covenant of grace and of "the Gospel preached beforehand unto Abraham," "the father of all them that believe."   Circumcision, like Baptism, spoke emphatically of purity, and of the need of cleansing by grace from the defilements of nature, before a sinner can have a place and portion with God and with His people.[1]

But circumcision by Divine appointment was administered to the infant children of the believer as well as to himself. It bore a message from God for both, not as individuals merely, but in their peculiar relations to each other and to the Lord.   It was a token of God's covenant with Abraham, the central promise of which was: "I will be a God unto thee, and to thy seed after thee."   Is there any reason to believe that the later ordinance of admission—"the circumcision of Christ," as Paul calls it [2]—had not according to the mind of Christ the same breadth and fulness of meaning and application as the earlier one ?

Certainly the burden of proof lies here upon those who maintain that it had not.   Unless an express statute of repeal and prohibition of the former privilege can be produced, the natural conclusion is that the old rule remained in force as regards the place of the infant children of the believer within the visible fellowship of faith to which their parent

---

[1] See above, pp. 48–51.   [2] Col. ii. 11 f.

belongs.   Seeing that "the Gospel," as we have seen, "was preached beforehand unto Abraham," and the covenant of grace established with him and his, and the Church of God visibly set up in the fellowship of his house, it would require very clear and strong evidence to prove that the sign of Gospel blessings, the token of the everlasting covenant, the ordinance of admission into the Church, "the circumcision of Christ," which corresponds to that which Isaac, the infant seed of Abraham, received, should be withheld from the infant seed of those now who, "being Christ's, are Abraham's seed, and heirs according to the promise" made to him.   No such evidence is forthcoming.   On the contrary, as we shall see in the next two parts of this work, there is not a little evidence, direct and indirect, from the Acts and the Epistles, that the old view and practice as regards the Church standing of the infant children of believers continued under apostolic guidance in the Church of Christ.

Meanwhile it is worth observing how this question stands at the stage in our discussion at which we are now arrived. From a historical standpoint, what were the circumstances of those to whom the Saviour's great commission was first addressed, as bearing upon the way in which they were likely to understand it ?   How would the command to baptize, in connection with a profession of discipleship, sound to "the eleven and those who were with them"?[1]

The increase of proselytes was, as shown above,[2] an outstanding feature of the time of our Lord, and of the generation preceding.   In almost every synagogue in the Holy Land, and still more in every synagogue of the Dispersion, there were "devout men" of Gentile birth who had "joined themselves to the Lord God of Israel," and, in varying degrees of closeness, to His professing people.   Numbers of such proselytes came up every year to Jerusalem, as was the case at the Pentecost after the Crucifixion, "from every nation

---

[1] In such a case Bengel's fundamental rule of Biblical exegesis applies with special force : " In exegesi sacrâ lector ponere se debet in illo tempore et loco quo oratio habita resve gesta est, et affectûs, vim verborum, contextum considerare." *In Matth.* xvi. 13.

[2] Pp. 114–117, 120 f.

under heaven," [1] to be present at the great annual feasts. Every one of these men, who was a proselyte in the full sense of the term, had been admitted to the congregation and assembly of Israel and of the Lord—the ἐκκλησία τοῦ κυρίου —by circumcision, "the seal of Abraham," as it was called; and every one of them who was the head of a family had brought his children in with him by the door of the same ordinance. "All his males had been circumcised." "He could not get in without them," as has been pointed out. "The law to this effect was quite clear and explicit: 'When a stranger shall sojourn with thee, and will keep the Passover to the Lord, let all his males be circumcised, and then let him come near and keep it.' [2] . . . The proselyte who, being a father, wants to come into the Hebrew Church by himself, is to be roundly informed that his profession of faith in the God of Abraham has a suspicious look : 'If your faith had been of the right kind, it would have moved you to seek admission for your household too. The Lord will not be the God of any man who does not desire Him to be the God of his seed with him. You cannot be suffered to have communion with us in the passover till you are circumcised, you and all the males of your house.' " [3]

All this was perfectly familiar to every member of the Jewish Church in our Saviour's time. It was looked upon as a matter of course. It had been so for the whole house of Israel in Palestine and in the Dispersion from time immemorial. Suppose, as is quite conceivable, that our Lord had appointed no new form of admission into His Church, but had simply retained the ancient one. The great commission would then have run : "Go ye and make disciples (or proselytes [4]) of all the nations, circumcising them into the

---

[1] Acts ii. 5.   [2] Ex. xii. 48.

[3] Binnie, *The Church*, Edin. 1882, p. 74.

[4] Justin Martyr and other writers of the sub-apostolic age often use the phrase "to become proselytes" as synonymous with "to become Christians," *e.g. Dial. cum Tryph.* c. xxviii. : "So short a time is left you in which to become proselytes. If Christ's coming shall have anticipated you, in vain you will repent, for He will not hear you;" c. cxxii. : "Christ and His proselytes, namely, we, Gentiles, whom He has illumined." (*Ante-Nicene Library*, ii. pp. 121, 254.)

name of the Father, and of the Son, and of the Holy Ghost, teaching them to observe," etc. Can there be any reasonable doubt that in that case the apostles would have administered the old ordinance upon the old principle, not only to the believing parent, but also to his infant seed, and that they would have acted rightly in so doing?

And when in point of fact the sole difference was that a gentler ordinance was substituted for circumcision, but one which held precisely the same place as regards admission to the Church, and which was equally a token of God's covenant, and "a sign and seal of the righteousness which is by faith," is there any reason to suppose that, without one hint of pro- hibition from Christ, the first disciples of their own accord excluded the children of believers from the position which they had hitherto held in the Church, and with which every Jew and proselyte, in "every country under heaven," was familiar from the beginning of his religious knowledge and experience?[1]

The argument now stated is, I believe, conclusive in itself alone; but it finds strong confirmation in the results regard- ing Jewish proselyte Baptism which have been arrived at, especially in the most recent times, by the majority of reliable investigators in that field. Their conclusion is that Baptism, as well as circumcision, was administered by the Jews in New Testament times to all proselytes. The two things were combined with a sacrifice in the Temple (or a vow to offer one when possible) to form the full ordinance of admission to the Jewish Church. Our Lord, therefore, simply singled out one of the three elements hitherto combined in the admission of proselytes as the most suitable for the initial ordinance of His Church, and left the other two to die out of themselves. Circumcision and Baptism evidently continued for a time side by side, just as the old seventh day Sabbath and the Lord's Day did. Paul did not "forbid the Jews which are among the Gentiles to circumcise their children," as was falsely reported of him; but he baptized families as well as individuals when the head of the family had believed.[2]

---

[1] Comp. Wardlaw, *Infant Baptism*, 3rd ed. p. 46 ff. Bannerman, *Church of Christ*, ii. p. 101 f.

[2] Acts xxii. 21; xvi. 15, 31-34; 1 Cor. i. 14-16. In all these cases the

According to the Rabbinical authorities, to some of which reference has already been made,[1] Baptism from time immemorial was looked upon as equally necessary with circumcision in the admission of a proselyte, and was administered both to females and to all infants whose parents made a profession of the Jewish faith. This view is reflected in the ancient Ethiopic version of the Gospels, in which our Lord's statement regarding the proselytizing zeal of the Pharisees in his days is translated : " Ye compass sea and land to baptize one proselyte." [2]   " A new Jewish name was given to the proselyte at circumcision, but he remained a ‎גר until he was baptized.   There was doubt whether he could be counted a real proselyte until baptism was added to circumcision. Little children were baptized with their parents, or with the surviving one if either were dead (Bab. Gem. on Ketubh. xi. 1). . . . Baptism makes the proselyte like a little child (Jebam. 22a, 48b, 97b).[3]   He receives therein the Holy Ghost and undergoes a new birth." [4]

" At the baptism and reception of a proselyte three persons, constituting a ' Beth Din ' or court of law, were in all cases required to be present.   In the case of ' a little proselyte,' it was said, ' they baptize him on the authority of a Beth Din ' (T. B. Kethuboth 11a).   But might this be done to a child without his intelligent consent ?   Yes, it was

word used for " family " is that which has the narrower meaning,—οἶκος, not οἰκία. See above, pp. 85–88. The fact in its bearing on the N. T. evidence for the Baptism of the infants of believers is referred to more fully in Part vi. chap. ii.

[1] See above, pp. 117–119.

[2] Winer, *Real. Wörterb. s. voce* " Proselyten."   Justin Martyr (born in Shechem or Nablûs, " a city of Samaria," about 114 A.D.) refers to the Jewish proselyte Baptism as combined with circumcision. " This circumcision," he says to his Jewish antagonist Trypho, supposed to be the famous Rabbi Tarphon, " is not necessary for all men, but for you alone.   Nor do we receive that useless baptism of cisterns, for it has nothing to do with this Baptism of life."   *Dial. cum Tryph.* c. xix. E. Tr. (*Ante-Nicene Series*) p. 110 ; comp. c. xiv. E. Tr. p. 104.

[3] The saying that " a newly made proselyte is like a new-born child " is quoted by Rabbi Jose, who flourished in the end of the first and beginning of the second century A.D.   Comp. C. Taylor, *Teaching of the Twelve Apostles, with Illustrations from the Talmud*, Camb. 1886, p. 58.

[4] Leyrer, *Proselyten*, S. 242 f.

replied, on the principle that one may act for a person to his advantage, though not to his disadvantage, without his knowledge and consent. The case supposed is explained to be that of a child who, having no father, comes, or is brought by his mother, to be made a proselyte. But when children were made proselytes with their father, the act of the father in bringing them was held to imply the assent of the children, independently of the authority of the court of three in attendance at the ceremony. In either case, ' whether his father has made him a proselyte, or a Beth Din have made him a proselyte,' the child may retract when he comes of age."[1]

3. In the ordinance of the Lord's Supper also Christ speaks

[1] C. Taylor, *ut supra*, p. 57. Grätz, *Gesch. der Juden*, 2te Ausg. iv. S. 110. Until towards the end of the 17th century the view of the Jewish teachers themselves was universally accepted by Christian scholars, viz. that proselyte baptism was of immemorial antiquity, and that it was certainly in general use before the time of Christ. The rise of the Anti-Pædobaptist theory after the Reformation naturally led to controversy upon the point. Both sides of the question have been advocated with much ability and with immense display of erudition. The ablest work on the side of those who deny the antiquity of the rite is probably that of Schneckenburger, *Ueber das Alter der jüdischen Proselyten-Taufe*. Of late years the balance of opinion among leading scholars has inclined decidedly to the older view. Delitzsch (in 2nd ed. of Herzog's *Real-Encycl.*), Zezschwitz (in his *Katechetik*), Edersheim (*Life and Times of the Messiah*, 2nd ed.), C. Taylor (*ut supra*), all hold substantially that position. Schürer, in his great work recently published, has thrown the full weight of his deservedly high authority in this field of research upon the same side. *Hist. of Jewish People*, ii. pp. 319-324.

It may be added, that even supposing that all the writers now named are mistaken in holding that Jewish proselyte baptism was in use in our Lord's time, and that therefore no direct argument can be drawn from it as regards the Baptism of the infants of believers in the Apostolic Church, two points would still be worthy of notice in this connection : (1) According to the most cautious and impartial scholars who have specially investigated the subject, the two elements of circumcision and baptism were associated together in the rite of admission for Jewish proselytes and their children from a very early date, although not till after the destruction of the Temple and the cessation of sacrifices did the latter element come to have the stress laid upon it which it has in the Talmudic teaching. Leyrer, *e.g.*, would date proselyte Baptism "*as an independent rite* of initiation " "certainly not earlier than the end of the first century," with not a few considerations pointing to a considerably later date. On the other hand, "Jewish prejudice and the continuity of the Rabbinic tradition, as a thing shut up in itself and firmly closed against outside influences, and especially against Christian ones, make the assumption of a direct and formal borrowing of Christian usages improbable " (*Proselyten*, S. 245-249).

An *indirect* influence from Christian usage, as suggested by Dean Plumptre,

first of all to the individual disciple, and speaks of his personal relation to Himself.

"This do in remembrance of Me." By taking his place at the Lord's Table, by what he himself does there, each communicant makes in the simplest yet most solemn way his own personal profession of faith in Christ and obedience to Him. No stranger to the Lord is invited to eat of this New Testament feast any more than of the passover in the Old Testament Church out of which it grew. It is a disciples' ordinance, instituted by Christ for such and such only. In it, on that night on which He was betrayed, our Lord embodied in expressive signs what He spoke of soon afterwards in His High-priestly prayer as already finished: "I glorified Thee on the earth, having accomplished the work which Thou hast given Me to do." He records it for each disciple in the words and actions of this ordinance.

"Take, eat; this is my body given for you. This cup is the new covenant in My blood, poured out for you; drink ye all of it."[1] This is what the Lord did for each believer. He took our nature upon Him, and died for our sins, according to the Scriptures, and rose from the dead in the power of an endless life to give to His people with His own hand all the fruits of His Passion, to be to them Himself the bread of life and the wine of heaven for evermore. The Saviour meets every true disciple here in the closest and most gracious fellowship, as One who has "done all things and given all things for us, before He asks us for anything."[2] Our salva-

seems very probable. "The Rabbis saw the new society, in proportion as the Gentile element in it became predominant, throwing off circumcision and relying on baptism only. . . . There was everything to lead them to give fresh prominence to what had been before subordinate. If the Nazarenes attracted men by their baptism, they would show that they had baptism as well as circumcision." (Art. "Proselytes," in Smith, ii. p. 944.) They thus developed and emphasized in the reception of proselytes and their children what had hitherto held a more subordinate position as one of the "divers baptisms," enjoined in, or arising out of, the Mosaic system on which the Pharisees laid such stress in our Lord's time (διάφοροι βαπτισμοί, Heb. ix. 10; comp. Mark vii. 4).

And (2) whether the practice of proselyte Baptism had established itself before the Christian era, or arose "as an independent rite of initiation" two or three generations after that date, it is perfectly clear at least that no difficulty was ever felt by those fellow-countrymen of the apostles who remained on the old Jewish ground as to baptizing the infants of converts to Judaism on the ground of their parents' faith.

[1] Matt. xxvi. 27 f.; Luke xxii. 19 f.   [2] Augustine.

tion rests on Him and on that finished work of atonement in which He is revealed, not on our obedience or deservings.[1] Each disciple in keeping this ordinance of Christ according to His command to him professes his own faith in these great central facts of redemption, and in the name of his Lord thus revealed as "the Christ, the Son of the living God." He takes for himself "the cup of salvation, and calls upon the name of the Lord" for all present and future blessing that he needs. He receives and rests upon Jesus Christ afresh for salvation, as He offers Himself afresh to him in this ordinance. And in this exercise of faith the Presence and blessing of the Lord are realized by each true disciple of His in a very special and gracious way.[2]

In all these respects the ordinance of the Supper, like that of Baptism, perfectly corresponds with what we have already seen to be our Lord's teaching as to the conditions of entrance into His Church on earth, and as to the relations between Himself and His disciples individually.

4. Both the sacraments of the New Testament look beyond the individual believer and his direct and personal relations to the Saviour. The union and fellowship which they represent and confirm are first with the Lord Himself, but also and necessarily with the brethren. The name in which they are administered is that in which the Church is assembled.

Baptism, in this aspect, denotes admission into the Church of Christ, as represented by the local congregation, in which the believer, or the believer together with his infant seed, now receives his place and his welcome. By finding the Lord he has also found brethren and sisters in the Lord. This is a token to him that it is so. The convert is baptized "into the name of the Father, the Son, and the Holy Spirit." But that is the name of God as revealed in Jesus Christ, the name in which the Church is gathered together, and in which it acts in all matters relating to its fellowship, or affecting its members as such.

---

[1] See Dr. Dale's striking remarks on the power of the Lord's Supper, when rightly viewed and used, to meet and correct false and perilous tendencies in Christian life and thought in every age of the Church. *Manual of Congregational Principles*, Lond. 1884, pp. 143–146.

[2] Compare a noble passage in Bruce's *Sermons on the Sacraments*, first published in 1590, (Wodrow ed.), Edin. 1843, pp. 28–30.

As an ordinance of Christ, and one in which He specially speaks to the soul, Baptism is most fitly administered where, according to His own express promise, He Himself is in the midst of His disciples; as an ordinance of admission into the fellowship of Christ's people, it is meet and right that it should be administered in their presence, with their visible concurrence, and with their prayers accompanying it.

In Old Testament times, after circumcision,—which, as in the case of our Lord and His forerunner, might take place at a distance from Jerusalem,—the children of believers were brought up to the temple, and presented to the Lord, with the appointed offerings, in the place "which He had chosen to put His name there."[1]   But under the New Testament, as we have seen, "the house of God" is to be recognised in the assembly of His people wherever met, and the Lord's Presence is to be found wherever two or three believers are gathered together in the name of Jesus.[2]   It is there, therefore, in the midst of the believing congregation and along with them, that the believing parents can now most fitly present their little ones to the Lord in His own ordinance for blessing.

On all these grounds it is evident that, in ordinary circumstances, it is by the public dispensation of Baptism that its true scope and meaning are best brought out, and its spiritual purposes attained.   When so administered, the "visible Word" in this sacrament is spoken most powerfully to the whole worshipping congregation, young and old alike.   Baptism is a standing and public witness to the reality of the forgiveness of sins and the cleansing efficacy of Christ's blood, and to the renewing and sanctifying power of the Holy Ghost, as sent by the Father and the Son, and working continually in the Church and in the world from the day of Pentecost onwards to the end of time.

As administered to the children of believers, Baptism represents and confirms to the parents and to the whole believing congregation that central blessing of the covenant of grace which was declared to Abraham: "I will be a God to thee,

[1] Luke ii. 21–39 ; Lev. xii. 6–8.   Comp. Bonar, *Leviticus*, p. 218 ff.
[2] See above, pp. 82–85.

and to thy seed after thee." It repeats in Scripture symbols the language of God's ancient promises to His people in connection with some of the chief renewals of that covenant in later days : " I will sprinkle clean water upon you, and ye shall be clean; from all your filthiness, and from all your idols, will I cleanse you. A new heart also will I give you, and a new spirit will I put within you; and I will take away the stony heart out of your flesh, and I will give you a heart of flesh. And I will put My Spirit within you, and cause you to walk in My statutes. . . . And ye shall be My people, and I will be your God." "Hear, O Jacob, My servant, and Israel, whom I have chosen; thus saith the Lord that made thee and formed thee from the womb. . . . I will pour water upon him that is thirsty, and streams upon the dry ground; I will pour My Spirit upon thy seed, and my blessing upon thine offspring; and they shall spring up among the grass, as willows by the water-courses. One shall say, I am the Lord's; and another shall call himself by the name of Jacob; and another shall subscribe with his hand unto the Lord, and surname himself by the name of Israel." [1]

Still more manifestly does the other sacrament of the New Testament look beyond the mere individual aspect of the believer's spiritual life, and bring before us his relations to the whole company or fellowship of believers, and their common relations to the Lord. Like the ordinance of the passover, out of which historically it took its rise, the Lord's Supper speaks of a great redemption, wrought by the hand of God for His people, and of the facts on which that redemption rests. In this sacrament, the Israel of God in all ages and all lands keep in joyful remembrance what was done for them once and for all long ago, the results of which remain for ever. In the ordinance of the Supper not one believer merely, but many, the whole worshipping congregation, join together as with one voice to " proclaim the Lord's death till He come," to " remember Him " as He revealed Himself after His Resurrection, as " the First and the Last, and the Living One; who was dead, and, behold, He is alive for evermore, and hath the keys of death and of Hades." [2]

[1] Ezek. xxxvi. 25–28 ; Isa. xliv. 1–5.   [2] 1 Cor. xi. 26 ; Rev. i. 18.

The Lord's Supper is thus a standing evidence throughout the world to the fact that the Lord Jesus Christ has a Church on earth to worship Him according to His will, and that there is a real communion between Him and His Church by the Spirit.   Around this ordinance in all countries under heaven, we see His disciples gather together, one with Him and with each other in all that is deepest and highest in their spiritual experience, on the common foundation of Christ known, and trusted, and loved, making confession with one accord before all men that He is "the Son of the living God," "the Christ, the Saviour of the world."

To meet and to have fellowship with the Lord Himself at His table is no doubt the first and highest blessing to be sought in the sacrament; but that is not all that the Saviour meant His disciples to find there.   He meant to draw them closer to each other, as well as to Himself; the signs and actions of the ordinance are specially fitted for this end.   To eat and drink together at a common table is a natural evidence and expression of family love and familiar friendship; and it is an act which tends to strengthen and deepen the feelings which are thereby expressed.   It was as the Head of the family of the disciples that the Saviour was wont to keep the passover with them according to Jewish custom.   As one family or household of faith, they sat down together to that last feast of the Old Testament, which passed without a break, before they rose from the table, into the first Lord's Supper of the New.   The essential character of the feast and the chief lessons of its symbols remained the same.   What Christ did, and bid His disciples do, with the passover bread and wine, they were to do with the like bread and wine in the Lord's Supper whenever it was celebrated: "And He took a loaf (λαβὼν ἄρτον), and when He had given thanks, He brake it, and gave to them, saying, This is My body, which is given for you: this do in remembrance of Me.   And the cup in like manner after supper, saying, This cup is the new covenant in My blood, even that which is poured out for you." [1]   Almost His first words, as it seems, to the disciples at the

[1] Luke xxii. 19 f.

table, and His action in rising from it and washing their feet spoke of brotherly love and mutual service.[1]

The order of communion generally observed in the Reformed Church, by keeping close to the example of the original institution, brings out this aspect of the truth taught in the ordinance in an impressive way. The communicants sit side by side with each other at a common table, the children of the congregation and other non-communicants being present and looking on. The bread and the cup pass among those at the Table from hand to hand. Each communicant both receives and gives the consecrated symbols. Each one breaks the bread in turn, and gives it to the brother or sister sitting next to him at the Table; and they again do the same. The disciples of the Lord Jesus, thus gathered together in His name, and doing with one accord the things which He commanded, are visibly one and yet many. The sacrament thus dispensed is "a visible word" from the Lord Himself to all who partake of it, and to all who look on, concerning unity and brotherly kindness in His Church. It represents and seals a brotherly covenant of mutual love and service among Christ's people.

2nd. Christ's great commission to His Church.

The nature of the great commission corresponds with that of the two sacraments. Alike they contemplate a world-wide Church. Disciples are to be made among all nations, and everywhere the Lord's presence is to be realized in connection with the observance of what He has commanded His disciples to do. Baptism and the Lord's Supper are fitted for a world-wide religion; they are not like the passover, which needed Jerusalem and a material altar and a sacrificing priest; and circumcision, which needed the temple and its offerings to complete its idea.[2]

[1] Luke xxii. 24–27 ; John xiii. 4–17.

[2] I may say here that I cannot agree with Prof. Candlish in what he says as to the uncertainty thrown upon the wording of our Lord's last commission, by the fact that the apostolic Church had difficulties about receiving the Gentiles into full fellowship with themselves without circumcision. Prof. Candlish's argument seems neither a sufficient nor a well-grounded one. He holds that while " we can hardly doubt " that the Evangelists have cast our

In the two sacraments of the New Testament we see first and chiefly what Christ is and has done for His people; but we see also what He calls them to be and to do for Him and for each other. In His ordinances, as in His word, He speaks to His disciples of Himself and of His work for them and in them; but He speaks also of the work which they are to do for Him and with Him, of what is really implied in being His disciple, and entering into that covenant fellowship with the Lord and with the brethren, which is the Church of Christ. So it has been ever since the visible Church of God was formally set up on earth in the days of Him who was "the father of all them that believe."

Lord's words on the subject into "a form substantially true, and faithful to their real meaning and intention," yet that if He had spoken so plainly as appears from Mark xvi. 15 and Matt. xxviii. 19, such doubts and scruples as are recorded in Acts xi. 2 f., xv. 1 ff., could not have arisen. *Kingdom of God*, p. 152 f. Weiss in his *Biblical Theol. of N. T.* (E. Tr. Edin. 1882, i. p. 139) takes the same view.

But, in point of fact, the objection raised by "them of the circumcision" to Peter's proceedings in the house of Cornelius was not to his "preaching of Christ to the Gentiles," as Dr. Candlish puts it, but to his "going in to men uncircumcised and eating with them" (Acts xi. 3). It was not settled by our Lord's words in Mark xvi. or Matt. xxviii. that His disciples were to enter into such intimate fellowship with the uncircumcised, nor that the nations were not to be brought into the Christian Church so far on the old terms. Was not Christianity just "Judaism with the Messiah come"? Circumcision and Baptism, as there is reason to believe, went together at this time in the admission of Jewish proselytes; why not in the admission of Christian ones? The great commission did not say that circumcision was to cease, although Baptism was to be used and to have more prominence than hitherto. Both ordinances had been administered side by side during Christ's lifetime. His disciples had baptized in His name (John iv. 1 f.); and circumcision had continued in their families as before. Their Master had never made light of it; why should they do so? Was it not a Divine ordinance? Had not Christ Himself been circumcised as well as baptized? The Gospel was, no doubt, to be preached to all nations after a full beginning had been made at Jerusalem (Luke xxiv. 47). The Gentiles were to be made proselytes to Christ; but why should they not enter by the same door with the Jews? The general terms of the great commission did not at all dispose of the particular difficulties which were certain to arise from the standpoint of the first disciples as soon as they began to preach the Gospel to others than "Jews and proselytes." Inferences from our Lord's words, which seem inevitable to us now, cannot be fairly said to be so when we place ourselves in the historical circumstances of the apostles. Comp. Meyer's reply to the same difficulties as those felt by Prof. Candlish, *Matthew*, E. Tr. ii. p. 301. See also Mr. Robert Mackintosh's remarks in his interesting and suggestive monograph, *Christ and the Jewish Law*, London 1886, p. 213.

God gave much to Abraham; but it was to fit him and his for much service. It was for high and world-wide ends that he was "chosen and called;" it was a great work in which he was found "faithful." Thus also in Baptism and the Lord's Supper Christ teaches and gives us many things; but it is for high and wide ends. And we on our part bind ourselves to certain things in His name.

This thought comes out especially in our Lord's parting words to His disciples, and in the great commission which He entrusted to them as representing the company of His believing people in all time. For what purposes was Christ to build His Church upon the rock, and to keep it so that the gates of Hades should never prevail against it? What are the chief ends for which His disciples are chosen of God the Father and given to Christ? In what work are they called to prove their faithfulness to Him?

The answer has been seen in part already in some of the great sayings of our Lord on which we have touched. The Church of Christ exists not merely as a society for worship; although in its assemblies the true worshippers in every land unite to worship the Father in spirit and in truth. It is not merely a society for moral and religious instruction, for spiritual edification and the communion of saints; although "where two or three are gathered together in Christ's name there He is in the midst of them" as their Mediator and Advocate with the Father, the source of all spiritual blessing and growth in grace and knowledge, the centre of Christian fellowship, He who hath all the gifts of the Holy Spirit to bestow upon His people. The Church has been established on earth not merely to guard her own purity of communion, and to seek the spiritual welfare of her members by the exercise of a loving yet authoritative discipline; although it is especially in connection with this, as we have seen,[1] that she receives the assurance of the Lord's presence in her assemblies, and of all needful gifts in answer to united prayer. These duties and privileges have been assigned to the Church by her Lord. All these ends are to be fulfilled by her. That they should be attained

---

[1] Above, pp. 188-193.

concerns most directly the spiritual life and well-being of her members.   And yet in another sense they are but means to a higher end.

The chief end of the Church is to be in this world what Christ Himself was, to do in it what He did, to carry on to final success the great work for which He came from heaven.

This is declared again and again in words of our Lord, which have been already under consideration.   It is one of the central thoughts in His High-Priestly prayer.   It finds expression in the first words of the risen Saviour to the disciples met in His name in the upper room at Jerusalem: "As the Father hath sent Me, even so send I you."   And with this high and comprehensive commission there was vouchsafed the earnest of the power needed for its per-formance: "And when He had said this, He breathed on them, and saith unto them: Receive ye the Holy Ghost; whose soever sins ye forgive, they are forgiven unto them; whose soever sins ye retain, they are retained."[1]   Along with this gift, as we saw before, another was bestowed, namely, a special insight into the meaning of the Scriptures bearing on the sufferings, death, and resurrection of the Messiah, and of the Gospel message for all the world as founded on these great facts; and a promise was added of further power from on high for the work committed to them, through the advent of the Holy Spirit, for which they were to wait in Jerusalem.[2] Lastly, in a solemn parting charge to His disciples before His ascension, "Jesus spake unto them, saying: All authority hath been given unto Me in heaven and on earth.   Go ye therefore and make disciples of all the nations, baptizing them into the name of the Father, and of the Son, and of the Holy Ghost; teaching them to observe all things whatsoever I commanded you; and, lo, I am with you alway, even unto the end of the world."[3]

In these memorable words which crown the group of pregnant utterances to which we have now referred, and in connection with which the purport of the great commission is best seen, the Church or company of believers, as has

---

[1] John xx. 21–23.   See the exposition of the passage above, pp. 192–201.
[2] Luke xxiv. 45–49.   [3] Matt. xxviii. 18–20.

been already shown, was solemnly put in trust by her risen Lord with the Gospel of the grace of God, the good tidings of forgiveness and salvation in the name of Jesus Christ, to be proclaimed by her with Divine authority among all the nations.[1] Christ's disciples as such are appointed by Him to be "witnesses of these things." He has made full provision by the mission of the Holy Spirit, the Paraclete, for their being sufficient and successful witnesses. "Ye shall receive power," the risen Saviour repeated as His parting assurance to the disciples, when, "being gathered in company with them,"[2] they asked Him concerning the future of His cause on the eve of the Ascension, "when the Holy Ghost is come upon you; and ye shall be My witnesses (ἔσεσθέ Μου μάρτυρες) both in Jerusalem and in all Judæa and Samaria, and unto the uttermost part of the earth."[3]

This witness for Christ is to be a witness, not of the lips only, but of the life. The mind and spirit of the Lord Jesus are to be seen in His disciples, living as He did in the world, but being not of it. "As the Father hath sent Me, even so send I you." "The Son of Man," our Lord said, repeating the saying at different stages of His ministry, "is come to seek and save that which was lost;" "not to be ministered unto, but to minister, and to give His life a ransom for many." "My meat is to do the will of Him that sent Me, and to accomplish His work."[4] The mind and heart of God the Father are revealed to us in the words and actions of the Lord Jesus Christ on earth, in what He says of the Good Shepherd and the wandering sheep, in the parables of the lost which we have in the fifteenth chapter of the third Gospel, in what He did and bore through all the years of His earthly life, "in His agony and bloody sweat, in His Cross and Passion." He that hath heard Christ hath heard the Father; He that hath seen Him hath seen the Father.

---

[1] See above, pp. 197–199.

[2] συναλιζόμενος, Acts i. 4. The term occurs here only in the New Testament. Meyer prefers the patristic rendering which the R. V. puts in the margin: "As He ate with them," deriving the word from ἅλς, salt.

[3] Luke xxiv. 48; Acts i. 8.

[4] Matt. x. 6; xv. 24; xviii. 11; xx. 28; Mark x. 45; Luke xv. 4 ff., 24; xix. 10; John iv. 34.

This mind, therefore, ought to be in the Church as a whole, and in all its members severally, which was in Christ Jesus. As He was, so ought we to be in this world. As He did, so we are called to do, to go everywhere making known the glad tidings of salvation, bringing back the lost to God in Christ, and then teaching and helping them to live as His redeemed and restored children should.[1]

The two divisions of the Church's work now indicated are set side by side in their connection in our Lord's last commission, in the form in which we have it in the first Gospel. Among all the nations, and throughout all time, " even to the consummation of the age," the Church is to be Christ's witness on earth, speaking of Him and for Him ; first of all, bringing all the nations to be His disciples ; and secondly, teaching them to observe all things whatsoever He has commanded. And it is in connection with this twofold charge that the Lord's own Presence is promised to be with her " all the days," in which she bears this testimony, and does this work.

Both of these two great sections of the work of the Church were no doubt included in the teaching which the apostles received from the risen Saviour during the forty days before His Ascension, when " He spoke to them the things concerning the kingdom of God." [2] That important phrase, as defined by Prof. Candlish, denotes " the gathering together of men under God's eternal law of righteous love by the vital power of His redeeming love in Jesus Christ, brought to bear upon them through the Holy Spirit." [3] It includes both " the process and the result of this gathering." Its purport coincides, therefore, in substance with the two parts of the great commission ; first, to make men disciples to Christ ; and secondly, to teach them to do His will in all things. " The kingdom of God," Dr. Candlish concludes, " as appears from a general survey of our Lord's teaching about it, is distinctively and comprehensively Christian ; it refers to Christianity in its living and practical aspect. . . . The idea of the kingdom

---

[1] Comp. Dr. Binnie's admirable chapter on "The Chief End of the Church," *The Church*, pp. 36–51.

[2] Acts i. 3.

[3] Candlish, *Kingdom of God*, p. 197.

of God has its chief value and use as affording an adequate category under which to unfold the body of Christian duty." [1]

Prof. Candlish fully admits and maintains that the conceptions of the Church and the kingdom agree in the two most essential points : First, as regards the persons included in them. "The subjects of Christ's kingdom are the same who are members of the Church invisible. This appears exegetically even from the Old Testament, where 'the congregation of the Lord' and the 'kingdom of priests' denote the same people ; and also from the passages in the New Testament where those Old Testament expressions are used. So the theological definitions agree in describing each not only as a company of men, but in its component parts as the same company." Secondly, the Church and the kingdom agree not only in referring to the same company of persons, but also as regards the way in which these persons have been gathered into one and are kept so. They are gathered together "in Christ," "into the name" of Jesus as the Christ, the Son of the living God, "by the vital power of God's redeeming love in Jesus Christ, brought to bear upon them through the Holy Spirit." [2]

It is unnecessary to refer here in detail to the aspects in which Prof. Candlish holds that the Church and the kingdom of God should be "distinguished from each other, although not separated." [3] It does not seem to me that he has been quite successful in bringing out the distinction in a clear and satisfactory way. But from the standpoint of our present discussion it may be enough to say that practically the kingdom of God in this world is just the Church at work. It denotes "all those throughout the world who profess the true religion, together with their children,"—that is, according to the Westminster Confession, "the catholic Church visible," [4] —regarded especially in their life and work, their influence

---

[1] *Kingdom of God*, pp. 195, 205.   [2] *Ib.* pp. 197, 203.
[3] *Ib.* p. 208.
[4] "The visible Church, which is also catholic or universal under the Gospel, —not confined to one nation, as before under the law,—consists of all those throughout the world that profess the true religion, together with their children ; and is the kingdom of the Lord Jesus Christ, the house and family of God, out of which there is no ordinary possibility of salvation." Westm. Conf. xxv. 2.

direct and indirect in the world. The chief conception of the Church in our Lord's teaching, as we have seen, is that of the קהל יהוה, the ἐκκλησία τοῦ κυρίου, in the widest sense. It is not bound to any special organization. It is not limited to any one organized Church, or even the sum of all such Churches. It is the "populus civitasque Christiana," — to use a fine expression of the old divines of the Reformed Church,—in its full influence, doing Christ's work in the world, seeking by His grace and Spirit to fulfil all righteousness, as He did, in all the relations of human life, and to lead others to do so, to be actually consecrated to God and His service, that the will of God may be done on earth as it is in heaven.[1]

---

[1] See Durham's dissertation "Concerning the Unity of the Catholic Visible Church," in his commentary on the Revelation (Glasgow, ed. 1788, pp. 553-6). "There is a unity amongst all professors in all parts of the world that live in the same time. They are all of this one Church ; and there is one integral catholic Church that is made up of them all. . . . All professing Christians, who possibly belong to no particular congregation, are of this Church ; for they are not of any particular Church, and yet cannot be without even the visible Church, but in that respect have a mother. This is the Church that the twelve apostles and their successors adorn. . . . All the apostles fed but one Church when they fed Christ's lambs anywhere. The Church so considered is most essentially the Church of Christ." Comp. Hudson, *Vindication of the essence and unity of the Church Catholic visible, and the priority thereof in regard of particular Churches*, Lond. 1650, pp. 25–76, 97–150, 216–253.

The difficulty of distinguishing between the two aspects of the Church on earth, which are indicated by the expressions "the Church invisible" and "visible," is illustrated by Mr. R. Mackintosh in his work already mentioned, *Christ and the Jewish Law*. In his able discussion of "the kingdom of God," Mr. Mackintosh seems in two successive sentences to identify it first with the Church visible and then with the Church invisible. "So far as its actual position in the world was concerned," he says, "the kingdom of God coincided with the circle of Christ's disciples. In history, measured similarly by its extent, it will mean much the same thing as the 'invisible Church' of Protestant theology ; only, while that is defined primarily by religious marks, as being the society which stands in inner fellowship with God, the kingdom of God is defined primarily by ethical marks as being the society which does the will of God" (p. 221). "The circle of Christ's disciples," however, even under His own eye during His earthly life, was by no means "the same thing as the invisible Church." In that circle were "Judas which betrayed Him," and other "disciples, who went back and walked no more with Jesus." There are some who are "in Christ," in a sense and for a time, who in the end are cast into the fire as dead branches, having no real union with the Vine. There are some who are "in His kingdom" for a season who shall finally be "gathered out of it" as "stumbling-blocks and they that do iniquity," and "cast into the furnace of fire." See above, pp. 208, 212, 216.

3rd. The position and functions in the Church assigned by Christ to His apostles.

Whatever else the apostles were to be, it is plain that they were to be office-bearers in the Church. During the period of our Lord's earthly ministry, they were the only individual disciples with respect to whom it was distinctly indicated that they were designed to hold that special position. "God hath set some in the Church," Paul wrote afterwards to the Corinthians, "first, apostles; secondly, prophets; thirdly, teachers . . . Are all apostles? Are all prophets? Are all teachers?"[1]

The twelve were to hold a foremost place as regards both the evangelistic and the pastoral work which needed to be done, both as to gathering men into the fellowship of Christ for the first time, and as to their spiritual nurture and growth within that fellowship. "Come ye after Me," our Lord said to the two whose names stand first in the list of the apostles, when He called them from their nets by the Sea of Galilee, "and I will make you fishers of men." "Fear not," He said again to Peter, after the miraculous draught of fishes, "from henceforth thou shalt catch men."[2] The apostles were to be shepherds of Christ's flock under Himself the Chief Shepherd, entering into the sheepfold by Him as the door;[3] having His command laid upon them, as given to Peter on his restoration to his old position among the twelve: "Feed My lambs. Be a shepherd to My dear sheep, and feed them."[4]

---

[1] 1 Cor. xii. 28 f. Comp. Eph. iv. 11, where the appointment is ascribed directly to Christ: "And He Himself gave (καὶ αὐτὸς ἔδωκε τοὺς μὲν ἀποστόλους) some to be apostles, and some evangelists, and some pastors and teachers."

[2] Matt. iv. 19; Luke v. 10.   [3] John x. 1 f., 7 f.

[4] Βόσκε τὰ ἀρνία μου. . . . Ποίμαινε τὰ προβάτιά μου. . . . Βόσκε τὰ προβάτιά μου, John xxi. 15–17. The Saviour's words imply much. They are *My* sheep, whom I entrust to your care. They are My *dear* sheep, to be *lovingly* as well as faithfully tended and fed. In ver. 16, B and C have προβάτια, while ℵ A D read πρόβατα; in ver. 17, A B C agree in reading προβάτια. We may hold the diminutive as certainly the right reading in the latter verse, while it is probable for the former also. The R. V. has πρόβατα in ver. 16, and προβάτια in ver. 17. Westcott and Hort put προβάτια in their text in both verses. It conveys the idea of tender solicitude and affection, rather than, as Godet suggests, a less advanced stage of strength and development than πρόβατα, although more than ἀρνία. The supposition of a climax of this sort is clearly an insufficient ground

Peter and the rest of the apostles, as we have seen, are to be stewards in Christ's house with the authority implied in the power o ithe keys, the power to bind and to loose.[1] A question put by Peter on another occasion as to the application of a parable regarding the duties of servants in a house in their master's absence, elicited from our Lord some striking words concerning the special responsibilities and rewards of those servants who should be set as stewards over others and over the household generally. " Blessed are those servants (δοῦλοι)," Christ had said, " whom the lord when he cometh shall find watching. Verily I say unto you, that he shall gird himself and make them sit down to meat, and shall come and serve them. . . . And Peter said, Lord, speakest Thou this parable unto us, or even unto all ? "[2] Could it be that so great a reward was held out to every servant in Christ's house ? Must it not be designed rather for those who held some special position in it, such as that to which the twelve had been called ?

The scope of the question, as has been pointed out,[3] corresponds closely to that of one which was put by Peter at another time as to the reward in store for the apostles who had left all to follow their Lord, which drew from Christ the assurance that hereafter they should " sit upon twelve thrones, judging the twelve tribes of Israel."[4]

Our Lord's response now is, so far, of a similar kind. All Christ's true servants should be rewarded ; but those of them who were set as stewards or overseers over the rest in their Lord's absence should receive a higher reward, according to their greater responsibility, if found faithful ; while, on the other hand, their punishment should be proportionately more severe, if they proved unfaithful. " And the Lord said : Who then (τίς ἄρα)[5] is the faithful and wise steward

for reversing the order of the R. V., as Godet is disposed to do, by putting πρόβατια in ver. 16, and πρόβατα in ver. 17. *L'Evangile de S. Jean*, 3me ed. iii. p. 685 f.

[1] See above, pp. 175 ff., 186 ff.　　　　　[2] Luke xii. 37–41.

[3] Godet, *L'Evangile de S. Luc*, 2me ed. ii. p. 136.

[4] Matt. xix. 27 f. ; Luke xxii. 30.

[5] " Jésus interroge réellement. Il invite Pierre à chercher lui même cet intendant (ce doit être lui et chaque apôtre). Matthieu, en conservant

(οἰκονόμος), whom his lord shall set over his household (θεραπείας) [1] to give them their portion of food in due season ? Blessed is that servant (δοῦλος) [2] whom his lord when he cometh shall find so doing. Of a truth I say unto you, that he will set him over all that he hath." [3]

The twelve, then, were unquestionably designed by Christ to be office-bearers, stewards or overseers, in His Church. We have seen in passages considered in last chapter, as well as in those now touched upon, that powers and functions of a pastoral kind, and in connection with discipline, were entrusted

---

(xxiv. 45–51) cette forme interrogative, tout en omettant la question de Pierre qui l'a motivée, rend un remarquable témoignage à la fidélité du récit de Luc." Godet, ii. 137.

[1] In Matthew οἰκετείας ; Lat. *famulitium*, the domestic establishment.

[2] The οἰκονόμος was a slave like the rest of the servants, although in a higher position.

[3] Ἐπὶ πᾶσι τοῖς ὑπάρχουσιν αὐτοῦ καταστήσει αὐτόν. Godet brings out with characteristic clearness the difference between the reward of the faithful servant (ver. 37) and that of the faithful steward (ver. 44). "The reward of the former is more familiar and endearing (plus intime). It is the expression of the personal affection of the master for the servant who has personally served him well and faithfully. The reward of the latter is more glorious. It is, so to speak, an official reward for the services he has rendered to the household (à la maison). It implies some high position of ministry in the kingdom of glory, given in return for work done in an influential position by the faithful servant during the economy of grace. This relation between the two things is indicated by the correspondence of the καταστήσει in ver. 42 with that in ver. 44. This utterance of Christ would seem to take for granted that the apostolate shall continue until the return of Christ ; and in truth it follows unquestionably from the image employed that there shall continue in the Church until the end a ministry of the Word established by Christ. The apostles felt this so strongly, that when the time came for them to leave the world they took care to establish ministers of the Word to fill their places in the Church. This ministry was a continuation, not indeed of all that the apostles were, but at least of one of their most indispensable functions, that of which Jesus speaks in this parable, the regular distribution of spiritual food to the flock ; comp. the Pastoral Epistles and 1 Pet. v. The theory which makes the pastorate emanate from the Church, as its representative organ, is therefore not Scriptural ; the office in question is rather an emanation from the apostolate, and thus mediately an institution of Jesus Himself. . . . It is by the will of Jesus that this ministry exists. He has established it by His mandatories; He vouchsafes to the Church in every age men who have the mission for the office and endows them with all needful gifts for this end. Hence their responsibility is the greater," ii. 137 f. The relation between the call of Christ to any believer to be a minister and the call of the Church will be considered under Parts V. and VI. Comp. Bannerman, *Church of Christ*, i. pp. 421–437. Binnie, *The Church*, p. 135.

to the apostles, the continuance of which in the Church after their death, " even unto the consummation of the age," was undoubtedly contemplated by our Lord. But the question remains, What was the essential nature of their office in itself ? Was the apostleship as such an ordinary or extraordinary office in the Church of Christ ? Was it designed by Him to be temporary only, or were the twelve to have successors, in such a sense that their office in itself, and not merely as regards some of the functions discharged by its original occupants, should be a permanent one in the Church ?

The more this point is calmly examined in the light of Scripture, the more evident it becomes that, from the very nature of the case, the apostolic office as instituted by Christ was unique in character and design, and essentially incapable of transmission.

1. The first and absolutely essential requisite in the case of any one who was to fill the office of an apostle was that he must have seen the Lord Jesus with the eyes of the flesh, and be personally qualified to be a witness to His resurrection from the dead.

Others among " the early disciples (ἀρχαῖοι μαθηταί) " [1] might be so far in the same position as regards direct and personal knowledge of " Christ after the flesh," but " the twelve " were His own selected and accredited witnesses. This primary requisite for the apostleship is stated by Peter in the clearest possible way, at the time when Matthias is chosen to fill the place of Judas. " Of the men, therefore, which have companied with us all the time that the Lord Jesus went in and out among us, beginning from the baptism of John unto the day that He was received up from us, of these must one become a witness with us of His resurrection." [2]

The same thought runs through all the recorded utterances of the original apostles which bear upon this point. " This Jesus did God raise up," Peter said, standing up with the eleven on the day of Pentecost, " whereof we all are witnesses." " Whom God raised from the dead," he repeats, in his own name and that of John, before the multitude in Solomon's porch, " whereof we are witnesses." " Peter and

---

[1] Acts xxi. 16.   [2] Acts i. 21 f.

the apostles answered and said," to the high priest and the Sanhedrin at Jerusalem, "The God of our fathers raised up Jesus, whom ye slew, hanging Him on a tree. Him did God exalt with His right hand to be a Prince and a Saviour for to give repentance to Israel and remission of sins. And we are witnesses of these things." "Him God raised up the third day," Peter said in his first address to a purely Gentile audience, "and gave Him to be made manifest not to all the people, but unto witnesses that were chosen before of God, even to us who did eat and drink with Him after He rose from the dead."[1]

It is needless to multiply evidence, but it is worth noting how strongly the one apparent exception, in the case of "the apostle of the Gentiles," really confirms the rule that this qualification was essential to make any one "an apostle of Christ." Paul had not seen the Lord in the way in which the original disciples had done so, either before His resurrection or during the forty days preceding His ascension. This defect, therefore, was supplied by an extraordinary revelation to him of the risen Saviour. "To this end have I appeared unto thee (ὤφθην σοι), to appoint thee a minister and a witness both of the things wherein thou hast seen Me (ὧν τε εἶδές με), and of the things wherein I will appear unto thee; delivering thee from the people, and from the Gentiles, unto whom I send thee (εἰς οὓς ἐγὼ ἀποστέλλω σε)."[2] That Paul saw Christ after His resurrection in as real a sense and in the same objective way as the other members of the apostolic college, he himself has not the slightest doubt: "He appeared to Cephas (ὤφθη Κηφᾷ); then to the twelve; then He appeared to above five hundred brethren at once . . . last of all, as unto one born out of due time, He appeared to me also (ὤφθη κἀμοί). For I am the least of the apostles, that am not meet to be called an apostle, because I persecuted the Church of God." "Am I not an apostle?" he says again; "Have not I seen (οὐχὶ ἑώρακα) Jesus Christ our Lord?"[3]

From the nature of the case, such eye and ear witnesses of Christ there could only be once and for all. In this capacity

---

[1] Acts ii. 32 ; iii. 15 ; v. 29–32 ; x. 40 f.
[2] Acts xxvi. 16 f.   [3] 1 Cor. xv. 5–9 ; ix. 1.

the apostles could not possibly have successors.   Their testimony is recorded for the Church of all time in the writings of
the New Testament, and in the historical facts of the rise, and
growth, and victory of Christianity after the death of Christ.

2. The same thing holds of the second great condition of the
apostleship, namely, a direct commission from the Lord Himself.

The twelve were called and "sent" by Christ, without the
intervention of human instrumentality, even as Christ was by
the Father.   The name "apostles" was expressly given to
them by Himself in connection with their original appointment: "He chose from among His disciples twelve, whom
also *He named* 'apostles.'"[1]   As Christ is the great "Apostle
and High Priest of our confession," so they are "His apostles."[2]

The fourth evangelist does not expressly mention the
formal appointment of the twelve by Christ, as the three
synoptists do.   But he takes it for granted, as soon as he
reaches the stage in our Lord's ministry to which it belongs.
"The twelve" appear in John's Gospel as a well-known
body, distinct from the rest of the "disciples."[3]   "Did not I
choose you the twelve?"[4]   In like manner Paul uses the
same phrase to denote the apostolic company when in point
of fact there were only ten present, Judas being dead and
Thomas absent: "He appeared unto Cephas, then to the
twelve."   We have an instance of the same sort in the ninth
chapter of Acts, where it is said that "Barnabas took Saul
and brought him to the apostles," *i.e.* introduced him to the
apostolic company as such, although, as we learn from his
own account in the first chapter of Galatians, only one representative of that body, namely Peter, was actually seen by
him at that time.[5]

---

[1] Luke vi. 13.   Comp. Matt. x. 1 f., 5 (τούτους τοὺς δώδεκα ἀπέστειλεν ὁ Ἰησοῦς) ;
Mark iii. 14 (ἐποίησε δώδεκα, ἵνα ὦσι μετ' αὐτοῦ, καὶ ἵνα ἀποστέλλῃ αὐτοὺς κηρύσσειν) ;
John xvii. 18 ; xx. 21.

[2] Heb. iii. 1 ; Acts i. 2 ; Eph. iii. 5.

[3] The first mention of them is in John vi. 67 f. ; but the number is implied in
ver. 13 : "They filled twelve baskets with the broken pieces from the five barley
loaves."   "La critique a demandé d'où venaient les douze corbeilles.   Le nombre
fait supposer que c'étaient les paniers de voyage des apôtres." Godet, ii. p. 479.

[4] Οὐκ ἐγὼ ὑμᾶς τοὺς δώδεκα ἐξελεξάμην, John vi. 70.

[5] 1 Cor. xv. 5 ; Acts ix. 57 ; Gal. i. 17.   "There is no difficulty in under-

The title, when first given by our Lord, must, as Bishop Light-foot has shown, have conveyed to the minds of the recipients, and of Christ's followers generally, the idea of some important mission to be entrusted to the twelve.   " Applied to persons, the word denotes more than ἄγγελος.   The 'apostle' is not only the messenger, but the delegate of the person who sends him.   He is entrusted with a mission, has power conferred upon him.   Beyond this the classical usage of the term gives no aid towards understanding the meaning of the Christian apostolate. . . . The term occurs but once in the LXX. in 1 Kings xiv. 6 as a translation of שָׁלוּחַ, where it has the general sense of a messenger, though with reference to a commission from God.[1]   With the later Jews, however, and it would appear also with the Jews of the Christian era, the word was in common use.   It was the title borne by those who were despatched from the mother city by the rulers of the race on any foreign mission, especially such as were charged with collecting the tribute paid to the temple service. After the destruction of Jerusalem the 'apostles' formed a sort of council about the Jewish patriarch, assisting him in his deliberations at home and executing his orders abroad." [2]

There could be no doubt, therefore, in the minds of the early disciples that the twelve whom Christ set solemnly apart from their number, and on whom He expressly bestowed this significant name, were designated thereby to some special and important work, and that all powers needful for the dischaige of it would be conferred upon them by their Lord.

standing 'the twelve' to be a designation of the apostolic college in the same way as 'the eleven' in Athens meant a body of officers. . . . Whether St. Paul includes James ('the Lord's brother') among 'the apostles' or not, it is im-possible to say.   It happens that the same uncertainty hangs over every other passage in which James is named with the apostles."   Principal Edwards, *First Corinthians*, 2nd ed. pp. 395, 397.

[1] It occurs in the words of the prophet Ahijah to the wife of Jeroboam : " I am sent to thee with heavy tidings," which the Alexandrian translators render : ἐγώ εἰμι ἀπόστολος πρὸς σὲ σκληρός.

[2] Lightfoot, *Galatians*, 5th ed. p. 92 f.   In illustration of the Jewish use of the term "apostle," Bishop Lightfoot refers to Eusebius (*Montf. Coll. Nov.* ii. 425); Jerome, *Comm. ad Gal.* i. 1 ; *Cod. Theodos.* xvi. Tit. viii. 14 ; Julian, *Epist.* 25 ; Epiphanius, *Hæres.* xxx. p. 128.   Comp. also Vitringa, *De Syn. Vet.* pp. 577, 586.

That a direct commission of this sort from Christ Himself was essential to make any one an apostle in the proper sense of the word as used in the New Testament, is signally confirmed—as in respect to the first condition—by the two cases which might seem at first sight to be exceptions to the rule.

In the election of Matthias, while the company of the disciples "put forward two" from the number of those who, from the beginning, had been eye-witnesses of Christ's earthly life, and who now could attest His resurrection, as in their judgment suitable for the place to be filled, the choice and the appointment to the apostolic office were put directly into the hand of the Lord Himself. "They prayed and said, Thou, Lord, which knowest the hearts of all men, show of these two the one whom Thou hast chosen to take the place in this ministry and apostleship (τὸν τόπον τῆς διακονίας ταύτης καὶ ἀποστολῆς) from which Judas fell away that he might go to his own place. And they gave lots for them; and the lot fell upon Matthias, and he was numbered with the eleven apostles."[1] In the case of Paul, there is nothing on which he insists more strongly than on the directness and Divine authority of His apostolic commission. He is in this respect "in no whit behind the very chiefest apostles." He "did not go up to Jerusalem" to receive his office from "them which were apostles before me." He is "Paul, an apostle, not from men, neither through man, but through Jesus Christ and God the Father, who raised Him from the dead."[2]

---

[1] Acts i. 23–26.

[2] 2 Cor. xii. 11 ; Gal. i. 1, 17 f. Bishop Lightfoot's dissertation on "the name and office of an apostle" is an extremely valuable one. It has been pronounced by Harnack, himself one of the highest authorities in this field, to be,—although open, in his view, to criticism on some points—on the whole, the best investigation of the question with which he is acquainted (*Texte u. Untersuchungen zur Gesch. der altchristl. Literatur*, Bd. ii. Heft 2, Leipzig 1884, S. 115). I am disposed to think, however, while agreeing with most of Dr. Lightfoot's conclusions on the subject, that he has not attached suffi-cient weight to the express statement of the third evangelist that Christ Him-self bestowed this distinctive name upon the twelve, nor to the facts above indicated regarding the appointment of Matthias and Paul to the apostleship. Dr. Lightfoot's treatment of the two passages which record the two last-named events and of that which narrates how Barnabas and Paul were set apart at

The analogy of the twelve tribes of Israel was preserved by the appointment of Matthias to be an apostle in the room of Judas. It was still more exactly carried out—not "broken in upon," as Dr. Lightfoot says (p. 95)—by the

Antioch "to the work which they had fulfilled," when they returned thither again (Acts xiv. 26), is not marked by his usual thoroughness and discrimination (*Galatians*, p. 98).

It seems to me that a clearer and broader line of distinction than appears in Dr. Lightfoot's essay must be drawn between "the apostles," properly so called,—"the apostles of Christ,"—and any others to whom in a laxer sense the term is applied in the New Testament. Dr. Lightfoot admits that "some uncertainty hangs over all the instances" which can be given of the use of the title "apostle" in Scripture as a term of office in reference to any save the twelve and Paul, with one solitary exception. "But the apostleship of Barnabas," he holds, "is beyond question" (p. 96). Now it is beyond question that Barnabas and Paul are together called "the apostles" in one passage of the Acts (xiv. 4 and 14). But it is by no means so clear that the former is ever included under that title again. What Bishop Lightfoot counts "similar language, held by St. Paul himself" regarding Barnabas, in Gal. ii. 9 and 1 Cor. ix. 5 f., amounts certainly to a cordial recognition by Paul of the gifts and work of Barnabas as specially associated with himself in the Gentile mission. This recognition is made in language of characteristic generosity and courtesy ; but it by no means amounts, either necessarily or on the most natural interpretation, to a recognition of Barnabas as "an apostle of Christ," in the sense in which the original apostles and Paul held that office.

On the contrary, in the passage in Galatians especially it seems clear that a distinction is made between "the apostleship of the circumcision" entrusted to Peter and "the apostleship of the Gentiles" to Paul, on the one hand, and, on the other, the general work among the circumcision and the Gentiles in which James the Lord's brother was specially associated with the twelve, and Barnabas with Paul (Gal. ii. 7–10).

In the only passage where Barnabas is expressly included along with Paul under the title "the apostles,"—and it is to be noted that he is never called an apostle when acting alone, — the use of the word is easily explained by its immediate connection with their being solemnly "sent forth" together by the Church at Antioch, under the guidance of the Spirit, on the first Gentile mission (Acts xiii. 3 f.). In that special relation, until they "had fulfilled the work" committed to them, and reported regarding it to the Church at Antioch (ὅθεν ἦσαν παραδεδομένοι τῇ χάριτι τοῦ θεοῦ εἰς τὸ ἔργον ὃ ἐπλή-ρωσαν, c. xiv. 26), and so exhausted their commission, both Paul and Barnabas were "apostles of the Church" in a similar sense—although with a higher charge—to that in which Epaphroditus was "the apostle of the Philippians," when entrusted by them with gifts and messages to Paul at Rome, and in which the brethren associated with Titus in the matter of the collection were "apostles of the Churches" in Macedonia (Phil. ii. 25 ; 2 Cor. viii. 23). It is noteworthy that the only inspired writer who in a single passage, and in a special connection includes Barnabas with Paul under the general term "apostles," is the same who records the fact that our Lord expressly con-

appointment of Paul "as of one born out of due time." For the twelve tribes were really made thirteen by the two sons of Joseph being raised to equal positions with their father's brethren; and Ephraim, the youngest born, proved like Paul the strongest and most fruitful of them all.

The wider use of the term "apostle" occurs in four or five cases in the New Testament, in all of which the nature of the special and temporary commission, which gave rise to the expression, is obvious from the context. Epaphroditus is "the apostle of the Philippians" when sent by them on a special errand to Paul at Rome. The representatives of the Macedonian believers sent by them along with Titus in charge of a certain collection are "the apostles of the Churches."[1] Among the Jews of the early centuries the term continued to denote those sent forth on any special mission among the synagogues of the Dispersion by the Sanhedrin or other central authority. Very naturally in the sub-apostolic period, as we see it in the recently discovered "Teaching of the Twelve Apostles,"[2] Christian missionaries or itinerant evangelists were sometimes spoken of as "apostles," men "sent forth" to preach the Gospel by the call and impulse of the Spirit in their hearts.[3] But all this does not in the least impair the force of the arguments for the essential distinction drawn in the New Testament between "the apostles of Christ," that is to say, the twelve and Paul, and all others who in a laxer sense of the word might be called "apostles."

---

ferred this title on the twelve, and who both in his Gospel and in the Acts uses it as his ordinary designation for the twelve, and for none besides them, with the exception of Paul, whose direct call by Christ and mission by Him to the Gentiles Luke so fully narrates (Acts ix. 6, 15 f.; xxii. 14 f., 21; xxvi. 16–18).

[1] See last note.

[2] Otherwise: "The Teaching of the Lord by the Twelve Apostles to the Gentiles." The title of the tract itself bears witness to the distinct and unique position of the twelve. Comp. Harnack, *Texte u. Untersuch.*, Bd. ii. Heft 1, S. 24 f. Manley, *Dissertation on the Presbyterate*, Camb. 1886, p. 39 f.

[3] *Teaching of the Twelve*, xi. 3. In an elaborate note (S. 118), Harnack points out that the following apostolic and sub-apostolic Fathers limit the title "apostle" strictly to the twelve and Paul, viz. Clement of Rome, Ignatius, Polycarp, and Justin Martyr.

3. A third distinction of the apostles of Christ is, that, by His express appointment, they were His representatives on earth in a sense and to an extent perfectly unique.

The power of the keys, as we have seen,[1] was given in a special manner to the twelve. They under Christ were to be the master - builders of the Church. No other names were to be inscribed on the foundations of the heavenly city, new Jerusalem, than those of "the twelve apostles of the Lamb."[2] The breath of the Spirit from Christ on the evening of His Resurrection, and the subsequent gifts of the Spirit at Pentecost, were received by "the eleven," not indeed exclusively, but in the peculiar measure and degree needful for their peculiar position and work in the Church and in the world. "Jesus was received up," Luke writes in the beginning of his "second treatise," "after that He had given commandment through the Holy Ghost unto the apostles whom He had chosen, to whom also He showed Himself alive after His passion by many proofs, appearing unto them by the space of forty days, and speaking of the things concerning the kingdom of God." To them especially the words were spoken: "Ye shall receive power when the Holy Ghost is come upon you; and ye shall be My witnesses both in Jerusalem and in all Judæa and Samaria, and unto the uttermost part of the earth."[3]

The nature and extent of the powers entrusted by Christ to His apostles appear clearly when we consider what is recorded regarding their use of these powers. We find the apostles everywhere speaking and writing in their official capacity, in a tone and with an authority "not of men, neither by men, but by Jesus Christ." We find them acting and claiming right to act in reference to the spiritual affairs of the Church throughout the world, in all variety of circumstances, with "the authority which the Lord gave us" (κατὰ τὴν ἐξουσίαν ἣν ὁ κύριος ἔδωκέ μοι),[4] and which is like the Lord's own when He was on the earth. We see them planting Churches, exercising discipline, writing catholic epistles, ordaining office-bearers in different places, empowering others

---

[1] See above, pp. 176 f., 184–187.
[2] Rev. xxi. 14.
[3] Acts i. 2 f., 8.
[4] 2 Cor. x. 8; xiii. 10.

for a time to act in their name, and then sending them to other work. " So ordain I in all the Churches." " If any man think himself to be a prophet or spiritual, let him take knowledge that the things which I write unto you are the commandment of the Lord." " As I gave order to the Churches of Galatia, so also do ye." " Though I have all boldness in Christ to enjoin thee that which is befitting, yet for love's sake I rather beseech thee." " For this cause left I thee in Crete, that thou shouldest set in order the things that were wanting, and appoint elders in every city as I gave thee charge. . . . When I shall send Artemas unto thee, or Tychicus, give diligence to come unto me to Nicopolis." [1]

We are constantly reminded by the whole spirit and tone of the utterances of the apostles in such matters—by what they say and what they take for granted—of Him whom they represent in His Church, and who spake " as One having authority, and not as the scribes."

4. Lastly, the apostolic commission, as entrusted to the twelve and to Paul, had attached to it certain visible seals.

The gifts of inspiration, the " signs, and wonders, and mighty works," to which Paul points the Christians among whom his apostolic position and authority had been challenged, were " the signs of the apostle " (τὰ σημεῖα τοῦ ἀποστόλου), the marks by which the apostle is Divinely attested. " These," Paul tells the Corinthians, " were wrought among you in all manner of perseverance (ἐν πάσῃ ὑπομονῇ)," shown forth with all possible stedfastness and fulness amid much opposition and many difficulties, so that those who refused to own his apostleship were without excuse.[2]

Other disciples, indeed, such as " the seventy," during the time of our Lord's public ministry, and others besides the twelve and Paul in the apostolic Church, possessed miraculous gifts, although not, as it seems, in the same degree,[3] and not, usually at least, after Pentecost, except through the intervention of the apostles and the laying on of their hands. But

---

[1] 1 Cor. vii. 17 ; xiv. 37 ; xvi. 1 ; Philem. 8 f. ; Tit. i. 5 ; iii. 12.

[2] 2 Cor. xii. 12 ; comp. Meyer *in loco.*

[3] Acts v. 12-16 ; ix. 40 ; xix. 11 f. ; xx. 9-12. " I thank God I speak with tongues more than you all," 1 Cor. xiv. 18.

none save the apostles, so far as we have evidence in Scripture, had the power of transmitting miraculous gifts to others, as we find was done repeatedly by members of the original apostolic college and by Paul.[1] These things were " the signs of the apostle" in the strict and proper sense of the word as used in the New Testament. They were seals, attached by Christ Himself to their unique and supreme commission in His Church, attesting it as such to all men and for all time.

In these four respects, then, the office of the apostles, as instituted by Christ, stood alone as one in which they had no companions, and in which, from the very nature of the case, they could have no successors. As Nitzsch expresses it in his powerful and conclusive reply to Möhler's *Symbolik*, " Christ allows no substitute but the Paraclete. And Paul, Peter and John suffer no successors to take their places; for by their voices heard from the Scriptures, and by their concrete historical work, they form the foundation still for all true building up of living Christianity. Personal powers and prerogatives which belonged to them as the first witnesses and ambassadors of Christ were simply personal; or they pertained to the members of that living fellowship with Christ which was first exemplified in the apostles, and hence continue in all time to pertain to the true spiritual Church, or to its appointed office-bearers (den verordneten Vorstehern), only according to the measure in which they follow the apostolic word, example, and spirit, or according to the degree in which they receive the gift of the Holy Ghost. . . . The grace of Christ works to-day only through the preaching and testimony of the apostles. They hold office still among us as the depositaries of the Divine Word in its original normative presentation; and every Christian tries the spirits of later times by their spirit, the doctrine of later days by their doctrine." [2] In this sense the apostles still sit on thrones judging all the tribes of the spiritual Israel.

A further question, of course, remains, which has been

---

[1] Acts vi. 6, 8 ; viii. 13–20 ; xix. 2–6.
[2] Nitzsch, *Protestantische Beantwortung der Symbolik Möhlers*, S. 207, 224. Comp. Bannerman, *Church of Christ*, ii. pp. 219–228. Jul. Müller, *Dogmatische Abhandlungen*, S. 629–635.

already touched upon in connection with some of our Lord's sayings, and which will be fully answered when we pass to the institutions of the apostolic Church, namely : Was it the will of Christ that a succession of ordinary office-bearers should be appointed to exercise permanent functions in the Church of the same kind as some of those exercised by the apostles ? But the question of the permanence of the apostolic office in itself is wholly different from that of the permanence of certain functions which, among others, were discharged for a time by the apostles.

4th. Before passing on to consider the historical development of the Church after the Ascension of Christ, and the conception of it which appears in the teaching of the apostles and other inspired writers of the New Testament, we may here recall and state briefly some of the chief results of our inquiry as regards the conception of the Church in our Lord's own teaching, whether by word or institution. From the passages already considered it appears that there are three distinct aspects in which the Church is presented to us in the Gospels.

1. In its first and highest aspect the Church comprehends all who have been given to Christ by the Father, viewed as forming one great whole. This is the Church catholic invisible, consisting of the whole number of God's elected and redeemed children, all "who have been, are, or shall be gathered into one in Christ" from all nations of men throughout all time.

This is the first and Divinest aspect of the Church. It is that which, as we have seen, comes out so strikingly in our Lord's High-priestly prayer and other kindred utterances of His to which our thoughts have been turned. In this aspect of the Church Christ Himself is all and in all. We see Him receiving the gift from the Father, gathering, keeping, and blessing all who have been given and drawn to Him by the Father. The Church is seen only in the closest union with and dependence on Christ, as the whole company of those thus chosen from the beginning, and in due time called and made faithful in Him.

Or, if we look for the Church at any given time on earth, it is the whole company of the redeemed now living among men, all who now and here in Christ's sight belong to His true Church below. This is the ἐκκλησία τοῦ κυρίου (the קהל יהוה) in the highest sense. Its members may cease to be a συναγωγή (an עדה), a gathered meeting. Their inward and real unity may not be able from circumstances to find almost any visible expression. They may be widely scattered, unseen, and unknown in great part to each other, as the hidden seven thousand in Israel were to Elijah. But they can never cease to be an ἐκκλησία, truly one in Christ their Lord, and seen to be so in the eyes of God, His Father and their Father, His God and their God.[1]

2. In a second and lower aspect the Church comprehends all professing believers on earth at any given time, together with their infant seed. This is the Church catholic visible. Here we have the outward and visible answer to Christ's call in the Gospel, men and families gathered together in His name, separating themselves so far from the world by a profession of faith in Christ and obedience to Him. Here elements of human sin and self-deception inevitably come in, as they did in the inner circle of our Lord's personal disciples. The profession does not always answer to the reality. There may be an outward connection with Christ for a time, which to the eyes even of true disciples seems close and true, but which ends in final separation and destruction, because there has never been any real or vital union with Him.[2]

3. We have the local Church, representing the Church universal in both its aspects, the higher and the lower at any given time, with an outward and visible unity more or less complete according to circumstances. It may be confined to one congregation, or may comprise several with more or less of organization, but it has at any rate a certain practical and visible unity from local or geographical circumstances. It is the Church of a town, or district, or country.

---

[1] See above, pp. 174, 206 f., 210, 217–222.
[2] See above, pp. 197–203, 208, 241 f., 250 f.

Its members might meet together, at least to a large extent. It is a Church which can act as one either directly or through its representatives speaking and acting in its name, as we have seen was the case with the congregation or assembly of Israel in Old Testament times.[1]

[1] See above, pp. 181 f., 239 f.

PARTS V. AND VI.

THE CHURCH IN THE ACTS, THE EPISTLES, AND THE REVELATION.

WE have seen that in the Gospels our Lord refers to His Church even towards the end of His public ministry as being, in some sense at least, a thing in the future : " On this rock *I will build* My Church ;" " I *will give* unto thee the keys," etc. ; " What things soever *ye shall bind* on earth," etc. In the Acts and the Epistles, on the other hand, from the day of Pentecost onwards, we find the Church of Christ a thing in the present, actually and historically existent, and constantly spoken of as such.[1] Beginning with the fifth chapter of Acts, the Epistle of James and the Epistles to the Thessalonians, the word " Church " (ἐκκλησία) occurs with increasing frequency alike in the narrative, the epistolary and the prophetic portions of the New Testament. In the latest apostolic epistles, and in the Book of the Revelation, the term and the conception which it embodies have special prominence.

It seems suitable at this stage in our discussion to give in a note[2] all the instances in which the word " Church " is used in the New Testament,—one hundred and fourteen in all,— classifying these under three general heads in accordance with the conclusions already reached as to the threefold aspect of the Church in the teaching of Christ Himself. It will be found that these three divisions embrace every subse- quent instance of the use of the expression in Scripture, with the exception of three examples of its classical use in the nineteenth chapter of Acts ; and this fact lends additional

---

[1] The term ἐκκλησία in the Received text of Acts ii. 47 is probably a gloss. But it is at least a correct expression of the fact that the Christian Church was now visibly in existence, growing and developing with each increase of converts.

[2] Note A in Appendix.

confirmation to the results of our investigation as to the purport of our Lord's teaching on this subject. A few brief exegetical remarks are added here and there where it seemed desirable to indicate the grounds of classification. Some of the more important passages will receive closer consideration when they come up again in their historical connection.

We turn now to the Church as it appears historically in the book of the Acts and in the rest of the New Testament.

The narrative of the Acts, as has often been pointed out, divides itself naturally into two sections. It leads us first from Jerusalem to Antioch (i.–xii.), and then from Antioch to Rome (xiii.–xxviii.). The historical progress of events corresponds precisely with the prophetic words of Christ to His disciples immediately before His Ascension. "Repentance and remission of sins must be preached in My Name unto all the nations, beginning from Jerusalem." "Ye shall receive power when the Holy Ghost is come upon you; and ye shall be My witnesses both in Jerusalem and in all Judæa and Samaria, and unto the uttermost part of the earth." [1]

In the first twelve chapters of the Acts we see the results of the preaching of the Gospel and of the power of the Holy Ghost in Jerusalem and the Holy Land, including Damascus. We pass from the Church of the upper chamber at Jerusalem, "where the eleven were gathered together and they that were with them," as described in the first chapter, to the picture in the end of the ninth chapter of "the Church throughout all Judæa and Galilee and Samaria," which "had peace, being edified, and walking in the fear of the Lord and in the comfort of the Holy Ghost was multiplied." [2] Towards the end of this period we get a glimpse of things beyond the limits of the Holy Land; [3] and questions connected with the admission of the Gentiles begin to rise up and threaten difficulty. [4] But throughout this first section of the Acts everything begins from Jerusalem and returns thither; the Church is still essentially on Hebrew

---

[1] Luke xxiv. 47 ; Acts i. 8.

[2] Acts ix. 31 ; the significance and importance of the reading ἡ ἐκκλησία (instead of αἱ ἐκκλησίαι), rightly adopted by the Revisers in this passage, will be referred to again.

[3] Acts xi. 19–30.

[4] x. 28, 45 ; xi. 1–3, 22–24.

ground, with the Jewish or Hebrew Christian element indisputably predominant.[1]

Besides what we have in the first part of the Acts, we learn much regarding the Hebrew Christian Church in the writings of "those who seemed to be pillars" in the fellowship of the disciples at Jerusalem, Peter, John, and James the Lord's brother, and in some of the earlier epistles of Paul.

---

[1] For a very thorough and conclusive defence of the historical trustworthiness of the book of Acts in view of the most recent investigations and results of German criticism, see K. Schmidt, *Die Apostelgeschichte unter dem Hauptgesichtspunkte ihrer Glaubwürdigkeit*, Erlangen 1882. Comp. Lechler, *apostolische u. nachapostolische Zeitalter*, 3te Aufl., Karlsruhe u. Leipzig 1885, S. 7-21. Eng. transl., Edin. 1886. See also Prof. Salmon's able discussion of the subject, *Introduction to the N. T.*, London 1885, pp. 366-407. The general grounds for relying on the truthfulness of the narrative in Acts are well summed up by Beyschlag, *Christl. Gemeindeverf. im Zeitalt. des N. T.*, S. 23 f.

PART V.

FROM JERUSALEM TO ANTIOCH: THE HEBREW CHRISTIAN CHURCH.

———◆———

CHAPTER I.

THE HEBREW CHRISTIAN CHURCH IN ITSELF, AS SEEN IN LIFE AND ACTION.

OUR first glimpse of the disciples of Christ after His Ascension shows them gathered together, men and women alike, in a large upper chamber or hall at Jerusalem. It is spoken of as a well-known place of meeting, "the upper chamber where they were continuing," and was, in all likelihood, the same "large upper room furnished" in which the eleven had kept the passover with their Master, and had partaken of the first Lord's Supper, the same also in which the risen Saviour had twice appeared to His disciples as a body.[1] As on the evening of the Resurrection, the company comprises "the eleven and them that were with them," "the number of the names together being about an hundred and twenty." They are "gathered together in the name" of Jesus Christ "with one accord" (ὁμοθυμαδόν),[2] one in their faith in Him as the Messiah foretold in the Scriptures,

———

[1] Εἰς τὸ ὑπερῷον ἀνέβησαν οὗ ἦσαν καταμένοντες, Acts i. 13 ; τὸ κατάλυμα . . . ἀνώγεον μέγα ἐστρωμένον, Luke xxii. 11 f. Its owner was evidently a friend and secret disciple of Christ before His death, and doubtless was now among the hundred and twenty. "The Master saith unto thee" was a sufficient password to ensure that all that he had should be at the disposal of those coming in that name. Comp. Luke xxiv. 33-36 ; John xx. 10 : ἀπῆλθον οὖν πάλιν πρὸς ἑαυτοὺς οἱ μαθηταί ; xx. 19, 26.

[2] Acts i. 14 ; ii. 1.

"the Son of the living God," declared and proved beyond all question to be such by His Resurrection from the dead and Ascension into heaven.[1] They wait according to His express command in Jerusalem until He "send forth the promise of His Father upon them" and they "be clothed with power from on high," until they be "baptized with the Holy Ghost not many days hence."[2]

In this interval of expectation, the members of the little company in the upper chamber betake themselves "with one accord" to prayer. They consider together the meaning and lessons of the great events which filled their minds, especially the betrayal and crucifixion of Christ, in the light of those Scriptures which bore upon the Messiah's time, and in the light also of their present circumstances and of the work to which they looked forward. In other words, they follow out the lines of study opened for them by the Lord in that very place on the evening of His Resurrection, when " He breathed on them, saying, Receive a gift of the Holy Ghost," and "opened their mind that they might understand the Scriptures," recalling His own former teaching regarding " the things written in the law of Moses and the prophets and the Psalms concerning Himself," and casting fresh light on the passages where "it was written that the Christ should suffer, and rise again from the dead the third day, and that repentance and remission of sins should be preached in His name unto all the nations, beginning from Jerusalem."[3]

As the result of this prayerful consideration of God's Word and Providence, and of their Master's indications of His will for them in the immediate future, it becomes plain to the disciples that one step at least, bearing upon the common interests of the people and cause of Christ, may and should be

---

[1] Comp. Paul's summary of the Gospel in the opening sentence of his Epistle to the Romans : εὐαγγέλιον θεοῦ ὅ προεπηγγείλατο διὰ τῶν προφητῶν αὐτοῦ ἐν γραφαῖς ἁγίαις περὶ τοῦ υἱοῦ αὐτοῦ, τοῦ γενομένου ἐκ σπέρματος Δαβὶδ κατὰ σάρκα, τοῦ ὁρισθέντος υἱοῦ θεοῦ ἐν δυνάμει κατὰ πνεῦμα ἁγιωσύνης ἐξ ἀναστάσεως νεκρῶν, Ἰησοῦ Χριστοῦ τοῦ Κυρίου ἡμῶν.

[2] Luke xxiv. 49 ; Acts i. 5.

[3] John xx. 22 ; Luke xxiv. 44-48. There is further evidence of the lines on which the disciples had thus searched the Scriptures together in Peter's speech at Pentecost.

taken by them before the sign from heaven came, which was to send them forth to work and witness-bearing in a wider sphere. They take united action accordingly, with solemn prayer and direct appeal to their unseen Lord, for the filling up of the blank made in the apostolic college by the treachery and death of Judas.[1]

1st. In all this we see the Church of Christ already showing itself in life and action to be what our Lord had foretold that it should be. We see it as a fellowship of believers gathered together in the name of Christ, one with each other because one with the common Lord and Saviour, built by Him upon a rock-fast foundation, finding guidance from His teaching and His gifts of the Spirit, drawing strength and courage from His unseen Presence in the midst of them, and receiving all needed wisdom and light from above as to present duty in answer to united prayer.

It was to this little company of believers thus waiting upon the Lord in prayer and study of the Scriptures, and in united action prompted by the Word, the Providence, and the Spirit of God, that the Holy Ghost came in power and majesty on the day of Pentecost. Not the apostles only, but all the disciples in the upper chamber that day, men and women alike, "were filled with the Holy Ghost, and spake with other tongues as the Spirit gave them utterance." [2] The fulfilment of the Lord's promise to them and their first fulfilment of His great commission to His Church went together. They were all "clothed with power from on high," and became at once Christ's witnesses to men "from every nation under heaven." What would otherwise have been the work

---

[1] Acts i. 15–26.

[2] Acts ii. 1–4. This universality of the Pentecostal gift appears both in the narrative and in the prophetic passage from the Old Testament to which Peter refers in the beginning of his address : "This is that which hath been spoken by the prophet Joel, And it shall be in the last days, saith God, I will pour forth of My Spirit upon all flesh, and your sons and your daughters shall prophesy, and your young men shall see visions, and your old men shall dream dreams ; yea, and on My servants and on My handmaidens in those days will I pour forth of My Spirit, and they shall prophesy" (vv. 16–18). Comp. Acts xxi. 9 ; 1 Cor. xi. 5.

of years of missions was done at once by the mighty power
of God working through an agency framed and fitted by His
Providence for the purposes of His grace through centuries of
gradual growth and manifold preparation. This was the
meaning of those great movements at which we glanced under
the heads of the Diaspora, the proselytes, and the synagogue
system. Jews and proselytes from all lands heard that day
from the lips of Christ's disciples, "every man in his own
language wherein he was born, the mighty works of God."[1]
As the pilgrims returned that summer from that marvellous
"feast of weeks, even of the first-fruits of harvest,"[2] at
Jerusalem, they carried back with them the message and the
power of the Gospel into all parts of the civilised world.

Meanwhile in Jerusalem itself the work went forward, as
we see in the record of the Acts, with that simple irresistible
movement, that *naturalness*, so to speak, which marks the
greatest works of God in other spheres. It was like the
coming of the spring time upon the earth, like the rising of
the tide in the ocean. The facts spoke; and the witnesses
to the facts rose up on every side. Some three thousand
souls were added to the little company of the upper room
at once, the first-fruits of the Gospel concerning Christ crucified and risen, as declared by the Apostle Peter in the power
of the Spirit on the morning of Pentecost, and of the great
inquiry meeting which followed, filling the hearts and hands
of "the eleven and them that were with them" with joyful
work throughout that long summer day. And as the growth
of the Church began, so it went steadily on; "The Lord
added to them—added together to the collective body—day
by day those that were being saved" (ὁ δὲ κύριος προσετίθει
τοὺς σωζομένους καθ' ἡμέραν ἐπὶ τὸ αὐτό).[3]

The word "Church" (ἐκκλησία), which occurs in the
Received text of the verse last cited, is no doubt, as already
noted, a gloss. But it is a correct interpretation of the facts
recorded; and it is to be observed that the more approved
reading (ἐπὶ τὸ αὐτό) brings out the same idea. The new
converts were "added together," "added to the united company." Hitherto, since the crucifixion of Christ, His dis-

[1] Acts ii. 5–11.   [2] Ex. xxxiv. 22 ; xxiii. 16.   [3] Acts ii. 37–41, 47.

ciples had been almost entirely withdrawn from public
view.   To the Sanhedrin it seemed no doubt that the
death of Jesus of Nazareth, as in the case of other religious
and political leaders whom they had known, had finally
scattered His followers.[1]   The gatherings in the upper
chamber had been in private.   But now, in the eyes of all
men, those who believe in Jesus as the Christ appear as a
unity, the several members knit together into one body.
" All that believed were together ($\mathring{\eta}\sigma a\nu$ $\mathring{\epsilon}\pi\grave{\iota}$ $\tau\grave{o}$ $a\mathring{v}\tau\acute{o}$), and had
all things common. . . . And the Lord added to the common
company ($\pi\rho o\sigma\epsilon\tau\acute{\iota}\theta\epsilon\iota$ $\mathring{\epsilon}\pi\grave{\iota}$ $\tau\grave{o}$ $a\mathring{v}\tau\acute{o}$) day by day those that were
being saved." [2]   We see here the disciples of Christ separat-
ing themselves so far, by necessity of their discipleship, from
their unbelieving fellow-countrymen, called out from them by
the Lord Jesus, through the power of His Spirit, to Himself
and to each other.   We see, in short, the Church of the
New Testament become clearly visible, as distinct from the
Jewish Church of the old economy.

The apostolic Church, when it counted its thousands in
Jerusalem, was essentially just what it was, when it could
count but its tens in the upper chamber.   It was essentially
a fellowship of believers in the Lord Jesus Christ through the
Spirit, united together for the purposes for which He had
called them to Himself.   Only now the restriction which the
Master had laid upon them for a little was removed by His
own hand.   He had " sent forth upon them the promise from
His Father."   They were "clothed with power from on
high," for all the work which He had given them to do.

At once, and as by instinct of its birth, we find the infant
Church under the new dispensation fulfilling what our Lord
had declared to be its chief end in the world, bearing witness
for Him, proclaiming the glad tidings of repentance and the
remission of sins in His name, making disciples from among
all the nations, and teaching them to observe all things
whatsoever He had commanded.   In this first and greatest
work of the Church the apostles are indeed foremost, as
the chosen and commissioned witnesses of Christ.   The
broad seal of the King Himself is set on their special

[1] Acts v. 36 f.   [2] Acts ii. 44, 47.

commission from the first. "Many wonders and signs," we
read in connection with the events of Pentecost, "were
done by the apostles."[1] They speak and act in the name of
Christ and His Church, doing so with a wisdom and power
which carry their own evidence with them, which, as their
Master had promised, "all their adversaries are unable to
withstand or to gainsay."[2] Yet their testimony, powerful as
it was, would have lacked more than half its force had it
not been accompanied and followed by that of others, such
as Stephen, Philip, Barnabas, Agabus, the "men of Cyprus
and Cyrene," and many other unnamed witnesses, and had
not every word been confirmed by "living epistles of Christ"
on every side "written by the Spirit of God, known and read
of all men."[3]

The preaching of the apostles to the multitudes consisted
essentially in an appeal to plain facts, with a few equally
plain inferences from them, followed up by a direct and
powerful appeal to conscience.

Take, for example, Peter's address on the day of Pentecost.
He starts from certain facts of present experience. Every
intelligent man in the crowd before him felt that these
needed an explanation, and that no credible explanation had
yet been found. "They were all amazed and perplexed,
saying one to another, What meaneth this?" "To what will
it lead"? (τί θέλει τοῦτο εἶναι;).[4] That was the feeling upper-
most in the minds of all the more serious portion of the
crowd as they saw and heard the extraordinary manifestations
of the Spirit among the disciples. The apostle's speech is
just an answer to that question. "Ye men of Judæa, and all
ye that dwell at Jerusalem, be this known,—be it explained
unto you,—and give ear unto my words."[5]

The whole address is an explanation of the astonishing
series of events and experiences which were filling the minds
of all earnest and candid men among the apostle's hearers
that day. How does he explain them?

[1] Acts ii. 43.
[2] Luke xxi. 15 ; Acts iv. 13 f., 19-21 ; v. 12 f., 29-33.
[3] 2 Cor. iii. 2 f. ; Acts viii. 4 ; xi. 19 f.
[4] Acts ii. 6 f., 12.   [4] τοῦτο ὑμῖν γνωστὸν ἔστω, Acts ii. 14.

He points, first, to the Word of God: "This is that which hath been spoken by the prophet Joel;" secondly, to the life of Christ, to His character, His mighty works, His crucifixion, as well known to all who listened to him: "Jesus of Nazareth, a man approved of God unto you by mighty works, and wonders, and signs, which God did by Him in the midst of you, even as you yourselves know, Him . . . ye by the hand of lawless men did crucify and slay."

Thirdly, the apostle declares Christ's Resurrection and Ascension, as foretold in the Scriptures, as proved now by eye-witnesses, namely, himself and the eleven standing up with him, and the other disciples grouped around. They were now joyfully risking their lives in proclaiming these things in Jerusalem. They were themselves changed, as all could see, by their knowledge of these great facts, by their faith in Christ risen, from what they had been but a few weeks ago,—trembling fugitives and deniers of their Master, —into men who could speak with such fearlessness and spiritual power as were seen in him that day.

Fourthly, the apostle appeals to the present evidence of the hand of God among them. He bids his audience consider "this which ye now see and hear."[1] The Worker was invisible; but who could doubt that the work was Divine? The mighty sound as of a whirlwind, heard far and wide over the city, like the blast of an archangel's trumpet, and summoning men together with as strange a power;[2] the tongues of fire; the wonder of the many languages spoken; the answer of each man's conscience, the answer of hundreds of hearts stirred to their depths by the message suddenly reaching them in a distant land in their own familiar tongue "wherein they were born;" the thrilling proclamation by so many voices of "the mighty works of God;" what human power could have brought about these things? And through whom was "this" wrought, "which they now saw and heard" and felt? "Were not all these which spoke Galilæans," followers of Jesus of Nazareth? To whom did the Spirit

---

[1] Ver. 33.

[2] Ἐγίνετο ἄφνω ἐκ τοῦ οὐρανοῦ ἦχος, ὥσπερ φερομένης πνοῆς βιαίας . . . γενομένης δὲ τῆς φωνῆς ταύτης συνῆλθε τὸ πλῆθος, Acts ii. 2, 6.

of God, thus marvellously "poured forth," bear witness in every ecstatic utterance ? Was it not to Him ?

The four great lines of evidence used by the apostle all converged on one point. They led inevitably to one conclusion; and the apostle gives it in a single emphatic sentence : "Therefore let all the house of Israel know assuredly that God hath made Him both Lord and Christ, this same Jesus whom ye crucified."[1]

The whole method of the address hitherto has been that of a direct appeal to facts. Its starting-point was the existence of certain facts, plain and patent to the senses and understanding of all present, for which an explanation was asked. The apostle gives it, in words that bear the stamp of truth and soberness, simply by bringing forward certain other facts, some of them of a historical, others of a moral and spiritual kind. Of these some were well known to all who heard him; others are now stated and proved by clear and convincing evidence. He sets these facts in their order. He shows the connection between them, and how they all harmonized with and confirmed and explained each other. What the whole amounted to was so plain, the inferences to be drawn from it were so inevitable, that they hardly needed to be stated in express terms. The hearts and consciences of the apostle's hearers were outstripping his words when he gathered up the results of his great argument in that one weighty concluding sentence. It was like a strong bolt hurled with a steady aim from some mighty engine of war, and going home full and fair to the centre of a shaking wall. Everything went down before it. "When they heard this they were pricked in their heart, and said unto Peter and the rest of the apostles, Brethren, what shall we do ? And Peter said unto them, Repent ye and be baptized every one of you in the name of Jesus Christ unto the remission of your sins, and ye shall receive the gift of the Holy Ghost. For to you is the promise, and to your children, and to all that are afar off, even as many as the Lord our God shall call unto Him."[2]

Observe how at this point the character of the address

---

[1] Ἀσφαλῶς οὖν γινωσκέτω πᾶς οἶκος Ἰσραὴλ, ὅτι καὶ Κύριον αὐτὸν καὶ Χριστὸν ὁ θεὸς ἐποίησε τοῦτον τὸν Ἰησοῦν ὃν ὑμεῖς ἐσταυρώσατε, ver. 36.

[2] Vv. 37–39.

changes. Hitherto it has been witness-bearing; now it passes into exhortation. The first appeal had been to facts,—facts of Scripture, of history, of past and present experience. These facts are first of all clearly and calmly stated by the apostle in fitting order. Until that was done, all the fiery impetuous eloquence natural to Peter was kept in check, with a self-control very different from what he had shown of old. The Spirit given to him by his ascended Lord was one " of power and love, and a sound mind." But now the first appeal had taken effect. The facts spoke for themselves to every open and truth-loving mind among the crowd. And now, from the vantage-ground thus gained, the full tide of warm entreaty and persuasion, of warning and promise, was poured in by the apostle upon his hearers. To recur to the figure already used, the heavy stroke of the battery first broke down the wall of unbelief, and then, wave upon wave, the besieging host went surging through the breach into the city till all was subdued. " With many other words he testified and exhorted them, saying, Save yourselves from this crooked generation." [1]

The main features of this first apostolic discourse are just in substance those of all others addressed to similar audiences during the period covered by the book of Acts. The first part of the great commission given by our Lord to the company of His believing people—namely, to declare the glad tidings and to make disciples—was fulfilled by the Church by thus bearing witness to the facts concerning Christ's Person and history, and by pointing to the evidence of the Presence and power of the Holy Ghost in the midst of them. What they had seen and heard and experienced, the apostles, and others such as Stephen and Philip, declared. They showed how their testimony answered to the testimony of God by word and deed in history, prophecy, and Psalm. They set these facts of Scripture alongside of facts of recent and present experience. They pointed to the life and death of Jesus of Nazareth. That He had lived and taught as a prophet, and wrought mighty works among the people; that He had been condemned by the rulers and elders of Israel for

[1] Ver. 40.

claiming to be the Christ, the Son of God; that He had been delivered up to the Gentiles, and had died upon the Cross,—of all these things their first hearers were fully aware from their own personal knowledge. That He had been " declared to be the Son of God with power by His resurrection from the dead,"—to this the apostles, as His chosen witnesses for this very end, bore unwavering testimony with great power.[1] Disciples in Judæa and Galilee, who, when Paul wrote his first Epistle to the Corinthians some quarter of a century after this, could still be counted by hundreds, added their testimony as eye and ear witnesses to the fact that the Lord was risen indeed, and had appeared unto them and unto many.[2]

Christ had ascended also to the right hand of God. The apostles had seen Him ascend, and bore witness. And He had shed forth this, which all men in Jerusalem, in one form or other, now saw and heard. Ere the day of Pentecost closed, not hundreds merely, but thousands, bore witness to the reality of the advent and the power of the Holy Ghost in the Church.

They bore a witness, which gathered strength as days and months went on, the witness of changed lives, of a new spiritual joy, and hope, and love to God and man, of which all around them could not but take knowledge. Pentecost itself, and the Pentecostal Church which sprang from it, were the conclusive evidence of the Resurrection and Ascension of Christ. They formed, and they form still, an evidence which, when fairly presented and fully weighed, no man " who is of the truth,"—to use our Lord's words before Pilate,[3]—no man of intelligent mind and open heart has ever been able to gainsay or to resist.[4]

2nd. Another outstanding characteristic of the apostolic Church is the way in which the Presence of Christ Himself was felt and realized in the midst of His disciples, met and

---

[1] Μεγάλη δυνάμει ἀπεδίδουν τὸ μαρτύριον οἱ ἀπόστολοι τῆς ἀναστάσεως τοῦ Κυρίου Ἰησοῦ, Acts iv. 33.

[2] 1 Cor. xv. 6.

[3] Πᾶς ὁ ὢν ἐκ τῆς ἀληθείας ἀκούει μου τῆς φωνῆς, John xviii. 37.

[4] Comp. Dykes, *From Jerusalem to Antioch*, 4th ed. pp. 75 f., 155 f.

acting in His name. Christ's promises that it should be so, and that especially through the coming and work of the Holy Spirit,[1] were signally fulfilled in the history of this period.

This truth meets us in the opening words of the book of Acts. Its author marks his sense of the historic unity and continuity of the work which he records in his two successive treatises: "The former treatise I made, O Theophilus, concerning all that Jesus began both to do and to teach until the day in which He was received up."[2] The beginnings of the acts and the teaching of Christ, these form the subject of the first part of Luke's history. In the second, while narrating "Acts of Apostles"[3] and other disciples of the Lord, he is recording as truly "Acts of Christ," the things which Jesus continued both to do and to teach to the apostles and by them.

In the first section of the Acts and the relative Epistles, we see the Saviour still "with His people all the days," "giving commandment through the Holy Ghost unto the apostles whom He had chosen," proving how "all power is committed unto Him on earth," as well as "in heaven," working by His Spirit in and through His disciples.

The Presence of Christ in the midst of the Church is not more clearly brought out in the history than is the fact that that Presence was revealed and made effectual by the Holy Spirit. Our Lord had foretold that it should be so. "He shall not speak for Himself. . . . He shall glorify Me; for He shall take of Mine and shall declare it unto you." It was "expedient" for the disciples and for Christ's cause on earth that His own visible Presence should be withdrawn, and that "the Paraclete" — the Advocate, the Helper and Strengthener—should come to them, "sent by Himself from the Father."[4] "Greater works" than those which marked Christ's own public ministry should His disciples do when

---

[1] Matt. xxviii. 20 ; John xiv. 18-23 ; xvi. 7-16.

[2] Acts i. 1 f.

[3] Πράξεις ἀποστόλων is the simplest and oldest title of the book.

[4] John xvi. 7, 13 f. See Canon Westcott's note on παράκλητος, *Gospel of St. John*, pp. 211-213.

this stage of things was reached. Yet the very words in which this promise is given show that these greater works are *His* also, though done by the hands and through the faith of disciples: "Whatsoever ye shall ask in My name, that *will I do*, that the Father may be glorified in the Son. If ye shall ask Me anything in My name, *that will I do*."[1] There is to be no absence on the Lord's part that would involve distance from His people or inaction as regards the guidance and work of His Church. It is "in His name" that His disciples are to gather together; in His name they are to pray, and to act in all matters that concern His cause and people. So meeting, they are to find that He is in the midst of them; so asking and acting, they shall have the petitions which they desire of Him. He will do the work through them.

We see the practical fulfilment of these promises in the narrative of the Acts. Far greater spiritual results followed the preaching of the Gospel after Pentecost than those which followed the preaching of our Lord Himself. More thousands of converts could be counted probably within a year from the Ascension than hundreds during the three years of the Saviour's earthly ministry. The unseen Leader was followed as He never had been when He companied with His disciples in the flesh. The voice of Christ risen and ascended was heard, and understood, and obeyed, although that same voice in other days fell so often upon dull and regardless ears.

Illustrations of this meet us in every scene in the history of the apostolic Church from the first. In the election of Matthias, while the company of disciples, on the proposal of Peter, "put forward" two men who seemed to them most fit, the actual appointment is placed directly in the hands of Christ Himself, as present unseen in the midst of them. He must choose this apostle as He had chosen the rest. "They prayed, and said, Thou, Lord, which knowest the hearts

---

[1] John xiv. 12–14. "The meaning of the phrase (ἐν τῷ ὀνόματί μου) is 'as being one with Me, even as I am revealed to you.' Its two correlatives are 'in Me' (vi. 56; xiv. 20; xv. 4 ff.; xvi. 33; comp. 1 John v. 20), and the Pauline 'in Christ.'" Westcott, *in loco*.

of all men, show of these two the one whom Thou hast chosen to take the place in this ministry and apostleship, from which Judas fell away, that he might go to his own place." [1]

In the first recorded instance of a miracle wrought by the hands of the apostles after Pentecost,—the healing of the lame man in the temple,—what Peter and John are chiefly concerned to prove, is that it is not they who have done this mighty work, but Christ. "Why fasten ye your eyes on us, as though by our own power or godliness we had made this man to walk?" It was "the Prince of life, whom God raised from the dead, whereof we are witnesses. And by faith in His name hath His name made this man strong whom ye behold and know." This was the special testimony of the Holy Spirit speaking through the apostles to the whole Sanhedrin. "Peter, filled with the Holy Ghost, said unto them, Ye rulers of the people and elders . . . be it known unto you, and to all the people of Israel, that in the name of Jesus Christ of Nazareth, whom ye crucified, whom God raised from the dead, even in Him doth this man stand here before you whole . . . and in none other is there salvation." [2]

Dr. Dykes shows in a striking way how exactly the *manner* of our Lord's own miracles reappears in this apostolic act. In this incident and others, such as the raising of Dorcas from the dead, we see Christ acting by His Spirit in the apostles, as He did of old in Galilee and Judæa. "This is the full New Testament significance of Pentecost. It is to be viewed as the resumption of work on earth by the Lord Jesus, the Church's Head and Life. It was His virtual return in spiritual power to do through His brethren such works as He had done in person, and greater works than these." [3] Only a few months before this event, "the blind and the lame came to Jesus in the temple; and He healed them." [4] The same great Healer was present in the

---

[1] Acts i. 24 f. On the point that the prayer is addressed to Christ, comp. Alford, *in loco.*

[2] Acts iii. 12, 15 f. ; iv. 8-10, 12.

[3] Dykes, *From Jerusalem to Antioch,* 4th ed. p. 125 f.   [4] Matt. xxi. 14.

same courts now, although unseen.   What Peter said afterwards to the palsied man at Lydda held as truly of him
who sat for alms at the beautiful gate of the temple: "Jesus
Christ healeth thee.   And straightway he arose.   And all
that dwelt at Lydda and in Sharon saw him, and they turned
to the Lord." [1]

In the healing of the lame man the likeness to what Christ
Himself had done, and to the spirit in which He had spoken,
was so clear and strong, that it forced itself on the unwilling
eyes of the rulers and elders of the Jews, before whom the
apostles stood to be examined.   It seemed to the Sanhedrin
as if Jesus of Nazareth was again in the midst of them,
speaking and acting as He was wont to do.   "When they
beheld the boldness of Peter and John, and had perceived
that they were unlearned and ignorant men, they marvelled;
and they took knowledge of them (ἐπεγίνωσκον αὐτούς,
recognised them) that they had been with Jesus." [2]   "It
is the very life of Christ Himself breathed into His saints
which forms the characteristic of their Christian life . . .
till they grow in supreme moments to be so like reproduc-
tions of that Christ whom the world refused as to vex
the world's conscience with the recollection of its rejected
Lord." [3]

Look at the first instance in which judgment falls upon
any professed member of the apostolic Church.   You have
there the same truth illustrated from another side.   It was
not Peter, as has often been pointed out, who executed judgment upon Ananias and Sapphira.   As to the first of the two,
the apostle did not predict, and in all likelihood did not look for
any such event as followed.   He simply unveiled and rebuked
the sin as one specially against the Holy Ghost, as a lie acted
in that Divine Presence which dwelt in the midst of Christ's
disciples gathered together in His name.   But the apostle's
words were awfully verified.   Even as in Old Testament
times fire came forth upon presumptuous offenders from the
Shekinah, the visible Presence of the Lord in the Holiest of
all,[4] so now swiftly and suddenly, as a thunderbolt from

---

[1] Acts ix. 34 f.   [2] Acts iv. 13.
[3] Dykes, p. 149.   [4] Lev. x. 1 ff.

heaven, the judgment of God came upon Ananias. "Hearing these words, he fell down, and gave up the ghost: and great fear came upon all that heard it." [1]

A space was given to his wife to repent of her share in the sin; although the awe which fell on the assembly kept the tidings from reaching her. Her coming in among the disciples unabashed was as if she had spoken. "And Peter answered unto her: Tell me whether ye sold the land for so much?" He foresees now what the result would be in her case also, if her guilt should prove the same; presently he foretells her doom. But he takes nothing for granted until opportunity for confession should be given. The bench of the apostles was like God's judgment-seat that day. It was, as in the Jewish saying, known even then, it may be, in the synagogues: "Where three elders of Israel give righteous judgment, the Shekinah is in the midst of them." The very form of Peter's question leaned to mercy. It might have suggested to Sapphira that her sin had come to light. The fatal money was lying, as it seems, where Ananias had laid it, at the apostles' feet, none venturing to lift it up. Peter may have pointed to it as he said, "Did ye sell the land for so much? And she said, Yea, for so much. But Peter said unto her, How is it that ye have agreed together to tempt the Spirit of the Lord?"

In the dead silence of awe and horror which must have fallen upon the assembly at the answer of the unhappy woman, and at the conviction which flashed upon all, that her husband's fate was overhanging her also, the tread of feet was distinctly heard without, like the sound of coming judgment, nigh even at the door. And the apostle went on: "Behold, the feet of them which have buried thy husband are at the door, and they shall carry thee out. And she fell down immediately at his feet, and gave up the ghost; and the young men came in, and found her dead, and they carried her out, and buried her by her husband. And great fear came upon the whole Church, and upon all that heard these things." [2]

This is the first instance in which the word Church (ἐκκλησία)

_____
[1] Acts v. 5.   [2] Acts v. 1-11.

occurs in the genuine text of the Acts. The connection is impressive. It shows that the Church or company of believers, separated from the world, and gathered together in the name of Christ, under the dispensation of the Holy Ghost, meets under solemn sanctions. The Gospel with which the Church is put in trust may be "a savour of death unto death." The real, although unseen, Presence of the Lord Jesus in the midst of His disciples, according to His promise, gives a sacredness to their assemblies which cannot be disregarded with impunity.

This was the first miracle of judgment, the first direct Divine visitation of death, seen in Israel since the days when fire fell from heaven at Elijah's bidding, and consumed the captains with their fifties, or since the open opposers of the truth in the time of the prophets of the exile died by the hand of God.[1] Never had the Saviour, while on earth, put forth His hand against the life of man. By deeds, as well as words, He had shown that "God sent not His Son into the world to judge the world, but that the world should be saved through Him."[2] But now He is exalted to the right hand of the Majesty in the heavens, "set as a king upon God's holy hill of Zion," with "all power given to Him in heaven and on earth," the "power to execute judgment also," as was done here in the eyes of all men, as shall be done in the day "when the Lord Jesus shall be revealed from heaven with the angels of His power in flaming fire, rendering vengeance to them that know not God, and to them that obey not the Gospel of our Lord Jesus, who shall suffer punishment, even eternal destruction, from the face of the Lord and from the glory of His might."[3]

This first open sin within the pale of the professing Church is visited by its unseen King and Lord with this open punishment from His own hand. Church discipline in the hands of Christ's disciples is a "power which the Lord has given for edification, and not for destruction (ϵἰς οἰκοδομὴν καὶ οὐκ

---

[1] 2 Kings i. 10 ff.; Jer. xxviii. 15 ff.; Ezek. xi. 1-4, 13.

[2] John iii. 17.

[3] Ps. ii. 6 f.; comp. Acts ii. 34 ff.; xiii. 33; Matt. xxviii. 18; John v. 27 2 Thess. i. 7 f.

εἰς καθαίρεσιν)." [1]   It works by spiritual means only, such
as those which our Lord indicated in the passage in the
18th chapter of Matthew already considered.   Its highest
censure is that the offending brother, after all efforts to
win him to repentance have failed, be shut out from the
fellowship of believers, and be to them "as the Gentile
and the publican."   Nothing further is done by Peter and
John in the case of the Samaritan soothsayer than to
declare this separation as henceforth subsisting, until repentance be manifested and forgiveness sought from God.[2]   But
here a warning was given once and for all as to the mind of
Christ concerning such sins as that of Ananias and his wife
within the fellowship of His professing people.   Their doom
is set as a beacon in the history of the Pentecostal Church, to
show how perilous a thing it is, and how fatal a thing it may
prove, "to tempt the Spirit of the Lord," and "to lie to the
Holy Ghost."   "A man that hath set at nought Moses' law,"
an inspired writer reminded a Hebrew Christian community
in the next generation, "dieth without compassion on the
word of two or three witnesses ; of how much sorer punishment, think ye, shall he be judged worthy who hath trodden
under foot the Son of God, . . . and hath done despite unto
the Spirit of grace ?" [3]   "Great fear came upon the whole
Church, and upon all that heard these things."   It was meant
that it should be so, and that the fear should remain in the
Church throughout all time.

It is needless to refer in detail to other illustrations of how
the personal Presence of Christ in and with His Church was
recognised by His disciples all through the period with which
we have now to do.   It is He whom the historian of the
Acts so often calls "the Lord" (ὁ Κύριος), as the apostles

---

[1] 2 Cor. x. 8 ; xiii. 10 ; comp. 1 Cor. v. 4 f., 12 f.

[2] Acts viii. 18–24.   The strong expression of horror and revulsion in Peter's
first words, before he passes to urge repentance and prayer upon Simon Magus,
suggests that the apostle must have recalled the scene of Ananias and Sapphira,
and feared lest a like fate from the hand of the Lord should follow this fresh sin
against the Holy Ghost.

[3] Heb. x. 28 f.   Dr. Dykes brings out in an impressive way some of the chief
lessons to be drawn from this incident in reference to the religious life of our
own times.   *From Jerusalem to Antioch*, pp. 174–179.

constantly do in their recorded addresses, transferring to Him in its fullest sense the Old Testament name of God in the form which the Alexandrian translation had made familiar everywhere.[1]   The Church in the upper chamber, as we have seen, prays to Him, and puts the choice of an apostle directly into His hands. " The Lord added to them day by day those that were being saved." [2]   The voice and hand of Christ drew each individual believer irresistibly to the company of believers in the midst of which His special Presence and blessing were to be found.   In all the work of the Church —to use the language in which the second Evangelist sums up the history after the Ascension—" the Lord " was seen to be " working with them, and confirming the Word with signs following. " [3]   The apostles declare constantly that these signs and mighty deeds are really wrought, not by themselves, but by Him.   And all men see and feel that they are done *as* He used to do them.   It is " the Lord " by " His angel " who delivers His servants from prison, and sends them seasonable words of encouragement and guidance in difficulty, and strikes down the strongest foes of His Church.   He is within sight of His disciples in the hour of special danger, when they have no help in man, and all other faces around are those of enemies.   They commit their spirits peacefully to Him, as felt to be close beside them, in the hour of death.[4]

The first sight of the Saviour after His Ascension is that vouchsafed to Stephen before the Sanhedrin.   The first words heard directly from Himself are those spoken to Saul on the road to Damascus.   Both the vision and the words bring out our Lord's intense, living sympathy with His disciples on earth.   They show us " the Son of Man who is in heaven," and yet " with His people all the days, even unto the end of the world."   When Stephen saw the Lord, His attitude was that of One, not sitting in calm sovereignty at the right hand of God, but risen to bend over His suffering servant, as of old

---

[1] See Weiss, *Biblical Theol. of the N. T.*, 3rd ed. E. Tr., Edin. 1882, i. pp. 180, 294 f.

[2] Acts ii. 47.   [3] Mark xvi. 20.

[4] Acts xii. 11, 17, 23 ; vi. 15 ; vii. 55 f., 59 f.

Christ bent over beds of pain on earth,—risen in sympathy and for effective help. The words which Saul of Tarsus heard from His lips were those of One who had been in the midst of the trembling disciples at Damascus, and *felt* the thrill of their suspense and anguish now, when the tramp of the fierce enemy was at the gate, bringing fiery trial and tortures for Christian men and women to " compel them to blaspheme." The Lord spoke to the persecutor as One who made their case thoroughly His own, using the very language which they would have used, " saying unto him in the Hebrew tongue : Saul, Saul, why persecutest thou Me ? " [1]

3rd. Another striking characteristic of the apostolic Church is the central and supreme place given to the Scriptures, as the record of Divine revelation, and as the infallible source of knowledge of the will of God and of Christ for the Church in all circumstances and at all times.

Far from trusting solely to the present impulses of the Spirit in individual believers, or to indications of the Lord's will received in meetings of the brethren, the apostolic Church is seen to betake itself at once to the written Word. The Holy Spirit, both when given in the way of earnest on the evening of the Resurrection and in His fulness at Pentecost, led the disciples directly to the record of His teaching in the past history of revelation. Our Lord's first gift to His disciples after His Resurrection was that of power " to understand the Scriptures ; " [2] and the gift was not suffered to lie idle. Just as the first recorded action of the apostolic Church was prayer, so her first recorded utterance was an appeal to the Scriptures, " to the law and to the testimony." By that rule the Church of God was to walk under the new dispensation as under the old.[3] " Brethren," Peter said when he rose to speak in the assembly of the disciples in the upper room after the Ascension, " it was needful that the Scripture should be fulfilled ($\check{\epsilon}\delta\epsilon\iota$ $\pi\lambda\eta\rho\omega\theta\hat{\eta}\nu\alpha\iota$ $\tau\grave{\eta}\nu$ $\gamma\rho\alpha\phi\acute{\eta}\nu$), which the Holy Ghost spake before by the mouth of David concerning Judas." [4]

---

[1] Acts ix. 1-6 ; xxvi. 11-15. [2] Luke xxiv. 45.
[3] Isa. viii. 20. [4] Acts i. 16.

The principles thus acted on by the Church in the upper chamber were consistently carried out in all the after stages of her historic development throughout the period now under consideration. The appeal to Scripture and the appeal to facts of recent and present experience go side by side, as we have seen, in the public addresses of the apostles to their fellow-countrymen. They do so equally in the fragments preserved of the preaching of Stephen, of Philip, and of Saul of Tarsus. Scripture evidence and personal testimony together formed the basis of evangelistic effort among the multitudes in Jerusalem. The Old Testament records and the oral teaching of the apostles held an equally important place in the training of the new converts.

In nothing, perhaps, have we a clearer proof of the fact that Christ's Presence was indeed in the midst of His disciples still, and that the Spirit of all wisdom and power was with them, than in the way in which the dangers were averted or overcome which beset the apostolic Church on every side during the first few months and years of its history. Among the most serious of these dangers were such as might have naturally arisen from the sudden influx of a vast multitude of new members; differing—many of them—from the little Galilæan company of the upper room in respect of country, language, and general culture; differing—all of them—in this, that they had not, like the first disciples, been under the personal teaching and influence of Jesus Himself. From the day of Pentecost onwards these new converts outnumbered the original disciples by thousands. They were frankly received from the first into the common fellowship, as brethren in full standing. It might have seemed that, in these circumstances, not a few changes in the general spirit and features of the society were inevitable. That such, in point of fact, was not the case,—that the "one accord," the unity of spirit and action which marked the little company in the upper chamber, prevailed as signally among "the multitude of them that believed" after Pentecost,—proves how powerful and how persistent were the forces by which the apostolic Church was moved and moulded.

The voice and hand of the unseen Leader, the grace and

guidance of the personal Spirit of truth, did not fail. They were as plainly to be recognised among the new converts as among those who, in contrast to them, were known now as "old disciples" (μαθηταὶ ἀρχαῖοι).[1]

This comes out clearly in the narrative from the first. Immediately after the account of what took place on the day of Pentecost we read : " And there were added unto them (the original company of disciples) in that day about three thousand souls. . . . And all that believed were together (ἦσαν ἐπὶ τὸ αὐτό), and had all things common. . . . And the Lord added to them (προσετίθει ἐπὶ τὸ αὐτό, continued tò add together,—to the collective company, those already gathered together into one) day by day such as were being saved." [2] That was among the first outward results which followed from His gracious dealing with every renewed soul. First of all came the great spiritual crisis in the history of each. As the historian of the Acts elsewhere expresses it, " they were *added*, as believers, *to the Lord*, multitudes both of men and women." [3] They became really one in Him. And then, by an unfailing instinct of their new spiritual life, the unity was manifested in ways which could be seen of men. " The Lord added to them," His hand gathered together into one company, " day by day such as were being saved."

The guiding hand of Christ, and the unerring instincts of the life which He implanted, were as clearly seen in this also, that the first thing which the new converts sought and found in the fellowship of the Church was " teaching." The narrative sums up the spiritual characteristics of those who received the Gospel at Pentecost in one suggestive sentence ; and in it the feature now named holds the foremost place. " They continued stedfastly in the apostle's teaching and fellowship, in the breaking of bread, and the prayers." [4]

---

[1] Acts xxi. 16.

[2] Acts ii. 41, 44–47.

[3] Acts v. 14. It is worth noting that the expression follows immediately after the first use of the term Church (ver. 11), and in connection with the incident of Ananias and Sapphira, which showed so plainly that men might be added outwardly to the Church, and might bring costly gifts to the apostles, without being truly added to the Lord.

[4] Acts ii. 42.

In the writings of the three, who stand out as "pillars" in the Pentecostal Church, we find special reference to this characteristic of healthful Christian life, which was so signally exemplified in their experience at this time.

The apostle Peter, in his first Epistle, speaks emphatically of the Scriptures as both the instrument of regeneration and "the great aliment of the new-born." "As new-born babes," he writes to believers in the Dispersion, "seek after the pure spiritual milk, that ye may grow thereby unto salvation, if ye have tasted that the Lord is gracious." [1] James, again, in his Epistle to Hebrew Christians, warns them against seeking to become, many of them, teachers. They had been begotten and brought forth by God through the word of truth. "Let every man be swift to hear, slow to speak. Receive with meekness the implanted word, which is able to save your souls. But be ye doers of the word, and not hearers only." [2] "Ye are strong," the apostle John writes to young believers, "and the Word of God abideth in you, and (so) ye have overcome the wicked one." "Whosoever goeth onward, and abideth not in the teaching of Christ, hath not God; he that abideth in the teaching, the same hath both the Father and the Son." [3]

For all this there had been a Providential discipline and preparation both on the part of the teachers and the taught. The Pentecostal converts were drawn chiefly from the multitude who came up to Jerusalem to worship at the feast. They were "devout men from every nation under heaven," "Jews and proselytes." Every one of them, therefore, had been trained more or less under the synagogue system. In many of them, doubtless, were to be seen the fruits of that system at its best. There were men in the crowd who heard Peter

---

[1] 1 Pet. ii. 2 f. "We learn a mode of living which has the savour of the new birth," Calvin says beautifully (vitæ ratio quæ novam genituram sapiat), "when we surrender ourselves to be brought up by God." There is no contrast here between the milk for babes and the meat for those of full age. The meaning is that in the Scriptures, or the Spirit speaking in the Scriptures, believers have the great source of spiritual nourishment, which they are to seek after as babes their natural food, and that they have there all that is needful for healthful life and growth. There is the same idea of "salvation" in this verse as in Acts ii. 47 (τοὺς σωζομένους), and as in Jas. i. 21 (τὸν ἔμφυτον λόγον τὸν δυνάμενον σῶσαι τὰς ψυχὰς ὑμῶν).

[2] Jas. i. 18–22 ; iii. 1.   [3] 1 John ii. 14 ; 2 John 9 f.

speak, such as Zacharias and Simeon, and Ananias of Damascus, such as the centurions of Capernaum and Cæsarea, such as the Ethiopian chamberlain. There were women like the mother of our Lord, like Elizabeth and the sisters of Bethany, like the ministering women from Galilee, like Lois and Eunice, like Lydia and Priscilla. Many a Jewish home there had been like that of Mary and Joseph at Nazareth, or that in which Timothy grew up at Lystra, where the children were trained in the fear and the love of God and in the knowledge of the holy Scriptures, knowing and feeling "the unfeigned faith" that dwelt in their parents, the spirit of grace and devoutness that breathed in their lives.

Many a scribe had taught in village synagogues of the Holy Land and the Dispersion, whose heart was "waiting for the consolation of Israel" and "looking for the promised redemption," and whose likeness might be traced in the picture, which Christ held up for His apostles to copy, of "a scribe who hath been made a disciple to the kingdom of heaven," and who was "as an householder, bringing forth out of his treasure things new and old." [1] Such men there were no doubt among the scribes of Jerusalem, and among the pilgrims who came up to worship there at the Passover when our Lord was crucified, and at the Pentecost which followed. Numbers of the Pentecostal converts had sat at the feet of such "wise men and scribes" in Israel, and had sacred memories of their words and lives, and of how they had "died in faith," "having served their own generation by the will of God," "not having received the promises, but having seen them and greeted them from afar." [2] They had learned from such scribes in the synagogues and the synagogue schools to reverence the Scriptures, to feel the spiritual power which

---

[1] Luke ii. 25, 38 ; Matt. xiii. 52.

[2] Acts xiii. 36 ; Heb. xi. 13 : Hilary, the deacon, in one of his commentaries makes an interesting reference to the thoroughness of the system by which the Jewish children were trained in Scripture knowledge. "This passed over by tradition to us ;" and he expresses regret that such teaching was not maintained in the Church of the fourth century as in earlier times. "Ii qui literis et lectionibus imbuendos infantes solebant imbuere, sicut mos Judæorum est, quorum traditio ad nos transitum fecit, quæ per negligentiam obsolevit." Ambrosiaster, *Comment. in Eph.* iv. 11.

accompanies God's word, to expect much from it. And now the Saviour's predictions at the close of His ministry were being visibly fulfilled. On the rock of a believing confession of Jesus as the Messiah the Son of the living God, proclaimed by the lips of that apostle who first publicly owned Him as such, the Lord Himself was building His Church, the true קהל ישׂראל. Into this Church He was visibly gathering the flower and fruit of that great synagogue system, through which for centuries His scattered people had received spiritual food, and had been gathered into one. In this Church, according to His promise, He was sending as His commissioned ambassadors (ἰδού, ἐγὼ ἀποστέλλω πρὸς ὑμᾶς) " prophets, and wise men, and scribes." [1] Ought not every true son of Israel to hear and obey them ? " They continued stedfastly in the apostles' teaching and fellowship, and in the breaking of bread, and the prayers."

The apostles on their part now saw, as never before, the reason of their three years' training under the eye of Christ Himself and in close fellowship with Him.[2] The Holy Spirit " brought to their remembrance," according to their Master's promise, " all that He had said to them " by word and deed, and " taught them all things," leading them to see the meaning of His words and of the things which He had done and suffered in their presence.[3] The remembrance of their own slowness to learn from the lips of Christ Himself would teach them patience with the brethren who sought now to learn from them concerning Him. As He had been among His disciples, so they strove now to be among those who waited on their teaching. No doubt they felt their own need of further guidance, and rejoiced to claim the fulfilment of the Lord's promise concerning the Holy Spirit, the Paraclete : " When He, the Spirit of truth is come, He shall guide you

---

[1] Matt. xxiii. 34.

[2] Comp. Acts i. 21 f. with Matt. x. 1 f.; Mark iii. 13 f.; Luke vi. 13, 17. The formal appointment of the Twelve to the apostleship towards the middle of our Lord's public ministry must, of course, be distinguished from their earlier personal call to discipleship. See Bruce, *Training of the Twelve*, 3rd ed. pp. 29-32, and compare the interesting summary of the main topics of Christ's teaching to the apostles given by Prof. Bruce at p. 530 f.

[3] John xiv. 26.

into all the truth . . . and He shall declare unto you the things that are to come. He shall glorify Me; for He shall take of Mine, and shall declare it unto you." [1] Like the Old Testament prophets, to whose spiritual experience Peter refers, in words which doubtless reflect his own experience and that of his fellow-apostles, when called to fill a similar place in the New Testament Church, "They sought and searched diligently: searching what, or what manner of time, the Spirit of Christ which was in them did signify, when it testified beforehand the sufferings of Christ, and the glories that should follow them." [2]

Such diligent searching and consideration of the Scriptures, and of the mind of Christ and of the Spirit, demanded much time. It is on this ground especially that the apostles ask to be relieved from the growing burden of the more outward affairs of the Church by the appointment of "the seven." "It is not fit," they said to the multitude of the disciples, "that we should forsake the Word of God and serve tables. Look ye out, therefore, brethren, from among you seven men of good report, full of the Spirit and of wisdom, whom we may appoint over this business. But we will continue stedfastly in prayer and in the ministry of the Word." [3]

From the glimpses of oral apostolic teaching which we have in the Acts and the Epistles, and from the nature of the case, we gather that this "ministry of the Word," as exercised towards those already Christians, divided itself into two distinct although closely related departments. These might be summed up in the two pregnant sentences which describe Paul's first preaching in the synagogues of Damascus after his conversion. "He proclaimed that Jesus is the Son of God;" and he "proved that this is the Christ." [4]

First, testimony was borne to the great facts of the personal history of the Lord Jesus by witnesses, some of whom, like "James the Lord's brother," had known Him from childhood; while others, like the eleven, had "companied with Him all the time of His public ministry, beginning from John's baptism until the day that He was received up." Instruction

---

[1] John xvi. 13 f.   [2] 1 Pet. i. 10 f.
[3] Acts vi. 2-4.   [4] Acts ix. 20, 22.

was given by "the apostles whom He had chosen" as to what
their Lord taught, and did, and suffered; as to what God did in
bearing witness to His Son from heaven, raising Him from the
dead, exalting Him at His right hand as a Prince and Saviour.

Secondly, proof was given by the apostles from the Old
Testament Scriptures that this was indeed the Messiah who
was to come.   They followed out the clues which the risen
Saviour had put into the hands of His disciples when,
"beginning from Moses and all the prophets, He interpreted
to them in all the Scriptures the things concerning Himself."[1]
They used the light given with the gift of the Spirit on the
evening of the Resurrection, when the Saviour "breathed on
them, saying, Receive ye of the Holy Ghost," and when He
"opened their mind that they might understand the Scriptures."   The apostles not only testified to the fact that
Jesus died and rose again; they "proved" that Jesus as the
Christ "died for our sins *according to the Scriptures* ($\kappa a\tau\grave{a}$ $\tau\grave{a}\varsigma$
$\gamma\rho a\phi\acute{a}\varsigma$); and that He was buried; and that He rose again
the third day *according to the Scriptures*. . . . Whether it
were I or they," Paul wrote in one of his earliest epistles,
speaking of the relation between him and the original
apostles, "so we preach, and so ye believed."[2]

We find clear evidence of this diligent searching into the
meaning of the things written in all the Scriptures concerning Christ in the first apostolic utterance after the
Ascension, the address of Peter to the little company in the
upper chamber.   We see it also in the preface to the third
Gospel.   The historian writes to Theophilus, "concerning
those matters which have been fully established among us[3]
($\tau\hat{\omega}\nu$ $\pi\epsilon\pi\lambda\eta\rho o\phi o\rho\eta\mu\acute{\epsilon}\nu\omega\nu$ $\grave{\epsilon}\nu$ $\dot{\eta}\mu\hat{\iota}\nu$ $\pi\rho a\gamma\mu\acute{a}\tau\omega\nu$), even as they

---

[1] Luke xxiv. 27.

[2] John xx. 22 ; Luke xxiv. 45 ff. ; 1 Cor. xv. 1-11.

[3] This rendering—which is that of the R. V. Margin, with most of the
Fathers and such modern exegetes as Calvin, Erasmus, Ewald, Alford, and
Meyer (5th ed.)—seems preferable to that of the Vulgate, "quæ in nobis com-
pletæ sunt," which is followed by the R. V. text.   Godet's criticisms of Meyer's
argument from 2 Tim. iv. 17 seem valid.   That particular text does not
support the conclusion in behalf of which Meyer cites it.   But the other
grounds adduced in favour of the conclusion appear sufficient to establish it
notwithstanding.   Godet, *L'Evangile de S. Luc*, 2nde ed. p. 70 f.

delivered them unto us which from the beginning were eye-witnesses and ministers of the Word [1] . . . that thou mightest know the certainty concerning the things wherein thou wast instructed " (κατηχήθης, taught by word of mouth).[2]

It was thus that the inner life of the apostolic Church grew strong. It was nourished and built up by the testimony of those who had been eye and ear witnesses of the teaching, the deeds, and the sufferings of Christ, and by that further "ministry of the Word" which opened to eager listeners the meaning of familiar Scriptures which they "had known from childhood," and heard "read in the synagogues every Sabbath day," "the things written in the law of Moses, and the prophets, and the Psalms concerning Christ." [3]

Along with such exposition of the Old Testament there were given by the apostles and others fitted by the Spirit for the work, words of practical guidance and exhortation, in which the teaching of Christ and of the ancient Scriptures was applied to present circumstances and duty. It was doubtless from his special gifts in this respect that Joseph of Cyprus "was by the apostles surnamed Barnabas, which is, being interpreted, Son of exhortation." [4]

The original disciples and the new converts were thus welded into one loving fellowship by the Spirit of God working through the ministry of the Word. "The multitude

---

[1] οἱ ἀπ' ἀρχῆς αὐτόπται καὶ ὑπηρέται γενόμενοι. "Serviteurs-devenus, dit littéralement le texte. Cette expression fait contraste avec la précédente. Ces hommes out commencé plus tard à être serviteurs de la parole ; ils ne le sont devenus que depuis la Pentecôte. C'est alors que leur rôle de témoins s'est transformé en celui de prédicateurs." Godet, p. 72 f.

[2] Luke i. 1–4.

[3] 2 Tim. iii. 15 ; Acts xv. 21 ; Luke xxiv. 44. "The written Gospel of the first period of the apostolic age was the Old Testament interpreted by the vivid recollections of the Saviour's ministry. The preaching of the apostles was the unfolding of the law and the prophets." Westcott, Introd. to Study of Gospels, 5th ed. p. 169.

[4] Acts iv. 36 ; comp. xi. 23, בַּר־נְבוּאָה, υἱὸς παρακλήσεως. How wide the compass of this gift might be, and how high those endowed with it might rise, we see in the author of the Epistle to the Hebrews, who puts his whole letter under the category of "the word of exhortation" (τοῦ λόγου τῆς παρακλήσεως), Heb. xiii. 22.

of them that believed were of one heart and soul." They
were "nourished," as the apostle desired that Timothy and
his hearers should be, "in the words of the faith, and of the
good and healthful teaching," "the healthful words of our
Lord Jesus Christ, and the teaching which is according to
godliness." [1] The effect was manifest in the thoroughly
healthful character of the life of the Church. Amid the
highest tide of spiritual enthusiasm everything like fanaticism
was avoided. Nothing is more striking in the narrative than
the sober self-control which marks the speech and conduct of
the leaders of the Church. The apostles are seen to be new
men in this as in other respects. Both in the private
meetings of the brethren and in public, in the temple courts
and before the Sanhedrin, they bear themselves in a spirit
and manner which are in the strongest possible contrast to
their former hesitations, mistakes, and stumblings as recorded
by the Evangelists. From the very height of the spiritual
excitement of the day of Pentecost, Peter speaks words of the
most clear and well-ordered argument. All the actions of
the Church under apostolic guidance are wise and well-
considered. The Spirit which the Risen Saviour gave to His
disciples when gathered together in His name, and seeking to
know and do His will in the world, was "a spirit not of fear,
but of power, and love, and a sound mind."

4th. Consider the relation of the members of the apostolic
Church of this period to each other, and the spirit which
prevailed among them.

Looking at the Hebrew Christian Church from this point
of view, we cannot fail to recognise the truthfulness of the
picture which our Lord had drawn of it beforehand in words
already considered. "One is your Teacher and your Master,
even the Christ; and all ye are brethren." "By this shall
all men know that ye are My disciples, if ye have love one to
another." [2] We see in the Pentecostal Church one great company of brethren, joined together in love and in an unwritten
brotherly covenant, listening daily to the voice of the unseen

---

[1] Acts iv. 32 ; 1 Tim. iv. 6 ; vi. 3 ; 2 Tim. iv. 3.
[2] Matt. xxiii. 8-10 ; John xiii. 35. See above, pp. 224-228.

Master, who was felt to be really present in the midst of them by His Word and Spirit as they met together in His name.

No paraphrase can equal the beauty and power of the simple words in which the historian of the Acts describes this aspect of the apostolic Church. "And all that believed were together, and had all things common; and they sold their possessions and goods, and parted them to all, according as any man had need. And day by day, continuing stedfastly with one accord in the temple, and breaking bread at home, they did take their food with gladness and singleness of heart, praising God, and having favour with all the people. . . . And the multitude of them that believed were of one heart and soul: and not one of them said that aught of the things which he possessed was his own; but they had all things common. And with great power gave the apostles their witness of the resurrection of the Lord Jesus: and great grace was upon them all. Neither was there among them any that lacked: for as many as were possessors of lands or houses sold them, and brought the prices of the things that were sold, and laid them at the apostles' feet: and distribution was made unto each, according as any one had need."[1]

"Thirty years later, from the midst of a Church often wet now with blood and tears, a Church which all over the Mediterranean lands had already begun its death-grapple with the pagan world,—fresh from its perilous labours, perhaps at the very side of its chief missionary as he lay chained in a Roman prison, Luke cast back his eyes on the sweet prime and glad day-dawn to draw this picture, which has ever since entranced the weary, fighting Church of God, and shines in our far retrospect, as it shone in his, with the light of a golden age."[2]

One emphatic word in the sentence that describes the spirit of the new converts at Pentecost, seems specially to refer to this beautiful aspect of the apostolic Church, its common life of brotherly love. "They continued stedfastly in the apostles' teaching and *in the fellowship* (τῇ κοινωνίᾳ)." It would be a mistake to limit the meaning of

---

[1] Acts ii. 44–47; iv. 32–35.

[2] Dykes, *From Jerusalem to Antioch*, 4th ed. p. 104.

this word here simply to Christian liberality. That may be its special though not its only reference in some of the Epistles, which speak of the history of a much later period. But here the term evidently has a broader and deeper significance. It describes what was a most real and ever memorable experience to every one who was "added to the Lord," and to the company of His disciples in Pentecostal times, namely, the wonderful atmosphere of *fellowship* in which they found themselves. The word embodies every manifestation of the warm brotherly love of the early disciples, their childlike joy in the Holy Ghost, their freedom and simplicity of heart.[1]

This spirit of fellowship found expression at Jerusalem in what has been called, in a somewhat misleading way, "the community of goods."

It was in reality just a strong effort, on the part of the members of the Church in Jerusalem, to carry out practically their glowing love to all the brethren, to give outward expression in the ordinary matters of daily life to their real unity with them through the Holy Spirit in the common Lord. They *were* all one family in Him, and they sought to live as such from day to day in a family fellowship (τῇ κοινωνίᾳ).

It is easy to see how naturally this thought arose and took this particular form of outward embodiment in the existing circumstances. During the public ministry of our Lord, He and the inner circle of His disciples formed one family, moving together from place to place, eating together, supported from a common purse, which was in the keeping of a trusted member of the Twelve. The bounds of this little company widened as time went on, and one and another heard and obeyed the special call of Christ: "Follow Me;" "Sell what thou hast and give to the poor, and come, follow Me." The women "who were with Him and the Twelve in Galilee, and ministered unto them of their substance," and "who

<hr />

[1] See Lechler, *Das apostolische u. das nachapostolische Zeitalter*, 3te Aufl., Karlsruhe u. Leipzig 1885, S. 39 f. Comp. Dr. Rigg on "The Fellowship of the Primitive Church," in *Comparative View of Church Organizations, Primitive and Protestant*, Lond. 1887, p. 11 f.

followed Him to Jerusalem," belonged to this family circle
of discipleship.   We see from the circumstances connected
with the first institution of the Lord's Supper, that Jesus
was wont to keep the Passover at Jerusalem as the head of
a household, with its members gathered round Him.   The
same relations seem to have been continued among " the
eleven, and them that were with them," in the upper
chamber after the Ascension, when the number usually
present is stated as " about a hundred and twenty." [1]   There
was still the common centre, the " home " of the brotherhood.
There were still, in all likelihood, a common purse and a
common table.   What more natural impulse for the disciples
after Pentecost than simply to widen the circle of the
common life, — the κοινωνία, — so as to take in the new
brethren and sisters into the fullest and closest fellowship
that was possible ?

Again, the converts of Pentecost were drawn largely from
the pilgrims who came from foreign lands to keep the feast
at Jerusalem.   The poorest Jews were often—then as now
—the most zealous in making such pilgrimages.   Many
of these converts would doubtless cling to the Church in
Jerusalem, after the scanty means which they brought with
them were exhausted.   Most of them were probably deprived
of the usual hospitalities of their fellow-countrymen to which
they had trusted.   It was the first form of persecution which
these young disciples had to bear for Christ's sake and the
Gospel.   Was it not fitting that their richer brethren in the
Lord should receive them joyfully to the common table, and
pour their money with an unstinted hand at the apostles' feet,
that "distribution might be made to each, according as any one
had need " ?

There was the case, too, of the apostles themselves.   Once
they had left all to follow Christ.   Now they were leaving
all for the sake of His cause and Church,—that they " might
give themselves continually to prayer, and to the ministry
of the Word " among the brethren, and to witness-bearing
to their fellow-countrymen.   There were also, as we learn,

[1] Matt. viii. 18–22 ; ix. 9 ; Mark x. 21 ; xiv. 12–16 ; xv. 40 f. ; Luke viii.
1-3 ; ix. 57–62 ; xxiv. 33 ; John xii. 4-6 ; xiii. 29.

at an early stage in the history, not a few widows connected
with the Christian community.[1]   There must have been aged
and feeble persons and young children, whose natural means
of subsistence had been withdrawn from them because of
their connection with the followers of Jesus of Nazareth, or
whose poverty and sickness specially appealed to Christian
sympathy.   Such cases might have been met in other
circumstances—as they were in point of fact in the apostolic Church at a later date—by some special organization.[2]
But all that was needful for them was abundantly supplied,
in the first place, by this irresistible outflow of Christian
love.

As regards the idea of there being here anything like
what is ordinarily meant by a "community of goods," two
things may be noted,—

1. It is plain that the whole movement was entirely
voluntary and spontaneous.   The Twelve never urged or
recommended this special mode of action.   No express
approval of it even on their part is recorded.   "Whiles it
remained," Peter said to Ananias, "did it not remain thine
own ?   And after it was sold, was it not in thy power ? "[3]
All that we hear of the apostles doing in the matter was to
receive the money brought to them, and to regulate and arrange
for the distribution.

2. The words of the narrative do not seem to imply that
there was an actual division of the property of all the disciples
into equal shares, or that it was held in common in a literal
sense.   It is certain at least that if such a state of things
did exist at first in Jerusalem it soon ceased there ; and
nothing like it is found anywhere else in the records of
the apostolic age.   What took place in the Pentecostal
Church seems to have been this : The necessities of the
poor and suffering were relieved.   The general spirit was
such that "not one of them said that aught of the things
which he possessed was his own,[4] for they had all things

---

[1] Acts vi. 1.   [2] Acts vi. 1-4; Rom. xvi. 1 f. ; 1 Tim. v. 9-16.
[3] Acts v. 4.
[4] The things were still his possession ($\tau\grave{\alpha}$ $\acute{\upsilon}\pi\acute{\alpha}\rho\chi o\nu\tau\alpha$ $\alpha\grave{\upsilon}\tau\tilde{\wp}$), although he did not
speak nor act as if they were so.   It has been truly pointed out that we hear of

common. . . . Neither was there among them any that lacked: for distribution was made to each according as any one had need." The richer disciples, in particular, regarded their possessions as common property, until all such cases of want were fully met. For this end they sold freely their possessions and goods, lands and houses, and poured the money thus obtained into a common treasury over which the apostles presided. Inquiry seems to have been made as far as possible into the different cases.[1] The burden of investigation and distribution which was thus brought upon the Twelve, was soon brought forward by them as a conclusive reason for having fit men specially "appointed over this business."

That private property with its rights and privileges continued to exist among the Christians at Jerusalem is plain from such passages as Acts xii. 12 and Rom. xv. 26. From the first of these we learn that Mary the mother of Mark, kinswoman of Barnabas, had servants, and a house of her own in the city. In the second of the passages to which I refer, the apostle Paul mentions incidentally that "it had pleased them of Macedonia and Achaia to make a certain contribution for the poor among the saints (εἰς τοὺς πτωχοὺς τῶν ἁγίων) that are at Jerusalem," and that he was on his way thither in charge of the money. This statement implies, as plainly as words can do, that all the believers there were not on the same level socially, but that there were both rich and poor members of the Church at Jerusalem.

At an earlier date we find the same apostle going up with Barnabas from Antioch to Jerusalem on a similar errand, although the contributions in this case had a somewhat wider destination.[2] The distinction between rich and poor is taken

---

none of the *poorer* disciples saying that the things which their richer brethren possessed were theirs. There is the widest possible difference between the spirit here described and that of many schemes of communism. It is one thing for a man to say to his friend, "What is mine is thine," and another for the friend to claim, "All that is thine must be mine."

[1] Acts ii. 44 f. ; iv. 32, 34 f.

[2] Acts xi. 29 f. ; xii. 25. The money was "for the relief of the brethren that dwelt in Judæa" under pressure of famine, and was "sent to the elders (there) by the hands of Barnabas and Saul." The capital was no doubt included

for granted in all the apostolic epistles, as one which continued to exist within the fellowship of believers, and which gave rise to relative duties of permanent obligation. In the epistle, for example, of James the Lord's brother, who filled so prominent a place in this very Church of Jerusalem, we find him assuming as a matter of course that there would be rich men and poor ones in every Christian assembly, and giving rules for the guidance of both.[1]

But although the movement now under consideration is wholly misinterpreted when it is regarded as akin to communistic schemes of later centuries, it is in itself of very great and permanent significance. It formed a distinctive part of the witness for Christ which His disciples were enabled to bear, " after that the Holy Ghost came upon them, both in Jerusalem, and in all Judæa and Samaria, and unto the uttermost part of the earth." [2] To the Church itself it taught the great lesson that the springs of Christian liberality within its own membership, when opened by the Lord's hand, are amply sufficient to meet all its temporal necessities, and to do so with the ease and overflow of a mighty perennial stream. The experience of the Pentecostal Church speaks courage and confidence in this matter to the Church of Christ in all ages ; wherever, as in the Church at Jerusalem, the Gospel is preached with the power of God's Spirit so as to awaken

in the scope of their mission, as well as the country districts and smaller towns. Jerusalem would naturally be the headquarters of the deputies during their visit, and it was "to Jerusalem" or "from" it to Antioch that "they returned when they had fulfilled their ministration." Comp. R. V. Margin, and Westcott and Hort on chap. xii. 25. It seems probable from this and other indications in the narrative, that although no formal arrangements for the relief of the poor were made in the first outburst of Christian love and liberality at and after Pentecost, the movement presently took the form of a common fund for the general purposes of the Church, and in particular for the behoof of the poor among the saints at Jerusalem and around it. This would correspond closely with the arrangement familiar to the original disciples when they lived in fellowship with their Master in Galilee and Judæa. The common store and purse, which we hear of then, were for certain recognised purposes, among which was the relief of the poor ; while yet John had "his own home," and Peter and the rest their houses, and boats, and other private property. Matt. viii. 14 ; xv. 34 ; xvi. 5 ; Mark i. 20, 29 ; vi. 38 ; viii. 5 ; Luke v. 3-11 ; xiii. 29 ; xxii. 36 ; John xiii. 29 ; xvi. 32 ; xix. 27 ; xx. 10 ; xxi. 3.

[1] Jas. i. 9-11 ; ii. 1-3, 15 f. ; v. 1-3.   [2] Acts i. 8.

and convert the souls of men, wherever there are believing prayer and the ministry of the Word so as to nourish and build up believers in faith, and holiness, and knowledge of the truth, there no outward straits need be feared by the fellowship of Christ's people on earth.[1]　"Where the Spirit of the Lord is, there is liberty," and there the hearts of the disciples are "enriched in everything unto all liberality."　Their givings to Christ's cause and for the needs of His people are like those of the apostolic Church, or like the offerings of the Israelites for the tabernacle in the wilderness, needing to be moderated and guided rather than stimulated.[2]

To the unbelieving world in Jerusalem, and soon throughout the Roman empire, the testimony borne by the apostolic Church in this aspect of its daily life was one which filled Jews and Gentiles alike with amazement.　The moral and spiritual facts thus presented could neither be overlooked nor denied.

This wonderful tide of unselfish love and liberality began to flow at Pentecost, but its effects were seen and felt wherever the Gospel was preached.　The passion for money, so deep-seated in the Jewish mind and heart, was utterly vanquished by this new principle of love to the Lord and to the brethren.　It was an illustration on a crucial point of the power of Christ made known by the Spirit.　It was assuredly not the least of "the signs following" by which "the Lord wrought with them everywhere, confirming the Word."　It

---

[1] Our own Church, in that portion of its history which has passed since 1843, has specially learned that lesson, and has been the means in God's Providence of teaching it to others.　Principal Cunningham, with whose honoured name these lectures are associated, bore emphatic testimony to this effect within a year of the Disruption, on his return from a first visit to the American Churches.　"I have seen," he said in the General Assembly of 1844, "much that is fitted to modify the impressions, which some of us may once have entertained, of the importance of State assistance to the Church of Christ and the cause of religion.　I have seen much, yea abundant, evidence that a vast deal of good, and good in the highest sense, may be done by Churches which have no State assistance ; and I have seen much to confirm me in the belief that there is nothing to which the energies of the Church of Christ, when animated by the Spirit of Christ, are not fully adequate."　Rainy and Mackenzie, *Life of Principal Cunningham*, London, 1871, p. 217.

[2] 2 Cor. iii. 17 ; ix. 11 ; Ex. xxxv. 20–29 ; xxxvi. 2–7.

was among the "greater works" than His, which He foretold His disciples should perform under the dispensation of
the Paraclete.[1] Hundreds were now found ready to do at
once, and with joy, for the sake of the unseen Saviour, what
the young ruler felt to be too hard for him when face to face
with Christ in the days of His flesh, to "sell all that he had
and give to the poor, and follow Jesus." And so, in the
midst of avaricious Pharisees[2] and worldly Sadducees and
Herodians, in the midst of Greeks and Romans with whom
Jewish greed had passed into a proverb, the apostolic Church
stood forth visibly "a new creature in Christ." With them
"old things had passed away; behold, all things were become new."[3]

In such ways as these the new life of the Pentecostal
Church found free and beautiful expression. The believers
"did take their food with gladness and singleness of heart,
praising God, and having favour with all the people."[4]
While such was the feeling of the general public in Jerusalem, the spirit and power which dwelt in the fellowship of
Christ's disciples were so manifestly of God and not of men,
that for a season their enemies, and the Jewish rulers in
particular, feared to lift their hands against them. Through
such fear and favour combined, their unseen Lord secured
that a time of peaceful growth and consolidation should be
given to His Church. Warnings soon came from Him,
showing that persecutions were in store for them, and showing
also where alone the secret of joy and strength lay. The
union must be in Christ and in the Holy Spirit,—not in the
Church merely. The flame of love must be kindled and fed
from above. It must be a real and spiritual, not an imitative
and earthly glow. The disciples met first in the upper
chamber under the shadow of such a warning. The roll of
the apostles, given in the first chapter of Acts, had been
purged since it was last recorded. A name was missing
from the list which we find in Luke's "former treatise."

---

[1] Mark xvi. 20 ; John xiv. 12 f.

[2] "And the Pharisees, which were lovers of money, heard all these things,
and they scoffed at Him," Luke xvi. 14.

[3] 2 Cor. v. 17.　　　　　　　　　　　　　　　　[4] Acts ii. 46 f.

A place was empty among the twelve. They were all "men of Galilee" now; the traitor was probably the only apostle from Judæa.[1]

Other warnings of like kind followed, in the incidents of Ananias and his wife at Jerusalem, and of Simon the sooth-sayer at Samaria.

"The eleven and they that were with them," when "the names together were about an hundred and twenty," were few in number; but they were united in faith and love, in earnest prayer and searching of the Scriptures. The emphatic and suggestive term ὁμοθυμαδόν, "with one accord," first meets us here in the New Testament. It is repeated to mark the same spirit of unity as still pervading the Church, when its membership had multiplied thirty-fold from the fruits of the day of Pentecost. The word occurs eleven times in the book of Acts,—seven of these being in reference to the Church,[2] — and only once again elsewhere. It expresses strongly and beautifully this great characteristic of the apostolic Church, that "the multitude of them that be-lieved were of one heart and soul," and that this inward unity could not but show itself outwardly in worship, and work, and witness-bearing in all manner of ways, some of which were new and strange, but wonderfully impressive and attractive.

In this our Lord's prayer for His disciples was visibly answered: "That they may all be one; even as Thou, Father, art in Me, and I in Thee, that they also may be in us: that the world may believe that Thou didst send Me, . . . that they may be perfected into one: that the world may know that Thou didst send Me, and lovedst them, even as Thou lovedst Me."[3] That perfect and ineffable oneness of heart and will in the Godhead was truly, although faintly, reflected in the apostolic Church; and the effect upon the world around was mighty. It was felt for generations. And wherever, in

[1] Luke vi. 13–16; Acts i. 11, 13. As to Judas Iscariot being from Judæa, see Bruce, *Training of the Twelve*, 2nd ed. pp. 33, 363 f.

[2] Acts i. 14; ii. 1, 46; iv. 24; v. 12; viii. 6; xv. 25. In the second of these instances, the preferable reading is ὁμοῦ, "together," instead of "with one accord."

[3] John xvii. 21, 23.

the history of the Church, seasons of great spiritual quickening and revival have been given by God, this experience of Pentecost has always been repeated. There has been a wonderful spirit of love and unity among all the brethren; and an awe and a silence, so to speak, have fallen for a time upon the world, as in the presence of something manifestly Divine. Believers in all ages may well plead and strive for the fulfilment of that petition of our Lord, and join in the prayer of an apostle who had himself seen and felt the unity of the Pentecostal Church: " Now the God of patience and of comfort grant you to be of the same mind one with another, according to Christ Jesus; that, with one accord (ὁμοθυμαδόν), ye may with one mouth glorify the God and Father of our Lord Jesus Christ." [1]

5th. The terms of admission to and exclusion from membership in the apostolic Church.

These were very simple, and founded upon principles almost self-evident. What had made a man to be recognised as a disciple of Jesus during our Lord's visible ministry on earth? Just these two things: first, that he professed belief in Jesus of Nazareth as the Messiah; and secondly, that he showed himself practically willing to obey His commands. In some instances, His commands required a literal following of His footsteps in Galilee and Judæa, as in the case of the twelve; in others, all that was asked was obedience to His precepts at home, as with the healed demoniac of Gadara. But, in every case, the essential points were that Jesus should be personally known and trusted as a Saviour, and that He should be openly acknowledged and obeyed as a Master. " Come unto Me," and " follow thou Me," were the two sentences which, on His lips, summed up the conditions of discipleship.[2] If these were really and from the heart complied with by any man, he was a true disciple of Christ. If there was a credible appearance of compliance with them, as in the case of Judas, the man was received into the company of the disciples, and was treated like the rest on the ground of his own profession,

[1] Rom. xv. 5 f.
[2] Matt. iv. 18–22; ix. 9; xix. 21; Mark i. 17 f.; ii. 14; John i. 35–43, etc.

seriously made, while there was nothing in his outward life, so far as appeared, to give the lie to it.[1]

This clear and simple principle was invariably acted upon in the apostolic Church, so far as the New Testament records carry us, with respect to the admission of new members. All who were "added to the Lord," "those that were being saved," were also "added day by day," under His guidance and the teaching of His Spirit, to the collective body of the disciples (ἐπὶ τὸ αὐτό), the fellowship of believers gathered together in His name.[2]

Those who could make Peter's confession from the heart, as he did at Cæsarea Philippi, had certainly entered into the true Church of Christ which He was now so manifestly building upon the rock. They had full right, therefore, to enter into the visible fellowship of His disciples. All who professed such faith in Jesus, and willingness to obey His commands, were joyfully welcomed into the Pentecostal Church. "They then that received his word (οἱ μὲν οὖν ἀποδεξάμενοι τὸν λόγον αὐτοῦ)"—the truth concerning Jesus as the Christ, the Son of God, of which Peter was the first preacher, as well as the first confessor among the disciples— "were baptized; and there were added unto them in that day about three thousand souls."[3]

No terms of admission except this simple "profession of faith in Christ and obedience to Him"[4] seem to have been proposed to applicants; and no test of sincerity required, beyond the very sufficient one involved in the circumstances of the apostolic Church and of the times, in which to profess allegiance to Christ implied a willingness to suffer, and even to die for Him. It was on this footing that the converts on the day of Pentecost were received forthwith into the fellowship of the Church by Baptism. The same rule seems to have been followed at all the subsequent stages of the history at which we hear of large additions being made to the mem-

---

[1] I may refer on this point to my little work, *Grounds and Methods of Admission to Sealing Ordinances*, Edin. 1882, pp. 25-30.

[2] Acts ii. 47 ; comp. ver. 40 ; v. 14 ; vi. 7.   [3] Acts ii. 41.

[4] "Baptism is not to be administered to any that are out of the visible Church till they profess their faith in Christ and obedience to Him," Westminster Shorter Catechism, Qu. 95.

bership of the Christian community. So it was evidently, for example, as regards the Baptisms under Philip in Samaria. The particular case, singled out by the historian, is plainly to be regarded as illustrating the method and principles of admission acted upon with respect to others. "Simon," the soothsayer, "also himself believed, and being baptized, he continued with Philip." The apparent conversion, and the profession of belief, proved in this instance not to be of a genuine kind; and Simon was publicly declared to have "neither part nor lot" with the disciples of Christ. But no blame whatever seems imputed to the evangelist for insufficient caution in dealing with the case. On the contrary, we find him soon afterwards, under the express guidance of the Spirit, proceeding on precisely the same principles in the admission of the Ethiopian treasurer, in whose case there was no time for probation at all, and no test of sincerity required, except what was involved in the fact that all considerations of a merely earthly sort were against his taking the step of publicly professing himself a disciple of Jesus. The same remarks apply to the Baptism of Cornelius and his friends at Cæsarea.[1]

As regards exclusion from the fellowship of the Church, our Lord Himself, as we have seen,[2] had given very distinct intimations of His mind. He had shown the serious nature of such a separation from communion, both by laying down in unusual detail the successive steps to be taken in reference to a brother who had trespassed, before recourse should be had to the final one of exclusion, and also by using the strong expressions regarding the offender when thus excluded, that he was to be held henceforth "as the Gentile and the publican." I need not repeat here what was said in connection with the exposition of the passage in question, but may simply observe that we have clear evidence in this first section of the history of the apostolic Church as to the sense in which such injunctions were understood and acted upon.

In the case of Ananias and his wife the purity of the

---

[1] Acts viii. 5–23, 26–40 ; x. 44–48 ; xi. 17 f. *Admission to Ordinances*, pp. 30–32.

[2] See above, pp. 177–194.

Church was vindicated, and discipline administered with awful severity by the hand of the unseen Lord.[1] In the case of the Samaritan soothsayer, a man who had been formally admitted to all the privileges of the Church was, in consequence of open and daring sin, authoritatively separated from its communion. He himself and his money were alike cast out by the indignant voice of the apostle into the region of death and corruption, in which all were perishing who had not yet truly come to repentance and faith in Christ. Simon was publicly declared to have neither part nor lot in the fellowship of Christ's people, to belong now in name, as all along in truth, not to the Church, but to the world, having thus openly proved himself to be a servant of the god of this world. He was "still in the gall of bitterness and bond of iniquity."[2]

We have here a good illustration of the right use by the apostle Peter of the keys of the kingdom of heaven, entrusted to him and other stewards of the Lord's house by Christ in words which we have already considered.[3] We see also the sense in which sins were to be forgiven and retained in the Church. Simon is solemnly shut out from Christian fellowship and privilege, because of open sin. But the conditions of forgiveness and restoration are clearly and authoritatively set before him : "Thy heart is not right before God. Repent therefore of this thy wickedness, and pray the Lord if perhaps the thought of thy heart shall be forgiven thee."

Such events led to wholesome awe and self-examination among the disciples of Christ, as when He said to those who sat with Him at His last Passover : "Verily, verily, I say unto you, that one of you shall betray Me. The disciples looked one on another, doubting of whom He spake."[4] Through such experiences as these the spiritual life of the apostolic Church deepened, and gathered reverence, without losing its gladness and freedom. They did not sensibly break the joyful confidence in the Lord and in each other, which so marked the early disciples, and further examples of which we shall see presently ; but they brought out more strongly one characteristic feature of the Hebrew Christian Church to

[1] See above, pp. 283–286.   [2] Acts viii. 20–23.
[3] See above, pp. 175–177.   [4] John xiii. 21 f.

which attention may be suitably called at this point. I mean its reverential fear of Christ. This is emphasized in the striking and suggestive sentence in which the history of this first period is summed up towards the end of the ninth chapter of Acts: "So the Church throughout all Judæa, and Galilee, and Samaria had peace, being edified; and walking in the fear of the Lord, and in the comfort of the Holy Ghost, was multiplied."[1]

These words are important in more respects than one. We must return to them when we come to consider the growth of the Church in numbers, and how far its inward unity found expression in its outward development and organization. Meanwhile observe how clearly they bring out one great characteristic of the apostolic Church of this period, namely, that all its worship and brotherly fellowship, its testimony and service, were pervaded with this spirit, the fear of the Lord Jesus as the Son of the living God.

That holy and loving fear of Jehovah, of which the Hebrew prophets and psalmists speak so often, had been the heart and life of Old Testament religion from the days of Abraham onward. "The fear of the Lord," God's people had found, "is a fountain of life. In the fear of the Lord is strong confidence, and His children shall have a place of refuge."[2] The *élite* of the Old Testament Church, those "who looked for the consolation of Israel," had now received the Redeemer promised to their fathers. They had joined themselves to the company of Christ's disciples, and had become the Christian Church of the Holy Land. And they carried this spirit of deep and loving reverence with them. The God of Abraham and of Israel, the God of their fathers, was now revealed to them in the Lord Jesus Christ. The fear of the Lord with them was what Paul expressly calls "the fear of Christ."[3] Saul of Tarsus had seen it in that Hebrew Christian Church of Judæa, Galilee, and Samaria. He learned it first for himself, on the Damascus road, in the presence of One around whom there shone a light above the brightness of the noonday sun; "and he, trembling and astonished, said: What shall I do, Lord? And the Lord said unto him: Arise,

---

[1] Acts ix. 31.   [2] Prov. xiv. 26 f.   [3] Eph. v. 21.

and go into Damascus; and there it shall be told thee of all things which are appointed for thee to do."[1]

The two leaders of the Church, with whom Paul tells us he was brought into special contact on his first visit to Jerusalem after his conversion, were the apostle Peter and James the Lord's brother. The fear of the Lord doubtless held as marked a place in their oral teaching as it does in their epistles.[2]

This was the spirit which was seen in such special measure in the apostolic Church of this first period of the history of the Acts, and which was deepened and strengthened by such manifestations of the Lord's presence, and of His will concerning the purity of His Church, as those to which we have now referred. It was not a spirit of bondage, but one of deep and loving reverence. The Son of the living God had been " manifested in the flesh, justified in the spirit, seen of angels, preached among the nations, believed on in the world, received up in glory."[3] He was withdrawn for a season from the eyes of His disciples, but was soon to come again, in like manner as the eleven had seen Him go into heaven. Meanwhile He was with them unseen, in the midst of their assemblies, making His presence known and felt as they sought to " do all the things that He had commanded," " with them all the days, even to the end of the world."

They learned of Him from apostles who had seen His face in the flesh, and they, too, had fellowship with the Father and with His Son Jesus Christ, and beheld His glory, glory as of the Only-begotten from the Father. They knew Him as one " full of grace and truth," full of majesty as well as of love.[4]

" So had the Church peace and was edified, and walking in the fear of the Lord, and in the comfort of the Holy Ghost, was multiplied."

6th. The position held in the apostolic Church during this period by women.

All through this section of the history, from the opening

---

[1] Acts xxii. 8 ff.

[2] Comp. 1 Pet. i. 17 ; ii. 13, 17 ; iii. 4, 15 ; iv. 17 ff.; v. 5 f.; Jas. i. 21 ; v. 6 f., 10, 15 ; v. 8 f.

[3] 1 Tim. iii. 16.　　　　　　　　　　　　　[4] John i. 14.

scene in the upper chamber at Jerusalem to the closing ones
in Peter's tour of visitation among the saints at Lydda and
Joppa, and in connection with his deliverance from Herod's
prison-house, believing women hold a significant place. It
has often, and justly, been pointed out how, among other
results of the moral revolution which Christianity wrought in
the world, it brought suddenly and powerfully to the front
what may be called "the feminine virtues."

On the lips of ethnic moralists, "virtue," as the word
itself implies, meant the qualities that make "a man."
Virtue with them was just manliness. But now in the life
of the Lord Jesus, as recorded in the Gospels, along with all
that forms the strength and glory of manhood, there were
revealed, in as full development, all the graces which belong
to the feminine side of human character, and which had
hitherto been held proof in a man of weakness and effeminacy.
Jesus of Nazareth claimed for Himself in the highest sense
the name of "the Son of Man," [1] as well as that of "the Son
of God." And there were seen in Him, "in loveliness of
perfect deeds," lowliness of mind, gentleness, patience, thoughtful and tender love, readiness to forgive, self-sacrifice to the
uttermost. These and kindred graces had been held inconsistent with "that stately group of virtues which made up the
antique ideal — foresight, fortitude, justice, and self-control.
It was their combination in Jesus which rectified the judgment
of humanity, and restored to us a symmetrical image of
character. . . . Manliness in Jesus is everywhere taken for
granted; womanliness in its best sense is made conspicuous.[2]
The cross of the Man of Sorrows confutes the ancient pre-
ferences of the world." [3]

[1] Comp. Dr. Bruce's note on this title, *Humiliation of Christ*, pp. 476–487 ;
Canon Westcott, *Gospel of St. John*, pp. 33–35 ; Dr. Smeaton, *Doct. of the
Atonement as taught by Christ Himself*, pp. 80–87, 402–406.

[2] See some suggestive remarks in Mackintosh's *Christ and the Jewish Law*,
as to the sense in which our Lord's ethic is in contrast to Old Testament
ethic : "Christ taught Jews. It was inevitable that He should lay more stress
on those Christian virtues, which they were hereditarily apt to disregard, than on
those to which they were already trained. It was inevitable that He should
often correct the assumptions which limited the Old Testament outlook, while
rarely affirming its attainments," pp. 98–102.

[3] Dykes, *From Jerusalem to Antioch*, 4th ed. p. 339. The Church in later

It was no wonder that the hearts of women were drawn to such a Saviour in the days of His earthly life. When we think how the quick intuitions of womanhood in moral and spiritual things, its swift instinctive recognition of truth and purity, holiness and love, when embodied in living character, often far outstrip the colder reasonings and conclusions of men, we shall easily understand how the best and purest of the daughters of Israel were among the first to see, or rather to feel in their inmost souls, the glory of Christ, and to receive Him as their Lord and Saviour. They failed, doubtless, in many cases to understand His words, or to attain to clear views of His Person and of the nature of His work on earth. But they knew that He was the Lord, *their* Lord, to be absolutely trusted and obeyed. They followed Him through good report and evil. And they loved Him with a love that was stronger than all womanly dread of harm and insult, or fear of death and the grave.

The evangelists tell us of no woman who ever came to Christ and went back from Him again, of none who betrayed or denied her Saviour, of none even who in any special manner forsook Him at the end.

From the beginning of the history of revelation, and especially in the Old Testament Church since its visible establishment in the days of Abraham, women had held a place of importance very different from that assigned to them in the ethnic religions of the East. In the long list of those who in the records of Scripture have " obtained a good report through faith," many of the brightest names are those of believing women, who, sometimes as judges and prophetesses raised up and guided by God, but more often as daughters, wives, and mothers, in quiet family circles, " wrought right-

centuries failed to see and study in the life of our Lord this perfect combination of all that makes the truest manhood and the truest womanhood in one. Thus it was that the fair, attractive form of the " Virgin Mother, full of grace," rose gradually into a place not hers ; and Christ, as Luther says, was " set afar off upon the rainbow," as " the Judge." Those who have studied that marvellous picture, Michael Angelo's " Last Judgment," in the Sistine, will remember a wonderfully powerful illustration of the tendency to which I refer. It has found what may be fairly called a blasphemous expression in one of the modern frescoes in the Vatican gallery, which depicts the coronation of the Virgin in heaven.

eousness and obtained promises, out of weakness were made
strong . . . received their dead by a resurrection; and others
were tortured, not accepting their deliverance, that they might
obtain a better resurrection."[1]

The Gospel history leads us first to the homes of those
who were the true heirs and representatives of the Old
Testament Church, walking in the fear of the Lord, and
" looking for the consolation of Israel."

In Elizabeth at Hebron, and Mary at Nazareth, we have
a picture of a Hebrew matron and a Hebrew maiden worthy
to be put beside those of Sarah and Miriam, Ruth and
Hannah, in the olden times of Israel. And as the history
goes on, and the Church is built by the unseen hand of
Christ upon the rock of personal relation to Himself, and
personal confession of Him before men, we get one glimpse
after another of pure and gracious womanly character, of
quick insight and readiness to serve, of women with all the
olden spirit of faith and devout reverence, rising up now in
the liberty wherewith Christ and His Spirit had made them
free, to serve the Lord and the brethren in new ways, with
gladness and singleness of heart, praising God and having
favour with all the people. We see in the Acts and the
Epistles how the position of women became more assured,
and how their ministry widened, and was more thankfully
owned and honoured in the Church.

It was at our Lord's own feet that the women of the
Gospels first found the place they could fill, and the work
they could do, for Him and for His cause. We see what
that place and work were in the case of Mary of Magdala,[2]

---

[1] Heb. xi. 33–35. Comp. 2 Macc. vii. 1–29, and Dr. John Ker's noble
sermon on "The Better Resurrection." *Sermons*, second series, Edin. 1887,
p. 336 ff.

[2] The name of Mary Magdalene has been most unfairly identified by the
Church of Rome—and the tradition survives in some Protestant circles where
the Bible should be better known—with "the woman which was in the city a
sinner," and who washed the feet of Christ in the Pharisee's house (Luke vii.
37–50). There is no Scripture ground whatever for holding that the two were
the same, nor for the supposition that our Lord ever placed one, who had
recently been an open profligate, in the position towards Himself which was
held by the ministering women who followed His steps in Galilee, and were
associated with His mother at the Cross. For the woman who washed His

Mary the mother of James and Joses, Salome, Joanna the wife of Herod's chamberlain, Susanna, and other ministering women who followed the Saviour to the end.[1] His visible presence was withdrawn from them after the Ascension, but they especially knew and felt how surely He was with His people still, unseen, according to His promise. They rejoiced to sit at His feet and hear His words still, as Mary did at Bethany, wherever two or three of His disciples were gathered together in His name. "These all with one accord," we read of the Church in the upper chamber, "continued stedfastly in prayer with the women, and Mary the mother of Jesus, and with His brethren."[2] They found happy service, as Martha did, in ministering to Christ in those whom He had called "His brethren and sisters," in the poor, the suffering, the bereaved, the aged,[3] and in the little ones whom He had called to come to Him in their mother's arms, and whom He bid those who loved Him feed as the lambs of His flock.[4]

feet with her tears at Simon's feast, for the woman of Samaria by the well, for her whom the Pharisees brought to Jesus for condemnation, a different path of service was appointed. Christ came to seek and save such lost ones, to call such sinners to repentance and to Himself. For all such He had gracious words of forgiveness, whenever they truly turned to Him as a Saviour from sin. "Neither do I condemn thee; go thy way: from henceforth sin no more." "Thy sins, which are many, are forgiven thee. Thy faith hath saved thee; go in peace." But our Lord gave them no call to any kind of service which would have brought them at once before the eyes of men, or into any prominence in the fellowship of His disciples. Their names are not once recorded in the pages of the Gospels. The significance of this fact is brought out with much beauty and delicacy of thought by Mrs. Charles in her poems on "The Unnamed Women of the Gospels" (*The Women of the Gospels*, Lond. 1868, pp. 53-63). See Dean Plumptre's article "Mary Magdalene," in Smith's *Bible Dictionary*, and comp. Luke vii. 37-50; xv. 1 f.; John iv. 7-29, 42; viii. 3-11. As regards the last-named passage,—the περικοπὴ περὶ μοιχαλίδος,—whatever the comparative weakness of the external attestation, few can fail to feel that the self-evidencing power of the narrative is almost proof sufficient, although it stood alone, that we have here indeed the words and the action of our Lord Himself. See Canon Westcott's note on the section in his *Gospel according to St. John*, p. 141 f.

[1] Mark xv. 40 f.; xvi. 1, 9; Luke viii. 2 f.; xxiii. 27, 49, 55; xxiv. 10. Comp. Schäfer, *Weibliche Diakonie*, Stuttgart 1887, 2te Aufl. S. 25 f.

[2] Acts i. 14.

[3] Matt. xii. 48 f.; xxv. 34-40; Mark iii. 33-35; John xii. 8.

[4] Luke xviii. 15 f. See above, p. 210, note.

Those women whom God in His Providence had brought into the position of the mother of the Lord herself, being "widows indeed and desolate," were treated from the first with a peculiar tenderness; and a special provision was made for their wants from the common treasury. It was the idea, whether well-founded or not, that "their widows were neglected in the daily ministration," which gave rise to the first murmuring of one section in the apostolic Church against another.[1]

It was to the widows among the saints in Joppa that the love of Dorcas specially turned. "She whom the people called, both in their homely Aramaic and in their Greek speech, by the name of 'the Gazelle,' because that loveliest of Syrian animals was from early times, to the poets of the East, a favourite emblem for a beautiful woman, has fitly bequeathed her name of Dorcas to express, not the gift of personal beauty in her sex, but the Christian ornament of meek and gracious charity. Dorcas was no deaconess; the age of Church organization had not yet come. But whatever she was, maid or widow, she had learned of Jesus Christ her Lord His best lesson,[2] and was enough of a woman to discover how she could most fitly practise it. By quiet feminine handiwork it was her wont to work for Christ.[3] Among the desolate and friendless of her own sex she found suitable objects for her unobtrusive aid. Her death was to the saints of Joppa a common grief. It brought out for the first time how much she had been to them. It was not the widows only who missed their benefactress, but the whole congregation lost one who was to them 'a living epistle' of Jesus Christ."[4]

The incident of the raising of Dorcas from the dead stands fittingly towards the close of the section which records the history of the Hebrew Christian Church, and immediately after the words which sum up the chief characteristics of its life and growth. It shows by what fruits of faith, by what

---

[1] Acts vi. 1 f.

[2] "She is called μαθητρία," Dr. Dykes notes, "a word of late Greek, only here used in the New Testament."

[3] "Comp. the Imperfect (ὅσα ἐποίει) in ver. 39."

[4] Dykes, *From Jerusalem to Antioch*, 4th ed. p. 340.

loving service the Church of the Holy Land was edified and multiplied. It shows also how dear to Christ Himself, and how highly honoured by Him, such ministering women were. When Dorcas was raised from the dead, and given back to the fellowship of the saints at Joppa, "a seal was set of purpose by the Lord on that new department of charitable labour within His Church which Dorcas had made so much her own." [1]

The very last scene in this first period of the apostolic Church is laid in a widow's house. [2] It is a time of peril and anxiety. Herod Agrippa, now sole ruler of Palestine, has "put forth his hands to afflict certain of the Church." His action is the more formidable because supported, at this juncture, by popular feeling among the Jews. [3] He has slain one of the foremost apostles, and has seized another, hitherto the most influential leader of the Christian community, the loss of whom would be a still heavier blow. Peter is in prison closely guarded, and on the eve of execution. His death might be expected to give the signal for another outburst of general persecution of all Christians without distinction of sex, such as followed the death of Stephen. To human eyes the future of the Church seemed at that moment as dark and threatening as it well could be. But the courage and self-devotion of a Christian woman stand out in face of the gathering storm. Mary, the mother of Mark, seems, like several of the ministering women from Galilee, to have been a person of some wealth and social position. Her house was within a few streets of the prison. In spite of the danger thereby brought upon herself, she made it a centre and meeting-place for the persecuted disciples. In its largest room "many were gathered together, and were praying," continuing in prayer all night. Very possibly, as has been suggested, her kinsman Barnabas was among them, and it may be also his fellow-deputy from Antioch, Saul of Tarsus. It is to Mary's house that Peter naturally turns first, on his deliverance out of prison; and in the picture which the narrative of his reception there gives us of the young servant girl Rhoda, with her instant recogni-

---

[1] Dykes, p. 342.   [2] Acts xii.   [3] Comp. vv. 3 and 11.

tion of the apostle's voice, and her eager message to the gathering of disciples within, we have another slight but suggestive glimpse of the position held by women in the apostolic Church.[1]

7th. What was the position held in the fellowship of the disciples during this period by the children of believers, the little ones to whose homes such new light and gladness had been brought by the Gospel ?

The strength and simplicity of faith, the union of childlike freedom and reverence of spirit which marked the Hebrew Christian community, recall strongly what we saw before to be characteristic of the patriarchal Church in the days of Abraham.[2] References to his name, and to God's covenant with him and his seed, are frequent, as was formerly pointed out, on the lips of the apostles in their first public addresses, after the Holy Spirit was given in fulness.[3] Was the visible fellowship of the Church to be narrower than it was in Abraham's time, and in the congregation of Israel and of the Lord since then ? Was there to be no acknowledged place in it for the infant seed of God's people, no token of His gracious covenant for them as heretofore ?

The burden of proof certainly lies with those who maintain the negative on this question. Beyond all controversy, there had been such a place and token assigned to the children of believers hitherto, under " the Gospel preached beforehand unto Abraham," and " the covenant confirmed beforehand by God," which the law, coming centuries after, " did not disannul," and to which, as regards conditions, " nothing was to be added." [4] The natural inference is, that the privileges accorded to the children of believers under that Gospel and that covenant were to be continued, unless expressly withdrawn. No such withdrawal is recorded, and all the indications of the mind of Christ and the practice of the apostolic

---

[1] On the general subject of the influence of Christianity on the position of women, see C. Schmidt, *Social Results of Early Christianity*, E. Tr., Lond. 1885, pp. 161 ff., 188 ff. Storr's *Divine Origin of Christianity indicated by its Historical Effects*, Lond. 1885, pp. 94–99, 300–308. Brace, *Gesta Christi*, 2nd ed. pp. 35 ff., 107 ff.

[2] See above, p. 57 f. [3] See above, p. 7 f. [4] Gal. iii. 8, 15–17.

Church, both positive and negative, point in the same direction as formerly.

" The blessing of Abraham," as an apostle, who was himself " an Hebrew of the Hebrews," wrote afterwards to a Gentile Christian Church, " has come upon the Gentiles in Christ Jesus, that we might receive the promise of the Spirit through faith." [1]   It came, first of all, upon the Jews and proselytes of Gentile birth at Jerusalem on the day of Pentecost.   That promise was declared then by Peter, the apostle of the circumcision, speaking to " devout men from all the nations, Jews and proselytes," to be " to you and to your children, and to all that are afar off, even as many as the Lord our God shall call unto Him." [2]

The Lord's call into the fellowship of His people on earth had hitherto unquestionably embraced the parent and his infant child ; " the sign of circumcision, a seal of the righteousness of faith," [3] was for them both.   The Saviour during His earthly life had shown special favour to the little ones by word and sign.   Once and again, He had given blessing to an unconscious child, expressly on the ground of the parent's faith. [4] He had recognised and acted upon that principle of representation, or covenant headship, so familiar to the Jewish mind, as we have seen, from Old Testament times. [5]   The father or mother was the head of the family.   The children were dealt with in respect of privilege and blessing as being one in many ways with the parents.   " This day is salvation come to this house " (τῷ οἴκῳ τούτῳ), our Lord said, when Zacchæus had received and confessed Him as his Saviour and

---

[1] Gal. iii. 14.

[2] 'Υμῖν γάρ ἐστιν ἡ ἐπαγγελία, καὶ τοῖς τέκνοις ὑμῶν, καὶ πᾶσι τοῖς εἰς μακράν, ὅσους ἂν προσκαλέσηται κύριος ὁ θεὸς ἡμῶν, Acts ii. 39.   " When God took Abraham into covenant, He said, ' I will be a God to thee and to thy seed ; ' and accordingly every Israelite had his son circumcised at eight days old.   Now it is proper for an Israelite, when he is by Baptism to come into a new dispensation of this covenant, to ask : What must be done with my children ?   Must they be thrown out, or taken in with me ?   Taken in, says Peter, by all means ; for the promise, that great promise, of God's being to you a God, is as much to you and to your children now as ever it was."   Matthew Henry, in loco.

[3] Rom. iv. 11.   [4] Mark vii. 29 ; ix. 23 f. ; John iv. 48 ff.

[5] See above, pp. 31–38, 64, 69, 101 f.

Master, "for that he also is a son of Abraham."[1] Christ
had "called" not only adults but babes in their mothers'
arms to Himself. "And they brought unto Him also their
babes that He should touch them; but when the disciples
saw it they rebuked them. But Jesus called them—the
babes—unto Him,[2] saying: Suffer the little children to
come unto Me, and forbid them not, for of such is the
kingdom of God." "And He took them in His arms,
and blessed them, laying His hands upon them."[3] Our
Lord counted it a "call" to the babes, although it reached
them only in and through their parents. He counted it as
"their coming," in some real sense, "unto Him," when they
were brought in their mothers' arms. He gave them, as
thus brought to Him, a visible sign of His special love, which
was never, so far as we know, given to any disciple of
riper years. Was there then to be no longer any token of
such privileges for the children of believers in the Church,
as there had been hitherto from the time when the Scripture first tells us clearly of the visible Church of God
being set up in this world at all?

It has been already pointed out how the command to
"make disciples of all the nations, baptizing them into the
name of the Father, the Son, and the Holy Ghost," would
sound to the first followers of Christ;[4] but it is worth while to
recall to our minds here a little more fully the situation of
the members of the Hebrew Christian Church in this respect.
The position of the infants of believers in the Old Testament
Church was to them not a theory, but a fact of everyday

---

[1] Luke xix. 9. Comp. the message by the angel to Cornelius: "He shall
speak unto thee words whereby thou shalt be saved, thou and all thy house (πᾶς
ὁ οἶκός σου)," Acts xi. 14; and Paul's assurance to the Philippian jailor: "Believe
on the Lord Jesus Christ and thou shalt be saved, thou and thy house (σὺ καὶ ὁ
οἶκός σου)," Acts xvi. 31. Observe that in all these cases the word which is
used for "house" or "family" is that which conveys the closest sense of
unity in that relation; and note the change of term in the very next verse
to that last cited, when the narrative goes on: "They spake the word of
the Lord to him, with all that were in his household" (οἰκία). See above,
pp. 85–88.

[2] προσεκαλέσατο αὐτά = τὰ βρέφη. Note the use of the same verb as in Acts
ii. 39, quoted at foot of last page.

[3] Luke xviii. 16–18; Mark x. 16.   [4] See above, pp. 233–237.

religious experience.   Those who listened to Peter's discourse at Pentecost were "devout men from every nation under heaven, Jews and proselytes."   Every devout Jewish father in that crowd had been himself circumcised in infancy, and had had his own child circumcised, pleading the promise to Abraham : " I will be a God to thee and to thy seed. This is the token of the covenant."   Every proselyte had received that ordinance for himself, and had then brought forward his little ones to receive it on the ground of his faith and profession, openly casting in his lot and theirs with the despised people of God.   His most memorable religious experiences were indissolubly linked with the momentous step which he then took, and with its outward sign.   As soon as he became a son of Abraham by faith in Abraham's God, he came himself, and brought his infant seed, to receive the sign and seal of the covenant, "the seal of Abraham," "the sign and seal of the faith which he—like Abraham— had, yet being uncircumcised."   Circumcision represented to him and his—just as Baptism does to a Hindu or Mohammedan convert to Christianity with his children now—the decisive breaking with the old life and its associations, and all things becoming new.

These men did not need any elaborate explanation about all this.   It was not to them a doctrine to be gathered from books, but an essential part of their own religious life and experience.   It could all be taken for granted by those who preached to them the glad tidings concerning the Christ.   It would indeed have been a new thing to them, a strange and startling innovation, if there had been no token of the covenant for the infant seed of believers now, when all the difference was that the Messiah had come, for whom Israel had been waiting so long, and had proved to be greater, more glorious, and more gracious far than they had dreamed. That the place and privileges of the children of God's people were to continue in His Church, if nothing was said to the contrary, was from their standpoint the most natural thing possible.

Suppose, as already suggested, that Christ had kept the old sacrament of admission, and had commanded the apostles : " Go ye into all the world and make disciples of all the nations, circumcising them in the name of the Father, and of the Son, and of the Holy Ghost." In that case no devout Jew or proselyte would ever have doubted that the children of the converts were to be circumcised as before. It presented just as little difficulty for Hebrew Christians when the Lord, without forbidding circumcision, singled out the easier and more gracious rite of Baptism as His appointed ordinance for admission into fellowship with Him and His. Baptism was already familiar to them as a sign of discipleship, not merely from "John's Baptism," but from its being already in use along with circumcision—as there seems good reason to believe—in the admission of proselytes with their children into the communion of the Old Testament Church.[1] The apostle's words needed no explanation when at Pentecost, in immediate connection with an exhortation to be baptized, he assured those sons of Abraham—some by nature as well as faith ; others by faith only—that the promise was " to them and to their children." The Messiah promised to their fathers had not come to cast the children of believers out of their ancient birthright. Only " in Christ there was to be neither male nor female ; " and the token of the covenant was to be a gentler and more gracious one, as became Him who " called the babes to Himself," and said : " Suffer the little children to come unto Me, and forbid them not, for of such is the kingdom of God." [2]

---

[1] See above, pp. 118 f., 235-238.

[2] It is worth noting that the term used by the narrator, in describing the Baptisms which followed Peter's address at Pentecost, is one which makes room for the children. "Then they that received his word were baptized ; and there were added unto them in that day about three thousand souls," Acts ii. 41. It is the term usually employed in Scripture when women and children, families as well as heads of families, are included in the enumeration. "Give me the souls," the King of Sodom says to Abraham, referring to all the captives, young and old, "and take the goods to thyself." "All the souls of the house of Jacob which came into Egypt were threescore and ten," i.e. including the "little ones" as well as the adults, "his sons and his sons' sons with him, his daughters and his sons' daughters, and all his seed," Gen. xiv. 21 ; xlvi. 5, 7, 27. So here it is not said that three thousand men were added, but so many men and heads of families as along with their little ones—baptized afterwards, in all likelihood as opportunity offered, "at home" (κατ' οἶκον)—might make up in all "about three thousand souls, added unto them" through that day's work.

Unless some positive prohibition of infant or family Baptisms had been given to the first disciples, their whole Providential training and previous religious experience made it inevitable that they should understand the terms of the great commission of Christ in this way. When the Anti-Pædobaptist, therefore, maintains that the command to "make disciples of all the nations, *baptizing* them," is narrower in its scope than a command to "make disciples, *circumcising* them," would have been, the burden of proof clearly lies with him. And no proof is forthcoming in the only two forms in which it could be received, namely, either an express revocation of the privileges hitherto accorded to the children of believers, or an express instance in any part of the New Testament of a child of believing parents growing up without Baptism and being baptized as an adult.[1]

It is important to observe that all the cases of individual Baptisms recorded in the New Testament are cases in which, if they occurred to-day, the ministers of every branch of the catholic Church, Reformed or un-Reformed, would baptize without hesitation, unless where, as with "the Society of Friends," the permanent obligation of the ordinance is denied. In all the Reformed Churches, in particular, there is full agreement regarding the proper conditions and results of Baptism in cases like those of the men and women who heard Peter's address at Pentecost, like those which our missionaries meet now in heathen lands. There should be just what is described in the narrative of the Acts : First, plain instruction in the leading facts and truths of the Gospel, these being pressed earnestly on the hearts and consciences of

---

[1] It is, of course, no proof whatever to quote half a text,—"He that believeth and is baptized shall be saved," Mark xvi. 16*a*,—and to argue that as infants cannot believe they ought not to be baptized. For (1) the argument would be equally valid that their incapacity for belief excludes them from salvation. And (2) the command was spoken to men who knew that adults were admitted to the Old Testament Church by circumcision and baptism only when they professed their faith in the God of Abraham, yet that the infant of a proselyte received the sign of admission equally with himself on the ground of the father's profession of faith. Abraham, as a believing man, had a right to "the sign and seal of the righteousness that is by faith" for his infant son as well as for himself. Why should it be otherwise now ? Comp. Bannerman, *Church of Christ*, ii. pp. 100–106.

the hearers; secondly, a believing reception of the truth and of the Saviour now made known to them; thirdly, some proof of sincerity, as was given in apostolic times by a public profession of faith in Christ at risk of persecution and death; fourthly, Baptism in the name of the Lord Jesus Christ, *i.e.* with profession of what makes a disciple, personal faith in Christ as a Divine Saviour, and in the leading truths taught by Him concerning the Father and Himself and the Holy Spirit; and lastly, stedfast continuance in faith and obedience, and in waiting upon the means of grace.

These are the principles on which our missionaries administer Baptism now in heathen and Mohammedan countries. The great majority of Baptisms in those fields are of that kind. They fill the foreground of our missionary reports. It is by such adult Baptisms that definite progress is marked. Following after these, less frequent at first and much less conspicuous from the nature of the circumstances, come the cases of household or family Baptism, where the convert happens to be the head of a young family and is not hindered—as may often happen—by domestic opposition from bringing his little ones for dedication to the Lord and for the sign of His covenant blessing. And so, too, in the Acts and the Epistles, we hear presently of cases of family Baptism, where Lydia or the jailor believes, and immediately, without mention of any one in the family believing except its head, we read: "She was baptized, and her house (ὁ οἶκος αὐτῆς);" "he was baptized, and all his, straightway (ἐβαπτίσθη αὐτὸς καὶ οἱ αὐτοῦ ἅπαντες παραχρῆμα)."[1]

This latter point is the only one about which, as regards the subjects of Baptism, a difference of opinion has arisen in the Church. Our Baptist—or more correctly Anti-Pædobaptist—brethren,[2] while agreeing with us in many much more important

---

[1] Acts xvi. 15, 34. Comp. 1 Cor. i. 14–16, and note the οἶκος in the last verse, as compared with οἰκία in chap. xvi. 15, where the members of the household of Stephanas in the wider sense are spoken of. See below, Part VI. chap. ii. 5.

[2] Our objection to the position of our "Baptist" friends really is that they do not baptize enough,—that they narrow the scope of our Lord's command in the great commission by omitting one important class of persons who ought to

and fundamental doctrines of Scripture, dissent from the belief and practice of the rest of Christendom on this point. There is no difference between us as to "believers' Baptism" in such circumstances as existed at Pentecost, and as exist now in heathen lands. We both agree that the children of parents who are not—either of them—believers ought not to be baptized.[1] The only question in dispute is: What is to be done with the infant children of believers? Our Anti-Pædobaptist brethren hold that there is no warrant for giving them any token of the covenant, nor for recognising them as having any place in the Church, until they grow up and make a personal profession of faith for themselves. The great majority of Christians in all ages, on the contrary, hold that there is sufficient Scripture evidence to prove that the infant seed of believers in the New Testament Church ought to receive the token of God's covenant of grace, as it is admitted they did in the Church under former dispensations. On the

be baptized, in accordance, as we believe, with the mind of Christ, and with the practice of the Church of God from the days of Abraham.

It is interesting to note how the strong Christian common sense of John Bunyan dealt with this matter. He was pastor of a church "which," as its present minister writes, "had from the beginning taken up a position of neutrality on this question." Their one decided and unanimous conviction about it apparently was that, whoever were right, the "close communion Baptists" at least were so clearly and so far wrong that they in Bedford "could not even recognise their congregations as Churches of Christ," nor transfer their members to them. Whether John Bunyan himself was theoretically in favour of the Baptism of the infants of believers or not may be disputed. There can be no doubt at least as to what his practice was. He had his own children baptized in infancy and by sprinkling. His youngest child Joseph was so baptized in Bedford in the end of 1672, after Bunyan had been for some time formally the pastor of the Nonconformist congregation there. "You ask me," he writes to his close communion opponents in the following year (1673), "how long is it since I was a Baptist? I must tell you I know none to whom that title is so proper as to the disciples of John. And since you would know by what name I would be distinguished from others, I tell you I would be and hope I am a 'Christian,' and choose, if God should count me worthy, to be called a Christian, a believer, or other such name which is approved by the Holy Ghost." Brown, *Life of Bunyan*, London 1885, pp. 235–241, 249. Comp. p. 421 f.

[1] I speak here from the standpoint of the Reformed Church. In cases of adoption, orphans, mission children, etc., Baptism is given on the ground of some Christian person standing to the children *in loco parentis*, and becoming responsible for their Christian education, becoming, in short, their "Godfather" or "God-mother" in the true and original sense of the phrase. Comp. "Admission to Ordinances," p. 40 ff.

grounds now indicated, and on others to which reference may be made again, I believe that this is the right view, that " Baptism is not to be administered to any that are out of the visible Church till they profess their faith in Christ and obedience to Him; but the infants of such as are members of the visible Church are to be baptized." [1]

[1] Westminster Shorter Catech. Qu. 95.

CHAPTER II.

THE first glimpse which we get of the disciples, after the
Ascension, in the narrative of the Acts, shows them
"all with one accord" in the upper room at Jerusalem,
"continuing stedfastly in prayer" and searching of the
Scriptures. Our last glimpse of them, after the Ascension, in
the Gospel of Luke, shows them "continually (διαπαντός) in
the temple,[1] blessing God."[2] Except when the Hebrew
Christians were absolutely driven from the temple and the
city by persecution, it was on these two lines that their
worship and their work for Christ were carried on through
all the period now under consideration, and indeed down to
the very latest account which we have in the Acts of the
Church at Jerusalem.[3]

The first public proclamation of the Gospel is made from the
doors of the upper chamber at Pentecost. But it is repeated
forthwith in the temple courts, whither the apostles "go up
at the hour of prayer." There "they taught the people and
proclaimed in Jesus the resurrection from the dead (διδάσκειν
. . . . καταγγέλλειν)." "Every day in the temple and at
home they ceased not to teach and preach (διδάσκοντες καὶ
εὐαγγελιζόμενοι) Jesus as the Christ." Of the whole body
of the disciples, from the day of Pentecost onwards, it is said:
"Day by day, continuing stedfastly with one accord in the
temple and breaking bread at home, they did take their food
with gladness and singleness of heart, praising God, and
having favour with all the people."[4]

---

[1] Κατὰ τοὺς καιροὺς δηλόνοτι τῶν συνάξεων, ὅτι εἶναι ἐν αὐτῷ ἰξῆν, Euth. Zig. as
cited by Meyer, in loco.
[2] Acts i. 14-20 ; Luke xxiv. 53.   [3] Acts xxi. 26 ; xxiv. 11 f., 18.
[4] Acts ii. 1 f. ; iii. 1, 11 f. ; iv. 2 ; v. 42 ; ii. 46 f.

In acting thus, the first disciples were following closely in the footsteps of their Lord. To "the eleven and them that were with them" the memory of His looks and words hallowed that upper chamber, the original "home" of the Church, and those cloisters named of Solomon where Jesus had been wont to walk, and where the people gathered round Him to hear His words.[1] In such places as these, the associations of the past lent help to faith in realizing the unseen Presence of the Master in the midst of His disciples as met in His name; and blessing received there, "day by day," in their worship and witness-bearing, gave assurance that "the Lord" was indeed "working with them, and confirming the word by signs following."

There were other and stronger grounds for acting in this way. Christ, as He said Himself to the high priest, when questioned about "His disciples and His teaching," had "spoken openly to the world; I ever taught in synagogues (ἐν συναγωγῇ), and in the temple, where all the Jews come together; and in secret spake I nothing."[2] He had no esoteric doctrine. The essential points of His teaching and of His claims had been proclaimed in the most public way. But yet, at the same time, He had "expounded all things privately to His own disciples," opening to them more clearly "the mysteries of the kingdom of heaven."[3] It was in the inner circle of His believing followers that our Lord taught them to pray, and instituted the ordinance of the Supper, saying to them, when alone with Himself in the upper chamber: "This do in remembrance of Me." "As He was" in those days, "so they were to be in the world" now. The temporary restriction, which bid them tarry in seclusion at Jerusalem, "until they should be clothed with power from on high," was now removed. They had "received power," according to Christ's parting promise, "through the Holy Ghost coming upon them," and were therefore to be "witnesses for Christ," first of all "in Jerusalem and in all Judæa."[4] As children of the light, they were no longer to hide in secret chambers "for fear of the Jews," as when

---

[1] John x. 23 ; Acts iii. 11 ; v. 12.
[2] John xviii. 20.
[3] Mark iv. 10, 34. .
[4] Luke xxiv. 49 ; Acts i. 8.

they did not know that the Lord was risen indeed, but to let
their light shine before men in face of day.

Further, the new life in Christ by the Spirit, which wrought
so mightily and in so many ways in the apostolic Church,
lent a powerful impulse to this twofold worship "in the
temple" and "at home." On the one hand, it bound the
disciples, as we have seen, in a wonderful way to each
other as forming one family and brotherhood in the Lord.
On the other hand, it brought them closer than ever, in some
respects, to their fellow-countrymen, and to all who looked for
"the Hope of Israel."[1] Their natural love for "their brethren and kinsfolk according to the flesh" grew the warmer,
the more tender, and the more intelligent, because they "had
found Him of whom Moses in the law and the prophets did
write," and knew Him to be a more glorious and gracious
One than they themselves had ever dreamed before, or than
their countrymen knew as yet.

The heart of the Hebrew Christian Church in the fresh-
ness of its first love, the "love which hopeth all things and
believeth all things," went out beyond the family of faith in
Christ to embrace the whole family of Israel. Ought not the
disciples to be as their Lord in this also? He went only
"to the lost sheep of the house of Israel," hardly turning
aside even to "the villages of the Samaritans." He bid them
"begin at Jerusalem."[2] Might not all Israel be saved, and
become in the fullest sense "children of Abraham, and of the
covenant which God made with their fathers, saying unto
Abraham, "And in thy seed shall all the families of the
earth be blessed?"[3]

In those earliest days, there seemed to be something like
an answering impulse in the hearts of many to whom the
Hebrew Christians turned in this spirit. There was no persecution at first. The disciples "had favour with all the
people." "The people magnified them."[4]

In such circumstances, it was most natural that the members of the Pentecostal Church should rejoice in all that they
had in common with their fellow-countrymen, and should

---

[1] Acts xxvi. 6 f. ; xxviii. 20.   [2] Matt. x. 5 f. ; xv. 24 ; Luke xxiv. 47.
[3] Acts iii. 25 f.   [4] Acts ii. 47 ; v. 13.

seek to draw closer all common ties. The most sacred of
these were to be found in the ancestral house of prayer,
and in the worship of the God of their fathers. The disciples of Jesus did not yet understand what His words meant,
when He spoke of His having "come to cast fire upon the
earth," and to bring, in one sense, "not peace, but rather
division." [1] They did not realize what a dividing line they
themselves had crossed, when they received and confessed
Jesus of Nazareth, as "the Son of God, and the King of
Israel;" nor how deep and vital a difference there would prove
to be between the children of Abraham who received, and the
children of Abraham who rejected the Christ, preached to them
in the power of the Holy Ghost sent down from heaven.
It was not they who were to separate from Israel, but those
calling themselves Israel who were to separate from them.
Those who had crucified the Saviour were soon to thrust His
disciples also from them with a ruthless and bloody hand.

Meanwhile there was but one outward distinction visible,
as regards the temple worship,—a slight but significant one.
The disciples of Jesus went up to the temple to worship—
as is noted in the first reference to their custom in this
matter—in one company.[2] They kept together, as it appears,
in the temple courts, seeking instinctively there also "to
breathe as it were a Christian atmosphere." [3] In other
respects, they were marked out among their fellow-countrymen, who frequented the temple, only by the unfailing regularity of their attendance at the appointed times of worship,
and by the spirit of gladness and freedom which showed itself
in all that they did.

The common prayers in which the converts of Pentecost
took part so assiduously [4] evidently include the prayers offered

[1] Luke xii. 49–53.
[2] Πάντες δὲ οἱ πιστεύσαντες ἦσαν ἐπὶ τὸ αὐτό . . . καθ' ἡμέραν τε προσκαρτεροῦντες ὁμοθυμαδὸν ἐν τῷ ἱερῷ, Acts ii. 44, 46.
[3] "Der Umstand dass sie eben ὁμοθυμαδόν, also in Gemeinschaft mit einander, den Tempel besuchten, dazu beitragen musste ihre Zusammengehörigkeit auch hier zu bethätigen, sich auch hier gleichsam eine christliche Atmosphäre zu schaffen." Lechler, Apost. u. nachapost. Zeitalter, 3te Ausg. S. 36. Comp. Dykes, From Jerusalem to Antioch, 4th ed. p. 106.
[4] Ἦσαν προσκαρτεροῦντες . . . ταῖς προσευχαῖς, Acts ii. 42. Comp. what Paul

daily in the temple and synagogues at stated hours, as well as
the prayers of the Christian assemblies in the upper room
and elsewhere. The example of the apostles in " going up
together to the temple at the hour of prayer," and praying
at such times at home when unable to join with others in
public, shows doubtless what was the general practice in the
apostolic Church.[1]   Some twenty-five years later, at the time
of Paul's last visit to Jerusalem, the Hebrew Christians there,
and those believers who came thither at the yearly Jewish
feasts, still came to worship in the temple, in spite of all that
persecution had done to drive them from it.   " Thou seest,
brother," James and the elders at Jerusalem said to the
apostle of the Gentiles, " how many thousands (lit. ' myriads ')
there are among the Jews of them which have believed ;
and they are all zealous for the law ($\zeta\eta\lambda\omega\tau\alpha\grave{\iota}\ \tau o\hat{\upsilon}\ v\acute{o}\mu o\upsilon$), and
they have been informed concerning thee that thou teachest
all the Jews which are among the Gentiles to forsake Moses,
telling them not to circumcise their children, neither to walk
after the customs." [2]   And the proposal made by them, and
accepted by Paul, as best fitted to remove such misappre-
hensions, is that he should join with his believing fellow-
countrymen in a special part of the old temple services.

Let us consider a little more closely the indications which
we have regarding the nature of the worship of the apostolic
Church, as it developed itself on these two lines, " in the
temple," or the synagogue, and " at home."

1st. " In the temple."

" Peter and John," we read in the third chapter of the
Acts, " were going up into the temple at the hour of prayer,
being the ninth hour."   It was the time when the evening

---

says of the special interest shown by Epaphras in the spiritual welfare of the
Colossians, $\pi\acute{\alpha}\nu\tau o\tau\epsilon\ \grave{\alpha}\gamma\omega\nu\iota\zeta\acute{o}\mu\epsilon\nu o\varsigma\ \pi\epsilon\rho\grave{\iota}\ \grave{\upsilon}\mu\hat{\omega}\nu\ \grave{\epsilon}\nu\ \tau\alpha\hat{\iota}\varsigma\ \pi\rho o\sigma\epsilon\upsilon\chi\alpha\hat{\iota}\varsigma$, Col. iv. 12.

[1] Acts iii. 1 ; x. 9.   Comp. Paul's statement regarding the vision of Christ
given him "while I was praying in the temple," xxii. 17.

[2] Acts xxi. 21.   The connection here makes it plain that the chief reference
is to the Hebrew Christians of Jerusalem and the Holy Land.   These are contrasted with the Jewish Christians in the Diaspora, of whose intercourse with
Paul their brethren in Palestine knew only through rumours, sedulously spread
($\kappa\alpha\tau\eta\chi\acute{\eta}\theta\eta\sigma\alpha\nu$) by his enemies.

sacrifice began to be offered; but neither here, nor anywhere else in the New Testament, is it called "the hour of sacrifice," as in corresponding references in the Hebrew Scriptures.[1] We have seen already how all that was best and highest in the religious life of Israel had, since the exile, come to centre in the synagogue rather than in the temple.[2] In the Pentateuch, as noted before, there is hardly one express injunction to pray, while precepts regarding sacrifices, and the duties and privileges of the priests, meet us on almost every page;[3] and in the later historical books of Scripture, everything centres round the temple in Jerusalem, with its priesthood and elaborate sacrificial system. The synagogue worship, on the other hand, needed neither sacrifice nor priest.

Now when we pass to the worship of our Lord's time, we find that a silent revolution has taken place. Not only is the institution of the synagogue with its eldership every-where in the foreground,—perfectly on a level, to say the least, in practical importance, with that of the temple with its priesthood; but a significant change is apparent as regards the temple worship itself. In it, too, those elements are now conspicuous which specially belonged to the syna-gogue, prayer, confession of sins, exposition of the Scriptures, and oral popular address.

Here, too, the teacher has to a great extent taken the place of the priest. The old sacrificial system indeed still goes on. Devout parents present their little ones in the temple, and offer sacrifice according to the law. The blood of the worshippers from Galilee is "mingled by Pilate with their sacrifices." Cleansed lepers show themselves to the priest, and offer for their cleansing as Moses appointed.[4]

But there is a manifest change with respect to the place and importance assigned to the material and ceremonial, as compared with the spiritual elements in worship. There is hearing of teachers, and asking them questions concerning Scripture, in the temple courts. The earliest scene recorded in any of the Gospels is that of a priest, making supplication in the holy place, "and the whole multitude of the people

[1] *E.g.* 1 Kings xviii. 29, 36. [2] See above, pp. 155 f., 161 f.
[3] See above, p. 156. [4] Luke i. 24 ; v. 14 ; xiii. 1.

praying without at the time of incense." Anna the prophetess "departs not from the temple, worshipping with fastings and supplications night and day." Pharisee and publican alike "go up to the temple to pray."[1] The daily hours of worship in the temple, although fixed by the burnt-offerings, were yet, in the language and hearts of the people, "the hours of prayer," and not "of sacrifice."

It is easy to see how these synagogue aspects—so to speak — of the temple worship must have had special attractions for the Hebrew Christians. None of the original apostles, and few at least of the other members of the hundred and twenty who formed the nucleus of the Pentecostal Church, belonged to Jerusalem.[2] They had been used, like their Master, to worship in the synagogue every Sabbath day, without the media either of sacrifices or priesthood. What their exact position now was toward the temple sacrifices, it is difficult to say with certainty. That they still continued generally to take part in them, and to regard that as the proper course for all Israelites by birth who were within reach of the temple, seems a natural inference from the case of Paul and the four believers who had taken the vow of the Nazarite, at the time of his last visit to Jerusalem.[3] In what light Paul himself, long before this time, had learned to look upon the temple sacrifices, so far as they bore upon the way of a sinner's acceptance with God, we see clearly from his earliest epistles, and from his attitude at Antioch and Jerusalem, in the great controversy as to the manner in which the Gentiles were to be admitted into the fellowship of the Church.[4]

That Stephen, at a still earlier date, had grasped and

[1] Luke i. 10, 13 : "Fear not, Zacharias, because thy supplication is heard ; " ii. 37 ; xviii. 10.

[2] "Are not all these which speak Galilæans ?" Acts ii. 7.

[3] The presentation in the temple of "the offering for every one of them," which, according to the Levitical rule, included a burnt-offering, a sin-offering, and a peace-offering, with other accompaniments (Lev. vii. 12 f.), was to be the proof in the eyes of the myriads of Hebrew Christians who were "zealots of the law," that "Paul himself also," like themselves, "was wont to walk orderly, keeping the law," Acts xxi. 23 f., 26.

[4] Rom. ii. 28 f. ; iii. 20–30 ; vii. 6 ; x. 4 ; xii. 1 ; Gal. ii. 3 ff. ; v. 3 f. ; vi. 15 f. ; 1 Cor. ix. 20 f.

taught the same truths, there can be little doubt.   They are
embodied, in all likelihood, in a perverted form, in the statement of the false witnesses before the Sanhedrin : " This man
ceaseth not to speak words against this holy place and the
law ; for we have heard him say that this Jesus of Nazareth
shall destroy this place, and shall change the customs which
Moses delivered unto us."[1]

In what light " the apostles of the circumcision," and other
leading teachers of the Hebrew Christian Church, regarded
the question of material sacrifices, when it came to be fully
considered and expounded by them, may be seen in the
Epistles of Peter and of John, of James and of Jude the
brother of James, and in the Epistle to the Hebrews.   In
none of these is any spiritual significance for believers attached
to the temple sacrifices or priesthood.   There is no reference
to them, save as furnishing figures to set forth New Testament
truths.   There is not the slightest indication that the writers
of those epistles held that the Christians, to whom they wrote,
were under any *obligation* whatever with respect to material
sacrifices or a human priesthood, whatever they might do
individually, as Paul at times did, on grounds of old association or expediency.

The apostle Peter, in his epistle " to the elect who are
sojourners of the Dispersion in Pontus, Galatia, Cappadocia,
Asia, and Bithynia," speaks of Christians being " redeemed
not with corruptible things, . . . but with precious blood
as of a lamb without blemish and without spot, even the
blood of Christ."   Believers are " an holy and royal priesthood, to offer up spiritual sacrifices, acceptable to God
through Jesus Christ."   " Christ His own self bare our
sins in His body upon the tree, that we having died to
sins might live unto righteousness ; by whose stripes ye
were healed."   " Christ suffered for sins once, the Righteous
for the unrighteous, that He might bring us to God."[2]   The
apostle knows nothing of any human priesthood among the
Christians to whom he writes, save that common to all
believers.   But he takes it for granted that, in all the
Churches, there will be elders or presbyters, with appointed

[1] Acts vi. 13 f.   [2] 1 Pet. i. 1, 18 f. ; ii. 5, 9, 24 ; iii. 18.

functions of oversight and pastoral care, similar to those
which had been entrusted to himself by Christ in words
which his language recalls. "The elders among you I
exhort, who am a fellow-elder. . . . Tend (shepherd) the
flock of God which is among you, exercising the oversight
(or doing a bishop's office therein), not of constraint, but
willingly, according unto God; nor yet for filthy lucre, but
of a ready mind; neither as lording it over the charge
allotted to you, but making yourselves ensamples to the
flock. And when the chief Shepherd shall be manifested,
ye shall receive the crown of glory that fadeth not away."[1]

The apostle John, in his first Epistle, speaks of "Jesus
Christ the Righteous" as "the Advocate with the Father,"
and "the propitiation for our sins, and not for ours only, but
also for the whole world." "The blood of Jesus, God's Son,
cleanseth us from all sin. . . . If we confess our sins, He
is faithful and righteous to forgive us our sins, and to cleanse
us from all unrighteousness." There is not the faintest hint of
any place being left now, as under the old economy, for the
mediation or intercession of an order of human priests, nor
for any visible sacrifice, in connection with the forgiveness
and cleansing of which the writer speaks. "Ye know that

---

[1] Ποιμάνατε τὸ ἐν ὑμῖν ποίμνιον τοῦ θεοῦ, ἐπισκοποῦντες . . . μηδ᾽ ὡς κατακυριεύοντες
τῶν κλήρων ἀλλὰ τύποι γινόμενοι τοῦ ποιμνίου, 1 Pet. v. 1–4. Comp. Luke xxii.
25-27 ; John xxi. 15–18. Comp. also Paul's charge to the presbyters of one of
the Churches to which this circular letter of Peter's was sent, the mother
Church of Asia. "He sent to Ephesus, and called to him the elders of the
Church, and said unto them : 'Take heed unto yourselves, and to all the
flock in the which the Holy Ghost hath made you bishops, to tend (ποιμαίνειν)
the Church of God, which He purchased with His own blood,'" Acts xx. 28.
We see from the narrative of the Acts, and the references in the Pauline
Epistles and the Apocalypse, that the Christian communities in Asia, Galatia,
etc., to which Peter wrote, although having their origin in almost every
case from the local Jewish synagogue, or proseucha, with its circle of proselytes, were made up chiefly of Gentile converts. It is quite in accordance
with this that several passages in Peter's epistle plainly take it for granted
that many, or most of those to whom he wrote, had been Gentiles, "called
out of darkness into His marvellous light, which in time past were no people,
but now are the people of God," ii. 9 f. Comp. i. 14 ; iii. 6 ; iv. 3 f. But the
apostle of the circumcision regards Jewish and Gentile believers as now one in
Christ, forming together the covenant people of God, the Christian Diaspora.
See Alford, *Prolegomena* to 1 Peter, iv. 122 f. Hatch in art. "Peter, Epistles
of," *Encycl. Brit.* 9th ed.

He was manifested to take away sins; and in Him is no sin."
" Hereby know we love, because He laid down His life for
us; and we ought to lay down our lives for the brethren."
" God sent His Son to be the propitiation for our sins." [1]

In the Apocalypse, the strongly Hebraic style and tone of
which strike even a careless reader, there is the same entire
absence of all reference to any sacrifice but that of Christ,
and to any priesthood save that of the risen Saviour,—who
appears in the opening vision with the symbols of priestly
as well as of kingly dignity,[2]—and that of all His true people.
" He loveth us, and loosed us from our sins by His blood, and
He made us to be a kingdom, to be priests unto His God and
Father." There is no temple in the New Testament seer's
vision of the New Jerusalem, and there are signs there of but
one sacrifice: " I saw in the midst of the throne a Lamb
standing as though it had been slain." There are no priests
with nearer access than others enjoy to the Holiest. The
titles of the foremost representatives of the Church of the
redeemed recall the fellowship of the synagogue, not the
hierarchy of the temple. " Round about the throne were
four and twenty seats, and upon the seats I saw four and
twenty elders sitting, clothed in white raiment; and they had
on their heads crowns of gold." [3]

James, the Lord's brother, the very ideal of a Hebrew
Christian of the most antique type,[4] writes to Hebrew
Christians, " to the twelve tribes which are of the Dispersion." With him " pure religion and undefiled (θρησκεία, the
' cultus exterior,' the outward expression and embodiment of
' religion ' in the more modern sense of our English word)
before our God and Father is this, to visit the fatherless and

---

[1] 1 John i. 7-9 ; ii. 1 f. ; iii. 5, 16 ; iv. 10.

[2] Rev. i. 13-16.

[3] Rev. i. 5 f.; v. 6 ; xxi. 22 ; iv. 4, 10 ; v. 5-14 ; vii. 11-14 ; xi. 16 f.

[4] Comp. the well-known description of him by Hegesippus preserved in Eusebius (ii. 23), with Lechler's comments upon it, *Apost. u. nachapost. Zeitalter*,
3te Ausg. S. 51-57 ; also Sorley's criticisms, *Jewish Christians and Judaism*,
Camb. 1881, p. 18 f. For an admirable summary of the evidence that "James,
the Lord's brother," was not identical with "James the little" (ὁ μικρός), the
son of Alphæus, and was not therefore one of the Twelve, see Bp. Lightfoot's dissertation on "The Brethren of the Lord," in his *Commentary on Galatians*,
5th ed. pp. 255-290.

widows in their affliction, and to keep himself unspotted from the world." [1]   He speaks of prayer and confession of sins among believers, of the singing of praise, of elders of the Church, who are to be sent for in cases of sickness to pray for and minister to the sick, of Christian assemblies in synagogue fashion, of the special responsibilities of teachers, of the duty of both hearing and doing the word.[2]   He says nothing whatever of priests or sacrifices. His only reference to an altar is to that on which "Abraham, our father," laid his son, proving thereby that his faith was not "barren" nor "dead," but as living and fruitful as when, long before, it was recorded of him that "Abraham believed God, and it was reckoned unto him for righteousness." [3]

"Jude, the brother of James," does not state expressly for what class of Christians his short letter is designed. It is sent to "them that are called, beloved in God the Father and kept for Jesus Christ," who have Him as "their only Master and Lord." But from the distinctly Hebraic tone of the Epistle, and its appeal, not merely to the Old Testament, but to Jewish traditions about Michael the archangel, and to the extra-canonical "Book of Enoch," we may reasonably infer that both the writer and those whom he addressed belonged to the Hebrew Christian Church. His only references to worship are to the duty of "prayer in the Holy Spirit," and to the distinctively Christian institution of the "love feasts." [4] The only teachers whom Jude expressly speaks of as such are

---

[1] Jas. i. 27.   "He is not herein affirming, as we sometimes hear, these offices to be the sum-total, nor yet the great essentials of religion, but declares them to be the body, the θρησκεία, of which godliness or the love of God is the informing soul. His intention is somewhat obscured to the English reader, from the fact that 'religious' and 'religion,' by which we have rendered θρῆσκος and θρησκεία, possessed a meaning once which they now possess no longer, and in that meaning are here employed. St. James would, in fact, claim for the Christian faith a superiority over the old dispensation, in that its very θρησκεία consists in acts of mercy, of love, of holiness, in that 'it has *light for its garment*, its very *robe being* righteousness;' herein how much nobler than that old, whose θρησκεία was merely ceremonial and formal, whatever inner truth it might embody." Trench, *N. T. Synonyms*, p. 192 f.   Comp. Coleridge, *Aids to Reflection*, ed. 1848, i. p. 14.

[2] Jas. i. 19–22; ii. 2 f.; iii. 13–16.   [3] Jas. ii. 20–23, 26.

[4] Jude 1, 4, 9, 12, 14, 20.

"the apostles of our Lord Jesus Christ." There may possibly be an allusion to teachers in what he says of some who, like Balaam, acted from selfish and sordid motives, and whose sin was like that of Korah, who at the love feasts of the believers were as "hidden rocks, shepherds that without fear feed themselves. . . . These are they who make separations, sensual, having not the Spirit."[1] There is as entire an absence of any reference to priesthood or sacrifices among the Christians to whom Jude wrote, as in the kindred Epistle of James.

Finally, embodying the fullest development of inspired teaching on the subject of sacrifice and priesthood, we have the "Epistle to the Hebrews." This heading, its oldest historic title, corresponds exactly with what we gather from the contents of the document itself; and beyond what it conveys it is very difficult to go with any confidence. Some Jewish Christian community is addressed by the author. It has had a distinct history of its own, to which he makes special appeal. But whether we should look for them in Rome, or Alexandria, or some seat of the Dispersion in the East, it is not easy to say. The word "Hebrews" must be taken here, of course, in its wider sense, as meaning Israelites of whatever tongue and country, in contradistinction to believers of Gentile origin, not in the narrower one, in which it refers to Jews of the Holy Land, not belonging to its Hellenistic districts, or at least Jews who were accustomed to speak Hebrew or Aramaic, and to use the Hebrew Scriptures.[2]

There is no reference whatever in this epistle to Gentile Christians. Among the special dangers to which its readers are exposed, are such as may arise from undue attention to

---

[1] Jude 17, 11 f., 19. The phrase in ver. 12, ἀφόβως ἑαυτοὺς ποιμαίνοντες, which the R. V. renders as above, might perhaps be more exactly translated "acting as shepherds to themselves without fear," or, as Dr. Salmon puts it, "not afraid to be their own shepherds." Comp. his note, *Introd. to N. T.* p. 600 f.

[2] Thus Saul of Tarsus, notwithstanding his Cilician birth and Roman citizenship, was "an Hebrew of Hebrews," Phil. iii. 5. And just as at Jerusalem there were separate synagogues for the Hellenists (comp. Acts vi. 9 with ix. 29), so at Rome, as appears from the inscriptions, there was a "synagogue of the Hebrews." Schürer, *Hist. of Jewish People*, Div. ii. vol. ii. p. 248. Comp. Rendall, *Theol. of Heb. Christians*, pp. 64-69.

" meats " and other unprofitable points alien from the message
of grace which they had received from their first teachers.[1]

In one passage, indeed, the Christian Hebrews seem even
" exhorted to sever all connection with their fellow-countrymen, still practising the ceremonial observances " of the tabernacle or temple system.[2]   They are at least clearly warned of
the danger of still " serving the tabernacle," *i.e.* allowing their
religious life to be governed by the principles and rules of a
system of things which had been superseded, inasmuch as
they thereby cut themselves off from the right or power
($\dot{\epsilon}\xi o u \sigma i a$) to share in the benefits of Christ's sacrifice.[3]   On
the other hand, many special features,[4] and the general tone
and style of the epistle, seem to show that the author, himself
probably a Hellenistic Jew, has before his mind readers who,
while children of Abraham, both in the flesh and the spirit,
belong to a Christian community of the Hellenistic type.[5]

There is no need for our present purpose to enter into the
details of the great argument of this epistle.   We simply
call attention to the fact that in this letter, written probably
before the fall of Jerusalem,[6] and written certainly to Hebrew
Christians, we have a full and clear exposition of the doctrine
of Christ's sacrifice and priesthood, of the abolition of the
Old Testament sacrificial system, of how believers now have
access as priests into the holiest by the blood of Jesus, and of
the nature of the spiritual sacrifices which they offer, and with
which God is well pleased.[7]

---

[1] Heb. xiii. 7 ff.   [2] Davidson, *Hebrews*, pp. 19, 253–257.

[3] Heb. xiii. 10–16.

[4] For example, the invariable use of the LXX. for quotations from the Old
Testament.

[5] Comp. Davidson, *Hebrews*, pp. 9 f., 15–18.

[6] It was while there were yet " priests, who offer the gifts according to the law,
and serve that which is the copy and shadow of the heavenly things," Heb. viii. 4 f.

[7] Heb. ii. 16 ff. ; v. 1–12 ; vii. 10, 22 ; xiii. 10–16. In one passage—the
only one in the whole N. T.—" the image is so far extended " that an " altar "
is also spoken of in connection with the spiritual offerings of believers, Heb.
xiii. 10.   Bp. Lightfoot's remarks on this point may be given, as those of an
exegete whose impartiality on such a question will be disputed by none.   He
protests against " transferring statements such as this from the region of
metaphor to the region of fact." . . . " It is surprising that some should have
interpreted $\theta u \sigma i \alpha \sigma \tau \dot{\eta} \rho i o v$ in Heb. xiii. 10 of the Lord's table.   There may be a
doubt as to the exact significance of the term in this passage, but an *actual*

As to the worship of the believers to whom the epistle is addressed, "the Word of God" holds the foremost place in it.[1] There are stated assemblies of the brethren, which the author calls by a name closely akin to the familiar word "synagogue," which were for mutual edification and exhortation, and which the author urges his readers with much earnestness "not to forsake, as the custom of some is." [2] They are exhorted also to remember former spiritual "leaders" (ἡγούμενοι) who in time past "spake unto them the Word of God, and, considering the issue of their life, to imitate their faith." They are bidden to beware of "divers and strange teachings" of a Judaistic sort, to "obey them that are your leaders (τοῖς ἡγουμένοις ὑμῶν, those now filling the places of the others deceased), and submit to them; for they watch in behalf of your souls, as they that shall give account." The epistle closes with greetings "to all your leaders (πάντας τοὺς ἡγουμένους ὑμῶν), and to all the saints." [3]

No more conclusive proof of the absence of anything like a separate priesthood and sacrificial rites from the institutions of the Hebrew Christian Church could well be given than the significant utterances, and the equally significant silence, of the Epistle to the Hebrews.[4]

---

altar is plainly not intended. This is shown by the context both before and after, *e.g.* ver. 9, the opposition of χάρις and βρώματα, ver. 15, the contrast implied in the mention of θυσία αἰνέσεως and καρπὸς χειλίων, and ver. 16, the naming εὐποιία καὶ κοινωνία as the kind of sacrifice with which God is well pleased. The sense which I have assigned to it (that it means the congregation assembled for common worship) appears to suit the language of the context; while at the same time it accords with the Christian phraseology of succeeding ages. So Clem. Alex. *Strom.* vii. 6; Ignat. *Eph.* iv.; *Magn.* 7, etc. Similarly Polycarp (c. iv.) speaks of the body of the widows as θυσιαστήριον θεοῦ." *Philippians*, 3rd ed. pp. 260, 263. Delitzsch, Alford, Davidson, and others, with more probability as it seems to me, hold that the altar here referred to is the cross of Christ.

[1] ii. 1-3; iv. 2, 11 f.; v. 12-14; vi. 5; xiii. 7, 22.
[2] Heb. x. 25: Τὴν ἐπισυναγωγὴν ἑαυτῶν μὴ ἐγκαταλείποντες, καθὼς ἔθος τισίν.
[3] Heb. xiii. 7-10, 17, 24.
[4] "If the sacerdotal office be understood to imply *the offering of sacrifices*, then the Epistle to the Hebrews leaves no place for a Christian priesthood." Bp. Lightfoot, "Essay on the Christian Ministry," in *Philippians*, 3rd ed. p. 264 f. See Dr. Bannerman's thorough discussion of the priestly and sacrificial theories in their Roman Catholic and Anglican forms, *Church of Christ*, ii. pp. 155-185.

How much of the truth regarding sacrifice and priesthood
under the New Testament dispensation, afterwards set forth
so luminously by the apostles and other teachers of the
Church in Jerusalem and in the Dispersion, was but dimly
seen even by themselves during the first months and years
after Pentecost, and how much more was altogether hid
from the " many thousands of Jews which had believed,"
it is impossible for us to say. The key to the whole subject
had been given to the apostles in many a pregnant utterance
of Christ, which shone out now in new light under the
promised teaching of the Holy Ghost. It was given to
them also in the speaking signs and actions of the Lord's
Supper, which were repeated and explained from day to day
in the assemblies of the Pentecostal Church by those who
were with the Son of God when He instituted the ordinance,
with ever-memorable words, on that night on which He was
betrayed. Andrew and John had heard their first teacher, the
Baptist, say of Jesus of Nazareth in His own presence : " Behold
the Lamb of God, which taketh away the sin of the world."
That significant testimony, which was twice repeated by the
Baptist, sent them at once to Christ. From them it passed
directly to Peter, Philip, Nathanael, and others of the twelve.[1]
The scene and the saying must often have been rehearsed and
pondered in the inner circle of the original disciples, and by
other followers of the Baptist who joined them after their
master's death.[2] They could hardly fail to ask the Lord
Himself concerning the meaning of John's testimony to
Him, and of His words to John regarding " the necessity
of His fulfilling all righteousness," at some of the times
when, " privately to His own disciples, He expounded all
things." [3]

Other deep sayings of Jesus concerning His sufferings and
death would naturally link themselves in the minds of the
apostles with the testimony of His Forerunner. " The Son
of Man came to give His life (His soul, τὴν ψυχὴν αὐτοῦ) a
ransom in room of many (λύτρον ἀντὶ πολλῶν)."[4] " As Moses
lifted up the serpent in the wilderness, even so must the Son

---

[1] John i. 29–37, 40–49.
[2] Matt. xiv. 12.
[3] Matt. iii. 15 ; Mark iv. 34.
[4] Matt. xx. 28 ; Mark x. 45.

of Man be lifted up, that whosoever believeth may in Him have eternal life." [1] " The bread which I will give is My flesh for the life of the world (ὑπὲρ τῆς τοῦ κόσμου ζωῆς)." " The Good Shepherd giveth His life for the sheep. . . . Therefore doth the Father love Me, because I lay down My life that I may take it again. . . . This commandment received I from My Father." " O My Father, if it be possible, let this cup pass away from Me ; nevertheless not as I will, but as Thou wilt. . . . O My Father, if this cannot pass away except I drink it, Thy will be done." [2]

In connection with the passover and the paschal lamb, " the fundamental sacrifice of the covenant people," [3] our Lord said to the twelve : " This (broken bread) is My body which is given for you. . . . This (cup) is My blood of the covenant (or in Luke's version : the new covenant in My blood), which is shed for many unto the remission of sins." When the apostle John records how, a few hours later, he beheld that blood actually poured out upon the cross, he adds a few words of comment, which show how he loved to trace the fulfilment of the symbolism of the paschal sacrifice in the death of Christ. " For these things came to pass that the Scripture might be fulfilled, A bone of Him shall not be broken." [4]

It was on such points as these passages suggest with respect to the meaning and results of His sufferings and death, that our Lord's unrecorded expositions of the Old Testament Scriptures specially turned, in His interviews with His

---

[1] John iii. 14 f. ; comp. xii. 32 f.

[2] John vi. 51 ; x. 11, 15–18 ; Matt. xxvi. 36–44 ; comp. x. 22 ; Mark x. 35 ; Luke xii. 50.

[3] Smeaton, *Doctrine of the Atonement as taught by Christ Himself*, Edin. 1868, p. 67.

[4] Matt. xxvi. 28 ; Mark xiv. 24 ; Luke xxii. 19 f. ; John xix. 33–36. The reference is to the legislation regarding the lamb of the passover in Ex. xii. 46 ; Num. ix. 12. Comp. Paul's express statement of the same thought : "For our passover also hath been sacrificed, even Christ," 1 Cor. v. 7. It is significant that the evangelist couples with his first quotation " another Scripture," in which the prophet describes Israel as awaking, through "a spirit of grace and supplication poured upon them " by Jehovah, to the perception that, by slaying One who specially represented the Lord and His cause, " they had pierced Jehovah " Himself. See Dods, *Post-Exilian Prophets*, p. 115. West-

followers after His resurrection. " Behoved it not the
Christ," He said to the two disciples on the road to
Emmaus, " to suffer these things, and to enter into His
glory ? And beginning from Moses, and from all the prophets,
He interpreted to them in all the Scriptures the things concerning Himself." Again, when on the evening of the first
Lord's day He met with " the eleven and them that were
with them " in the upper room at Jerusalem, " He said unto
them : These are My words which I spake unto you while I
was yet with you, how that all things must needs be fulfilled
which are written in the law of Moses, and the prophets, and
the Psalms concerning Me . . . that the Christ should suffer,
and rise again from the dead the third day, and that repentance and remission of sins should be preached in His name.
. . . And they worshipped Him," the evangelist goes on
after briefly recording Christ's ascension, " and returned to
Jerusalem with great joy, and were continually in the
temple blessing God." [1]   Must not part at least of their
joy, and of the attraction to the temple, have arisen from
the glimpses which they had now attained of the meaning
of " the things written in the law of Moses," and in the old
sacrificial system, concerning the Christ and His appointed
sufferings ?

On the day of Pentecost the Holy Spirit had come to the
apostles in power, to " guide them into all the truth,"
according to the Saviour's promise ; yet still it was only
step by step " as they were able to bear it," [2] and as they

---

cott on John xix. 36. Rendall, *Theol. of Heb. Christians*, pp. 122-152.
Note also the significant way in which John prefaces his account of Christ's
feeding the five thousand, and of His subsequent discourse at Capernaum on
the bread of life, with the statement: " Now the passover, the feast of the Jews
(ἡ ἑορτὴ τῶν Ἰουδαίων), was at hand." What seems the underlying thought is well
put by Prof. Bruce : " The passover was nigh, and—so we may bring out John's
meaning—Jesus was thinking of it, though He went not up to the feast that
season. He thought of the paschal lamb, and how He, the true Paschal Lamb,
would ere long be slain ' for the life of the world,' and He gave expression to
the deep thoughts of His heart in the symbolic miracle I am about to relate,
and in the mystic discourse which followed." *Training of the Twelve*, 2nd ed.
p. 121 ; comp. Godet, ii. p. 473.

[1] Luke xxiv. 26 f., 44 ff., 52 f.
[2] John xiv. 25 f. ; xvi. 12 f.

were prepared by one event in Providence after another to receive and use aright the fuller revelation.   Graciously and gently, as His manner was of old, the unseen Lord led His disciples onwards in those early years of the apostolic Church, making the new to rise for them gradually out of the old. Christ still "opened to them the Scripture" by His Spirit from day to day, as they searched it together "at home," and opened it to them also by His Spirit in the temple from the ancient ordinances of His Father's house.   "Day by day, they were breaking bread at home," "proclaiming the Lord's death," [1] showing forth His sacrifice of Himself upon the cross, repeating joyfully His own words : "This is My body, which is given for you."   "This is My blood of the covenant, which is shed for many unto the remission of sins."

For those early disciples, nothing could come in the place of that one offering, or be a substitute for the Lord's own appointed memorial of it.   But when they passed, "day by day," from the Christian gatherings "at home" into the temple courts at the hours of sacrifice, truths, once undreamt of, must have come out more and more in grand if still dim outline, as they saw those acted parables of the laver and the altar, concerning sin and atonement, and purification by water and by blood.

The eleven could scarcely fail to remember at such times one incident in the Saviour's last visit to Jerusalem.   After His triumphal reception as He came towards the city, " He entered," the second evangelist tells us, " into Jerusalem, into the temple ; and when He had looked round about upon all things (περιβλεψάμενος πάντα), it being now eventide, He went out unto Bethany with the twelve." [2]

What was implied in that deep and searching look, which seems so to have impressed those who saw it, with what thoughts and feelings our Lord stood in silence by the altar at the hour of the evening sacrifice, we may in some sort imagine when we think who He was, and how He knew all things that were to befall Him in Jerusalem, and what

---

[1] Acts ii. 46 ; 1 Cor. xi. 23 : τὸν θάνατον τοῦ κυρίου καταγγίλλοντις.
[2] Mark xi. 11.

should be a few days hence, "about the ninth hour," in which he now beheld the lamb slain and offered, as had been done for centuries, on that great altar of burnt-offering.[1]   The shadows of Gethsemane and of the Cross fell athwart the path of the Master then.   They lay all behind His disciples now : " Our passover hath been sacrificed, even Christ."   Even with the light of the Resurrection and Ascension, with the light of the teaching of the Risen Lord concerning Himself, and with the Spirit " taking of the things of Christ and showing them to them," the apostles' insight into the meaning of Christ's sufferings, and their bearing on the salvation of men, was very different from His perfect knowledge.   Still it must have been for them, too, a thrilling experience to stand silently in the temple courts at the hours of sacrifice, and find point after point in that grand system of prophetic ordinances opening out day by day with new significance and power.

In Bunyan's allegory of *The Holy War*, he tells how the citizens of Mansoul, when pardoned after their rebellion, were feasted at the Prince's table, and thereafter had certain riddles set before them.   " These riddles were made upon the King Shaddai and Emmanuel His Son, and upon His wars and doings with Mansoul. . . . And when they read in the scheme wherein the riddles were writ, and looked in the Face of the Prince, things looked so like the one to the other that Mansoul could not forbear to say : This is the Lamb !   This is the sacrifice !   This is the Rock !   This is the red Heifer ! This is the Door, and this is the Way ! "   The first disciples, at this time, were fresh from " looking in the Face of the Prince."   Can we wonder that they loved to look also into the scheme of things wherein that Face had been so long reflected, and had been seen with joy by the true children of Abraham,—although " seeing it afar off " and " as in a mirror, in a riddle,"—to be full of grace and truth ?[2]

The great truths concerning Christ's sacrifice and priesthood, and their relation to the temple worship and Jewish priesthood, which were afterwards set forth in the first Epistle

---

[1] John xiii. 1-4 ; Matt. xxvi. 2 ; xxvii. 46-51.
[2] John viii. 56 ; 1 Cor. xiii. 12.

of Peter, the Apocalypse, and the Epistle to the Hebrews, opened doubtless only by degrees upon the apostles themselves, — more swiftly, perhaps, upon Hellenists such as Stephen. They passed slowly from them to the general Christian consciousness of the Church, especially as regards the intellectual apprehension of them, and the practical inferences as to conduct which were to be drawn from them. But, from the first, a certain change must have been *felt* by all the Hebrew Christians to have taken place in their spiritual relation to the old sacrificial system,—a change which was real and operative, although many of the disciples, no doubt, were hardly conscious that it had come about, and could not have defined its nature; and none were aware of the consequences to which it would lead in the end.

That a certain element of separation had come in between them and their non-Christian fellow-countrymen, was unconsciously indicated, as already noticed, by the disciples going up in one company to worship in the temple courts, and keeping together there.[1] Yet, in other respects, they felt nearest to their brethren according to the flesh when calling along with them upon the God of Abraham, Isaac, and Jacob, the God of their fathers. They were still strong in hope that all the seed of Abraham would speedily own the Lord Jesus as "the Son of God, the King of Israel." Their heart's desire and prayer in His name in the temple was, that all Israel might be saved, and the fulness of the Gentiles come, and that "the holy and beautiful house, where their fathers praised God," might thus become in their day "an house of prayer for all nations."[2]

The relation of the Hebrew Christians to the synagogue congregations, in which they had all hitherto been members, does not appear so expressly in this first section of the book of Acts as it does in the second; but it can be brought out by fair inference, and from various indications, more or less direct.

In the first place, the natural presumption certainly is, if nothing be said to the contrary, that the first members of the Pentecostal Church would follow the example of their Lord when on earth, with respect to the synagogue, as well as the temple. "His custom was" to join in the synagogue services "on the Sabbath day" from His youth up. The synagogues of northern Palestine had formed the chief sphere of His public ministry. "I have spoken openly to the world," He said to the high priest when questioned as to His teaching; "I ever taught in synagogue (ἐν συναγωγῇ) and in the temple, where all the Jews come together." [1] In our Lord's parting words to His disciples, He had taken it for granted that they would maintain their old connection with their synagogues, and that its violent termination would be felt as a special trial, and one which, if it came upon them unprepared, might be a stumbling-block to faith.

We might, therefore, be surprised at first that we have so little positive evidence in the earlier chapters of the Acts that the Hebrew Christians continued to attend the synagogue services, as compared with the frequent references to their going up to the temple. But these chapters, it is to be kept in mind, refer almost exclusively to Jerusalem; and there the synagogues, although numerous, were naturally overshadowed by the temple. A closer examination of the narrative, moreover, discloses evidence that the disciples of Christ in Jerusalem and around it were still to be found in the synagogues, to which they had hitherto belonged.

When Paul speaks from the castle stairs in Jerusalem to his fellow-countrymen, he recounts what the Lord said to him while praying in the temple: "Make haste and get thee quickly out of Jerusalem, because they will not receive of thee testimony concerning Me. And I said, Lord, they themselves know that I imprisoned and beat in every synagogue them that believed on Thee." [2]

The reference here obviously is to what the Jews of Jerusalem knew for themselves had been done by Saul of Tarsus, when urging on the persecution that arose about Stephen, in the city and its immediate neighbourhood; and it

---

[1] Matt. iv. 23; ix. 35; xiii. 54; Mark i. 39, etc.; Luke iv. 15 f., etc.; John xviii. 20.

[2] Acts xxii. 18 f.

clearly implies that the Christians were still to be found " in every synagogue."

The apostle repeats his statement in yet clearer terms before Agrippa and Festus : "This I also did in Jerusalem : and I both shut up many of the saints in prison, having received authority from the chief priests ; and when they were put to death, I gave my vote against them. And punishing them oftentimes in all the synagogues, I strove to make them blaspheme ; and being exceedingly mad against them, I persecuted them even unto foreign cities." [1] A similar relation between the Hebrew Christians and the synagogues of the place in which they lived evidently existed in the " foreign cities," to which Saul's persecuting zeal afterwards impelled him to journey. He asks of the high priest " letters to Damascus unto the synagogues, that if he found any that were of the Way, whether men or women, he might bring them bound to Jerusalem." [2] It seems a fair inference from this statement that the Christians in Damascus, as well as in Jerusalem, habitually attended the synagogues, and were under the oversight, or at least within the ken, of the synagogue elders.

Again, Ananias, through whom Saul was received into the Christian Church, is described by him as " a devout man according to the law, well reported of by all the Jews that dwelt in Damascus." [3] This he certainly could not have been, had he failed in that regular attendance in the synagogue, which was held by all Jews of that age to be an essential part of the duty of every devout Israelite. The fact referred to by James in the council at Jerusalem, that " Moses hath in every city them that preach him, being read in the synagogues every Sabbath," is adduced by him as a reason for urging the Gentile Christians to have special regard on certain points for the feelings and customs of their fellow-believers of Hebrew descent; and it clearly implies that the latter, at least, were in the habit of " hearing Moses in the synagogue " still " every Sabbath." [4] Lastly, there can be no doubt that

---

[1] Acts xxvi. 10 f.   [2] Acts ix. 1 f.   [3] Acts xxii. 12.
[4] Acts xv. 21. Comp. Lechler, *Apost. u. nachap. Zeitalter*, 3te Ausg. S. 46.

the "myriads" of Hebrew Christians in Jerusalem and Judæa, whom James and the elders of the Church there described as being "all zealots of the law," and "walking after the customs," were regular attenders of the synagogue, as well as of the temple services.   And Paul accepted, and endorsed by action, the statement, made in his behalf by the representatives of the mother Church of Hebrew Christendom, that he on his part did not "teach the Jews which are among the Gentiles to forsake Moses," nor to cease "to walk after the customs," "but himself also," as he had opportunity, "walked," in these respects, "orderly, keeping the law." [1]

What the nature of the synagogue worship was we have already seen.[2]   In most of its prayers, in the reading of the Old Testament Scriptures, in the chanting of the Psalms, every Hebrew Christian could join with heart and mind. But, more especially, the opportunities furnished by the synagogues, as well as the temple, were eagerly used by the apostolic Church for carrying out the first half of the great commission, for preaching the Gospel and making disciples.   The first believers felt it to be their duty and their joy thus to be Christ's witnesses, "beginning from Jerusalem."   The gatherings at the hours of prayer in the broad courts of the temple, the freedom of speech in the synagogue, the call of its rulers "after the reading of the law and the prophets," to any deemed competent to speak "a word of exhortation for the people,"[3] were hailed by the apostles, by men like Stephen and Philip the evangelist, and by many a warm-hearted unnamed disciple, like those who were scattered abroad by the first general persecution, as so many openings given them by the Lord for telling the good news concerning Him, of which their hearts were full.   "Every day in the temple and at home," we hear of

---

[1] Acts xxi. 20-24.   Comp. Paul's own statement before Felix, that he had "come up to Jerusalem to worship; and neither in the temple did they find me disputing with any man, or stirring up a crowd, nor in the synagogues, nor in the city," xxiv. 11 f.   This certainly implies that it would have been as natural for a Christian Hebrew, who came to Jerusalem for purposes of worship, to be found in some one of the synagogues of the city as in the temple, where, in point of fact, Paul was found.

[2] See above, pp. 130-133.   [3] Acts xiii. 15.

the apostles,—and their example was doubtless followed from the first by others according to their gifts and opportunities, —"they ceased not to teach and to preach Jesus as the Christ. . . . And the Word of God increased, and the number of disciples multiplied in Jerusalem exceedingly." So we read of Saul of Tarsus, that after his conversion, "straightway in the synagogues he proclaimed Jesus, that He is the Son of God."[1]

The first persecutions arose just in connection with this witness-bearing of the apostolic Church, in the temple courts and in the synagogues. It was "as the apostles spake unto the people in Solomon's porch," that "the priests, and the captain of the temple, and the Sadducees came upon them, being sore troubled because they taught the people, and proclaimed in Jesus the resurrection from the dead, and laid hands on them, and put them in ward." The chosen champions of the Hellenistic synagogues in Jerusalem engage in disputation with Stephen, and are "not able to withstand the wisdom and the Spirit by which he spake." Then they suborn false witnesses, and "stir up the people and the elders and the scribes," and "bring him into the Sanhedrin."[2]

2nd. Meanwhile the life of the Church was deepening and gathering strength in the calmer and sweeter atmosphere of the purely Christian gatherings "at home."

The phrase itself (κατ᾽ οἶκον) is a beautiful and suggestive one.[3] In going to the temple to pray, and to bear witness for Christ, as opportunity might offer, the disciples, as we have seen, went in one company, and kept for the most part together.

Although little if at all realized at first, there was an element of separation as well as of union in their relation to their fellow-countrymen, even in their common resort to the temple and the synagogue. In spite of themselves, they did not feel so entirely "at home" there as they once had been. That little rift was soon to deepen and widen, against the will of the Hebrew believers, into a great and

[1] Acts v. 42 ; vi. 1, 7 ; ix. 20.   [2] Acts iv. 1 f. ; vi. 9 f.
[3] Acts ii. 46 ; v. 42. Comp. Rom. xvi. 5 ; 1 Cor. xvi. 19 ; Col. iv. 15 ; Philem. 2.

well-nigh impassable gulf. But "at home," the disciples
found all the peace and freedom, the loving intercourse, the
perfect sympathy, the glad, fearless confidence in each other,
which the word implies. In that hallowed upper chamber
where they met at first, with its thrilling memories of the
Lord's visible presence, and of the Spirit's first coming in
power, in the "home" to which the beloved disciple took
the mother of Jesus, in the house of Mary, the kinswoman
of Barnabas, and in many another centre gladly opened to
meet the needs of the growing thousands of the Church,
there was in full measure that joyful unbroken "fellowship"
in praise and prayer, in word and ordinance, which filled
so great a place in the new experience of the converts of
Pentecost, and which did so much to foster and strengthen in
the infant Church "the unity of the Spirit in the bond of
peace and love." [1]

Here the Lord's presence was never sought in vain. His
disciples were met as such. Avowedly, and "with one
accord," they were "gathered together in His name;" and
He was indeed "there, in the midst of them," from day
to day in grace and power. To this sacred inner circle,
made up of believers in the Lord Jesus Christ, together
with their children,—of those who had been "called out"
by the Spirit of God from the company of the rejectors of
the Saviour, and "called together" in Him,—the hearts of
the first disciples always turned as to "their own company,"
"their own people," "the brethren." [2] It was emphatically
"the Church at home," the centre of spiritual fellowship
($\dot{\eta}$ κοινωνία) in word and deed, in worship and Christian
service.

We see this twofold development of the life of the
Hebrew Christian Church, as regards its worship, most clearly

---

[1] See above, pp. 297-299, 304-307.

[2] The first words of Peter's first address in the Church of the upper chamber
give the keynote, which runs through the whole inner history of these early
years : "Ανδρις αδελφοί. Brethren! It is taken up at once by those who
"received his word" under the teaching of the Holy Ghost at Pentecost:
"They said unto Peter and the rest of the apostles, Brethren, what shall we
do?" Acts i. 16 ; ii. 37. Comp. iv. 23 : απολυθέντες δὲ ἦλθον πρὸς τοὺς ἰδίους ;
vi. 3 ; ix. 17 ; xi. 1, 29 ; xii. 17.

at Jerusalem, because the historian of the Acts, in the first section of his treatise, tells us comparatively little of what happened anywhere else. But the same process no doubt went on wherever, through our Lord's personal ministry or that of the twelve and the seventy under His guidance, or through pilgrims returning from Pentecost, a nucleus had already been formed of those "Churches of Judæa which were in Christ," to whom Saul of Tarsus—although well known in Jerusalem itself—"was still unknown by face" for years after his conversion. "The Churches of God, which are in Judæa in Christ Jesus," Paul wrote in his earliest epistle, had "suffered like things of the Jews," in the way of persecution, to those which the Thessalonian converts suffered at the hands of their Gentile fellow-countrymen.[1] In each isolated group of believers in Judæa, Samaria, and Galilee, in each congregation comprehended in that Church of the Holy Land, which is spoken of towards the end of this period as forming a collective unity,[2] this twofold life doubtless showed itself, clinging on the one hand with a touching loyalty to the synagogue, with its sacred associations and ancestral ways, until forced from it sooner or later by persistent persecutions; and, on the other hand, developing itself more freely, under the guidance of Christ's Word and Spirit, in the ἐκκλησία κατ' οἶκον, "the Church at home."

What, then, were the elements of the worship of the apostolic Church in this specifically Christian form of its development?

They are all indicated in the comprehensive summary given us of the characteristics of the Christian community, as seen especially in the converts of Pentecost. "They continued stedfastly in the apostle's teaching and in the fellowship, in the breaking of bread, and the prayers. . . . All that believed were together. . . . And day by day continuing stedfastly with one accord in the temple, and breaking bread at home (κατ' οἶκον), they did take their food with gladness and singleness of heart, praising God, and having favour with all the people."[3]

[1] Gal. i. 22; 1 Thess. ii. 14. [2] See above, p. 311. [3] Acts ii. 42, 44-47.

The inner life of the Church, after the Ascension of her Lord, went on, as it had begun, in an atmosphere of prayer and praise. From the opening scene of the hundred and twenty in the upper chamber, "all with one accord continuing stedfastly in prayer," to the closing scene in this section of the history, where we see "many gathered together" in the house of Mary "praying," the voice of united prayer rises continually in the apostolic Church. It is the unfailing resource in every difficulty and emergency in the Church's affairs,—in the choice of an apostle, in the training of young converts, in the appointment of the seven, in the consolidation of the Church among the Samaritans, for the success of the apostles' ministry in Jerusalem, when Peter and John are forbidden by the Sanhedrin to speak in the name of Jesus, when Peter is lying chained in Herod's prison, to be put to death on the morrow.[1]

Only a few fragments of these prayers are recorded, but they are enough to give us some idea of their general character. They are simple fervent utterances, breathing the Old Testament spirit of reverence and faith, combining direct petition with adoration and thanksgiving.[2]

Utterances of pure praise are also spoken of,—a setting forth by the Spirit of the "mighty works of God," "speaking with tongues and magnifying God;"[3] but of these none have been expressly handed down to us. Christ and His apostles had been wont to sing together; and Hebrew Christians, with the treasury of the Psalter in their hands and memories, and with their hearts filled with the Holy Ghost and gladness, would certainly not forget His example, nor the precept which James, the Lord's brother, wrote afterwards to the twelve tribes in the Dispersion: "Is any cheerful among you? Let him sing praise."[4]

---

[1] Acts i. 24 ; ii. 42 ; iv. 23 f., 31 ; vi. 4, 6 ; viii. 15 ; xii. 5, 12.

[2] Acts i. 24 f.; iv. 24–30.   [3] Acts ii. 4, 11, 47; x. 46; comp. xi. 15 ff.

[4] Matt. xxvi. 30 ; Jas. v. 13. On the place and significance of the Psalms in the apostolic and post-apostolic Church, I may refer to my little work, *Worship of the Presbyterian Church*, Edin. 1884, p. 21 f. The fact that so many of the Psalms seem to have been set, according to the traditional headings, to the melodies of well-known vintage and harvest songs, like that beginning "Destroy it not, for a blessing is in it" (Ps. lxv. 8), would fit them the better to give

The " Magnificat," the " Benedictus," and the " Nunc Dimittis," show us on what lines the praise of Hebrew believers, when " filled with the Spirit," was likely to shape itself when it went beyond the Psalter. Augustine calls Mary, the mother of our Lord, " nostra tympanistria." She led the song of the New Testament Church with her " Magnificat," as Miriam did that of Israel with her timbrel by the Red Sea. Of what sort the first " hymns and spiritual songs" of the apostolic Church were, we may gather, further, from such rhythmical passages as Eph. v. 14 and 1 Tim. iii. 16, which there seems reason to ascribe to this source. Like these passages, the unrecorded utterances of the first singers of the Hebrew and Gentile Christian Churches probably moved closely in the circle of the great foundation truths concerning Christ, " who He was, and from whom He came, and how He redeemed us." [1]

But the central and highest place in the worship of the Church at home was given, as before noted,[2] to " the ministry of the Word." First in the list of the spiritual characteristics of the converts of Pentecost it is recorded, that " they continued stedfastly in the apostles' teaching." [3]

As to the significance and effect of this something has been already said.[4] It may be noted further in this connection, that there is a clear distinction made in the narrative between " preaching " and " teaching," between the proclamation of the Gospel, the design of which is to make men disciples of Christ, and the instruction, the spiritual nurture and edification of those who are already disciples. It was under these two

expression to the feelings of the Hebrew believers at a time when they "rejoiced before the Lord, according to the joy in harvest." See Robertson Smith, *Old Testament in Jewish Church*, p. 190 f.

[1] Compare in this respect the earliest hymns of the post-apostolic Church, such as the " Gloria in Excelsis," the " Ter Sanctus," and the " Te Deum." Compare also Pliny's reference to the antiphonal singing of the Christians in Bithynia (A.D. 112): "On an appointed day ('stato die,' no doubt the Lord's day) they are wont to meet together before dawn to sing a hymn responsively to Christ as God (carmen Christo quasi Deo dicere secum invicem)." *Epist.* x. 97. See Bishop Lightfoot's note on Col. iii. 16, and his *Apost. Fathers—Ignatius*, i. pp. 31, 51.

[2] See above, p. 288 f.

[3] ἡ διακονία τοῦ λόγου, Acts vi. 4 ; comp. ver. 2.   [4] See above, pp. 291–297.

divisions, corresponding to the two parts of Christ's great commission to His Church, that "the ministry of the Word" was carried on.[1] The two could not, of course, be kept apart by any hard line of separation; it was natural and inevitable to pass from the one to the other. Foundation truths regarding the Saviour and the way of salvation needed constantly to be repeated, illustrated, and enforced, even in the case of those who had already professed to receive them. But, as a rule, the proclamation of the Gospel, the bearing witness to Jesus as the Son of God and the Messiah foretold in Scripture, took place in the temple courts and in the synagogues; whereas the gatherings of the Church at home formed the natural sphere for teaching and learning "all the things which Jesus had commanded;" for searching the Scriptures in the lines opened to the disciples by the risen Saviour, and followed out in the upper room before Pentecost; for utterances of the Spirit by prophets, such as Agabus, in reference to future events or present duty; and for the purposes of Christian edification generally.

In this "ministry of the Word," in the private assemblies of the brethren, as well as in speaking to mixed audiences in the temple precincts, the apostles held the foremost place. They were "from the beginning" the chief "eye-witnesses and ministers of the word, . . . concerning the things wherein catechumens were instructed."[2] The converts of Pentecost "continued stedfastly in the teaching of the apostles." It was the apostles' own sense of the weight and responsibility

---

[1] The distinction is embodied in a variety of expressions. On the one hand, we have Christ's command: Κηρύξατε τὸ εὐαγγέλιον πάσῃ τῇ κτίσει. Μαθητεύσατε πάντα τὰ ἔθνη (Mark xvi. 15; Matt. xxviii. 19), and the record of how it was fulfilled in every page of the history of the apostolic Church: Ἐκήρυξαν πανταχοῦ: Διεμαρτύρατο κ. παρεκάλει: καταγγέλλειν: εὐαγγελιζόμενοι τὸν Χριστὸν Ἰ., κ.τ.λ. (Mark xvi. 20; Acts ii. 40; iv. 2; v. 42, etc.). On the other hand, we have Christ's further commands: Διδάσκοντες αὐτοὺς τηρεῖν πάντα ὅσα ἐνετειλάμην ὑμῖν: βόσκε τὰ ἀρνία μου: ποίμαινε, βόσκε τὰ πρόβατα μου (Matt. xxviii. 20; John xxi. 15–17), and the fulfilment of these precepts also in the Church: ἦσαν προσκαρτεροῦντες τῇ διδαχῇ τῶν ἀποστόλων: διδάσκειν τὸν λαὸν κ. καταγγέλλειν: οὐκ ἐπαύοντο διδάσκοντες κ. εὐαγγελιζόμενοι τὸν Χ. Ἰ.: ἡ ἐκκλησία . . . οἰκοδομουμένη κ. πορευομένη τῷ φόβῳ τοῦ κυρίου κ. τῇ παρακλήσει τοῦ Ἁγίου πνεύματος, κ.τ.λ. (Acts ii. 42; iv. 2; v. 42; ix. 31, etc.)

[2] Luke i. 2–4.

of this special function of theirs which led, as we shall see more in detail presently, to the first steps being taken towards further organization in the Church. "It is not fit," they said to the multitude of the disciples, "that we should forsake the Word of God and serve tables. . . . We will continue sted-fastly in prayer and in the ministry of the Word." [1]

But from the very first the work of proclaiming the Gospel and of edifying the Church is not carried on by the twelve alone. The gifts of the Holy Ghost at Pentecost are bestowed on the whole company of disciples in the upper chamber. "They were all filled with the Holy Spirit, and began to speak with other tongues, as the Spirit gave them utterance," "speaking the mighty works of God," so that men of all nations received the message "each in his own language." [2] This one particular characteristic of the "first speaking with tongues" may, indeed, have been a sign distinguishing the first advent of the Spirit in connection with that representative gathering of "men from every nation under heaven." It does not appear to have accompanied the "glossolalia" in the Church at Corinth, to which Paul refers so often in his first epistle to the Corinthians. There is in fact no evidence whatever of its being continued or repeated at any other point in the history of the apostolic Church, with one possible exception, namely, in the account of what took place in the house of Cornelius, when the same apostle who spoke to the multitude of Jews and proselytes at Pentecost preached for the first time the same Gospel to the Gentiles. [3] But whether with or without

---

[1] Acts vi. 2, 4.

[2] Acts ii. 4, 6-8, 11. Cremer holds that ver. 4 is to be understood as meaning "they began to speak with other languages," but hesitates to con-clude that this implies a speaking foreign languages, not learned in the usual way. He prefers the hypothesis of "a language produced by the Holy Ghost, specially for intercourse with God, which blended in one comprehensive expression, the various languages of mankind." *Lexicon of N. T. Greek*, 3rd ed. p. 163 f.

[3] The fact of the Gentiles "speaking with tongues" through the pouring out of the Holy Spirit upon them, "even as on us at the beginning," is referred to by Peter both at the time and afterwards in such a way as to give the impression that the phenomena of Pentecost had remained unique hitherto in the experi-ence of the Hebrew Christian Church, and that now for the first time did they

the special signs which marked the coming of the Holy
Ghost at Pentecost, there was no restriction of His gifts to
the twelve alone.   After Peter and John had returned from
being examined and threatened by the Sanhedrin "to their
own company," . . . "They, when they heard the report of
the apostles, lifted up their voice to God with one accord," . . .
"And when they had prayed, the place was shaken wherein
they were gathered together; and they were all filled with
the Holy Ghost, and they spake the Word of God with
boldness. . . . And with great power gave the apostles their
witness of the resurrection of the Lord Jesus: and great grace
was upon them all." [1]

The prediction of Joel regarding the Messianic times,
which Peter had cited in his first address to the multitude,
was fulfilled continually in the experience of the Hebrew
Christian Church.   "Their sons and their daughters did
prophesy."

From the scantiness of our materials for information a
good deal of obscurity rests upon several questions as to the
nature of these prophesyings, and as to the points of resem-
blance and difference between the prophets and prophetesses
of the New Testament and those of the Old.   One thing,
however, may be noted here, that the chief, though probably
not the exclusive sphere for the exercise of prophetic gifts

fully recur.   The speaking with tongues at Cæsarea may not, indeed, have gone
beyond such rapturous and ecstatic utterances as we hear of at Corinth.   But
it may, on the other hand, have been in all respects parallel with the "glossolalia" of Pentecost, and have included utterances in language and dialects
hitherto unknown to the speakers.   It may have been on this account that
the repetition now of the Pentecostal gifts in their entirety was hailed by the
apostle as such an unmistakeable sign and seal from heaven, a clear token that
it was the will of God that these Gentiles should be admitted at once to the
same privileges as had been vouchsafed to Jewish believers in connection with
the first advent of the Spirit at Pentecost.   This would explain the more easily
how it was at once accepted in that light also by "them that were of the
circumcision" at Jerusalem, when Peter "expounded the matter unto them"
in his own defence.   Comp. Acts x. 45–47 with xi. 15–18.   "It was the
Pentecost of the Gentiles. . . . God would put the alien and so long 'unclean'
nations on a platform no less high than that of the Jerusalem mother Church.
He would authenticate by as solemn a Baptism from heaven their admission
into the household and kingdom of His Son."   Dykes, *From Jerusalem to
Antioch*, 4th ed. p. 379 f.

    [1] Acts iv. 23 f., 31, 33.

in apostolic times, was in the Christian assemblies "at home." Save in the case of predictions of judgment by the apostles themselves, it is in that sphere alone that we have any instances recorded of Christian prophesyings at all. Agabus and the other "prophets which came down from Jerusalem unto Antioch" evidently spoke there, as they had been wont to do in the mother Church, in the meetings of the disciples. This holds good also of the second appearance of Agabus in the history, when he came down from Judæa and joined in the fellowship of the disciples at Cæsarea, in the house of "Philip the evangelist," who "had four daughters, virgins, which did prophesy." [1]

The apostle Paul himself heard both the recorded utterances of this prophet from Jerusalem. He had the best means of knowing the nature and design of prophecy, both in the Hebrew Christian and in the Gentile Churches, and no doubt speaks with respect to both when he says : " He that prophesieth speaketh unto men edification, and exhortation, and comfort ($\lambda a\lambda\epsilon\hat{\iota}$ $o\hat{\iota}\kappa o\delta o\mu\dot{\eta}v$ κ. $\pi a\rho\acute{a}\kappa\lambda\eta\sigma\iota v$ κ. $\pi a\rho a\mu\upsilon\theta\acute{\iota}av$). He that speaketh in a tongue edifieth himself ; but he that prophesieth, edifieth the Church. . . . Prophesying is for a sign, not to the unbelieving, but to them that believe." [2]

Closely akin to the gift of prophecy, if not absolutely blending into it, were spiritual gifts such as those possessed by Joseph of Cyprus, which gained for him from the apostles at Jerusalem the name of " Barnabas," "a son of exhortation." He seems not to have been endowed, like Paul, with eloquence, or with the power of giving closely-reasoned addresses.[3] The special gift which distinguished Barnabas in the Christian assemblies was that of warm and loving counsel and appeal, "that word of exhortation growing into a word of comfort, which only the Holy Ghost can give to the preacher." [4] It was this gift which Barnabas used with such

[1] Acts xi. 27 f. Comp. xiii. 1 f. ; xxi. 8-11.

[2] 1 Cor. xiv. 3 f., 22.

[3] Observe the impression made by the two respectively upon the barbarous people of Lycaonia. "They called Barnabas Jupiter and Paul Mercury, because he was the chief speaker," Acts xiv. 12.

[4] "Both these ideas," Dr. Dykes adds, "must be held fast in the $\pi a\rho\acute{a}\kappa\lambda\eta\sigma\iota\varsigma$,

happy effects among the new converts from the Gentiles in
the Church at Antioch, when "he exhorted them all (παρεκάλει πάντας) that with purpose of heart they would cleave
unto the Lord. For he was a good man, and full of the
Holy Ghost and of faith." And then, seeing the need at
Antioch of gifts and attainments beyond what he himself
possessed, with characteristic humility and singleness of heart,
Barnabas "went forth to Tarsus to seek for Saul . . . and
it came to pass that even for a whole year they were
gathered together with the Church (ἐν τῇ ἐκκλησίᾳ), and
taught much people (διδάξαι ὄχλον ἱκανόν)." [1]

Less known disciples exercised kindred gifts "for edification, exhortation, and comfort," "as the Spirit gave them
utterance" in the free and kindly atmosphere of the Church
at home. "The fellowship" into which the converts of
Pentecost were welcomed, and in which they abode so stedfastly, was one which took voice, and uttered itself in words
as well as deeds of Christian love and helpfulness. "The
teaching of the apostles" came first. As "faithful and wise
stewards," whom their Lord had "set over His household,"
they themselves "gave them their portion of food in due
season," [2] and took the guidance and oversight of all that
was done in this sphere. But many besides Barnabas came
forward to lay spiritual contributions as well as money at
the apostles' feet. In respect of spiritual gifts and religious
experience, of insight into the meaning of the Word and
the Providence of God, as well as in respect of more outward matters, "all that believed were together, were of one
heart and soul, and had all things common." [3]

Now it is true, as has been urged, that these characteristics
and developments of the worship of the Hebrew Christian

---

from which the Holy Spirit borrows His most characteristic New Testament
title." *From Jerusalem to Antioch*, 4th ed. p. 335.

[1] Acts xi. 23 f., 26.   [2] Luke xii. 42.

[3] Acts ii. 42–47 ; iv. 31-37. The spirit and practice of the apostolic Church
in this respect are reflected in an interesting way in one of the precepts
given to catechumens in the *Teaching of the Twelve Apostles*. "Thou
shalt seek out from day to day the faces of the saints, that thou mayest be
refreshed by their words," iv. 2. Harnack, *Texte u. Untersuchungen*, ii. 1,
S. 14.

Church arose from the presence and working of the Holy Spirit in and with the apostles and the other believers. But it is true also—and it has not been sufficiently considered by many writers—that the Spirit was guiding them in ways marked out beforehand by the Word and the Providence of God.[1] The spiritual life of the Church availed itself of these forms and modes of worship, doing so naturally, as it were, and without constraint, under the impulse of that Spirit of the Lord, who is the Spirit of freedom. But the forms themselves had been moulded and proved for centuries in the Holy Land and the Diaspora. The men who took part in the services of the first Christian assemblies had been trained and prepared to do so by personal and hereditary experience. Whether Jews or proselytes, they had done the like, or seen and heard it done by others, ever since they first learned to call for themselves upon the name of the God of Abraham, and Isaac, and Israel. The worship of the apostolic Church at home was just in substance the worship of the Hebrew synagogue or proseucha.

Two new institutions were added to what the first disciples and the converts of Pentecost had been used to in the synagogue services, Baptism and the Lord's Supper. But these, as we have seen, grew directly out of previous ordinances of Divine

---

[1] Rothe, *e.g.*, holds that the Christians had no cultus of their own in the proper sense until after the destruction of Jerusalem. See his *De primordiis cultûs Christianorum*, Bonn 1851. Even Lechler puts the case in a one-sided way when he says : "Der urchristliche Gemeinde Gottesdienst hat sich ohne ausdrückliche Einsetzung des Erlösers, ohne gesetzliche Vorschrift, ohne bewussten Plan, von innen heraus, so zu sagen autonom gemacht ; er ist das freie Erzeugniss der Triebkraft des Geistes, wie Harnack [Th. Harnack, *Christl. Gemeinde Gottesdienst im apost. u. altkath. Zeitalter*, S. 111 ff.] mit vollem Recht bemerkt," *Apost. u. nachap. Zeitalt.*, 3te Ausg. S. 41. Dr. Dykes also fails to give due consideration to the facts to which I refer. "The characteristic of the earliest believers," he says, "was that they had no model, worked without precedent, and let rules arise as they were required. . . . Life shaped forms for itself as it wanted them. The Church took its external mould under the slow pressure of Providence. Through the inward impulse of Christ's Spirit it grew as living things grow, freely, variously, everywhere." *From Jerusalem to Antioch*, p. 464 f. Dean Plumptre arrives at a sounder conclusion : "It would hardly be an exaggeration to say that the worship of the Church was identical with that of the synagogue, modified (1) by the new truths, (2) by the new institution of the Supper of the Lord, (3) by the spiritual charismata." Art. "Synagogue," in Smith's *Bible Dict.* iii. p. 1400a.

appointment in the Old Testament Church. And there was a new life from above breathing through all the elements of the service. But these elements themselves were the same. There was praise in the hallowed words of the Hebrew Psalter, sung or chanted to familiar and long-descended melodies; praise also in warm and rapturous utterances by the Spirit, which yet, so far as we can gather from such fragments as have reached us, clothed themselves for the most part in grave and Scriptural language drawn from the Old Testament prophets and psalmists.[1] There was prayer at every gathering of the Hebrew believers to the Lord God of their fathers. There were the reading and exposition of the Old Testament, of "the things written in Moses, and the Psalms, and the Prophets concerning the Christ." There were opportunities for free speech on Scripture questions, and for the interchange of spiritual experiences, for "the word of exhortation to the people" by fitting men.

These were just the features of the synagogue services with which every disciple of Jewish birth had been familiar from childhood, with which every proselyte from the Gentiles associated the dawn of his religious life and its happiest experiences. The men who first stood up at the call of the apostles, or with an assenting sign from them, to read the Scriptures, to pray or to offer a word of exhortation in the gatherings of the Hebrew Christian Church, were the very men who had been used to do the same at the call of the rulers of the synagogues, in which they had hitherto been wont to worship every Sabbath day. They were such as Nicodemus, Joseph of Arimathæa, Barnabas, and Manaen the foster-brother of the tetrarch. Some of these men, like the two first named and Saul of Tarsus, had themselves been "rulers of the Jews" and "teachers of Israel" in the synagogue and Sanhedrin. They had been used to take their place as a matter of course on the seat set apart for "the doctors," "the wise men and scribes," the "teachers of Israel."[2] The loving deference of their brethren naturally

---

[1] Comp. the "prayer-hymn," as it has been called, in Acts iv. 24–30. Lechler, S. 119 ; and see above, p. 354 f.

[2] Matt. xxvii. 57 ; Mark xv. 43 ; xxiii. 50 f. ; Luke ii. 46 ; John iii. 1 f.,

set such men from the first in a like position in the Christian assemblies. They were obviously fitted to fill it aright by their approved gifts and by their Providential preparation and training, all now quickened and turned to the highest account by the breath of the Spirit of God. Such "leaders among the brethren"[1] proved themselves in the temple courts and in the meetings of the Church at home to be "scribes made disciples unto the kingdom of heaven, bringing forth out of their treasure things new and old."[2]

The seal of the Divine blessing was signally given to the words of these men. The crown was set upon the old synagogue system of worship by the Lord raising up in connection with it, among His disciples, "prophets" such as were seen in Israel in the days when that system first arose by the rivers of Babylon, and among those who returned to the Holy Land with Ezra and Nehemiah. The Saviour's promise at the close of His own earthly ministry was manifestly fulfilled: "Behold, I send unto you prophets, and wise men, and scribes."[3] They might be opposed and rejected, as the Lord had foretold, when they spoke in the Jewish synagogue gatherings. There was all the more reason why the disciples of Christ should joyfully welcome and honour them in theirs.

The name "synagogue," and the technical terms of its service, continued for years, and indeed for generations, on Hebrew Christian ground, and in the language of leaders of the Church, such as James, the Lord's brother, to be used as the natural and appropriate names for the Christian assembly and its arrangements for worship. "My brethren," James writes to the twelve tribes which are of the Dispersion, "hold not the faith of our Lord Jesus Christ, the Lord of glory, with respect of persons. For if there come into your synagogue a man with a gold ring in fine clothing . . . and ye say, Sit thou here in a good place, and say to the poor, Stand thou there, or sit here under my footstool, do ye not

---

10 ; vii. 50 f. ; xix. 38 f. ; Acts xiii. 1 f. Such action on the part of Paul and Barnabas in the synagogue of Antioch, in Pisidia, would explain how the rulers recognised them at once as men to whom an opportunity of speech, a "facultas docendi," should be given. Acts xiii. 14 f.

[1] ἄνδρας ἡγουμένους ἐν τοῖς ἀδελφοῖς, Acts xv. 22. Comp. ver. 32.
[2] Matt. xiii. 52.   [3] Matt. xxiii. 34.

make distinctions, and become judges with evil thoughts?"
He warns his readers against the very abuses to which the
freedom of speech granted within certain limits by the Jewish
synagogue system was specially liable, and to which the same
system in the Jewish Christian Church was likewise exposed.
"Be not many teachers, my brethren, knowing that we shall
receive heavier judgment. . . . If any stumbleth not in word,
the same is a perfect man. . . . Let every man be swift to
hear, slow to speak, slow to wrath. . . . Who is a wise man
(σοφός) and understanding among you? Let him show by
his good life his works in meekness of wisdom. . . . For
where jealousy and faction are, there is confusion and every
vile deed."[1] So, too, the author of the Epistle to the Hebrews
urges the Jewish Christians to whom he wrote: "Forsake
not the assembling of yourselves together (τὴν ἐπισυναγωγὴν
ἑαυτῶν), as the custom of some is; but exhort one another,
and so much the more as ye see the day drawing nigh."[2]

3rd. Observance of the two Christian sacraments, and of
the Lord's Day.

1. Baptism.

We have already considered the nature and meaning of this
ordinance of Christ, and who were the subjects of it in the

[1] Jas. i. 19 ; ii. 1-3 ; iii. 1 f., 13, 16. See above, pp. 130-133. "Even in
patristic literature συναγωγή is sometimes used for the Christian congregation
(Harnack, *Zeitschr. für wissenschaftl. Theol.* 1876, S. 104 ff., and his note on
Hermas' *Mandat.* xi. 9, in Gebhardt and Harnack's ed. of the *Patr. Apostol.*).
In Christian Palestinian Aramaic, כנישתא, which answers to the Greek
συναγωγή, seems to have been the usual word for Church (see Land, *Anecdota
Syriaca*, iv. p. 217. Zahn, *Tatian's Diatessaron*, p. 335). Schürer, ii. p. 58.
"Nam profecto," Augustine says in reference to the conduct of the Jews in
putting the disciples of Christ out of the synagogues, "quia non erat ullus alius
populus Dei quam illud semen Abrahæ, si agnoscerent et reciperent Christum,
tanquam rami naturales in olea permanerent (Rom. xi. 17) ; nec aliæ fierent
Ecclesiæ Christi, aliæ synagogæ Judæorum ; eædem quippe essent, si in eodem
esse voluissent," *Tract. in Joann.* xciii. 2.

[2] Heb. x. 25. See above, pp. 339-341. It may be added here, that the
injunction to mutual "exhortation" (παρακαλοῦντες), given also in iii. 13.
"Exhort one another day by day," corresponds exactly both in phrase and
substance to the synagogue usage as we have seen it carried out by the
Hebrew Christians at Jerusalem. "Jeder ist an seinem Theil durch Wort
u. Vorbild zur Erbauung der Gemeinde beizutragen verpflichtet," Delitzsch,
Hebräerbrief, S. 491.

apostolic Church.[1] Let us consider now the place which it holds in the history of this period, the manner in which it is spoken of, and the indications which we have regarding the mode in which Baptism was administered and the persons by whom it was dispensed.

(1.) It is evident at the first glance how closely Baptism is associated, from the earliest mention of it in the Acts, with the coming and work of the Holy Ghost. The apostle Peter in his address at Pentecost holds out "the gift of the Holy Ghost" to all who should "repent and be baptized in the name of Jesus Christ unto the remission of their sins; for to you is the promise, and to your children. . . . Then they that received his word were baptized; and there were added to them in that day about three thousand souls."[2] Baptism was thus the outward sign of the inward change of heart and spirit wrought by the Holy Ghost in every man who truly "received the word" concerning "the name of Jesus Christ" as it was proclaimed by the apostles. It accompanied and sealed his public confession of faith in Christ and obedience to Him. Baptism with water "in the name of the Lord Jesus," or in the threefold name of God as revealed in and by Him, was the fitting embodiment in well-known Scriptural symbols of the new and blessed relation into which the believer and his house were now brought with God in Christ as the Giver of the Holy Spirit. It was "a visible Word" from the Lord, as when He said to one who had "received Him joyfully:" "This day is salvation come to this house; forasmuch as he also is a son of Abraham." "The promise," and the sign of the promise, "was to him and to his children." "The blessing of Abraham had come upon him in Christ Jesus, that he might receive the promise of the Spirit through faith," receiving it for himself and for all family duties and relations.[3]

The true connection between the sign and the thing signified—between Baptism with water and Baptism with the Spirit—is brought out with unmistakeable clearness in the account of "the Pentecost of the Gentiles" in the house of

---

[1] See above, pp. 319-327. [2] Acts ii. 38, 41.
[3] Luke xix. 6, 9 ; Acts ii. 39 ; Gal. iii. 14.

Cornelius at Cæsarea. "As I began to speak," Peter said when reporting the matter to the Church at Jerusalem, "the Holy Ghost fell on them, even as on us at the beginning. And I remembered the word of the Lord, how that He said, John indeed baptized with water, but ye shall be baptized with the Holy Ghost. If, then, God gave unto them the like gift as He did also unto us when we believed on the Lord Jesus Christ, who was I that I could withstand God ? " [1]

Nothing could be plainer than the teaching of this passage, as of that which records the Baptism of Simon the soothsayer. There is no essential connection between the external rite of Baptism and the inward work of the Holy Spirit. The one may be where the other is not. They stand to each other as the sign and the thing signified. Cornelius and his friends had received neither the Old Testament nor the New Testament ordinance of admission into the Church of God. They were neither circumcised nor baptized. Yet beyond all question, as the apostle felt, they were "acceptable to God," members of Christ's Church and " in fullest communion with the Head, since they have been introduced into fellowship by Christ's own hand, and sealed with His seal. Who can forbid the water, where He has not withheld the Spirit ? " [2] Baptism with water was not the means, nor even the accompaniment, of these men's receiving the Baptism with the Spirit. But it followed as a fitting sign and seal where the substance of the blessing had been so manifestly and richly given. "Wherever, therefore, we find the fruits of the Holy Spirit of Christ, there on the authority of an apostle we are bound to recognise the Church of Christ—'ubi Christus ibi ecclesia.' Churches which unchurch communions of believing and holy men because their ecclesiastical order is (supposed to be) not valid nor their episcopal descent continuous, appear on these principles to be guilty, not only of folly, but of schism. They misunderstand and then they rend the spiritual body of Christ. But if hierarchism and high-churchism accord ill with the transactions at Cæsarea, it fares little better with the

[1] Acts xi. 15–17 ; comp. i. 5.

[2] τὸ ὕδωρ . . . τὸ πνεῦμα, Acts x. 47. Dykes, *From Jerusalem to Antioch*, 4th ed. p. 380.

ultra-spiritualism of those who despise Church order or deem
of no account the due administration of the holy sacraments.
Never save on that solitary occasion did the special gift of the
Holy Ghost precede the Baptism of a convert. Even on that
occasion the exceptional presence of the thing signified did
not render superfluous the observance of the sign. God is
not bound even to His own order ; nor can Baptism possess
any magical virtue to confer what God conferred without it.
Yet the Church even then followed in the steps of her Lord,
ratifying by her outward act what He had already done by
inward grace." [1]

We may compare with this passage another which, though
it belongs in point of date to the second section of the Acts,
yet refers to men who were probably Hebrew Christians, and
who in point of religious training and experience belonged to
the Church of the first days. At the beginning of Paul's
work in Ephesus, he " found there certain disciples," men
recognised as believers in Jesus and in fellowship with the
infant Church of the place. " And he said unto them, Did
ye receive a gift of the Holy Ghost when ye believed ? And
they said unto him, Nay, we did not so much as hear whether
there is such a bestowment of the Holy Ghost.[2] And he
said, Into what then were ye baptized ? And they said,
Into John's Baptism." On the apostle's explaining to them
in what relation John's preaching and Baptism stood to faith
in Jesus, " they were baptized into the name of the Lord Jesus.
And when Paul had laid his hands upon them, the Holy Ghost
came on them, and they spake with tongues and prophesied."

It will be seen at once in what an interesting and suggestive

---

[1] Dykes, p. 381. The fact to be referred to presently (p. 374), that
Peter left the administration of the sacrament of Baptism in the house of
Cornelius to the six brethren from Joppa, is in perfect accordance with the subordinate position to be assigned to the ordinance. The apostle had declared to
the centurion "words whereby he should be saved, he and all his house"
(c. xi. 14). By preaching the Gospel, Peter had done by God's blessing the
essential spiritual work, and had seen the seal of the Holy Ghost set upon it
from heaven. The mere outward rite, which expressed and embodied in
symbol what had taken place, might well be left to other hands. Comp. 1 Cor.
i. 14-17.

[2] εἰ πνεῦμα ἅγιον ἐλάβετε πιστεύσαντες . . . . ἀλλ' οὐδὲ εἰ πνεῦμα ἅγιόν ἐστιν
ἠκούσαμεν, Acts xix. 2. See above, pp. 195 f., 271 f.

light this sets the sacrament of Baptism as administered to
the infant seed of God's people.   The believing father and
mother are placed in a new position with new responsibilities,
through God's gift to them of children.   They are called
accordingly to cast themselves afresh by faith upon the covenant grace of God in Christ, and upon the foundation promise of the covenant : "I will be a God unto thee and to thy
seed after thee."   They feel their special need of the gifts
and power of the Holy Spirit for themselves and for their
child, that they may have grace and wisdom to take this little
one and nurse and train it for the Lord.   Their heart's desire
and prayer for the child is that from the very first he may be
" washed and sanctified and justified in the name of the Lord
Jesus Christ and in the Spirit of our God." [1]   The Lord's
answer to such desires and petitions of His servants is given
in the apostle's assurance to those children of Abraham to
whom he spoke at Pentecost, and in the ordinance in direct
connection with which his words were spoken : " The promise is to you and to your children."   Baptism is the sign
and seal of the promise in this special relation in which you
stand now.   You are to receive it as such.   " If ye are
Christ's, then are ye Abraham's seed, and heirs according to
the promise."   " The blessing of Abraham has come upon the
Gentiles in Christ Jesus that ye might receive the promise of
the Spirit—for yourselves and for your children—through
faith."   " Ask, and ye shall receive."   " If ye shall ask anything in My name, I will do it."   " If ye being evil know
how to give good gifts unto your children, how much more
shall your heavenly Father give the Holy Spirit to them
that ask Him." [2]

(2.) What was the mode of Baptism in the apostolic Church ?

From the nature of the case, and from the whole spirit of
the narrative in the passages which refer to the administration
of Baptism, it is evident that this question, from the standpoint of Scripture, is an entirely subordinate one.   The
questions to which importance is attached by our Lord and
His apostles are such as these : Into what name and unto

[1] 1 Cor. vi. 11.

[2] Gen. xvii. 7 ; Acts ii. 38 f. ; Gal. iii. 14, 29 ; Matt. vii. 11 ; Luke xi. 13.

what gifts is any one baptized ?   In what spirit and on what grounds ought the applicant to seek the ordinance for himself and those that are his ?   What are the true answers to these questions we have already seen.   Further, we learn from the analogy of the Old Testament ordinances for puri- fication, and from such words as those of Peter lately cited, that Baptism is to be with water, as the Scriptural symbol of the Holy Spirit in His purifying and renewing power. But as to how the element is to be applied, and how much of it is to be used in Baptism, no express rule is given; and no instance is recorded in the New Testament where the precise mode can be said to be more than a matter of probable inference.[1]   The natural conclusion is, that the mode is simply a question of Christian expediency, to be decided according to circumstances and in conformity with the two great New Testament canons for the minor arrange- ments of worship.   " Let all things be done unto edification : "

[1] One may still occasionally hear strong assertions, that to " baptize " means to immerse and nothing but to immerse; that " the mode here is the ordin- ance," and that no one therefore is or ever was baptized who was not immersed. That view has passed into an accepted tradition in some quarters; but like many other traditions it is quite unreliable, and has been conclusively dis- proved.   The question is not as to the use of the word βαπτίζω and its cognates in the classics, but in Hellenistic Greek, such as that of the LXX., of the New Testament, and of most of the Greek fathers of the early centuries. Now it is quite clear that these writers repeatedly speak of sprinklings and pourings of different sorts as " baptisms," e.g. the sprinkling of the " water of purification," of the ashes of the heifer, of the blood of lambs, etc. ; and further, that they often use the word " baptize " in a general sense, as meaning to wash or purify in any way, whether by sprinkling, pouring, or immersion. There are other Greek words which mean to " immerse and nothing but immerse," such as καταδύω and ἐνδύω ; and it is worth noting that the early ecclesiastical writers sometimes use these terms when they wish to call attention to the point that the Baptism of which they speak took place by immersion, as was in point of fact the general custom in the post-apostolic age.   The very fact that they do so is a proof that Baptism might be by other modes.   These terms might have been used by our Lord and His apostles to show the mode of Bap- tism which Christians were to use.   In that case there could have been no difference of opinion.   But the N. T. does not use these words in reference to the ordinance.   It uses the words " baptize " and " baptism," which in that age were undoubtedly used in several senses, and very often to denote " washing " or " purifying " generally.   Comp. President Beecher, *Baptism with reference to its Import and Modes*, New York 1849, pp. 160-168, 171-176, 188, 197-203, 263, 308-316.   Bannerman, *Church of Christ*, ii. pp. 121-127.   Cremer, *Biblico- Theol. Lexicon of N. T. Greek*, 3rd English ed. p. 127.

"Let all things be done in seemly form, and according to order."[1]

One thing seems very clear from the accounts of cases of Baptism that meet us both in the first and second sections of the Acts, that the ordinance must have been administered in some way in which it could be easily done. We never hear of any difficulties or delays. The three thousand are baptized at Pentecost, in a city which has no natural water supply but from wells, at the height of the dry season, when water is always most scarce and precious, and at a time when Jerusalem was crowded with pilgrims, and all the reservoirs would be carefully guarded. There may have been, in some way which we cannot explain, some means of immersing those thousands who were added to the Church in that day ; but we are not told that they were immersed, and the circumstances seem much against it.[2]

Saul of Tarsus, but that moment restored from three days of fasting and prostration, "stood up," on the bidding of Ananias, "and was baptized ; and he took food, and was strengthened."[3]

There is a crowded meeting in the house of Cornelius ; in all likelihood of both sexes, "many being come together" of the centurion's "kinsmen and near friends." Peter preaches the Gospel to them. The Holy Ghost is poured out "on all them which heard the word." The apostle asks, "Can any

---

[1] 1 Cor. xiv. 26, 40. Comp. my little work, *The Worship of the Presbyterian Church*, Edin. 1884, pp. 3–6.

[2] "Why might they not be baptized in the brook Kedron," Dr. Carson asks, "going farther up the stream if it was polluted near the city ?" (*Baptism in its Mode and Subjects*, p. 167). For a very plain reason. Because the brook Kedron at Jerusalem, as its very name (ὁ χείμαρρος) implies, is, and always has been, a "winter-torrent," and flows only for a few months in the wet season. At Pentecost, and for months before it, there is not a drop of water in it. It is commonly used as a bridle-road. There was no resource in that quarter, and no stream that would have served the purpose nearer than the Jordan. The conclusion of one of the latest commentators is a more reasonable one : "Die Taufe ist wohl nicht als in Form einer eigentlichen Massentaufe erfolgt zu denken, sondern als allmählich u. an verschiedenen Orten im Laufe des Pfingsttags (u. zwar gemäss Διδαχὴ τῶν ἀποστ. vii. 2, 3, unter Anwendung teils des Immersions teils des Adspersionsritus), zum Vollzug gelangt." Zöckler, *Apostelgeschichte*, Nördlingen 1886, S. 164.

[3] Acts ix. 18 f.

man forbid the water, that these should not be baptized which have received of the Holy Ghost as well as we?"[1] And the converts, men and women, are baptized then and there, as it appears, by the six brethren who came with Peter from Joppa, without difficulty or inconvenience. The Philippian jailor is converted at midnight. Roman prisons in a provincial town were not likely to be supplied with luxurious appliances for bathing. There was no time for preparation. Yet there seems to have been no more difficulty about producing all the water needful for the Baptism of several persons, than there was in bringing water to wash the stripes of the apostle and his companion. "He took them the same hour of the night and washed their stripes; and was baptized, he and all his, immediately."[2]

In such cases as these, there is, to say the least, a strong probability, rising in some instances—that of Cornelius, for example—almost to a moral certainty, that the application of water was in some simple way, as by sprinkling or pouring. John's baptisms at Jordan, on the other hand, were probably by immersion. And in the case of the Ethiopian treasurer, whom Philip baptized "on the way that goeth down from Jerusalem unto Gaza, which is desert," the ordinance may have been administered by immersion, or by the candidate standing in a shallow pool, while the evangelist poured water on his head,[3] as in some of the earliest Christian pictures in the catacombs,—that, for instance, in the cemetery of St. Calixtus, which is held by De Rossi to belong to the second century.[4]

All Scripture evidence bearing on the question of the mode of Baptism, leads us to the conclusion that the view held in all the Reformed Churches, except the "Baptist"

---

[1] Μήτι τὸ ὕδωρ κωλῦσαι δύναταί τις τοῦ μὴ βαπτισθῆναι τούτους. "The expression is interesting," Dean Alford remarks on the verse, "as showing that the practice was *to bring the water to the candidates, not the candidates to the water*. This, which would be implied by the word under any circumstances, is rendered certain when we remember that they were assembled *in the house*."

[2] Acts xvi. 33.   [3] Chap. viii. 26, 36-39.

[4] See Marriott's art. "Baptism," in Smith and Cheetham's *Dict. of Christ. Antiquities*, i. p. 168 ff. Comp. the passage as to mode of Baptism from the recently discovered "Teaching of the Apostles," quoted below.

denomination, is the correct one, that baptism by immersion,
although perfectly lawful, is not necessary, and is very generally inexpedient.   It is never enjoined in Scripture; and it
cannot be proved from Scripture that it was even the common
mode in the New Testament times.   In several instances in
the apostolic history, as we have seen, the strong presumption
is that the ordinance was administered in some other way
than by immersion.   An interesting confirmation of this
view is given by the very earliest reference to the mode of
Baptism which meets us when we pass beyond the New
Testament writings.   "The Teaching of the Twelve Apostles"
is variously dated by the most competent scholars as belonging to the end of the first century or first half of the second.
There is general agreement that it proceeded from some
Jewish Christian community, whether in Egypt or Syria,
being "an intensely Jewish document."[1]   It is the more
fitted to assist our interpretation of the Scripture account of
the practices of the Jewish Christian Church during the
period covered by the Acts.   The author of this "genuine
fragment of the earliest tradition of the Church," as it has
been called by one of our greatest living authorities on such
subjects,[2] testifies to the existence in his time, "in the primitive age in which Christianity had but just separated itself
from the parent stock of Judaism," of at least two modes of
Baptism, by immersion and by pouring or affusion, and he
evinces not the slightest doubt that the one is as valid as
the other.   After speaking of the preliminary instructions
needful for converts from heathenism, he says: "And as
touching Baptism, thus baptize ye: when ye have first recited

---

[1] Salmon, *Lecture on Non-Canonical Books*, Lond. 1886, p. 57.   There is
much to be said in favour of Dr. Salmon's theory, adopted and further
developed by Harnack, "that the author of the 'Didache' has taken a
Jewish manual of instruction for proselytes, and has adapted it for Christian
use, by additions of his own; in particular, by insertions from the Sermon
on the Mount."   In such a Jewish handbook there would probably be rules
for Baptism, Fasting, Prayer, the First-Fruits, Care of the Poor, etc., corresponding to what we have in the Jewish Christian Manual, the "Teaching
of the Apostles."   See Harnack, *Die Apostel-Lehre u. die jüdischen Beiden
Wege*, Leipzig 1886, S. 27-32.   C. Taylor, *Teaching of the Twelve Apostles*,
Camb. 1886, pp. 6-30.

[2] Dr. Taylor, *ut supra*, p. 118.

all these things, baptize unto the name of the Father, and of the Son, and of the Holy Ghost in living water. But if thou have not living water, baptize into other water; and if thou canst not in cold, then in warm. And if thou have not either, pour forth water thrice upon the head unto the name of the Father, and Son, and Holy Ghost." [1]

(3.) By whom was Baptism administered?

During the time of Christ's public work, although He Himself did not baptize, His apostles did so in His name, in cases where men through His ministry had been "made disciples." [2]

The twelve probably continued to administer the ordinance, so far as this did not interfere with what they regarded as their

---

[1] "Teaching of the Twelve Apostles," c. vii. I quote from Dr. C. Taylor's translation. It is evident from this passage that at the time and in the circle of its author, the normal or favourite mode of baptism was by immersion in "living," *i.e.* fresh and running water; but that where water was scarce, as in a private house, a prison, or a catacomb, it was held equally lawful to baptize by pouring or sprinkling water on the head in the name of the Trinity. Comp. Schaff, *Oldest Church Manual*, Edin. 1885, p. 32 f. "We learn here that in the post-apostolic age a degree of freedom prevailed on the mode of Baptism, which was afterwards somewhat restricted. From this fact we may reason *a fortiori* that the same freedom existed already in the apostolic age. It cannot be supposed that the twelve apostles were less liberal than the writer of the 'Didache,' who wrote as it were in their name," p. 34. The term βαπτίζω, almost invariably in classic Greek and often in Hellenistic, means to immerse, although in the latter especially, as already shown, it is often used in other senses. Baptism by immersion must be always held — as it is by all branches of the Church — to be a perfectly lawful mode of administering the ordinance; and as an ecclesiastical custom it is interesting from its antiquity. It became almost universal in the early Church, when persecution ceased in the third century and beginning of the fourth, and it became possible to erect great baptisteries, and have suitable arrangements, with curtains, etc., for the convenient Baptism of men and women. The catechumens were baptized "in a state of absolute nakedness" in great numbers at Easter and other feasts of the Church, with elaborate ritual of all sorts. Immersion, generally three times repeated, lent itself readily to such ceremonial and to the allegorizing tendencies of the patristic writers. It was identified in the most absolute way with regeneration; and the significance of this precise mode of Baptism came to be insisted on in language of the wildest extravagance. Comp. Marriott, art. "Baptism," *ut supra*, pp. 157-164. Any one who considers the language used on this subject, even by such a man as Chrysostom, will not wonder at the way in which "the pool of regeneration and justification" was spoken of by less enlightened writers of the patristic period. See Isaac Taylor, *Ancient Christianity*, 2nd ed. i. pp. 236-239.

[2] John iv. 1 f.

highest functions, "the ministry of the Word and prayer."
Their view of the relative importance of the different clauses
in our Lord's great commission was like that of the apostle
of the Gentiles when he said : "Christ sent me not to baptize,
but to preach the Gospel." [1] Christ's parting charge was
addressed, as we have seen, to the Church as such, the whole
company of the believers.   When once there was sufficient
evidence that the great end had been accomplished, that men
had been really "made disciples" through the preaching of
the Gospel, it was simply a matter of order and arrangement
by whose hands this subordinate part of the commission
should be carried out, and the converts formally received into
fellowship by Baptism.

In all likelihood there were few out of the hundred and
twenty original disciples who had not work of this kind to do
when the fruits of Peter's address on the day of Pentecost
were being gathered in.   Philip, "one of the seven,"—whose
later name, "the evangelist," was probably a result of his work
at Samaria,—baptizes the Ethiopian chamberlain with his
own hand.   Those who received the Gospel from Philip at
Samaria "were baptized, both men and women," either by
himself or by his assistants, before the arrival of the apostolic
deputies from Jerusalem.   Peter, on the conversion of the
centurion and his friends at Cæsarea, entrusts their Baptism
to other hands, probably those of the six representatives of
the Church at Joppa who had accompanied him.   Saul of
Tarsus is baptized in his lodging at Damascus by "a certain
disciple there named Ananias." [2]   The mother Church of
Gentile Christendom was founded by the efforts of private
disciples "telling the good news of the Lord Jesus" ($\epsilon\dot{v}a\gamma$-
$\gamma\epsilon\lambda\iota\zeta\acute{o}\mu\epsilon\nu o\iota$ $\tau\grave{o}\nu$ $K\acute{v}\rho\iota o\nu$ $'I\eta\sigma o\hat{v}\nu$).   The men of Cyprus and
Cyrene, who first crossed the line in Antioch and "spake
unto the Greeks also," so that "a great number believed and
turned unto the Lord," doubtless baptized these believers
forthwith upon their profession of faith.   There is no indication whatever that Barnabas, on his arrival in the Syrian
capital, found anything yet to be done as regards the
admission of the converts into full communion.   It was to

---

[1] 1 Cor. i. 17.   [2] Acts viii. 12–16, 38 ; xxi. 8 ; ix. 10, 18.

their further instruction in Christian truth that he and Saul specially devoted themselves for the next year.[1]

2. The Lord's Supper.

This ordinance appears twice over in the earliest description of the life of the Pentecostal Church. The first converts "continued stedfastly . . . . . in the breaking of the bread (τῇ κλάσει τοῦ ἄρτου), and the prayers." And with respect to "all that believed," we read that "day by day continuing stedfastly with one accord in the temple, and breaking bread at home (κλῶντές τε κατ᾽ οἶκον ἄρτον), they did take their food (τροφῆς) with gladness and singleness of heart, praising God, and having favour with all the people." [2] It seems clear that these statements imply that sort of twofold fellowship afterwards known under the designations of, the "love feast" (ἀγάπη) and the "eucharist," and referred to under the former of these names in the New Testament by one of the leaders of the Hebrew Christian Church, Jude the brother of James, and also—according to the most probable reading—in the Second Epistle of Peter.[3] There was close and loving fellowship between all the disciples as brethren and sisters in one family. The token and pledge of this was the common table at which they took their food together daily. And this loving intercourse was fitly closed for the day with the Lord's Supper as the sign and seal of their fellowship with the common Lord and Saviour, unseen but really present in the midst of His disciples to bless them with all the gifts and blessings won for them by His life and death. Christ's own ordinance of remembrance was the crown and consummation of their communion (ἡ κοινωνία) with Him and with each other.[4] It soon came to bear that name as its fitting designation. We find the word and the idea of this twofold

---

[1] Chap. xi. 19-26.   [2] Chap. ii. 42, 46 f.

[3] Jude 12 ; 2 Pet. ii. 13.

[4] "The Lord's Supper," in the wider sense, covered both the "love feast" and the eucharist, the former rising into the latter before abuses such as those censured by Paul in the Church at Corinth led to the separation of the two. It was "substantially a reproduction of Christ's last night with His apostles," in which the joyful fellowship of the Paschal meal rose into the new covenant ordinance of the bread and the cup blessed by the Lord. See Bp. Lightfoot, *Ignatius*, i. 386. Meyer on 1 Cor. xi. 20, E. Tr. i. p. 335.

communion specially linked with the Lord's Supper in one of Paul's earliest epistles.[1]

We have no information regarding the question of who presided at the Table, or first broke the bread and gave the cup to his brethren. From the standpoint of the apostolic Church such points were of as little importance as the question by whose hand a convert should be baptized, or that of the precise mode in which the water should be applied, or the amount of it to be used in the ordinance. These were simply questions of arrangement to be settled by Christian common sense. The precedent of the first Lord's Supper was no doubt followed as nearly as circumstances would allow. One of the twelve would naturally preside in the meetings for worship in the upper room, or at any assembly for the breaking of bread where apostles were present. But the Pentecostal Church soon numbered its thousands; and from the first different languages were represented in it. The meetings of the disciples were held in different houses in Jerusalem.[2] Fellow-countrymen would doubtless keep together to "hear in their own tongue wherein they were born the mighty works of God."[3] Each little gathering had its own natural or appointed leaders, who took the initiative when in each different centre the ordinance of communion was observed, and the bread was broken, and the cup passed from hand to hand.[4]

---

[1] Τὸ ποτήριον τῆς εὐλογίας ὃ εὐλεγοῦμεν οὐχὶ κοινωνία τοῦ αἵματος τοῦ Χριστοῦ ἐστι ; τὸν ἄρτον ὃν κλῶμεν, οὐχὶ κοινωνία τοῦ σώματος τοῦ Χριστοῦ ἐστιν ; ὅτι εἷς ἄρτος, ἓν σῶμα οἱ πολλοί ἐσμεν· οἱ γὰρ πάντες ἐκ τοῦ ἑνὸς ἄρτου μετέχομεν, 1 Cor. x. 16 f. "Le Plur. κλῶμεν, nous rompons, ou bien rapelle la participation morale de toute l'église à cet acte qu' accomplissait le président en souvenir de Jésus rompant le pain aux disciples, ou bien suppose une forme telle que celle qui existe dans les églises ou chaque communiant rompt lui-même un morceau du pain qui passe de l'un à l'autre. Le terme de κοινωνία, communion, est répeté à l'occasion du pain ; c'est en effet la notion qui réunit les deux actes en un seul et d'où est provenu le nom ordinaire du sacrement, la Communion." Godet, La première Epitre aux Corinthens, Paris et Neuchatel 1887, ii. p. 99.

[2] See above, pp. 318, 351 f.   [3] Acts ii. 5–11.

[4] Comp. "All that believed were . . . breaking bread at home," ii. 44 ff., with "When we were gathered together to break bread . . . when he was gone up and had broken the bread," xx. 7–11. "The bread which we break," 1 Cor. x. 16, with Godet's remarks on the passage given in note above. See also Dean Stanley, Corinthians, 2nd ed. p. 173. Plumptre, art. "Lord's Supper," in Smith, ii. p. 140 f.

Songs of praise, and words of comfort and of exhortation, mingled with these feasts of love and of remembrance in the Hebrew Christian Church. The disciples "did take their food with gladness and singleness of heart, praising God." They "had their songs," such as were of old in Israel, "as in the night, when a holy solemnity was kept; and gladness of heart, as when one goeth with a pipe to come unto the mountain of the Lord, to the Rock of Israel."[1] They had the ancient Paschal Psalms of the Hallel, in which the eleven had joined with the Lord Himself at the first Lord's Supper, and new songs of praise, and words of prayer and thanksgiving, as the Spirit gave them utterance. The familiar forms of blessing used at the Passover would be repeated at such times with new and deeper meaning. "Therefore we are bound to give thanks, to praise, to glorify, to honour, to magnify Him that hath done for our fathers and for us all these wonders; who hath brought us from bondage to freedom, from sorrow to rejoicing, from mourning to a good day, from darkness to a great light, from affliction to redemption, therefore must we say before Him, Hallelujah, praise ye the Lord."[2] This fellowship at a common table rising into fellowship in the holiest things, in Word and Sacrament, "was in its essence nothing else than a prolongation of that Divine communion of daily family life which His followers had kept with the Son of God while He was on earth. That family fellowship of Jesus Christ with His own had been to them the seal of a deeper soul fellowship with One whom they loved as their Saviour. At the Table it was so still. He had expressly consecrated table intercourse into a badge of unity, a memorial of His Passion and a seal of discipleship. By 'the breaking of bread,' therefore, there were naturally expressed, first, the continuity of their intercourse with One in whom, though now they saw Him not, yet believing they still rejoiced; secondly, their own fraternity as the children of One whom the Son had taught them to call 'our Father;' and thirdly, their expectation of His speedy return who had

[1] Isa. xxx. 29.
[2] Lightfoot, cited by Dean Plumptre, art. "Lord's Supper," in Smith, ii. p. 139 f.

only gone away that He might make the Father's great house above ready for all the family. Let us try to forget if we can the abuses which after a while, and among the Greeks, darkened this primitive love feast, and led to the separation of the Holy Supper from what had become an unholy repast. Let us endeavour, as often as we renew the sacred rite, to catch its tender and homely interest. It is a reminiscence of days when men did eat and drink with the Eternal God in flesh. It is a pledge that all who love Jesus Christ are still members in Him of one 'household of faith.' Above all, it leads us to associate the religious sanctity of our inner life as a life in Christ with whatsoever we daily do, 'whether we eat or drink' (1 Cor. x. 31)." [1]

3. The Lord's Day.

The day of Christ's resurrection appears more distinctly in the second section of the Acts than in the first as the stated time for Christian assemblies, and especially as that for "the breaking of bread;" but during the first fifty days of the history of the apostolic Church it had gathered round itself the most sacred and indissoluble associations. The first day of the week recalled the deepest, the most thrilling and joyful experiences of the original disciples, those which had filled the never-to-be-forgotten time between the Resurrection and the Ascension of their Lord. It had been singled out by Himself in the most unmistakeable way as the day on which, above all others, He was pleased to meet with His disciples, and to bless them.[2] It represented the central facts of the Gospel which had come in such power to the converts of Pentecost, the whole burden of the apostles' message, "Jesus and the Resurrection."

Undoubtedly all the members of the Pentecostal Church still kept the old seventh-day Sabbath with their fellow-countrymen. For all the Hebrew believers it had the strength of a lifetime of religious habits and associations. It was the day on which every synagogue in town and country was open, and the temple courts were fullest of worshippers. The original

---

[1] Dykes, p. 107 f. Comp. Neander, *Planting and Training of the Christian Church*, 3rd ed., E. Tr. i. p. 27.

[2] See below, p. 381 f.

disciples had kept the Sabbath for years with Christ Himself, sitting with Him on those very synagogue seats, listening to Him as He spoke from the platform of the teachers before the roll of the law and the prophets, or as He taught the multitudes in the temple.   They knew how often He had striven to clear it from abuse, and had uttered weighty and memorable words regarding its true meaning and the spirit in which it should be kept.   He had not acted nor spoken so regarding any institution which belonged merely to the Mosaic system, such as the Passover or the Feast of Tabernacles. Superstitions and abuses had grown up about these institutions also like rank weeds, in the schools of the Rabbis, and in the practice of their followers; but Christ had not paused to clear those weeds away.   But with respect to the two great ordinances of the Sabbath and of marriage, both of which had a distinct place in the Scripture records concerning man in his primeval state, with respect to " those two ordinances of Eden which alone survived the Fall," [1] our Lord had acted very differently. He had come forth repeatedly in a marked way, and at the cost of malignant opposition, to vindicate the true ideal of the day of rest, and of the union of man and wife in marriage.[2]   With respect to both He had gone back with a peculiar emphasis to the original institution of the ordinance by God.[3]

When the Saviour spoke to the apostles, towards the end of His public ministry, of what should happen after His death, at the time of the destruction of Jerusalem, when " there should not be left one stone " of the temple " upon another

---

[1] Dr. Candlish.

[2] Regarding the Sabbath : Matt. xii. 1–8, 10–14 ; Mark ii. 23–28 ; iii. 1–6 ; Luke vi. 2–5, 6–11 ; xiii. 11–17 ; xiv. 1–6 ; John v. 8–18 ; vii. 21–24 ; ix. 14–16, 24–33.   Regarding marriage : Matt. v. 31 f. ; xix. iii. 11 ; Mark x. 2–12, 29 f.; Luke xviii. 29 f.; John iv. 16–18.

[3] "The Sabbath was made for man, and not man for the Sabbath," Mark ii. 27 ; comp. Gen. i. 26 f.; ii. 2 f.   " Have ye not read that He which made them from the beginning made them male and female, and said, For this cause shall a man leave his father and mother, and shall cleave unto his wife, and the twain shall become one flesh ?   What therefore God hath joined together let not man put asunder. . . .   Moses for your hardness of heart suffered you to put away your wives ; but from the beginning it hath not been so."   Matt. xix. 4–6, 8 ; comp. Gen. ii. 18, 21–24.   Comp. Bannerman, *Church of Christ*, i. pp. 394– 397, "The Christian Sabbath."

that should not be thrown down," He took it for granted that there would still be then a day of sacred rest and worship which His followers would be bound to keep. "Pray ye," He said, "that your flight be not in the winter, neither on a Sabbath (μηδὲ σαββάτῳ)." [1] Just as certainly as the ordinances of nature would continue, as there would be winter then, so also would there still be the ordinance of a day of rest, a Sabbath. Christ bade His disciples make it matter of prayer that they might not be forced to flee during "the inclemency of the one season or the sacredness of the other." [2]

It could not possibly suggest itself to any of the disciples, when they heard our Lord's words concerning the judgments which were to come upon Jerusalem, that there could ever be any other day the sacred associations of which would surpass those of the Sabbath they had been wont to keep. But now in the history of the Church of Christ, since the time when the eleven sat with Him upon Olivet, over against the temple, and heard Him foretell its overthrow, there had been the Crucifixion, the Resurrection, the Ascension, and Pentecost. All these stupendous events had risen like a mighty mountain range, summit beyond summit, high above all the tamer experiences of their old religious life, changing the look and the relations of all their past history. The disciples of the risen and ascended Saviour were in a new world, [3] with new landmarks now to which their eyes were turned, and by which their feet were guided into yet untrodden paths, that led them whither they knew not, with new springs of living water making glad their way from step to step. And among the changes,—and like many of them, and those not the least important, rather *felt* as yet than recognised or understood,—there was this: Just as there had come in an element of separation between the Hebrew Christians and their unbelieving fellow-countrymen, an element real and influential, although coming in against the will and almost

---

[1] Matt. xxiv. 2, 20. [2] Bannerman, *ut supra*, p. 401 f.

[3] As one of the apostolic Fathers expresses it : "We ourselves having received the promise, iniquity being done away, and all things made new by the Lord, and we made able to work righteousness . . . God has made the beginning of another world (ἄλλου κόσμου ἀρχήν)." Ep. Barn. xv. 4, 7. Comp. the apostle's words in 2 Cor. v. 17 ; Gal. vi. 15 f.

without the knowledge of the disciples, so, too, there had fallen for them a shadow over the ancient Sabbath, a shadow which was felt the more because of the surpassing brightness that now rested upon the day which followed. The one was on the dark, the other on the sunlit side of the mountain range; and the faces of Christ's disciples were toward the sun-rising.[1] The seventh day had terrible memories for "the eleven and them that were with them," memories of unfaithfulness and unbelief, of desolation and despair. It had been the darkest day of the "Triduum mœstosum." The first day of the week had brought light from heaven, and gladness never to pass away, "the light of the knowledge of the glory of God in the face of Jesus Christ." It could never again be to any of the first disciples as a common day.

More than this. The day of Christ's resurrection had been singled out, and sealed by Himself, ever since, in the most marked and significant way as the day on which especially He would meet with His disciples, and expected that they should be gathered together to meet with Him. Out of some twelve or thirteen recorded appearances of Christ to the disciples between His Resurrection and Ascension, six at least took place on the first day of the week.[2] One of the twelve is not with the rest who were gathered together in Jerusalem on the day on which Christ rose from the dead, and does not therefore see the Lord when He appeared in the midst of His assembled disciples. They met doubtless for worship as they had been wont to do on the seventh day of that week, but Jesus did not come to them. Not until the Resurrection day returned, and the disciples again met together, "and Thomas with them," did the risen Saviour again meet with them, and reveal Himself to the doubting apostle. Other interviews,

[1] "The pilgrim (after he had been received into 'the House Beautiful') they laid in a large upper chamber, whose window opened toward the sun-rising; and the name of the chamber was Peace; where he slept till break of day, and then he awoke and sang." *Pilgrim's Progress.*

[2] To Mary Magdalene, Mark xvi. 9; John xx. 14-18; to the other women, Matt. xxviii. 9; to the two on the road to Emmaus, Mark xvi. 12; Luke xxiv. 13-31; to Peter, Luke xxiv. 34; 1 Cor. xv. 5; to the disciples without Thomas, Luke xxiv. 36 ff.; John xx. 19-25; to the disciples with Thomas, John xx. 26-29.

such as that with the five hundred in Galilee, with respect to which no special note of the time is recorded, may very possibly have taken place also on the first day of the week. It was unquestionably the day on which Christ Himself during the forty days taught His disciples specially to expect His presence and blessing.[1]

The crown was put upon the sacred and inalienable position of this day above all others in the apostolic Church by the Advent of the Holy Spirit. The day of Christ's Resurrection was to be as closely associated in the minds of the disciples with the coming and work of the Paraclete as with the presence of the Lord Himself in the midst of their assemblies. Pentecost that year fell on the first day of the week.[2] By this time none of the disciples had failed to learn the lesson taught before to Thomas. " When the day of Pentecost was now come, they were all together in one place." And to the Church thus gathered together with one accord in the name of the Lord Jesus, on the 'day of His Resurrection, the Holy Spirit was sent in power and majesty.[3]

---

[1] It seems to have been held by some in the sub-apostolic and post-apostolic age that our Lord's Ascension as well as His Resurrection took place on the first day of the week. Thus in the Epistle of Barnabas the author, in arguing against Judaistic tendencies, cites Isa. i. 13, and goes on : "Ye perceive how God speaks : Your present Sabbaths are not acceptable to Me, but that is which I have made, when giving rest to all things I shall make a beginning of the eighth day, that is, a beginning of another world. Wherefore also we keep the eighth day with joyfulness, the day, too, on which Jesus rose again from the dead, and, having manifested Himself, ascended into the heavens (ἐν ᾗ καὶ ὁ Ἰησοῦς ἀνέστη ἐκ τῶν νεκρῶν, καὶ φανερωθεὶς ἀνέβη εἰς τοὺς οὐρανούς), Ep. Barn. xv. 8. See Zahn, Geschichte des Sonntags, Hannover 1878, S. 61. Hefele, Patr. Apost. ed. 4, S. 41, and his Sendschreiben des Ap. Barn. S. 112 f. Whether the passage above cited really puts the Ascension on the first day of the week depends on the punctuation adopted. Dressel puts a full stop after ἐκ νεκρῶν, in which he is followed by Dr. Roberts and Principal Donaldson in the Ante-Nicene Library, i. p. 128. Canon Barry agrees with Hefele and Zahn, art. "Lord's Day," in Smith and Cheetham's Dict. of Christ. Antiq. ii. p. 1043. Comp. "The Teaching of the Apostles," in Syriac Documents, p. 38, in Ante-Nicene Library, xx., Edin. 1871. But see Bp. Lightfoot's estimate of the value of these "Documents," which were first published in Dr. Cureton's posthumous work, Ancient Syriac Documents, Lond. 1864. Lightfoot, Ignatius, i. p. 69 ; comp. his Philippians, p. 209.

[2] Canon Barry, art. "Lord's Day," in Dict. of Christ. Ant. ii. p. 1043. Hessey, art. "Lord's Day," in Smith's Bible Dict. ii. p. 136.

[3] Acts ii. 1–4.

By this great series of facts and events, far more powerful in their successive testimony than words, a threefold seal was set upon the first day of the week as the great day of the new dispensation. On this day God the Father had given assurance unto all men concerning His Son and His holy servant Jesus by raising Him from the dead. The risen Redeemer had made it plain by many unmistakeable tokens, that on this day above all others it was His good pleasure to reveal Himself to His disciples. And on this day the Holy Ghost had been given. The threefold name of God into which believers were baptized, in which the Church assembled together, was written full and clear upon this day, separating it from all the rest. The day of Christ's Resurrection as kept by His disciples for Him was the constant memorial and representative in the worship of the Pentecostal Church of that to which the apostles bore witness in word, proclaiming Christ as risen from the dead and as the giver of the Holy Spirit. It preached Jesus and the Resurrection, and the power and fruits of the Resurrection.

On all these grounds it is easy to understand how the first day of the week rose swiftly and silently, and as it were by the natural laws of the new world in which the disciples of the risen Saviour now moved, to the position, which we find it holding as a matter of course in the second section of the history, of the acknowledged day for Christian assemblies, and especially for the fellowship of the common table and of the Lord's Supper.

Alongside of the Lord's Day, as already noted, all the members of the Hebrew Christian Church kept the old Day of Rest, although doubtless in that spirit of freedom which breathed in the teaching and example of Christ Himself. The place of the Sabbath in " the ten words " was sufficient of itself to secure that it should be kept. Our Lord had foretold in the plainest terms that the temple should be utterly destroyed. When that came to pass, as the disciples must have felt on pondering His words, it would be impossible to continue the sacrifices, and the priest's office would practically be abolished. But Christ had never given the slightest

indication that a time would ever come when the law of the
ten words was to lose its authority over the consciences of
men, or when one was to be taken out of the number.
The ten commandments had no connection with the temple,
nor with sacrifices and priesthood. They rested on reasons
that arose out of the essential and permanent relations of
man with his Maker, and of man with his fellows.[1] The
place of the ten commandments in the Sinaitic legislation
made this plain to every member of the Hebrew Church.
Before any other statutes were given, " God spake all these
words," speaking them not through Moses, but directly to
the people met in solemn assembly, and " He added no
more ; and He wrote them upon two tables of stone, and
delivered them unto Moses." [2] These ten commandments
only were written with the finger of God on the tables of
stone, as He had written that law in substance also on the
hearts of all men. They only were kept within the ark
beneath the mercy-seat in the inmost shrine of the Holiest of

---

[1] All the four commandments of the first table, as has often been pointed out,
are very closely connected with each other. They all deal with the worship of
God ; its *object*,—" no other gods before Me ; " its *means*,—" not by idols or any
way not appointed in His word ; " its *manner*,—" with reverence and godly fear ; "
its *time*,—"especially one day in seven as a day of holy rest and service."
How the Sabbath was to be kept in the Old Testament Church is indicated
in the brief but suggestive commentary in the twenty-third chapter of Leviticus, where the Sabbath stands in a place by itself before and apart from all
" the set feasts of the Lord, even holy convocations which ye shall proclaim in
their appointed season." " The seventh day is a rest day of solemn rest, an holy
convocation ; ye shall do no manner of work ; it is a rest day unto Jehovah in
all your dwellings," Lev. xxiii. 3 ; comp. Isa. lviii. 13 f.   No doubt the Sabbath
had a special place in the national covenant of Israel with God, as " a sign
between Me and the children of Israel for ever ; " and it was a special reason for
Israel's keeping the Sabbath that God had redeemed them from the bondage of
Egypt (Ex. xxxi. 13–17 ; Deut. v. 15) ; as in all ages each fresh experience of
redemption is a new reason for keeping God's commandments.   But this
is not in the least inconsistent with the original ground of this commandment in the creation rest of God, and in His marking out the true
relation for man between work and rest, and setting His blessing on the
rest day.

[2] "These words the Lord spake unto all your assembly (אֶל־כָּל־קְהַלְכֶם) in
the Mount, out of the midst of the fire, of the cloud, and of the thick darkness,
with a great voice ; and He added no more : and He wrote them upon two
tables of stone, and delivered them unto me," Deut. v. 22 ; comp. Ex. xx.
1–22 ; xxxi. 18.

all, while all later legislation found its place in the roll without the ark.[1]

So far from giving the slightest hint that the ten commandments were to lose this exceptional position of sanctity and
authority, or that one of them was to be taken out of the
list, our Lord repeatedly appeals to them as the supreme
standard of right and wrong: "If thou wouldest enter into
life, keep the commandments." "Why do ye transgress the
commandment of God because of your tradition ? For God
said : Honour thy father and mother." [2] And of all the
commandments, not even excepting the fifth and seventh,
the one which Christ most often selects for vindication from
corruption and abuse, is that which embodies the ordinance
of the day of rest. He takes it for granted, as we have
already seen, that the keeping of a Sabbath is to continue in
His Church at the time of the fall of Jerusalem, more than
a generation after His own death.[3]

It is in a Hebrew Christian document, proceeding from
one of the foremost leaders of the Church in Jerusalem,
that we first meet the name "the Lord's Day," as applied
to the day of Christ's Resurrection, and associated with the

---

[1] Ex. xxv. 21 ; xl. 20 ; 1 Kings viii. 9 ; Rom. ii. 14 f. "The position of
the Sabbath in the decalogue (where nothing is placed which was of merely
Jewish concern, and which was not of fundamental importance) is a presumption of perpetuity for every candid mind. The much disputed question
of the ethical nature of the Sabbath law is not of so great moment as has
been imagined. Moral or not, the weekly rest is to all men and at all times
of vital importance ; therefore practically, if not philosophically, of ethical
value. The fourth commandment certainly differs from the others in this
respect, that it is not written on the natural conscience. The utmost length
reason could go would be to determine that rest is needful. Whether rest
should be periodical or at irregular intervals, on the seventh day or on the
tenth, as in revolutionary France, with its mania for the decimal system, the
light of nature could not teach. But the decalogue settles that point, and
settles it for ever for all who believe in the Divine origin of the Mosaic legislation. The fourth commandment is a revelation for all time of God's mind on
the universally important question of the proper relation between labour and
rest." Bruce, *Training of the Twelve*, 3rd ed. p. 94. Comp. Bannerman,
Church of Christ, i. pp. 397-401 ; and as to the union of a moral and a positive
element in the fourth commandment, p. 393. See also Fairbairn, *Typol.* 6th
ed. ii. pp. 124-152.

[2] Matt. xv. 3 f. ; xix. 17 ff.

[3] See above, pp. 379-381. Comp. Fairbairn, *Revelation of Law in Scripture*,
pp. 235-242.

last appearance of the risen Saviour on earth—an appearance made, like the first, upon that day.[1]   The title reminds us of the claim constantly made in the name of God, both in the legislative and the prophetic portions of the Old Testament, with respect to the ancient day of rest.   " It is the Sabbath of the Lord thy God."   " Ye shall keep My Sabbaths, and reverence My sanctuary: I am the Lord your God."   " If thou turn away thy foot from the Sabbath, from doing thy pleasure on My holy day; and call the Sabbath a delight, the holy of the Lord, honourable . . . then shalt thou delight thyself in the Lord." [2]   All days are the Lòrd's; and all, so far as He Himself is concerned, are alike holy and blessed.   When, therefore, in the beginning of the record of revelation, we read of one day in the seven that " God blessed and sanctified it," and find that He claims it henceforth as " His holy day," we see at once that this must have reference to man as made in the image of God, and for fellowship with Him, that " the Sabbath was made for man," that it was on his account, in his highest interests, that the day was set apart from the rest of the week, and crowned with special blessing from God.   And so, too, in the later Scriptures, when we find the day of

---

[1] ἐγενόμην ἐν πνεύματι ἐν τῇ Κυριακῇ ἡμέρᾳ, Rev. i. 10. Dr. Hessey refutes conclusively the various and conflicting interpretations of this phrase which have been given by writers who departed from " the general consent both of Christian antiquity and of modern divines, which refers it to the weekly festival of our Lord's Resurrection." Art. "Lord's Day," in Smith's *Bible Dict.* ii. p. 135a.   The most plausible of these divergent interpretations is perhaps that of Augusti, who understood it of the Day of Judgment, ἡ ἡμέρα τοῦ Κυρίου. This view has more recently been advocated by the late justly revered Dr. Beck of Tübingen, *Offenbarung Johannis*, Gütersloh 1884, S. 70 f. One is surprised to find that Bishop Lightfoot, in his latest work, indicates a leaning to the idea that by ἡ κυριακὴ ἡμέρα in Rev. i. 10, "the day of judgment is intended," and that he adds, "If this be so, the passage before us [*Ign. ad Magn.* ix.] is the earliest extant example of its occurrence in this sense [*i.e.* Κυριακή = ' the Lord's Day '], *Ignatius*, ii. p. 129." This last statement, although published in 1885, must surely have been written before the appearance of the Διδαχή in 1883. See the passage quoted from it on next page. Dr. Lightfoot himself places the Διδαχή " in the later decades of the first century." *Ignatius*, i. p. 739. Comp. his paper read at the Carlisle Church Congress in 1884, and published in the *Expositor*, Jan. 1885, p. 6 f.

[2] Ex. xx. 10; Lev. xix. 30; xxvi. 2; Isa. lviii. 13 f.   Comp. Ezek. xx. 12 f., 16, 24; xxii. 8, 26; xliv. 24.

Christ's Resurrection singled out from the rest as we have
seen, and crowned with special blessing, and called "the
Lord's Day," and the only day so called in the New
Testament, we may surely gather that it was Divinely
meant to hold a like place of honour to that held by the
ancient rest day in the former dispensation, and that it has
been Divinely separated and sanctified for the highest ends,
as in the Old Testament "the Lord's House" was separated
from common dwellings, and in the New Testament the Lord's
Supper (τὸ Κυριακὸν δεῖπνον) is separated from an ordinary
meal.

It is noteworthy in this connection that the same phrase
meets us at once in what is probably the earliest extra-
canonical utterance from the circle of the Jewish Christian
Church, namely, the "Teaching of the Twelve Apostles;" but
it meets us there with an interesting variation.   Christians
are there exhorted: "On each Lord's Day of the Lord (κατὰ
Κυριακὴν δὲ Κυρίου) be ye gathered together, and break bread,
and give thanks." [1]   The very phrase reminds us that there
had been, and for the Hebrew Christians there still was,
another "Lord's Day," a "Sabbath unto the Lord in all
their dwellings."   But a higher and holier consecration
rested now upon the day on which they met to break bread
and give thanks, the Lord's Day of the Lord Jesus.[2]

What precisely was to be the relation between the new
Lord's Day and the old "day of holy convocations," and "Rest
day unto Jehovah in Israel," was a point which was not
naturally raised for the apostolic Church in the first period
of its history.   Deeper and more vital questions had the
chief place in the minds and hearts of these early disciples.
In many lesser matters they *felt* their way rather than saw
it, and in this among the rest.   The Lord Himself was in
the midst of His Church and people, of that they were
joyfully assured; He was leading them, like Israel of old, by
a right way, although it was a way that they knew not.
One step at a time was enough for them to see, as they

[1] *Teaching of the Apostles*, xiv. 1.

[2] It is hardly fair, therefore, to call the phrase in question "a pleonasm," as
is done by Harnack, *Texte*, ii. 1, S. 53.

went forward following Christ in gladness and singleness of heart. Of the members of the Pentecostal Church, as of our forefathers in the times of Prelatic persecution, it might be said in the words of a Scottish poet :—

> " With them each day was holy ; every hour
> They stood prepared to die, a people doomed
> To death ; old men, and youths, and simple maids,
> With them each day was holy ; but that morn
> On which the angel said, ' See where the Lord
> Was laid,' joyous arose ; to die that day was bliss." [1]

As regards the Sabbath and the Lord's Day, it was' clear that the privilege and duty of weekly rest remained for the followers of Jesus as before, and that practically they and their households, the stranger within their gates, their servants and their cattle, could rest only on the seventh day. Law and custom provided for that in the Holy Land, and to some extent over all the Roman Empire, wherever a Jewish settlement had established itself. The Hebrew Christians accordingly kept both days from the first ; although more and more distinctly and consciously, as time went on, the power and gladness of the new life of the Church gathered round " the Lord's Day of the Lord," the day of Christ's Resurrection, and of the Advent of the Holy Ghost ; whereas the old Hebrew Sabbath, the day of the disciples' fear and faithlessness, while Christ lay in the grave, came to be kept more as a day of preparation, and it might be of fasting.[2]

The practical relation of this Sabbath and the Lord's Day upon Jewish Christian ground has been well stated by Canon Barry : " The idea of Christian worship would attach mainly

---

[1] Graham, *The Sabbath.*

[2] In the Eastern Church the festal aspect of the Sabbath, as a day of rest and refreshment, generally prevailed, except on what was called "the great Sabbath," namely, the day before the anniversary of our Lord's Resurrection (Easter Eve), which was always kept as a fast. In several parts of the West, on the other hand, especially in the Church of Rome, the custom was to fast regularly on the seventh day of the week. This is referred to by Tertullian (*De Jejuniis*, xiv.), and at considerable length by Augustine in his very interesting letter to Casulanus on the question : " Utrum liceat Sabbato jejunare ? " Ep. xxxvi. Aug. *Opera*, ed. Migne, ii. 136, E. Tr. (Dods' ed.) i. pp. 112-125. Comp. Barry, art. "Sabbath," in Smith and Cheetham's *Dict. of Christ. Ant.* ii. p. 1824 ff.

to the one ; the obligation of rest would continue attached to
the other ; although a certain interchange of characteristics
would grow up, as worship necessitated rest, and rest naturally suggested worship." It might be added, that for years
at least the rest of the Jewish Sabbath brought full facilities
of worship to the Hebrew Christians. So long as the synagogues and the temple courts were not closed against them,
they resorted thither, " as their custom was," every Sabbath
day. " Under these circumstances the two days would be
regarded as festivals, perhaps at first almost co-ordinate ;
afterwards the dignity of the Lord's Day must have continually increased, and that of the Sabbath as continually
decreased." [1] That the Hebrew Christians, so long as they
kept the spirit of the apostolic Church, did not shrink from

---

[1] Barry, art. "Lord's Day," *ut supra*, p. 1045*a*. Comp. the well-known
passage in the Epistle of Ignatius to the Magnesians in the shorter Greek
version—"the Middle Version," according to Bishop Lightfoot's nomenclature.
The Christian community at Antioch was of mixed origin, and believers of
Gentile descent probably formed the majority from the first. Yet the Jewish
Christian element was strongly represented also in the Church of the Syrian
capital ; and Ignatius seems to speak here from the standpoint of believers who,
like Saul of Tarsus, Barnabas, Menahem, and others of the first teachers of the
Church at Antioch, were Jews by birth and religious training. " If those,"
he says, " who were brought up in the ancient order of things (ἐν παλαιοῖς
πράγμασιν) have come to the possession of a new hope, no longer observing the
Sabbath, but living in the observance of the Lord's Day (μηκέτι σαββατίζοντες,
ἀλλὰ κατὰ Κυριακὴν ζῶντες," *i.e.* as Bishop Lightfoot remarks, "not merely in
the observance of it, but in the appropriation of all those ideas and associations which are involved in its observance), on which also our life has sprung
up again by Him and by His death, how shall we be able to live apart from
Him ?" *ad Magn.* c. ix. Lightfoot, *Ignatius*, ii. p. 129. The commentary
on this, which is furnished by the longer Greek recension of the same passage,
is interesting : " But let every one of you keep the Sabbath after a spiritual
manner, rejoicing in meditation on the law, admiring the workmanship of God,
and not [like the Jews] eating things prepared the day before, nor using luke-
warm drinks, and walking within a prescribed space, nor finding delight in
dancing and plaudits, which have no sense in them. And after the observance
of the Sabbath [μετὰ δὲ τὸ σαββατίσαι], let every friend of Christ keep the Lord's
Day as a festival, the Resurrection Day, the queen and chief of all the days (τὴν
ἀναστάσιμον, τὴν βασιλίδα, τὴν ὑπάτην τῶν πασῶν ἡμερῶν)," *ad Magn.* c. ix.,
E. Tr. *Ante-Nicene Library*, i. p. 180 f. Comp. the "Apostolical Constitutions,"
v. 15, 18, 20 ; vii. 23, 36 ; viii. 33 ; *Ante-Nicene Library*, xvii. pp. 134, 143,
186, 196 f., 246. The date of the main part of the "Apostolic Constitutions"
is assigned by Harnack to the middle or end of the second century. *Texte u.
Untersuch.* ii. 5, S. 55.

the ancient name which our Lord had used of the day of rest, as His disciples were to observe it more than a generation after His death, may be gathered from the use of it about that very time in the Epistle to the Hebrews. " There remaineth therefore a Sabbath rest (or 'a Sabbath keeping,' ἀπολείπεται σαββατισμός; not merely κατάπαυσις, as in previous context) for the people of God. For He that hath entered into His rest hath Himself also rested from His works, as God did [in the Creation-rest] from His. Let us therefore give diligence to enter into that rest, that no man fall after the same example of disobedience." The word fitly described the redemption rest into which our Lord entered on the morning of His resurrection, in which His disciples are called to share here, and which leads on to the holy rest and service, the " Sabbath keeping" of heaven. " The Rest of the people of God," as an eminent recent commentator on the Hebrews expounds chap. iv. 9, " is like the keeping of a Sabbath." This idea was suggested by God's resting on the seventh day (ver. 4). The comparison was not unfamiliar to Jewish theology : " The Israelites said, O Lord of the whole world, show us a type of the world to come. God answered them, That type is the Sabbath." And of Ps. xcii. it is said : " A Psalm for the Sabbath day, because it refers to the world to come, which is all Sabbath, and a rest unto eternal life" (Rabbinical passages quoted in the Commentaries). " This Rest is left for the people of God. The epistle adheres to the Old Testament idea that believers form a people, and that Christ sanctified the people with His blood (xiii. 12). . . . Israel as the people of God fell short of the rest at the Exodus; they shall, as the people of God, with all that cleave to them (Isa. xiv. 1), enter the true Rest and Sabbath keeping. It was a point with the author to identify Christian Hebrews with the people of God." [1] The word which described that " Rest and Sabbath keeping " might well therefore be used of the Christian Sabbath, the day of holy rest and worship on earth.[2] " The Lord's Day," as Canon Barry

---

[1] Davidson, *Hebrews*, Edin. 1882, p. 95. Comp. Garden, "Sabbath" in Smith's *Bible Dict.* iii. p. 1072.

[2] Heb. iv. 9–11. I agree with Dean Alford, following Ebrard, Stark, Alting,

expresses it, "grew up naturally from the apostles' time, gradually assuming the character of the one distinctively Christian festival, and drawing to itself, as by an irresistible gravitation, the periodical rest which is enjoined in the fourth commandment, on grounds applicable to man as man, and which was provided for under the Mosaic law by the special observance of the Sabbath." To use the words of Principal Fairbairn, by whom the same thought has been somewhat more thoroughly and consistently developed: "The primeval character and destination of the Sabbath remain. As Baptism in the Spirit is 'Christ's circumcision' (Col. ii. 11 f.), so the Lord's Day is His Sabbath; and to be 'in the Spirit on the Lord's Day,' worshipping and serving Him in the truth of His Gospel, is to carry out the intent of the fourth commandment." [1]

4. Entire absence of the sacerdotal and the sacrificial in the worship of the Hebrew Christian Church.

This fact has already been brought out in connection with the attitude of the first disciples to the temple worship, and the teaching of the apostles and other leaders of the Hebrew Christian community with respect to the priesthood and sacrifice of Christ.[2] But the point is of such practical importance that we may return to it here for a moment, before passing from the general subject of the worship of the Hebrew Christian Church. The more carefully we study the statements and indications bearing on the observance of Christian ordinances which meet us in this part of the history, the more inevitably are we shut up to the conclusion that no separate priesthood and no sacrificial rites had any place in the worship of the apostolic Church, any more than in that of the synagogue to which it was so closely conformed; in particular, no sacrificial theory of the Lord's Supper has the

---

Owen, and others, that ὁ εἰσελθών in ver. 10 is best referred to Christ : "'For He that entered into His (own or God's) rest, Himself also rested from His works, like as God rested from His own,' and therefore our Forerunner having entered this Sabbatism, it is reserved for us, the people of God, to enter into it with and because of Him." Alford, *in loco.*

[1] Barry, art. "Lord's Day," *ut supra,* p. 1052*a.* Fairbairn, *Revelation of Law in Scripture,* p. 474.

[2] See above, pp. 335-347.

slightest support in the New Testament records of the Hebrew Christian period.

It is mentioned incidentally in one passage of the Acts, in reference to a time when, after the appointment of "the seven," "the Word of God increased, and the number of the disciples multiplied in Jerusalem greatly," that "a great company of the priests also were obedient to the faith."[1] It was most natural that this should be hailed as an encouraging proof of the progress of the Gospel; for the Jewish priests as a class had hitherto been its most bigoted opponents. But there is no trace whatever of any special position in the Church being assigned to these converted priests as such. They would have received none in the synagogue.[2] As Christians, those who had formerly executed the office of priests are never once called by that name. They took their places humbly and gladly alongside of their fellow-disciples in the ranks of the New Testament priesthood of all believers, at the feet of the High Priest of their confession, even Jesus.[3] What the teaching of the apostles and of apostolic men was concerning the priesthood and the sacrifice of Christ, and concerning the position and privileges of all His people as made "an elect race, a royal priesthood" in Him, we may see in the epistles of the apostles of the circumcision, in the book of the Revelation, and in the Epistle to the Hebrews. In these writings we have the explanation of the fact that there was no other priesthood named or known in the apostolic Church.[4] The fact itself stands out clear and unquestionable to all candid readers of the history of this period.

In the words of Bishop Lightfoot: "The kingdom of

---

[1] Πολύς τε ὄχλος τῶν ἱερίων ὑπήκουον τῇ πίστει, Acts vi. 7.

[2] See above, pp. 137 f., 155, 160.

[3] Heb. iii. 1. How little reason there is for ascribing the growth of sacerdotalism in the post-apostolic Church to the influence of such priestly converts, or of the Jewish Christians generally, has been well shown by Bishop Lightfoot: "The earliest Jewish Christian writings contain no traces of sacerdotalism. . . . Indeed, the overwhelming argument against ascribing the growth of sacerdotal views to Jewish influence lies in the fact that there is a singular absence of distinct sacerdotalism during the first century and a half, when alone on any showing Judaism was powerful enough to impress itself on the belief of the Church at large." Lightfoot, *Philippians*, 3rd ed. p. 258.

[4] See above, pp. 336–341.

Christ is in the fullest sense free, comprehensive, universal. It displays this character not only in the acceptance of all comers who seek admission irrespective of race, or caste, or sex, but also in the instruction and treatment of those who are already its members. . . . Above all, it has no sacerdotal system. It interposes no sacrificial tribe or class between God and man, by whose intervention alone God is reconciled and man forgiven. Each individual member holds personal communion with the Divine Head. To Him immediately he is responsible, and from Him directly he obtains pardon and draws strength. . . . The priestly functions and privileges of the Christian people are never regarded as transferred or even delegated to these officers [of the Church]. They are called stewards or messengers of God, servants or ministers of the Church, and the like; but the sacerdotal title is never once conferred upon them. The only priests under the Gospel, designated as such in the New Testament, are the saints, the members of the Christian brotherhood. . . . The sacerdotal view of the Ministry is a new principle, which is nowhere enunciated in the New Testament, but which notwithstanding has worked its way into general recognition, and seriously modified the character of later Christianity." [1]

[1] Lightfoot, *Philippians*, pp. 179, 182, 243. By no living writer has the Scriptural doctrine on this subject been more powerfully stated and defended than by Bishop Lightfoot in this "Dissertation." It is to be regretted that he should so far have qualified his admirable statements and reasonings by one hesitating clause near the beginning of his essay, and two or three sentences to the same effect near the end. See Note B, "Bishop Lightfoot's attitude towards the sacerdotal theory of the Christian ministry.'

CHAPTER III.

EVERY fellowship or society of men, meeting for common objects and for united action, must have leaders and rules of some kind. This arises from the nature of men and things. If the society be small in numbers and with little to do, the position of the leader or leaders may be temporary and informal, and the rules unwritten and elastic. But *some* one to take the initiative, and *some* rules or common understandings which amount practically to rules, there must always be. The necessity for further and firmer organization makes itself felt as soon as the society grows in numbers, and addresses itself to any definite and sustained action.

This natural law finds illustration in the case of the apostolic Church. Its organization, at first simple and rudimentary, is seen to widen and strengthen itself in accordance with the growth of the society, the emergencies of its history, and the necessities for varied action which arise. Only the development of the organization in this case goes forward with a singular ease and certainty. There is an absence of mistakes. There is no retracing of steps, tentatively taken, which have proved to lead in a wrong direction, as in the early history of infant societies and commonwealths generally. In this fact we have evidence again that a higher wisdom than man's was present to guide the course of the apostolic Church, and that the hand of God in Providence and history had made the right path plain in the sphere of organization as in that of worship. Every step was taken, as we shall see, with prayer on the part of the disciples for guidance and blessing from the unseen Lord, in whose name they met. So doing, His leadership never failed them.

Let us glance for a little at the facts recorded regarding the growth and expansion of the apostolic Church during this first period ; and then note how the organization kept pace with the growth from stage to stage.

1st. The Churches to be organized.

At the date of the Ascension, the fellowship of Christ's disciples was made up of the little company which met statedly in the upper room at Jerusalem, numbering about a hundred and twenty, and of the other disciples in Judæa, Samaria, and Galilee, who were the fruits of the personal ministry of Jesus, the Twelve and the Seventy, prior to the Crucifixion. What the number of these disciples beyond Jerusalem may have been it is impossible to say. But that it must have been considerable, various statements in the Gospels as to the results of Christ's preaching lead us to believe.[1] Our Lord's command to His disciples, mentioned by the first two Evangelists, to meet Him in Galilee on " the mountain where He had appointed them," [2] His actual interviews with them there, as recorded by the first and fourth Evangelist and implied by the second,[3] all go to prove that Galilee, which had been the chief sphere of Christ's teaching, was also the centre where His disciples were to be found in largest numbers at the time of His Ascension. This is confirmed by Paul's reference in First Corinthians to one of the appearances of the Risen Saviour at which upwards of five hundred brethren were present. This incident is in all likelihood identical with the interview in Galilee " on the mountain where Jesus had appointed them," at which, as Matthew tells us, " *they* (the disciples as a body) worshipped Him, but some doubted." [4] The number mentioned by Paul is more than four times as great as that of the disciples who were wont to meet in the upper room at Jerusalem ; and the " doubts," natural to men who saw

---

[1] Matt. iv. 23–25 ; viii. 1 ; ix. 35–38 ; xix. 16 ; xx. 29 ; with the parallels in the other Synoptic Gospels ; John iv. 1 f., 39–53 ; vii. 31 ; x. 42 ; xi. 45–50 ; xii. 11, 19–23, 42 f.

[2] Matt. xxviii. 16 ; comp. Mark xvi. 7 ; Matt. xxvi. 32 ; xxviii. 7, 10.

[3] Matt. xxviii. 16–20 ; Mark xvi. 7 ; John xxi.

[4] Matt. xxviii. 17.

the Risen Lord for the first time, would not have been so, in the case of "the eleven and them that were with them," after the repeated appearances of the Saviour in Jerusalem on the Resurrection evening and the Lord's Day which followed.

Of the growth of the Church in Judæa, Galilee, and Samaria, we have some incidental glimpses at a later stage ; to these we shall advert again. The narrative of the Acts, after a general reference to repeated interviews between the Lord and the apostles during the "forty days,"[1] turns back with the Eleven after the Ascension from Olivet to the little company in the upper room where the disciples awaited the promised coming of the Holy Ghost. The history begins at Jerusalem, and for the greater part of the first section does not pass beyond it.

First, then, let us look at the Church in Jerusalem in its successive stages of growth.

After the Advent of the Spirit the growth in numbers was rapid and continuous.

1. As the result of the preaching of the Gospel on the Day of Pentecost, "there were added unto them about three thousand souls."[2]

This, of course, must not be taken as a permanent addition to the Church in Jerusalem merely. A number of the pilgrims from the Diaspora, who received the truth that day, doubtless returned, after a longer or shorter stay in Jerusalem, to their homes, and formed the nucleus of some of those Christian communities in the Dispersion to which the Epistle of James was afterwards sent. At least as large a proportion probably of the converts of Pentecost had come up from Judæa and Galilee to keep the feast in the Holy City. They went back also after a time carrying with them the new life and the gifts of the Spirit which they had received, and joined themselves to those who had already become disciples of Christ in the scenes of His earthly ministry beyond Jerusalem.

With all these deductions from the full number of three thousand, it still, no doubt, represented a very considerable

---

[1] Acts i. 3. [2] Acts ii. 41.

increase of the permanent membership of the Church in Jerusalem. And more followed :

2. " The Lord added to them day by day such as were being saved." [1] There was a steady and continuous influx of converts from the Day of Pentecost onwards.

3. After Peter's address in connection with the healing of the lame man in the temple it is noted : " Many of them that heard the word believed, and the number of the men— apart from women and children—came to be about five thousand." [2]

4. Again, after a period during which " they "—the disciples generally—" spake the Word of God with boldness," and " the apostles gave their witness to the resurrection of Christ with great power ; signs and wonders also being wrought by their hands among the people," the historian records as the general result that " believers were the more added to the Lord, multitudes both of men and women." [3] This growing success led to a second attempt by the Sanhedrin to check the progress of the truth.[4] But the attempt failed, and then followed :

5. Another period,—how long, it is not said,—during which the counsels of Gamaliel practically prevailed, and the Church was " let alone." The apostles used this opportunity with zeal and energy. " Every day in the temple and at home they ceased not to teach and to preach Jesus as the Christ." [5] The consequence was that the time was one marked for the Church by steady and continuous growth. " In these days, the number of the disciples was multiplying." [6] This led to the appointment of " the seven " to relieve the apostles, by a division of labour, from a burden which growing numbers made too heavy for them. And the result again by God's blessing was—

6. A further expansion of the Church of a very rapid and signal kind—" The Word of God increased ; and the number of the disciples multiplied in Jerusalem exceedingly ; and a great company of the priests were obedient to the faith." [7]

---

[1] Acts ii. 47.   [2] Chap. iv. 4.   [3] Chap. iv. 31–33 ; v. 12–14.
[4] Chap. v. 17–31.   [5] Chap. v. 42.
[6] Πληθυνόντων τῶν μαθητῶν, vi. 1.   [7] Chap. vi. 7.

This was the crowning stage of the unbroken development of the Church in Jerusalem. There followed " the tribulation that arose about Stephen." The apostles, sheltered doubtless by faithful friends, remained in or near Jerusalem. But the members of the Church generally " were all scattered abroad throughout the regions of Judæa and Samaria." [1] The persecution, however, although fierce while it lasted, does not seem to have been of long continuance. The mainspring of it was broken by the conversion of Saul of Tarsus. Other Providential events, such as the collision with the Roman Emperor on matters connected with the temple worship,[2] turned the minds of the Jewish rulers in a new direction. The strong national and patriotic feelings of the Hebrew Christians, whose homes were in Jerusalem or its neighbourhood, would induce them to return to the city as soon as God's hand seemed to open the way for their doing so. The fact that the leaders of the Christian community in Jerusalem had held their ground there through the worst of the storm must have tended to quicken this movement.

The Church which gathered again round the apostles after the persecution was doubtless at first much weaker in numbers than it had been before. But it had its full share in the time of refreshment and blessing described towards the close of the first section of the narrative—" Then the Church throughout all Judæa, and Galilee, and Samaria had peace, being edified; and walking in the fear of the Lord, and in the comfort of the Holy Ghost, was multiplied." [3] The last reference which we have, after a long interval, to the numbers of the Church in the capital, is one which recalls the triumphant results of earlier years. " Thou seest, brother," the elders at Jerusalem said to Paul on his last visit to the city, " how many myriads there are among the Jews of them which have believed; and they are all zealots of the law." [4]

The language of this last passage, however, must not be limited to the Church in Jerusalem merely. It plainly includes all Jewish Christians from different parts of Palestine

---

[1] Acts viii. 1 ; xi. 19 f.
[2] See the graphic account of this in Archdeacon Farrar's *St. Paul*, i. pp. 243–255.
[3] Chap. ix. 31.   [4] Chap. xxi. 20.

who had come up to Jerusalem for the feast, as distinguished
from representatives of "the Jews which are among the
Gentiles." [1]

Secondly, looking now for a little, as this feature in the last
statistical reference naturally leads us to do, at the progress
of the Hebrew Christian Church beyond Jerusalem from the
time of the Ascension onwards, we have—

1. The disciples in Judæa, Samaria, and Galilee, who were
the fruits of Christ's personal ministry and that of the apostles
and "the Seventy" during His earthly life. In Galilee
especially, as noted above,[2] these must have amounted to a
considerable number.

2. The ranks of these "old disciples" throughout the Holy
Land were reinforced by the converts of Pentecost. "The
Galileans also went to the feast." "Dwellers in Judæa"
were among the multitude who heard Peter speak on that
memorable day. His first words expressly appealed to them,
as forming a distinct and prominent element in the crowd:
"Ye men of Judæa, and all ye that dwell at Jerusalem, be
this known unto you."

Many returned that summer to their homes in northern
and southern Palestine, bringing with them the power of the
new life and the gifts of the Holy Ghost. The pulse of that
life beat most strongly in Jerusalem under the personal
ministry of the apostles. But wherever the converts of
Pentecost went, the good news concerning the Christ was told,
and disciples were made and drew together. And the life
spread from every new centre where the Gospel was proclaimed and received.

3. The multitudes who came "from the cities round about
Jerusalem" bringing sick folks and demoniacs for healing,
doubtless received spiritual blessing as well as temporal.[3]

4. The immediate effect of the persecution which fell upon
the Church in connection with the martyrdom of Stephen was
to scatter the believers "throughout the regions of Judæa and
Samaria," ... "and they went about preaching the Word,"—
εὐαγγελιζόμενοι τὸν λόγον, telling the message of the Gospel.[4]

---

[1] See above, p. 332.   [2] See above, p. 395.
[3] Acts v. 16.   [4] Acts viii. 1, 4.

The witness for Christ by word and deed, borne by these confessors, must have been the means of adding largely to the number of the disciples already existing in Judæa and Samaria.   One instance only is recorded in detail :

5. Philip preaches in Samaria, with the result that "the multitudes gave heed with one accord;" and "when they believed the good tidings concerning the kingdom of God and the name of Jesus Christ, they were baptized, both men and women."[1]   The work here demanded special attention, both from its being on so great a scale, and also from its taking place among a people who stood in such peculiar relations to the Jews as the Samaritans did.

6. The apostles therefore send a deputation of their number from Jerusalem, who confirm and complete the work begun by the evangelist, and, on their way homewards, carry it on upon the same lines by " preaching the Gospel to many villages of the Samaritans."[2]   The significance of this apostolic oversight of the Churches we may consider again ; meanwhile we simply note the fresh stage in the growth and expansion of the apostolic Church.

7. Philip "preaches the Gospel to all the cities" of the sea-coast "from Azotus till he came to Cæsarea."   That large and important city seems to have become his headquarters for further work.   We find him there with his family some twenty years afterwards in the midst of a Christian community of some considerable size.[3]

The result of all this work of evangelization beyond Jerusalem is seen in the subsequent history in two successive stages of development.

(1.) The scattered disciples drew together into little companies or congregations.   As such they went up together "with one accord " to the synagogues, as the disciples in Jerusalem did to the temple and to the synagogues there ; and like them also they met for worship, to edify one another, and to break bread " at home."

Such little companies, when considered separately, formed " the Churches of Judæa which were in Christ," of which the

---

[1] Acts viii. 6, 12.   [2] Chap. viii. 14 ff., 25.
[3] Chap. viii. 40 ; xxi. 8-16.

apostle Paul speaks to the Galatians, and to the members of which he was "still unknown by face" after his first visit to Peter and James at Jerusalem; they only heard say: "He that once persecuted us now preacheth the faith of which he once made havoc."[1] They, too, had their experience of persecution, whether spreading from Jerusalem through the country districts, or breaking out there from causes similar to those which gave rise to it in the capital.[2] "Ye, brethren," Paul wrote in his earliest epistle, that to the Thessalonians, "became imitators of the Churches of God which are in Judæa in Christ Jesus; for ye also suffered the same things of your own countrymen, even as they did of the Jews."

(2.) We have these "brethren" and "Churches" in Judæa and Northern Palestine regarded as forming one Christian fellowship or Church, enjoying common privileges, and knit together in ways which we shall consider presently. "So the Church throughout all Judæa, and Galilee, and Samaria had peace (ἡ μὲν οὖν ἐκκλησία καθ' ὅλης τῆς Ἰουδαίας, καὶ Γαλιλαίας καὶ Σαμαρείας εἶχεν εἰρήνην), being edified; and walking in the fear of the Lord, and in the comfort of the Holy Ghost, was multiplied."[3]

To what extent its numbers were multiplied we may gather from the statement of the elders of Jerusalem to Paul as to the "tens of thousands among the Jews which had believed."[4]

So much concerning the growth and ultimate dimensions of the Church which had to be organized on Hebrew Christian ground.

Let us now consider—

2nd. The successive steps in organization.

The beginnings of organization had been given by Christ

---

[1] Gal. i. 22 f.

[2] 1 Thess. ii. 14. Comp. Acts xi. 1, 29: "The brethren in Judæa," "which dwelt in Judæa." The persecutions which followed believers from Jerusalem to their first places of refuge, may have led to their pushing on farther, with the same results as regards the spread of the Church, to Damascus and the regions of Syria (Ananias has heard by many fugitives of this man, ix. 3; x. 13, 25), to Phœnicia, Cyprus, and Antioch, xi. 19.

[3] Acts ix. 31.   [4] Chap. xxi. 20.

Himself in the sense and to the extent pointed out in a former part of this work.[1]

1. For the little company which met before Pentecost at Jerusalem " the Twelve " formed a sufficient centre of unity and guidance. The first action of the Church in the upper chamber was to complete the number of the apostolic college, broken by the fate of Judas.

The proposal came from Peter, still as in former days the readiest spokesman of the Twelve, and now fully restored to the confidence of his fellow-disciples. Whether the suggestion originated with him or not, he at least is the first to bring it forward in a definite and practical shape. Certainly there is no trace of official superiority either in the words of the historian or in his own. " In these days Peter stood up in the midst of the brethren, and there was a multitude of persons gathered together, about an hundred and twenty."[2] The very first words of the apostle remind us of those two great doctrines of the brotherhood of all believers, and the authority of Scripture as the supreme source of guidance for all believers, which hold so marked a place in his epistles : " Brethren, it was needful that the Scripture should be fulfilled which the Holy Ghost spake before by the mouth of David concerning Judas."[3] The proposal thus introduced led to the first election to office in the apostolic Church.

There seems no ground for holding—as some have done—that the action was a hasty one, taken before the Spirit had come upon the disciples in His fulness, and that Paul was the man really designed by the Lord to fill the vacant place in the apostolic college, and to keep it in accordance with the analogy of the twelve tribes of Israel. On the contrary, there seems every reason to regard this election of Matthias as a right and seasonable step, to which the disciples in the upper room were led under the guidance of the Spirit through a

---

[1] See above, pp. 251–254, 263.

[2] " He did not ' sit down,' " says an old commentator, " as one that ' gave laws,' or had any supremacy over the rest, but stood up, as one that had only a motion to make, in which he paid a deference to his brethren, standing up when he spake to them," Matth. Henry.

[3] Acts i. 15 f.: "''Ανδρες ἀδελφοί ist ehrsamer und feierlicher als das einfache vertrauliche ἀδελφοί; cf. ii. 29, 37 ; vii. 2, al." Meyer, in loco.

prayerful consideration of the Word and the Providence of God. And as regards the position designed for Paul, it has already been pointed out that his being added to the apostolic company made the correspondence with the tribes of Israel all the closer. For in reality the number of the tribes was thirteen ; and Ephraim, the youngest and the latest added, proved to be, like Paul among the apostles, the strongest and most fruitful of them all.

Further, with one exception,—the appeal to the lot,—everything in connection with the appointment of Matthias was done in a way obviously fitted and intended to be a pattern to the Church in after times as regards the principles on which such matters should be conducted, and the spirit in which they should be gone about. This explains the minuteness of the narrative. We find the same principles and spirit exemplified in subsequent appointments to office which are recorded or referred to in the Acts.

The chief points in the transaction are—

(1.) The election is placed in the hands, not of the eleven merely, but of the whole company of the disciples.

(2.) The way having been prepared by united prayer and study of the Scriptures, the matter is brought before the meeting by one already in office.

(3.) A clear statement is made of the occasion for the election, of the indications of God's will in His Word and Providence bearing upon it, and of the qualifications needful for this particular " office " or " ministry." [1]

(4.) Two men are chosen accordingly by the company of disciples from their own number, whom they " put forward " (ἔστησαν δύο) as being in their judgment suitable for the office.

(5.) The formal admission to office is conducted apparently by those who already held that office,[2] and is again associated with solemn prayer for Divine guidance and blessing.

---

[1] Τὴν ἐπισκοπὴν αὐτοῦ λαβέτω ἕτερος, in Acts i. 20, is a literal quotation from the LXX. of Ps. cix. 8, except that λαβέτω is put for λάβοι. Ἐπισκοπή (פְּקֻדָּה) is used here in the general sense of " office," or " charge to be fulfilled," just as διακονία is in the sense of " ministry " or " service " in vv. 17 and 25.

[2] The " putting forward " of the two seems to indicate, as in chap. vi. 6, where

One peculiarity only marks the procedure, namely, that the final choice between the two, selected as being, either of them, fit to be appointed, is made by the use of the lot in Old Testament fashion, and with direct appeal to Christ.

This feature never meets us again in any of the elections of office-bearers subsequently recorded in the New Testament. Its occurrence here is easily explained if we consider other Scripture references to the use of the lot with prayer as a solemn religious ordinance under the ancient dispensation, and realize the position of this little company of Hebrew believers in this transition period between the Old and the New, and at this unique crisis of the Church's history.[1]

Around this little company of "early disciples," with the apostles at their head, the converts of Pentecost gathered in that spirit of loyalty and teachableness to which reference has already been made. For a while matters went on of themselves, so to speak, in a sort of provisional way. The wonderful new life in Christ, the fruits of the Spirit on every side, the loving brotherly fellowship among all who believed in the Lord Jesus, the testimony to be borne for Him,—these were the great things that filled every heart. The life, and work, and witness of the Church came first. Anything in the shape of organization was wholly secondary in importance.

Yet from the first, in a fellowship of this sort, the members of which were now counted by thousands, rules and arrangements of some kind, however informal and elastic, there must have been ; as to times and places of meeting, for example, whether in the upper room, in the temple courts, or in the houses of disciples,—as to the administration of Baptism and the breaking of bread. Some of the brethren, besides the Twelve, must have taken the lead in making these arrangements, and others in carrying them out, and attending to the

---

the same phrase is used with a fuller explanation of what followed, that those chosen by the members of the Church were set before the apostles for their approval, and the description of the way in which Matthias was "numbered together with the eleven apostles" (συγκατεψηφίσθη μετὰ τῶν ἕνδεκα ἀποστόλων), naturally suggests that he was formally received and welcomed by them into their number. There is no mention of any imposition of hands any more than in the account of the appointment of the original apostles by our Lord.

[1] Comp. 1 Sam. xiv. 41 ; Prov. xvi. 33.

practical details involved. The hereditary Hebrew reverence for age and experience, instincts of order, habits formed among the Jewish people by long experience of representative government both in Church and State, doubtless came in strongly to help in this. Younger men (οἱ νεώτεροι, νεανίσκοι) volunteered for duties like those of the chazzan in the synagogue.[1]

2. Elders associated with the apostles in Jerusalem, and appearing by themselves elsewhere.

The Twelve formed the acknowledged centre of unity and guidance in the apostolic Church from the beginning. With them from the first it seems probable that, more or less formally, "elders" (πρεσβύτεροι) were associated. They appear by name in the history towards the end of the first section of the Acts, and repeatedly thereafter, as men who were in charge of the affairs of the Hebrew Christian Church, and were its recognised representatives.

In Jerusalem, when the apostles are present, the elders are mentioned as associated with and acting along with them.[2] But in the earliest express reference, which is in connection with a deputation from the Church at Antioch, the elders appear alone. Prophets from Jerusalem had come to Antioch. One of them foretold in the Christian assemblies there that a famine was impending over the whole Roman world. On hearing this, "the disciples, every man according to his ability, determined to send relief (or for ministry, εἰς διακονίαν) unto the brethren that dwelt in Judæa ; which also they did, sending it to the elders (ἀποστείλαντες πρὸς τοὺς πρεσβυτέρους) by the hands of Barnabas and Saul."[3] The commission of the deputies from Antioch was for the relief of distress among the believers, not merely in the capital (which in fact is not mentioned), but in the lesser towns and country districts of Judæa, where the pressure of the famine was likely to be more severe. They are directed therefore to address themselves to a class of men whom, it is taken for granted, they would find in all those "Churches of Judæa

---

[1] Acts v. 6, 10 ; comp. 1 Pet. v. 5. Comp. Neander, *Planting of Christian Church*, 3rd ed. E. Tr. i. p. 35 f.

[2] Acts xv. 2, 4, 6-22 ; xvi. 4.

[3] Acts xi. 29 f.

which were in Christ," to whom Saul of Tarsus was "still
unknown by face," although he had spent some time in
Jerusalem, only they had heard the good report of the
change which had taken place in him, and of his services to
the common cause in Syria and Cilicia.[1]

These elders appear in this passage as office-bearers whose
position was everywhere understood, as the responsible representatives of the Churches, the natural organs for communication with "the brethren that dwelt in Judæa."[2]   That
"Barnabas and Saul when they had fulfilled their ministration" among these Judæan disciples "returned from,". or as
many ancient authorities read, "to Jerusalem,"[3] is not in
the least inconsistent with the plain statement in chap. xi. 29 f.
No deputies to Judæa were likely to fail to visit Jerusalem
ere their return, although their special mission might lie in the
country districts.   Moreover, there was a particular reason
for noting that the deputies from Antioch returned to that
city *viâ* Jerusalem.   The capital was the home of John
Mark, whom his kinsman Barnabas was desirous of enlisting
for work at Antioch.   "They returned" thither "from Jerusalem, taking with them John whose surname was Mark."[4]

Our information regarding "the Churches of Judæa" is so
scanty that we cannot be surprised that it includes no notice

[1] Gal. i. 21–24 ; cf. Lechler, S. 203. Barnabas and Saul would, no doubt,
use the opportunities afforded by this journey through the country districts of
Judæa for preaching the Gospel. This is probably the time referred to by Paul,
in his speech before Agrippa, when, describing the different fields in which he had
laboured as a witness for Christ, he says that he "declared both to them at
Damascus first and at Jerusalem, and throughout all the country of Judæa, and
also to the Gentiles, that they should repent and turn unto God, doing works
worthy of repentance," Acts xxvi. 20.

[2] Bishop Lightfoot regards the second persecution (that in which James the
son of Zebedee was put to death), and the dispersion of the Twelve from
Jerusalem in connection with it, as the probable occasion of the "adoption
of the usual government of the synagogue," and so of the first appointment
of elders. He seems to overlook the facts that the elders are spoken of as
already existing, not in *Jerusalem* merely, but in *Judæa*, and that the deputation
from Antioch, with their commission "to the elders," appears to have been
appointed *before* the persecution arose, in connection with the prediction of
Agabus respecting the famine. Lightfoot, *Philippians*, 3rd ed. p. 191. *Galatians,* 5th ed. p. 123, note.

[3] Acts xii. 25.

[4] Chap. xii. 12, 25.

(like that in Acts xiv. 23-27) of the appointment of the elders there, to whose charge the contributions from Antioch were entrusted by the deputies. It may be asked, however, How comes it that we have no account of the first ordination of elders in the Church at Jerusalem, in reference to which the narrative is so much more detailed ?

The true explanation is in all likelihood a very simple one, namely, that among the disciples in Jerusalem there was a sufficient number of elders from the first.

The original disciples, and those " devout men, Jews and proselytes," who received the Gospel and joined themselves to their fellowship at Pentecost, had all belonged to synagogues in the Holy Land or the Dispersion. Every synagogue, as we saw, had its council of elders, regularly ordained to the office by the laying on of hands. It is morally certain that a number of the converts of Pentecost had already for years filled the office of elder, and were well known to have discharged its duties with acceptance. Men holding that position, and of the spirit which characterized its best occupants, were more likely than others to come from the city and neighbourhood, and from other lands, to be present in the temple courts on the day of Pentecost, and to be found among the " devout men " who received the Gospel as proclaimed by Peter. Such Jewish elders would take their natural place, and fall into their familiar functions, in the different Christian gatherings in Jerusalem κατ' οἶκον very much as a matter of course. There was no need and no thought of any fresh ordination.

Their brethren of the same synagogue in Jerusalem, from the same Judæan district, of the same tongue and country of the Dispersion, and now one with them in the Gospel, would gather round such men as their natural leaders in religious things. They would instinctively look to them for elders' work, and call on them to do it. Such rulers and teachers in Israel as Joseph of Arimathæa, Nicodemus, and Barnabas had been faithful and honoured men, apt to teach, and found fit for the oversight of the flock before, and much more were they felt to be so now, when the Holy Spirit had come upon them in power with His gracious gifts. The ancient institution of the eldership would thus pass by the most simple and natural process from the Church of the Old Testament to that of the New.[1]

In a similar way, doubtless, many of "the elders," whom the deputies from Antioch met among "the brethren that dwelt in Judæa," came to hold that position in the Christian assemblies. Others, after experience of their gifts in the capacity of private members of the Church, may have been "put forward" by the brethren, as Joseph and Matthias were,[2] and ordained in the accustomed way by the existing eldership, or by the hands of apostles and other representatives of the Church in Jerusalem, as they, like Peter, "passed through all quarters," visiting and confirming the Churches.[3] Both Barnabas and Saul had had full opportunity of knowing the practice of the Church in Jerusalem and "throughout all Judæa" ($\dot{\eta}$ $\dot{\epsilon}\kappa\kappa\lambda\eta\sigma\acute{\iota}a$ $\kappa a\theta$' $\ddot{o}\lambda\eta\varsigma$ $\tau\hat{\eta}\varsigma$ $'Iov\delta a\acute{\iota}a\varsigma$),[4] as well as that of the Church of Antioch in this matter. They followed familiar precedents in their ordination of elders in the Gentile, or mixed Jewish and Gentile, Churches of Lystra, Derbe, Iconium, and the Pisidian Antioch.[5]

This view of the origin of the eldership in the apostolic Church is confirmed by all the references to it which we find in the relative Epistles. The word "bishop" ($\dot{\epsilon}\pi\acute{\iota}\sigma\kappa o\pi o\varsigma$) does not meet us until a much later date. It does so, as we shall see subsequently, only on Gentile Christian ground, and, in its technical sense, only in the utterances of the apostle of the Gentiles,[6] once in an address at Ephesus, and three times in his epistles, and always as a synonym for

---

[1] Comp. Baur, *Church History of the First Three Centuries*, 3rd ed. E. Tr. ii. p. 16. Baur rightly recognises the fact that "the statements in the Acts seem to presuppose as a matter of course that, in addition to the apostles, there were also presbyters at the head of the first Christian Churches after the analogy of the Jewish synagogue," and that as regards Jerusalem in particular, before the appointment of the seven, "this Church already possessed presbyters;" but he offers no explanation of how this came about. The natural explanation seems to be the one given above.

[2] Acts i. 23.   [3] Chap. viii. 14; ix. 32.

[4] Chap. ix. 31.   [5] Chap. xiv. 23–27.

[6] The apostle Peter uses the name $\dot{\epsilon}\pi\acute{\iota}\sigma\kappa o\pi o\varsigma$ once of Christ "the Shepherd and Overseer of souls," 1 Pet. ii. 25. He uses the verb $\dot{\epsilon}\pi\iota\sigma\kappa o\pi\hat{\epsilon}\iota\nu$, "to take the oversight," once of the elders of the Christian communities to whom he wrote, chap. v. 2.

" elder." It is worth noting that when these epistles—that to the Philippians and the Pastoral Epistles—came to be translated into Aramaic for Hebrew Christians who still used, at least by preference, their ancient speech, the term ἐπίσκοπος was invariably rendered by " kashisho " or " elder," and ἐπισκοπή, " a bishop's office," by " kashishkuto " or " eldership." [1] Bishops disappear altogether from the Peshito, the oldest translation of the New Testament, in every case in which the term was used by Paul in his letters to Greek-speaking Churches.[2]

On the other hand, the term " elder " is the only technical one used for the ordinary permanent office-bearers of the Christian community, both in the Holy Land and the Diaspora, by those " who seemed to be pillars " in the Church at Jerusalem. Peter writes to the Christians of " the Dispersion in Pontus, Galatia, Cappadocia, Asia, and Bithynia." He takes it for granted, just as the Church at Antioch did with respect to " the brethren that dwelt in Judæa," that in every Christian community there would be " elders " holding an established position, and with a recognised work of oversight and pastoral care to do among their fellow-believers. " The elders among you I exhort, who am a fellow-elder. . . . Tend the flock of God which is among you, exercising the oversight . . . not lording it over the charge allotted to you, but making yourself ensamples to the flock." [3] James, the Lord's brother, sends his epistle to " the twelve tribes which are of the Dispersion," who " hold the faith of our Lord Jesus Christ, the Lord of glory." He takes it as a matter of course that just as the believers to whom he writes, although exposed to persecution and oppression from their fellow-countrymen, assemble regularly for worship in their Christian " synagogue,"

---

[1] ܩܫܝܫܐ in Phil. i. 1 (Plur.); 1 Tim. iii. 2; and Tit. i. 7; and

ܩܫܝܫܘܬܐ in 1 Tim. iii. 1.

[2] The term ܐܦܣܩܘܦܐ, "episkkopo," is retained only (in the Plural) in Paul's address to the elders of Ephesus, Acts xx. 28.

[3] Acts ix. 29 f. ; 1 Pet. i. 1 ; v. 1-3.

so within reach of every sick person among them are "the elders of the Church," to whom he is exhorted to send that they may "pray over him, anointing him with oil in the name of the Lord." [1]   John, the other member of " The Three," who held the foremost place among the leaders of the original Hebrew Christian community at Jerusalem, like Peter, calls himself an elder; and in his great vision of heaven in the Apocalypse, four and twenty elders seated on golden thrones before God, appear as the highest representatives of the Church of the redeemed above. [2]

As regards the nature of the office of elder in the Hebrew Christian Church, the natural presumption, apart from evidence, would be that it continued in substance what it had been hitherto under the Jewish synagogue system in its best days, with suitable modifications and developments in accordance with the free spirit of the Gospel, and the Providential circumstances in which the Christian congregations found themselves placed.   This presumption is confirmed by all the evidence, direct and indirect, bearing upon the point in the New Testament documents which belong to this period of the history.   In them all it is taken for granted —as in the passages above referred to—that the position and general functions of the eldership are those of a well-known and well-understood institution.   "The elders ($οἱ\ πρεσ$-$βύτεροι$) " appear, without introduction or explanation, as the permanent and responsible representatives of the Church in every locality of a wide district such as Judæa, to whose charge commissions from a distance are addressed.   The apostle Peter applies to them the name of "shepherds" or "pastors," which was a familiar title of the synagogue elders. [3]

---

[1] Jas. i. 1 ; ii. 1 f. ; v. 13.   "So finden wir auch im Jacobus-briefe, diesem Spiegel uralter jüdisch-christlicher Verhältnisse der Diaspora, die unter starkem socialen Druck ihrer Volksgenossen lebenden Juden-christen in eigner Synagoge, und dem entsprechend unter eignen Aeltesten ; beide Begriffe sind vermöge ihres historischen Ursprungs einander correlat."   Beyschlag, *Christl. Gemeinde-verf. im Zeitalter des N. T.*, S. 40.

[2] 2 John 1 ; 3 John 1 ; Rev. iv. 4, 10 ; v. 5 f., etc.   The sense in which the word "angel" is used in the seven epistles in the Revelation will be considered again.   See Part vi. chap. iv.

[3] Vitringa, *De Syn. Vet.* pp. 621-640.   See above, p. 135 f.

As himself a fellow-elder (συμπρεσβύτερος), he gives them
the same exhortation which Christ gave to him, bidding them
do a shepherd's duty to the flock of God which was among
them, tending and feeding the lambs and the sheep, exercising
the oversight, or doing a bishop's work among them (ποιμάνατε . . . ἐπισκοποῦντες), not of constraint, but willingly,
nor yet for filthy lucre, but of a ready mind. So doing,
their reward shall be great from the hand of "the Chief
Shepherd," — "the Shepherd and Overseer of your souls,"
as the apostle had previously called Him (Ποιμὴν κ. Ἐπίσκοπος).[1]

James refers to "the elders of the Church" as having
among their ordinary duties those of visiting and praying
with the sick. In the Epistle to the Hebrews, "the leaders"
of the Christian community (οἱ ἡγούμενοι ὑμῶν, a term also
applied to the Jewish elders [2]) "speak to them the Word of
God," and "watch in behalf of their souls, as those that shall
give account." The believers are exhorted to "obey their
leaders," and "submit to them." Salutations are sent to
"your leaders," as being distinct from, and in position above,
the ordinary members of the Church, "all the saints." In
other words, these leaders hold precisely the position and
discharge precisely the functions attributed by Peter and
James to those office-bearers whom they expressly call "the
elders which are among you," "the elders of the Church."[3]

3. Appointment of "the seven."

The circumstances which led to this step, the manner in
which it was carried out, and the results which followed, are
all so carefully noted in the narrative of the Acts as to

---

[1] Acts xi. 29 f. ; 1 Pet. ii. 25 ; v. 1–4. Comp. John xxi. 15–17.

[2] See Vitringa, *l.c.* p. 647 f. Leyrer, art. "Synagogen der Juden," in Herzog,
xv. S. 312.

[3] Jas. v. 14 f. ; Heb. xiii. 7 f., 17, 24. Comp. the designation of Judas
and Silas in the Church at Jerusalem, "men who were leaders among the
brethren" (ἄνδρες ἡγούμενοι ἐν τοῖς ἀδελφοῖς, Acts xv. 22). Meyer sums up the
functions of the elders of the apostolic Church with his usual discrimination
and clearness in his commentary on Acts xi. 30 : "Die Presbyter, nach
Synagogenweise (זקנים) verordnet, waren die ordentlichen Lehraufseher
(Ordner und Leiter, aber auch zum Lehren bestimmt) der einzelnen Gemeinden, und sind im ganzen N. T. identisch mit den ἐπισκόποις, welche erst in
der nachapostolischen Zeit als Inhaber der *Ober*aufsicht mit Unterordnung

show clearly how much importance was attached to this event in the history of the Hebrew Christian Church. "In these days, when the number of the disciples was multiplying, there arose a murmuring of the Hellenists against the Hebrews, because their widows were neglected in the daily ministration (ἐν τῇ διακονίᾳ τῇ καθημερινῇ). And the twelve called the multitude of the disciples unto them, and said, It is not fit that we should forsake the Word of God, and serve tables (διακονεῖν τραπέζαις). Look ye out therefore, brethren, from among you seven men of good report, full of the Spirit and of wisdom, whom we may appoint over this business. But we will continue stedfastly in prayer, and in the ministry of the Word (τῇ διακονίᾳ τοῦ λόγου). And the saying pleased the whole multitude : and they chose Stephen, a man full of faith and of the Holy Spirit, and Philip, and Prochorus, and Nicanor, and Timon, and Parmenas, and Nicolas, a proselyte of Antioch ; whom they set before the apostles (οὓς ἔστησαν ἐνώπιον τῶν ἀποστόλων); and when they had prayed, they laid their hands upon them. And the Word of God increased ; and the numbers of the disciples multiplied in Jerusalem exceedingly ; and a great company of the priests were obedient to the faith." [1]

The increase in numbers alone would have justified the measures taken ; but the need for them was the more pressing because of the differences of language, nationality, and training represented by the two words "Hellenists" and "Hebrews." [2] The great majority of the members of the Church in Jerusalem were Hebrews. All the apostles probably belonged to that section.[3] So did those rulers of the Jews and elders of syna-

---

der Presbyter geltend wurden. . . . Uebrigens erscheinen die Presbyter hier nicht als *Armenpfleger* (gegen Lange, *Apost. Zeitalt.* ii. S. 146), sondern die Gelder werden ihnen als dem *Gemeindevorstande* übersandt. 'Omnia enim rite et ordine administrari opportuit,' Beza." Meyer, *Apostelgesch.* 3te Ausg. S. 243 f.

[1] Acts vi. 1–7.

[2] See above, p. 108 f. It is easy to conceive how the difference of language alone might lead to misunderstandings and suspicions. Many Hellenists might not be able to express themselves freely in the unfamiliar Aramaic, or to catch precisely what was said in that tongue in their presence. Men who feel themselves at a disadvantage in such ways are always prone to fancy that an advantage is being taken of them.

[3] The names of two of them, Andrew and Philip, seem to indicate some

gogues,—such as Nicodemus and Joseph of Arimathæa,—who being ordinarily resident in Jerusalem had joined themselves to the company of the disciples there, and from the first held positions of influence among them. It was to such men of weight and experience in affairs that the apostles would naturally turn for counsel and help in making the general arrangements necessary for disposing of the money "laid" so liberally "at their feet," and in the oversight of the common tables which seem to have been established. The actual "distribution made to each, according as any had need," and the other manual work required, was done by the younger brethren (οἱ νεώτεροι).[1] And those whom the twelve, and other leading men associated with them, would naturally call first to their assistance were youths from their own circle of relatives and acquaintances, and therefore Hebrews.

In these circumstances it is easy to explain how misunderstandings and suspicions arose on the part of the minority of Hellenists at Jerusalem, and why they "murmured against the Hebrews," and accused them of partiality to brethren and sisters of their own tongue, and country, and synagogue. They did not allege that Hellenistic believers who were able to come forward and state their own claims were dealt with unfairly, but that "their widows," speaking perhaps a foreign tongue, and shrinking in their affliction from publicity, "were overlooked" (παρεθεωροῦντο).[2]

This is the first dissension among brethren recorded in the Acts,—the first break in the harmony of the apostolic Church, of which hitherto it could be said that they were "all of one heart and one soul." It is noteworthy that it arose in con-

---

Hellenistic connection; and it has been noted that it was to them that the Greek proselytes, who sought to see Jesus at the feast, made their application, as if more confident of a kindly reception from these two apostles than from the rest of the twelve. But the Bethsaida to which Peter, Andrew, and Philip belonged was not a Hellenistic town. There seems no ground for identifying it with Bethsaida-Julias, at the north-east end of the lake. And other considerations, on which we cannot enter here, make it improbable that any of the twelve were Hellenists in the proper sense of the term.

[1] Acts iv. 34 f.; v. 6, 10.

[2] Comp. the exhortation given at a later date to Jewish Christians by one of the leaders of the Church in Jerusalem "to visit the fatherless and widows in their affliction," Jas. i. 27.

nection with a great increase in the number of the disciples, and in connection with the outward and temporal affairs of the Church ; just as did the first instances of hypocrisy and deadly sin among professing believers.[1]   Such difficulties and occasions of stumbling have often arisen in like circumstances in the subsequent history of the Church of Christ; and men have often sought to meet them in wrong ways.   It has been held that the Church ought to be in the strictest sense "a pure communion," and that when hypocrisy and worldliness are manifested within her pale, it is the duty of true believers to come out and be separate from her, and to set up small societies with a higher standard and more easily kept pure. In a modified and more modern form this view has lent strength to the theory that the visible Church ought never to be larger than a single congregation, able to meet for worship in one place.[2]   It is instructive to observe on what principles and in what spirit such emergencies were met in apostolic times.

This was the first crisis arising within the Pentecostal Church, as distinguished from opposition and persecution from without.   The dangers which it brought were very great. The rising spirit of jealousy and distrust between Hebrew and Hellenist might have led to the most serious divisions.   Had it been by this means that "the Church which was in Jerusalem" was first "scattered abroad," instead of through "the tribulation that arose about Stephen," the result, as regards the furtherance of the Gospel, would have been different

---

[1] The cases of Judas, and of Ananias and Sapphira.

[2] "There is nothing," says Calvin on this passage, "which we ought more to desire than that God would increase His Church and gather His people into one, as much as may be, in every place.   But the corruption of our nature hinders this from being an unmixed blessing.   For many inconveniences arise in connection with additions made to the Church."   Then, after speaking of the entrance of false disciples in the crowd, and of the likelihood of controversies and disputes arising in every large body of men from diversity of temperament, training, etc., he goes on : "Such scandals as these lead many to choose to themselves a handful in place of the Church, shrinking from and even abhorring a crowd.   But no vexation, no trouble of this sort, ought so to weigh with us as to keep us from heartily rejoicing over every increase to the Church, from striving earnestly to enlarge its bounds, and from seeking always, so far as in us lies, to be at one with the whole body of the faithful."   *Comment. in Nov. Test.*, ed. Tholuck, iv. p. 101.   Comp. the author's *Admission to Sealing Ordinances*, pp. 5–20.

indeed. What Gamaliel had lately hinted to the Sanhedrin as the possible issue of this popular movement, as of former ones, if only it were let alone,—what perhaps he desired in his heart to see,—would have seemed to be fulfilled. Even as the followers of Theudas and Judas of Galilee had been " scattered and brought to nought," so " this counsel and work," had it also been " of men " only, would have been overthrown.[1]

Never were the guidance of the unseen Lord and the power of His Spirit more manifest than in the words and action of the apostles at this crisis, and in the response with which their appeal was met on the part of the Church as a whole. The Christian wisdom and self-control displayed by the twelve are most noteworthy.[2] They throw no blame either upon their volunteer-assistants or upon the murmuring Hellenists. They go at once to the root of the evil, the want of a proper division of labour, and of more adequate arrangements for this special business of distribution. Something of implied rebuke there may be in the indication conveyed in the apostles' words, that the true ground of complaint was that the spiritual interests of the Church were suffering through the pressure of more outward work, which had been allowed to fall upon the twelve. But they pass from that at once to the practical remedy. There must be further organization to meet the felt and acknowledged need. Suitable men must be chosen and set apart for the special charge of the whole department of the Church's work in connection with which complaints of neglect —whether well founded or not—had been made. It may be added that the manner in which the whole multitude of the disciples responded to the words of the apostles was a signal proof of the truly Christian spirit which animated the Church

---

[1] Acts v. 36–39.

[2] Even M. Renan, after stigmatizing the apostles as being "little, narrow, ignorant, as devoid of experience as men could possibly be, . . . of an un-bounded credulity, . . . sitting immoveable at Jerusalem upon their seat of honour," etc., cannot withhold his tribute of admiration here : " Le tact qui guida en tout ceci la primitive Eglise fut admirable. Ces hommes simples et bons jeterent avec une science profonde, parce qu'elle venait du cœur, les bases de la grande chose chrétienne par excellence, la charité. Rien ne leur avait donné le modele de telles institutions. . . . On sent que la pensée encore vivante de Jésus remplit ses disciples et les dirige en tous leur actes avec une merveilleuse lucidité." *Les Apôtres*, pp. 56 f., 120 f.

at large. "The Hebrews" formed the great majority of those who chose, but the men chosen by them were to a large extent, if not all—to judge from their names—of the Hellenistic section of the Church. It was a delicately conveyed rebuke, if the complaints of the minority were really unfounded. It was a full proof at least, if there were some grounds for complaint, that the neglect had been entirely unintentional. The Hebrews were perfectly willing to trust "their widows" to the care of the Hellenists, with full confidence in their brotherly love and faithfulness.

The general scope of the office thus created is pretty clearly defined by the words employed in this passage. It was to embrace all that was involved in the work of "the daily ministration" (ἡ διακονία ἡ καθημερινή) and "the serving, or ministry, of tables" (διακονεῖν τραπέζαις). Viewing these expressions in the light of what has been already said regarding the common or family life of the Church, and the common fund from which distribution was made, after suitable inquiry, according to the necessities of the disciples,[1] it seems plain that the functions now assigned to "the seven" related to the care of the poor and needy within the Church, the distribution of money from its treasury, and generally the charge of its outward affairs in their more practical aspects and details. "For ministry" (εἰς διακονίαν) is the phrase used soon afterwards to denote the temporal relief sent by deputies from Antioch to "the brethren that dwelt in Judæa" in time of famine. Jerusalem was included in the mission of this deputation, and at the head of it was Joseph of Cyprus, who had taken part there in the appointment of the seven "for the ministry of tables."[2] A "table" is the natural and Scriptural symbol for the whole temporal requirements of a family. "To serve tables" in the apostolic Church meant to concern oneself about the daily temporal wants of the household of faith, the brotherhood of the disciples of Jesus. The duties entrusted to "the seven," in short, were just in substance those assigned to the office-bearers known as "deacons" in the times of Justin Martyr and other early patristic writers, and there seems no ground for reasonable

---

[1] See above, pp. 299–303. [2] Acts xi. 29 ; comp. xii. 25.

doubt, on a survey of the whole evidence, that the unbroken tradition of such writers from Irenæus [1] onwards is correct in declaring this to be the origin of the deaconship in the Christian Church.

The precise number proposed by the apostles for this office was probably suggested by the familiar Jewish municipal institution of the local Sanhedrin, or " the seven good men of the city." These were " men of good report," and of business capacity, to whom were entrusted by the community all matters relating to public property, such as the sale of synagogue buildings and furniture, copies of the Scriptures, etc. [2] Like these Jewish officials, the seven first deacons had no doubt the help of subordinates in matters of detail. The proposal of the apostles was that men should be chosen who were fit to be " appointed over this business " ($οὓς$ $καταστή$-$σομεν$ $ἐπὶ$ $τῆς$ $χρείας$ $ταύτης$). The expression itself suggests that others were to be under them in the matter. " The seven " were to be at the head of the work. They were to be specially responsible for making the practical arrangements necessary, and seeing that these were efficiently carried out. But the younger men ($οἱ$ $νεώτεροι$), who had been ready to do any lowly service hitherto at the bidding of the apostles, would fall naturally into the place of assistants to the

---

[1] Iren. *Adv. Hær.* i. 26. 3 ; iii. 12. 10 ; iv. 15. 1, E. Tr. (*Ante-Nicene Lib.*) i. pp. 97, 307 f., 419. Irenæus was a pupil of Polycarp, who was a personal disciple of the apostle John, one of the "pillars" of the Church in Jerusalem when the seven were appointed, and afterwards resident in Ephesus where "deacons" were appointed in accordance with Paul's instructions to Timothy, 1 Tim. iii. 8-13. Polycarp, in his letter, written about A.D. 116, to the Church at Philippi, which was then governed by "presbyters and deacons," as in Paul's time it was by "bishops and deacons" (Phil. i. 1), speaks of the deacons as a well-known class of office-bearers, and refers to their duties in terms which perfectly correspond with the view given above. Polyc. *Ad Philipp.* c. v. Comp. Bp. Lightfoot, *Philippians*, 2nd ed. p. 186. *Ignatius and Polycarp*, ii. 914 f. The author of the "Teaching of the Apostles," our earliest extra-canonical witness regarding the polity of the Jewish Christian Churches, refers in like manner to "deacons" as a familiar class of office-bearers existing along with "bishops" in every congregation, and speaks of their election and qualifications in language which recalls that of Acts vi. : "Elect therefore unto yourselves bishops and deacons worthy of the Lord ; men meek and not lovers of money, truthful and approved," chap. xv. 1. See Harnack, *Texte*, ii. 1, S. 56 ff.

[2] Hausrath, *N. T. Times*, 2nd ed. E. Tr. i. p. 83. Lumby, *Acts*, p. 153.

deacons in gathering up the contributions of the faithful, and distributing these under the direction of the seven.

The apostles sought relief from the excessive burden laid upon them, as Moses had done in somewhat similar circumstances in the wilderness, by a division of labour.[1] They handed over this special department of practical work to the seven and their young assistants, with the view of concentrating their own strength in a more effective way on the higher objects of their spiritual ministry. But there is no reason to suppose that this implied that the twelve meant henceforth to resign that general oversight of the affairs of the Church in all their aspects which had been hitherto taken by them. And nothing is more plain than that the apostle Paul held it to be quite consistent with the position and functions of one, who was " not a whit behind the very chiefest apostles," to take the general oversight of collections in the Churches, and to give careful directions in the matter, although leaving to others the local arrangements needful for the actual gathering of the money, and associating others chosen by the Churches with himself in charge of the fund until it was handed over to " James and all the elders " at Jerusalem.[2]

The very next reference in the book of Acts to matters such as those with which " the seven " were put in charge is in connection with the collection made at Antioch " for ministration (εἰς διακονίαν) to the brethren that dwelt in Judæa." The money raised for this purpose is sent by the hands of Barnabas and Saul " to the elders " in Judæa, as the highest permanent representatives of the Churches there in all their interests, outward as well as spiritual, and as the governing body in each congregation. The share of the collection which went to the capital was doubtless laid at the feet of the apostles—if any of the twelve were then in the city—as well as of the elders associated with them, before " Barnabas and Saul returned from Jerusalem [to Antioch] when they had fulfilled their ministration " [3] [πληρώσαντες τὴν διακονίαν].

---

[1] See above, pp. 102, 150.

[2] Acts xxi. 18 f. ; Rom. xv. 25-28 ; 1 Cor. xvi. 1-4 ; 2 Cor. viii. 4 ff., 19-23 ; ix. 1-5 ; xi. 5.

[3] Acts xii. 25.

It may have appeared uncertain to the Church at Antioch whether any of the twelve would be found in Jerusalem when the deputation arrived there. When Paul made his first visit to the capital after his conversion, Peter seems to have been the only representative of the apostles, strictly so called, then in the city.[1] But there was no doubt at all in the mind of the Church at Antioch but that " elders " would be accessible in every Christian community which had been formed in Judæa, whether in town or country ; and it is " to the elders " accordingly that the deputies receive their commission. It seems probable that throughout the country districts of Judæa, elders were as yet the only office-bearers generally recognised in the assemblies of the Hebrew Christians. In the great Church of the capital, with its multitudinous membership and overflowing treasury, there had been already a fuller organization and further division of labour by the appointment of deacons. The actual distribution of the money in the city would naturally be entrusted by the elders there to the survivors of the original seven, with those who may afterwards have been added to their number. In the country districts this would be done by the elders themselves, with such help as was needful from " the younger men." [2]

[1] Gal. i. 18 f.

[2] The fact that the contributions from Antioch were delivered in the first place by the deputies "to the elders" in Judæa is thus not in the least inconsistent—as has been sometimes alleged, e.g. by Prof. Lindsay, Acts, p. 84 f.—with the view that "deacons" had already been appointed in Jerusalem. The functions involved, although related, are quite distinct. "The presbyters," as Meyer says rightly, "do not appear here as *having special charge of the poor ;* but the money is sent to them as the *governing body in the Church.* The funds are handed over to them in order that they may portion them out for distribution by the different persons to whom the personal care of the poor was entrusted." "The presbyterate retained the oversight and general guidance of the diaconate ; but the latter arose out of the former through the emergency described in chap. vi., not *vice versâ.*" *Apostelgesch.* 3te Ausg. S. 136, 243 f. To draw an illustration from the experiences of modern Church life : Suppose a sum of money sent to the "session" of any of our congregations for behoof of the poor. The best mode of dealing with the money would naturally be considered by the "Deacons' Court," *i.e.* the elders and deacons meeting together for the management of the temporal affairs of the Church ; and the actual distribution of it would be made by the deacons in their respective districts.

The office of deacon in the Church was so far a new one, although formed upon Jewish analogies. It was not like that of elder, which passed over naturally and at once from the synagogue, and the nature and general functions of which needed no explanation to any Jewish Christian or proselyte accustomed to the synagogue worship and polity. The care of the poor and needy in Israel had been laid upon the people by God as a religious duty from the times of the earliest legislation. It had been powerfully enforced from age to age by inspired men, and by influential teachers in the synagogues and schools since the period of inspiration came to an end.[1] All the members of the Pentecostal Church were familiar with various arrangements made in the interests of the poor and afflicted; but none of these corresponded to the institution of the deaconship as here described, although it combined elements present in several of them. In New Testament times, in every Jewish community of any size which had the right of self-government, there were officials[2] who went from door to door at stated times collecting for the poor either in money (collectors of the box) or in kind (collectors of the dish or platter).[3] From the fund or store thus gathered, distribution was made under the direction of the "rulers." But these collectors as such had no place among the officials of the synagogue proper, although part of their work might in point of fact be done within the synagogue buildings. They were appointed and paid by the civil Sanhedrin or Jewish magistrates, by whom the amount to be contributed by each member of the community was often fixed. The duties also of these collectors were of a quite subordinate sort, including the details of the work, but not its arrangement and oversight, answering to what might be done as a rule by "the younger men" (οἱ νεώτεροι) in the apostolic Church, rather than by the seven who were "appointed over this business." There seems no

---

[1] See Vitringa, *De Syn. Vet.* pp. 806–809.

[2] Known as נַבָּאֵי צְדָקָה or נַבָּאֵי הָעִיר, "collectors of righteousness" (*i.e.* alms), or "of the city."

[3] נבאי חקופה and נבאי תמחוי. See Vitringa, *De Syn. Vet.* pp. 211 f., 543–547. Schürer, *Hist. of Jewish People*, Div. ii. vol. ii. p. 66.

ground therefore to suppose, as some have done,[1] that these "city collectors" formed the pattern which was followed in the institution of the deacons of the Hebrew Christian Church.

Collections were made also in various ways in connection with the synagogues. Two boxes commonly stood in all the synagogues of the Diaspora, one for alms for the poor of the place, and the other for contributions for the poor of the Holy Land. Reference is made repeatedly in the Gospel narratives to similar provision for receiving the gifts of the worshippers in the synagogues of Palestine and in the temple courts.[2] The general arrangements with respect to these collections, and to the disposal of the funds thus raised, were made by the elders of the congregation who had the oversight of its financial as well as religious affairs; and the practical arrangements for gathering and distributing the money were sometimes entrusted to special collectors, but more commonly were left in the hands of the Chazzan or attendant.[3] In many cases, especially in the smaller synagogues, a somewhat miscellaneous congeries of duties devolved upon this useful official.[4] Instances of this give a certain plausibility to the view of Hausrath and others, that the position of "the seven" was like that of the Chazzan of the synagogue, and that their number possibly corresponded to that of the separate centres of Christian worship, which existed at this time in Jerusalem.[5] But although it may be

[1] See, e.g., Hausrath, N. T. Times, 2nd ed. E. Tr. i. p. 86.   Comp. Vitringa. ut supra, p. 932 f.

[2] Vitringa, pp. 212, 809-815; Mark xii. 41-44; Luke xxi. 1-4; John viii. 20.   In Matt. vi. 2 our Lord censures the ostentation of the Pharisees who were wont to "sound a trumpet before them in the synagogues and in the streets" when they "did alms."

[3] When the collection was made on the Sabbath, the scruples which prevailed among the Jews under Rabbinical teaching against handling money on that day were overcome by the Chazzan taking a promise to pay from the members of the congregation instead of the actual coin, Vitringa, p. 811 ff.   The rule against giving or receiving money on the Sabbath is referred to by Philo, Leg. ad Caium.

[4] See above, p. 148.

[5] See Zöckler, Apostelgesch. S. 179.   Vitringa holds that the "deacons" of the Pauline Epistles and of the early post-apostolic Church corresponded to the Chazzans of the synagogue, but that "the seven" were appointed to

perfectly true that there were cases in which a synagogue officer, being a man of proved honesty and tact, had a good deal of what might be called "deacons' work" entrusted to him, yet his position cannot be fairly said to correspond in essentials with that of "the seven." The difference is obvious between the single synagogue attendant, with his multifarious and often menial duties, and the body of responsible men, set apart to office in the Church with prayer and the laying on of hands, and appointed collectively over one distinct department of the Church's work. The office of the Chazzan, as stated in connection with our consideration of the synagogue system, was essentially that of the beadle, church officer, or caretaker of modern times. The name ($\dot{v}\pi\eta\rho\acute{e}\tau\eta\varsigma$) applied to the synagogue attendant in the New Testament is the term commonly used in the Gospels and Acts for an apparitor, lictor, or temple attendant.[1] It is never used in reference to "the seven" in the Acts, nor in reference to the "deacons" of the apostolic Epistles.

On the other hand, the office, the origin of which is so carefully narrated in the passage now under consideration, is a lower one indeed than that of "the ministry of the Word," and the oversight of the flock in spiritual things; but it is an office distinctly in the Church and not outside of it, and one of importance and honour. The men who are to fill it are chosen on the ground of distinctively Christian qualifica-

---

an extraordinary and temporary office, distinct from that of "deacon," as curators of the poor in the Hellenistic section of the Pentecostal community at Jerusalem, *De Syn. Vet.* pp. 920–932. Ritschl, again, although speaking with some hesitation on the subject, is disposed to regard the office of "the seven" as comprising the duties assigned to both "elders" and "deacons" at a later period in the apostolic Church. In their appointment he sees implicitly the foundation of both of these offices as afterwards separately developed, *Entstehung der alt. kath. Kirche*, 2te Aufl. S. 354–357. Lechler agrees in substance with Ritschl, *Apost. u. Nachap. Zeitalt.* 3te Ausg. S. 78 f. Others, such as J. H. Böhmer in earlier, and Professor Lindsay in later times, have held that this was the first appointment in the apostolic Church of the office-bearers who appear soon afterwards (c. xi. 30) as "elders." None of these theories seem to me to meet all the facts of the case.

[1] Matt. v. 25; xxvi. 58; Mark xiv. 54, 65; Luke iv. 20; John vii. 32; xviii. 3; etc.; Acts v. 22, 26. It is used also in reference to John Mark when acting as personal attendant to Barnabas and Saul on their first missionary journey, Acts xiii. 5.

tions, as well as on those of trustworthiness and capacity for affairs. They are put in charge of what formed, as we have already seen, a most important part of the fellowship (ἡ κοινωνία) of the Pentecostal Church, the practical expression of the spirit of Christian brotherhood by the relief of every one among them who was in need.

The view of the office of " the seven" now given will be found to be confirmed if we examine a little more closely the qualifications required, and the mode in which the appointment was made.

As to the qualifications for the office:

First, those to be appointed must be members of the Church.

"Look ye out, brethren, from among you seven men." It was not a matter for " them that are without," however upright and reliable in the ordinary relations between man and man; nor was it to be delegated to a paid agency. It was work among brethren and sisters, to be done by brethren in a spirit of brotherly love and willing service.

Secondly, there must be several brethren joined together in the common charge.

This was now the third time in the experience of the apostles that the love of money, or of advantages arising from it, and that in connection with a common fund, had led to most unhappy results. The temptations of the common purse, which Judas bore in the original circle of the disciples, had been the first occasion of his sin and fall. It was in connection with contributions to the treasury of the Church that Ananias and his wife had gone astray. And now this first dissension within the Christian brotherhood after Pentecost had arisen from certain disciples seeing or supposing that they and theirs were not getting their full share of the benefits of the common fund. This charge was a burden too great, and associated with temptations too insidious, to allow of its being left with safety in the hands of one man. There must be joint responsibility, and united " oversight of this business " of apportionment and distribution from the common store.

Thirdly, those appointed to this office must be " men of

good report " (ἄνδρες μαρτυρούμενοι), of well-established character for honesty and uprightness.

Any deficiency or uncertainty in this respect, the mere fact of any of the seven not being known to the Church generally in this capacity, would have been a preliminary bar to his election. It is easy to see how the circumstances of the Church gave special weight to this consideration. The apostles put it first in their statement of the personal qualifications necessary. There was a spirit of jealousy and suspicion rising among the Hellenists. Let them choose men who would be owned on all sides as above suspicion, men whom they themselves could trust.

Fourthly, " men full of the Spirit." Those who were to fill this office must be believers in whom were manifestly seen the fruits of that new Divine life which came to the Church with the advent of the Holy Ghost at Pentecost, in whom all impulses of selfishness and partiality were taken away by the presence and power of the Holy Spirit of God, and who would do the work entrusted to them faithfully and gladly from love to the Lord and the brethren.

Fifthly, " men full of wisdom."

Besides proved integrity and a Christian spirit, certain natural gifts were essential for the right discharge of the duties of the deaconship. The office demanded practical sagacity, discrimination, and prudence. Such qualities, when quickened and consecrated by the breath of the Divine Spirit, form the very features of that " wisdom from above " of which one of the chief leaders of the Church at Jerusalem afterwards wrote to the Jewish Christians of the Dispersion: " The wisdom that is from above is first pure, then peaceable, gentle, easy to be entreated, full of mercy and good fruits, without partiality, and without hypocrisy." [1]

The facts recorded in the subsequent history regarding Stephen and Philip furnish no valid objection to the view now given of the office of deacon, as one in itself essentially distinct from the ministry of the Word and the oversight of the flock. That two out of the seven men first set apart to the deaconship in Jerusalem should have afterwards developed

[1] Jas. iii. 17.

gifts obviously fitting them for different and higher work in the cause of Christ, and should, under the guidance of the Spirit and the Providence of God, have done such work with signal success, constitutes no argument whatever against the conclusions as to the true nature and functions of the deacon's office in itself to which we have been led by the direct evidence bearing on the subject. There was nothing in the fact of the seven having been set apart specially for service in the deaconship to hinder them from using freely, like the other disciples, as they had opportunity, all spiritual gifts of utterance and exhortation which might be in them. On the contrary, the confidence shown them by their brethren, and the experience gained daily among "the poor of the saints which were at Jerusalem," in visiting the sick and dying, "the fatherless and widows in their affliction," were fitted to be spiritually helpful and stimulating to themselves in many ways. "They that have served well as deacons," was the testimony some thirty years later of one who had known both Stephen and Philip, "gain to themselves a good standing and great boldness in the faith which is in Christ Jesus."[1]

In those Reformed Churches in which at this day the deaconship exists in practical efficiency as an office which has to do essentially with the outward and temporal affairs of the Church, and especially with the care of the poor and needy, no facts are more familiar than these,—that the office itself gives many valuable opportunities for spiritual work to every man who holds it; that it opens to him a wider sphere of Christian usefulness and influence than he had as a private member of the Church; and that by the use and improvement of such opportunities men are constantly rising from the ranks of our deacons to fill with acceptance and success higher positions among the elders, the evangelists, and the pastors and teachers of the Church.[2]

---

[1] 1 Tim. iii. 13. Comp. Rothe, *Pastoralbriefe*, 2te Aufl. i. 8, S. 68.

[2] See Mr. Macpherson's interesting sketch of "The Deaconship since the Reformation" in *Cath. Presbyt.* ix. pp. 443–450. The New Testament conception of the deaconship has unfortunately been lost in the Church of Rome and the Church of England. With them the "deacon" is an "assistant clergyman." His chief public duties are to read the lessons and prayers in the Church, to preach, to baptize, and to "instruct the youth in the Catechism." A faint

As to the mode of appointment, observe—

1. The proposal came not from any individual apostle, but from "the twelve" acting as a body.

We do not even hear of Peter coming forward, with his wonted readiness, as the spokesman of the rest. It was no longer possible now, when the membership of the Church was counted by thousands, that all the disciples should be consulted from the first, as in the case of the election of Matthias in the upper chamber. The mind of the twelve had no doubt been ripened and gathered through previous conference among themselves, and probably with other "leaders among the brethren," and through prayerful consideration of the crisis which had arisen in all its aspects. The suggestion, from whomsoever it first came, had approved itself to all the apostles. The proposal had taken definite shape, and is made now by "the twelve" in their collective capacity. From this point onward action is taken in precisely the same way as in the election of Matthias, already considered,[1] with one exception, namely, that there is now no use of the lot.

2. The emergency, and the method proposed for meeting it, are brought by the apostles before the members of the Church generally, in a full meeting called for the purpose. The nature of the proposal is clearly explained to the meeting; and their unanimous approval of it is expressly recorded, "The saying pleased the whole multitude of the disciples." The initiative now passes into their hands.

3. The members of the Church choose the seven men from among themselves whom they count fittest for this office, and "put them before the apostles."

4. The apostles, concurring in the choice, set these brethren apart to the office with solemn prayer and laying on of hands, as the custom was in the ordination of elders in the synagogues.

---

reminiscence of the work of "the seven" may be seen in the Anglican "office for the ordering of Deacons," in the concluding clause : "Furthermore, it is his office, where provision is so made, to search for the sick, poor, and impotent people of the parish, to intimate their estates, names, and places where they dwell unto the curate, that, by his exhortation, they may be relieved with the alms of the parishioners or others." Comp. *Life of Dr. Arnold*, 7th ed. pp. 470, 494.

[1] See above, pp. 402–404.

All these facts taken together seem to prove beyond doubt
that we have here the first recorded appointment of ordinary
office-bearers in the Christian community, that the nature of
the office was as stated above, that it was in one sense a new
one, and that therefore the grounds on which it was established,
and the mode in which the first deacons were appointed, were
carefully put on record for the future guidance of the Church,
but that the office was framed on the lines of well-known
Jewish institutions and arrangements, and embodied principles
with which every member of the Pentecostal Church, as having
been previously connected with some synagogue congregation,
was thoroughly familiar. In one of its main aspects, the
deaconship in the Hebrew Christian Church was just a practical embodiment of that care for the poor and needy in the
congregation of the Lord, and for the stranger within their
gates, as a religious duty and privilege, which was no new
thing in Israel, but which was now developed in a new
and higher form, inspired and consecrated by the Spirit of
Christ and of loving Christian fellowship.

3rd. General results as regards organization.

Looking back now upon the section of the history of
the apostolic Church which we have traversed, the general
results of our survey of the evidence available under the
two heads of worship and organization may be summed
up as follows. Both in its worship and polity the Hebrew
Christian Church was conformed in all essential respects to
the model of the Hebrew synagogue. We have seen already
how clearly this comes out as regards its worship. We are
now so far in a position to see that the same thing holds as
unmistakeably with regard to its organization. The form of
polity which had been universally established for centuries in
the Jewish Church, both in the Holy Land and the Diaspora,
which in its central institution of the eldership and in many
of its leading principles went back to the earliest days of the
history of Israel, was " simply accepted and perpetuated by
the apostles." [1]

---

[1] " This, then, is the reason why you do not find distinct traces in the New
Testament of the creation of the Presbyterian form of Church government.

The few modifications which they made were in perfect accordance with the principles and spirit of the system. What was to a certain extent new, as in the appointment of "the seven," grew naturally out of the old.

The institution of the deaconship furnishes an admirable illustration of the remark last made. It was rather, as we have seen, a happy combination and elevation of existing elements into a higher unity, than a new creation in the strict sense of the word. And the whole manner of the appointment was in the closest accordance with recognised precedents in the synagogue system. We have already noted the main principles embodied in the office itself as a collegiate one, and in the successive steps by which the first deacons were set apart to it,[1]—the principle of representation and common responsibility,—of free election by the members of the community,—of admission to office by those who were themselves already office-bearers, with the customary token of this in the imposition of hands,—that all power of jurisdiction and oversight in any department of public work should be entrusted, not to one man merely, but to several, associated together for the purpose. With every one of these principles, both as to theory and practice, every member of a Jewish synagogue was perfectly familiar. And all the members of the Hebrew Christian Church had been members of synagogues,—most of them from their earliest childhood, like their fathers before them. There was therefore for them no breach of historic continuity, as, under the guidance of the Spirit of Christ and of God speaking through the apostles, the old passed gradually and almost insensibly into the new, and the Churches of Christ rose out of the congregations of Israel and of the Lord in which these "devout men, Jews and

---

The apostles could not create what had been in use some hundreds of years before they were born. They themselves were all of them Presbyterians before they were Christians. And these are the two facts, the knowledge of which makes us intelligent Presbyterians : First, that the form of government in the Church before Christ came was Presbyterian ; and secondly, that this form of government was not abolished nor altered, but simply accepted and perpetuated by the apostles. It was extended to all groups of people who received Christ.' Dr. Marcus Dods, *Presbyterianism older than Christianity*, p. 22.

[1] See above, pp. 423 f., 426.

proselytes," together with their children, had worshipped and found spiritual nurture and blessing hitherto.

1. The synagogue system in the Hebrew Christian Church, in its more congregational aspects.

In cases where a whole synagogue, or the majority of its office-bearers and members, embraced the Gospel,[1] the change in the experience of the congregation as regards the form and order of worship and government, even to the minutest outward details, must have been hardly perceptible. They still met, both on the Sabbath and the Lord's day, in the familiar place called by the old name, to worship the God of their fathers. The same eldership took the oversight of the congregation. The same men came forward at their call " before the ark," where the rolls of the law and the prophets were kept, to read the Scriptures, to lead in prayer, or to give " a word of exhortation to the people." The same familiar psalms were chanted. Only the worshippers had " found Him of whom Moses in the law and the prophets and psalmists did write," Jesus of Nazareth, the Son of David and the Son of God. They heard of Him in their synagogue, of His life and teaching, His death and resurrection, from the lips of " eye-witnesses and ministers of the Word." They realized His own Divine presence in the midst of them, and heard and felt how God had fulfilled the promise made of old to their fathers by sending now in full measure to their children " the blessing of Abraham " in the mission of Christ and the gift of the Holy Ghost.[2] Through all the old familiar forms the Hebrew Christians felt the power of a new and glorious life. It met them in " the teaching of the apostles," " the fellowship " of the brethren, " the breaking of the bread, and in the prayers " and praises of the Church.[3] The Lord fulfilled His promise and sent them, as in the best days of Israel, " prophets, and wise men, and scribes." [4] As Paul himself, " an Hebrew of the Hebrews," wrote afterwards to a Church which grew directly,

---

[1] Instances of this sort are recorded. See Selden, *De Syned. Vet. Heb.* lib. iii., Londini 1655, p. 318 f. Vitringa, *De Syn. Vet.* p. 448 f. Comp. Acts xviii. 10–12 ; xviii. 8 ; Jas. ii. 2. Hatch, *Organiz. of Early Christ. Churches*, p. 59 ff.

[2] Acts iii. 24–26 ; Gal. iii. 14.   [3] Acts ii. 42.   [4] Matt. xxiii. 34.

like most of the Pauline Churches, out of a Jewish synagogue, and only separated from it at length by constraint: " Christ gave some to be apostles, and some prophets, and some evangelists, and some pastors and teachers ; for the perfecting of the saints unto the work of ministering unto the building up of the body of Christ." [1]   But no utterance of apostles or New Testament prophets ever called upon any Hebrew Christian to leave his synagogue, if the synagogue would receive Jesus as the Messiah promised of old, or even tolerate in their meetings the proclamation of Christian truth from the ancient Scriptures. And when it proved necessary, in face of growing opposition and blasphemy, to " separate the disciples," along with those of " the synagogue rulers which believed," as Paul ultimately did at Corinth and at Ephesus, and to meet for worship elsewhere, there is not the slightest evidence that any other organization was set up among the believers in the Christian synagogue than just what they had been familiar with from childhood in the Hebrew one, from which persecution had now driven them against their will, and no doubt with hopes of returning to it in happier days, when their brethren and kinsfolk according to the flesh should repent and believe the Gospel. [2]

For the apostles to have done otherwise, without an express command from Christ Himself, or some clear revelation of His will by the Holy Spirit, would have been to run counter to all the teaching of God's Providence in His dealings with Israel for centuries.   God's voice in the history of His chosen people had spoken plainly in this matter.   " His name had been recorded " in their " houses of prayer " and " of meeting " since the days of the Exile and the Return.   According to His ancient promise, He had " met with them and blessed them " wherever, from the time of Ezekiel and Ezra, Nehemiah and Malachi, [3] they had gathered themselves together to hear His Word and confess their sins, to pray and to praise the

---

[1] Acts xviii. 19 ff., 24–27 ; xix. 1–9 ; Eph. iv. 11 f.   Even if, as is now generally held, our " Epistle to the Ephesians " was originally sent as a circular letter to the Churches of Asia, it had special reference to the Christians of Ephesus, as forming the mother Church of the province.

[2] Acts xviii. 4–11 ; xix. 8–10 ; Rom. ix. 1–5 ; x. 1 ff.

[3] " He shows himself a true prophet when he contrasts the worthless ministry of

name of their covenant God. His hand had prepared and tested the framework for the polity of a world-wide Church in that synagogue system by which the scattered nation in the Dispersion, as well as in the Holy Land, had been able everywhere to spread and prosper in spite of opposition and persecution, and to hold their ground even against the power of Rome.[1]

So far from the apostles having any command of Christ to discard the ancient system of worship and polity, there were not a few sayings of His which pointed in the opposite direction. He had promised to raise up " prophets, and wise men, and scribes," *i.e.* teachers of the kind most honoured in Israel since the Exile, along with others of the old prophetic type, commissioned by Himself to labour especially " in the synagogues." He had spoken words of sympathy to His disciples regarding the special trial which, He foretold, was in store for them, in that their fellow-countrymen would " put them out of the synagogues " in which they had hitherto worshipped.[2]

Our Lord's two great utterances regarding His own Church in its future development, as recorded by the first evangelist, correspond closely, as we saw before,[3] with the two main conceptions of the fellowship of God's people which had gradually formed themselves in the religious consciousness of Israel in Old Testament times, under the progressive teaching of the Word and the Providence of God. Every devout Israelite was familiar with the conception of " the whole congregation or assembly of Israel," and " of the Lord," made up of all who were united in faith and obedience to the God of Abraham, the one true and living God. This great " ecclesia " had its centre and seat of authority in Jerusalem, and especially in the temple. It was there that the " elders of Israel " met in council in the great Sanhedrin, and in the schools of the teachers and masters of Israel. " Out of

the unwilling priests with the 'pure offering' of prayer and praise that rises from all corners of the Hebrew Dispersion." Robertson Smith, art. " Malachi," in *Encycl. Britann.* 9th ed. xv. p. 314*b*.

[1] See above, pp. 148 ff., 160 f.
[2] Matt. xxiii. 34 ; John xvi. 2. See above, pp. 144 f., 226 f.
[3] See above, pp. 161 f., 180 f., 264 ff.

Zion went forth the law, and the Word of the Lord from Jerusalem."

Equally familiar to the Hebrew mind was the conception of the local " ecclesia," as the representative in each place of the authority and fellowship of " the congregation of the Lord." These became visible and accessible to the individual Israelite in the synagogue or synagogues of the local Jewish community to which he belonged, and in the eldership ($\text{ܩ}\text{ܫ}\text{ܝ}\text{ܫ}\text{ܐ}$, $\gamma\epsilon\rho\text{ov}\sigma\acute{\iota}a$) which had the oversight of each synagogue separately, and often, as in Alexandria, of all of them collectively.[1]

2. Relations of members and congregations of the Hebrew Christian Church to one another : unity of the Church as a whole.

What we have been considering hitherto in connection with worship and organization, has belonged for the most part to the sphere of the second conception above mentioned, that, namely, of the local religious community, as brought out especially in the narrative regarding the Church at Jerusalem. Let us see now whether, and to what extent, we find in the New Testament sources available for this period anything which corresponds to the Hebrew conception of the whole congregation or assembly of Israel and of the Lord. What do we learn in the first section of the Acts and the other canonical documents which bear upon the subject regarding the relation of the scattered believers and groups of believers, the Christian congregations or communities in different places,

---

[1] Comp. Beyschlag's remarks in his chapter on "die Gemeinde-idee Jesu." After referring to our Lord's use of the word ἐκκλησία in the two great passages in Matthew, he goes on : " Ein Formbegriff den bereits das Judenthum ausgeprägt hatte, und zwar in derselben zwiefachen weiteren und engeren Fassung in der wir ihn in Jesu Munde finden, und der darum um so weniger als ein bereits von ihm angewandter anzuzweifeln ist. Ebenso wie er (Matt. xvi. 18) seine künftige Gemeinde als eine über den ganzen Erdkreis hin zu bauende denkt, so dachte schon das Judenthum das ganze israelitische Volk als eine grosse im Tempel anbetende Gemeindeversammlung ; und ebenso wie er (Matt. xviii. 17 f.), seine Gemeinde überall, wo zwei oder drei in Seinem Namen versammelt seien, als Ortsgemeinde in selbstständige Erscheinung treten lasst, hatte auch schon das Judenthum die grosse einheitliche Volksgemeinde in der Vielheit der überall wo sich ein Versammlungshaus erhob, in selbstständige Erscheinung tretenden Synagogengemeinden." *Christl. Gemeindeverf. im Zeitalt. des N. T.* S. 10.

to each other?   Had they any common relations and responsibilities ?   If so, how were these conceived of by themselves,
and in what forms were they expressed and embodied ?

The answers to these questions may be summed up in three
sentences.

The Hebrew Christian Church was, and felt itself to be,
essentially one.   It is constantly spoken of as one.   It acted
and had suitable means for acting as one.

(1.) The apostolic Church of this first period was one, and
felt itself to be so.

Nothing comes out more clearly in the early chapters of
Acts than the unity of the Church of those days.   The fact,
and the sense of it which prevailed among the disciples, are
alike set forth often and powerfully in the narrative.   As
already observed, the keynote of this whole first period of
the history is the emphatic word ὁμοθυμαδόν, " with one
accord." [1]

Until the Advent of the Spirit, the little company of
a hundred and twenty " were all together in one place." [2]
When growing numbers, from the day of Pentecost onward,
made it impossible for them to have but one place of meeting,
the unity of mind and heart was still unbroken.   It grew
only the deeper and stronger.   " All that believed were
together " still, as opportunity offered, " in the temple " and
" from house to house," and " had all things common."   " The
multitude of them that believed were of one heart and soul
. . . and great grace was upon them all." [3]   They were, and
felt themselves to be, one in the Lord, one in the new life in
the Holy Spirit, the Spirit of Christ and of God, one in faith
and love, in hope and joy.

Strong as the old Hebrew sense of the unity of Israel had
been, and strongly as it continued to be felt by Hebrew
Christians, such as the apostle Paul, this new consciousness
of their being one with Christ, and with all His true disciples,
was stronger still.   It arose out of the central fact in the
whole spiritual experience of each believer, namely, that he
had been brought, by the power of the Holy Spirit, into
the closest personal relation to the Lord Jesus, that he had

[1] See above, pp. 298, 306 f.   [2] Acts i. 14 ; ii. 1.   [3] Chap. ii. 44 ; iv. 32 f.

received, and was daily receiving, Him afresh as his Saviour and Master, that he had come to "know the only true God, and Jesus Christ whom He hath sent." This real experimental knowledge of God in Christ was for him even here "eternal life." [1] It had changed the look and the relations of everything round about him. "The darkness had passed away, and the true light was shining more and more." To walk in this blessed fellowship with the Lord Jesus in the light was consciously "the way of salvation." And it was not a solitary way. Others around him had the same experience, and showed the same evidence of it. Some of the ancient Paschal Psalms, which were doubtless often on the lips of disciples who had sung them with the Lord Himself, expressed the feelings of each :

> That stone is made head corner-stone which builders did despise :
> This is the doing of the Lord, and wondrous in our eyes.
> God is the Lord, who unto us hath made light to arise :
> Bind ye unto the altar's horns with cords the sacrifice.
>
> . . . .
>
> I'll of salvation take the cup ; on God's name will I call ;
> I'll pay my vows now to the Lord, before His people all.
> Within the courts of God's own House, within the midst of thee,
> O city of Jerusalem, praise to the Lord give ye.[2]

All alike felt that they belonged to each other, because they belonged to the same Lord and Saviour, and that it was His will that they should associate themselves together in His name in every possible way, so that their unity should be seen and known of all men. Each disciple individually had first of all been "added to the Lord," and had thereby set foot on the way of salvation ; "and the Lord continued adding to their company day by day those that were being saved" (προσετίθει τοὺς σωζομένους καθ' ἡμέραν ἐπὶ τὸ αὐτό).[3] Each fresh day of blessing added new brethren to their gatherings, and to the fellowship of the Church in all its forms. The Spirit, who dwelt in and guided the believers at Pentecost, was as far as possible from being a source of separation or indi-

---

[1] John xvii. 3.
[2] Ps. cxvi. 13 f. ; cxviii. 22, Scottish Metrical Version. Comp. 1 Pet. ii. 2-9.
[3] Acts ii. 41, 47 ; v. 12-14.

vidualism. One of the first and fairest fruits of the Spirit was
seen in this, that all in whose hearts His grace was felt were
drawn into the closest outward as well as inward unity.

Our Lord Himself set His seal upon this sense of unity, in
words which no disciple would have ventured to use, unless
he had received them directly from Him. The lesson of the
oneness of believers with Christ, and with each other in Him,
was the first which Saul of Tarsus learned from the lips of
the ascended Saviour. When struck down to the ground by
the great light from heaven that shone around him at mid-
day on the road to Damascus, " he heard a voice, saying
unto him : Saul, Saul, why persecutest thou Me ? . . . And
he said : Who art Thou, Lord ? And the Lord said : I am
Jesus whom thou persecutest." [1]

Those humble and defenceless men and women, whom Saul
persecuted to the death, " punishing them oftentimes in all
the synagogues, and striving to make them blaspheme "
their Lord,[2] were right indeed to " hold fast His word and
not deny His name," right in that unconquerable conviction that the Lord Jesus was theirs and that they were
His. The Son of God Himself bore witness from heaven that
they were in the most real sense *one* with Him, and He with
them. It was of this that Paul the apostle wrote afterwards,
in many a deep similitude, in his later epistles ; but it is all
summed up in one brief comprehensive phrase, which runs
through all his writings from the earliest to the last, " in
Christ " ($\dot{\epsilon}\nu$ $X\rho\iota\sigma\tau\hat{\omega}$). He uses the words once and again in
reference to those little groups and gatherings of Christians
in the country districts of Judæa on whom also that fiery
persecution fell which was everywhere associated with the
name of Saul of Tarsus ($\dot{o}$ $\delta\iota\dot{\omega}\kappa\omega\nu$ $\dot{\eta}\mu\hat{a}s$), but to whom he
himself " was unknown by face " until long after his con-
version, " the Churches of Judæa which were in Christ,"—
" the Churches of God, which are in Judæa in Christ Jesus,
. . . which suffered such things of the Jews." [3]

This, then, was the great central bond of union between
the members of the apostolic Church. They were and felt

---

[1] Acts xxvi. 14 f. [2] Chap. xxvi. 11.
[3] Gal. i. 22 f. ; 1 Thess. ii. 14.

themselves to be one in Christ Jesus. It is essential to the right discussion of the part of our subject now in hand that we should at the outset give its proper place to this fundamental fact. It follows from the nature of the case that this real and essential unity which existed among the members of the Hebrew Christian Church would find ways of expressing itself outwardly, just as the unity of "the congregation of Israel" did in earlier times. Further, we should expect that the lines of development would be similar at least in both cases, but that the deeper and stronger consciousness of unity would create for itself new forms of expression where the old ones proved insufficient. We might have been sure that this would be so, even had the evidence as to what actually took place been much scantier than it is.

(2.) The apostolic Church of this period is constantly spoken of as one.

In the first twelve chapters of Acts the word "Church" (ἐκκλησία) occurs nine times : and in every case it is in the Singular, not the Plural.[1] We have seen how rapid and steady was the growth of the Church in and around Jerusalem during all that first period in its history which ends with the death of Stephen. From the day of Pentecost onward its membership was reckoned by thousands. The successive additions of large numbers at one time, and the intervening seasons of quiet and continuous growth, are carefully noted by the historian.[2] The disciples, during all this period, had their appointed meetings in public, as we saw before, in connection with the worship of the temple and synagogues. They had also their more private gatherings in the upper room and in the houses of different disciples, for the purposes of distinctively Christian worship.[3]

These latter assemblies were certainly "Churches in the house" (ἐκκλησίαι κατ' οἶκον), in the sense in which we find the phrase used in the Pauline epistles. Yet during the whole of the first twelve chapters of Acts the word used to denote the fellowship or society of the Hebrew Christians,

---

[1] See Note A, "Use of the word ἐκκλησία in the N. T."
[2] See above, p. 396 ff.   [3] See above, pp. 351 ff.

in its actual historical development in Jerusalem and around it, is "Church" in the Singular (ἡ ἐκκλησία). "Great fear came upon the whole Church." "There arose a great persecution against the Church which was in Jerusalem." "Saul laid waste the Church, entering into every house (κατὰ τοὺς οἴκους εἰσπορευόμενος,—the different houses especially which had been places of Christian assembly), and haling men and women." "The report came to the ears of the Church which was at Jerusalem ; and they sent forth Barnabas as far as Antioch," etc.[1]

The only instances of the use of the word "Church" in the Plural, in connection with the Hebrew Christian period, are in the two verses already quoted from Paul's first Epistle to the Thessalonians, and his Epistle to the Galatians. There the apostle is speaking of those scattered groups and congregations of believers whom he first came to know face to face when he went among them as one of the deputies bringing relief from Antioch to "the brethren which dwelt in Judæa." It was at a time when the Christians there had been sorely broken by persecution and weakened by famine. The apostle refers to them, not as "the Church," but "the Churches of Judæa," and speaks of their special sufferings ; but, in the same breath, he asserts their high calling, and their inward abiding unity. They are "the Churches of Judæa which are in Christ," "the Churches of God which are in Judæa in Christ Jesus." And in view of that real spiritual unity, in another early epistle, he includes these scattered groups of believers also in the one word "Church," when speaking of his attitude towards all the Hebrew Christians at this period : "I am the least of the apostles, that am not meet to be called an apostle, because I persecuted the Church of God."[2]

---

[1] Acts v. 11 ; viii. 1, 3–11, 22, etc.

[2] Gal. i. 22 ; 1 Thess. ii. 14 ; 1 Cor. xv. 9. The first instance of the use of ἐκκλησία in the Plural in the book of Acts falls within the second great section of the history, and refers to Gentile, or mixed Jewish and Gentile, Churches beyond the bounds of Palestine. It is in connection with the result of Paul's missionary labours in Syria and Cilicia, xv. 41. There is one earlier reference to Churches, which probably consisted of single congregations only, the phrase being used in the Distrib. Sing. κατ' ἐκκλησίαν, xiv. 23.

It is interesting to notice also, with respect to these
" Churches of Judæa," that a time of rest from persecution
seems to have enabled the inward unity in their case to find
more outward expression.   The rapid unbroken development
of the Church at Jerusalem received a severe check from
" the tribulation that arose about Stephen."   The apostles,
indeed, remained in or near Jerusalem ; but the disciples
generally were scattered from it for a time.   It is expressly
said that they betook themselves first to the neighbouring
" regions of Judæa and Samaria," and that " they went
everywhere preaching the Word."   One result of this, to
which we have already adverted, was that the Gospel spread
greatly in places, such as the cities of Samaria, where it was
only partially known before.[1]   Another result naturally was
that, as the persecution slackened and ceased in Jerusalem,
and the disciples returned to it, the bonds of brotherly union
between believers in the city and country districts were
greatly strengthened and multiplied.   Old links were drawn
closer, and new ones formed.   The place of these separate
groups and gatherings of brethren in the general body of
" the faithful in Christ Jesus " was more recognised.   The
real unity was made more visible to all men, " that the
world might believe."   In what forms, and by what special
methods, this was done, we shall consider presently.   Meanwhile, it is worth noting that in the next reference in the
book of Acts to the Christians of the Holy Land generally,
after the persecution had come to an end, we find them all
spoken of as forming one great collective unity, in connection
with their common use of the means of grace : " So the
Church throughout all Judæa, and Galilee, and Samaria had
peace, being edified ; and walking in the fear of the Lord,
and in the comfort (or exhortation) of the Holy Ghost, was
multiplied." [2]

The references to the unity of the Church in the group of
New Testament documents, which specially connect themselves with the Hebrew Christian portion of its history, are
in perfect accordance with what appears in the narrative of

[1] See above, pp. 400 ff.   [2] Acts ix. 31.

the Acts. In the First Epistle of Peter,[1] and in that of James, the Lord's brother, we cannot fail to see how the old Hebrew idea of the post - exilic times, as to the unity of Israel in its twelve tribes scattered abroad, is transferred to the members of the Christian "Dispersion" in all lands. These form "an elect race, a royal priesthood, a holy nation, a people for God's own possession, . . . which in time past were no people, but now are the people of God." They are "living stones," resting on "the Lord, a living Stone, rejected indeed of men, but with God elect, precious," and in Him "built up a spiritual house," "the house of God."[2] Believers form "the brotherhood," "your brotherhood which is in the world" (ἡ ἐν κόσμῳ ὑμῶν ἀδελφότης).[3] They are "the flock of God."[4]

In the Apocalypse, while the seven Churches of Asia are in the foreground, much as the Church at Jerusalem is in the first section of the history, behind and above them, from the first to the last verse in the book rises the conception of one great company of "the saints" and "servants of Jesus Christ" in earth and heaven, a perfect number from all the tribes of Israel, and a countless multitude from all nations of the earth, united through the love and the work of Christ to form "a kingdom and priests unto His God and Father." On each separate believer there is written by the hand of Christ "the name of the City of God, the New Jerusalem," as well as "Mine own new name." And the unity of all who are Christ's is set forth in the crowning vision of "the Bride, the Lamb's wife," as "the holy City, New Jerusalem, coming

---

[1] This epistle is written, indeed, to Christian communities of mixed origin, and in which the Gentile Christians apparently formed the majority (see above, p. 335 f.). But the writer is a relevant witness to the consciousness of the Hebrew Christian Church in this matter, and to the teaching of the "pillar apostles" at Jerusalem.

[2] It is interesting to note how often the two great figures of the Rock and the Shepherd with his sheep, used by our Lord in speaking to Peter regarding His Church, reappear in this epistle, 1 Pet. ii. 4-8, 25 ; v. 2-4. See above, pp. 170-175, 251.

[3] Here again the apostle but reproduces his Master's teaching in the original circle of the twelve, as to His disciples forming one brotherhood, a true "communitas fratrum," an ἀδιλφότης. See above, pp. 224 f., 227 f.

[4] Comp. Jas. i. 1 ; ii. 1 ; 1 Pet. i. 1 f., 22 ; ii. 5 ff., 9 f., 17 ; iv. 17 ; v. 2, 9, 14.

down out of heaven from God, prepared as a bride adorned for her husband."[1]

All through the Epistle to the Hebrews the essential unity of the Church of God in all ages is stated, and taken for granted, in the most striking way. The Jewish believers to whom the author writes are "the Christian Israel." "They are in his view 'the people of God.' They have been sanctified to be God's worshipping people through the blood of the new covenant, the offering of the Son. . . . The people of God is not a number of individuals, as when we speak of 'people;' it is a unity such as Israel was. This unity continues."[2] The principles of God's dealings with His people in the Old Testament times, and the privileges bestowed on them then, hold with respect to His people now. " Unto us was the Gospel preached, as well as unto them (καὶ γάρ ἐσμεν εὐηγγελισμένοι καθάπερ κἀκεῖνοι)." The rest offered to them was, in substance, the very "rest which remaineth for the people of God," into which believers now are to "give diligence to enter." Moses shared in "the reproach of Christ." Abraham, and other believers in patriarchal times, "looked for" the abiding city of God, "the heavenly Jerusalem." " The House of God " is spoken of as one from first to last in human history.[3]

Messianic utterances in the Psalms and Isaiah are ascribed in the Epistle to the Hebrews directly to Jesus, as being His words to believers now. " In the first passage ('I will declare Thy name unto my brethren, in the midst of the Church will I sing Thy praise'[4]) the Messiah expresses His consciousness that believing men are His brethren, for He and they are all members of one great congregation or Church, and He declares to them the name and praise of God,—His name and praise as the God of salvation, as the

---

[1] Rev. i. 1-6 ; iii. 12 ; iv. 4 ; v. 8, 9 ; vi. 11 ; vii. 3-15 ; viii. 3 ; xiii. 7-10 ; xiv. 12 ; xv. 2-4 ; xvii. 14 ; xix. 1-10 ; xxi. 1-11 ; xxii. 3-5, 9, 14-21. Comp. Milligan, *Revelation of St. John*, Lond. 1886, p. 158 f.

[2] Davidson, *Hebrews*, pp. 22, 203 f.

[3] Heb. iv. 2, 6-11 ; iii. 1-6 ; xi. 10, 16-26 ; xii. 22.

[4] Heb. ii. 12. 'Εν μίσῳ ἐκκλησίας ὑμνήσω σε is the LXX. rendering of Ps. xxii. 22 : בְּתוֹךְ קָהָל אֲהַלְלֶךָּ.

Psalm shows (comp. Heb. v. 8 f.). In the second, He expresses His faith in God, like any one of His believing brethren (Heb. xii. 2). And in the third, He presents Himself before God, or calls attention to Himself among men, as on the same footing with the children whom God has given Him. The children are God's children in the spiritual sense, whom He has given to Him (John xvii. 6), and as one with whom He presents Himself."[1] It is worthy of note that in this great epistle, which above all others supplies the key to the true relations of the Old Testament to the New, the term " Church " (ἐκκλησία) in the two passages in which it occurs[2] has unquestionably the catholic or universal, not the local sense. It means " the whole congregation of Israel," "the congregation of the Lord." In other words, the conception of the Church, which meets us in Hebrews, is that in which the unity of the whole body, throughout all its parts, is most strongly brought out. It is " the Church of the first-born who are enrolled in heaven."

(3.) The Hebrew Christian Church acted as one, and had suitable means for doing so.

Throughout the whole history of this period, we find the apostolic Church acting as one, and apparently feeling no difficulty as to the lines and methods by which such action should proceed. It is taken especially through the apostles, as the recognised leaders and representatives of the Church ; in one instance, already noted, " the elders " or presbyters, without mention of the apostles, stand out as the responsible representatives of the Church, and the organs of its action ; in other cases, neither apostles nor elders are named separately, but the action is simply spoken of as taken by " the Church." In such circumstances, " united action may well be held to supply the place of unity expressed in definite forms."[3]

---

[1] Davidson, *Hebrews*, p. 68.

[2] Heb. ii. 12 ; xii. 23. See the exposition of the latter verse in Note A.

[3] " Was insbesondere den Gesamtverband der Kirche betrifft, so müssen wir uns, wie Niedner gegen Rothe mit Recht bemerkt (*Kirchengesch.* S. 152, Anm. 1), vor dem Irrthum hüten ' dass einheitliches Handeln kein Ersatz sei für einheitliche Formen.' So lange die Apostel das Ganze leiteten, bestand allerdings nicht ein sachlicher Verband in gewissen Ämtern und Stellen, Einrichtungen und Formen bestehend, wohl aber ein lebendiger und persönlicher,

The seat and centre of unity for the Hebrew Christian Church, as hitherto for " the whole congregation of Israel," was felt from the first to be in Jerusalem. It was " from Jerusalem," according to Christ's own appointment, that " His witnesses " were to go forth " to all Judæa and Samaria, and to the uttermost part of the earth." In Jerusalem the Advent of the Spirit took place, and the disciples were first " clothed with power from on high." Galilee had been the cradle of the Gospel. But the strong and gifted Church of Jerusalem, counting its members by thousands, and with the continuous teaching of the apostles in the midst of it, became the nursing mother of the faith throughout all the Holy Land and beyond it. Here the pulse of spiritual life was strongest, and the sense of oneness with all the brethren in the Lord, and of responsibility for their welfare, was most strongly developed. Accordingly, it is from Jerusalem that we find united action first taken for the oversight of the Church at large, and for the furtherance of the spiritual interests of new converts, wherever these might be found.

The first recorded instance of such action had reference to the first Christian community of any size formed outside of Jerusalem. " When the apostles, which were at Jerusalem, heard that Samaria had received the Word of God, they sent unto them Peter and John." [1] It is to be noted that again, as in the appointment of the deacons, the twelve act not individually, but as a body, doubtless after united prayer and conference, and that the foremost members of the apostolic college, as regards personal gifts and influence, were subject to the authority of the apostolic company as a whole. The sending of Peter and John " to inspect, to advise, and to sanction so important a step as the foundation of a Samaritan Church, implied neither jealousy of Philip nor any incompetency on his part. The apostles were the responsible chiefs of the whole body. They were bound to see to its welfare, and in every way to aid its progress.

aber darum nicht unwirklicher und erst zukünftiger Einheitspunkt und Zusammenhalt für die einzelnen Gemeinden." Lechler, *Apost. u. nachapost. Zeitalter*, 3te Aufl. S. 92. [Translation, vol. i. p. 107. Edinburgh : T. & T. Clark.]

[1] Acts viii. 14.

" It was of the utmost moment that a branch Church, formed among an alien and hostile people, should not fall out of the unity of brotherhood with the mother Church at Jerusalem.[1] Besides, it is plain that the formal recognition of the converted Samaritans, as members of the kingdom of Christ, was expressly reserved for the apostolic deputies. Baptism had put them in the position of the hundred and twenty before Pentecost ; but the full bestowal of spiritual influence, evidenced by visible or audible tokens like the gift of tongues,[2] took place only when, after solemn prayer for the assembled brethren, Peter and John laid their hands successively on the head of each." [3] It was the Samaritan Pentecost, the seal set by Christ Himself, acting through His foremost representatives, on the reception of these despised aliens into the highest privileges of His people. The Samaritan converts were thus visibly brought into the unity of the Church, on a footing of perfect equality with the brethren in Jerusalem and Judæa. This was further assured to them by their being received into the privilege of "the apostles' teaching," as well as into the fellowship of spiritual gifts. Peter and John "testified and spoke unto them the Word of the Lord," and "preached the Gospel to many villages of the Samaritans." [4]

In like manner, when the Gospel, in the case of Cornelius and his friends, crossed another and yet stronger barrier of prejudice and nationality, the matter was taken up at once with anxious interest, not in Jerusalem merely, but by the Christian community throughout Southern Palestine, as being one which concerned the whole Church. "Now the apostles, and *the brethren that were in Judæa*, heard that the Gentiles also had received the Word of God." [5] There

---

[1] "Ita scilicet Ecclesiæ suæ unitatem fovet [Deus], dum alii aliis manûs porrigunt ; nec homines tantum vicissim inter se, sed totas quoque Ecclesias conciliat," Calvin, *in loco*. See the rest of his admirable exposition of these verses, which is referred to both by Dr. Dykes and Dean Alford. The latter, with his usual candour, admits that there is no ground for trying to make out any apostolic institution of "confirmation" from this passage, or from any other in the New Testament.

[2] Comp. the case of Cornelius before Baptism, Acts x. 44-48.

[3] Dykes, *From Jerusalem to Antioch*, 4th ed. p. 263 f.

[4] Acts viii. 14-25.   [5] Chap. x. 45 ; xi. 1.

was no need in this case to send a special deputation to inquire into the facts. The most prominent member of the apostolic company had been the chief actor in the scenes which occurred in the house of the Roman centurion. Peter himself comes up from Cæsarea to Jerusalem, to give account of what had taken place. His statement is anticipated by the eager challenge of one section of the Church. "They that were of the circumcision,"—those Hebrew Christians who were pre-eminently "zealots of the law,"—"contended with him, saying: Thou wentest in to men uncircumcised, and didst eat with them."[1] The apostle meets this inquiry into his conduct, not as an unwarranted or unreasonable demand on the part of the Church, but as one which was natural and right in itself, and which he was bound fully to satisfy. "Peter began and expounded the matter unto them in order," explaining both what he had actually done, and on what grounds he had been led to do it. The result was that all the objectors were silenced; the Church, as a whole, was fully satisfied with the apostle's action in the matter; and the question of the admission of uncircumcised men to the full privileges of the Church, on the conditions of faith and repentance alone, was settled in point of principle.[2]

---

[1] Acts xi. 2 f. ; xxi. 20.

[2] It is not very easy to decide whether the events at Cæsarea (chap. x.), or those at Antioch (chap. xi. 20), occurred first. On the whole, I am disposed to hold with Meyer, that the order in which they occur in the narrative is the order of time, that, at least, the discussion regarding Peter's procedure at Cæsarea took place before the news of what had been done at Antioch reached Jerusalem. This best explains the gentleness with which the action of the men of Cyprus and Cyrene is dealt with, both by the Church at Jerusalem and by Barnabas at Antioch. If so much difficulty was felt about what was done by Peter, the most distinguished of the twelve, and a Hebrew of the Hebrews, how much more would this have been the case had the question first come before the Church at Jerusalem through the action of certain unknown Hellenists, with no revelation from heaven beforehand, and apparently no speaking with tongues afterwards, to attest the Divine approval,—had the whole matter reached Jerusalem only by report, with all manner of additions and exaggerations, and with no trusted leader, such as Peter, to give the true account from personal knowledge of the facts! But now there was an authoritative precedent to go by. The only point of importance to be ascertained at Antioch was, whether the work was a genuine one, bearing the seal of the Lord's approval, as in the case of Cornelius. If so, the question of

So also as regards the foundation of what proved to be the mother Church of Gentile Christendom. At Antioch for the first time, not by any acknowledged leader of the Church, but by unnamed and private members, "the Lord Jesus had been preached," not to Hellenists merely, but "to the Greeks;[1] and the hand of the Lord was with them, and a great number that believed turned unto the Lord. And the report concerning them came to the ears of the Church which was in Jerusalem, and they sent forth Barnabas as far as Antioch." We see here the same keen and active sense of the unity of the Church, and of responsibility for its welfare, wherever men were "added to the Lord" through the preaching of the Gospel. We see wise and well-considered measures taken, with a view to maintain harmony and friendly communication between the most distant portions of the Christian brotherhood and the original centre of the Church. It was not necessary for this purpose that an apostle should be sent to Antioch. The seal of the miraculous gifts of the Spirit had already been set on the reception of the Gentiles as such into the Church in the house of Cornelius; and what the foremost of the apostles had done there had been carefully weighed and approved by the whole Church at Jerusalem. No more suitable deputy, in the circumstances, could have been chosen than Barnabas. He was among those most trusted and honoured in the Pentecostal Church, with its predominantly Hebrew membership. Yet he was himself a Hellenist, and a fellow-countryman of those "men of Cyprus and Cyrene" who had been the founders of the new community at Antioch. And "he was a good man, and full of the Holy Ghost and of faith."

It deserves special notice that the selection and mission of Barnabas are described as resulting from the action, not of the apostles and elders merely, but of the Church as a whole.

principle had been already settled. There remained only questions of expediency and practical arrangement, with a view to brotherly fellowship between disciples of Jewish and Gentile origin respectively. These questions were not without serious difficulties of a practical kind, as later events at Antioch showed; but, for dealing with them successfully, a man of the gifts and spirit of Barnabas was singularly well qualified.

[1] Πρὸς τοὺς Ἕλληνας, Acts xi. 20 ff.

The mind of the Church was no doubt ripened and gathered, as in the election of Matthias and of the deacons, through common counsel and representative action, in which the apostles, or as many of them as were then at Jerusalem, took a leading part. But the final action was in the name of the Church as such; and the commission with which Barnabas came to Antioch, and in virtue of which he summoned Saul to his aid from Tarsus, carried with it the weight and authority of the whole Church. Other deputations, more or less formal, of gifted men from the Church at Jerusalem, came to Antioch subsequently. It was from one of these that the utterance came which led to the first return deputation from Antioch to the Church of Judæa.[1]

The results of this first-exercise of loving oversight by the mother Church at Jerusalem, as regards the newly formed society at Antioch, were of the happiest kind. When Barnabas "was come, and had seen the grace of God, he was glad, and he exhorted them all that with purpose of heart they would cleave unto the Lord: and much people was added unto the Lord." In Barnabas, and still more in Saul of Tarsus, whom he was the means of bringing among them, the infant Church at Antioch received from the hands of the parent Church the very gifts of which, at that stage in its history, it had most need, men eminently fitted for "the perfecting of the saints, for the work of ministering, for the building up of the body of Christ." It was to this work of consolidation, instruction, and edification, as distinguished from that of further evangelization, that Barnabas and Saul gave their main strength in Antioch. "It came to pass that even for a whole year they were gathered together with the Church, and taught much people; and that the disciples were called Christians first in Antioch." [2]

How deep the sense of gratitude was among the disciples at Antioch, and how strongly they, too, felt the bond of union between themselves and the Church of the Holy Land, may be seen in what they in their turn do for the good of its members. Agabus, a man of prophetic gifts, who had recently come with others from Jerusalem, "stood up" at Antioch,

---

[1] Acts xi. 27; Gal. ii. 11 f.   [2] Acts xi. 26.

evidently in one of the assemblies of the Church, and foretold "that there should be a great famine over all the world." Such a visitation would obviously press with special severity upon the poor and persecuted Christians in Palestine. Accordingly, "the disciples, every man according to his ability, determined to send relief unto the brethren that dwelt in Judæa; which also they did, sending it to the elders by the hand of Barnabas and Saul," the two most honoured ministers of the Church in Antioch.[1] Thus by reciprocal giving and receiving, by interchange of messengers and brotherly help, both in spiritual things and outward, the unity of the apostolic Church, from its centre in Jerusalem to its farthest outpost in the midst of heathendom, was from the first manifested and strengthened.

Another glimpse into the forms and methods by which the real unity of the Church in its Hebrew Christian period found outward expression, is given us in the account of Peter's "visitation of the saints throughout all parts," in connection with which he came to Lydda and Joppa.[2] It was at a time when, through various Providential circumstances and events, the Church throughout the Holy Land had rest from persecution, and increased steadily in numbers and in spiritual strength. Peter used this opportunity for "passing through all parts" ($\delta\iota\epsilon\rho\chi\acute{o}\mu\epsilon\nu o\nu$ $\delta\iota\grave{a}$ $\pi\acute{a}\nu\tau\omega\nu$),[3] confirming the disciples in the faith, seeing to their welfare in all things, promoting brotherly fellowship with each other, and with the Church as a whole. "Out of Peter's journey of apostolic inspection only two incidents have been preserved, one at Lydda and one at Joppa. It is plain, however, that his tour may have embraced a considerable tract of country before he arrived at Lydda. That town lay only some eighteen miles from the capital, on the direct road to Cæsarea; but it could not have been his first halt, for we are told that he arrived there while he was passing through among all the saints. It is probable enough that he had already visited the central highlands, or even Samaria and Galilee, before he turned back to over-

---

[1] Acts xi. 27–30.   [2] Chap. ix. 32–43.

[3] Or "through all the saints," if we supply $\tau\tilde{\omega}\nu$ $\dot{a}\gamma\acute{\iota}\omega\nu$, as Meyer, Alford, and Dykes do, instead of with the A. V. and R. V., $\tau\tilde{\omega}\nu$ $\tau\acute{o}\pi\omega\nu$.

take the coast plain. There, however, the interest of his tour culminated." [1]

It is a fair inference that what we are told here of one apostle is but a specimen of the activity of the others. They did not remain, as a brilliant but most unreliable French writer of our day puts it, "sitting idly on their seats of honour in Jerusalem." [2] On the contrary, on Paul's first visit to the city after his conversion, probably during this very period of peace, he seems to have found no apostle there save Peter, and saw also, of "them that seemed to be pillars," only James, the Lord's brother. [3] On his second visit some years after, John was apparently the only additional member of the apostolic college who was then in or near Jerusalem. [4] Christ had given the apostles a distinct injunction to begin their work at Jerusalem; and accordingly, until they had clear evidence that it was His will that they should leave the city, it formed the chief sphere of the labours of the twelve. But from the first, while Jerusalem remained the headquarters of the apostolic company, wherever their services were specially needed, whether in Samaria, in the centre of the country, or among the thickly planted villages of the maritime plains on its western border, there we find the apostles labouring. And so, too, at a later period, beyond the limits of the Holy Land, in Antioch and Babylon, among the seven Churches of Asia, among the twelve tribes in the Dispersion, among the elect sojourners in Pontus, Galatia, Cappadocia, Asia, and Bithynia, we have evidence of a like oversight being exercised, and like efforts used by the apostles and other leaders of the Hebrew

---

[1] Dykes, *From Jerusalem to Antioch,* 4th ed. p. 335 f.

[2] "Les diacres firent bien plus que les apôtres, immobiles à Jérusalem sur leur siége d'honneur." Renan, *Les Apôtres,* p. 120.

[3] Comp. Acts ix. 26 f. with Gal. i. 18 f. "Brought him to the apostles," in the former passage, may simply mean "introduced him to the apostolic company;" and εἰ μή, in the latter, may naturally be taken in an adversative, not an exceptive sense. It does not necessarily imply that James was of the number of the apostles properly so called, any more than the same phrase in Luke iv. 26 f. implies that Sarepta was a city in Israel, or Naaman an Israelitish leper. "Funfzehn tage blieb Paulus beim Petrus; einen zweiten aber von den aposteln sah er nicht, nur sah er noch den Jacobus den bruder des Herrn." Holsten, *Evangelium des Paulus,* Berlin 1880, S. 8.

[4] Gal. ii. 1 f., 9 f

Christian Church, in person or by letter, with respect to some particular portion of the Church, or in behalf of the general interests of the whole.[1]

It has been shown that the polity everywhere adopted by the Hebrew Christian Church, under the guidance of the apostles, was the Presbyterian system of the synagogue, with a few modifications and developments, as in the institution of the deaconship, to meet the new circumstances of the Christian community.[2] That system furnished at once an elastic and well-tried organization, singularly well fitted to embody and express, whether in a larger or more limited sphere, the sense of unity and common brotherhood so strongly felt by the Pentecostal believers. Its representative principle, its familiar and effective methods of communication from all parts of the Diaspora to the centre at Jerusalem by deputies for financial and religious purposes, supplied the very lines and precedents according to which we see the unity of the apostolic Church expressed, and united action taken, in this first period of its history. It was thus that the isolated "Churches of Judæa, which were in Christ," and "suffered such things from the Jews," were knit together into a closer outward union when the persecution ceased, and the result was brought about which the historian sums up in those brief but suggestive words already cited: "So the Church throughout all Judæa, and Galilee, and Samaria had peace, being edified; and walking in the fear of the Lord, and in the comfort of the Holy Ghost, was multiplied."[3] It is a beautiful picture of the Hebrew Church of Christ in the Holy Land, with its inward unity and brotherhood in the Lord manifesting itself, as God gave opportunity, on the familiar lines of that strong and simple system which had come to the first disciples as an inheritance through centuries of providential training in Israel, with the deep, reverential faith of the Old Testament saints, with the old religious care for the poor, the widow, the fatherless, and the stranger finding fresh and fuller forms of expression, edifying one another in love, through the exhortation and comfort of the Holy Ghost.

[1] Gal. ii. 11 ; Jas. i. 1 ; 1 Pet. i. 1 ; v. 13 ; Jude 3 ; 3 John 9 f. ; Rev. i. 4. Comp. Lechler, *Apost. u. nachapost. Zeitalter*, S. 89. [Transl. T. & T. Clark, Edin.]
[2] See above, pp. 427–432, 436.   [3] Gal. i. 22 ; 1 Thess. ii. 14 Acts ix. 31.

PART VI.

FROM ANTIOCH TO ROME: THE GENTILE CHRISTIAN CHURCH.

———◆———

CHAPTER I.

PREPARATION AND TRANSITION.

THE section of the history on which we now enter may be called the period of the Gentile Christian Church. Or, more precisely: it is the period of transition from mixed Jewish and Gentile Churches or congregations to Churches in which the great majority of the members were, in point of fact, of Gentile origin, but in which the old distinction of Jewish and Gentile Christians was becoming more and more fully merged in the deeper unity of the Church of Christ.

As regards the Acts, this is the period of the great missionary journeys of Paul and his companions in the work of the Gospel. We follow the footsteps of the apostle of the Gentiles from one scene of labour to another, in Asia and Europe. The centre of interest and of action passes from Antioch to Corinth, to Ephesus, to Rome. Thus the parting words of the risen Saviour to His disciples were fulfilled. The book of Acts records how the witness in the power of the Holy Ghost concerning Christ spread from Jerusalem to "all Judæa and Samaria," and thence "unto the uttermost parts of the earth." Step by step, we trace the progress of the Gospel and the spread of the Church, until we leave the apostle Paul "preaching the kingdom of God, and teaching the things concerning the Lord Jesus Christ with all boldness," in that mighty city, where he had so long desired to be, where "the uttermost parts of the earth" met in Rome.[1]

As regards the Epistles, this is the period specially covered by the letters of Paul to the various Churches in Asia and Europe, of which he had been the founder, or the care of which lay in some special manner upon him. We have also the remarkable group of letters known as "the Pastoral Epistles," addressed to individuals, but bearing specially on the condition of the Gentile Christian Churches at a comparatively late stage in their history. Something may be gathered also from Peter's letter to the Christian Diaspora, in which he writes to a wide circle of Churches with many of which Paul also had had to do. Our knowledge of the period is filled in and crowned by the Apocalypse, the fourth Gospel, and the Epistles of John.

During almost the whole of this period we are beyond the limits of the Holy Land, moving in the regions of the Dispersion among the Gentiles. Close relations, indeed, are maintained with the Hebrew Christian Church. Its influence is strongly felt. There is abundant evidence of the continuance and unbroken power of the sense of unity among all the brethren in Christ wherever they might be. A right to see to and care for each other's welfare is taken for granted everywhere. Both in the narrative and the Epistles we see messengers and communications of all sorts constantly passing between the Gentile Christian communities in Asia Minor and Europe on the one hand, and the Church in Palestine and the further East on the other. Peter comes to Antioch. He writes from Babylon to the Christians scattered throughout the provinces of Asia Minor, in whose Christian experience Pauline influences had hitherto probably been the strongest factor. "The apostle of the circumcision" sends greetings to them from "the Church that is in Babylon, elect together with you."[2] Paul, on the other hand, comes again and again to Jerusalem, on errands of brotherly love from the Gentile Churches, and in connection with questions bearing

---

[1] Acts i. 8 ; xxviii. 31.

[2] 1 Pet. v. 13; comp. Huther in Meyer's series on the exposition of the passage, 3te Aufl. S. 228 ff.

on their interests. Among " his fellow-workers " at Rome
and elsewhere,—" men which have been a comfort unto him,"
—are not a few who are expressly described by him as
being " of the circumcision." Timothy, his own child in the
faith, is circumcised by Paul's own direction to fit him for
greater usefulness among the fellow-countrymen of his mother.
Deputies from Jerusalem, more or less formally commissioned,
—representatives at least of Hebrew Christian feeling,—
intervene, as being assured of full right to do so, in matters
connected with the spiritual welfare of the Churches in
Antioch, Galatia, Corinth, and elsewhere.[1] But still we are
made to recognise that this is now the history of the Church
on Gentile ground.

In almost every instance the work begins in the Jewish
synagogue or proseucha ; and a certain number of devout Jews
and proselytes form the nucleus of the Christian community
in the place. But the Gentile Christian element grows more
and more predominant, and questions and tendencies arising
from extra-Jewish sources come more and more to the front ;
till, in the latest New Testament writings, the questions about
the relation of Gentile believers to the Jewish law, which
hold so large a place in the second section of the Acts, and
in the earlier Pauline Epistles, and to which allusion is made
even in the Pastoral ones, pass out of sight altogether, and
" the brief antithesis in John i. 17 sounds like a distant
memory of a battle long since fought through." [2]

From the thirteenth chapter of Acts onward the horizon
of the narrative suddenly widens. The first verses of the
chapter describe the solemn sanctions under which Barnabas
and Saul, after labouring for more than a year among the
prophets and teachers of the Church at Antioch, are " separated,"
and " sent forth to the work to which the Holy Ghost has
called them,"—a work which proves to be, as they themselves

[1] Col. iv. 11 ; Acts xvi. 1-3 ; xi. 27 ff. ; xii. 25 ; xiii. 1, 13 ; chap. xv.
throughout, etc. Some of those Hebrew Christians who intervened in the dis-
cussions at Antioch are stigmatized by Paul as "false brethren " (Gal. ii. 4) ;
but still it was as "brethren " that they were received, as such they claimed
and were accorded a right to take part in the concerns of the common brotherhood.

[2] Reuss, *Hist. of N. T.*, E. Tr. Edin. 1884, p. 221.

reported it to the Church on their return, nothing less decisive than " the opening of the door of faith unto the Gentiles." [1] Yet, although this event seems at first sight to happen suddenly, on looking back it becomes clear for how long, and in how many ways, under the guidance of the Spirit and the hand of the unseen Lord, the preparation for this had been going on, and that the end had been reached by many successive steps. These are recorded by the historian with a care and minuteness which show the importance attached to them in his mind. In fact, from the sixth chapter to the end of the twelfth, the narrative is really that of the transition from the Hebrew to the Gentile Christian period of the history.

In the opening section of the book of Acts we saw what were the life, and work, and worship of the Church in Jerusalem, how the community of believers there grew and multiplied, how it was built up and strengthened by the teaching of the apostles and the ordinances of Christ, by Christian fellowship with one another in word and deed. We saw how the organization of the Church was formed, and adjusted to the new circumstances, on the familiar lines of the synagogue system. Patterns and precedents were thus established, on which the disciples could take action wherever the hand of God in Providence might lead them afterwards. Persecution, by scattering the Church now, would only spread it. The seed already had its wings, and would spring up quickly, wherever the breath of the storm might waft it in a new Diaspora. The presence of the apostles in Jerusalem was less needful than at first. The Church there was fully organized, and could stand alone. The twelve were more and more set free for journeys of visitation " among all the saints," and for evangelistic work in wider and more distant spheres.

From the sixth chapter, accordingly, the narrative tells how the Gospel passed gradually from Jerusalem to Samaria, and to the regions beyond. We see one barrier after another of prejudice and nationality broken down. One instrument after another is prepared for the work, and used in it. First

[1] Acts xiii. 1-4 ; xiv. 26 f.

of all, the Hellenistic—that is, the freer—element in the
Church at Jerusalem comes more to the front in the election
of the seven deacons.   Every one of these, if we may judge
from their names,[1] was of Hellenistic origin and training ; one
of them is expressly said to have been " a proselyte of Antioch."
The preaching of Stephen tells especially in the Hellenistic
synagogues in Jerusalem.   The points which roused the
keenest opposition seem to have been his declaration that,
through Jesus of Nazareth, the holy city and the temple
were no longer to hold the position of exclusive sanctity
which had been theirs hitherto, and further statements to the
effect that great changes were to ensue with respect to " the
law " and " the customs which Moses had delivered " to the
Jews.[2]   Stephen's defence before the Sanhedrin is the longest
address recorded in the Acts.   " It forms what may be called
the Apology to the Jews for the universalism of Christianity,
and for the wider extension of the preaching of the disciples." [3]

Among Stephen's converts from Hellenistic circles in Jerusalem were, in all likelihood, those " men of Cyprus and
Cyrene," who, being driven from the city by the subsequent
persecution, travelled as far as Antioch, and were the first to
" preach the Lord Jesus to the Greeks " in the Syrian capital.
Before this had taken place, Philip, another Hellenist, had
preached Christ in Samaria ; and the work there had been
carefully tested and confirmed by a deputation from the
apostles.[4]   The Baptism of the Ethiopian treasurer may be
held to be a further step in the same direction ; although his
case was that of a man already taught to worship at Jerusalem and to study the Old Testament Scriptures, so that he

---

[1] The criterion, however, is not a very certain one.
[2] Acts vi. 1, 5–14.   [3] Lumby, *Acts*, pp. xv.–xvii.
[4] Acts vi. 9 ; xi. 19 f. ; viii. 5–25.   Archdeacon Farrar finds the special significance of the admission of the eunuch in his physical condition, which brought
him under the prohibition of the Deuteronomic law (Deut. xxiii. 1).   "This law
forbade him to become a member of the Jewish Church ; but Philip admitted
him into that Christian communion in which there is neither Jew nor Greek,
neither male nor female, neither bond nor free," *St. Paul*, i. 262 f.   But compare Isa. lvi. 3–6, a passage which follows almost immediately after the one
which the Ethiopian and the evangelist had read together, and which promises
to the eunuchs, "who join themselves to the Lord, . . . a memorial and a name
in His house, and within His walls, an everlasting name that shall not be cut off."

may have been practically in the same position as the proselytes from Libya, who heard Peter's address at Pentecost.[1]
After receiving the Ethiopian into the Church, the evangelist
passed northward from Azotus, preaching in all the towns
of the sea-coast, until he came to Cæsarea, and found, apparently, his permanent sphere of labour in what was then
the most Gentile city within the bounds of the Holy Land.[2]
Thither also, probably about the same time as that in which
the Hellenists were preaching the Gospel to the Greeks at
Antioch, the apostle Peter is brought by a notable chain
of providences, ending in a direct revelation from heaven,
and an express command by the Spirit of God. He preaches
Christ in the house of the Roman centurion Cornelius; and
he and his friends, "men uncircumcised," and Gentiles in the
full sense of the word, are received into the fellowship of
the Church by Baptism.[3]

The door of entrance for the Gentiles had thus been formally
opened by the hand of the foremost representative of the
apostolic college. The step excited, as we saw in last chapter,
the keenest interest and concern throughout the Hebrew
Christian community. Peter's action was challenged at once
on his return to Jerusalem, and was only approved after full
consideration by the Church of all the facts of the case, and
especially of the evidence that the seal of God had been

---

[1] Acts viii. 26–39 ; ii. 10.

[2] Cæsarea was at this time the political capital of the country, as Jerusalem
was the religious one. (Thus Tacitus, speaking of events before the fall of
Jerusalem, says : "Discessere, Mucianus Antiochiam, Vespasianus Cæsaream :
illa Syriæ, hæc Judeæ caput est," *Hist.* ii. 79.) It was the official residence of
the Roman procurators, and the headquarters of the imperial troops for the province. Gentiles formed the majority of the population. The Jewish minority were
chiefly Hellenists. Hence the LXX. was used in the synagogues ; and Hebrew
visitors were startled by hearing the "Shema" repeated in Greek. (Schürer,
Hist. of Jewish People, i. p. 85 ff., ii. pp. 284–287.) Philip, as himself a Hellenist,
would be the better fitted for such a field of labour, and would enter upon it the
more hopefully after his recent experience in Samaria and in the case of the
Ethiopian treasurer. Those Jews who received the Gospel here from the lips of
the evangelist, and those Gentiles on whom the Holy Ghost fell while the apostle
spoke in the house of Cornelius, would probably combine more readily in one
Church at Cæsarea than converts of such mixed origin would have done in any
other part of Palestine. Acts viii. 40 ; x. 1–48 ; xxi. 8–16.

[3] Acts x. 44–48 ; xi. 1–3.

visibly set on what was done by a Pentecostal outpouring of the Holy Ghost. The question of the admission of Gentiles as such to the full privileges of the disciples of Christ had thus been already raised under the most favourable circumstances, and settled in point of principle, before the news reached Jerusalem that Gentiles had been received in large numbers into the Church at Antioch. Hence, as already pointed out, the way was providentially prepared for the wise and generous treatment of the case of Antioch by the mother Church and her deputy Barnabas.[1]

Still the original apostles did not apparently hold that the time had yet come for them to go forth to direct aggressive effort among the Gentiles. Apart from all lingering scruples in their minds as to the principles involved in such a course, there were serious practical difficulties, as we may see again, to prevent them from adopting it readily. And meanwhile, besides the general oversight of the Hebrew Christian Church in Palestine, their hands were full of most hopeful work among "their brethren and kinsfolk according to the flesh," the thousands of pilgrims from the Jewish Dispersion, whom every Passover, and Pentecost, and feast of tabernacles brought to Jerusalem. It would have needed, it seemed to them, a more clear indication of the mind of God than had, up to this point, been given, to warrant their turning as yet from Israel to the Gentiles. Peter himself "tarried certain days" at Cæsarea, and took part along with Philip—unless his arrival at Cæsarea was of later date—in the work of consolidating the first mixed congregation of Jews and Gentiles, in which the latter, in all likelihood, formed the majority.[2] We find

---

[1] See above, pp. 443-446.

[2] This work seems to have been shared in subsequently by other representatives, both of the Hebrew and Hellenistic sections of the Church at Jerusalem besides Peter and Philip. Agabus, who was among the first to follow Barnabas to Antioch, appears also at Cæsarea. Mnason of Cyprus, "an early disciple," who had his fixed residence, apparently, at Jerusalem, was in close relations with the Church in the Gentile seaport. The apostle of the Gentiles and his companions in travel "tarry many days" in that congenial sphere, under the hospitable roof of Philip, when Paul is on his way to Jerusalem for the last time. The same Judæan prophet, whose first recorded utterance at Antioch had been the means of Paul's first visit to the brethren in Judæa as a representative from a Gentile Christian Church, now warns him that bonds and afflictions await him

Peter afterwards in the Church at Antioch holding brotherly fellowship with Gentile Christians, on the same terms which he had been blamed, at first, for according to the Gentiles at Cæsarea, "entering in to men uncircumcised and eating with them."[1] But he does not seem, so far as our information goes, to have engaged in independent mission work among the Gentiles. Peter appears to have felt at this time what Paul says regarding him, in writing to the Galatians with respect to this very question, as it came up at a later period, that "he had been" especially "entrusted with the Gospel of the circumcision," and that his first and chief duty was to be faithful in the discharge of the functions of that "apostleship of the circumcision" to which he had been called, and in which he had hitherto been so signally blessed of God.[2]

Never more clearly than at this great turning-point in the history of the apostolic Church do we recognise the presence and the guiding hand of One wiser and stronger far than His best servants on earth. The narrative which we are following is not a record merely of "acts of apostles," as its traditional heading puts it, but, as its inspired author indicates in his opening sentence, it is a history of "the things which Jesus" Himself continued "both to do and to teach." While apostles hesitated and held back, Christ's work went steadily forward, without break or failure, towards the mighty future which He had foretold for it "in the uttermost parts of the earth." It did so by many different yet converging lines. We have glanced at some of these already. Let us look now a little more closely at the two special lines of development and preparation which met in Antioch, before we consider the great forward movement of the Church which took place from that centre,—a movement the commencement of which marks the beginning of the second section of the narrative of the Acts, while the history of its progress and results fills the rest of the book from the thirteenth chapter to the end.

in Jerusalem. When the apostle will not be dissuaded from going on thither, a loving band of disciples from Cæsarea escort him to his destination, and provide for his comfort there. Acts xxi. 8–16.

[1] Acts x. 28 ; xi. 3 ; Gal. ii. 12.

[2] Gal. ii. 7–9. The attitude of the original apostles in this matter, and the causes which led to it, are well described by Professor Lindsay, *Acts*, ii. pp. 26–30.

1st. How had the Christian community at Antioch been prepared to be a centre of missions to the heathen, to become the mother Church of Gentile Christendom ?

2nd. How had the apostle of the Gentiles been prepared for his work ?

1st. At the time when the events took place which are recorded in the thirteenth chapter of Acts, the Church at Antioch had been in existence for about seven years.[1] The first missionaries who reached the Syrian capital "spoke the Word to none save only to Jews." But there were some of them, men of Cyprus and Cyrene, who, when they were come to Antioch, spake unto the Greeks also, preaching the Lord Jesus. And the hand of the Lord was with them, and a great number that believed turned unto the Lord.[2] The membership of the Church at Antioch was thus, from the first, of a mixed character, consisting partly of Jewish and partly of Gentile converts; but the latter evidently formed the majority. The state of matters already existing at Cæsarea was thus reproduced here on a larger scale. Subsequently Barnabas is sent to Antioch from Jerusalem. Through his labours and those of others, " much people ($ὄχλος$ $ἱκανός$) was added unto the Lord." Thereafter Saul is brought by Barnabas from Tarsus ; "and it came to pass that even for a whole year they were gathered together with the Church, and taught much people ($ὄχλον$ $ἱκανόν$), and that the disciples were called Christians first in Antioch."[3]

---

[1] The crucifixion of our Lord took place in the spring of A.D. 33. The first twelve chapters cover a period of about as many years. The Emperor Tiberius died in the spring of A.D. 37. The martyrdom of Stephen, and the persecution which followed, fall within the season of disorder which occurred in the empire in A.D. 37–38, when the reins of government were slackened in Judæa and elsewhere. The Church at Antioch was founded by fugitives from this persecution. Settled government was restored when Petronius became legate of Syria in A.D. 39 ; and in the next year the energies of the Jews were wholly absorbed in repelling Caligula's proposal to profane the temple. The death of Herod Agrippa I. determines the date of the second persecution and the martyrdom of James as being A.D. 44. The famine under Claudius was probably felt in the Holy Land in the following year. Paul's first missionary journey from Antioch took place some time after his return from visiting the Churches of Judæa as a deputy from Antioch in connection with this famine ; it must have been, therefore, about A.D. 46 or 47.

[2] Acts xi. 19–21.   [3] Chap. xi. 24 ff.

The thirteenth chapter of Acts opens with a reference to "prophets and teachers," statedly ministering "in the Church which was at Antioch." Five of the leading names are given, seemingly in the order of distinction, according to the position which they were felt to hold in the Christian community there from their age, services, and gifts.[1] It does not appear that the enumeration was meant to be an exhaustive one. Agabus and other "prophets from Jerusalem," of whom we hear in the last preceding reference to Antioch as taking part in the Christian assemblies there, are not mentioned in this list. It cannot be supposed to include the "many others also," who were associated with Paul and Barnabas at Antioch in "teaching and preaching the Word of the Lord," as noted in the fifteenth chapter. Part of the commission of the two missionaries from Antioch, when sent forth thence on their first evangelistic journey together, was to provide the newly planted Churches with regular office-bearers in the form of an ordained eldership in each congregation (χειροτονήσαντες αὐτοῖς πρεσβυτέρους κατ᾿ ἐκκλησίαν). The disciples at Antioch, as we have seen, took it for granted, in sending deputies to Judæa, that they would find such elderships everywhere established among the brethren there. It seems a fair and natural inference from these facts to conclude that elders

---

[1] Comp. the order in which the first and last named in this list continue to be spoken of in the narrative, until ver. 13. "The signs of an apostle" were so manifest, as regards Paul, in the incident of Elymas and the proconsul in Paphos, that henceforth Barnabas cheerfully takes the second place. It is no longer "Barnabas and Saul," but "Paul and Barnabas," or "Paul and his company,"—οἱ περὶ τὸν Παῦλον, the Homeric phrase for a chief or leader with his followers. Henceforth in the Acts the original order of the names is always reversed, with two exceptions only,—the scene at Lystra, where the connection explains the order, and the Council at Jerusalem, described in the fifteenth chapter. In that assembly, Barnabas, as the older man and better known in the Hebrew Christian Church, spoke first. He is put first also in the official utterance of the Council, the letter to the Churches in Antioch, Syria, and Cilicia. "Our beloved Barnabas and Paul" reverts to the old Jerusalem order of precedence. It was not that which the Church at Antioch would have used, after the first journey of their two missionaries. In their commission to the Council, they "appoint that Paul and Barnabas and certain other of them should go up to Jerusalem unto the apostles and elders about this question." Acts xiii. 13, 43, 46, 50 ; xiv. 12 ff., 19 f. ; xv. 2, 12, 22, 25, etc.

were already appointed, or had been received from the synagogue in the Church of Antioch itself.[1]

From all these notices it is plain that the Christian community in Antioch, at the end of the first seven years of its history, was a large and flourishing one. It had been checked, seemingly, by no persecution. It gathered within its pale men of different nationalities, who had hitherto been of different religions. Founded by zealous members of the Pentecostal Church of Jerusalem, who had suffered persecution and banishment gladly for Christ's sake and the Gospel, the Church at Antioch had enjoyed the continuous services for several years of a number of men with special gifts for edification, exhortation, and teaching.[2] It was able, from the number of its members, contributing " every man according to his ability," to raise a sum of money sufficient to afford substantial relief to " the brethren that dwelt in Judæa " in a time of famine. It must have spread over several districts of the city, holding its meetings in different centres, and thereby becoming visible, and an object of attention, even to the careless eyes of the general population.

From the time when Antioch was founded, some three hundred years before the birth of Christ, Jews had been settled there in very large numbers, and with special privileges. Their synagogues in the city were numerous, and famous for their wealth. The Church in Antioch is always spoken of in the Singular ;[3] but this, as in the case of " the Church at Jerusalem," and "the Church throughout all Judæa, Samaria, and Galilee," evidently implies a unity made up of a number of local assemblies or congregations. It is out of the question to suppose that, if the disciples of Jesus had been represented in Antioch by so many persons only

---

[1] Acts xi. 27–30 ; xv. 35 ; xiv. 23. Comp. above, pp. 405–408.

[2] "One a Cypriote," says Professor Lumby, in reference to the prophets and teachers at Antioch who are named in the beginning of chap. xiii. ; "another a Cyrenian, another a Jew, but from his double name accustomed to mix among non-Jews, one a connection of the Idumean house of Herod, and Saul the heaven-appointed apostle of the Gentiles,—the list may be deemed in some sort typical of 'all the world,' into which the Gospel was now to go forth." *Acts*, p. 239.

[3] Acts xiii. 1 ; xiv. 27 ; xv. 3.

as could meet ordinarily for worship in a single congregation, they could ever have been distinguished by the populace
from the Jews of the city, or thought worthy of a separate
name. For Antioch, the capital of the province of Syria and
the seat of its imperial legate, was at this time " the third
metropolis of the world," " a second Rome." It counted its
inhabitants by hundreds of thousands.[1] In such a city, the
disciples of Christ must have grown to be a very considerable
community, before they attracted so much general attention
as it is evident they had now done in Antioch. They had
not here been hunted into fame by persecution, either on the
part of the Roman authorities or the synagogue rulers. Yet
the careless and pleasure-loving populace of the city had
learned to distinguish them from the Jews, and to embody
the distinction in a new name, and one which described the
disciples so correctly as that of " Christians." [2]

The name itself bore witness to another great characteristic
of the Church at Antioch, that here first, on a large scale, the

[1] Archdeacon Farrar—following M. Renan—estimates the population of
Antioch at this time as being about 500,000. See his eloquent description of
the moral and spiritual corruption of the city and of the significance of the
name "Christian," "a word which, more than any other that was ever invented,
marks the watershed of all human history." *St. Paul*, i. pp. 288–303.

[2] Ἐγίνετο . . . χρηματίσαι πρῶτον ἐν Ἀντιοχείᾳ τοὺς μαθητὰς Χριστιανούς, Acts
xi. 26. It was a Greek translation of a Hebrew word, with a Latin termination,—reminding one of how these three languages met in the inscription on
the cross. " The Greek adjective from Χριστός would have been Χριστεῖος. It is
true that ηνός and ινός are Greek terminations, but *anus* is mainly Roman, and
there can be little doubt that it is due—not to the Doric dialect !—but to the
prevalence of Roman terminology at Antioch." Farrar, *St. Paul*, i. p. 296 f.
Ewald holds that it was probably first given by the Roman magistrates in
Antioch, and points out that in the only N. T. passage in which the word is
used by an apostle (1 Pet. iv. 10) the reference is to persecution by the Roman
civil authorities, *Gesch. des Volks Israels*, vi. S. 408. Comp. Lightfoot, *Ignatius*,
i. pp. 401–404. " We take the explanation to be this," says Principal Brown,
"that ' Christ ' was so constantly upon the lips of the disciples and their
preachers, that those with whom they came in contact talked of them as
those ' Christ-people,' or Christians." *Romans*, Edin. 1883, p. x. An interesting parallel to this may be found in the annals of the Scottish Reformation, in
the first half of the sixteenth century. It is recorded, in reference to the arrest
of the martyrs of Perth who were put to death in 1544, that the name by which
they were commonly called in derision by their enemies in the town was "the
Christers," because they spoke so much of Christ. Calderwood, *Hist. of Kirk
of Scotland*, i. p. 175.

old and deep drawn lines of separation between Jew and
Gentile were lost sight of in the deeper and higher unity of
the Gospel and the Spirit of Christ.   It was here that Paul
first saw and realized what he wrote of in after days to the
Churches of Galatia and Colossæ, a spiritual brotherhood
in the Lord, in which there was "not Greek and Jew, circumcision and uncircumcision, barbarian, Scythian, bondman,
freeman ; but Christ is all and in all." [1]   The features of
such a time have been well portrayed by an eminent living
minister, who has himself shared in the work and the joy of
more than one great season of spiritual revival in the Churches
of Christ in Britain : "Any one who has ever been· privileged to witness a widespread quickening in the religious life
of a community, or to come close to any large number of
people, who have simultaneously and recently received the
good news of salvation as a new thing, and for them most
certainly a true thing, will not forget the unmistakeable and
inimitable stamp of Divine gladness set upon men's faces, or
the sweet simple affection with which brothers and sisters in
Jesus greet one another, the tender sense of new pardoned
guilt, the devout susceptibility to the Divine Word, the
frank personal clinging to Jesus as to One quite near, the
elevation above their usual carefulness and each petty vexation of daily life, which are the beautiful marks of such a
time.   All this Barnabas had seen some years before.   He
had been present in Jerusalem, when the first unction of
holy joy came from the Lord in heaven.   He was himself
one of those who had been carried away most completely with
the enthusiastic love of those early days.   Now at Antioch,
in a heathen city, in the very stew of pagan uncleanness, he
found himself, to his surprise, in the midst of the same
wonderful young life in God.   The very same fresh childlike sense of reconciliation and peace, the same pure
devout joy, were filling the new - born Gentile Church,
which had at first filled the new - born Hebrew Church.
He recognised the grace of God in Jesus Christ, and was
glad.   Misgivings about Gentile unfitness, or the uncleanness of uncircumcised men, ·could not live in such an

[1] Col. iii. 11 ; Gal. iii. 28 ; vi. 15.

atmosphere. The life was the life of Christ; the air was the air of heaven." [1]

All that savoured of separation disappeared of itself in such an atmosphere in the case of all open-hearted members of the Hebrew Christian Church who came to Antioch. Peter, " an Hebrew of the Hebrews," and " the apostle of the circumcision," felt that the seal of God was upon the fellowship of the disciples here, as certainly as when the Holy Ghost fell on those to whom he spoke at Cæsarea, and he " heard them speak with tongues and magnify God." " When he came to Antioch, he did eat with the Gentiles." Barnabas, Saul of Tarsus, and other Jewish Christians, whether Hellenists or Hebrews, did the same.[2] It was no small part of the preparation, whereby the Church in Antioch was fitted to be the first great centre of missions to the Gentiles, that in it, for years, the social and religious diffi-culties of mixed congregations had been practically solved by the spirit of Christian love and brotherly forbearance. It had been proved in Antioch,—and every missionary sent out from it could bear personal witness to the fact,—that Jewish and Gentile believers could live together as brethren, eating at one table in loving fellowship, partaking of one bread and cup of the Lord.

The first united action of which we hear, on the part of the disciples at Antioch, was one in which they showed their thankfulness for spiritual benefits received from the Hebrew Christian Church, and their sense of spiritual unity with them, by sending temporal help in time of famine to the brethren in Judæa. The next common action recorded of them is in behalf of those who were in yet deeper poverty and need in the great heathen world. It was only to be expected that, in a Christian community, so largely composed of disciples of Gentile birth, the longing on their part for the salvation of their brethren and kinsfolk according to the flesh should soon make itself felt, and should move the whole Church to special prayer and effort. The Christians of Antioch lived in a city wholly given to idolatry, and that of

---

[1] Dykes, *From Jerusalem to Antioch*, 4th ed. p. 408 f.
[2] Acts x. 44 ff. ; Gal. ii. 11–14.

the most corrupt and licentious sort, in the midst of a population which, as a whole, at this time was frivolous, immoral, and debased, beyond even that of Rome itself.[1] Yet the Gospel had proved, and was every day proving itself in Antioch, to be "the power of God unto salvation to every one that believed, to the Jew first, and also to the Greek." [2] Why should it not be so beyond the limits of the city ?

It was most natural that the idea of a mission, which should address itself to Gentiles, as well as to Jews and proselytes, should first arise and take practical shape here. In no other Church probably, at this date, would it have been so warmly welcomed as at Antioch. In no other city would so many believing hearts have been lifted up to God in earnest and intelligent prayer when Paul and Barnabas "were committed to the grace of God for the work which they fulfilled" in the first Gentile mission.[3] The thing was of God. The first evangelists to the heathen were "separated and sent forth by the Holy Ghost, for the work whereunto He had called them," as is brought out with such care in the narrative. But God works by fitting means, and prepares His instruments for special ends ; and we see this principle of the Divine government strikingly illustrated in the way in which the Church of Antioch was prepared, and led to stretch out hands of love, not only towards Judæa and Jerusalem, but towards the vast heathen world, and to become a fruitful mother of Churches drawn from among the Gentiles.

---

[1] Some of the points in M. Renan's vivid, but not exaggerated, description of the morals of Antioch will not bear reproduction. Two or three of his graphic touches may be given. "La légérité syrienne, le charlatanisme babylonien, toutes les impostures de l'Asie, se confondant à cette limite des deux mondes, avaient fait d'Antioche la capitale du mensonge, la sentine de toutes les infamies. . . . L'avilissement des âmes y était effroyable. . . . Ce fleuve de boue, qui, sortant par l'embouchure de l'Oronte, venait inonder Rome, avait là sa source principale." Les Apôtres, p. 218 ff. The allusion in the last sentence is, of course, to the well-known line of Juvenal :—

"Jampridem Syrus in Tiberim defluxit Orontes."

[2] Rom. i. 16. Paul had seen its power in Antioch, before he wrote thus to believers living in Rome.

[3] Acts xiii. 2 f. ; xiv. 26.

2nd. How had the apostle of the Gentiles been prepared for his work ?

It is impossible here even to name all the different elements which entered into the Providential preparation of Saul of Tarsus " for the work which he fulfilled ; " much more is it impossible to enter into the details of the subject in any one of its aspects. To the apostle himself, as he looked back upon it afterwards, his whole previous history seemed one long preparation, under the hand of God, for the great mission among the Gentiles, to which he was formally " separated " at the bidding of the Holy Ghost in the Church at Antioch. " It was the good pleasure of God," he said, " who separated me even from my mother's womb, and called me through His grace, to reveal His Son in me, that I might preach Him among the Gentiles." [1] His birth as " an Hebrew of the Hebrews," " a Pharisee and a son of Pharisees," his Roman citizenship, the Hellenistic surroundings and influence of Greek literary and commercial life at Tarsus, his training in Jerusalem at the feet of Gamaliel, his position as a trusted leader in the counsels and action of the Sanhedrin,—all this varied experience and education, not in schools merely, but in practical knowledge of the world, of men and of affairs, combined with natural gifts and capacities of the highest kind, to fit the future apostle for his work.[2]

Saul of Tarsus mingled doubtless in the keen debates, in which men of his own synagogue in Jerusalem — " the synagogue of Cilicians "—" disputed with Stephen, and were not able to withstand the wisdom and the spirit by which he spake." [3] That wonderful address before the Sanhedrin must have impressed a mind like that of Saul, so well fitted to appreciate its reasonings, and to feel the force of its appeals.[4]

[1] Gal. i. 15 f.

[2] Many of these points are admirably handled in Stalker's *Life of St. Paul*, ed. 1885, pp. 21-45.

[3] Acts vi. 9 f.

[4] It has often been pointed out that there are distinct coincidences between the method, the leading ideas, and expressions of St. Stephen's speech on the one hand, and those of Paul's letters and addresses on the other. See Farrar, *St. Paul*, i. p. 163.

He had seen the martyr's face, "as it were the face of an angel," calm, confident, and rejoicing, lighted up with heavenly radiance, amid all the savage fury of his adversaries. He had heard Stephen speak of what he saw, as he "looked up stedfastly into heaven," had heard his dying prayer to the Lord Jesus for himself and for his murderers, and had seen how "he fell asleep."[1] These things, and other like scenes of the persecution, must surely have haunted Saul, even before his conversion; after it, it is plain, they often returned upon him.[2] He could not bring himself, as it seems, actually to lay hands on Stephen. Who can say with what strain put upon his natural feelings he stood by, "consenting unto his death, and kept the raiment of them that slew him," thinking he "did God service" thereby? Yet, if it were right to do this, it was right to do more. Saul's next step, therefore, was to throw himself, heart and hand, into the work of rooting out this blasphemous heresy, as he deemed it, which had arisen in Israel concerning Jesus of Nazareth. It may have been in part from a half-conscious desire to stifle thought, and crush down doubts and questionings which arose within him, as he recalled the martyr's look and words, that Saul of Tarsus flung himself so fiercely into the whirl of excitement and energetic action, in which he lived during the months that followed Stephen's death. Persecution became the very breath of his life. "Saul, yet breathing threatening and slaughter against the disciples of the Lord, went unto the high priest," and "unto the whole presbytery" (δ $\dot{a}\rho\chi\iota\epsilon$-$\rho\epsilon\dot{v}\varsigma$ $\kappa\alpha\dot{\iota}$ . . . $\pi\hat{a}\nu$ $\tau\dot{o}$ $\pi\rho\epsilon\sigma\beta\upsilon\tau\dot{\epsilon}\rho\iota o\nu$, $\pi\alpha\rho$' $\hat{\omega}\nu$ $\dot{\epsilon}\pi\iota\sigma\tau o\lambda\dot{a}\varsigma$ $\delta\epsilon\xi\dot{a}\mu\epsilon\nu o\varsigma$), and obtained from them written "authority and commission" to persecute "them of the way," even "unto foreign cities."[3]

Then came the turning-point of Saul's life, his "seeing Jesus Christ our Lord" on the road to Damascus. The wolf thirsting for blood, "breathing slaughter," was at the very door of the sheepfold, crouching, as it were, for the fatal

[1] Acts vi. 15 ; vii. 54-60.
[2] Acts xxii. 19 f. ; xxvi. 10 f. ; Gal. i. 13 ; 1 Cor. xv. 9 ; 1 Tim. i. 13.
[3] Acts ix. 1 f. ; xxii. 5 ; xxvi. 11 f.

spring, when he was suddenly grasped by the strong hand of the Good Shepherd, and not struck down merely, but changed from a raging enemy, first into a humble follower of Christ, and then into the best and tenderest of the under shepherds of His flock; "de lupo, ovis; de ove, pastor." "I was apprehended, I was laid hold on," — as he describes the event himself in one emphatic phrase,—"by Christ Jesus." [1]

There followed three memorable days during which Saul "conferred not with flesh and blood." For three days, in fasting and darkness, he was like Moses on the mount, encompassed with a cloud, and communing alone with God. What inward struggles, what deep convictions of sin, what repentance towards God, and seeking after the grace of God in Christ, what mighty and far-reaching changes in Saul's whole spiritual being, made up for him the real history of those three days, who can tell? A veil has been thrown, in great measure, over this period of the apostle's life, as over the kindred period of his sojourn in Arabia, which came shortly after. We may gather something of the process from the result, and from indications in his Epistles. The latter part of the seventh chapter of the Romans, for example, shows how Paul passed from a false use of the law of God to the true, and from that to Christ. But to enter on this subject, deeply interesting and attractive as it is, would be foreign to our present purpose. [2] Enough to say that the practical link between the two states of feeling described in that chapter, and exemplified in the apostle's own experience in Damascus, — between crying out under the burden of sin and death on the one hand, and rejoicing

---

[1] Κατελήφθην ὑπὸ Χριστοῦ Ἰησοῦ, Phil. iii. 12.

[2] See the powerful and suggestive treatment of this subject by Principal Rainy in "Paul the Apostle," the first of the "Evangelical Succession" lectures, Edin. 1882, pp. 15–29. See also Stalker, *Life of St. Paul*, ed. 1885, pp. 52–63, 72–84. I differ from Dr. Rainy, and agree with Mr. Stalker,—as will be seen from what I have said above,—regarding the light thrown on Saul's mental attitude before his conversion by our Lord's words, "It is hard for thee to kick against the goad." Comp. the fine passage on this point in Pfleiderer, *Influence of the Apostle Paul on the Development of Christianity* (Hibbert Lect. 1885), p. 34 ff.

in Christ Jesus as our Lord and Saviour on the other,—is to be found in three words of the message which the Lord gave to Ananias concerning Saul of Tarsus: "Behold, he prayeth."[1] Light was arising in his soul out of darkness, the struggle was ending in victory, when true prayer began, the prayer of faith, and in the name of Jesus. And, while he was yet speaking in prayer, the answer was given from above. "He saw in a vision a man, named Ananias, coming in, and laying his hands on him, that he might receive his sight." The very name — meaning "the Lord is gracious"—may have seemed to Saul, as "an Hebrew of the Hebrews," a special token for good.[2]

After Saul's first bold confession and testimony for Christ in the synagogues of Damascus, he withdrew, for a period apparently of considerable length, into the solitudes of Arabia.[3] This season of retirement and study, although fruitful doubtless in the highest spiritual results to Saul himself, was not marked by any outward events which have been recorded. From Arabia, he returned for a time to Damascus. "Then, after three years," he tells the Galatians, "I went up to Jerusalem to become acquainted with Cephas, and tarried with him fifteen days; . . . and I saw also James, the Lord's brother."[4]

---

[1] Ἰδοὺ γὰρ, προσεύχεται, Acts ix. 11.   [2] Chap. ix. 13.

[3] "Immediately I conferred not with flesh and blood; neither went I up to Jerusalem to them which were apostles before me; but I went away into Arabia; and again I returned unto Damascus," Gal. i. 16 f. The place where Paul's Arabian sojourn should be inserted in the condensed narrative of the ninth chapter of Acts, is probably after ver. 21 or 22. It cannot well be after ver. 25, in view of his own statement: "I returned *again* to Damascus." This was after the interval referred to in the first clause of ver. 23; and the fact of his absence from the city during that interval, removes the difficulty of understanding how the Jews allowed "many days to be fulfilled" before "they took counsel together to kill him." On Saul's first appearance in the synagogue, to give testimony that "Jesus of Nazareth was the Son of God," the Jews were overawed and paralysed by the amazing character of the event. Before they had recovered from this first stupor, the bold witness was gone. But when, "after many days," he returned to Damascus, "increased in strength," and thoroughly able now to "prove" from Scripture "that this is the Christ," we cannot wonder that the irritation and alarm of the Jews led them to "take counsel together to kill him."

[4] Gal. i. 18 f. Regarding the force of the εἰ μή in this passage, see above p. 448.

It is easy to understand of what importance this personal and confidential intercourse with Peter and James must have been to Saul of Tarsus, as regards his preparation for his future work. He too, like "them which were apostles before him," had now "*seen* the Lord Jesus," and "heard the voice of His mouth," but not, as they had, in the days of His humiliation. No better eye and ear witnesses to the facts of the life and death, the resurrection and ascension of Jesus, could have been found than just the two with whom Saul held close converse during that memorable fortnight at Jerusalem. Peter could tell him of all the things concerning the Master, which were known in the inmost circle of the apostles, beginning from the baptism of John until the day when Peter went first into the open sepulchre, and, first of the Twelve, met with the risen Lord, and onward until the day when He was taken up from them on the Mount of Olives. James, the Lord's brother, could go back to an even earlier date, and tell of things known only in the home at Nazareth, how God sent forth His Son made of a woman, made under the law, how from the first He had "grown in wisdom as in age and in favour with God and man," how none of His brethren could "convict Him of sin," in that "He did always the things that were pleasing to his Father," how yet they had doubted, and held aloof from full recognition of His claims, until the resurrection removed all doubts, and "He appeared unto James."[1]

---

[1] Luke ii. 51 f. ; John viii. 29, 46 ; 1 Cor. xv. 7. An additional evidence in support of the view which distinguishes James, the Lord's brother, from the Twelve may be found in the fact that Paul, in this passage, when enumerating in order the successive appearances of the risen Saviour, places the appearance to James after both the interview with "the Twelve" and that with the five hundred. James was called "the Just" by Jews as well as Hebrew Christians. Comp. Hegesippus in Euseb. ii. 23 ; Origen, *Contra Cels.* i. 47. "No man was less likely to have been deceived or to have deceived." Edwards, *First Cor.* 2nd ed. p. 397.

Holsten supposes that James was specially seen by Paul "because of the position which the brother of the Lord already held in the Church at Jerusalem." There can be no doubt that his personal weight of character, and his peculiar relation to the Saviour, must have given him a position of special influence in the Apostolic Church from the first. But the facts above referred to, and the allusion in 1 Cor. xv. 7 to our Lord's interview with

It is worth noting that both at Damascus, on his return from Arabia, and at Jerusalem, on this first visit after his conversion, Saul sought earnestly and perseveringly to find entrance as a witness for Christ among the Jews; but his efforts met with little success. Everywhere, but especially among the Hellenists of his own synagogue in Jerusalem, he was regarded as a renegade of no ordinary stamp. The hope and pride with which his fellow-countrymen had once looked upon him, as the foremost pupil of Gamaliel, and a rising leader in the national cause, were changed into feelings of the bitterest enmity. "They went about to kill him." [1]

The conviction was forced on the mind of Saul, much against his will, that this door of usefulness was hopelessly closed against him. He still abode in Damascus, knowing that the Jews plotted against him, and "watched the gates day and night that they might kill him," until "his disciples took him by night, and let him down through the wall, lowering him in a basket."

In Jerusalem he yielded only when the Lord's voice in vision lent authority to the urgency of brethren in the city who saw his danger. He was "brought down" by them to Cæsarea, and "sent forth" to his native Tarsus.[2] His experience there seems to have been of a somewhat similar kind. We hear at least of no marked success, until at the invitation of Barnabas he came with him to the great Gentile city on the Orontes. There, for the first time, Saul found himself in the midst of a Church which was drawn chiefly from the Gentiles, and in which Jew and Gentile were walking lovingly together

---

James after the Resurrection, suggest other reasons. It is a piece of perfectly gratuitous theorizing, without the slightest foundation in the facts, so far as recorded, when Holsten goes on to suppose that Paul told his Gospel for the heathen to Peter at this time, and that the latter, being startled by the announcement, called in James to the conference, "against Paul's original intention." *Evang. des Paulus*, Berlin 1880, S. 8 f.

[1] Acts ix. 23 f., 29. It must surely be simply by inadvertence that Arch-deacon Farrar speaks of those Hellenists, who "disputed against Paul" at Jerusalem, and "went about to kill him," as "Jews who had embraced Christianity," and as "Christians, circumcised and Judaic." *St. Paul*, i. p. 126.

[2] Acts ix. 24 f., 30. Comp. xxii. 17-21; Gal. i. 21; 2 Cor. xi. 32 f.

as yet, according to the rule, which he himself gave afterwards for "the Israel of God," that in Christ Jesus "neither
is circumcision anything, nor uncircumcision, but a new
creature."[1]

There, for the first time, so far as our records bear, since
his conversion, the Lord set before him an open door for the
work of the Gospel, and there, accordingly, "even for a whole
year, Barnabas and Saul were gathered together with the
Church, and taught much people."[2]   Thus by the discipline
of disappointment and of hope deferred, by successive lessons
in humility, obedience, and self-denial faithfully learned, the
future apostle of the Gentiles had been prepared for the great
enterprise, to which he was now to be sent forth from
Antioch.

That some arduous but honourable and successful work
for Christ in a wide field was in store for Saul, had been once
and again revealed to himself from the time of his conversion
onwards, and was doubtless understood, to some extent,
among the disciples in Damascus, Jerusalem, and elsewhere.
That the work in question bore especially on the spread of
the Gospel among the Gentiles, was known to Barnabas and
others who had been especially brought into contact with
Saul; and this probably led to his being thought of at once,
when the new field among the Greeks opened at Antioch.[3]
The bitterness of Saul's disappointment, in having to give up
all prospect of being a means of blessing to his brethren and
kinsfolk in Jerusalem, was softened by a direct revelation
from Christ, that a great future was before him, to which the
Lord Himself was to "send him forth" in far distant regions
"among the Gentiles."[4]   But what form this work, among
the heathen and their rulers, was to take, in what way,
and from what centre, he was to be sent forth to it, and
in what relation it was to stand to work among "the
children of Israel," which was linked with it in the

---

[1] Gal. v. 6; vi. 15 f.   [2] Acts xi. 26.

[3] See Acts ix. 15 f. Compare Paul's abbreviated statement of this message
to the Jewish mob from the castle steps in Jerusalem (xxii. 15) with the
fuller summary of all the revelations from this period, bearing on his apostolic
commission, which he gave before Agrippa (xxvi. 16 ff.).

[4] Acts xxii. 17–21.

revelations to Ananias and to Saul himself, remained as yet unrevealed.

But now, at last, after these years of waiting and preparation, the hour had come. The converging lines, on which the great unseen Worker had been carrying forward His purposes of grace, met in Antioch. The Christian community there was by this time sufficiently established and built up in faith, and love, and knowledge of the truth, for its share in the work. The Church of Antioch was strong enough now to spare two of its leading teachers for a wider enterprise. And, on the other hand, that one of the two had been fully prepared for the work, whose name was soon to hold the foremost place in the heart and on the lips of the brethren at Antioch, although hitherto he had willingly seen others preferred there in honour to himself. As "a vessel of election to bear the name of the Lord Jesus before the Gentiles," [1] Saul of Tarsus had been shaped and moulded hitherto under the Lord's hand, through long and manifold discipline. He had been tested and refined in the furnace of trial. Like "the captain of his salvation," he "learned obedience by the things which he suffered." And now he was "a vessel unto honour, sanctified, and meet for the Master's use" in many lands.[2]

3rd. How the great commission of Christ to His Church was taken up afresh at Antioch.

As the prophets and teachers of the Church at Antioch "ministered to the Lord and fasted," the command came from the Holy Spirit, speaking by the lips of some man of prophetic gifts in their assembly: "Separate Me Barnabas and Saul for the work whereunto I have called them. Then, when they had fasted and prayed, and laid their hands on them, they sent them away. So they, being sent forth by the Holy Ghost, went down to Seleucia, and from thence they sailed to Cyprus." [3]

We have noted already what a spirit of intelligent and

---

[1] Σκεῦος ἐκλογῆς ἐστί μοι οὗτος, Acts ix. 15.

[2] Heb. ii. 10 ; v. 8 ; 2 Tim. ii. 21.

[3] Acts xiii. 1–4.

energetic Christian love and zeal characterized the members of the Church at Antioch,—how, before this time, they had shown themselves prompt to take action in the interests of Christ's cause beyond their own borders, and to look not to their own things merely, but the things of others. Antioch was at this date the most advanced post of Christianity, pushed far out from the Holy Land into the very centre of heathendom. There could not fail to be in such a Church not a little serious thought and prayer, especially among its leading men, regarding their responsibility and duty, not only with respect to their heathen fellow-countrymen in and around the city, who had proved themselves already so open to the Gospel, but with respect to the vast heathen world beyond, lying in darkness and sin. It seems probable that the special services mentioned in the passage above cited—the earnest waiting on the Lord, the concentration of spirit, and withdrawal from sources of outward distraction, which are implied in New Testament fasting — had some reference to this momentous problem, and the need of further light regarding it. The answer given by God seems to show the nature of the requests, which had gone up to Him from the hearts of the believers in Antioch. " As they ministered to the Lord and fasted, the Holy Ghost " spoke in their assembly, calling the men suited, above all others, to go as evangelists to the Gentile world, and leading the Church to recognise the call, and to act upon it.

We have here the first formal appointment of missionaries in the apostolic Church. Let us note the connection and significance of the successive steps by which it took place.

1. The initiative, if we may so speak, comes from above. The call of the Holy Spirit to the work forms the primary and essential element in the commission of Barnabas and Saul;[1] and this is received in connection with special and united waiting on the Lord, on the part of those called, and other believers in Antioch.

---

[1] 'Αφορίσατε δή Μοι τὸν Βαρνάβαν καὶ τὸν Σαῦλον εἰς τὸ ἔργον ὃ προσκέκλημαι αὐτούς. " The middle force of προσκέκλημαι, though not possible to be represented in a translation, should not be lost sight of. The Holy Ghost says: I have called them *for Myself*." Lumby, *Acts*, p. 239.

2. The call is a twofold one. It is addressed not merely to the future missionaries themselves, but to the Church, in which they had hitherto been teachers. Both parties were to take fitting action in the matter, each, in their mutual relations, recognising and obeying the call of the Spirit. "The Holy Ghost said (to the Church): Separate Me Barnabas and Saul for the work whereunto I have called them." It was a direct and personal call to the men themselves, recognised by them inwardly as such. But it was not left to their individual impulse to leave the position which they now held at Antioch, and to go forth of themselves at the inward call of the Holy Ghost. They must be separated and set apart to the work to which He had called them, by the Church to which they belonged.

3. The Church, accordingly, acting through its representatives, the prophets and teachers, proceeds to give effect to the call by formally setting apart Barnabas and Saul to the work in question. This was done with solemn prayer and special services, in which, as it appears, the membership of the Church generally took part, "committing" the two brethren "to the grace of God for the work which they were to fulfil."[1]

It was accompanied, as in the appointment of the deacons in Jerusalem, with "the laying on of hands," an action familiar to every Jew and proselyte of Antioch in connection with the ordination of elders in the synagogues.

4. The result is, that the missionaries, as the historian emphatically repeats, are "sent forth by the Holy Ghost," but are "sent" also by the Church, to which in due time they return to give in their report of "all things that God had done with them, and how that He had opened a door of faith unto the Gentiles."[2]

The two great agencies, which Christ had said to His disciples that He would use for the establishment of His cause and kingdom on the earth, were the Holy Spirit, the Helper and Teacher, "whom He would send unto them from the Father," and the Church, which He was to "build for Himself upon the rock, and against which the gates of Hades

[1] Acts xiii. 3 ; xiv. 26.   [2] Acts xiii. 3 f. ; xiv. 27.

should not prevail." [1] In this opening scene in the second section of the Acts, we see these two agencies, distinct from each other, yet in the closest relations, and acting harmoniously together for the spread of the Gospel.

It was thus that Christ's great commission to His disciples was taken up afresh at Antioch. The rest of the book of Acts records the results that followed. Into the historical progress and details of these we cannot enter; but it may be suitable to indicate here, in the most summary way, the main steps in the advance of the Gospel, and the chief fields in which the Church of Christ was established during this second period.

I. Paul's first missionary journey; Paul and Barnabas in Cyprus; conversion of the Roman proconsul. The Gospel passes from the Jews to the Gentiles in Antioch of Pisidia; planting and organization of Churches in cities of Lycaonia; organization in Antioch; preaching in Pamphylia. Acts xiii. and xiv.

II. Questions raised by admission of Gentiles into Church, and by existence of mixed congregations, dealt with in Council of Jerusalem. Acts xv.; Gal. ii.

III. Paul's second missionary journey. Acts xv. 36; xviii. 22. Paul (and Silas ?) in Syria and Cilicia; in Lycaonia, where Timothy joins (chap. xvi. 1 ff.); in Phrygia and Galatia; through Mysia to Troas, where Luke joins,[2] and the "we sections" of the narrative begin (chap. xvi. 10). Paul and his companions enter Europe. The Gospel in Macedonia; Philippi, Thessalonica, Berœa (chap. xvi. 11–40; xvii. 1–14). The Gospel in Greece; Athens, Corinth, Cenchrea (chap. xvii. 15–34; xviii. 1–18; Rom. xvi. 1 f.). Paul, Aquila, and Priscilla in Ephesus (chap. xviii. 18–21).

IV. Apollos in Ephesus and Achaia; Acts xviii. 24–28; xix. 1; 1 Cor. i. 12; iii. 5 f.; iv. 6; xvi. 12.

V. Paul's third missionary journey. Acts xviii. 23; xix.

[1] John xv. 26; xvi. 7; Matt. xvi. 18.
[2] Possibly Silas also,—Paul having "chosen," and sent for him as his companion on his dissension with Barnabas, but having started from Antioch in Syria without waiting for him. See K. Schmidt's ingenious argument to this effect. *Apostelgesch.* S. 108.

20 ; xxi. 1–14. Paul again in Galatia and Phrygia; in Ephesus for about three years (chap. xx. 31). Gospel spreads through all the Roman province of Asia (chap. xix. 10, 26). Timothy and Erastus sent by Paul into Macedonia (chap. xix. 22). Paul again in Macedonia and Greece ; in Illyricum (Rom. xv. 19) ; again in Troas ; in Miletus. Charge to the elders of the Church of Ephesus. Paul and his company in Tyre and Cæsarea.

VI. Paul in Jerusalem, bringing contributions from the Gentile Christian Churches ; on his defence ; in Cæsarea again as a prisoner for some three years, but with access to the Gentile Christian Church there (Acts xxi. 15–40 ; xxii. ; xxiii. ; xxiv. ; xxv. ; xxvi.). Paul on his way to Rome ; work in Melita; work in Rome (chap. xxvii. ; xxviii.). Epistles of the first imprisonment.

VII. Glimpses of Paul and his fellow-workers after his release from first imprisonment at Rome ; in Ephesus (1 Tim. i. 3 ; iv. 13 ; 2 Tim. i. 18 ; iv. 12) ; in Miletus, Troas, Corinth (2 Tim. iv. 13, 20) ; in Crete, Nicopolis, Macedonia, Dalmatia, Galatia (Titus i. 5 ; iii. 12 f. ; 1 Tim. i. 3 ; 2 Tim. iv. 10).

VIII. Paul at Rome in second imprisonment, yet having opportunities still to " proclaim Christ's message fully so that all the Gentiles might hear " (2 Tim. iv. 17) ; and, whatever befalls him, " the Word of God is not bound " in Rome (2 Tim. ii. 9).

IX. A few glimpses from a yet later period regarding the state of the Church of Ephesus, and the region associated with it, may be obtained from the Apocalypse, the fourth Gospel, and the Epistles of John.

How, then, does the apostolic Church come before us in the period to which we now pass, during the years of the great missionary movements, by which the Gospel was carried by successive stages from Antioch to Corinth, to Ephesus, to Rome, and during the later time, of which we see something in the Pastoral Epistles, and in the writings of the apostle John ? We may deal with the subject on the same general plan as in Part V., although our limits will not allow of so much detail, and some sections must be omitted.

CHAPTER II.

THE GENTILE CHRISTIAN CHURCH IN ITSELF; ITS LIFE AND WORK
AND GENERAL CHARACTERISTICS.

IN itself, as regards its general spirit and leading characteristics, the apostolic Church of this period is found to
be essentially the same as we have seen it on Hebrew Christian
ground. It is still, in the first place, and above all else, a
fellowship of believers, associated together in the name of the
Lord Jesus Christ, and under the teaching of the Holy Spirit,
for the purposes for which Christ has called them into union
with Himself and with each other. The life of the Church
is manifestly the same in its nature and source, although we
see it now to some extent taking fresh forms, and adapting
itself differently to different circumstances and emergencies
in Providence. The action of the Church is guided by the
same principles, and directed towards the same great ends;
but the principles find embodiment and are put into practice
in new ways. There are, in short, the unfailing marks of all
healthful life, namely, vigorous growth, and free, harmonious
development according to its own laws.

1st. Witness for Christ in word and deed; nature of the
Gospel preached to the Gentiles; methods and results.
The chief end of the Church's work is still, as before, to
bear witness for Christ, and to bring men to receive and obey
the Gospel. Christianity had been founded in Antioch chiefly,
as we saw in last chapter, through the witness-bearing of
private disciples. They were members of the Hebrew Christian Church, driven from the Holy Land by persecution; and
at first " they spake the Word to none save only to Jews." It
was, accordingly, from the circle of the synagogues in Antioch,
as elsewhere, that the first converts were made. But some

warm-hearted Hellenists, when they reached the great Gentile city, and saw its sins and needs, were led to cross that line. "They spake unto the Greeks also, telling the good tidings of the Lord Jesus;" and the witness carried such Divine power with it, that "a great number of them turned in faith unto the Lord."[1] By the continuance of such simple witness-bearing, often, doubtless, from unlettered lips, as well as by the labours of the "prophets and teachers," the Church of Christ spread and grew strong at Antioch. There, as in Jerusalem at the beginning, the fruits of the Gospel were the best evidence to all men of its Divine origin and authority. "The fruits of the Spirit," seen in changed lives, "and the kingdom of God" manifestly established "in righteousness, peace, and joy in the Holy Ghost," were the best means for preparing men's hearts to receive the message of salvation, spoken in the power of the same Spirit.

Jew and Gentile had been separated hitherto in Antioch by older and deeper differences than any that had existed between the converts of Pentecost. But these differences all melted away under the transforming heat and light of the Gospel and the Spirit of Christ. Those who had been drawn to Christ from the synagogues, and those who had turned to Him from idols, were so visibly "one in the Lord," that even the careless heathen "took knowledge of them," and felt that none of the old titles would suit any longer, but that this new community, which had suddenly appeared in the midst of them, must be called by a new name, even that of Him of whom its members spoke so much.[2] Men fresh from the experience of Pentecostal times in Jerusalem "saw the grace of God" at Antioch, and "were glad," and joined themselves to the fellowship of the brethren there, exhorting them only to "cleave with purpose of heart unto the Lord," from whom such grace came.[3] They saw the same simplicity of faith and joy in the Lord, the same spirit of unity and brotherly love,

---

[1] Εὐαγγελιζόμενοι τὸν Κύριον Ἰησοῦν . . . πολύς τι ἀριθμὸς ὁ πιστεύσας ἐπέστρεψεν ἐπὶ τὸν Κύριον, Acts viii. 4 ; xi. 19.

[2] Compare the corresponding fact, on a small scale, from "Reformation Times in Scotland," cited above, p. 461, note.

[3] Acts xi. 23 f.; Gal. ii. 12 ff.

of practical sympathy and helpfulness towards all the brethren who had need and were in affliction.

The second section of the history of the apostolic Church opens with a scene which recalls vividly what is told us of the little company in the upper chamber at Jerusalem, just before the advent of the Holy Spirit at Pentecost. A number of Christians at Antioch had met " with one accord," along with their leading teachers, for special waiting upon the Lord. There, at the bidding of the Holy Ghost, the great commission was taken up afresh, and in a deliberate, and, so to say, normal way, the work of Christian missions was begun.[1]

What was the nature of the message which was borne by the missionaries from Antioch into the regions beyond, we learn from the reports of Paul's speeches in the Acts, and from what he calls " his Gospel" in his own epistles. There is perfect harmony between the accounts given of it in these two different sources. " The Gospel" which Paul preached unto the heathen, and which " those who seemed to be pillars " in the Church at Jerusalem found, when it was " laid before them " by himself, to need no alteration or addition from them,[2] was always in substance just the message which Peter declared on the day of Pentecost. It was the same message which, when carried from Jerusalem to Antioch by the fugitives from the persecution, and spoken there by feebler lips than those of apostles, but brought home by the hand of the Lord, had wrought such great things among the Gentiles in the Syrian capital. It was " the good tidings concerning the Lord Jesus."[3]

The practical rule on which Paul and his companions in labour acted as regards the starting-point of their mission was that which he states in the first chapter of his Epistle to the Romans: " To the Jew first, and also to the Greek."[4] In the view of the apostle of the Gentiles, as well as of " the Twelve," the right of the first-born still belonged to the Jew, until he should openly and deliberately " despise his birthright." Apart even from the Lord's command to " begin at Jerusalem," and from the strong affection towards his fellow-countrymen and desire for their salvation which animated one who always felt

---

[1] See above, pp. 472-475.
[3] Acts xi. 20 ; Rom. i. 1-5 ; 1 Cor. i. 2-9 ; xv. 1-11, etc.
[2] Gal. ii. 2-10.
[4] Rom. i. 16.

himself to be " of the seed of Abraham," " an Hebrew of the
Hebrews," this was obviously in itself the wisest course for
all the ends of the Gentile mission. The Jewish Dispersion,
as we saw in Part III., had already been a notable means of
spiritual blessing to the Gentiles.[1] Hitherto, indeed, the
work had been confined within comparatively narrow limits.
But still, around almost every synagogue throughout the
empire, there had been gathered a certain number of persons,
—more or fewer, and more or less closely connected with the
ordinary congregation—who were not of the stock of Abraham,
but who had come through Jewish influence and teaching to
worship the true God, and to study the Jewish Scriptures
as a revelation of His will. Might not all this be but an
earnest of far greater things now ? If Israel in the Dispersion would only be true to their high calling, might not " the
blessing of Abraham come," through them, " upon the Gentiles
in Christ Jesus, that they both together might receive the
promise of the Spirit through faith " ? [2] Many a devout heart
in Israel, in the temple courts and in the synagogues, had
prayed for such a future.[3] There were " voices of the prophets read every Sabbath day " in the synagogues of the Dispersion, and known in pious homes like that in which Timothy
was trained, which seemed to promise the fulfilment of such
a hope.[4] In the beginning of the Gospel, Simeon had declared
by the Spirit, in the temple, concerning the Saviour, that He
should be " a light for revelation to the Gentiles, and the
glory of Thy people Israel." The words seem more than once
referred to by Paul, and are recorded by that evangelist who
was closely associated with him during his missionary labours,
and who is held to have been a native of Antioch, from which
they began.[5] Might not that light shine out from every

---

[1] See above, pp. 114–117, 157 f.   [2] Gal. iii. 7–14.

[3] "God be merciful unto us and bless us, and cause His face to shine upon
us, *that Thy way may be known upon earth, Thy saving health among all nations.*
Let the peoples praise Thee, O God, let all the peoples praise Thee." Ps.
lxvii. 1–3. Comp. Ps. xlvii. 8 ; lxviii. 28–35, etc.

[4] Acts xiii. 27 (in Paul's first recorded address on the Gentile mission); 2 Tim.
i. 5 ; iii. 15 ; Ps. lxxxvii. 3–6 ; Isa. ii. 1–5 ; xix. 23–25 ; xlii. 5–7 ; Jer. xxxi.
35 f.; Micah iv. 1 f.; Hag. ii. 6–9.

[5] Luke ii. 31 f. Comp. Acts xiii. 47 ; xxvi. 23.

synagogue of the Diaspora ? Might it not be the crowning
"glory of God's people Israel," "our twelve tribes earnestly
serving God night and day," [1] to be His great instrument
for the evangelization of the world, that so " in Abraham
and in his seed all the families of the earth should be
blessed " ?

It was not to be so for Israel, as a nation, at this time.
Prophetic utterances, which pointed to this darker issue,
seem more and more to have weighed upon the mind of
Paul, as his work went on. But how natural that he should
cling, as long as might be, to "the larger hope" for his
brethren and kinsfolk according to the flesh, and that it
should quicken and stimulate his efforts, as he turned
unweariedly, in each new sphere of labour, "to the Jew
first" ! [2] It was at all events his part to go on step by
step, as the Lord opened up the way. It was at least right
that the opportunity of receiving the Gospel for themselves,
and being in their collective capacity the means of spreading
the Gospel among the Gentiles, should be offered first to
Israel in each of the great seats of the Dispersion, in Antioch,
Ephesus, Corinth, and Rome. If the children of Abraham
in these great representative centres of Jewish life despised
their birthright, and refused the work of "a prophet unto
the nations" for good, then the apostle might well turn
finally to the Gentiles. [3]

From one utterance of Paul's after another in the Acts,
and from a striking section in the Epistle to the Romans,
we may gather with what deep and thrilling feelings he
pondered these things, as he beheld the purposes of God
towards Israel and the Gentiles gradually unfolding before
him in the facts of history and the experiences of his own
ministry, and as he recognised the meaning of the facts, and
the great principles of Divine sovereignty, election, and grace,
which were embodied in them, reading all in the light which
the Holy Spirit shed upon the Word and the Providence of
God. Yes, Israel, as a people, had stumbled and fallen, as
the prophets had foretold, but not for ever ; and meanwhile,

---

[1] Acts xxvi. 7.   [2] Zech. viii. 20–23 ; xiv. 16–21.
[3] This point is well developed by K. Schmidt, *Apostelgesch.* S. 480–486.

"by their fall, salvation had come unto the Gentiles, for to
provoke them to jealousy. Their fall was the riches of the
world, and their loss the riches of the Gentiles; how much
more their fulness? . . . 'The receiving of them' into the
fold of Christ, 'the grafting of them in again into their own
olive tree,' should, when it came at last, be 'as life from the
dead.'"[1]

Yet even now there was "a remnant, an election of grace,"
from among the children of Abraham, according to the flesh.
It was only "in part"—although, alas, the largest part—
"that a hardening had befallen Israel, until the fulness of
the Gentiles be come in; and so all Israel shall be saved."
There was a chosen company, like Obadiah and the seven
thousand in Israel in Elijah's time, to whom the apostle's
heart went out with a special warmth of love. They were
"brethren," both "according to the flesh" and "in the Lord."
"The election obtained that which Israel (the majority of the
nation) seeketh for; and the rest were hardened, according as
it is written, God gave them a spirit of stupor . . . unto
this very day."[2]   Those who formed this "election of grace"
did obtain the birthright, which should have been the portion
of "all Israel." They both received themselves "the blessing
of Abraham in Christ Jesus," and were most effective helpers
to the apostle afterwards, in spreading that blessing among
the Gentiles. Paul did not spend his strength in vain when
labouring in every place, first of all, in the synagogue,
although amid much opposition and disappointment. The
only case in which no success in this field seems indicated,
is that of the synagogue in Athens. And there, it is to be
noted as an exceptional fact, the apostle began work simultaneously in both spheres, and appears from the first to have
given his main strength to the heathen. But, as a rule, in
every Church planted by Paul during this period, there were
more or fewer believers of Jewish origin, and others who
had been proselytes under synagogue training. Among the
apostle's best helpers in each Christian community on Gentile

---

[1] Acts ix. 20, 29; xiii. 16 f., 26 f., 46; xvi. 3; xviii. 6; xxii. 1 ff.; xxiv.
17; xxvi. 6 f.; xxviii. 17–20, 25–28; Rom. ix.; x.; xi.
[2] Rom. ix. 6–8, 27; xi. 2–5, 7 f., 26.

ground, not a few were like the three Jewish Christians, of whom he makes such emphatic mention in writing from Rome to Colossæ : " Aristarchus, Mark, and Jesus, which is called Justus, who are of the circumcision; these only are my fellow-workers unto the kingdom of God, men that have been a comfort unto me." [1]

The Jewish synagogue or proseucha, in every place to which the missionaries came, was the natural starting-point for their work. It gave a vantage ground, which was not needlessly to be thrown away. It was sure to afford some points of contact with those Gentiles, who were most open to the Gospel, through the proselytes, in the stricter or looser sense of the term, who had gathered round the local Jewish community.

Besides working in the synagogue, until driven out by persecution, Paul and his associates made known the Gospel to Jews and Gentiles in the open air, in the market-place, in rooms hired or lent for their meetings, from house to house, and by whatever other way was open to them for the purpose.[2]·

Whether specially designed for a synagogue audience or a Gentile one, the apostolic addresses, which have reached us from this period,[3] are all framed on the same general lines. They consist essentially of an appeal to facts and to conscience, with an appeal to the Old Testament Scriptures, where these were known, and to natural religion, where the hearers have hitherto been without a written revelation. In other words, the same method is employed which was used by the Apostle Peter on Hebrew Christian ground; only it is adapted now to the circumstances, not merely of Jewish, but of mixed or purely heathen audiences.

The substance of Paul's message to his fellow-countrymen, and to those who, although of Gentile birth, had already come to fear God and know something of His Word, could not be

---

[1] Col. iv. 10 f.

[2] Acts xiii. 42 ff. ; xiv. 1 ff., 7 f., 13 ; xvi. 13 ; xvii. 17, 22 ; xviii. 7 ; xix. 7 f. ; xx. 8, 20. Comp. Lechler, *Apost. u. nachapost. Zeitalter*, 3te Aufl. S. 104–107, E. Tr. Edin. 1886, i. pp. 132–135.

[3] Some of these are mere fragments or notes of speeches ; all of them, probably, are more or less summarized.

more clearly summed up than in the two sentences which describe his work in Damascus. "Straightway in the synagogues he proclaimed Jesus, that He is the Son of God." Thereafter, as "Saul increased the more in strength," —possibly after his return from Arabia,—"He confounded the Jews which dwelt at Damascus, proving that this is the Christ." [1] It was Peter's confession in both its clauses, taken up afresh by this powerful voice, this new and most un-challengeable witness. The rock, on which our Lord was to build His Church, stands out as strongly in the case of the future apostle of the Gentiles as it did in that of him who, under Christ, was the chief master builder in Pentecostal times. [2]

The confession meant even more on the lips of Paul than it had done on those of the earlier apostle. The twelve, in whose name Peter spoke, had learned first of all that Jesus of Nazareth was "the Messiah," "He of whom Moses in the law and the prophets did write." They trusted and followed Him as such, with a growing conviction that He was absolutely trustworthy, "the Holy One of God." [3] To the end of their Lord's earthly life, His disciples *felt* rather than *saw* the higher truths concerning His Person. But Saul of Tarsus had been led at once to the second and loftiest clause in that good confession. Mighty and terrible events had befallen since Peter said to Jesus: "Thou art the Son of the living God." In the light of the judgment hall and the Cross, the words stood out now in a new way. Their meaning could not possibly be mistaken by men who knew how the conflict between Jesus of Nazareth and the rulers of Israel had shaped itself, and on what it had turned in the end. Once and again, the Jews had sought to stone Jesus during His public ministry, "because He called God His own Father, making Himself equal with God." It was the very point on which, according to the concurrent testi-mony of all the four evangelists, He was condemned before the high priest and the Sanhedrin: "He hath spoken blas-

---

[1] Acts ix. 20, 22. See above, p. 468.
[2] See above, pp. 170–174.
[3] John i. 41 f., 45 ; vi. 67 ff. ; Mark viii. 29.

phemy ; what further need have we of witnesses ? . . . He is worthy of death." "We have a law," His accusers said to the Roman procurator, "and by that law He ought to die, because He made Himself the Son of God." It was the name cast in His teeth on the Cross. "If Thou be the Son of God, come down from the Cross. . . . He trusted in God, let Him deliver Him now, if He desireth Him; for He said, I am the Son of God." "We remember," the chief priests said to Pilate, "that that deceiver said, while He was yet alive, After three days I rise again. Command, therefore, that the sepulchre be made sure until the third day." [1]

It was on a charge of blasphemy in connection with this name, "the Son of God," that Jesus of Nazareth had been put to death. Every member of the Sanhedrin knew it; and Saul of Tarsus had sat in the Sanhedrin. It was for the honour of the great and holy name of the Lord God of Israel that "he verily thought with himself that he ought" to persecute to the death all who joined the name of Jesus of Nazareth with the name of Jehovah. Wherever the report went concerning the followers of Jesus,—"this sect which is everywhere spoken against," as the leaders of the Jewish community in Rome said,—all Jews knew that it was the charge of blasphemy that was brought against them. The charge had been appealed on both sides, if we may so speak, to the tribunal of God Himself. Was Jesus of Nazareth a blasphemer, or was He what He said ? The answer came from "the Throne of the Majesty in the heavens" on the morning of the third day. It was as Paul wrote afterwards in the first sentence of his greatest Epistle : "The Gospel of God is concerning His Son, who was born of the seed of David, according to the flesh, but declared to be the Son of God with power, according to the spirit of holiness, by the Resurrection from the dead : even Jesus Christ our Lord, through whom we received grace and apostleship unto obedience of faith among all the nations for His name's sake." [2]

---

[1] Matt. xxvi. 63-66 ; xxvii. 40-43, 54; Mark xiv. 61-64 ; xv. 39; Luke xxii. 70 f. ; John v. 18 ; xix. 7 ; Matt. xxvii. 63 f.

[2] Rom. i. 1-5.

We have seen already that the original apostles were witnesses, first of all and chiefly to Christ's Resurrection. That one stupendous fact proved His Divinity. It settled for ever the whole controversy between Jesus and the rulers of Israel, as to who He was, and from whom He came. And now another witness was qualified to speak to this. "Last of all, as unto one born out of due time, He appeared to me also." [1] Paul had seen and heard Jesus of Nazareth risen from the dead, clad with light as a garment, even the light of God-head, before one gleam of which all creatures were cast to the earth. Nothing henceforth could ever shake his belief in this truth, which he knew as he knew that he lived himself. Other things might be dim to him, or altogether dark as yet. He needed much time and earnest study, ere he could speak of them as he did in after years. But one mighty truth stood out from the first clear as that "light, above the brightness of the sun," in which it was revealed to him on the Damascus road, namely, the Divinity of "the Lord, even Jesus who appeared unto him in the way." On this he could take his stand, as on a rock of adamant, against the whole world. At the bidding of the messenger sent him by the Lord, "Saul arose, and was baptized," "calling upon His name," receiving the assurance of the forgiveness of his sins, and the gift of the Holy Ghost. "And straightway in the synagogues he proclaimed Jesus, that He is the Son of God." [2] Then as he went on "increasing the more in strength," in the gifts of the Spirit, and in knowledge and grasp of the Scripture statements bearing on the subject, he advanced from simple testimony to reasoning from facts of testimony, and from the Word of God. "He confounded the Jews which dwelt at Damascus, proving (συμβιβάζων) that this is the Christ." He proved it, as the word implies, by "putting things side by side," [3] making comparisons and drawing conclusions. He did so with all the power and the resources of a mind trained, as his had been, in the highest learning of the Jewish schools, under the guidance of the foremost teacher of his day. Paul set the life, and death,

---

[1] 1 Cor. xv. 8.   [2] Acts ix. 17–20 ; xxii. 15 f.
[3] Lumby, *Acts*, p. 199.

and resurrection of Jesus of Nazareth alongside of the picture, drawn by the prophets, of what the Messiah should be, and do, and suffer, and drew the irresistible conclusion: "This is He that should come."

Such was the method which Paul seems always to have followed on his missionary journeys, wherever he could assume some knowledge of the Jewish Scriptures on the part of those to whom he spoke. In Thessalonica, for example, where the number of persons of Gentile origin who frequented the synagogue seems to have been unusually great: "for three Sabbath days he reasoned with them from the Scriptures, opening and setting forth (παρατιθέμενος) that it behoved the Christ to suffer, and to rise again from the dead, and that this Jesus, whom, said he, I proclaim unto you, is the Christ. And some of them were persuaded, and consorted with Paul and Silas; and of the devout Greeks a great multitude, and of the chief women not a few." [1]

It was most natural that Paul, in ordinary circumstances, should begin with what formed the second part of his work at Damascus, the proof from Scripture, and from the facts of our Lord's earthly life, that Jesus was the Christ. This was the path by which our Lord Himself had led His first disciples in Galilee and Judæa, step by step, to know Him first as "the Christ," and then as "the Son of the living God." At what stage in the mission, in any particular place, it might be best to pass on, from the proof that Jesus was the Messiah, to the further proof that He was the Son of God, would depend on the circumstances of each case. To begin with that second thesis would probably, in most cases, have closed the doors of the synagogue at once against the preacher.

How such discourses, as are indicated in outline in the passage last cited, were filled up in detail, may be seen in the specimen instance given us of Paul's preaching in the synagogue of Antioch in Pisidia.[2]

Starting, probably, from the portions of "the law and the

---

[1] Acts xvii. 1-4.
[2] Acts xiii. 14-41. There are minute touches in the account of this scene which seem to show that it came from an eye and ear witness. Comp. *e.g.* xiii. 16 with xx. 34 ; xxi. 40 ; xxvi. 1.

prophets," which had just been read in the hearing of the congregation,[1] the apostle divides his address into three distinct parts. Each of these forms a separate stage in the discourse, and begins with a fresh appeal to the audience. (1) Vv. 16–25, " Men of Israel, and ye that fear God (proselytes), hearken ! The God of this people Israel chose our fathers." (2) Vv. 26–37, " Brethren, children of the stock of Abraham, and those among you that fear God, to us is the word of this salvation sent forth." (3) Vv. 38–41, " Be it known unto you, therefore, brethren, that through this man is proclaimed unto you remission of sins ; and by Him every one that believeth is justified from all things, from which ye could not be justified by the law of Moses."

1. In the first division of his speech Paul sets forth Jesus as the promised Son of David. He begins with a glance at the history of Israel up to the time of David, with special reference to God's grace to the people, in spite of their sins and unbelief. Then, coming to the main purpose of his discourse, the apostle proclaims to them Jesus, as the promised Saviour of the seed of David. John, the last of the prophets,—of whom something was known in every seat of the Dispersion,—bore witness to Him, as Samuel, the first in the prophetic series, did to David, preaching repentance to all Israel, and pointing to One greater than he, who was to come.

2. The apostle shows what " this salvation " is, and in whom it is revealed. He proclaims unto them Jesus, that He is the Son of God, as well as the Son of David, conveying the doctrine, however, in the form least likely to rouse Jewish monotheistic opposition, stating the fact of the Resurrection, which implied it, and citing the title given to the Messiah in

---

[1] An ingenious and certainly plausible theory would identify these portions with Deut. i. and Isa. i., which occur together in the arrangement for public reading of the Scriptures in one of the oldest synagogue orders of service. This is done on the ground of three unusual words, which occur in the opening sentences of the apostle's address, and which are found also in these two chapters, and hardly anywhere else, — one of them, indeed, in no other passage. Comp., however, Schürer's statement that there was in New Testament times no " lectio continua " of the prophets, but that a choice of the passage to be read was always open, ii. p. 81.

the second Psalm. God's grace was seen here, as of old,
against the dark background of Israel's sin. The representatives of Israel in Jerusalem recognised neither the Messiah,
when He came, nor " the voices of the prophets " concerning
Him, which had been heard again in this very synagogue
to-day. Yet, by God's overruling hand, they fulfilled them
in bringing about the condemnation, and death, and burial of
Jesus. " But God raised Him from the dead," proving
thereby that this was indeed " His Holy One," the
" Saviour " promised to the fathers. And then the apostle
brings forward the evidence of this stupendous fact : first, the
evidence of eye-witnesses ; secondly, that of personal Christian experience ; thirdly, that of the prophets. Personal
disciples of the Lord Jesus, who came up with Him from
Galilee to Jerusalem, saw Him after His resurrection for
many days. They are now His chosen witnesses to the
people. We also, who speak now, bear witness to this
good tidings, that God hath fulfilled all the promises in
raising up Jesus. We risk our lives gladly in this cause,
enduring all hardship, and facing all danger, in making this
Gospel known. And thus it behoved the Christ to die and
to rise again, for thus it was foretold in Scripture ; and
the apostle adds a brief exposition of two or three leading
passages in the Psalms, bearing on the point.

3. Lastly, the apostle preaches unto them the good tidings
of the forgiveness of sins, and a full and free justification
through this crucified and risen Saviour, the Son of David
and the Son of God. The law of Moses, however men might
labour to keep it, could not bring them these blessings.
Sacrifices offered in the temple could not make the offerer
perfect, as pertaining to the conscience. The hearts of many
of the more earnest of Paul's hearers, doubtless, bore witness
to the truth of his words, and thrilled in answer to the
assurance given by one who was felt to speak what he knew
from personal experience, when he declared that whosoever
believed in Jesus was " justified from all things, from which
ye could not be justified by the law of Moses."

The apostle ended with a solemn warning as to the danger
of despising this offered salvation. It was specially needed,

as he knew well from what had befallen him in the past, by the Jews who heard him. Probably the looks and gestures of many in the synagogue showed already that they were on the point of breaking out in open opposition. It was the Gentiles chiefly, here as elsewhere, who received the Word with gladness.[1]

It is interesting to compare with this discourse what we learn of Paul's method of bringing the Gospel before purely heathen audiences. At Lystra a miracle of healing, wrought by the apostle, gave rise to an attempt on the part of the people to pay Divine honours to Paul and Barnabas. Of the "sayings," with which the missionaries restrained the crowd from doing this, only a few are recorded; but from these we see plainly that the method of argument used was still the same. The starting-point was equally an appeal to facts within the cognizance of the hearers, only the facts themselves were necessarily of a different kind. At Lystra, Paul and Barnabas appeal to the testimony of natural reason and conscience as to the vanity of idol - worship, and the existence of One Supreme Creator and Ruler of all. They point to the witness borne by the works of God to His eternal power and Godhead, to His goodwill and fatherly care for men. They appeal, in short, to the voice of God, speaking for Himself in the hearts of their hearers, to His voice in nature, and in the history of nations, since they could not here appeal to His clearer utterances in His written Word. Paul and Barnabas had already " preached the Gospel " in Lystra (ἦσαν εὐαγγελιζόμενοι ἐκεῖ). They ended, doubtless, as at Athens, where Paul's address is given more fully, by urging repentance towards God in the light of a coming judgment, and by "preaching Jesus and the Resurrection." [2]

The method employed by the apostolic missionaries to the Gentiles is still more strikingly illustrated in Paul's wonderful address to the Athenians on the Areopagus; but on this we must forbear to enter.[3]

---

[1] Comp. K. Schmidt, *Apostelgesch.* S. 454–478, 484 f. Stier, *Reden der Apostel*, 2te Aufl. S. 244–272, E. Tr. Edin. 1869, p. 205 ff.

[2] Acts xiv. 7, 15–18.

[3] See Stier's excellent exposition, *Reden der Apostel*, 2te Aufl. S. 73–105,

It was, therefore, one and the same Gospel, which Paul proclaimed both to Jew and Gentile; and the method by which he sought to commend it to their acceptance was essentially the same. In every case he strove to start from ground common to himself and his hearers, whether his argument was drawn chiefly from the sphere of natural or of revealed religion. And his appeal was always made to facts of testimony, of history, and of moral and spiritual consciousness. In these respects, as already indicated, there is perfect harmony, in all essential points, between Paul and those who "did the work of an evangelist" in the apostolic Church in the first period of its history. The Epistles of Paul bear abundant evidence to this, apart altogether from the narrative of the Acts.[1] In writing to Corinthians,—to give but one instance out of many,—Paul states what were the primary truths which he had preached at Corinth, and expressly testifies that the essential features of his Gospel and of the Gospel of the original apostles were the same: "Now I make known unto you, brethren, the Gospel which I preached unto you, which also ye received, wherein also ye stand; by which also ye are saved; I make known, I say, in what words I preached it unto you[2] . . . for I delivered unto you first of all that which also I received, how that Christ died for our sins according to the Scriptures; and that He was buried, and that He hath been raised on the third day according to the Scriptures; and that He appeared to Cephas, then to the twelve. . . . Whether then it be I or they, so we preach, and so ye believed."[3]

The two great articles, therefore, in this one apostolic Gospel are: first, "that Christ died for our sins according to the Scriptures;" and secondly, "that He hath been raised from

E. Tr. p. 284 ff. Conybeare and Howson, *St. Paul*, i. pp. 443-449. Meyer, *Apostelgesch.* 3te Ausg. S. 359 f., E. Tr. Edin. 1877, ii. p. 112 ff.

[1] Comp. Lechler, *Apost. u. nachap. Zeitalt.* 3te Ausg. S. 16 f., E. Tr. i. 18 ff.

[2] Τίνι λόγῳ εὐηγγελισάμην ὑμῖν—"with what word." The apostle states the *form* in which he put the Gospel. He made it known by declaring the facts of Christ's death and resurrection. The Gospel itself, the good tidings of salvation, was "the life and soul of the facts." Comp. Principal Edwards' *First Corinthians*, 2nd ed. p. 390.

[3] 1 Cor. xv. 1-11.

the dead according to the Scriptures." These two stupendous facts, the death and resurrection of Christ, were proclaimed to all men. They were proved by the evidence of eye-witnesses. They were shown to be in accordance with the Scriptures, to have been foretold by "voices of the prophets, read in the synagogues every Sabbath day." Then the significance of these facts was set forth and pressed home on the hearts and consciences of the hearers. These great events convey a message from God to men, which meets the deepest needs and cravings of every human soul. The perfect correspondence, and the effect of the message when received, prove it to be Divine. "The Gospel is the power of God unto salvation to every one that believeth, to the Jew first, and also to the Greek." [1]

The results which followed the proclamation of this Gospel were due, as Paul himself tells us, not to "excellency of speech, or man's wisdom," but to the "demonstration of the Spirit and the power of God." [2] As regards his own preaching, it is in the very instance, at Athens, in which we see most to admire in the tact and persuasive eloquence of the speaker, that the amount of practical success attained was most disappointing. God prepared fitting instruments for His work; and the fruit of that preparation was very manifest in the way in which the work was done. "The training of the Twelve" for their future ministry, carried on year after year by their Master, was not in vain. How manifold and long-continued Paul's preparation for the apostleship of the Gentiles had been was indicated in last chapter. The results of it stand out clearly in every address of his, and every epistle. But it was the Gospel itself, brought home to heart and conscience by the Holy Ghost, which was the power of God unto salvation to every one that believed, whether Jew or Greek. And the apostolic Gospel was summed up in the great revelation of the righteousness and grace of God in Christ crucified for our sins, and Christ risen from the dead, according to the Scriptures.

We may recognise, indeed, a certain difference in emphasis, and in the development of different parts of the message, as

[1] Rom. i. 16.   [2] 1 Cor. ii. 1–5.

declared by the original apostles and by Paul. Forgiveness
and the Cross are more clearly brought together by the
latter. He speaks, even from the first, more expressly to
Jews and proselytes, concerning " justification from all
things, from which ye could not be justified by the law
of Moses." On the other hand, in the apostolic addresses
recorded in the first section of the Acts, the Resurrection of
the Lord Jesus, as was most natural, fills all the foreground.
Peter and the eleven in Jerusalem preached repentance and
the forgiveness of sins, and the gifts of the Holy Spirit, in
and through Christ risen from the dead and exalted by the
right hand of God the Father.[1] In the Epistles of Peter and
John, written years afterwards, we see a similar progress and
development of doctrine as, at an earlier stage, in the case of
Paul. " The sufferings of Christ " are now linked more
expressly with " the glories that should follow them." The
redemption from sin is ascribed to " the precious blood of
Christ, as of a lamb without blemish and without spot." " He
Himself bare our sins in His body upon the tree, that we,
having died unto sin, might live unto righteousness." It is
" the blood of Jesus, God's Son, that cleanseth us from all
sin." " Jesus Christ the righteous " is set forth in His death
as " the propitiation for our sins, and not for ours only, but
also for the whole world." [2] Paul also preaches " Jesus and
the Resurrection." His latest message from Rome to Timothy,
his " true child in the faith," was, " Remember Jesus Christ,
risen from the dead, of the seed of David, according to my
Gospel." [3] But from the first, as it has been truly said, " it
is from the Cross that Paul's thoughts of Christ take wing." [4]
They rise to wonderful heights in heavenly places with the
risen Lord; but they ever return again to the point from
which they rose. " We preach Christ crucified, unto Jews a
stumbling-block, and unto Gentiles foolishness; but unto them
that are called, both Jews and Greeks, Christ the power of
God, and the wisdom of God." " Far be it from me to glory,

---

[1] Acts ii. 32–39 ; v. 31 f.   [2] 1 Pet. i. 11, 18 f.; ii. 24; 1 John i. 7 ; ii. 1 f.
[3] Acts xvii. 18 ; 2 Tim. ii. 8.
[4] Rainy, " Paul the Apostle," p. 31, in *Evangelical Succession Lectures*, Edin.
1882.

save in the Cross of our Lord Jesus Christ, through which the world hath been crucified unto me, and I unto the world." [1]

This is not the place to point out how natural it was that there should be this difference between Paul and the Twelve in this matter, and how strongly the fact that it exists, confirms the history of the different experiences through which they were respectively led to "receive grace and apostleship" from the Lord. [2] It is enough for our present purpose to repeat, what we have already shown, that the Gospel message itself was one and the same, as carried to the circumcision by the Twelve, and to the Gentiles by their apostle, although with a certain difference in accent and emphasis, in the way and to the extent now indicated.

It was on the broad and sure foundation of this one apostolic Gospel that "the Churches of the Gentiles," as Paul calls them, [3] were founded and built up by him, as a wise master builder, and by other evangelists and teachers, who laboured in his spirit. And the same fruits followed, wherever their message concerning Christ was received, as had been seen in Pentecostal days at Jerusalem. The same new life and joy in the Holy Ghost, the same brotherly fellowship, were manifest in every Gentile Christian Church. The same gifts of the Holy Spirit were received. Paul himself had shared in the fellowship of the original Christian community at Jerusalem during the fifteen days spent by

[1] 1 Cor. i. 23 f.; Gal. vi. 14.

[2] "It is not exactly the Christ of the Gospels who comes before us in the writings of Paul. No doubt he lets us see that the vision, which the Gospels set before us, was also before his mind; and words of our Lord, delivered in His earthly ministry, and preserved by those who heard Him, were precious to Paul, and were reverently reproduced to guide the Churches, as need required. Still, the Christ of Paul is the Lord who met him by the way. It is Christ dead, risen, and ascended; it is Christ, with the reason and the result of His finished work made plain; Christ, with the significance for believers of all His wonderful history shining out from Him: *Christus vestitus Evangelio.* . . . No longer is He hedged about by the necessities of mortal life; no longer tied by earthly bonds to some places, and some men, and one nation. He is glorified; all fulness dwells in Him; in Him all the purposes of God are seen to centre." See the whole of this fine and suggestive passage in Dr. Rainy's Lecture, cited above, p. 29 f.

[3] Rom. xvi. 4.

him under Peter's roof, in the inmost circle of the Hebrew Christian Church; again when, with Barnabas, he visited " the brethren which dwelt in Judæa; " and yet again at the Council in Jerusalem. Some three years after that last visit, and not twenty-five years after Pentecost, he wrote his earliest epistle. In it he speaks of the Thessalonians, as " imitators ($\mu\iota\mu\eta\tau\alpha\grave{\iota}$ $\dot{\epsilon}\gamma\epsilon\nu\acute{\eta}\theta\eta\tau\epsilon$) of the Churches of God which are in Judæa in Christ Jesus." The immediate reference, indeed, is to fellowship in sufferings; but it is clearly implied that the sufferings were borne in both instances in the same spirit; and what that was, in the case of the Thessalonians, the apostle states in the opening sentences of his letter: " Our Gospel came not unto you in word only, but also in power, and in the Holy Ghost, and in much assurance . . . and ye became imitators of us and of the Lord, having received the word in much affliction with joy of the Holy Ghost." " The letters of the Apostle Paul," Lechler says truly, " are full of such notes of holy gladness, coming not only from his own heart, but from the hearts of the Churches founded by him."[1] We hear them rising from the narrative of the Acts also wherever it speaks of the first-fruits of the Gospel among the Gentiles.[2]

All the great characteristics which marked the apostolic Church on Hebrew Christian ground, reappear in this second period of its history, in the field of Gentile Christendom.

2nd. We have still the Presence of Christ Himself in the midst of the Church, speaking and acting in and through His servants.

It is " the hand of the Lord " which is " upon Elymas," the first open opponent of the Gospel in the Gentile mission. It is " the teaching of the Lord " that is received by the proconsul. At Iconium, Paul and Barnabas " speak boldly in the Lord, which bare witness unto the word of His grace, granting signs and wonders to be done by their hands." " I will not dare "—Paul said, looking abroad, after years of mission work,

---

[1] 1 Thess. ii. 14 ; i. 5 f. Lechler, *Apost. u. nachap. Zeitalt.* 3te Aufl. S. 34, E. Tr. i. p. 40.

[2] Comp. *e.g.* Acts xiii. 48, 52 ; xv. 3 ; xvi. 34.

upon the world in which the Gospel was now being preached by
many voices " to every creature under heaven "—" to speak of
any things save those which Christ wrought through me, for
the obedience of the Gentiles, by word and deed, so that from
Jerusalem, and round about even unto Illyricum, I have fully
preached the Gospel of Christ." [1]   Christ's presence abides
with the newly organized Churches of Lycaonia, when their
first teachers had to leave them with little hope of seeing the
faces of the brethren again in this world.   " They commended them to the Lord, on whom they had believed." [2]
His presence and power are felt, according to His promise,
wherever, on Gentile as on Hebrew ground, " two or three
of His disciples are gathered together in His name."   " In
the name of our Lord Jesus," Paul writes to the Church at
Corinth regarding the exercise of discipline in the case of a
brother who had sinned,—the very connection in which the
original promise was given,[3]—" ye being gathered together,
and my spirit, with the power of our Lord Jesus, to deliver
such a one unto Satan for the destruction of the flesh, that
the spirit may be saved in the day of the Lord Jesus." [4]

What was thus known and realized throughout the Gentile
Churches in the facts of Christian experience, was developed in
doctrinal form by the apostle of the Gentiles, especially in his
later epistles.   We see this in what he says of " the building
of God," "the House of the living God," "the household of God,
built upon the foundation of the apostles and prophets, Christ
Jesus Himself being the chief corner-stone, in whom each
several building, fitly framed together, groweth into a holy
temple in the Lord ; in whom ye also are builded together for
a habitation of God in the Spirit." [5]   Such truths regarding the
relation of Christ to his Church are embodied in those images
of vital union so powerfully used by Paul,—the Bridegroom
and the Bride, the Head and the members of the body, etc.[6]

[1] Acts xiii. 11 f. ; xiv. 3 ; Rom. xv. 18 f.

[2] Acts xiv. 23.   Comp. xiii. 52.

[3] See above, pp. 177 ff., 185–190, 193.

[4] 1 Cor. v. 4 f.   Comp. chaps. iv. 17 ; xi. 23 ; xiv. 37 ; 2 Cor. xiii. 3 ; Acts
xvi. 7–10 ; xxiii. 11.

[5] 1 Cor. iii. 9 ; xi. 17 ; Eph. ii. 19–22.

[6] Rom. xii. 4 f. ; Eph. iv. 15 f. ; v. 29–32 ; Col. i. 18, 24–28.

But upon this wide and interesting field we cannot enter here.[1]

3rd. The Word of God holds still the supreme place in the Church, as the one authoritative standard of appeal in all matters of faith and duty.

We have seen how the Scriptures form the starting-point of every address of the apostle of the Gentiles wherever he could take for granted that his audience had some acquaintance with the Old Testament. The teaching of Paul and Barnabas in the Church at Antioch, during the time which they devoted to the systematic instruction of the converts there, consisted, doubtless, like that of the twelve at Jerusalem after Pentecost, in an exposition of "the things written in Moses and the Psalms and the prophets concerning the Christ," read in the light of what eye and ear witnesses could tell of the words and deeds and sufferings of the Lord Jesus.[2] The mother Church of Gentile Christendom was thus itself grounded and built up in the faith for years, before its two leading teachers could be spared for mission work. After their first Evangelistic tour, Paul and Barnabas betook themselves again, "for no little time," to their former work at Antioch. They returned to it a third time after the Church there had been shaken by controversy, and "tarried in Antioch, teaching and preaching the Word of the Lord, with many others also."[3]

The same process of regular Scripture teaching went on in every little community won to Christ from among the heathen. One of the most admirable parts of the Jewish synagogue system, its thorough training of the young in the knowledge of God's Word, "passed over," as a Christian writer of the fourth century says, "by tradition to us."[4] Children in Christian households among the Gentiles were everywhere "trained up in the nurture and admonition of the Lord," learning His command-

---

[1] See Bannerman, *Church of Christ*, i. pp. 194–200, 203–210. Beyschlag, *Christl. Gemeindeverf. im Zeitalt. des N. T.*, S. 51 ff.

[2] Comp. Dykes, *From Jerusalem to Antioch*, p. 409 f.

[3] Acts xi. 26 ; xii. 24 f. ; xiii. 1 ; xiv. 28 ; xv. 1 f., 35.

[4] Hilary the deacon, quoted above, p. 292. See also pp. 142 f., 159 f.

ments.[1] The amount of knowledge of the Old Testament, which Paul, Peter, and John take for granted in the case of every one of the Gentile Christian Churches to whom they write, is sufficient proof of the universality and the thoroughness of the instruction in the Hebrew Scriptures (of course in the Greek translation), which was given and received in every part of Gentile Christendom.

Alongside of the Old Testament Scriptures are now set, first, the oral Gospel, of which Luke speaks, "the things" concerning the life and teaching, the death and resurrection of the Lord Jesus, "as they delivered them unto us who, from the beginning, were eye - witnesses and ministers of the Word;"[2] and secondly, the writings of the apostles. No utterance of the Spirit in ordinary believers, not even on the part of those who claimed prophetic gifts, is allowed to rank in point of authority with the letters of "the apostles of the Lord." "If any man thinketh himself to be a prophet or spiritual," Paul wrote to the Church in which spiritual gifts of an extraordinary sort were most abundant, "let him take knowledge of the things that I write unto you, that they are the commandment of the Lord." "We received, not the spirit of the world, but the Spirit which is of God; that we might know the things that are freely given to us by God; which things also we speak, not in words which man's wisdom teacheth, but which the Spirit teacheth. . . . We have the mind of Christ." "I adjure you by the Lord that this Epistle be read unto all the brethren." "If any man obeyeth not our word by this Epistle, note that man, that ye have no company with him." "When this Epistle hath been read among you, cause that it be read also in the Church of the Laodiceans; and that ye also read the Epistle from Laodicea." "The Revelation of Jesus Christ, which God gave Him to show unto His servants. . . . Blessed is he that readeth, and they that hear the words of this prophecy, and keep the things which are written therein."[3]

It was thus that the second part of Christ's great com-

---

[1] Eph. vi. 1-4.　Comp. 2 Tim. iii. 14-17.　　　　　　　　　[2] Luke i. 1-4.
[3] 1 Cor. ii. 12-16; xiv. 37; 1 Thess. v. 27; 2 Thess. iii. 14 f.; Col. iv. 16; Rev. i. 1-3; xxii. 18 f.　Comp. Bannerman, *Inspiration*, pp. 370-375, 386 f., 395.

mission was carried out in the Churches of the Gentiles, and believers were " taught to observe all things, whatsoever He commanded them ; " so doing, His disciples found that " He was with them all the days, even unto the end of the world."

4th. The living voice of the Church itself is now heard, speaking to all believers concerning present truth and duty, in the name of its Lord, and with an accent of authority ; and its utterances are received everywhere as carrying a peculiar weight, and deserving, *primâ facie*, to be obeyed.

This is one of the fruits of growing faith on the part of the Church in its unseen Lord and in the Holy Spirit, and of growing experience of the certainty of the two great facts, already noted,—that Christ was really present with His people always when " gathered together in His name," and that in the written Word of God, along with the oral Gospel and teaching of the apostles, interpreted by the Spirit, the Church had a sufficient and unfailing rule for its guidance at all times. Throughout this second period of the history there is a manifest growth in Christian manhood on the part of the apostolic Church. Great questions, doctrinal and practical, are dealt with and decided aright in a spirit of believing courage, not in the light of any new revelation, but by careful application of the mind of the Church to interpret for itself the meaning of the Word and the Providence of God, to grasp and apply Scripture principles, already given, to new circumstances and emergencies. The means by which this is done, in dependence on the Lord's promised guidance, are simply the ordinary methods of conference and debate, and gradual ripening of the judgment of the Church through representative institutions, such as those with which all Hebrew Christians and their fathers before them had been long familiar under the synagogue system. Questions are extricated from local entanglements, and referred for consideration and decision to the assembly of " the apostles and elders at Jerusalem," in the light of open, brotherly discussion, and under the guidance of the leading minds of the Church.[1] The decision thus reached is authoritative, and obedience is claimed for it, as sent forth to the

[1] Regarding the different steps in the transaction, see below, chap. iv. 3rd.

believers elsewhere, in virtue of the authority of the
assembly or council of the Church by which it was enacted.
As Paul and his company passed through the Churches, " they
delivered them the decrees for to keep, which were ordained
of the apostles and elders that were at Jerusalem." [1] The
decision was authoritative because coming from such a
representative assembly, acting as the ordinance of Christ for
such ends in His House.   The voice of the Holy Spirit,
speaking in the Scriptures, and speaking also in the work of
grace among the Gentiles, was distinctly heard by the office-
bearers of the Church met in Christ's name " to consider of
this matter ; " and they were well assured, therefore, that their
decision, reached after considerable difference of opinion, and
by the ordinary means open to the Church in all ages, was in
accordance with His will.   " It seemed good to the Holy
Ghost (as speaking in the Word, and setting His seal on the
conversion of the Gentiles), and to us (as interpreting His mind
thus conveyed to us, and ' having come at last to one accord '
in our interpretation [2]), to lay upon you no greater burden
than these necessary things." [3]   They are assured that Christ's
Presence has been " in the midst of them " when thus
" gathered together in His name," and that His promise has
been fulfilled, that " what things they have bound on earth
have been bound in heaven, and what things they have loosed
on earth have been loosed in heaven." [4]

5th. The position held by women in the Gentile Christian
Church.

From this important and interesting subject we must
resolutely turn for the present.   Two general remarks only
may be made.   In the second as in the first period of the
history, there is the warmest and fullest recognition of the
place and services of believing women in the Church.   The
lists of greetings in the Pauline Epistles alone would be
enough to prove this.   Yet certain differences appear in
the Gentile Christian period, both in the way of lines

---

[1] Acts xvi. 4 f.   [2] *Εδοξεν ημιν, γενομενοις ομοθυμαδον*, Acts xv. 25.
[3] Acts xv. 2-6, 22 f., 28 ; comp. 1 Cor. xi. 16 ; 1 Tim. iii. 15.
[4] See above, pp. 176 f., 185-190.

being indicated, beyond which spiritual enthusiasm and consciousness of new gifts were not to carry Christian women, and also in the way of more formal recognition and organization of women's work in the Church.

Our limits forbĭd our entering on either of these aspects of difference. With regard to the first, it might easily be shown, from a true exegesis of the passages in which it appears, that the restrictions laid by the apostle Paul, in particular, upon the public ministry of women are grounded by him not on temporary social customs, but on deeper and more abiding reasons connected with woman's physical constitution, and her relation to man as created.[1]

With respect to the further development and organization of women's work in the Church, we have the beginnings of deaconess work distinctly indicated. " Phœbe, a deaconess of the Church that is at Cenchreæ " (οὖσα διάκονος τῆς ἐκκλησίας τῆς ἐν Κεγχρεαῖς), goes to Rome (or to Ephesus [2]) with warm and special commendation of her services from Paul.

In first Timothy, in the midst of a section treating of the qualifications of deacons, we read : "Women in like manner must be grave, not slanderers, temperate, faithful in all things." The connection makes it almost certain that the reference is to women having to do with duties similar to those of the deacons, whether as being members of their families, and so their natural assistants in ministering to women in distress or sickness, or whether formally set apart to the work.as deaconesses.[3]

---

[1] See Meyer on 1 Cor. xi. 3 and xiv. 33-36, E. Tr. i. pp. 320-330 ; ii. 30 ff.; Weiss in Meyer's series on 1 Tim. ii. 11-14, 5te Aufl. S. 123-129. Comp. Godet's exposition of these passages in his article on " Woman's share in the Ministry of the Word," *Contemp. Review*, Jan. 1884, pp. 49-55 ; also Dean Plumptre's paper in the same vol. p. 45 f.

[2] See below, p. 523. Dean Howson says truly in reference to this passage and 1 Tim. iii. 11 : "As to Bible authority for women-deacons among the ministries of the Church, the case for them is stronger than for the existence of bishops" (in the Prelatic sense). *The Diaconate of Women in the Anglican Church*, p. 44.

[3] 1 Tim. iii. 11. It is interesting to note in Pliny's letter to Trajan, written not fifty years after the Pastoral Epistles, another glimpse of such helpful and faithful women. " There were two female servants, who were called ' helpers ' (quæ ministræ dicebantur, ' doubtless Pliny's own translation of

Widows of a certain age, and of approved Christian character, were enrolled in an official list, with a view to their being assisted or maintained by the Church, and also, as appears probable from the context, made serviceable in suitable ministries, especially among those of their own sex.[1]

6th. Position of the infant children of believers.

What their position was in the Hebrew Christian Church we have already seen. It remained what it had been since the visible Church was first distinctly set up in this world. The infant seed of God's people were not understood to be cast out now from their ancient heritage, under the covenant of grace, and "the Gospel preached beforehand unto Abraham." The promise, and the covenant sign and seal of the promise, were held to be to believers and to their children still. There would be a strong presumption that this continued to be the case in the second stage of the history,—even were there no more direct evidence bearing upon the point,—from the close genetic connection between the Hebrew Church and those Christian communities of mixed or Gentile origin, which arose chiefly through the labours of Paul and his companions. But there are several important facts, now to be noted, which lead to the same conclusion.

1. Negatively. Throughout the whole of this second period, both in the Acts and the Epistles, we do not meet with a single instance of the theory of our Anti-Pædobaptist brethren being put into practice.

There are, indeed, repeated references to adult Baptisms ; but these prove nothing as regards the point in dispute. They were simply cases of grown-up persons, hitherto Jews or heathen, who received Christian Baptism on their profession of faith in Christ. Any missionary, belonging to any branch of the Reformed Church, would baptize such persons as a matter of course. But although in Acts and the Pauline

---

the Greek διάκονοι, "deaconesses," which he heard'); these I thought it needful to put to the torture, to find out what truth there might be in the allegations against the Christians. But I found nothing but a perverse and excessive superstition." *Ep.* 96. Lightfoot, *Ignatius*, i. p. 53.

[1] 1 Tim. v. 9–16. Comp. Lightfoot, *Ignatius*, ii. pp. 322 ff., 913.

Epistles we have the history of the apostolic Church for some thirty-five years after the resurrection, with glimpses of a later date in other New Testament writings, yet we have not a single case of a child of Christian parents growing up without Baptism and being baptized as an adult. For more than a generation Christian family life had gone on in the homes of the apostolic Church. It seems strange—from an Anti-Pædobaptist standpoint—that there should be no reference whatever, direct or indirect, to what, on the theory in question, must have been of constant occurrence, namely, that children, "brought up" from infancy by Christian parents "in the nurture and admonition of the Lord," should make public profession of their faith, and be received into the Church, to which (*ex hyp.*) they had been hitherto strangers, by the door of Baptism.

2. Alongside of this negative evidence, there is a corresponding fact of a positive kind on the side of the view which has generally prevailed in Christendom, namely, that in this portion of the history we have repeated instances of family Baptisms, as distinct from individual ones.

These family Baptisms are referred to in precisely the way in which we should expect them to appear, on the supposition that the former practice of the Church was to continue as regards the privileges of the infant seed of believers. In the field of the Gentile mission, as in our missions to the Jews and the heathen now, the cases of adult Baptism were more numerous, and of greater importance, as regards the impression made in the Jewish or Gentile community from which the converts were drawn. Each case of this sort told with power in the circle in which the man or woman had hitherto moved.

That the convert, if he happened to be the head of a family, took his infant children with him into his new religious position, was a thing that in itself made little impression on others. Hence both in modern missionary reports, and in the much briefer notes which have reached us regarding the foundation of the Pauline Churches, adult Baptisms are naturally set in the foreground, and family ones mentioned much more incidentally.

But both in the Acts and in Paul's Epistles such family

Baptisms are referred to, and that as forming a distinct class by themselves.

The first convert through the Pauline mission in Europe was Lydia. She was a proselyte,[1] accustomed to attend the Jewish proseucha at Philippi, and familiar with Jewish rules as to the position of children in the Church. She seems to have been, like Mary the mother of Mark, at Jerusalem, a woman of some wealth, able to show hospitality, and probably, like her, the widowed head of a family. Her trade was a lucrative one ; and her house was of a size suitable for the meetings of " the brethren " in Philippi. The steps in her own conversion are carefully noted. " She heard " the evangelists " speak " in the proseucha. " The Lord opened her heart, to give heed unto the things which were spoken by Paul." She was " judged " by Paul and his fellow-labourers " to be faithful to the Lord." And the result was : " She was baptized, and her family (ἐβαπτίσθη, καὶ ὁ οἶκος αὐτῆς)." [2]

There is not the slightest indication that any one in the family believed, or was of age to believe, and to be " judged faithful to the Lord," except its head and representative. The natural conclusion is that, as in the Old Testament Church, with the usages of which regarding the circumcision and baptism of proselytes and their children Lydia was familiar, the children received the token of God's gracious covenant, and of " the Gospel preached beforehand unto Abraham," on the ground of their parents' faith.

Look at the next case of individual conversion. The jailor at Philippi is rescued from suicide by Paul's interposition. He falls down before Paul and Silas in deep spiritual concern, and asks : " What must I do to be saved ? " The missionaries had seen in the house of Lydia how blessing comes to the family when it comes to its head ; " and they said, Believe in the Lord Jesus, and thou shalt be saved, thou and thy house (σωθήσῃ σὺ, καὶ ὁ οἶκός σου)." The words recall those spoken by our Lord regarding the conversion of Zacchæus, recorded by Luke in his " former treatise : " " This day is salvation come to this house (τῷ οἴκῳ

---

[1] Σιβομίνη τὸν Θεόν, Acts xvi. 14.   [2] Acts xvi. 13-15.

τούτῳ), forasmuch as he also is a son of Abraham." [1]
When the Philippian jailor became by faith a son of Abraham, he became an heir of the promise given to Abraham:
" I will be a God to thee and to thy seed." " The promise
was to him and to his children." His faith is to be a
means of blessing to them; it brings them with himself
within the fellowship of the visible Church. And in token
of this, the outward sign of admission to that fellowship
is given alike to the believer and to his infant seed, as in
the case of Abraham. " He was baptized, he and all his,
immediately (ἐβαπτίσθη αὐτὸς, καὶ οἱ αὐτοῦ πάντες, παραχρῆμα). And he brought them up into his house (εἰς τὸν
οἶκον, his own house, or, possibly, the family room), and set a
table before them, and rejoiced greatly, with all his house, he
having believed in God (ἠγαλλιάσατο πανοικὶ, πεπιστευκὼς
τῷ Θεῷ)." [2]

It will be observed that there is no mention in this whole
passage of any one having believed, except the jailor himself,
although " he and all his were baptized." This is the more
noteworthy because it is distinctly stated that the evangelists
preached the Gospel that night to a wider circle than that of the
jailor's family. " They spake the word of the Lord unto him,
with all who were in his household " (ἐν τῇ οἰκίᾳ αὐτοῦ), i.e.
all who made up the establishment of the prison, the attend-
ants and under-keepers, as well as the prisoners, who had
been already impressed by the way in which, " about midnight,
Paul and Silas were praying and singing hymns unto God." [3]
It does not appear, however, that any except the jailor were
brought to full decision that night, or gave, at least, such
evidence of faith in Christ as would have warranted the
apostle in baptizing them forthwith. But with respect to
the jailor himself there was no difficulty. " He believed in
God, and he was baptized, he and all his, immediately."

The author of the book of Acts, and most of its first

---

[1] Luke xix. 9.　　　　　　　　　　　　　[2] Acts xvi. 27–34.
[3] Vv. 25, 32. Regarding the distinction between οἶκος and οἰκία, see above,
pp. 85–88. We may be sure that Luke, in particular, one of whose characteristics
among the New Testament writers is his scrupulous accuracy in the use of
language, would not have used two different words here, in two successive
verses, to denote the same thing.

readers, were Jews or proselytes, familiar all their lives with the fact of infant membership in the Church on the ground of the parents' faith. Can there be any doubt as to how they would understand this statement about the jailor, and the previous one about Lydia? Suppose that the Old Testament sacrament of admission had been continued in the Church of the new dispensation. We should, in that case, have read: "He believed in God, and he was circumcised, he and all his, immediately." Could there have been any reasonable doubt as to whether these words included the infant seed of the believer or not?

The same distinction between individual and family Baptisms meets us in the same natural and incidental way in Paul's first Epistle to the Church at Corinth. The apostle is speaking to the Christians there regarding the divisions which prevailed among them, so that one said, "I am of Paul;" and another, "I of Christ." "Is Christ divided?" he asks. "Was Paul crucified for you? Or were ye baptized into the name of Paul? I thank God that I baptized none of you, save Crispus and Gaius; lest any man should say that ye were baptized into my name." These were the only cases in which the apostle himself had baptized adults at Corinth. But there had been there, as at Philippi, Baptisms of a different sort, namely, family Baptisms; and at one of these Paul had himself officiated. "And I baptized also the family of Stephanas (τὸν Στεφανᾶ οἶκον); besides, I know not whether I baptized any other." [1]

3. The general principle on which the Baptism of the infant seed of believers rests is very clearly laid down by the apostle in the same Epistle in which he refers to the Baptism of the family of Stephanas.

In the seventh chapter of First Corinthians Paul deals with

---

[1] 1 Cor. i. 12–16. Whether during the five or six years that elapsed between the Baptism of the family of Stephanas and the date of First Corinthians any of the children baptized had reached an age at which they could aid in "ministering to the saints," must remain uncertain. But it is worth noting that "the household of Stephanas," who "helped in the work and laboured," are designated by a different and wider term than is applied to "the family of Stephanas" which Paul baptized. The οἰκία Στιφανᾶ, like "the household of Chloe," no doubt included slaves or freedmen (1 Cor. xvi. 15 f.; i. 11).

cases in which one of two persons joined in marriage has received the Gospel and the other not. "A brother has an unbelieving wife; a sister an unbelieving husband." Let not the Christian husband or wife think that their union is an unholy one, and seek to break it on that ground. "For the unbelieving husband is sanctified (ἡγίασται) in the wife, and the unbelieving wife is sanctified in the brother; else were your children unclean (ἀκάθαρτα); but now are they holy (ἅγια)." [1]

The Church at Corinth had arisen, like almost all the Pauline Churches, out of the local synagogue. Several of its leading men had been Jewish office-bearers. No one familiar with the Old Testament and with synagogue usages could have any difficulty in understanding the apostle's argument, and the terms in which it was conveyed.[2] "Holy" and "unclean" have their ordinary Old Testament sense. They mean set apart for God, consecrated to Him, within the fellowship of His covenant people, or the reverse. All Christian parents at Corinth knew from the teaching of the apostle, and the practice of the Church under his guidance, that their children, even although only one of the parents might be a believer, were counted "holy" in that sense of the word. They were set apart for God, entitled to a place and name within the fellowship of His people on earth, and treated as such.[3] In other words, the Church membership of the infants of believers was an admitted and familiar truth in the Christian community at Corinth, as in every congregation of the

---

[1] 1 Cor. vii. 12–14.

[2] "Loquitur apostolus cum tritissimâ notione gentis Judaicæ religionis, cui בקדושה, *in sanctitate*, idem sonat quod *intra professionem Judaicæ religionis;* et לא בקדושה, *non in sanctitate*, idem quod *in Ethnicismo*. Instantia hujus rei apud scriptores Hebræorum sunt infinitæ; satis sit hæc una. Disputatur semel iterumque a magistris de fœminâ ethnicâ ad religionem Judaicam jam conversâ, sobolem quidem concipiente לא בקדושה, *non in sanctitate*, *i.e.* dum adhuc esset in Ethnicismo, pariente autem בקדושה, *in sanctitate*, *i.e.* factâ jam Proselytissâ." Lightfoot, *Opera Posthuma*, Ultrajecti, 1699, p. 107.

[3] "Supposing the obsignatory theory of Baptism to be the apostle's theory, the principle on which infant Baptism rests is contained in this verse. For if infants are either children of God, or in the covenant, why not give them the symbol and seal of their privilege?" Principal Edwards, *First Corinthians*, 2nd ed. p. 172.

Old Testament Church.   The apostle takes that for granted,
and argues from it.   "If your children, who, from their age,
are not yet able to believe, are notwithstanding (as you all
know) not 'unclean,' but 'holy' in God's sight, in virtue of
their union with you their believing parent, why should you
not be also assured that your husband, or wife, who does not yet
believe, is likewise 'set apart for God,' in virtue of his or her
union with you, in which they desire to remain?   That wish
on their part is a token for good, which you should hail as a
sign that the outward union may be made a means, by God's
grace, to a deeper and truer union 'in the Lord,' that 'thou
shalt save thy husband, shalt save thy wife.' "[1]

It is obvious how absolutely as a matter of course the
apostle, in this passage, treats the Church membership of
infants, where even one parent only is a believer.   He makes
it the foundation of his whole argument.   It seems equally
obvious that if infants were recognised as members of the
Christian Church in virtue of their parents' faith, they had a
right to receive the sign of membership, and that family
Baptisms, in such cases as those of Lydia, the jailor, and
Stephanas, must have been matters of course in the Pauline
Churches, just as the circumcision and baptism of the children
of a proselyte to Judaism were in every synagogue.   "For
my part," says one of the most eminent of living interpreters
of First Corinthians, "I cannot regard the expressions used by
Paul in this passage as intelligible except upon the supposition
of the existence of the custom of infant Baptism."[2]

---

[1] 1 Cor. vii. 14–16.   See Godet's excellent exposition of the passage, *Première
Epitre aux Corinthiens*, Paris 1886, i. pp. 312–317, E. Tr. Edin. 1886.   Bannerman, *Church of Christ*, ii. p. 90 f.; comp. Calvin, *in loco*.

[2] "Pour moi, je ne trouve les expressions de Paul intelligibles que dans la
supposition de l'existence de cet usage."   Godet, i. 317.

M. Godet shows, with his usual lucidity and force, how incompatible the
apostle's statements and reasonings are with the doctrine of Baptismal regeneration.   "Paul sees in the Baptism of these infants, not the *source*, but the *proof*
of the fact, the seal of their condition of 'holiness.'   His meaning is not that
they are made holy by their Baptism, but that their Baptism was the sign and
proof that they were holy already. . . . Just as the Jewish children did not
become children of Abraham by circumcision, but it was their birth from parents
who were children of Abraham which gave them a title to receive circumcision ;
so is it with the children of Christians.   Their consecration to God does not

4. The apostle expressly describes Baptism as being " the circumcision of Christ."

" In whom (Christ) ye were also circumcised with a circumcision not made with hands, in the putting off of the body of the flesh, in the circumcision of Christ; having been buried with Him in Baptism, wherein ye were also raised with Him through faith in the working of God, who raised Him from the dead." [1] In their union to Christ, as regards the substance and reality of the blessing, in Baptism, as regards its Divinely appointed sign and seal, members of the Christian Church have what circumcision was to the members of the Old Testament Church. Baptism is to the believer now what circumcision was to Abraham and his children. It is "the circumcision of Christ." The apostle had special reasons for making this express statement in writing to this particular Church. " The Colossians seem to have been exposed to the influence of two fundamental errors: first, the belief that they were under the influence, or at any rate needed the assistance, of intermediate intelligences; secondly, the persuasion that circumcision, the symbol of purification appointed by God, must still be necessary. Both are, in fact, met by the single clause καὶ ἐστε—πεπληρ.; this, however, is further expanded in two explanatory relatival clauses, ὅς ἐστιν κ.τ.λ. being directed against the first error, ἐν ᾧ κ.τ.λ. against the second." [2]

In Jewish Christian circles, and in the families of those who had been proselytes, the two ordinances probably continued to go together, as there is reason to believe they had done before this time in the synagogues. Paul did not teach the Christian Jews of the Dispersion—as was falsely alleged against him—" not to circumcise their children," as well as

---

depend upon their Baptism; but their fitness for Baptism arises from the solidarity of life which unites them to their parents, and, through them, to the covenant of grace founded in Christ, in the fellowship of which their parents live. Until the point is reached at which the children of Christians make their own decision for or against the salvation which is offered to them, they receive the benefit of this provisional position, and are brought, with the family as a whole, into close contact with the holy influences which animate the body of Christ," i. p. 316.

[1] Col. ii. 11 f.
[2] Bishop Ellicott, *Colossians*, p. 155 ; comp. Calvin, *in loco*.

to baptize them.[1]   But he taught them Baptism was "the circumcision of Christ," and that the Lord's own ordinance included all—and more than all—that the seal of Abraham's covenant conveyed.   They and theirs "were circumcised with the circumcision of Christ when they were buried with Him in Baptism, in and with whom also they were raised again, through faith in the working of God who raised Him from the dead."[2]

The Baptism of the infant seed of believers in the Gentile Christian Churches, in so far as these were of mixed origin, as almost all of them were, had no doubt a history much like that of the Lord's Day in relation to the seventh-day Sabbath. The ordinance of Christ took its place, first beside, then above, and lastly instead of the older institution out of which, to some extent, it arose.[3]

[1] Acts xxi. 21. See above, pp. 332, 334, 350.

[2] Col. ii. 11 f. It seems better to regard the ἐν ᾧ in ver. 12 as referring to Christ, and parallel with the ἐν ᾧ in ver. 11, than to render "wherein." So Meyer, Ewald, Huther, etc., following Chrysostom and most of the patristic interpreters. Whether or not any reference is implied in the apostle's language here and in Rom. vi. 3 ff. to the customary manner of Baptism, as being by immersion, is a point on which good exegetes differ, and is in itself of no great importance. Comp. on the one side Meyer, Ellicott, and Lightfoot, and on the other Eadie, Beecher, Williams, and Wardlaw. See above, pp. 369–373 ; also Bannerman, *Church of Christ*, ii. pp. 46–49.

[3] As regards post-apostolic practice, we find infant Baptism proceeding as a matter of course, alongside of that of adult converts, as soon as we get any information on the subject. It is referred to in this way by Irenæus, born early in the second century. (Dodwell, Marriott, and others put his birth in A.D. 97 ; Bishop Lightfoot puts it *circa* 120.) He was a native of Asia Minor, and had learned much in his youth from Polycarp, who was a personal disciple of the apostle John. (Iren. *Adv. Hær.* ii. 22. 4; comp. iii. 17. 1.) In the next generation, towards the close of the second century, Tertullian speaks in the clearest terms of infant Baptism as the practice of the Church in his time, and does not give the slightest hint that in his view it was an innovation or unscriptural, although, with characteristic boldness, he argues against it as *inexpedient* for children ("Cunctatio Baptismi *utilior* est"). It is worth observing the exact ground which he takes. Baptism, he held, in every case, washed away all previous sins. "We enter the font once ; once are sins washed away. . . . Why then should that innocent age hasten to the remission of sins ? Men act more prudently in worldly matters. Why should the Divine heritage be entrusted to those to whom we would not commit the keeping of their earthly goods ?" He goes on to argue in the same way that Baptism should be delayed in the case of all persons exposed to special temptations, such as the unmarried and widows (*De Baptismo*, c. xv. 18). Tertullian is the

first Anti-Pædobaptist on record ; and he is such confessedly in the interests of his theory of Baptismal regeneration. "His whole argument rests upon false premisses. . . . His protest against infant Baptism fell without an echo" (Schaff). Origen, born *circa* 185 A.D., gives equally clear testimony that the Baptism of the infants of believers was the universal custom of the Church in his time, and states expressly that it had been so from the time of the apostles. "Ecclesia ab apostolis traditionem accepit etiam parvulis Baptismum dare." *Comment. in Ep. ad Rom.* v. 6. See Marriott, art. "Baptism," in *Dict. of Christ. Antiq.* i. p. 169 f. Bannerman, *Church of Christ*, ii. p. 127. Van Dyke, "Baptism of Infants," in *Presb. Review*, 1885, p. 33 ff.

CHAPTER III.

OUR limits forbid our entering fully on this department of the subject. Only a few points can be indicated briefly.

It is instructive to note the place and importance assigned to Christ's appointed ordinances, in the Gentile as in the Hebrew Christian Church, even in those days which were so marked by the presence and power of the Holy Ghost and by the abundance of spiritual gifts.

1st. Among ordinances of edification in the Christian assemblies, as we saw with respect to the aggressive work of the Church,[1] the Word of God and the ministry of the Word still hold the central place.

We have the reading of the Old Testament Scriptures, and of apostolic letters, in the meetings of the Churches. Towards the close of the New Testament period the synoptic Gospels begin to take the place of the oral witness of the apostles, and of such private notes and summaries of their testimony as Luke refers to in the preface to his Gospel.[2] The first three evangelists gave the facts concerning the life and ministry of Christ "even as they delivered them unto us, which from the beginning were eye-witnesses and ministers of the Word." They put each of their readers in a position to make with intelligence Peter's confession that Jesus is "the Christ, the Son of the living God." The fourth evangelist, again, coming at the very end of the period, and assuming in those for whom he wrote a certain amount of knowledge of the Gospel history, gave a fuller revelation of the name of Christ, based

[1] See above, pp. 497-499.

[2] 1 Thess. v. 27 ; 2 Thess. iii. 14 ; 2 Cor. ix. 9 ff. ; Col. iv. 16 f.; Heb. xiii. 22 ; Rev. i. 3, 11 ; 3 John 9 ; Luke i. 1-4.

on that same fundamental confession. He opened to the
Church the higher aspects of the Person, life, and teaching of
our Lord, and the corresponding duties and privileges of His
disciples. "These things are written that ye may believe
that Jesus is the Christ, the Son of God ; and that, believing,
ye may have life in His name. . . . That ye may know that
ye have eternal life." [1]

Correspondent with these higher truths, unfolded in the
fourth Gospel, are the wonderful progress and development of
doctrine in the later apostolic Epistles, such as those to the
Ephesians and Colossians, as compared with the simple
addresses in the Acts, and the stress laid—especially in the
Pastoral Epistles and those of John—upon "sound teaching,"
"walking in the truth," avoiding false teachers, etc.[2] In this
connection we may note the increasing emphasis laid on the
importance of "pastors and teachers, for the perfecting of the
saints, for the work of ministry, for the building up of the
body of Christ." Presbyters are to be "apt to teach."
"Special honour" is to be given to those presbyters who,
besides "ruling well," "labour in the Word and in teaching."
The verse which follows seems to point to pecuniary support
in particular as included in this "special honour," in order
that these teaching presbyters should be able to devote
themselves fully to their most important work. Timothy
is to see to it that the deposit of apostolic doctrine received
by him from Paul is "committed to faithful men, who shall
be able to teach others also." [3]

Alongside of this more official teaching, there were still no
doubt what existed so largely in the earlier portion of this
period in the Church at Corinth,—opportunities for what in

---

[1] John xx. 31 ; 1 John v. 13. Reuss sums up "the theology of the
fourth Gospel" from John iii. 16 and 1 John iv. 9, as follows: "First, theological premisses : God and the Son. Secondly, historical premisses : The sending (Incarnation) and the world (natural condition and separation or judgment).
Thirdly, the mystical theology itself : Faith and life. In further analysis of
these ideas we have the trilogy of Light, Love, and Life, which are the
essence of God, offered by the Son, and received by the elect." *Hist. of N. T.*,
E. Tr. Edin. 1884, p. 223.

[2] Rom. xvi. 17 ; 1 Tim. i. 3 f. ; iv. 6, 16 ; vi. 3 ; 2 Tim. i. 13 ; iv. 2 ff. ;
Titus i. 9 f. ; ii. 1 f., 7 f. ; 1 John iv. 1 ff. ; 2 John 9 ff. ; 3 John 3 f.

[3] Eph. iv. 11 f. ; 1 Tim. iii. 2 ; v. 17 f. ; 2 Tim. ii. 2.

modern phrase would be called "open meetings," in which all who possessed spiritual gifts were free to use them, and every man might bring his "Psalm and interpretation and teaching" for the common good of the brethren, provided only that "all things be done unto edifying" and "in seemly form and according to order."[1]

2nd. Baptism and the Lord's Supper.

It is impossible here to enter into an exposition of the passages in which reference is made to the sacraments during this second section of the history.

Generally, what was said in reference to the Hebrew Christian Church holds good here also, both as to the manner in which these two ordinances of Christ were dispensed and the place which they held in the life of the Church.[2]

3rd. The Lord's Day.

We saw before, in connection with the worship of the Hebrew Christian Church, what a unique position the day of Christ's Resurrection had come to hold for the first disciples, how it had been set apart and hallowed by the seal of the Father, the Son, and the Spirit. There is abundant evidence that it held a like position, and one which, in some respects, was even more distinctly defined, in the Gentile Christian Churches. The stated meetings of the disciples for worship take place on that day. The ordinance of the Lord's Supper, which in the Pentecostal Church seems, at first at least, to have been celebrated daily, appears now to be observed as a rule on the Resurrection day.[3] Paul—although "he was hastening, if it were possible for him, to be at Jerusalem the day of Pentecost"[4]—waits over the week at Troas, in order that he may meet with the brethren in worship "on the first day of the week, when the disciples were gathered together to break bread." Before the dispensation of the ordinance, the apostle gave a somewhat lengthened discourse (διελέγετο αὐτοῖς . . . διαλεγομένυ τοῦ Παύλου ἐπὶ πλεῖον); and, after "the breaking of the bread," there followed a meeting of a more conversational kind, apparently in connection with a meal

---

[1] 1 Cor. xiv. 26, 33, 40.   [2] See above, pp. 364–378.
[3] See Plumptre, art. "The Lord's Supper," in Smith, ii. p. 142 f.
[4] Acts xx. 16.

of Christian fellowship or love-feast.[1] In like manner, "having found the disciples" at Tyre, Paul and his company "tarry there seven days," so as to include at least one first day of the week, and only "when they had accomplished the days," do they "depart and go on their journey," being "brought on their way" by the disciples in a body, "with wives and children." So, too, at Puteoli, "where we found brethren, and were entreated to tarry with them seven days."[2]

The apostle "gives order" to the Church at Corinth, and to "the Churches of Galatia," that "upon the first day of the week" each of the disciples should set aside what he could afford from his weekly income towards "the collection for the saints at Jerusalem." The special day of weekly worship, therefore, was to be regarded by Christians, both in Asia and Europe, as the most suitable one for making offerings, according to their means, to the cause of Christ.[3]

That the apostle Paul, when among Jews or Jewish Christians, as on his visits to Jerusalem, observed the old seventh day Sabbath, as well as the Lord's Day, is in every way probable from what we know of his practice in similar matters, and from his own statement: "To the Jews I became as a Jew, that I might gain Jews; to them that are under the law, as under the law, not being myself under the law, that I might gain them that are under the law."[4] The only reference in his epistles to the relation of Gentile Christians to the old Sabbath is in Col. ii. 16 f., the passage in which he speaks of Baptism as being "the circumcision of Christ." "Let no man therefore judge you in meat, or in drink, or in respect of a feast day, or a new moon, or a Sabbath ($\dot{\epsilon}\nu$ $\mu\dot{\epsilon}\rho\epsilon\iota$ $\sigma\alpha\beta$-$\beta\dot{\alpha}\tau\omega\nu$, in respect of Sabbaths); which are a shadow of the things to come: but the body is Christ's."

Now it is true, and should be noted, that the Article is wanting here, and that the word "Sabbath" is in the Plural, and that it is never used elsewhere in the New Testament in the Plural to denote the weekly Sabbath, except with the Article.[5]

---

[1] Acts xx. 7–11. Comp. *Teaching of the Apostles*, xiv. 1.
[2] Acts xxi. 4 f. ; xxviii. 14.   [3] 1 Cor. xvi. 1 ff.   [4] 1 Cor. ix. 20 f.
Archdeacon Stopford, *Scripture Account of the Sabbath* (in reply to Dr. Whately), Lond. 1837, p. 162.

The phrase, therefore, was probably designed to embrace all Jewish Sabbatic observances, such as those of the seventh month,[1] the seventh year, and the year of jubilee.[2] But there can be little doubt that it included also the Jewish Sabbath in the ordinary sense, that in which the word was most familiar to the Gentile Christians at Colossæ. The meaning and scope of the injunction are very clear from the connection in which it stands, and especially from the immediately preceding reference to circumcision and Baptism. Paul, as we have seen,[3] did not forbid the Jewish Christians at Colossæ, or anywhere else, to circumcise their children. But when there was danger, as now among the Colossians, from Judaizing influences, he taught expressly that there was no *necessity* for retaining the ancient rite, seeing that Baptism was "the circumcision of Christ." And when "they of the circumcision" passed from suggestions about the *expediency* of the step, to urge, as at Antioch, "Except ye be circumcised, ye cannot be saved," the apostle "gave place to such in the way of subjection, no, not for an hour; that the truth of the Gospel might continue with you."[4] In like manner, when Judaizing teachers at Colossæ, or in Galatia, or in Rome sought to lead or force the Gentile converts to "observe days, and months, and seasons, and years," Paul stood forth at once in behalf of perfect liberty of conscience in all such matters. "Be not entangled again in a yoke of bondage." "One man esteemeth one day above another; another esteemeth every day alike. Let each be fully assured in his own mind. He

---

[1] The great day of Atonement may have been specially in the apostle's mind. It was "the Fast," κατ' ἐξοχήν, to all Jews and Jewish Christians, and observed in all parts of the Diaspora, as it is to this day, with singular strictness. The Divine ordinance regarding it ran in most express terms: "It is a statute for ever throughout your generations in all your dwellings. It shall be unto you a Sabbath of solemn rest, and ye shall afflict your souls : in the ninth day of the month at even, from even unto even, ye shall keep your Sabbath," Lev. xxiii. 26-32.

[2] See Garden, art. "Sabbath," in Smith, iii. pp. 1066 f., 1072. Haldane, in his essay on "The Sanctification of the Sabbath," regards the reference as being to these Sabbatic observances only, apart from the weekly Sabbath. But this seems an unfair limitation of the natural meaning of the apostle's words, *Romans* (Appendix), iii. pp. 418-420.

[3] See above, pp. 350, 509 f.   [4] Acts xv. 15 ; Gal. ii. 5.

that regardeth the day regardeth it unto the Lord. . . . Why dost thou judge thy brother?" But, on the other hand, " Let no man judge you . . . in respect of a feast day, or a new moon, or a Sabbath; which are a shadow of the things to come: but the body is Christ's." [1]

In so far as the seventh day Sabbath had become a part of the Mosaic system,—although in itself, like circumcision, it was "not of Moses, but of the fathers,"—and had gathered round it special and temporary enactments as to mode of observance and penalties for non-observance, it had certain typical or symbolical aspects in which it pointed forward to "the things to come," to blessings to be revealed in Christ. It spoke, in particular, of the true spiritual rest to be found in Him and in His finished work of atonement, of "the Sabbath rest that remaineth for the people of God." This made it the more fitting that there should be a change as regards the actual day to be kept as the day of rest, in order that the primary and permanent elements in the institution of the Sabbath should be extricated, so to speak, from their temporary accompaniments in the Jewish Church under the Mosaic dispensation, and brought into direct relation to the Person and work of our Lord, as they are in the great Christian ordinance of the Lord's Day. [2]

Hence, while not judging, and sometimes joining with, those brethren who still kept the old sacred day "unto the Lord," as well as the day of His Resurrection, it was to the latter that Paul himself turned, as being specifically "of Christ." On it he joined with the disciples in every place, in their stated assemblies for worship, and for "proclaiming the Lord's death till He come," in the sacrament of communion. And in all the Churches he "gave order" that the weekly freewill offerings should be laid in store on the first day of the week. It was the day above all others for thank-offerings and thanksgivings to God "for His unspeakable gift." [3]

---

[1] Gal. v. 1; Rom. xiv. 5 f.; Col. ii. 16 f.

[2] See Fairbairn, *Typology*, 6th ed. ii. pp. 144–153; Owen, *Works* (Goold's ed.), xix. pp. 395–402.

[3] It deserves notice that this injunction to "observe" the first day of the week as regards offerings for Christian purposes is given by the apostle to those very

Towards the close of this period of the history, the crowning honour is set upon the first day of the week by the last
appearance of the risen Saviour, vouchsafed to the apostle
John in Patmos, and by the distinguishing name, now
expressly given it, of " the Lord's Day."   The event and the
name are recorded by one who had been " a pillar " in the
Hebrew Christian Church ; but the message of the Revelation
is addressed to the Churches of Asia, and, in particular, to
Ephesus, where Pauline influences had been strongest hitherto,
and where Paul himself had laboured so long.   To the significance of the name reference has already been made.[1]   John
uses it as a title well known, and familiar in all the Gentile
Christian Churches to whom he wrote, as much so as that of
the Lord's Supper, or the Lord's House.   It fitly and conclusively closes the Scripture evidence regarding the place and
honour to be assigned to the Lord's day, as one of holy rest
and service and blessing,—that day meets us as such in the
beginning of the last book of Scripture, as it does in the
beginning of the first.   Like a golden thread it binds all
together from Genesis to Revelation, leading us from the
history of the Paradise which was lost to the apostle's
vision of Paradise restored.[2]

Churches of Galatia with respect to whom in another connection, and in a different sense, he expressed his fears as to their "observing days, and months,
and seasons, and years."

[1] See above, pp. 385–388.

[2] Gen. ii. 2 f.; Rev. i. 10 ; ii. 7 ; xxi. 1–7 ; xxii. 1–5, 17.

"The Christian Sunday is still the great circumstantial proof of the Resurrection upon the first day of the week.   What teaching could change our day of
worship, a day hallowed from childhood, and made sacred by the traditions of
our fathers ?   Yet something happened in Judæa on that first day of the week
which naturally, spontaneously, without conflict, and without discussion, so
readily that hardly a trace remains of the process by which it was accomplished,
did change the whole religious habit and the most sacred associations of Jews
exceedingly tenacious of the old traditions.   There is nothing accidental in
history ; the light which put the glory of the Sabbath into the shade was the
glory of the risen Lord."   See the whole of this eloquent passage, Newman
Smyth, *Old Faiths in New Light*, Lond. 1882, pp. 327–330.

CHAPTER IV.

ORGANIZATION OF THE APOSTOLIC CHURCH DURING THE SECOND PERIOD OF ITS HISTORY.

CONSIDER the circumstances and the constituent elements of the Churches to be organized.

As already pointed out, it is on Gentile Christian ground that the word itself (ἐκκλησία) meets us, for the first time, in the Plural.[1] We hear now not only, as hitherto, of "the Church," but of "Churches." The change corresponds with the difference in circumstances and situation. During this missionary period, the Gospel was carried through regions of great extent, and widely separated from each other. Little Christian communities were formed by the preaching of Paul and others in remote districts, and left to hold their ground alone in the midst of a heathen population, exposed to persecution now from Jewish and now from Gentile sources. Individual believers in such circumstances must have felt themselves to be indeed "strangers, scattered abroad." Little groups of believers, who met at evening, or before daybreak, in the open air, or in an upper room, must often have had a painful sense of isolation and practical severance from their brethren in the faith. Christians who belonged to "the Churches of the Gentiles" were, as a rule, in a very different position, as regards numbers and opportunities of intercourse with fellow-Christians beyond their own immediate circle, than the members of "the Church at Jerusalem," or "the Church throughout all Judæa, Galilee, and Samaria."

How strong, notwithstanding, was the underlying sense of unity, and in what ways practical expression was given to this in the language, action, and institutions of the apostolic Church, we shall see presently. Meanwhile the actual

[1] See above, p. 436 f.

position of things is to be noted, as bearing on the question of the organization of the Gentile Christian Churches. Most of these were probably, at first at least, ἐκκλησίαι, in the sense of being separate congregations, meeting, as a rule, in one place for worship, and needing to be organized as such only. That the term ἐκκλησία occurs for the first time, and occurs so often in this period, in the Plural, is one proof of the fact.

In several instances, however, it is clear, on a survey of the evidence, that a Church which is spoken of in the Singular, and which is seen in the narrative to act as one, must, like the Church at Jerusalem, have embraced several congregations. This holds of all the great centres of Paul's missionary operations during this period, of Antioch, Corinth, and Ephesus.

With regard to Antioch, the evidence for this statement has been already indicated, and we need not return to it now.[1]

Corinth, the populous capital of the Roman province of Achaia, became also " the metropolis of Christianity in Hellas proper." [2] Paul had access in the synagogue there both to Jews and Greeks. He was joined in his work by Silas and Timothy, being helped also by Aquila and Priscilla. Together they laboured continuously in Corinth for a year and six months, encouraged by an express assurance from the Lord that He would be specially with the apostle in his ministry here, and " that he had much people in this city."

At an early stage in the work, " the chief ruler of the synagogue, and all his family," received the Gospel; and this event was the means of many conversions. The attitude of the proconsul shielded the growing Church from persecution. Apollos, after being fully instructed in Christian truth, took up the work in Corinth after Paul left it; and his labours there were signally successful. " He powerfully confuted the Jews, and that publicly, showing by the Scriptures that Jesus was the Christ." Paul himself testifies that " God gave the increase " in connection with the work of Apollos at Corinth, as manifestly as with his own. He was " a minister " by whom

---

[1] See above pp. 460–464.   [2] Lechler, S. 109, E. Tr. i. p. 128.

also many " believed, as God gave to every man." A number of his converts were even disposed to exalt him above the apostle himself. Judaizing teachers were also busy in this important centre of Christian life. There was room among the members of the Church there for four distinct parties, each with watchwords of their own, and gathering round representatives of different tendencies.[1]

In view of all these facts, and of others which might be adduced, it is impossible to believe that "the Church of God at Corinth" was confined to a single assembly, meeting only in the house of Titus Justus,—where Paul consolidated the first Christian congregation, when the disciples had to separate from the synagogue,—or in that of "Gaius mine host and of the whole Church," or in that of "Erastus, the treasurer of the city," or of Stephanas, or any other of the leading men whose houses, in different parts of the city, were no doubt open for Christian assemblies κατ' οἶκον.[2]

With respect to Ephesus, the evidence is still more clear that several congregations are covered by the one designation "the Church in Ephesus," and that their office-bearers were regarded as representatives of one collective body.[3]

The Gospel was preached at Ephesus by Paul towards the end of his second missionary journey. The work there was carried on, in his absence, by Aquila and Priscilla. It was at Ephesus that Apollos first gave proof of his gifts for Christian service, as "an eloquent man, and mighty in the Scriptures." "Being fervent in spirit, he spake and taught carefully the things concerning Jesus; and spoke boldly in the synagogue." The progress of the work, and its need, in various ways, of completion and establishment, soon drew the apostle of the Gentiles again to the great commercial city.

---

[1] Acts xviii. 4–18, 24–28 ; xix. 1 ; xx. 2 f.; 1 Cor. i. 2, 10-16 ; iii. 3–10.

[2] Acts xviii. 7 ; Rom. xvi. 23 ; 1 Cor. i. 16 ; xvi. 15. The injunction to the Corinthians: "Let the women keep silence in the Churches" (ἐν ταῖς ἐκκλησίαις, chap. xiv. 34), may possibly refer to different meetings of the same congregation ; but it seems a more natural interpretation to understand the reference to be to different congregations of the one Christian community at Corinth ; wherever Church meetings were held in the city, the women were to refrain from speaking in them.

[3] Acts xx. 17, 28 ; Rev. i. 11 ; ii. 1-5.

Ephesus became the centre of Paul's labours for about three years. Within three months of his second visit, the disciples were formally separated from the Jewish community, and Christian gatherings held daily in the lecture-hall of one Tyrannus.

From the narrative in the nineteenth chapter of Acts, from Paul's address to the Ephesian presbyters in the twentieth, and from statements in his epistles, it is plain that for the apostle this was a period of the most energetic activity, both among the members of the large Jewish colony in the city, and among its crowded Gentile population.[1] The success was on a scale correspondent to the efforts put forth. "The Word of God grew mightily and prevailed," not only in the great city itself, but throughout the whole province, with every part of which it had so many political and commercial links of connection.

The extent to which Christianity spread during this period, in and from Ephesus, is attested both by friends and foes. "This continued," says the narrator, referring to the daily meetings begun in the hall of Tyrannus, "for the space of two years, so that all they which dwelt in Asia heard the word of the Lord, both Jews and Greeks." "A great door and effectual is opened unto me," Paul wrote from Ephesus to the Corinthians, in explanation of his long continuance in that city ; "and there are many adversaries." We learn from the same epistle that Apollos also was at this time labouring in Ephesus, and probably, in part at least, for the same reason, was likewise unwilling to leave it, even at the urgent request of the apostle that he should go to Corinth.[2] The idolatrous practices of Ephesus were so far affected that the interests of some of the leading trades of the place were seriously endangered ; and meanwhile Paul's position and influence had risen so high that some of the most powerful personages in the province, " the chief officers of Asia," were ready to protect and befriend

---

[1] "By the space of three years he ceased not to admonish men day and night with tears." He " taught believers ($\dot{v}\mu\tilde{a}s$) publicly, and from house to house ($\delta\eta\mu o\sigma\dot{\iota}\alpha$ $\varkappa\alpha\dot{\iota}$ $\varkappa\alpha\tau'$ $o\ddot{\iota}\varkappa o v s$), testifying both to Jews and Greeks repentance toward God, and faith toward our Lord Jesus Christ," Acts xx. 20 f., 31.

[2] Acts xix. 10 ; 1 Cor. xvi. 8 f., 12.

him. Demetrius, the silversmith, appealed to facts well known to all his audience, when he said to the meeting of his own workmen and artisans in similar employments: "Ye see and hear that not alone at Ephesus, but almost throughout all Asia, this Paul hath persuaded and turned away much people, . . . so that there is danger that the temple of the great goddess Diana be made of no account, and that she should even be deposed from her magnificence, whom all Asia and the world worshippeth." [1]

It is impossible to suppose that "the Church in Ephesus," the fruit of labours which had been so energetic and long continued, and which filled such a place in the public mind of the Ephesian people, was confined within the limits of a single assembly. The Christians of the city, long before the end of Paul's three years' ministry there, must have had several regular centres of meeting, such as the hall of Tyrannus, the house of Aquila, and the dwelling-places of other believers, in which the apostle was wont to teach in his labours κατ' οἴκους. One of these stated meetings is referred to by Paul, when writing from Ephesus to Corinth. He sends Christian greetings from Aquila and Prisca, and from "the Church that is in their house." [2] Yet when reference is made to the Christians of Ephesus as a whole, they are never spoken of as "the Churches," but as "the Church" in that city. The office-bearers, whom the apostle summoned to meet him at Miletus, were "the presbyters," not "of the Churches," but "of the Church at Ephesus." "The flock, in which the Holy Ghost had made them bishops," and in tending which they were "tending the Church of God," was one flock, although cared for and fed by them, as good under-shepherds, in different meeting-places throughout the city.[3]

[1] Acts xix. 24–27, 31. Comp. Conybeare and Howson, ii. p. 97.

[2] 1 Cor. xvi. 19. Comp. Rom. xvi. 5. If, as there is some reason to believe, our sixteenth chapter of Romans is really a postscript intended for the Christian community at Ephesus, and added by the apostle to the copy of the Epistle to the Romans which was sent to the mother Church of Asia, then we have additional information, both as to the large number of Paul's fellow-workers in the Gospel in Ephesus and as to the different centres in which Christian assemblies were held in the city (Rom. xvi. 5, 9–12, 15). Comp. Farrar, *St. Paul*, ii. p. 170 f.

[3] Acts xx. 17, 28.

What were the constituent elements of these Churches, whether larger or smaller in extent ?

Recall for a moment the method of evangelization pursued by Paul and his fellow-labourers.[1] In every place they turned " to the Jew first." The local synagogue, or proseucha, offered in so many ways, as we saw, the best vantage ground for beginning their work, both in the interests of the Jew and the Gentile, that it was never neglected by the first missionaries of the apostolic Church. The results of the work in this field varied greatly. In some cases there was very considerable success among the purely Jewish members of the synagogue congregation. In Berœa the majority of the converts were Jews; and the synagogue may have been turned into a Christian place of worship. So also in Corinth, where a considerable section of the Jewish community seem to have received the Gospel along with " Crispus, the ruler of the synagogue, and all his house." [2] The more usual result, as in the Pisidian Antioch and in Thessalonica, was the conversion of some Jews, but of a much larger number of " devout Greeks," especially " women of honourable estate," and other Gentiles who had not hitherto been under the ordinary influence of the synagogue.

In every case, with the possible exception of Athens,[3] the congregation which was formed, as the fruit of the labours of Paul and his companions, was a mixed one, consisting of Jews and Gentiles in varying proportions. The latter element, so far as we can gather from the indications in Acts and in the relative epistles, was, as a rule, the preponderating one in point of numbers, even from the first; and as time went on, the majority on the side of the Gentiles would naturally tend to increase.

On the other hand, it is clear from a number of significant facts, such as the familiarity with the Jewish Scriptures which the apostles, in writing to Churches of mixed origin, invariably

---

[1] See above, pp. 479–483.

[2] Acts xvii. 10 ff.; xviii. 4–8. The violence of the opposition of the unbelieving Jews in Corinth seems to have arisen largely from their seeing the effects of the Gospel among their fellow-countrymen. Paul was succeeding in " persuading men (i.e. Jews) to worship God contrary to the law " (ver. 12 f.).

[3] See above, p. 482.

take for granted on the part of their readers, that a very
large proportion of the Gentile Christian members of these
communities had been more or less under synagogue training.
It is further to be kept in mind that many things tended to
give to the Jewish Christian members of these Churches a
weight and influence among their brethren, much greater than
would have arisen from their numbers alone.   The truth of
our Lord's words to the Samaritan woman was thankfully
owned in all the Churches of the Gentiles.   They felt that
" salvation was from the Jews."   " The Gentiles had been
made partakers of their spiritual things, and their debtors
they were." [1]   These Jewish Christians represented to them
in a special way their first evangelists and teachers.   To the
ears of the Gentile believers these brethren spoke with the
accent of the apostles, and prophets, and the disciples scattered
abroad from Jerusalem, who had first preached the Gospel
unto them in the power of the Holy Ghost, since whose
coming and work among them all things had become new.

The Jewish Christians in " the Churches of the Gentiles,"
in this early formative period, had the place and rights of
the first-born generally accorded to them.   By birth and
training, by family connections with the Holy Land, they
stood nearer, in a sense, than the rest of their fellow-
worshippers to the Lord Himself, and to the hallowed circle
of those who had companied with Him in Galilee and Judæa.
Gentile believers, as in Antioch and Galatia, were apt sometimes to attach too much weight to such advantages, and to
yield too readily to the influence of Judaizing teachers who
could speak, as even Paul could not, of personal intercourse
with the Twelve, and could report the words and ways of
those who " had known Christ after the flesh." [2]   But, for the
most part, the Jewish Christians, in the Churches planted by
Paul, were men worthy of the confidence which their fellow-
disciples naturally placed in them.   They were like those
whom the apostle names with such warmth of affection in
writing from Rome to the Colossians : " They of the circumcision, my fellow-workers unto the kingdom of God, men that

[1] John iv. 22 ; Rom. xv. 27.
[2] Acts xv. 1 f. ; Gal. ii. 12 f.; iv. 9 f., 17; vi. 12 f. ; 2 Cor. v.16 ; xi. 4 f., 12 f., 22.

have been a comfort unto me."[1] In Christian communities such as those of Antioch and Ephesus, in the days of their first love and brotherly unity, such Jewish believers formed a sort of spiritual aristocracy, in the true sense of the term. Theirs was the natural and unsought leadership of the best and fittest to lead, the more readily accorded because on all sides there was so much of the "love that seeketh not her own," and of single-hearted desire for the good of Christ's cause and Church.

It was the *élite* of the synagogue who were drawn to Christ by the preaching of Paul. In every centre of the Diaspora there were men and women like those "devout Jews from every country" to whom Peter spoke at Pentecost. They had waited and prayed for years for "the Consolation, the Redemption of Israel;" and now they hailed the good tidings concerning the Christ, in the spirit in which Simeon and Anna had done so in the beginning of the Gospel. And with them were "devout Greeks and women of honourable estate." These had been led to the synagogue by religious instincts and cravings, for the satisfaction of which they had found something in its services, and much in its Scriptures; and now they found everything in Christ and in fellowship with His disciples.

Such converts, whether Jews or proselytes, must have formed the life and strength of the Pauline Churches. From their previous religious experience and training, from their knowledge of the Scriptures, from their practical familiarity with the modes and requisites of true spiritual worship, and with the working of a representative ecclesiastical system, such believers were the natural leaders and helpers of the rest in all meetings of the brethren, whether for worship or for the affairs of the Church. It must have been from this source especially that the first office-bearers of the Christian communities on Gentile ground were drawn.

Even were we to ignore the historical connection of the Gentile Christian Church with the Hebrew Christian, and to begin our study of its organization and administration with the thirteenth chapter of Acts and the Pauline Epistles, we should be at once reminded of the general features and spirit

[1] Col. iv. 11.

of the synagogue system. This impression would only be strengthened by a closer examination of the subject. The direct evidence drawn from the second period of the history alone is sufficient to prove the substantial identity of the two systems of ecclesiastical polity. But the proof becomes irresistible when we apply the law of growth and continuity, and observe how every New Testament writer, whether addressing himself especially to Christians of Jewish or of Gentile origin, asserts or assumes the unity of the Church of the Old Testament with that to which his readers belonged. Illustrations of this have met us, to some extent already,[1] and will meet us again. Meanwhile let us note that all the Churches of the Gentiles were founded by men who had been teachers or members of the Hebrew Christian Church. They were built on the same foundation by the hands of "the apostles and prophets" from Jerusalem.[2] The same Gospel was preached, as we have seen, by Paul and by the Twelve,[3] and the same practical results followed from its reception. The Christian communities established among the Gentiles stood in the closest relations of brotherly love and sympathy with the mother Church of the Holy Land. Prophets and teachers passed freely from the one to the other. There was a mutual giving and receiving both of spiritual and temporal gifts. A special—sometimes even an undue—weight was attached in Gentile Churches to the words of brethren who "came down from Judæa," who "came from James." Jewish Christians were felt everywhere, on grounds already indicated, to have something of the right of the first-born, with "the excellency of dignity, and the excellency of power."

In such circumstances, the natural presumption would be, supposing all positive information to be absent, that the Gentile Christian communities were organized on the same general principles as the Hebrew Christian ones. This, as already said, becomes matter of certainty, when we combine the different lines of proof now referred to, and consider the direct evidence regarding the organization of the apostolic Church during this period. In entering upon this field, we

[1] See above, pp. 361–364, 440 f.   [2] Eph. ii. 20.
[3] See above, pp. 479–484, 491-494.

are met at once by two great characteristics of the synagogue system : its elasticity and freedom on the one hand, and its power of order and control vested in distinct office-bearers on the other.

First, The elasticity and freedom of the system.

It rests upon a broad and popular basis. The organization is always such as is consistent with a full and frank recognition of. the individual rights of all the members of the community. Along with this there is a corresponding enforcement of individual responsibility for the welfare of the whole Church and for its corporate action. Opportunities and encouragements are freely given to every member of the Church to use and develop all gifts for edification and service which may be possessed by him. This is done in the face of all risks of disorder and mistake, such as arose in the department of worship in the Church at Corinth. A living and practical interest is fostered and taken for granted on the part of each believer in the common affairs and common welfare of the Christian society, both in its local and catholic form. Means are used to inform the minds of all the brethren with respect to all matters of importance with respect to which any step has to be taken. Their concurrence is carefully noted.[1]

Secondly, In the apostolic Church, as in the synagogue system, there is a power of order and control vested in distinct office-bearers.

This power is often held in reserve and kept in the background. Especially when, as in the Church meetings at Corinth, disorders arose from the abuse of gifts good in themselves, the exercise of which it was desired not to discourage but to regulate, we find the apostle Paul appealing to the offenders themselves as Christian men and women by suitable motives, and refraining, with characteristic tact and delicacy, from any direct use of his own authority, and from any reference to the authority vested in the office-bearers of the Church.[2]

---

[1] Acts xiv. 27 ; xv. 3 f , 12, 22, 30, 40 ; xviii. 27, etc. ; 1 Cor. v. 3 f. ; 2 Cor. ii. 5 f., etc.

[2] By Baur and others this has been made an argument to prove that there were no regular office-bearers among the Corinthians at the date of Paul's letters to them. Such writers " forget," as Beyschlag answers well, " that the office-

But the existence of distinct offices and office-bearers in the Churches of Gentile Christendom is perfectly clear, from the evidence, from the very beginning of this period of the history. It is evident also that, as in the synagogue system, the office-bearers were clothed with a real authority, not dependent merely on the consent at the time of the community in which they held office,—that there were, in short, in the apostolic Church of this period those who were " rulers," in the proper sense of the word, and those over whom rule of a certain kind was exercised. The proof of this is manifest from the records of the planting of the Gentile Christian Churches and from the relative Epistles. It grows more distinct and strong, as we might expect, when the reference is to Churches of considerable size and of long standing, and when the date is one at which miraculous gifts grew fewer, and the profusion of charismata, which was abused at Corinth, gave place to a more normal state of things. This is seen, for instance, in Paul's address to the presbyters of the Church at Ephesus, and in the pastoral Epistles.

We have noted already the importance attached during the period now under consideration to human instrumentality and

bearers, in any case, could have done nothing effectual in the matter unless they were supported by the general feeling of the membership ; and that it is in the most thorough accordance with the whole bent of the apostle's mind and heart that he should seek to come to a direct understanding with the whole Church, as such. . . . A numerous community, such as was formed by the Christians at Corinth, scattered through a metropolis, the population of which was counted by hundreds of thousands, had obviously more need of stated office-bearers than other and smaller Churches where we know they were appointed. The κυβερνήσεις and ἀντιλήψεις, to which Paul refers in 1 Cor. xii. 28, could not work in any efficient way without being recognised as such by the Church ; and just in proportion to the size and scattered condition of the Christian community in Corinth is it unreasonable to deny the existence of such recognized rulers on the ground of a mere argument e *silentio*. It is highly improbable that this Church at the time of the first Epistle, five years after its original foundation, was still without a body of stated office-bearers. And in addition to all this, we have the testimony of Clemens Romanus [before the end of the first century] writing precisely to this Church at Corinth, who, with special reference to the Corinthians, expressly ascribes the institution of the office of rulers and helpers to the apostolic initiative."—*Christliche Gemeindeverf.* S. 656. Comp. Dale, *Congreg. Principles*, pp. 64–67. Dr. Rigg's argument against this view seems weak and inconclusive, *Church Organization*, pp. 32–37.

to stated ordinances in the department of worship.[1]   The same
thing is true with respect to ordinances and appointments
relating to the spiritual oversight of the Church, its discipline,
the general administration of its affairs, and orderly procedure
in its assemblies.   Careful provision is made for the interests
of this whole department of Church life and action.   General
principles are laid down, especially by the apostle Paul, bearing
upon this field, and capable of wide and varied application.
" God is not a God of confusion," he reminds the Corinthians,
" but of peace, as in all the Churches of the saints."   " Let all
things be done in seemly form, and according to order."   " I
beseech you, brethren,—ye know the household of Stephanas,
that they have set themselves to minister unto the saints,
εἰς διακονίαν τοῖς ἁγίοις,—that ye also be in subjection unto
such, and to every one that helpeth in the work and laboureth.
. . .   Acknowledge ye, therefore, them that are such."
" Ye are the body of Christ, and severally members thereof ;
and God hath set some in the Church, first apostles, secondly
prophets, thirdly teachers, . . helps, governments, divers kinds of
tongues."   Christ, as the risen and ascended Lord, " gave some
to be apostles ; and some prophets ; and some evangelists ; and
some shepherds and teachers (τοὺς δὲ ποιμένας κ. διδασκάλους),
for the perfecting of the saints, unto the work of ministering
(εἰς ἔργον διακονίας), unto the building up of the body of
Christ ; till we all attain unto the unity of the faith, and of
the knowledge of the Son of God, unto a full-grown man, unto
the measure of the stature of the fulness of Christ."[2]

Let us consider how such principles were put into practical
operation in the apostolic Church on Gentile Christian ground.

1st. Appointment of elders or presbyters.

In the first missionary journey of Paul and Barnabas, they
passed from Antioch in Pisidia to Iconium ; thence to Lystra ;
and thence to Derbe in Lycaonia.   How much time they spent
in each of these centres of labour is not definitely stated ;
but it was evidently considerable, especially in some cases.[3]

---

[1] See above, p. 512.
[2] 1 Cor. xiv. 26, 33, 40 ; xvi. 15–18 ; xii. 28 ; Eph. iv. 11–13.
[3] In Antioch "almost the whole city" was moved by the missionaries.   From

From all the indications in the narrative, some of which are noted below, the missionaries must have made a stay of several months at least in each place; and the interval between the first planting of the Churches and the return of Paul and Barnabas to them for the purposes mentioned towards the end of the fourteenth chapter of Acts, cannot well have been less than from eighteen months to two years. About three years is the time usually allotted by the best commentators for the whole journey from the date of the missionaries leaving Antioch in Syria to that of their return thither.

Derbe, in which Paul and Barnabas met with much success, and apparently little or no persecution, formed the furthest limit of their first evangelistic tour. They had travelled far eastward, behind the great mountain range of the Taurus. The well-known pass, called "The Cilician Gates," was close before them. It would have led at once to Paul's native city of Tarsus, from which the return to Antioch in Syria, either by sea, or by the coast road, would have been easy and safe. But, instead of adopting this course, the two apostolic missionaries turned back again on their former route; to Lystra, where Paul had been stoned and left for dead; to Iconium, where both of them had with difficulty escaped from like outrage; to the Pisidian Antioch, where also they had met with organized persecution from the Jewish and Gentile authorities, and from which they had been violently expelled. The objects which Paul and Barnabas had at heart in this second visit, and for the sake of which they deliberately faced anew all the dangers of this perilous road, are very distinctly

their work there "the word of the Lord was spread abroad throughout all the region." In Iconium, a large and influential town where several Roman roads met, "they tarried long time, speaking boldly in the Lord, which bare witness unto the word of His grace." Lystra and Derbe seem to have been used by Paul and Barnabas as centres for preaching the Gospel "unto the region that lieth round about." Their stay in Lystra, in particular, was long enough to allow the tidings of their success in that district to reach the Jewish community not only in Iconium, some forty miles off, but in Antioch, which lay ninety miles further to the north-west, and to allow the Jews in both of these cities to combine in raising organized opposition to the work in Lystra, "some of them coming a hundred and thirty miles for the purpose" (Lindsay, *Acts*, ii. p. 58). In Derbe, after they had been driven from Lystra by persecution, Paul and Barnabas "made many disciples." Acts xiii. 14-52; xiv. 1-21.

stated in the narrative. They returned in order that they might "confirm the souls of the disciples," that they might give them suitable counsel and encouragement in view of the persecutions to which they were exposed, and especially that they might organize the Christian communities, in each centre where converts had been made, by the appointment of elders. "And when they had appointed for them elders in every Church, having prayed with fasting, they commended them to the Lord, on whom they had believed." [1]

There could hardly be a more striking proof of the importance attached by Paul and his fellow-labourers to the right organization of the Churches of the Gentiles, and of their conviction that the steps which they took in this respect were in accordance with the mind and will of Christ for the spiritual good of His people. So far at least as regards this primary office of the eldership, the organization of the Church of Christ was not a matter to be left to chance, or to develop itself on different lines, according to circumstances and the predilections of the first converts in each locality. Whether the founders of these infant societies would ever be able to return to them again, after this second visit, was very doubtful. It might well be, as Paul said afterwards in similar circumstances to the elders of Ephesus, that "they all should see his face no more." [2]   But, for the maintenance and propagation of this fundamental office of oversight and administration in the Church, the presence of an apostle was unnecessary. "These elderships, once established, were self-acting," [3] in the Christian Church, as in the Jewish synagogue. They could take all needful steps, with the concurrence of the members of the congregation, to add to their number, or to form other elderships in congregations which might spring up in neighbouring localities around the mother Church. The blessing of Christ, and all needful gifts of the Spirit, might be confidently looked for from Him in connection with His own ordinances for government and pastoral care in the Church, not, save in exceptional circumstances, apart from these, nor if oppor-

---

[1] Χειροτονήσαντες δὲ αὐτοῖς πρεσβυτέρους κατ' ἐκκλησίαν, προσευξάμενοι μετὰ νηστειῶν, Acts xiv. 21 ff.

[2] Acts xx. 25–38.   [3] Lindsay, *Acts*, ii. p. 59. See above, pp. 134 ff., 138 ff.

tunities for obtaining them were wilfully neglected. It was only after, at much personal risk, Paul and Barnabas had secured the appointment of elders in each of the Churches which they had been the means of founding among the Gentiles, and after special and solemn services in connection with their being set apart to office, that the eldership and the flock under their charge were together, in their mutual relations, finally " commended to the Lord on whom they had believed."

Similar action is, in all likelihood, covered by the general expressions used in reference to subsequent tours of visitation by Paul and his fellow-labourers among Christian communities which had been in existence for some time ; as when, after associating Silas with himself, " he went through Syria and Cilicia, confirming the Churches." It is expressly included in the apostle's instructions to Titus, when left on a temporary mission in a district where the Churches were as yet in an unorganized condition. " For this cause left I thee in Crete, that thou shouldest set in order the things that were wanting" (or " left undone," A. V. marg.), " and appoint elders in every city, as I gave thee charge." [1]

It is interesting to observe, with respect to the first organization of the Churches of Gentile Christendom, that, in connection apparently with Paul's third visit to Lystra, the eldership or presbytery of that place,—which had been appointed on his second visit, as above noted,—solemnly set apart Timothy for special service as a fellow-worker with the apostle in the field of the Gentile mission. He was a young man, well instructed in the Scriptures from his childhood, who had received the Gospel, along with older members of his family, probably on Paul's first visit. He was now " well reported of by the brethren that were at Lystra and Iconium," having done Christian work apparently at both places. In his ordination to office the action of laying on of hands was used,

---

[1] Acts xv. 41 ; comp. xvi. 4 f.; xix. 1, etc.; Tit. i. 5 ; iii. 12. Titus was probably a Christian of Antioch. He was, at all events, one who had been closely associated with the apostle during his earlier missionary journeys, and knew well the methods adopted by him in the organization of "the Churches of the Gentiles."

as in ordinations to the eldership in the synagogue, and as had been done when Barnabas and Saul were "separated unto the work" of the Gentile mission, at the bidding of the Holy Ghost, by the prophets and teachers of the Church at Antioch.

Paul speaks of this memorable event in the history of Timothy in his first letter to him, alluding to prophetic utterances in the Church, which had been given in connection with it, and which seem to have had to do with the call to special service being first addressed to him, and with his acceptance of it,—"according to the prophecies, which led the way to thee, that by them thou mayest war the good warfare." "Till I come, give heed unto reading, to exhortation, to teaching. Neglect not the gift that is in thee, which was given thee by prophecy, with the laying on of the hands of the presbytery."[1] The apostle himself,—as may perhaps be gathered from another reference in his second letter to Timothy, and as was in every way likely in the circumstances,—apparently took part in the services, probably presiding at them, and joined with the presbytery in the laying on of hands on one who was "his true and beloved child in the faith."[2]

From beginning to end, therefore, of the second period of the history of the apostolic Church, the appointment of elders is regarded everywhere as the first necessity in the matter of organization. We have seen that it was so in all the Churches of Pisidia and Lycaonia, and in every city of Crete. Elders appear in the second section of the Acts, equally with the first, as the recognized and responsible representatives and guides of the Church in every locality. It is in this capacity that the elders of Ephesus are appealed to by Paul on what he regards as his last visit to that region. It is taken for granted in the Epistle of James and in the first Epistle of Peter, that elders are to be found in office among all the twelve tribes of the Christian Dispersion, and that whether

---

[1] Acts xvi. 1–4 ; 1 Tim. i. 18 (R. V. marg.) ; iv. 13 f.

[2] 1 Tim. i. 2 ; 2 Tim. i. 2, 6 f. Comp. Bannerman, *Church of Christ*, ii. pp. 284–288. For an admirable vindication of the authenticity and genuineness of the Epistles to Timothy and Titus, see Prof. Salmon's *Introd. to N. T.*, pp. 488–511.

the Jewish or the Gentile element predominated,—the latter
probably being the case, as a rule, in the Churches of " Pontus,
Galatia, Cappadocia, Asia, and Bithynia." They are referred
to, under equivalent titles, as existing in the Churches at
Thessalonica, at Philippi, at Rome, (probably) at Corinth
and Colossæ,[1] and in the Jewish Christian communities to
which the author of the Epistle to the Hebrews addresses
himself.[2]

1. Mode of appointment.

From all our sources of information it appears that the
principles on which the appointment of elders was made
during the second section of the history of the apostolic
Church, were those which we saw exemplified in the appointment of the seven deacons at Jerusalem. The elders are
chosen from the membership of the congregation in which
they are to serve, after some experience had of their Christian
character and gifts for the office. They are chosen, as it
appears, by the members themselves, or indicated, with the
concurrence of the brethren, by men of prophetic powers,[3] or
by the first founders of the Church on a subsequent visit for
purposes of organization. They are formally ordained, or set
apart to office, by men already holding similar or higher office
in the Church. This is always done with religious services
of a special kind, and generally, as it seems, with the laying
on of hands in synagogue fashion.

All these points, except that of the imposition of hands,
are more or less distinctly brought out in the very first reference to the appointment of elders in the Gentile Churches.[4]

(1.) The appointment of presbyters in the Churches of

---

[1] For Corinth, see note at p. 529. For Colossæ, comp. Col. iv. 17 with
Philem. 2. Archippus had received a definite "ministry in the Lord" at
Colossæ, and had been definitely set apart to it (ἣν παρέλαβες). This ministry
was one in which Paul counted him as "a fellow-soldier." The phrase does not
suggest the deaconship. It was in all likelihood the same office of spiritual
oversight and pastoral care of which the apostle spoke to the presbyters of
Ephesus, the mother Church of the whole region in which Colossæ lay. Comp.
Beyschlag, S. 69 f.

[2] Acts xx. 17, 28 ff.; 1 Tim. i. 3; iii. 1 f., 5; v. 17–20; Jas. v. 14; 1 Pet.
i. 1; v. 1–4; Rom. xii. 7 f.; Heb. xiii. 7; xvii. 24.

[3] As in the case of Timothy. See last page.

[4] Acts xiv. 21–23.

Lycaonia and Pisidia was made, as already noted, not on the first visit of Paul and Barnabas, but on the second. A period of from one to two years was interposed between the foundation of the Christian community in each place and its formal organization. Time and opportunity were thus given to develop and prove the Christian character and different gifts, natural and spiritual, of all the converts. Paul and Barnabas, in short, acted in this matter on the principles laid down at a later date in the Pastoral Epistles respecting the appointment of office-bearers. "Not a novice (νεόφυτος, a new convert), lest, being puffed up, he fall into the condemnation of the devil. Moreover, he must have a good testimony from them that are without." "Let the deacons also first be proved, and then let them serve as deacons, if they be blameless." "Lay hands hastily on no man." [1]

Timothy, as the apostle testifies in his last letter to him, had hitherto "been a follower" of Paul's "teaching, conduct, purpose," as he had known them "at Antioch, at Iconium, at Lystra." He is now exhorted to "abide in the things which he had learned, knowing of whom he had learned them." In this matter of the organization of the Church, Timothy had learned his first lessons as an eye-witness to the establishment of the first Christian eldership in his native city of Lystra and in the neighbouring Iconium. He knew that the apostle's practice corresponded to the rules which he now received for his own guidance and that of the "faithful men" to whom he was to "commit the things which he had learned from Paul among many witnesses," and who would thus be "able to teach others also." [2]

(2.) It seems a fair inference, from all the circumstances of the case, that the choice of the presbyters in each congregation was entrusted to the members of the Church. It can hardly be said that the words of the narrative in themselves assert this; [3] although that has been strongly maintained by many very competent interpreters both in earlier and later times. [4] The judgment of the Revisers is, I think, on the

---

[1] 1 Tim. iii. 6 f.; v. 22; Tit. i. 5 f.   [2] 2 Tim. ii. 2; iii. 10 f., 14.

[3] Χειροτονήσαντες αὐτοῖς πρεσβυτέρους κατ᾽ ἐκκλησίαν.

[4] Erasmus: "Cum suffragiis creassent presbyteros." So Meyer and Beyschlag.

whole, to be accepted as the right one. According to it, the term here, and in 2 Cor. viii. 19, means simply to appoint, without determining the manner in which it is done. Still the fact that the original meaning of the term was to appoint or elect by show of hands, is favourable so far to the view that the appointment of the elders was by the choice of the members of the Church in which they were to hold office. There can be little doubt that this was the method by which the messengers of the Church at Corinth were appointed, as referred to in the only other passage in the New Testament in which the word occurs.

Other considerations point more decisively in the same direction. The very object of the delay from the first to the second visit was to give time for the members of the Church to know and test the qualifications of the brethren who might seem fittest for office. They only could say who had been "proved and found blameless," "having a good testimony from them that are without," and who among them were "apt to teach." The confidence always shown by the Apostle Paul in the powers of self-government inherent in the members of the Christian communities which he founded; his reliance on the gifts of the Holy Ghost bestowed on them in the form of wisdom and knowledge and discernment of spirits; his practice of leaving the appointment of their representatives in important matters to the choice of the Churches themselves,— these are all facts which strengthen the presumption that the elders in the Pauline Churches were appointed by the choice, or at least with the full concurrence, of the members generally. This was the rule, as we saw, in the Jewish synagogues.[1] Lastly, the argument from precedent and analogy in the previous history of the Apostolic Church is so strong—when taken with the considerations already noted—as to be practically conclusive. Both in the appointment of an apostle, and in that of the seven deacons, the election was made by the

---

Dean Alford holds that the term here implies election by the members, "not necessarily as the meaning of the word, but by analogy of chap. vi. 2-6. . . . The apostles ordained the presbyters whom the Churches elected."

[1] 1 Cor. xvi. 3 ; 2 Cor. viii. 4, 11, 19-24 ; ix. 1-5, 13 ; Phil. ii. 25 ; iv. 3, 15-18 ; 1 Thess. v. 12 f., 21 ; comp. 1 John iv. 1. See above, p. 134 f.

whole body of the disciples, although the confirmation of the choice was referred directly to the Lord in the one case and to the apostolic company in the other.[1] There is every probability that, in this third recorded instance of an appointment to stated office in the Apostolic Church, as in the two former ones, the initiative as regards choice lay with the members of the Christian community as a body.[2]

(3.) The presbyters are formally set apart to their office by men already in office in the Church, with solemn religious services.

Paul and Barnabas "appointed for them elders in every Church, having prayed with fasting."[3] We recognize the same leading features in this transaction as in the appointment of the seven deacons, and in the separation of Barnabas and Saul to the Gentile mission. Certain men are separated for a special office, or special service, by the call of the Spirit, acting in and through the Church. They are set apart to the work with solemn prayer and special waiting upon God by those already in office, and are sent forth to their work accordingly, whether in a wider or narrower sphere, by the Holy Spirit and by the Church, acting in unity. Hence the presbyters at Ephesus are "the presbyters of the Church;" and yet it was "the Holy Ghost who had set them as bishops therein, to tend the flock, and the Church of God, which He purchased with His own blood."[4]

"Laying on of hands" is not expressly mentioned in the case of the first elderships in the Pauline Churches, as it is in

---

[1] See above, pp. 403 f., 423, 426.

[2] It may be noted, in addition, that on no point is the testimony of the patristic writers of the first three centuries more unanimous than on this, that from the time of the apostles, the members of every Church had the right of a free choice,—or, at the very least, a substantial voice,—in the appointment of their office-bearers. See Blondel's thorough discussion of the subject in his great work, *Apologia pro sententia Hieronymi de Episcopis et Presbyteris*, Amstel. 1646. Sect. iii. "De plebis in electionibus jure," pp. 379–438. Comp. Principal Cunningham, *Works*, iv. pp. 306–321, "Rights of the Christian People." See also the passage from the Life of Severus quoted above, p. 135, note.

[3] Χειροτονήσαντες . . . προσευξάμενοι μετὰ νηστειῶν. The Aorists imply that the religious exercises were at the time of the ordination and in connection with it.

[4] Acts xx. 17–28.

connection with the ordination of the deacons, and in the setting apart of the missionaries at Antioch. The omission may show that it was not regarded as entering into the essence of the transaction, but only as a suitable accompaniment.[1] But, in point of fact, imposition of hands was, in all likelihood, used here too, although not recorded. We hear of a second ordination at Lystra in connection with which this action is distinctly named. What was done by the eldership there at the ordination of Timothy, on Paul's third visit to the place, was not probably omitted when the elders were themselves ordained at his second visit. It is taken for granted as a usual feature of such appointments to office in the apostle's injunction to Timothy : " Lay hands hastily on no man." [2]

2. Nature and functions of the elder's office ; qualifications required.

It strongly confirms the conclusions, to which we have already come, regarding the genetic connection between the Jewish synagogue and the Christian Church, to find that in the second section of the Acts, as in the first, an acquaintance with the general nature and functions of the elder's office is everywhere taken for granted. Presbyters appear, as a matter of course, in the Christian community of Ephesus, the mother Church of Proconsular Asia, just as we saw them do in the Christian community of Jerusalem, the mother Church of the Holy Land, and among the Churches of Judæa to which relief was sent from Antioch. The fact and the date of the first appointment of elders in the Pauline Churches are noted in the narrative, but there is no such careful explanation of " the business, over which they are appointed," and the position which they are to hold, as is given in the account of the first ordination to the deaconship, which was in many respects a new office.

Now, this is precisely what we should expect upon that interpretation of the history to which we have been already

---

[1] "Manûs autem impositio non, sicut Baptismus, repeti non potest. Quid est enim aliud nisi oratio super hominem." Augustine, *De Bapt. Contra Donatistas*, iii. 16. Comp. Bannerman, *Church of Christ*, ii. pp. 421–424, " Imposition of Hands in Ordination ;" Hatch, *Organiz. of Christ. Churches*, pp. 130–135 ; also my little work, *Admission to Ordinances*, p. 56 f.

[2] Acts xvi. 1-4 ; 1 Tim. ii. 18 ; iv. 13 f. ; v. 22 ; 2 Tim. iii. 10 f.

led. The Christian Church, with respect to its polity as with respect to its worship, on Gentile as on Hebrew ground, grew out of the Jewish synagogue. There was no breach in the continuous development of God's providential education of His people in this matter during the centuries which had passed over Israel in the Dispersion. There was no loss of the lessons learned through generations as to the worth of "a regulated, a self-regulating freedom," [1] as to how liberty might be combined with order in worship and in discussion, as to the strength, elasticity, and practical resources of the Presbyterian system. That time-honoured institution of the eldership passed without a break or jar from the Church of the Old Testament into the Churches of the Gentiles. It took its place there, from the first, under apostolic guidance, as it had done before in the Church of the Holy Land, as the basis of a representative polity, the centre of organized life, and the means of united action in the Christian society. It did so most naturally and simply,—if we regard the process from a merely human standpoint,—in virtue of the two facts already noted, namely, that all the founders of the Gentile Churches were themselves Jewish Christians, and that the nucleus and strength of each of the Pauline congregations were formed by persons who had been connected with the synagogue or proseucha of the place, as Jews or proselytes whose influence in the infant Church—from causes before explained—was far more powerful than in proportion to their numbers, and from whom the first office-bearers of the congregation were almost certain to be chosen. [2]

There was little need, in such circumstances, to explain the

---

[1] Rainy, *Three Lectures on the Church of Scotland*, ed. 1883, p. 36.

[2] See above, pp. 524–527. "Diese wesentliche Zusammenstimmung der paulinischen Gemeindeordnung mit der urapostolischen kann nur die etwa befremden, welche die Kirche, anstatt aus der Neuschöpfung Gottes in Christo, vielmehr aus dem Streit des Judaismus und Paulinismus meinen herleiten zu sollen. Sie hat ihre ganz natürliche Gründe an der Naturgemässheit der synagogalen Vorbilder, an der jüdischen Bildung auch des Heidenapostels, an dem nicht rein-hellenischen, sondern immer doch jüdisch-untermischten Character seiner Gemeinden und deren unleugbarer Entstehung aus Abzweigungen der Diaspora synagoge ; endlich, an der Einheit des Geistes, bei der Mannigfaltigkeit der Gaben, welche auch zwischen Paulus und den Uraposteln waltete (Gal. ii. 7–9)." Beyschlag, *Christl. Gemeindeverf.* S. 82.

nature of the institution of the eldership.   Those who knew
from practical experience what a pious and gifted elder, " a
scribe made a disciple unto the kingdom of heaven," had been
in the synagogue, knew in substance what a man like Crispus
at Corinth would be, when baptized with the Spirit of Christ,
and set apart, with others like-minded, for service as an elder
in His Church, to " tend the flock of God, exercising the
oversight, not of constraint, but willingly, according to God."[1]
At the same time, the references to the subject, direct and
indirect, in the Acts and relative Epistles, are so numerous
that there is no difficulty in arriving, even from these
sources alone, at a clear view of the nature and functions of
the office of elder in the apostolic Church in this period of
its history.

(1.) It is a spiritual office, and the primary requisite in
those who are to fill it is that they be spiritual men, true and
consistent Christians.

This comes out very clearly in what is said of elders or
bishops[2] in the Pastoral Epistles.   These letters belong, as
is now generally admitted by all who maintain their authenticity, to the very latest period in the life of Paul,—a period
beyond what is covered by the Acts.[3]   The Epistle to Titus is
addressed to one of the apostle's helpers in the Gentile
mission, whom he had left behind in Crete after a personal
visit there.   It had seemingly been a brief one, but long
enough to show Paul that many things were wanting in the

---

[1] Matt. xiii. 52 ; Acts xviii. 8 ; 1 Pet. v. 1 f.

[2] The identity of " elder " and " bishop " in the New Testament both as to
name and office may be assumed here.   The evidence for it is indicated below.
The point used to be strongly contested by advocates of the Prelatic theory.
It is not matter of controversy now among competent scholars who admit the
authority of the Acts, the Epistle of James, First Peter, and the Pastoral
Epistles, as evidence for the practice of the Apostolic Church.   Harnack with
one or two others who have recently disputed the point, from a very different
position than the Prelatic one, base their arguments upon a denial that these
documents belong to the first century.   See, e.g., Harnack's article in *Expositor*
for May 1887, pp. 322, 334, 338.   Comp. Kühl, *Gemeindeordn. in den
Pastoralbriefen*, Berlin 1885, S. 25 f., 87 f., and Principal Rainy's article,
" Presbyters and Bishops," in *Theol. Review*, Nov. 1886, p. 14 f.

[3] The only feasible alternatives are the theory of a second Roman imprisonment, and that which gives up the Pauline authorship altogether, and ascribes
the Epistles to a disciple of the apostle, writing after his death under his name.

Christianity of the island. In particular, the groups of believers in different parts of Crete were as yet, so far as appears, wholly unorganized. The first duty laid upon Titus, therefore, is to see that this defect was supplied by the appointment of elders in every city, in the manner enjoined upon him by the apostle. This, as we saw above, was in Paul's eyes the primary requisite in the organization of the Churches.[1] The appointment of deacons was not of such pressing importance ; and no reference is made to it here, any more than in the fourteenth chapter of Acts. It could be safely left with the local elderships to make suitable arrangements for the care of the poor, and for the oversight of the temporal affairs of the congregation, whether by looking to that department themselves in the meantime, or by having fit men ordained to the deaconship, as in Jerusalem, where the growth of the Church required that step.

The First Epistle to Timothy, although belonging to the same period, and referring to the same type of false doctrine, as the Epistle to Titus, has to do with a more advanced stage of Church life. In Ephesus, and around it, ecclesiastical organization was more fully developed. Both presbyters and deacons had been generally appointed. The office of spiritual oversight, in particular,—that of presbyter or bishop,—was of long standing, and had become to many an object of honourable ambition.[2] The apostle's main design in asking Timothy to tarry for a season in Ephesus, while he himself went into Macedonia, had reference not to the organization of the Church, but to its doctrine. He apprehended danger from certain tendencies among the teachers of the Church in and

---

[1] Tit. i. 5 ; Acts xiv. 21–23. See above, pp. 531–534. One special reason, as appears plainly from the Epistle to Titus, of the apostle's anxiety to have the Cretan Churches organized, was his apprehension of evils likely to arise there from the influence of false teachers (i. 10 ff.). In view of this danger, Paul urges the appointment of presbyter-bishops who shall be " God's stewards holding to the faithful word which is according to the teaching, able both to exhort in the sound doctrine, and to convict the gainsayers." Having enforced the need of teaching gifts, and still more of consistent Christian character, on the part of the elders in five verses of the first chapter, the apostle turns from the subject of organization altogether, and devotes the rest of the Epistle to the truth to be taught, and the evils in doctrine and life to be opposed in the Cretan Churches.

[2] 1 Tim. iii. 1.

around Ephesus, the nature of which he specifies.[1] It was on this account that he had exhorted Timothy to remain for a little in the great commercial centre of Asia Minor, and to seek to counteract these growing evils. From doctrinal references he passes to speak of how public prayer should be offered in the congregation, and of the place to be taken and the spirit evinced by its female members. Not till the third chapter does Paul come to the subject of organization, and then it is not, as in Titus, to enjoin the appointment of elders as a thing hitherto neglected, but to speak of how candidates for the two offices of bishop and deacon—the nature of which is assumed to be well known—should be tested, and what are the qualifications to which primary importance should be attached. In the fourth chapter the subject of doctrine again receives prominence. There is in it but one passing allusion to an act of a presbytery, which marked a memorable step in Timothy's own experience. Doctrinal and practical statements are combined in the rest of the Epistle. In the last chapter there is no reference whatever to organization; but in the fifth, light is thrown on various points connected with arrangements for the care of the poor and the afflicted in the Christian community, and there are two or three references to the position and duties of elders. In Second Timothy there is not a single direct reference to organization of any sort.

Two things must strike every intelligent reader of the two earlier Pastoral Epistles, as regards the brief sections which speak of presbyter bishops: First, how the apostle, like other New Testament writers, takes it for granted that this office of elder is no new creation but a familiar institution, needing no explanation, as regards its essential nature, to those to whom he writes; and, secondly, that the point which Paul urges most strongly upon his deputies in Ephesus and Crete is the supreme importance of the moral and spiritual qualifications for the work of the eldership. He refers in general terms to elders' duties under the two categories,—well known in every synagogue,—of ruling and teaching.[2] He emphasizes the

---

[1] 1 Tim. i. 3 f., 6 f.
[2] 1 Tim. iii. 2, 4 f.; v. 17 f. ; Titus i. 9.   See above, pp. 141-145.

latter as specially needed in present circumstances. But it is
on what an elder ought to be in personal character and life
that the apostle dwells with the most earnest minuteness.[1]

In the teaching of the Apostle of the Gentiles, and in the
practice of the Gentile Churches, we find the same principles
as to the twofold call to office in the Church set forth and
applied as in the Hebrew Christian community. But on this
we cannot enter now.[2]

(2.) The office of elder in the Gentile Christian Church was
a collegiate one, and included the functions of ruling, of oversight or episcopal care, and of teaching.

In other words, the eldership in the Apostolic Church, in
the second as in the first period of its history, was, in all
essentials, what it had been under the synagogue system, save
that all was touched and quickened with the new life which
marked the dispensation of the Spirit. We have traced the
historic genesis of this fact already.[3] A very slight survey of
the evidence afforded by the names and exhortations given to
the elders of the apostolic Church on Gentile ground, and by
the other references direct and indirect to their functions, will
show how complete the correspondence in question is.

Take Leyrer's summary of the titles and functions of the
synagogue elders, in his admirable monograph, "The Synagogues of the Jews," [4] and compare these with the names and
duties of the office-bearers of the Christian Church in Acts
and the relative Epistles. "At the head of the synagogue
stood a college of זְקֵנִים πρεσβύτεροι (Luke vii. 3), also מְמֻנִּים,
מְמֻנִּים from מנה Po. = προεστῶτες, ἄρχοντες, ἀρχισυνάγωγοι
(Mark v. 22; Luke vii. 3 ff.; Acts xiii. 15), פַּרְנָס, פַּרְנָסִים,
ποίμενες (from פַּרְנֵס, pascere politice et ecclesiastice, cf. Acts xx.
28; 1 Pet. v. 2; Vitr. p. 621 ff.; Buxt. Lex. Talm. p. 1821),
also מנהיג ἡγούμενος (Abarb. in Jes. iii. 1; Heb. xiii. 17),

---

[1] 1 Tim. iii. 2-7; xv. 19-22, 24 f.; Titus i. 6-8. Comp. Weiss, Briefe an
Timoth. u. Tit. (Meyer's series), 5te Aufl. S. 143 f.; Kühl, Gemeindeordn. in
den Pastoralbriefen, S. 7, 16, 29.

[2] See above, pp. 473-475; comp. 1 Cor. xii. 28 f.; Eph. iv. 8-12; Beyschlag,
Christl. Gemeindeverf. S. 81 f.; Bannerman, Church of Christ, i. pp.
421-439.

[3] See above, pp. 415 ff., 449.

[4] Leyrer, Synagogen der Juden, in Herzog, xv. S. 312.

and נְדוֹלֵי הַקָּהָל. These formed, under the presidency of the ἀρχισυνάγωγος κατ᾽ ἐξοχήν (Luke viii. 41, 49; xiii. 14; comp.
Matt. ix. 18; Mark v. 35 ff.; John vii. 48; Acts xviii. 8, 17;
רֹאשׁ הַכְּנֶסֶת, M. Jom. vii. 1; Sot. vii. 7, ר' הַצִּבּוּר, ר' הַקָּהָל, Chald.
רִישׁ כְּנוּשְׁתָּא), a consulting college, which had the charge of order
and discipline in the synagogue, punished offerders by admonition and exclusion (hence ἀποσυνάγωγος, John ix. 22; xii.
42; xvi. 2), and managed also the care of the poor. . . . Its
members were also, no doubt, members of the local synedria
(Vitr. p. 553 ff.; Maim. h. Taan. i. 17); but those of its
number who were trained in the knowledge of the Scriptures,
were, at the same time, as can be inferred from several
passages in Philo and from 1 Tim. v. 17,[1] the members of the
congregation who specially officiated in public worship. They
were consecrated to their office by χειροθεσία, probably by the
ἀρχισυνάγωγος and the rest of the elders (Acts vi. 6; xiii. 3,
etc.)."

The conclusion, even were there no further evidence of
historic connection, would be irresistible. These names and
functions correspond at every point with those which meet us
in the Acts and the Epistles in reference to the elders or
overseers (bishops) of the apostolic Church, both on Hebrew
Christian and Gentile Christian ground.

3. Relation of the elders to each other.

(1.) As already noted, the office of elder in the apostolic
Church, as in the synagogue, was a collegiate one.

Several elders, as we have seen, were appointed in every
congregation. Unless by an apostle in special circumstances,
and possibly, in like circumstances, by an apostolic deputy,
such as Timothy, no act of government or discipline, no
setting apart to office is recorded in the New Testament as
done by one man; and there is no instance whatever in the
New Testament of a Church stately governed by a single
ruler. These functions are entrusted only to a collective
body. The decision or action is that of the Church or its
representatives. The principles of Old Testament Presby-

---

[1] Comp. Clem. Rom. ad Cor. xlii., xliv., liv., lxiii., also the very ancient
Homily known as his Second Epistle to the Corinthians, xvii. 19; Bishop
Lightfoot, St. Clement of Rome, Lond. 1877, pp. 303 f., 333, 389.

terianism are faithfully carried out. What concerns all in
the Christian community is done, as far as possible, with the
voice and concurrence of all. "For this purpose a college of
elders is appointed, that the responsibility may be divided."[1]

(2.) A difference of gifts and training is recognised among
those who belonged to the one order of the eldership.

This corresponded to the distinction in the synagogue
presbyteries between the ordinary members of the court, who
did a shepherd's work of guidance and oversight (פרנסים), and
those who were trained teachers, "wise men and scribes."[2]
All presbyters in the apostolic Church were overseers of the
flock, and did a shepherd's office therein, guarding and tending
it, caring for its welfare, purity, and increase. In seeking to
attain these ends, there was a wise division of labour. Each
member of the eldership, as of the Church at large, was to
use and cultivate the special gifts of nature and of grace
which God had given him. "According as each hath received
a gift, ministering it among yourselves, as good stewards of
the manifold grace of God; if any man speaketh, speaking as
it were oracles of God; if any man ministereth, ministering
as of the strength which God supplieth." "Having gifts
differing according to the grace that was given to us, whether
prophecy, let us prophesy according to the proportion of our
faith; or ministry, let us give ourselves to our ministry; or
he that teacheth, to his teaching; or he that exhorteth, to his
exhorting: he that giveth, let him do it with liberality; he
that ruleth, with diligence; he that showeth mercy, with
cheerfulness."[3]   Neither in the synagogue nor the Church
were all elders alike "apt to teach." That qualification grew
more and more desirable as time went on. The extension of

---

[1] See above, pp. 99 f., 103, 134 f. "The apostolic plan of assigning a plurality of
rulers to every Church, and the prelatic plan of assigning a plurality of Churches
to one ruler, are as contrary as can be imagined." Binnie, *The Church*, p. 127 f.

[2] See above, pp. 141–144.

[3] 1 Pet. iv. 10 f; Rom. xii. 6 ff. Comp. the interesting "Report on the
Eldership" given in at the Third General Council of the Alliance of the
Reformed Churches holding the Presbyterian system, with the papers on the
subject by Prof. Chancellor, and James A. Campbell, Esq., M.P., and the
discussion that followed. *Minutes and Proceedings of Council at Belfast*, pp.
374–401. Append. pp. 131–136.

the Church made it less and less possible that each particular congregation should receive the benefit of direct apostolic instruction. The apostles themselves, and men endowed with extraordinary gifts through the laying on of the apostles' hands, were removed by death. And false prophets and teachers arose " to draw away the disciples after them." [1] Hence the growing emphasis laid in the later Epistles of Paul on the importance of having such teaching presbyters in every eldership. They were to be recognised as among the choicest gifts of Christ to His Church on earth; and suitable provision was to be made for their support. " Having ascended on high, He Himself gave some . . . shepherds and teachers [2] for the perfecting of the saints, unto the work of ministering unto the building up of the body of Christ." " Let the elders that rule well be counted worthy of double honour, especially those who labour in the Word and in teaching. For the Scripture saith, Thou shalt not muzzle the ox when he treadeth out the corn. And, The labourer is worthy of his hire." [3]

[1] Acts xx. 30 ; comp. Matt. xxiv. 11 ; 1 John iv. 1 ; 2 John 7 ff.

[2] τοὺς δὲ ποιμίνας κ. διδασκάλους. The form of expression indicates that 'the two words describe the same office under different aspects." Bishop Lightfoot, *Philippians*, 3rd ed. p. 192. Comp. Dodwell's valuable dissertation, " De Presbyteris doctoribus," in Migne's *Patrol.* v. pp. 35–38.

[3] Eph. iv. 11 f. ; 1 Tim. v. 17–19. The τιμή, from the connection, seems clearly to *include* support from the Church. Comp. 1 Cor. ix. 4–14 ; and, as regards the stress laid on teaching gifts, 1 Tim. iii. 2 ; iv. 13, 16 ; vi. 3 ff., 20 f.; 2 Tim. ii. 2, 24 ; Tit. i. 9 ff.

Dr. Dale treats this whole question of the eldership, according to the apostolic idea of the office, with great ability and candour. He admits frankly that the diaconate, in modern Congregational, or Independent Churches, has come to be, " in perhaps the majority of cases, a board of elders," with " deacons," in the New Testament sense of the word, intermixed, and that it would be better if the two orders were clearly distinguished, both in name and function, according to the apostolic model. Practical evils, as he points out with great force, arise from the present confused condition of things for all the three parties first involved,—the presiding elder or " minister," those who ought to be recognised as elders, and the " deacons " proper ; and so the Church as a whole suffers seriously.

The title " ruling-elder," as Dr. Dale rightly says, is ambiguous, and open to the objection " that it seems to restrain these particular elders from the right to use what powers they may possess for instructing and exhorting their brethren." The designation " lay-elder " is still more objectionable and misleading, unless it be taken simply as indicating the fact that the office-bearer so called is not a professional teacher, and is in the same position with the ordinary members of the Church as regards his secular occupation. But from the standpoint of

(3.) Presidents of presbyteries.

In the meetings of the elderships of single congregations, and in the larger and more representative assemblies, as when "the presbyters of the Church at Ephesus" met together for common counsel and action regarding the affairs of the Christian community in that great city, or when "the apostles and elders which were at Jerusalem came together to consider of this matter" of the admission of the Gentiles, some one must have acted as president.[1] Every council or conference must have a chairman or president of some kind, whether appointed at each meeting, or for a longer term, or for life.

The analogy of the synagogue elderships would naturally be followed in the Church in this as in other respects.[2] By apostolic injunction, "special honour" was to be given to those presbyters who, besides "ruling well," laboured in the Word and in teaching. This would naturally lead to such a "minister of the Word" presiding, as a rule, in the meetings of the congregation, and of its eldership, as the scribe or Rabbi had been wont to do in a village synagogue. Where a congregation enjoyed the services of several elders of teaching gifts, or where representatives of several congregations met in conference, considerations of seniority, or acknowledged fitness for the work specially in hand, would determine who should fill the chair. Often it might seem best on

Scripture and of the Reformed Church, those elders who do not publicly "labour in the Word and in teaching" hold a spiritual office in the Church equally with the trained teacher or "minister of the Word." They have been chosen by their fellow-worshippers, in connection with solemn prayer for the guidance of the Holy Spirit, to take the oversight in the flock of God which is among them, to do a shepherd's work in guiding and tending the sheep and the lambs of Christ, to share in administering the government and discipline of the house of God. And they have been solemnly ordained and admitted to this office in the name of Christ the Head of the Church by the eldership of the congregation, the members of which have called them to it, recognising in them, as they believe, the higher Divine call to this service for Christ. See Dale, *Congreg. Principles*, pp. 114–119; comp. Binnie, *The Church*, pp. 122–130. Bannerman, *Church of Christ*, ii. pp. 305–308.

[1] Acts xv. 6 ; xx. 17, 28 ; 1 Tim. iv. 14.

[2] See above, pp. 138–141. Dr. Lightfoot remarks in connection with this point that "the 'threefold order' of the Christian ministry as a whole seems to have no counterpart in the synagogue" (*Philippians*, 3rd ed. p. 205). It might be added with equal truth, that it seems to have no counterpart in the apostolic Church.

various grounds to have a standing president. In times of difficulty or persecution, some Christian teacher of impressive personality, and of sound and tried judgment, might be felt on all sides to be the leader whom God had raised up for the Church, and who must preside in her counsels. A good instance of this may be found in the position held in the Church at Jerusalem, in the second section of its history, by James the Lord's brother.

Although not, as we have seen reason to conclude, one of the apostles, James had stood in a quite unique relation to Christ after the flesh. He seems to have been the eldest of " the brethren of the Lord," the natural head and representative, according to Eastern ideas, of the family of Jesus. As such, probably, James was singled out by the Saviour for a special interview after the Resurrection.[1] His spiritual gifts and weight of character increased the reverence naturally accorded in the Pentecostal Church to one whose relations to the Lord Jesus had been so close and sacred. The apostles gradually left Jerusalem on missionary errands ; so that we find at one time Peter only in the city, and at a later date apparently none of the twelve remaining there. But James still continued in the original seat of the Hebrew Christian Church, standing out now alone of " those who seemed to be pillars " in it at the time of Paul's first and second visits to Jerusalem. Add to all this the special influence which his " devoutness according to the law " gave him with the unbelieving Jews, and which is indicated by his title of " James the Righteous ; " and it is easy to understand the prominence which James has in several passages in the second section of the Acts, and in two or three references made by Paul to the Church at Jerusalem.[2] Setting only the apostles aside, he was undoubtedly the most honoured and influential member of the Hebrew Christian community, the man who would, as a matter of course, be expected to preside and take the lead in any meeting of importance in connection with the affairs of the Church.[3]

---

[1] 1 Cor. xv. 7.   [2] Acts xii. 17 ; xv.; Gal. i. 19 ; ii. 9, 12 ; 1 Cor. ix. 5.
[3] Parallels could easily be given from the history of the Reformed Church. "Calvin was moderator of the presbytery of Geneva as long as he lived,

On the other hand, there is not the slightest evidence that James the Lord's brother held any position different in rank or order from the other presbyters of the Church at Jerusalem with whom he acted. In the earliest passage bearing on the point, we find that the commission from Antioch for relief of the brethren in Jerusalem and Judæa is not addressed to James, nor even "to James and the elders who are with him," but simply "to the elders." It is to "the apostles and elders at Jerusalem" that the appeal is made from Antioch regarding the admission of Gentile converts. It is "the apostles and the elders" who are "gathered together to consider of this matter." Who presided at the council is not stated. James, as well as Peter, took a leading part in the discussion; and his proposal was finally accepted by "the apostles and the elders, with the whole Church." But the official letter and "the decrees" run in the name of "the apostles and elders that were at Jerusalem," the president, whoever he may have been, not being referred to in the slightest degree.[1]

The last reference to James in the Acts is in connection with Paul's last visit to Jerusalem. After being warmly received by the brethren of the Hebrew Christian Church generally, the apostle reports regarding the Gentile mission to a more formal meeting of the office-bearers. "On the day following, Paul went in with us unto James; and all the elders were present. And when he had saluted them, he rehearsed, one by one, the things which God had wrought among the Gentiles by his ministry. And they, when they heard it, glorified God; and they said unto him," etc. It seems clear that James presided in this meeting; but it will be observed that the report is given not to James, but to the elders in their collective capacity as a presbytery, and that their answer is made on that footing. They explain the position of the Hebrew Christian Church, and propose that Paul should

probably just because no other man would take the chair while he was present. After his death, Beza, to whom a similar mark of respect would have been conceded by his colleagues, declined it, as likely to lead to injurious results." Cunningham, *Works*, ii. p. 236.

[1] Acts xi. 30; xv. 2, 4-7, 13-23; xvi. 4. Bishop Lightfoot sums up the evidence on this point on the whole very fairly, *Philippians*, 3rd ed. p. 195 f.

take certain steps with the view of removing prejudices against him which were entertained by some of its members, adding a well-timed statement so as to guard the freedom of the Gentile Christian communities, whom the apostle and his companions then present specially represented. "As touching the Gentiles which have believed, we wrote, giving judgment that they should keep themselves from things sacrificed to idols, and from blood, and from what is strangled, and from fornication."[1] It is worth noting here how distinctly the eldership or presbytery of Jerusalem, although meeting now without the presence of a single member of the original twelve, identify themselves with the eldership which came to the decision which they quote. They refer to that judgment as theirs, and as still valid, citing its technical language, and make a practical proposal to the apostle with the view of carrying out its spirit and purpose. They do not seem to feel that their authority is at all weaker than it was then for all who come within their jurisdiction; and the president simply acts as the mouthpiece of the court.[2]

If, as seems probable, the apostle Paul was present when

[1] Acts xxi. 17–25; xv. 29.

[2] There is an interesting passage in a commentator of the fourth century to the effect that the original custom in the Church was for the oldest presbyter to take the chair, and be "the bishop" κατ' ἐξοχήν ("primi presbyteri episcopi appellabantur, ut recedente eo, sequens ei succederet"); but that, unsuitable men coming to preside by this system of rotation, a change was made, so that the presidency should go by merit and not merely by seniority ("sed quia cœperunt sequentes presbyteri indigni inveniri ad primatûs tenendos, immutata est ratio, ut non ordo sed meritum crearet episcopum"). Ambrosiaster, *Comment. in Eph.* iv. 12.

The variety of arrangement, compatible with Presbyterian principles, as regards such a president, may be illustrated from the practice of our own Church. In the "Kirk-session," or congregational eldership, the "minister" is the perpetual president; and none except a "minister of the Word" in full standing may preside. In the "Deacons' Court," or joint meeting of elders and deacons, the pastor presides *ex officio*, if present; but in his absence the chair may be taken by any member of the court. In the Presbytery or Synod,—representing the eldership of the district or province,—the moderator is usually appointed for six months, or a year, being chosen by rotation or free election from the ministers of the congregations within the bounds. In the General Assembly or Supreme Court of the Church, the moderator holds office during the sittings of the House, but has certain functions which continue for a year. Comp. Bannerman, *Church of Christ*, ii. p. 262 ff. Turrettin, *Opera*, Edin. 1847, iii. p. 170. Loc. xviii. Quæst. xxi. 3. 2.

Timothy, "his own son in the faith," was solemnly set apart, "with the laying on of the hands of the presbytery," to special service in the Church, "according to the prophecies which led the way to him," there can be little doubt that the elders of the Church at Lystra would call upon the apostle to preside at their meeting, and to lead them in the customary act of the imposition of hands; yet he speaks of it as the act "of the presbytery" as such.[1] Whether or not it was on the same occasion that some special χάρισμα was conferred on Timothy by the laying on of Paul's hands, as referred to in the Second Epistle,[2] is uncertain; and the point is of no importance in this connection. It is perfectly clear that the act of the presbytery in setting their young brother apart to special service in the manner customary in every synagogue was complete in itself, and is spoken of by the apostle as such in connection with Timothy's ministerial duties at Ephesus. It is in a different connection and in another epistle that Paul alludes to the fact of his young companion in labour having received some of those special "gifts," such as "workings of miracles, discernment of spirits, the word of wisdom or knowledge," which were ordinarily given by the laying on of an apostle's hands, and which Timothy is exhorted to "stir up" and improve.[3] Whenever an apostle was present at the meetings of such a local eldership as that of Lystra, or in larger and more influential presbyteries, like that of Ephesus, his presidency would be gladly welcomed as a special privilege, without any idea that his absence would invalidate the proceedings of the court under a less eminent president.[4]

---

[1] 1 Tim. i. 18; iv. 14. See above, p. 533 f. [2] 2 Tim. i. 6.

[3] 1 Cor. xii. 8 ff.; comp. Bannerman, *Church of Christ*, ii. pp. 284–288; Binnie, *The Church*, 136 f.

[4] "The imaginary picture drawn by St. Paul, when he directs the punishment of the Corinthian offender, vividly represents his position in this respect. The members of the Church are gathered together, the elders, we may suppose, being seated apart on a dais or tribune; he himself, as president, directs their deliberations, collects their votes, pronounces sentence on the guilty man (1 Cor. v. 3 ff.). How the absence of the apostolic president was actually supplied in this instance we do not know. But a council was held; he did direct their verdict 'in spirit, though not in person;' and 'the majority' condemned the offender (2 Cor. ii. 6). In the same way St. Peter, giving directions to the elders, claims a place among them. The title 'fellow-presbyter,' which he applies to himself, would doubt-

That a leading presbyter might sometimes "love the first seat" among his brethren, and make an unwarrantable use of the influence and authority connected with it, was to be expected, human nature being what it is even in Christian men.   Instances of this kind were to be found in the annals of the Jewish synagogue elderships, and of "the presbytery of Israel" in Jerusalem.[1]   In what is perhaps the latest document of the New Testament, the Third Epistle of John, the aged apostle speaks with strong reprehension of ambitious tendencies of this sort on the part of leading men in some of the Churches of Asia.   "I wrote somewhat unto the Church; but Diotrephes, who loveth to have the pre-eminence among them (or over them: ὁ φιλοπρωτεύων αὐτῶν), receiveth us not.   Therefore, if I come, I will bring to remembrance his works which he doeth, prating against us with wicked words; and not content therewith, neither doth he himself receive the brethren, and them that would he forbiddeth, and casteth them out of the Church.   Beloved, imitate not that which is evil, but that which is good." [2]

less recall to the memory of his readers the occasions when he himself had presided with the elders and guided their deliberations (1 Pet. v. 1)." Bishop Lightfoot, *Philippians*, p. 196.

[1] Matt. xxiii. 6 f.; Vitringa, *De Syn. Vet.* p. 832 f.

[2] 3 John 9-11. Bishop Lightfoot and others have tried to frame some link of connection between the Ignatian form of prelacy and the apostle John. They argue that the first appearance of a definite distinction between presbyters and bishops is to be found early in the second century in some of the Churches of Asia Minor; that John, who, according to tradition, spent his closing years at Ephesus, must have seen at least the beginnings of the change, and may have sanctioned it, cannot, at least, have disapproved of it. Otherwise, should we not have heard that he opposed it ? And how could writers of the second and third centuries say that "the sequence of bishops" in proconsular Asia could be traced back to the authority of John ? "This," as Dr. Rainy observes, "is a fair enough speculation for men who conceive that prelatic institutions constituted an appreciable providential gain to the Church, and who think they can carry the date of these institutions high enough up to reach the close of John's lifetime. It is not, and it never can be, more than a speculation" (*Theol. Review*, Nov. 1886, p. 6). And, on the other hand, it is surely noteworthy that the very last utterances of the apostle John, recorded in Scripture, are to be found in the two short letters in which he, like Peter, styles himself a presbyter, and in which he passes emphatic censure on the conduct of a leader in one of the Churches in Asia, "who loved to have the primacy among them" ("Is qui amat primatum gerere in iis," D.V.). Comp. Litton, *Church of Christ*, p. 425, and the language used by Ignatius regarding the position and dignity of bishops.

2nd. Deacons in the Gentile Christian Church.

Office-bearers of this class do not appear so early, nor so often as elders, in the notices which we have regarding the organization of the Pauline Churches. This fact is easily explained from the nature of the case, and from the circumstances of the Gentile Christian communities. The care of the poor and afflicted, and the care of the Church's treasury, did not demand a separate organization so soon or so imperatively as the requirements of spiritual oversight and teaching. Paul and his companions risked much, as we saw, in order to establish regular elderships at the earliest suitable time in the Churches of Lycaonia and Pisidia.[1] But we do not hear of any appointment of deacons there. Neither does Titus receive any injunction to have deacons ordained in the cities of Crete, where Christianity was of comparatively recent growth. In such cases, especially where the congregations were small, deacons' work might be left for a time in the hands of the elders, according to the practice of the synagogue, with such arrangements as to collectors, etc., as were usual there.[2] When growing numbers made the need of a further division of labour to be practically felt, the local eldership might be trusted to take suitable steps for an election and ordination of deacons, after the example of the mother Church at Jerusalem, and in accordance with the directions given to Timothy for Ephesus and the surrounding districts, where Churches had been longer established, and the membership was larger.

Only one of the smaller Pauline Churches, so far as we know, that of Philippi, was organized apparently from an early date with both presbyter-bishops and deacons. It is interesting to note the fact that, perhaps as the result of this, the Philippian Church was specially distinguished both for its systematic liberality and for the effective way in which the contributions of its members were conveyed to the proper quarter.[3]

In writing to the Corinthians regarding the Church, under the figure of the body and its members, the apostle refers to those whom "God has set in the Church, first apostles,

---

[1] See above, pp. 530-533.   [2] See above, pp. 417-422.

[3] Phil. i. 1 ; ii. 25 ; iv. 15-19.

secondly prophets, thirdly teachers, then miracles, then gifts of healings, helps, governments (ἀντιλήψεις, κυβερνήσεις), divers kinds of tongues." Setting aside the extraordinary offices of apostle and prophet, and the extraordinary gifts of a miraculous sort, we have here the three departments of teaching, helping, and ruling, which are certainly of permanent necessity in the Church, and which seem to correspond with the sphere of the presbyter-bishops, all of whom ruled, and some received special honour as being also "apt to teach," and of the deacons. This is confirmed, as regards the deacons, by comparison with Paul's address to the elders of the Church at Ephesus. There the apostle uses the same term in reference to his design in working with his own hands, that he might be able both to support himself and "to help the weak (ἀντιλαμβάνεσθαι τῶν ἀσθενούντων)," and that in this he might "give an example" to the Church in its office-bearers and members to do likewise, remembering the words of the Lord Jesus as to the blessedness of giving.[1] Whether deacons had been formally appointed among the Corinthians at the date of Paul's first letter to them, we do not know. Possibly the chief dependence as yet was on volunteer assistants, as in the early history of the Pentecostal Church.[2] But several considerations seem to indicate a certain amount of organization in this department. We hear of the members of the household of Stephanas, who "had set themselves to minister unto the saints (εἰς διακονίαν τοῖς ἁγίοις)," and for whom Paul bespeaks "submission" on the part of the members of the Church as for men in a recognised and so far official position, and "for every one that helpeth with them in the work and laboureth." Further, we hear of "a deaconess of the Church at Cenchreæ," the eastern harbour of Corinth, of whose work the apostle speaks in high terms; and it seems probable that such "helpers" were known in the mother Church of Corinth also.[3]

---

[1] 1 Cor. xii. 27 f.; Acts xx. 33 ff.; comp. Edwards, *First Corinthians*, 2nd ed. p. 335.

[2] See above, pp. 413–417 ff.

[3] 1 Cor. xvi. 15 f.; Rom. xvi. 1. Comp. Beyschlag, *Christl. Gemeindeverf.* S. 74 f. When Clement of Rome wrote to the Corinthians, in the end of the

As regards the qualifications for the deaconship, these might still be summed up, as at the appointment of "the seven," under the three comprehensive requirements : "Men of good report, full of the Holy Ghost and of wisdom." [1] In the apostle's instruction to Timothy regarding the appointment of deacons in the region of which Ephesus was the centre, the chief emphasis, as in the case of the presbyters, is laid on moral and spiritual qualifications. Above all else, let care be taken that those placed in this office be earnest and consistent Christian men, well established in the faith, with a certain weight and sobriety of character. Let special regard be had also to the special duties and temptations connected with the deaconship. There is no such requirement, as in the case of the presbyters, that they should be "apt to teach," or to "take the oversight of the Church of God." But let the deacons be men able to keep guard over their tongues, as being brought into contact with the business of the Church, and with the affairs of its members in straitened circumstances. Let them not speak to the poor, and receive their confidences, as Christian friends and office-bearers, and then speak of them outside with another tongue, the tongue of the tatler (μὴ διαλόγους). Let them be free from all tendency to excess in wine, and from the love of money, which might so easily be a snare to those who, along with the presbyters, were in charge of the funds of the Church, and who had specially to do with their distribution among the poor and afflicted. Such qualifications were needful also in all women who assisted in the work of the deacons, whether members of their own family, wives and daughters, or deaconesses such as Phœbe.[2]

3rd. Unity of the Church; relation of different local Churches to each other and to the Christian society as a whole.

During this second period of the history, as during the first, it might be truly said that the apostolic Church was and felt itself to be one, and is spoken of as such ; it acted as one, and had suitable means for doing so.

first century, the Church there, like that at Philippi, and those organized by Timothy, had its presbyter-bishops and deacons.

[1] See above, pp. 423–427.   [2] 1 Tim. iii. 8–13.

1. Unity felt and expressed.

The same living sense of unity and common brotherhood continued among the members of the Church generally, whether on Gentile Christian or Hebrew Christian ground. Reference has already been made to events and incidents which illustrate this. Brethren "who came from Judæa," whether prophets and teachers or belonging to the ordinary membership, interested themselves at once in the affairs of the Church at Antioch, Galatia, Corinth, or Rome; and their right to do so is admitted as a matter of course.[1]

The fact of this unity between the disciples of Christ is seen in the history. It is both asserted and explained in the addresses and Epistles of Paul. Sometimes this is done in connection with the truth of the unity of the Church of God in all ages. This is brought out as strongly in the writings of the apostle of the Gentiles as in those of the apostle of the circumcision and other leaders of the Hebrew Christian Church.[2] The olive tree of the Church has been one from the beginning. The Jews, as a nation, have been broken off because of unbelief, but shall one day be grafted in again "into their own olive tree." The Gentiles, "being a wild olive," were "grafted in, contrary to nature," and "became partakers with the Jews of the root and fatness of the olive tree." They were once "separate from Christ, aliens from the commonwealth of Israel, strangers from the covenants of the promise. But now, in Christ Jesus, ye that once were far off are made nigh in the blood of Christ. . . . He made both one, and brake down the middle wall of partition. . . . So then ye are no more strangers and sojourners, but fellow-citizens with the saints and of the household of God, being built upon the foundation of the apostles and prophets, Jesus Christ Himself being the chief corner-stone, . . . builded together for a habitation of God in the Spirit."[3] At other times the unity of all believers is brought out both for doctrinal and practical purposes under striking and suggestive figures— the body and its members ; "Christ the Head of His body, the Church;" the bridegroom and the bride, one in a mysterious

---

[1] See above, pp. 525 ff.   [2] See above, pp. 438–441.
[3] Rom. xi. 17–24 ; Eph. ii. 11 f., 17–22.

marriage union; "the house of God, which is the Church of the living God," in which, however, as in every great house, there are vessels of wood and earth, as well as of gold and silver, "some unto honour and some unto dishonour."[1]

2. The apostolic Church, during this second part of its history, acted as one, and had suitable means for doing so.

Such a deep and strong sense of unity as appears in the New Testament writings which bear on this period must, by necessity of nature, have found ways of expressing itself, even had the Gentile Christian Church arisen as a new creation under the hands of Paul with no vital or historical connection with the Church of the Old Testament. We have seen how far this is from being the case, and how the principles and results of the synagogue system in the Diaspora are every-where taken for granted by Paul and his fellow-labourers in the field of the Gentile mission. How those principles and results bore on the matter now before us has been indicated to some extent already.[2] Further illustrations meet us repeatedly in the second part of the Acts and the relative Epistles; the most instructive instance of the kind referred to is furnished by what is generally known as the Synod or Council of Jerusalem.

The minuteness of the narrative in the Acts regarding this assembly, and the character of Paul's references in Galatians to the crisis which led to it, show the importance of the whole transaction itself and its results.[3] Upon the doctrinal aspects of the question at issue we must not enter. Enough to say that the Council of Jerusalem settled the principles on which the Gentiles in all lands and ages were to be admitted to the fellowship of the Church of God, and that it vindicated and set forth afresh the one Divine way of salvation for sinners of mankind. It secured, as Paul said to the Gentile Christians of Galatia, "that the truth of the Gospel should continue with

---

[1] Eph. i. 22 ; iv. 12-16 ; v. 23-32 ; Col. i. 18, 24 ; 1 Tim. iii. 15 ; 2 Tim. ii. 20; comp. a fine passage in Heidegger on the language of Scripture as to the unity of the Church, *Corpus Theol. Christ.* ii. Locus xxvi. 1.

[2] See above, pp. 441-449.

[3] That these two independent accounts are in essential harmony with each other has been conclusively shown by Bishop Lightfoot (*Galatians*, 5th ed. pp. 102-110, 123-128, 305-311) and Lechler (*Apost. u. nachap. Zeitalter*, 3te Ausg. S. 164-195); comp. Hatch, art. "Paul," in *Encycl. Britann.* 9th ed. p. 418.

you," that " the freedom wherewith Christ set you free " should not be limited by any " yoke of bondage." [1] But we must confine ourselves to considering the light thrown here upon the constitution of the apostolic Church, and the methods used under apostolic guidance for the orderly settlement of doctrinal and practical questions which might arise within it from time to time.

The controversy began through " certain men who came down from Judæa and taught the brethren " in Antioch, " saying, Except ye be circumcised after the custom of Moses, ye cannot be saved." They did this persistently, observing at first a measure of secrecy, and using underhand methods.[2] They claimed, it seems, the authority of the leading name in the mother Church at Jerusalem in support of their views, and availed themselves in an unscrupulous spirit of all the feelings of reverence which prevailed among the Gentile Christians for the Hebrew Christian Church, and especially for those who had known Christ after the flesh.[3] The movement, insidiously begun by these men, had thus many elements of strength. " Paul and Barnabas had no small dissension and questioning with them," with no conclusive success. It was agreed, therefore, to refer the whole matter for decision " to the apostles and elders " at Jerusalem. " The brethren appointed that Paul and Barnabas, and certain others of them, should go up to Jerusalem unto the apostles and elders about this question." [4]

The step was in perfect accordance with Jewish precedent, which would make " those that came from James " the more ready to concur in it. Not a year probably passed without some question of a religious sort being referred from some of the synagogues of Antioch to " the presbytery of Israel " in Jerusalem for solution. Neither in the synagogue nor in the apostolic Church did the appeal lie in such circumstances either to the mass of the members generally, or to a single authority, such as the president of the Sanhedrin

[1] Gal. ii. 5 ; v. 1.
[2] Acts xv. 1: ἰδίδασκον; Gal. ii. 4 : τοὺς παρισάκτους ψιυδαδέλφους, οἵτινες παρισῆλθον κατασκοπῆσαι τὴν ἰλιυθιρίαν ἡμῶν.
[3] Gal. ii. 12. See above, pp. 524–527.   [4] Acts xv. 2.

in the one case, or the supposed head of the apostolic college—such as Peter—in the other. It was not even, in the instance before us, to the apostolic college as such, but "to the apostles and presbyters that were at Jerusalem," meeting on one common platform for deliberation, discussion, and decision. Care and thought were evidently used in the choice of deputies.[1] The view of "the party of the circumcision" was sure to find many advocates among those that were "zealots of the law" at Jerusalem.[2] It was probably represented also by some of the "certain others." We know from Gal. ii. 1, 3 that this clause included Titus, a Gentile convert and uncircumcised. From his vigour of character, and success in Christian work, there could not have been a better representative of those believers whose position was now challenged, who were Gentiles in the full sense, yet endowed with gifts of the Spirit, and manifestly blessed by God in the service of His Church.

It is to be observed, that while the whole question might have been authoritatively determined, either, first, by an express revelation to Paul or any of the prophets at Antioch, or, secondly, by a definite utterance from any of the apostles at Jerusalem in their inspired capacity, no such " word of the Lord" was given.[3] The office-bearers and members of the Church at Antioch in the first place, and the apostles and presbyters at Jerusalem in the second, were left to act simply as ordinary uninspired Christians are meant to do in like circumstances.

Good results followed at once from the resolution to refer the question at issue to Jerusalem. The dissension and dis-

---

[1] Οἱ ἐκ περιτομῆς, Acts xi. 2 ; ζηλωταὶ τοῦ νόμου, xxi. 20.

[2] Ἔταξαν. The term, the tense, and the connection show that the appointment of deputies was a definite and deliberate act of the Church as such, probably in a general meeting of the members with their office-bearers, at which both sides were represented.

[3] The only " revelation " given was one to Paul at Antioch, to the effect that it was right to refer the matter to Jerusalem. The seal of Divine approval was thus put on the method of procedure adopted by the brethren at Antioch. In that sense the deputation "went up by revelation." For the rest, both at Antioch and Jerusalem the Church was left to the ordinary means open to the Church in all ages for ascertaining the mind of Christ for His people concerning any question of truth or duty. Gal. ii. 1 f. ; Acts xv. 2, 7, 25.

putation came, for the time at least, to an end.   The deputation are "brought on their way by the Church" as a whole,
all parties apparently uniting in a spirit of harmony to seek
light in this way, and to abide by the decision given by the
apostles and elders.[1]   The company on their way to Jerusalem "pass through both Phœnicia and Samaria, declaring[2]
the conversion of the Gentiles; and they caused great joy to
all the brethren."   There was unanimous approval of what
had been done, regarding the admission of the Gentiles in all
these Churches.   The deputies were able, therefore, to report
their views also at Jerusalem, and to represent them there.
At Jerusalem there was a public reception "by the Church,
and the apostles and the elders," at which Paul and Barnabas
"rehearsed all things that God had done with them."   In
this general gathering of the Christian community with
its office-bearers, signs of opposition appeared.   When the
deputies stated how the Gentile converts had been received
into the Church, a protest was entered by "certain of the
sect of the Pharisees who believed."   They did not question
the truth of what had been told them regarding the conversion of the Gentiles, nor deny that the hand of God in
these events should be thankfully acknowledged.   But they
held that, with respect to the new converts, "it was needful to circumcise them, and to charge them to keep the law
of Moses."[3]   The whole question, which the deputies were
commissioned to submit to the apostles and elders, was thus
raised at once.   It was not to be debated further in the
more miscellaneous and popular gathering, which had met to
welcome the brethren from Antioch.   A regular assembly, or

---

[1] Acts xv. 2 f. ; comp. ver. 30 f.

[2] 'Εκδιηγούμενοι = giving the account in full detail.

[3] Acts xv. 3 ff.   The proposal is marked by a certain moderation of tone as
compared with that of the Judaizers at Antioch.   The leaders of the Pharisaic
party in the Church at Jerusalem do not adopt the extreme position that the
Gentiles could not be saved without circumcision.   Whether from conviction or
policy, they take a lower ground, on which they could rally far more sup-
porters, namely, that "it behoved," in the circumstances, whether as a matter
of necessity or merely of high expediency, that the Gentile converts should be
circumcised, and urged to keep the law of Moses.   It was a position in support
of which a great deal could be said.

council, of the office-bearers of the Church was called "to consider of this matter."

In the interval probably between these two public meetings, Paul had various interviews, "privately, with them of reputation," the apostles and other "leading men among the brethren." At these conferences, in which Barnabas and Titus seem also to have taken part, Paul "laid before them the Gospel which he preached among the Gentiles," entering into explanations not so suitable for a public assembly. The result was that the leaders of the Hebrew Christian Church became completely satisfied, and prepared to guide the minds of others, and to support the apostle of the Gentiles in the cordial spirit which they showed in the council.[1]

"The apostles and the elders were gathered together to consider of this matter." It does not appear from the narrative that any save office-bearers, or members of the deputation, took any direct part in the proceedings of the council, and "the decrees," in which their decision was embodied, are spoken of as "ordained by the apostles and elders that were at Jerusalem."[2] It seems probable, however, that a number of the members of the Church were

---

[1] Gal. ii. 2–10 ; Acts xv. 22–26.

[2] Acts xvi. 4. The heading of the official letter also (Acts xv. 23), according to the reading adopted by the Revisers (on the authority of A B C D ℵ, with Irenæus and other early sources), does not make separate mention of the members of the Church, although their concurrence is noted in the preceding verse: "The apostles and the elder brethren (οἱ ἀπόστολοι κ. οἱ πρεσβύτεροι ἀδελφοί ; the American company of Revisers render : 'The apostles and the elders, brethren '), unto the brethren which are of the Gentiles in Antioch and Cilicia." It seems probable, as Dean Alford observes, "that the words καὶ οἱ were inserted to bring the decree into exact harmony with the beginning of ver. 22. In this the first official mention of πρεσβύτεροι (after chap. xi. 30), it is very natural that the import of the term should be thus given by attaching ἀδελφοί to it." Any apprehensions, such as De Wette expresses, that the words καὶ οἱ were omitted in the great uncials from a hierarchical tendency, may be allayed by noting the indignation with which Dean Burgon denounces the Revisers for a reading and rendering which " have set up lay-elders in the first Christian council, and erected this hitherto unheard-of order of persons, co-ordinate with the apostles, into a supreme court of reference for decision of difficult ecclesiastical causes." It is "a very grave offence," "a foul blot," "a clear misrepresentation of sacred fact." It gives us "a hopelessly mutilated English Bible," etc. etc. Quarterly Review, July 1885, p. 214 ff.

present as interested hearers,[1] and the final decision, and the practical step of sending a deputation to Antioch to explain the grounds of it to the brethren there, commended themselves to "the whole Church," so that their unanimous concurrence is specially noted as a circumstance which lent additional weight to the judgment of the council.[2]

Even in the calmer atmosphere of a representative assembly there was "much questioning," and much time seems to have been spent before a decision was reached. Both sides, no doubt, were fully argued. We have only an outline of the two chief speeches, and indications of the nature of two others, which principally moulded and decided the mind of the council. It is interesting to observe, although we must refrain from entering on the subject here,—the different lines taken by these four speakers,—Peter, the deputies from Antioch, and James the Lord's brother ; each making his own contribution to the discussion, and to the right conclusion from a somewhat different standpoint, and from a different personal experience. Again, as in instances formerly noted,[3] we see the right use of the great rule for the guidance of every court in Christ's Church. The right course is found by His servants "gathered together in His name," by earnest consideration of the teaching of God in His Word and Providence, by faithful application of general Scripture principles to the present circumstances of the Church, however different these may be from former ones, and however unwelcome, on the ground of natural feelings and old associations, the consistent carrying out of those principles may be.

The discussion was summed up, and the arguments already adduced by the apostle of the circumcision and the representatives of the Gentile Churches were confirmed by James the

---

[1] The statement in ver. 12, "all the multitude kept silence," may very possibly include the audience generally, who probably expressed their feelings of approval or dissent in a way that occasionally made silence desirable.

[2] "It seemed good to the apostles and the elders, with the whole Church, to choose men out of their company, and send them to Antioch with Paul and Barnabas, namely, Judas called Barsabas, and Silas, leaders among the brethren : and they wrote thus by them," etc., Acts xv. 22 f., 27.

[3] See above, pp. 402 ff., 426 f., 472–475.

Lord's brother.   He proved from the Old Testament Scriptures that God had *designed* from the beginning that the Gentiles should be included in His Church, even as he had *shown* this in the case of Cornelius, to which Peter had referred.   James ended with a wise and temperate proposal as to the form which the decision of the council should take.   This was agreed to, with the addition,—suggested possibly by the deputies as a step which would greatly conduce to peace among the brethren at Antioch,—that they should not merely send a letter, but an influential deputation from Jerusalem, to explain and enforce the decision of the council by word of mouth.   The resolution which the representatives of the apostolic Church, "having come to one accord," unanimously adopted, was to this effect: It "vindicated the truth of the Gospel," which Paul preached, and the freedom of the Gentile converts in all essentials.   It laid no new burden upon them as necessary to salvation or to Church fellowship.   But it asked them meanwhile to forbear from three things the use of which jarred greatly upon the feelings and associations of Jewish Christians,—from "things sacrificed to idols, and from blood, and from things strangled."   To these things a fourth was added, not in itself indifferent, like the rest, but counted so by public sentiment among the Gentiles in that age, and inextricably mixed up with their heathen worship and idolatrous feasts, namely, fornication.[1]

This well-weighed resolution, the result of such careful and

---

[1] Acts xv. 20 f., 29.   The order of the four in the official letter is more careful than in the draft form of the resolution, so to speak, in the speech of James. But he gives the reason for the forbearance asked,—which would be further explained at Antioch by Judas and Silas,—namely, that "Moses hath (still) in every city them that preach him, being read in the synagogues every Sabbath." Jews and Jewish Christians still met for worship in the same synagogue.   Of course in a *Jewish* synagogue no Christian explanation could, as a rule, be given of the light in which these Mosaic statutes were now to be regarded.   When an opportunity was obtained for Christians to speak there, it was used for declaring more vital truths,—"that Jesus is the Christ, the Son of God."   The reason for the precept, therefore, shows for how long it was to be binding, viz. as long as Moses was ordinarily read in the synagogues to Jews and Christians together. While that state of things lasted, it was needful that the Gentile believers should bear this burden for the sake of Jewish brethren in the Lord, and their fellow-countrymen.   It was a particular and temporary application of the universal and abiding law of Christian love.

prolonged deliberation on the part of the apostles and elders at Jerusalem with representatives of the Gentile Christians, was embodied in a carefully framed official letter, and sent to the Churches from whom the appeal had come, or who were held to be represented in the matter. It was addressed "to the brethren which are of the Gentiles in Antioch, and Syria, and Cilicia," as an authoritative decision of the point at issue, and was accepted by the Churches as such. Paul and Silas and Timothy, "as they went through the cities, delivered them the decrees for to keep, which had been ordained of the apostles and elders that were at Jerusalem. So the Churches were strengthened in the faith, and increased in number daily." [1]

This whole transaction furnishes an interesting and instructive illustration of the way in which the principles of the synagogue system were carried out, as circumstances required, in the apostolic Church during the second period of its history.

In the successive steps, so carefully recorded in the narrative, we see how the unity of the Church through all its parts was preserved and strengthened by the application of the principle of representation, and how the mind of the local Christian community was ruled by the mind of the Church as a whole, gathered and expressed by such a representative assembly as the Council of Jerusalem. Such a council or synod of office-bearers, "gathered together in the name of Christ," and guiding themselves by the voice of the Holy Spirit in Scripture, and the voice of God in His providence and His grace, was the highest earthly authority or court of appeal in the apostolic Church. It follows from the nature of the case that, if the eldership of the Church at Antioch had given judgment on the case themselves, as they might have done,—say, by a majority, against the view held by Paul and Barnabas,—the minority might have appealed to "the apostles and the elders at Jerusalem" to review and reverse the erroneous decision. We have here, in short, a very clear and suggestive example both of the union of office-bearers from different congregations for purposes of common counsel and

[1] Acts xv. 40 f.; xvi. 4 f.

government, but of the subordination of lower to higher Church courts.[1]

How the unity of the Church was represented and maintained in important centres of Christianity by the local eldership, may be seen from Paul's words to the presbyters at Ephesus, when he believed that he was speaking to them for the last time. That the Christians in this great city formed several congregations was shown above.[2] Yet it was one flock which "the presbyters of the Church at Ephesus" tended, although it met in separate folds. The presbyters as a body are addressed by the apostle as the highest earthly representatives of "all the flock, in the which the Holy Ghost hath made you bishops." They are solemnly put in charge with the care of "the Church of God" which is among them, both as to life and doctrine. They are warned against inroads of evil from without, and that from among their own number false teachers shall arise "to draw away the disciples after them." In view of all these duties and dangers, the apostle "commends them to God,[3] and to the Word of His grace."[4]

---

[1] Comp. Bannerman, *Church of Christ*, ii. pp. 325–329. Comp. Dr. Binnie's remarks as to the practical value of a Church polity framed on the lines of such New Testament precedents. *The Church*, p. 132.

[2] See p. 522 f.

[3] Or, "to the Lord," according to the reading noted on margin by R. V., and put in text by Westcott and Hort. Comp. the parting words to the Churches of Lycaonia after the first ordination of presbyters there, Acts xiv. 23.

[4] Acts xx. 17–35. It is interesting to compare the apostle's farewell charge to the eldership of the Church at Ephesus with our Lord's Epistle in the Revelation, by the hand of the apostle John, "to the angel of the Church in Ephesus" (Rev. ii. 1–6). The time is thirty or forty years later. Some of the evils foretold have arisen, and some of the warnings are again enforced. The tone of Paul's address to the Ephesian presbytery corresponds with what seems, on the whole, the most probable explanation of the symbolic phrase, "the angel of the Church" (ἄγγελος τῆς ἐκκλησίας), namely, that it denotes those sent with Christ's message and for His work in an official capacity in the local Christian community,—as Bishop Stillingfleet puts it, "the consessus or order of presbyters in that Church" (*Irenicum*, 2nd ed. p. 289). Comp. Durham, *Revelation*, pp. 65 ff., 82, 238–249 ; Bannerman, *Church of Christ*, ii. p. 290 f. The only other feasible interpretation seems that of Augustine, adopted by Bishop Lightfoot and other good exegetes, that "the angel" is the personification of the Church, "its spirit, or idea." "Laudatur angelus ecclesiæ quæ est Ephesi, quem nemo recte intelligens dubitat ipsius ecclesiæ gestare personam," Aug. *Ad Donatistas post Coll.* xxii. *Opera* (ed. Migne), ix. p. 675. Lightfoot, *Philippians*, p. 197 f.

Our limits forbid us to speak of other forms, in which the sense of unity throughout the apostolic Church, both on Hebrew Christian and Gentile Christian ground, found expression during this period, such as the arrangements for collections, and the "Catholic Epistles." We can only refer in a few sentences to the subject of the apostolic deputies or delegates, such as Timothy, Titus, Tychicus, Epaphroditus, and others. These men were sent forth by Paul—we do not hear of other apostles adopting the same plan, although it seems probable that they did so [1]—on special errands of various kinds, particularly to different districts where he himself had been, when it was impossible for him to remain in the locality or to return to it. In his place, in such cases, he sent a delegate, with suitable instructions, and clothed with special authority for a certain time. The commission was always a temporary one; and the bearer of it, on having fulfilled his trust, was to return to the apostle.[2] Such deputies were, in fact, his "apostles," in the sense in which the name was applied by the Jews to the special messengers of the Sanhedrin for religious or financial purposes,[3] in the sense in which Epaphroditus was for a time an "apostle" of the Church at Philippi, and those associated with Titus in the charge of the collection for the saints were "apostles of the Churches at Macedonia," when entrusted by them with a special mission in their name.[4]

[1] Comp. 1 Pet. v. 13 with 2 Tim. iv. 11.

[2] 1 Cor. iv. 17 ; xvi. 10 f.; 2 Cor. vii. 6–8, 13 ff.; viii. 4–23; Eph. vi. 21 f.; Col. i. 7 f.; iv. 7–10; 1 Tim. i. 3 f.; 2 Tim. iv. 9–13; Tit. i. 5; iii. 12 f.

[3] See above, p. 257 f.

[4] 1 Cor. xvi. 3; 2 Cor. viii. 23; Phil. ii. 25; iv. 18. I prefer not using the name "evangelist" to denote these apostolic deputies, as is done by Dr. Bannerman and some other good authorities. The term is never applied in Scripture to any of the men in question, except in one passage, in which Timothy, among other exhortations regarding different parts of his ministerial work, is charged "to do the work of an evangelist" (2 Tim. iv. 5). Philip is once called "the evangelist," apparently from the success of the Gospel in his hands at Samaria (Acts xxi. 8; comp. viii. 5–8; xii. 35, 40). But it is not clear that he, who is the only person to whom the name seems applied as a distinctive title, had the powers of an apostolic delegate. Men fitted to "do the work of an evangelist," in places where the Gospel had never been proclaimed, were among the gifts of Christ to His Church, specially needed in those days, and specially given by Him. Such gifts are to be thankfully recognised and honoured

Two things are very clear from the Scripture evidence bearing on this point: (1) The position of these apostolic deputies was essentially different both from that of the later diocesan bishop, and of the earliest representative of a form of prelatic or monarchical episcopacy, the Ignatian bishop.[1]

"Among irrelevant and inconclusive arguments on this subject," says Professor Sanday in his able and candid discussion of the "Origin of the Christian Ministry," "I should include that which sees in Timothy and Titus the direct and lineal ancestor of our modern bishops. No doubt we must look, not at names, but at things. Names are, however, the indications of things. And in the case of institutions, the only means we have of tracing continuity is by following the course of the name. Institutions are in this respect like persons. We are told that every particle of our bodies changes, if I am not mistaken, once in seven years. Yet personal identity survives, and is marked by the name. In like manner, the name of an institution may change its contents; these may be added to, or subtracted from, or transformed in one way or another; but the process is a historical one, and the track of its history follows the course of its name. Now it is true that Timothy and Titus are called 'bishops,' but in authorities so late as to be practically worthless. And, on the other hand, they are represented in the epistles addressed to them, not as being bishops themselves, but as appointing other persons to be bishops. It is to those other persons that we must look to see what the attributes of a bishop were; and it is by comparing the different

by the Church in all ages, whether in connection with the ordinary ministry of the Word, or in the field of Home and Foreign Missions. But the work of an evangelist, or missionary, in charge of the Gospel in a heathen land, or of an ordained or unordained preacher doing the work of an evangelist in some line of special effort at home, seems different from that of the deputies entrusted with temporary commissions of various kinds by Paul, although evangelistic work properly so called, as opportunity offered, might be included in their commission. It seems better, therefore, not to use the names as equivalent. Comp. Bannerman, *Church of Christ*, ii. 235 f.

[1] See Hatch, *Organization of Early Christian Churches*, pp. 190–208; *Growth of Church Institutions*, Lond. 1887, pp. 8–19. Bannerman, *Church of Christ*, ii. pp. 234–244, 271 ff.

instances in which the name occurs that we must trace their development."[1]

(2) The position and work of the apostolic deputies furnish a valuable and suggestive precedent, which has not been followed in all branches of the Reformed Church as it might have been, with respect to the importance of entrusting special powers at times to men of special gifts for organization and administration. Such men, under suitable safeguards against prelatic developments, may act, and have acted, most usefully as eyes and hands to the ordinary elderships of the Church, as superintendents or overseers of special departments over wide districts, or in responsible and honourable missions in the general interests of the Church and the cause of Christ at home and abroad.[2] Such men sent forth with special temporary commissions in apostolic times, as under the ancient synagogue system, did not a little to maintain and express the essential unity of the apostolic Church in the second portion of its history.

We have traced the growth and development of the Church of Christ, so far as our limits would allow, to the close of the New Testament period. Of the shortcomings of the work no one can be more conscious than its author. He can at least say that he has honestly sought to see and to speak the truth regarding this great subject, as set forth in Scripture. May the result be for the glory of God, and for the good of His Church on earth.

"Now unto Him that is able to do exceeding abundantly above all that we ask or think, according to the power that worketh in us, unto Him be the glory in the Church, and in Christ Jesus, unto all generations for ever and ever. Amen."[3]

---

[1] Sanday, *Expositor*, Feb. 1887, p. 112 f.

[2] Comp. Bannerman, *Church of Christ*, ii. pp. 262–264. Rigg, *Church Organization*, pp. 221–228, 235 f. It may be noted that the value of Dr. Rigg's "comparison of the ecclesiastical principles of Wesleyan Methodism with 'regular' Presbyterian Churches" is lessened by what seems an unfortunate lack of reliable information regarding the latter part of his subject.

[3] Eph. iii. 20 f.

APPENDIX.

—o—

NOTE A, p. 267 f.

USE OF THE TERM ἐκκλησία IN THE NEW TESTAMENT.

The instances are classified under three heads, in accordance with the threefold aspect of the Church, as seen in our Lord's teaching.[1]

I. *The Church Catholic Invisible.*

1. "Upon this rock I will build my Church; and the gates of Hades shall not prevail against it," Matt. xvi. 18. See above, pp. 173–176.

2. "The Church of God, which He purchased (ἣν περιεποιήσατο = acquired, made His own possession) with His own blood," Acts xx. 28. Comp. Ex. xv. 16. "Till Thy people pass over, O Lord; till the people pass over which Thou hast purchased" (קָנִיתָ = acquired for Thyself. Dillmann: "das Du erworben"). Comp. also Titus ii. 14: λαὸν περιούσιον = "a people for His own possession."

3. "The Church which is His body, the fulness of Him that filleth all in all," Eph. i. 22 f.

4. "That now unto the principalities and the powers in the heavenly places might be made known through the Church the manifold wisdom of God, according to the eternal purpose which He purposed in Christ Jesus our Lord," Eph. iii. 10 f.

5. "Unto Him be the glory in the Church and in Christ Jesus unto all generations for ever and ever. Amen," Eph. iii. 21.

---

[1] See above, pp. 264–268. The fact that these are *aspects* of the Church explains the difficulty of being certain under which head some of the instances should be ranked.

6–11. " For the husband is the head of the wife, as Christ also is the Head of the Church, being Himself the Saviour of the body. But as the Church is subject to Christ, so let the wives also be to their husbands in everything. Husbands, love your wives, even as Christ also loved the Church, and gave Himself up for it; that He might sanctify it, having cleansed it by the washing of water with the Word, that He might present the Church to Himself a glorious [Church], not having spot or wrinkle or any such thing. . . . No man ever hated his own flesh, but nourisheth it and cherisheth it, even as Christ also the Church; because we are members of His body . . . and the twain shall become one flesh. This mystery is great; but I speak in regard of Christ and of the Church," Eph. v. 23–32.

12. " And He is the Head of the body, the Church; who is the beginning, the first-born from the dead; that in all things He might have the pre-eminence. For it was the good pleasure of the Father that in Him should all the fulness dwell," Col. i. 18 f.

13. " The afflictions of Christ in my flesh, for His body's sake, which is the Church; whereof I was made a minister, according to the dispensation of God which was given me to you-ward, to fulfil the Word of God," Col. i. 24 f.

14. " Ye are come unto Mount Zion, and unto the city of the living God, the heavenly Jerusalem, and to countless hosts, the joyful assembly of angels, and to the Church of the first-born who are enrolled in heaven, and to God the Judge of all, and to the spirits of just men made perfect, and to Jesus the Mediator of the new covenant, and to the blood of sprinkling that speaketh better than that of Abel," Heb. xii. 22 ff. I agree with the arrangement and rendering of the R. V. margin here, except that I insert " to " before " the Church of the first-born," as before the other datives. Not to mention other arguments for this rendering, it is clear that it only brings out the full force of the " and," which occurs so often and so impressively in this passage. Each time it introduces a new element in the picture: " Ye are come unto Mount Zion, *and* . . . *and* . . . *and*" (seven times repeated).

II. *The Church Catholic Visible.*[1]

1. "And great fear came upon the whole Church, and upon all that heard these things," Acts v. 11. This instance might perhaps be better put under III. Cremer, however, and other competent writers, prefer to regard it as referring to the whole Church of Christ as then existing on earth, in the Holy Land and the Diaspora.

2. "But Saul laid waste the Church," Acts viii. 3. The same remark holds good here. It was the Christian community generally, including those in foreign cities, that Saul persecuted,—all who at that time professed faith in Christ, and obedience to Him, together with their children. Comp. 1 Cor. xv. 9.

3. "Gaius, mine host, and of the whole Church, saluteth you," Rom. xvi. 23. A kindly hyperbole. It was not merely to the local community, but to the universal Church of Christ, that this hospitality went forth,—to all who belonged to Christ in every place. So Cremer, etc.

4. "Unto the Church of God, which is at Corinth, them that are sanctified in Christ Jesus, called to be saints, with all that call upon the name of our Lord Jesus Christ in every place, their Lord and ours," 1 Cor. i. 2. Comp. Meyer, *in loco*, and 2 Cor. i. 1.

5. "Give no occasion of stumbling, either to Jews, or to Greeks, or to the Church of God," 1 Cor. x. 32.

6. "Or despise ye the Church of God," 1 Cor. xi. 22. See Meyer and Cremer.

7. "God hath set some in the Church, first apostles, secondly prophets," etc., 1 Cor. xii. 28.

8. "I persecuted the Church of God," 1 Cor. xv. 9.

9. "As touching zeal, persecuting the Church," Phil. iii. 6.

10. "If a man knoweth not how to rule his own house, how shall he take care of the Church of God?" 1 Tim. iii. 5. Ἐκκλησία Θεοῦ, without the article, might mean the local Christian community in which the elder or bishop is set for purposes of oversight; but ἐκκλησία in ver. 15, also without

[1] See above, p. 265.

the article, seems to point to the wider meaning here also. See Cremer, *in voce.*

11. "That thou mayest know how men ought to behave themselves in the House of God, which is the Church of the living God, the pillar and ground of the truth," 1 Tim. iii. 15.

12. "In the midst of the Church will I sing Thy praise," Heb. ii. 12.[1] This may perhaps refer rather to the whole Church of the redeemed in heaven and earth, all those whose names are "enrolled in heaven," as in chap. xii. 23. In that case it ought to be placed under I.

III. *The Local Church.*

1 and 2. "And if he refuse to hear them, tell it unto the Church; and if he refuse to hear the Church also, let him be unto thee as the Gentile and the publican," Matt. xviii. 17. For exposition, see above, pp. 180–183.

[3. "And the Lord added to the Church daily those that were being saved," Acts ii. 47. This would fall either under this head or—as Cremer prefers to classify it—under II.— were it not rather to be regarded as a gloss.[2]]

4. "And there arose on that day a great persecution against the Church which was in Jerusalem; and they were all scattered abroad," etc., Acts viii. 1.

5. "So the Church throughout all Judæa and Galilee and Samaria had peace, being edified; and . . . was multiplied," ix. 31.

6. "The report concerning them came to the ears of the Church which was in Jerusalem; and they sent forth Barnabas," xi. 22.

7. "Even for a whole year they were gathered together with the Church, and taught much people," xi. 26.

8. "Herod the king put forth his hands to afflict certain of the Church," xii. 1.

9. "Peter was kept in the prison; but prayer was made earnestly of the Church unto God for him."

10. "There were at Antioch, in the Church that was there, prophets and teachers," xiii. 1.

---

[1] See above, p. 440 f.   [2] See above, pp. 266, 273 f.

11. "When they had appointed for them elders in every Church," xiv. 23.

12. "When they had gathered the Church together, they rehearsed all things," xiv. 27.

13. "Being brought on their way by the Church," xv. 3.

14. "They were received by the Church, with the apostles and the elders," xv. 4.

15. "It seemed good to the apostles and the elders with the whole Church," xv. 22.

16. "Confirming the Churches," xv. 41.

17. "So the Churches were strengthened in the faith, and increased in number daily," xvi. 5.

18. "He went up and saluted the Church," xviii. 22.

19. "He called the elders of the Church," xx. 17.

20. "A deaconess of the Church that is at Cenchræa," Rom. xvi. 1.

21–23. "The Churches of the Gentiles. . . . The Church that is in their house. . . . All the Churches of Christ salute you," Rom. xvi. 4 f., 16.

24. "As I teach in every Church," 1 Cor. iv. 17.

25. "Those who are of no account in the Church," vi. 4. Cremer makes this the Church catholic.

26. "So ordain I in all the Churches," vii. 17.

27. "We have no such custom, neither the Churches of God," xi. 16.

28. "When ye come together in the Church" (ἐν ἐκκλησίᾳ = in congregation, R. V. margin = in a Church meeting), xi. 18.

29. "Howbeit in the Church (ἐν ἐκκλησίᾳ) I had rather speak five words," etc., xiv. 19.

30–37. "Edifieth the Church. . . . That the Church may receive edifying. . . . The edifying of the Church. . . . If the whole Church be assembled together. . . . Keep silence in the Church. . . . As in all the Churches of the saints. . . . Let the women keep silence in the Churches. . . . It is shameful for a woman to speak in the Church," xiv. 4 f.; xii. 23, 28, 34, 35. The first three of these Cremer claims for the Church catholic.

38–40. "I gave order to the Churches of Galatia. . . . The

Churches of Asia. . . . The Church that is in their house,"
xvi. 1, 19.

41. "The Church of God which is at Corinth, with all the
saints which are in the whole of Achaia," 2 Cor. i. 1.

42–49. "The Churches of Macedonia. . . . Through all the
Churches. . .'. Appointed by the Churches to travel with us.
. . . The apostles of the Churches. . . . In the face of the
Churches. . . . I robbed other Churches. . . . Anxiety for all
the Churches. . . . The rest of the Churches," viii. 1, 10, 19,
23 f.; xi. 8, 28 ; xii. 13.

50, 51. "The Churches of Galatia. . . . The Churches of
Judæa, which were in Christ," Gal. i. 2, 22.

52. "No Church had fellowship with me in the matter of
giving and receiving, but ye only," Phil. iv. 15.

53, 54. "The Church that is in their house. . . . The
Church of the Laodiceans," Col. iv. 15 f.

55, 56. "The Church of the Thessalonians in God the
Father and the Lord Jesus Christ. . . . Ye became imitators
of the Churches of God which are in Judæa in Christ Jesus,"
1 Thess. i. 1 ; ii. 14.

57, 58. "The Church of the Thessalonians in God our
Father and the Lord Jesus Christ. . . . In the Churches of
God," 2 Thess. i. 1, 4.

59. "Let not the Church be burdened," 1 Tim. v. 16.

60. "The Church in thy house," Philem. 2.

61. "Let him call for the elders of the Church," Jas. v. 14.

62. "Who bare witness to thy love before the Church;"
i.e. probably in some assembly of the Church in which John
was present. Comp. Westcott on 3 John 6.

63, 64, "I wrote somewhat unto the Church (viz. that to
which Gaius belonged); but Diotrephes, etc., casteth them
out of the Church," 3 John 9 f.

65–84. "The seven Churches which are in Asia, do. do.
do. do. The Church in Ephesus. . . . The Churches. . . .
The Church in Smyrna, etc. etc. I, Jesus, have sent mine
angel to testify unto you these things for the Churches,"
Rev. i. 4, 11, 20 (*bis*) ; ii. 1, 7 f., 11 f., 17 f., 23, 29 ; iii. 6 f.,
13 f., 22 ; xxii. 16.

NOTE B, p. 393.

BISHOP LIGHTFOOT'S ATTITUDE TOWARDS THE SACERDOTAL THEORY OF THE CHRISTIAN MINISTRY.

Nothing could be more effective or satisfactory than Dr. Lightfoot's treatment of the sacerdotal theory throughout his dissertation as a ·whole. But he qualifies his statements and arguments slightly, but unfortunately, in two places.

First of all, at the outset of his discussion, after describing the ideal of the Christian Church in a passage quoted above,[1] Bishop Lightfoot notes the difference between the ideal, considered in itself, and the means which may be necessary to its realization on earth, and states that every society among men must have officers and rules of some sort, that the Church of Christ forms no exception to this universal law, and must therefore have rulers and teachers of some sort, to whom in a special way is committed "the ministry of reconciliation." This is a sound and undeniable position;[2] but to it is appended the very questionable rider, that such rulers and teachers "may, *in some sense*, be designated a priesthood."[3]

After this we go on in great harmony with Dr. Lightfoot, so far as the priestly theory is concerned, to almost the end of his essay. The one unfortunate clause seems contradicted by much that follows. The author at least shows most convincingly that "the sense in which the Christian ministry may be designated a priesthood" is an improper and dangerous one, without the slightest support in the language of the New Testament.[4] "Sacerdotalism"—if it be understood to imply "the offering of sacrifices"—"contradicts the general tenor of the Gospel." "The Epistle to the Hebrews leaves no place for a Christian priesthood."[5] The evidence of the languages of modern Europe "shows that the sacerdotal idea was imported and not original" in the consciousness of Christen-

---

[1] See above, p. 373 ; Bp. Lightfoot, *Philippians*, 3rd ed. p. 179.
[2] Comp. the remarks made in this work at p. 394.
[3] P. 180. [4] Pp. 182 ff., 243 f. [5] Pp. 243, 264 f.

dom.[1] It is unknown in the teaching of the apostolic fathers. Ignatius himself, "the champion of Episcopacy, never regards the ministry as a sacerdotal office. . . . While these letters teem with passages enjoining the strictest obedience to bishops, while their language is frequently so strong as to be almost profane, this Ignatian writer[2] never once appeals to sacerdotal claims, though such an appeal would have made his case more than doubly strong."[3]

Sacerdotal terms begin to be applied to the ministry by Tertullian, Hippolytus, and Origen. They "are hovering on the borders of the new domain, into which Cyprian boldly transfers himself." With them "the Christian minister is regarded as a priest, because he is the mouthpiece, the representative, of a priestly race. . . . The clergy are spoken of as separate from the laity, only because the Church has, for convenience, entrusted to them the performance of certain sacerdotal functions, belonging properly to the whole congregation. . . . So long as this important aspect is kept in view," Dr. Lightfoot adds, "so long as the priesthood of the ministry is regarded as springing from the priesthood of the whole body, the teaching of the apostles has not been *directly* violated. *But still it was not a safe nomenclature which assigned the terms sacerdos, ἱερεύς, and the like to the ministry as a special* designation. *The appearance of this phenomenon marks the period of transition from the universal sacerdotalism of the New Testament to the particular sacerdotalism of a later age.*"[4]

---

[1] P. 244.

[2] Dr. Lightfoot refers here to the seven Epistles which he now regards as the product of the genuine Ignatius, although at the date of the earlier editions of his commentary on Philippians he still regarded them as "interpolated and forged," yet originating not later than 150 A.D., and therefore "among the most important of early Christian documents," p. 232.

[3] P. 249.

[4] Pp. 253–6. The italics are mine, except as regards the epithet "special." The passage is a significant one to all who are familiar with "the appearance of this phenomenon" in the Anglican prayer-book on the most favourable construction of its terms. One can hardly wonder that a canon of St. Paul's, even before he became bishop of Durham, should feel the stress of the dilemma between faithfulness to history and its lessons on the one hand, and respect for the formularies of his Church on the other. Several courses might naturally suggest themselves in the circumstances. The course adopted, for example, by

Cyprian was "the first champion of undisguised sacerdotalism." It is an instructive coincidence, but Dr. Lightfoot,
although with characteristic candour he notes the fact, does
not draw the inferences which will suggest themselves to
many minds,—that the parallel development of the organization of the Church in the direction of prelatic Episcopacy,
which had been going on apparently from the time of
Ignatius, received its consummation also—until taken up
afresh by the bishops of Rome[1]—from the hands of Cyprian.
" As Cyprian crowned the edifice of episcopal power, so also
was he the first to put forward, without relief or disguise,
these sacerdotal assumptions ; and so uncompromising was the
tone in which he asserted them, that nothing was left to his
successors but to enforce his principles and reiterate his
language." Dr. Lightfoot regards the view as " correct in the
main " which ascribes " this divergence from primitive truth "
not to Jewish Christian, but to Gentile influences. The
sacerdotalism which was so fully developed by Cyprian was
" imported into Christianity by the ever-increasing mass of
heathen converts, who were incapable of shaking off their sacerdotal prejudices, and appreciating the free spirit of the Gospel."

the Reformed Episcopal Church of America is a courageous and consistent one.
They expunge the term "priest," as applicable to a Christian minister, from
their liturgy altogether, and "condemn and reject as an erroneous and strange
doctrine, contrary to God's Word," the view "that Christian ministers are
'priests,' in another sense than that in which all believers are 'a royal priesthood,'" ("Declaration of Principles of the Reformed Episcopal Church," prefixed
to their "Book of Common Prayer," Philad. 1874). Dr. Lightfoot's way of escape
seems to be the theory of "a wider and looser sense, in which this unsafe
nomenclature," he thinks, "cannot well be withheld from the ministry of the
Church of Christ" (p. 265).

[1] "Whence were all those theocratic institutions and aristocratic forms
derived, in which the [Roman] Catholic Church found ready to her hand the
elements of her future organization ? . . . The true centre and living pillar
of [Roman] Catholicism, the organizing and animating principle of the whole
body corporate, is the episcopate. Now, the early idea of the episcopate [e.g. in
the Ignatian letters] was that the bishop was to be to the individual community
of Christians, concretely and visibly, what the Jewish Messianic idea in its
Christian development represented Christ as being for the Church general in
His heavenly dignity. And thus, in the first beginnings of the episcopal constitution, we see before us the whole Papal hierarchy of the Middle Ages."
Baur, Church Hist. of the First Three Centuries, 3rd ed. E. T. (Theol. Transl.
Fund Library), 1878, p. 112.

. . . "The only High Priest under the Gospel, recognised by the apostolic writings, is our Lord Himself." Hence, for a considerable time, a scruple was felt as to applying this title to the bishop even after his presbyters, equally against the tenor of the New Testament, had become "priests." But the scruple was at length set aside. One step on a false path as usual led to another. The analogy of the Jewish hierarchy was too strong to be resisted. The bishop became the "pontifex," or "summus sacerdos." "Thus the analogy of the sacrifices, and the correspondence of the threefold order, supplied the material on which the sacerdotal feeling worked, and in this way, by the union of Gentile sentiment with the ordinances of the old dispensation, the doctrine of an exclusive priesthood found its way into the Church of Christ." [1]

Secondly, at the close of all this conclusive demonstration from Scripture and Church history as to the errors and evils of the priestly theory, and its attendant phraseology, we find Dr. Lightfoot returning, although in a very few sentences, to that unfortunate idea of "a wider and looser acceptation of the word priesthood in which it cannot well be withheld from the ministry of the Church of Christ." If we define a priest as "one who represents God to man and man to God, and who is called by God," for "no man taketh this honour to himself;" or, more generally still, as "an officer appointed to minister for men in things pertaining to God," [2]—then we may call Christian ministers "priests." In other words, if we give a vague and arbitrary definition of priest, perfectly different from the distinct sense in which the term is used in Scripture, and which would apply equally well so far as it goes to apostles, prophets, elders, and even deacons (especially in the Anglican view of the last-named office), then, remembering all that this essay tells us of the origin and growth of sacerdotalism in the Church of Christ, we may use this "unsafe nomenclature" with respect to the Christian ministry. "Only in this case," Dr. Lightfoot thinks, "the meaning of the terms should be clearly apprehended; and it might have been better if the later Christian vocabulary had conformed to the silence of the apostolic writers, so that the possibility of confusion would

[1] Pp. 256 f., 262.   [2] P. 265 ; comp. p. 243, note.

have been avoided." Nearly eighteen centuries of Church history have shown how "the possibility of confusion," and worse than confusion, from this source is, in point of fact, a certainty.

Two rather vague sentences, which seem to point in the direction of the necessity of "apostolical succession" in connection with "the threefold ministry," or at least to "our jealous adhesion to it," and suspicion of the Church standing of "Christian communities differently organized," are then balanced by an admirable and vigorous statement of the doctrine that the ministry is not essential to the *existence* of the Church, however closely connected with its *well-being*. "It may be a general rule, it may be under ordinary circumstances a practically universal law, that the highest acts of congregational worship shall be performed through the principal officers of the congregation. But an emergency may arise, when the spirit and not the letter must decide. The Christian idea will then interpose, and interpret our duty. The higher ordinance of the universal priesthood will overrule all special limitations. The layman will assume functions which are otherwise restricted to the ordained minister." [1]   And then the essay closes with an eloquent reference to the way in which the apostolic ideal of the Church and the ministry "was forgotten within a few generations," and yet in spite of human imperfections and errors, the promise of Christ's Presence was fulfilled in the continuous history of the Church.

It is to be regretted that the few unsatisfactory sentences to which I have referred should occur in an essay which, as a whole, is so valuable in its bearing on this question. They have not sufficed to avert some abuse from Dr. Lightfoot—for which he was probably prepared—for his "Protestantism;" but they are certain to be taken advantage of by the sacerdotalists of the Church of England, who always seek the shadow of great names. Such men will ignore the whole of Dr. Lightfoot's powerful argument against sacerdotalism, and shelter themselves under his hesitating approval of a certain amount of sacerdotal phraseology.

[1] P. 265 f. ; comp. the remarks in this work, pp. 201–203.

History often repeats itself in a curious way. We have
an illustration of this in the present case in connection
with an even greater name than that of the present eminent
Bishop of Durham. Hooker, when defending the position of
the Church of England in his *Ecclesiastical Polity,* evidently
feels himself hard pressed by the vigorous onset of Cartwright
and others upon this weak point, the sacerdotal phraseology
of the Prayer-Book. He tries to minimize the importance of
the question, and makes one concession after another. He
admits that "when learned men declare what the word
'priest' doth *properly* signify, according to the mind of the
first imposer of that name, their ordinary scholies do well
expound it to imply *sacrifice.*"[1] He admits, in language
which Dr. Lightfoot seems almost to repeat: "In truth, the
word 'presbyter' doth seem more fit, and in propriety of
speech more agreeable than 'priest,' with the drift of the
whole Gospel of Jesus Christ. . . . Seeing we receive the
adoption and state of sons by their ministry whom God hath
chosen out for that purpose, seeing also that when we are the
sons of God our continuance is still under their care which
were our progenitors, what better title could there be given
them than the reverend name of presbyters, or fatherly
guides? The Holy Ghost throughout the body of the New
Testament doth not anywhere call them 'priests.'"

Hooker's only refuge, like that of Dr. Lightfoot, is to
plead that an improper sense of the word may be allowed.
St. Paul in one passage calls "fish" "flesh," because "it hath
a proportionable correspondence to flesh, although it be in
nature another thing." Why may not we, then, call a
Christian minister a "priest," "although he be in nature
another thing"? "The Fathers of the Church of Christ
with like security of speech call usually the ministry of the
Gospel 'priesthood,' in regard of that which the Gospel hath
proportionable to ancient sacrifices, namely, the communion
of the blessed Body and Blood of Christ, although it have
properly now no sacrifice. As for the people, when they hear

---

[1] Hooker's note on this is: "'Ιερῦσαι, θυσιάσαι. Hesych. *s.v.* ἱερῦσαι.
'Christus homo dicitur quia natus est; Propheta quia futura revelavit;
Sacerdos quia pro nobis hostiam se obtulit.' Isid. Orig. iii. 2."

the name, it draweth no more their minds to any cogitation
of sacrifice than the name of a senator or alderman causeth
them to think upon old age, or to imagine that every one so
termed must needs be ancient, because years were respected
in the first nomination of both." [1]

How little truth there is in this last plea of Hooker's, that
hearing constantly the word " priest," " draweth the people's
minds to no cogitation of sacrifice," is plain from the history
and literature of sacerdotalism in the Church of England
from the time of Laud to that of Dr. Newman and Dr.
Manning. Some twenty years ago the Dean of Canterbury
could declare publicly, that " the majority of the members of
Convocation are assertors of exclusive sacerdotalism." [2] And
no one who is at all familiar with the teaching of the High
Church and Ritualistic party for the last half century, both from
pulpit and press, and with its results, can fail to see how
effectively for practical purposes the argument can be used
with the common people, that because the Prayer-Book calls
ministers priests, therefore they really are priests, and offer a
true and proper sacrifice at the altar.[3] Take two instances
only out of a multitude that might be given. The first is
from the writings of a respected bishop of the Scotch Episcopal
Church. It contrasts rather amusingly with Hooker's statement cited above, that " the Gospel hath properly now no
sacrifice." " If we deny," says Bishop Jolly, " that there is
any proper material sacrifice in the Christian Church, we pull
down proper priesthood, and open a door to Socinianism. . . .
While the Church of England retains the Christian priesthood, she retains by implication the Christian sacrifice; for
every priest must have somewhat to offer: sacrifice and priesthood being correlative terms, they stand or fall together." [4]

The other instance is a passage taken, almost at random,

---

[1] Hooker, *Eccles. Pol.* v. 78. 2, 3.

[2] Dean Alford, " The Union of Christendom in its Home Aspect," *Contemp.
Review*, Feb. 1868.

[3] " The English of the Prayer-Book, till it is conformed to the English of the
Bible, will continue to convey to the congregations which use it, a view of the
Christian ministry which the authors of the Prayer-Book would have been the
first to repudiate." Binnie, *The Church*, p. 143.

[4] Bishop Jolly, *The Christian Sacrifice in the Eucharist*, 2nd ed. p. 139.

from a volume entitled *Essays on the Reunion of Christendom*, edited by the Rev. F. G. Lee, the Secretary of the A.P.U.C., with a Preface by the late Dr. Pusey: " The marvel is that Roman Catholics do not see the wisdom of aiding us to the uttermost. Admitting that we are but a lay body, with no pretensions to the name of a Church, we yet in our belief,—however mistaken,—that we are one, are doing in England that which they cannot do. *We are teaching men to believe that God is to be worshipped under the form of Bread*, and they are learning the lesson from us which they have refused to learn from the Roman teachers who have been among us for the last three hundred years. . . . How many English Protestants have Roman priests brought to confession compared with the Anglican clergy? Could they have overcome the English dislike to ' mummery ' as we are overcoming it ? " [1]

---

[1] *Essays on Reunion*, vii. p. 179 f.

INDEX OF SUBJECTS AND AUTHORS.

———